OPERA ON RECORD 2

Also by Alan Blyth

WAGNER'S RING: AN INTRODUCTION

Edited by Alan Blyth

OPERA ON RECORD
REMEMBERING BRITTEN

Opera on Record 2

Edited by Alan Blyth
Discographies compiled by
Malcolm Walker

Beaufort Books Inc.
New York

Library of Congress Cataloging in Publication Data
Main entry under title:

Opera on record 2.
   No more published in U.S.
   Includes index.
   1. Operas – Discography.   2. Sound recordings – Reviews.
I. Blyth, Alan.
ML156.4.0460552 1984   789.9′13621   83-21420

ISBN 0 8253 0212 9

Published in the United States by Beaufort Books, Inc., New York.

Printed in Great Britain   First American Edition

10   9   8   7   6   5   4   3   2   1

Contents

Introduction

ALAN BLYTH

The chapters in this volume, unlike those in its predecessor, are almost all
original commissions. Only the contributions from Harold Rosenthal and
Edward Greenfield derive from articles in *Opera* (although *Les Contes
d'Hoffman*, *Samson et Dalila* and *Die lustige Witwe* have appeared in the
magazine's pages since I commissioned them). That is largely because we are
here dealing with, on the whole, more esoteric works, not exactly on the
fringe of the repertory but not in many cases central to it. Reviews of *Opera
on Record* frequently criticized me for not including *Dido and Aeneas*, *Die
Entführung aus dem Serail* and *Wozzeck*. Well, I hope their inclusion here
amply makes up for what may have seemed a serious sin of omission in the
earlier volume. For obvious reasons there are this time more composite
chapters, involving their authors in a vast amount of research both into the
music (editions and so on) and into the relevant discography. By and large,
because of the nature of the operas covered, there is probably more musi-
cology, somewhat less 'gramophology' than in volume one. I am certain that
chapters such as those by Stanley Sadie on Handel, Max Loppert on Gluck,
David Cairns on Berlioz, Robin Holloway on Berg will be read as much for
what they tell us about the works concerned as what they report on the
records, and those, for instance like Robert Henderson on *Hoffman*, are
authoritative words on pieces with difficulties over editions.

Inevitably, comments on the first volume dwelt on the discrepancy of
approach between authors. I was reproved for not giving sufficient editorial
guidance. As I said in the introduction to that book, each opera and its
discography dictate the way it should be examined and in almost every case
that will be different. As before I have preferred to leave the writer to decide
his approach for himself, offering guidelines only when they have been
requested. Ronald Crichton pointed out, most pertinently, that 'ability to
write, collecting mania and musical judgement do not always go hand in
hand'. I hope that at least something of each of those characteristics is to be
found in every chapter this time.

As regards the presentation of items and numbers, I have inevitably learnt
some lessons from previous experience. However, the basic approach is the
same as before. As far as possible in the text, the numbers for items have

been given in brackets according to the following principle. The number is that of the original 78rpm records, where applicable. After a semicolon there is the most recent LP reissue, or that which is considered most readily accessible. With the help of Eric Hughes of the National Sound Archive and of John Hughes, I hope that this information is as up-to-date and accurate as possible at time of going to press. Since the previous volume, the business of reissues has happily been expanded still further, with many important singers now covered comprehensively. Besides the issues from the larger companies, most importantly EMI/Electrola with their huge archives (Continental issues beginning with a 1C, 2C etc prefix, according to country of origin), the smaller companies have continued to work unceasingly on reissues. The chief among them are the Austrian firm of Preiser, with its Lebendige Vergangenheit (LV prefix) and Court Opera (CO) series, Rubini Records (GV) masterminded by Syd Gray, and Charles Haynes's Pearl catalogue (GEMM). Then there are the American or Canadian firms Rococo, Club 99 and OASI, whose records are available intermittently from specialist dealers in Britain. Only where 78s have not been reissued from any of these sources have older, deleted numbers been resorted to. Some numbers of 'private' and 'off-the-air' issues emanating from live performances have now been included in the discographies, but their distribution is inevitably haphazard. As regards the big companies only the numbers of their records are given: the rest of the information is readily available in the *Gramophone* catalogue or those of its Continental and American equivalents.

As regards 78rpm numbering, this is the same as in *Opera on Record*. All those numbers without prefixes are those of the acoustic Gramophone and Typewriter (G&T), Gramophone Company, Monarch, Amour, Grammophon etc. labels (an exception is made in the *Huguenots* chapter, mostly concerned with old discs, where Vivian Liff's meticulous detail has been retained). Where titles were reissued on double-sided DB (twelve-inch) or DA (ten-inch) series, these numbers have been preferred. Other early labels have been shortened thus: Fono. for Fonotipia; Od. for Odeon; Poly. for Polydor; Parlo. for Parlophone/Parlophon; Col. for Columbia; and H&D for Pathé 'hill-and-dale' records made by the vertical cut process. HMV prefixes are: DB, DA, D, E, C, B; Columbia prefixes are L, LX, DX. Columbia ten-inch DBs have 'Col.' before them to indicate they are not HMV DBs. Discs originally issued by Victor in the USA but later issued in Britain are given their British numbering. Most points of doubt in the electrical era of 78s can usually be clarified by reference to the still-invaluable *World Encyclopedia of Recorded Music* by Clough and Cuming (original volume with three supplements). More details of numbers and items can be found in the eleven volumes of *Voices of the Past*, though most are at present out of print. It remains to thank my contributors once again for their hours and hours of fruitful labour, and for the knowledge and wise opinions dispensed therefrom, enlightening and useful, I hope, to those who read their words; Malcolm Walker for again providing so much exhaustive detail in his discographies. Record collectors without whose assistance this volume would have been impossible to compile include John Hughes, Edward and Peter Lack, Vivian Liff, George Stuart, Arthur Carton, Christopher Norton-Welsh and Brian Gould. The help and advice given by Derek Lewis, BBC Record Librarian has, as always, been invaluable. Kevin McDermott and Valerie Hudson, as editors, have been a constant source of encouragement. I would also like to thank my colleagues Robert Henderson and Max Loppert for their editorial advice, although all decisions have, in the last resort, been mine, and I take responsibility for any lacunae or mistakes to be found within.

THE DISCOGRAPHIES

The policy adopted in the discographies in regard to issuing companies plus record and cassette numbers has been to quote both the UK and US information citing the most up-to-date or, in the case of deleted recordings, the most recent details. Where a recording was not released in either of these two countries we have quoted the relevant country in question.

SYMBOLS USED

* denotes 78 rpm disc(s); ⓜ mono; ④ cassette; © electronically reprocessed stereo.

Country of origin is indicated only where otherwise unclear. For complete information on country of origin, see list of record companies and labels.

Dido and Aeneas

GRAHAM SHEFFIELD

In an age in which the performance of baroque music is increasingly dominated by the use of original instruments (or modern copies) and by so-called
'authentic' performance practices, it seemed strange that until recently no
one had recorded a *Dido and Aeneas* that made a consistent attempt to apply
such ideas to Purcell's opera. By contrast there are several scholarly recordings, but, sadly, the most erudite of these falls victim to the old adage 'the
letter killeth, the spirit giveth life'. So we are fortunate that two *Didos* are
now available which not only pay more than lip-service to seventeenth-
century performing practice, but also happen to be among the more satisfying
performances on record.

Dido was almost certainly commissioned for, and first performed by,
largely amateur forces, namely the young gentlewomen of Josiah Priest's
boarding school in Chelsea. The date was 1689 when England was far from
being accustomed to continuously sung music-drama. There is no definitive
edition since no autograph or contemporary printing of the music is known
to survive, 'only the printed libretti from 1689 and 1700 which do not always
agree with each other and which depart in various ways from a group of
eighteenth-century manuscript copies of the score which quite often differ
among themselves'.* The three published editions are by Edward Dent,
Thurston Dart/Margaret Laurie (The Purcell Society Edition) and Benjamin
Britten/Imogen Holst. All are responsible and respectable and the majority
of the recordings under consideration are based on one of these editions or
an amalgam of them.

No music for the end of the Grove Scene has survived, although the words,
'Then since our Charmes have sped . . .' together with an indication for a
dance, exist in the 1689 libretto. Dent supplies no solution, but both of the
other editions do. Musical and theatrical considerations demand that the
words be set and a dance included. By no means all of the recordings oblige.

By virtue of its length, around an hour, *Dido and Aeneas* lends itself to
LP recording. It fits comfortably on to one disc and does not invite the
idiosyncratic or foolhardy bedfellows it has often acquired in the theatre.

* Roger Savage – *Early Music*, 1976, Volume 4, pp 393–406. Producing *Dido and Aeneas*.

Excluding the two most recent recordings, there have been two performances on 78s and ten on LP, including one in Russian (!) that I haven't located; it gives no pleasure to report that, notwithstanding the differences in edition and approach, these all sound remarkably alike. The blame for this, if blame there is, lies not at the door of the singers but of the conductors, and, more fundamentally than that, at the door of what can loosely be termed the English musical tradition. Bizarre though it may seem, there is a parallel to be drawn with the fate of the Gilbert and Sullivan operettas. Productions of these, amateur and professional, have tended to become so institutionalized and hidebound by dubious traditions that the original ambience and dramatic purpose have become heavily obscured. Handel's *Messiah* is another work which still often suffers a similar fate.

Dido and Aeneas is, dare one say it, comparatively simple to perform adequately, and within the technical competence and financial limitations of most companies; it also contains a substantial role for chorus. Hence, following Edward Dent's edition in 1925, it has become very popular with amateur operatic societies. The performing styles then prevalent have tended to attach themselves to Purcell's piece, in professional as well as amateur renderings, and gently but inexorably to throttle it. On record we often need listen no further than the opening of the overture to perceive the ponderous, over-blown response of most conductors to the opera. The Sorceress and attendant witches provide another pitfall. The Sorceress is frequently drawn as an absurd pantomime dame surrounded by snivelling wizened crones with silly voices.

How refreshing it was then, despite certain idiosyncracies, to discover the 1979 performance of *Dido and Aeneas* conducted by Joel Cohen, the only conductor of the work on disc, incidentally, not born in the Commonwealth. Cohen also plays a continuo lute and sings the part of the Sailor (about which the most charitable thing one can say is that he is vigorous). His written introduction makes the general approach clear, echoing much of what is hinted at above. He wishes to get away from the misguided application of nineteenth-century grand opera conventions to Purcell's compressed small-scale opera. 'Our intention in this performance,' he says, 'is not to search for some kind of definitive (and unattainable) historical authenticity but rather to recreate *Dido and Aeneas* using our experience of seventeenth-century music – English and French masques, Lullian ballet, early Italian opera – as a general framework. We arrive thus at a different orchestral sound, other ideas about tempi, even unconventional thoughts about characterization (the two witches, for example, so often sung in our time by sinister operatic mezzo-sopranos, are unquestionably intended as comic roles for light, adolescent voices).' The result, as one might expect, is a *Dido* fundamentally different from any other previous recording. To begin with, there is the distinctive sound of a small baroque group playing in period fashion. Unspecified parts for flute and oboe are added, as well as percussion in a couple of dances. One of these is an unscheduled instrumental repeat with tambourine of 'Fear no danger'. String tone is never over-nourished, but only rarely the reverse (introduction to Act 2, scene i). Some tempi are unexpected – exceedingly slow 'ho-hos' from the witches for example, and a bizarre mid-dance hiatus in the Witches' Dance – but as a rule, Cohen settles on speeds in accord with his small-scale approach. His rhythmic feel is taut and incisive; crisp French rhythms are employed where appropriate with beneficial effect (Echo Dance and the Dances of Witches and Sailors). The stately tempo for 'To the hills and the vales' lends great poise to the Triumphing Dance that follows, without the customary Meyerbeerian overtones.

The biggest surprise of the disc is the sex-change undergone by the Sorceress, translated into a tenor. There seems little historical justification for this except for the tenuous link with seventeenth-century roles in Venetian opera; but the practical result is curiously felicitous. Images of Lady Bracknell thankfully recede, while the light adolescent tone of the attendant witches (the first one sounds like a baroque violin) contributes to the force of evil being put across simply by virtue of its understatement.

The Dido, D'Anna Fortunato, is one of the two best on record. Hers is a clean, unaffected interpretation; through restrained colorations of tone, she imparts a fragile, vulnerable quality to the doomed queen that is most poignant. Cohen's sympathetic, gentle, but not stagnant tempi in the set-piece arias do much to assist her.

Of the other soloists, Nancy Armstrong (Belinda) also responds to the words with sensitivity and an absence of affectation, but her 'Haste to Town' is excessive: just one example of her occasional rhythmic unsteadiness and a tendency to rush. On these two points, Cohen's direction is not beyond reproach either.

A lack of clearly focused tone mars the Aeneas of Mark Baker, but otherwise his reading is distinguished by its mellowness and youth – qualities conspicuously absent from some of his rivals in the part. The Spirit is effectively cast as a counter-tenor (Ken Fitch). The chorus – a small group placed very close to the microphone – is inclined to stiffness of enunciation and phrasing, but does produce a very beautiful echo chorus. This is the only recording in which the soloists are drawn from the chorus. One would have thought, in a performance like this, that some conclusion would have been added to Act 2, scene ii, but that is not the case.

The hunt for authenticity can, of course, be taken to ludicrous extremes; hence the comment in Cohen's introduction about 'unattainable authenticity'. In *Dido* one would ultimately have to involve several young schoolgirls somewhere in Chelsea. But, whimsy apart, there is much to be said for youth in the work, for avoiding both over-sophistication and a self-conscious mannered style. The work needs a restrained musical aesthetic in keeping with its domestic scale. All this Cohen achieves, and if once or twice he goes too far in his desire to obliterate the nineteenth century, we must forgive him for the sake of his thoughtful, provocative and unencumbered performance.

Andrew Parrott's 1980 *Dido* (digitally recorded and authentically played) is also thoughtful and provocative, as one would perhaps expect from this imaginative musician. However, despite some strong positive features (among them a finely judged and paced closing scene) the performance promises more than it delivers and the result remains strangely unfulfilling. The enterprise is more professional and polished than Cohen's, and less idiosyncratic, but some of his exuberant spirit is missing, and the exuberance that is present is often misplaced: choral witches that sound like demented cats, a distressingly raucous and frankly ghastly Sorceress, an unwarranted infernal cacophony at the end of Act 2, scene i, and some over-exaggerated hairpin dynamics from the orchestra. When the chorus are not giving an impression of feline malady, they assume a tone far too suave and velvety for my taste ('When Monarchs unite', 'Fear no danger'). David Thomas, as Aeneas, is in strong voice, but ultimately he fails to bring home the emotional dilemma that Aeneas faces during the opera. The Sailor (Rachel Bevan) also fails to make any great impact.

Elsewhere on this record, there is much that pleases. Judith Nelson (Belinda) is admirable, so is Judith Rees as the Second Woman; she gives a soft, liquid rendering of 'Oft she visits'. Also in good form are the Taverner Players; apart from the reservation expressed above, they play with a refreshing cleanness of attack and concern for detail. The dances are subtly characterized and finely shaded.

For his part, Andrew Parrott chooses tempi with care and discretion. 'Ah Belinda' is somewhat statuesque and lacking in flow, but elsewhere, there is little with which to take issue. Happily, the Lament is not overweighted as in so many of his colleagues' performances. On the whole the recitatives and ariosos are given stylishly and flexibly.

Although there is no mention on the sleeve of an edition (despite the fact that the record was produced in association with the Open University) we do have the benefit of the two optional guitar dances, and there is a dance (a hornpipe from the *Married Beau*) but no chorus to round off Act 2, scene ii.

Emma Kirkby as Dido is excellent, this record's greatest asset. At the outset, I had reservations; her tone is surely too reedy and, like the orchestra, she falls victim to some unattractive hairpin dynamics on certain long held notes, but after the first aria matters improve immeasurably. Miss Kirkby's light, pure, youthful soprano is ideally suited to the recitatives and her interpretation of the Lament is the more telling for its simplicity and sense of dignified resignation.

The modest success of the recordings conducted by Cohen and Parrott does not wholly disqualify the other eleven versions of *Dido*, which are by no means without their individual virtues, despite the important general stylistic reservations outlined above.

The earliest appeared late in 1935 using the edition by Edward Dent. One is immediately struck by the fact that, apart from the sound quality and the manner of string playing, the performance is not unlike that encountered in more recent recordings. Indeed, Clarence Raybould and the Boyd Neel Orchestra could well enlighten one or two of their modern counterparts in terms of dramatic shape and pace. The approach is traditional and tempi are on occasion lumpy (a singularly moderato 'moderato' in the overture), but a springy Triumphing Dance and a vigorous Echo Dance are more indicative of the performance's quality. An over-brisk 'Cupid only throws the dart', with consequent lack of clarity, caused me to raise an eyebrow, as did a nasty *accelerando* at the end of 'To the hills and the vales'. On the credit side Boris Ord contributes a stylish harpsichord continuo, probably worked out in some detail together with Dent.

The singing, if not uniformly satisfactory, does have its attractions. The A Capella singers acquit themselves creditably with a particularly sensitive 'In our deep vaulted cell'. A shaky opening chorus and a rhythmically flat 'Harm's our delight' are the only clouds in the choral sky. Of the soloists, Roy Henderson stands out as a most impressive Aeneas, with a relaxed but firm approach to his line and a true awareness of the emotional possibilities of the scene in which he decides to leave Carthage, as well as the dramatic possibilities of his final encounter with Dido.

Mary Jarred (the Sorceress) is the best of the women, her powerful and well-centred voice managing to sound duly sinister without resort to gimmickry. Sydney Northcote is a lively Sailor from north of the border, but Mary Hamlin as Belinda is unexceptional. Dido, too, in the person of a twenty-year-old Nancy Evans, has her problems. While she gives a characterful, dramatic reading, the flaws in her major arias are too apparent to overlook; the quality of voice is too chesty, the dynamic and tone colour unvaried and, by today's standards, her *portamenti* and her habit of singing for effect just under a note make for uncomfortable listening. The top Gs at 'Remember me' do not emerge with ease.

Ten years later, in 1945, the second recording of *Dido* appeared, conducted by Constant Lambert. Once again, Edward Dent's edition was used. As Benjamin Britten did later, Lambert clearly showed a composer's sympathy and understanding for the music of his illustrious predecessor. Both Britten and Lambert seem to have been seduced by the potential richness of the music – compare for example the G minor Chacony as edited and conducted by Britten (Decca SXL 6405) and the overture of *Dido* conducted by Lambert. Both have that imposing thrustful 'stringy' quality which calls to mind Elgar's arrangements and performances of Bach and Handel. In Lambert's case the grandiose impression continues throughout the performance often at the expense of rhythmic vitality (e.g. 'When monarchs unite' and the whole of Act 2, scene ii). By contrast, 'Cupid only throws the dart', always a contentious chorus for tempi, is too quick and Love's pursuit of her conquest is relentless. The important harpsichord (another idiomatic performance by Boris Ord) is placed well forward – acceptable in general but distracting in the Echo Dance at the end of Act 2, scene i.

Lambert's cast is a distinguished one: Joan Hammond, Isobel Baillie, Dennis Noble and Edith Coates in the leading roles. Of these it is Baillie who carries off the honours, achieving a good, springy rhythm for 'Shake the cloud' and constantly reminding us of the great virtue of clean, pure singing. Dennis Noble's Aeneas is strongly portrayed but betrays a hint of loose tone at 'If not for mine, for empire's sake. . .'. As the Sorceress, Edith Coates is overpowering; her jolly attendants (Edna Hobson and Gladys Ripley) emanate from the St Trinian's school. I wish I could feel that Joan Hammond was an ideal Dido. She is, and sounds like a soprano, always to be preferred, and her singing is sturdy and dramatic. Her first aria shows a thrustful kind of languor, even a touch of impatience at her virgin state, and she displays effective hooded tone on the long melisma at 'languish'. But overall, her interpretation, like that of so many others, lacks classic restraint; the Lament, too bold and assertive, failed to move me. The chorus is adequate if not inspired, but unfortunately suffers from drooping pitch as well as drooping wings at the end of the opera.

Stature, musicality and theatricality are three words which immediately come to mind when considering the 1951 *Dido and Aeneas* conducted by Geraint Jones, the first on LP. The reading is both thoughtful and compelling, though I have several scruples as to the manner of performance. A highly charged overture, albeit over-reliant on *mezzo forte*, leads into a first scene where one is struck by the unorthodox Belinda of Elisabeth Schwarzkopf. The character she draws is certainly not that of a pert, provocative soubrette, but frankly her super-sophisticated, almost precious, way with words and with a vocal line militates against proper flow in this music. No one can doubt the integrity behind her interpretation, but too often she sounds as though she is singing lieder by Hugo Wolf, over-colouring the tone and neglecting hard consonants in the interests of a smooth line, with a resultant loss in impact. In addition to Belinda, Schwarzkopf also takes the parts of Second Lady and Attendant Spirit. In the latter guise, the individuality of her voice confuses the issue – much better, surely, to have chosen one of the witches to take this role.

Kirsten Flagstad, in 1951 very near the end of her career, sings Dido; legend has it that she was paid for her labours in beer by Bernard Miles, who was the inspiration behind both the recording and a number of live performances. I must confess to having returned several times to Flagstad's arias before putting pen to paper. Ultimately, as with the performance of the opera as a whole, the dignity and authority of her singing overcome any recurrent doubts – but only just. The line is sometimes uneven, the *portamenti* are unattractive; so is the tendency to sing beneath the note. But who will deny that this is a compelling reading? The parting duet between her and Aeneas is truly dramatic.

Aeneas himself is grandly drawn by Thomas Hemsley; although he is inclined to self-indulgence, perhaps in an attempt to make much of little, his control, for example at 'Let Dido smile', is impeccable. The Sorceress, Arda

Mandikian, is spiteful and chilling without degenerating into the absurd. Fortunately the witches, Sheila Rex and Anna Pollak, as well as the chorus, take their cue from her. Credit for the performance's positive qualities must go to the conductor Geraint Jones. One is constantly reminded of his sympathy for this music. His tempi are for the most part appropriate (an exception is an unusually brisk opening to the grove scene) and he draws expressive, lively playing from the Mermaid Orchestra. An effective departure from normal practice is the *pianissimo* climax to the orchestral postlude of Dido's first aria. A commendably firm cello continuo is provided by Raymond Clark. If the Mermaid Singers lack the balance and polish of more eminent ensembles, they are never dull. The difficult tests of 'Great minds' and 'With drooping wings' are overcome with sustained singing and attention to the shape of the phrases.

The closing verses of Act 2, scene ii (for which no music has survived) are set here to a passage from Purcell's 'Welcome Song for His Majesty on his return from Newcastle, 1682' together with an air from *The Virtuous Wife* as the final dance. This is the first version to fill this lacuna.

Another recording of *Dido* followed within the year: it requires little comment. The conductor was Jackson Gregory who, according to the record sleeve, prepared his own performing edition from existing manuscripts. It corresponds quite closely to Dent. The impression here is one of great enthusiasm from Gregory for the score. He clearly had sound ideas about performing style in early music. Sadly, however, either he did not possess the authority or his cast lacked the ability to transform these ideas into successful practice. Nobody is helped by the cramped, muddy sound (all three earlier recordings are better) or by some dreadful tape joins.

The Dido (Eleanor Houston) sings with a very quick vibrato but without great commitment. Adele Leigh (as Belinda) performs brightly enough, but Henry Cummings is an inflexible Aeneas. The cast's chief assets lie in the firm, focused singing of Evelyn Cuthill as the Sorceress (despite considerable shortcomings in 'Our next motion') and of Heather Harper (her recording debut?) as First Witch.

On the debit side, a fundamentally good sense of pace is disfigured by frequent large and unwarranted *rallentandi*. The singing overall lacks fluency, the orchestra sounds homespun; the chorus begins adequately but rhythmic insecurity and uncertainty of pitch soon raise their ugly heads. The harpsichord continuo, we are told, is improvised throughout; the number of inaccuracies makes this abundantly clear.

Sir Anthony Lewis's *Dido and Aeneas*, which first appeared in 1961, has much to commend it. A scholarly reading, it nevertheless wears its scholarship lightly and communicates a strong sense of atmosphere. The edition used is that by Thurston Dart, who provides an excellent harpsichord continuo, constantly helping to point the text, to add weight where necessary and to reveal the strength of Purcell's harmony.

Commentators have often remarked that there has never been an entirely

satisfactory recording of *Dido*, but throughout this first act, there is every
indication that this performance will realize that long-awaited ideal. Patricia
Clark draws a bright-toned, confident Belinda. The chorus is well drilled and
recorded and shows a welcome relish for Nahum Tate's maligned verses.
Lewis's innate feeling for the Purcellian style and for the theatre is everywhere in evidence. The score flows effortlessly from one number to the next.
Tempi and, significantly, pauses are all well judged. Dances are crisply and
tautly played.

Many of these qualities are present throughout the performance, reinforced by strong contributions from John Mitchinson (Sailor) and Raimund
Herincx (Aeneas). The latter creates a character of greater strength and
robustness than usual, producing a more bass than baritonal sound. The
sound itself, however, is placed too far back in the voice and is consequently
inclined to lack clarity.

Whatever the other merits of this performance, most collectors will seek
it for Janet Baker's Dido. It is a more eloquent reading than her later one
under Steuart Bedford. Her singing here is uncomplicated, unencumbered
and affecting. There is no trace of lugubriousness in either 'Ah Belinda' or
the Lament. The impression, paradoxical though it may seem, is of lightness
and yet great depth of emotion. Decorations flow naturally from the line;
every nuance of the text is observed and all is poise, shape and control. A
small point; the strict observance of Dart's quavers at 'Remember me'
(𝅘𝅥 | 𝅘𝅥 𝅘𝅥 𝅘𝅥) adds a pathetic, pleading quality to the phrase that no
other interpreter has ever quite matched.

Where, then, lies the drawback to this record? In a word – witches. If your
taste in witches is for grotesque distortion and the absurd, you will not object
to this travesty of Purcell's music. It is all the more unfortunate and incomprehensible in view of the success of other aspects of this performance. The
Sorceress, Monica Sinclair, slithers and snarls through her part, rarely resorting to conventional singing. She reduces her role to a figure of ridicule
– a Humperdinckian broomstick harridan. The choruses are just as absurd
with vowels and consonants relentlessly pulled out of shape ('Ham's our
delight'). The attendant witches are less objectionable; they perform with
zest, but without bluster or loss of impact.

In 1975 Janet Baker headed the cast in her second recording. Steuart
Bedford conducted, and the edition used was that by Benjamin Britten and
Imogen Holst. Sadly, the qualities outlined above in her 1962 recording are
no longer in evidence. In general her approach is more stately, her tone
more full-bottomed and her character so strong-willed and lacking in vulnerability as almost to preclude influence by Belinda and her attendants.
Given the expansive tempi set by Bedford for 'Ah Belinda' and 'When I am
laid in earth', it is not surprising that an oppressive vibrato creeps into the
voice in order to sustain the line. Sir Peter Pears is unhappily cast as Aeneas,
sounding more like an elderly restoration roué than a young virile Trojan

prince. All the intelligence and musicianship he can bring to bear cannot in this instance hide a fundamentally unsteady line and a pinched tone.

The Belinda of Norma Burrowes is an unqualified delight: 'Pursue thy conquest love' is wonderfully alert and 'Thanks to these lonesome vales' deliciously decorated. Felicity Lott's rendering of 'Oft she visits' should also not escape notice. Another positive feature is the manner in which the Sorceress and employees manage successfully to convey gleeful malice without unwarranted eccentricity. Anna Reynolds sounds most sinister, her words intelligently articulated. Felicity Palmer and Alfreda Hodgson provide well-contrasted support. Unfortunately someone decided on a boy treble False Spirit, an expedient with slight historical justification and one that is made even less satisfactory because of the stiff inadequacy of the boy chosen.

This being the Britten/Holst edition, the evil trio close Act 2, scene ii with music from *The Indian Queen* (1695), together with a chorus from the *Welcome Song* (1687) and a dance from *Sir Antony Love* (1690). The London Opera Chorus acquit themselves with distinction, the Aldeburgh Festival Strings with merit (The Triumphing Dance is a shade untidy). On the rostrum Steuart Bedford's approach is undeniably invigorating but, in comparison with Sir Anthony Lewis, less instinctive, and with Raymond Leppard (see below) less shapely. One or two of the tempi are somewhat relentless and clinical. There is a horrid 'tierce de picardie' in the harpsichord on the very last chord, actually written into the Britten/Holst score; it is symptomatic of some over-intrusive harpsichord figuration.

It would perhaps have been surprising if Alfred Deller had not conducted a recording of *Dido*. In 1965 one appeared. As a performer Deller had an intuitive grasp of the Purcellian style, but as a conductor (he would probably have admitted this himself in private) he was rarely able to communicate this affinity to colleagues. In a sense, therefore, it is no surprise that this is not a satisfactory performance, lacking dramatic and musical thrust. It falls down on too many fundamental details which Deller should have corrected. The orchestral playing is careless, the oversized chorus sings without strong rhythmic feeling, and many of the tempi are wrong-headed. 'To the hills and the vales' and 'When monarchs unite' are two examples of elephantine leaden-footedness; there is a nasty intrusive 'y' in tri-y-umph.

Mary Thomas simply does not possess the vocal armoury for Dido; her interpretation suffers from inept phrasing, lack of tonal variety and uncertain intonation. She too distorts her syllables – 'prest with torment' emerging mysteriously as 'rest with tormint'. The Sorceress, witches and evil spirits are appalling; Maurice Bevan's Aeneas is curiously dull and one-dimensional. Two bright spots are a pleasing, crisp Belinda from Honor Sheppard (in contrast to her First Witch) and a splendid Sailor from Robert Tear (he is also 'boozing' in Bedford's and Barbirolli's recordings), though it was not a happy notion to make him sing the Spirit as well, particularly since there is no additional music for the end of Act 2, scene ii to separate his two appearances.

Sir John Barbirolli was the next conductor to tackle Purcell's elusive score – a strange combination one might think, akin, say, to asking Elgar to conduct a Dufay mass. The resulting effort is predictably an amalgam of styles and ideas, a scholarly edition (by Neville Boyling based on a manuscript discovered at Tatton Park in the early sixties) complete with double dotting and ornamentation married to modern instruments and an expansive, languorous romantic interpretation. The adagio in the overture provides a hint of what is to come: sultry self-indulgence at the first sign of a slow tempo marking (here with some uncharacteristic lapses in string ensemble). Barbirolli, however, is alive to the rhythmic vitality inherent in the score and does inspire several felicitous moments – a particularly lilting 'Fear no danger' and a marvellously invigorating Triumphing Dance. But offset these against some extremely ponderous tempi elsewhere ('Cupid only throws the dart' and the opening of the Grove Scene) and one can sense the overall drawbacks of his interpretation. An unexpected bonus from the slow tempi is that we are allowed to relish to the full the colourful harpsichord continuo of Raymond Leppard, who busies himself filling out with great imagination the long spaces between beats.

Victoria de los Angeles is Dido, a reading of unusual warmth, sung with obvious relish. Unfortunately the sound itself is extremely plush, even lugubrious and the singer shows little understanding of a suitable style for the music. Line and intervals are unclean – appropriate in Canteloube but not here, and distortion of vowels makes for uncomfortable listening (another intrusive 'y', this time at 'When I yam laid').

The Aeneas, Peter Glossop, is one of the most successful on record, vividly capturing the bluff geniality of the character, rather out of his depth with temperamental queens and inconvenient spirits. His singing is strong and unmannered with only one obvious blemish, a damaging break in the phrase 'Let Dido smile and I'll defy – the feeble stroke of destiny'. The remainder of the cast is variable, an incisive Sorceress from Patricia Johnson (with only a few swooning portamenti) while her acolytes (witches and chorus) avoid undue crassness. There is a surprisingly dull Belinda from Heather Harper and a crisply articulated Sailor from the ubiquitous tar, Robert Tear. The False Spirit is taken most pungently by a mezzo (Sybil Michelow). The Ambrosian Singers perform with zest, but the resonant acoustic tends to obstruct clean textures. There is no added ending to Act 2, scene ii.

On paper, the recording issued on the Archiv label in 1967 looks promising, with an authoritative and sympathetic conductor in Sir Charles Mackerras, and a strong cast including Barry McDaniel, Sheila Armstrong, Patricia Johnson, Nigel Rogers and Tatiana Troyanos. The Hamburg Radio Chamber Orchestra and the Hamburg Monteverdi Choir are both much respected. Considerable thought has also gone into the edition used, basically that of Neville Boyling (as with Barbirolli) based on the Tatton Park manuscript, but incorporating various suggestions by Mackerras. In addition, the pair of dances with guitar together with the conclusion to Act 2, scene ii indicated in the original libretto are both included. (This is the only recording, apart from Andrew Parrott's, to include the guitar dances.) The music is arranged by Neville Boyling from other works by Purcell. Strange that it was not used on Barbirolli's record, but in the event, it proves curiously ineffective.

With this weight of scholarship allied to Mackerras's undoubted theatrical instinct, one might reasonably have expected great achievements. Expectations, however, are not all fulfilled, and the performance given sounds tired, well considered but dull and uninspired. It attempts a theatrical ambience but sounds undramatic, and, unforgivably, wears its scholarship like a weight around the neck. The vocal lines are heavily ornamented, but all too often the cast (Aeneas in particular) place them too self-consciously, failing to allow them to grow naturally from the music. Several of Mackerras's speeds are ill-judged (either choppy or too slow), and frequent *rallentandi* obliterate any sense of forward movement. Passages of recitative are especially prone to this.

Notwithstanding these stylistic reservations, some individual performances merit attention: Sheila Armstrong is an engaging Belinda. Patricia Johnson, making her second recording of the Sorceress, is just as imposing and incisive as with Barbirolli, and here she is assisted by an effective cavernous acoustic (for Act 2, scene i) and tempi that do not encourage intrusive *portamenti*. Other positive contributions come from Nigel Rogers as the Sailor and Paul Esswood as the Spirit.

By comparison with, say, Peter Glossop, Barry McDaniel is a sophisticated Aeneas, his tone silky and finely honed. Yet, aside from the question of ornamentation mentioned above, his approach seems cool and detached. The same criticism can be levelled at Tatiana Troyanos as Dido. The coolness is caused principally by lack of distinct diction. The voice itself is rich, languid and dusky, imbued with emotion certainly, but, as with so many Didos, the kind of emotion more commensurate with nineteenth-century operatic heroines. The exceptionally slow tempi for her two major arias do not help. Lack of clear diction is also a shortcoming of the Monteverdi Choir of Hamburg: theirs is altogether a disappointing effort, marred too by woolly tone and lapses in intonation and balance.

Troyanos also heads the cast in Raymond Leppard's 1977 performance, and her voice here is lent added weight and resonance by the acoustic and by the closeness of the recording. The result, however, is more successful because of Leppard's highly charged, dramatic approach and also because the performance style here is universally rich, whereas in Mackerras's version Troyanos sounded at musical odds with her colleagues. Her words are clearer this time and her encounters with Aeneas are electrifying. Robustness is the keynote of the work so far as Leppard is concerned. His full-blooded intentions are apparent from the outset. The overture is a summons to attention and from that moment on, whatever one's reservations about Leppard are, the excitement never slackens. One of Leppard's great merits is his preoccupation with rhythm; this is everywhere apparent, from the ebb and flow of the recitative to the dances and choruses, which are full of spring and vitality. The orchestral playing throughout is first rate. A few tempi do appear odd: a curiously plodding 'When monarchs unite', a sluggish 'Harm's our delight', and a very sedate 'Cupid only throws the dart'.

Not for the first time the infernal members of the cast conjure up problems. The opening to Act 2, scene i is chilling and the Sorceress (Patricia Kern) characterful without being hammy, but also without ever suggesting the venom that Patricia Johnson brought to her readings. By contrast, the attendant witches are frightfully South Kensington. Felicity Palmer (Belinda) suffers by comparison with Sheila Armstrong in purity of tone, but is otherwise an asset. Richard Stilwell is a sturdy, robust Aeneas, but in his big conscience scene at the end of Act 2, scene ii, he lacks control. Perhaps he was put off by the sudden appearance of a chamber organ to accompany the Spirit (Alfreda Hodgson). Philip Langridge is a somewhat strait-laced Sailor. The edition Leppard uses is not specified; there is no conclusion to Act 2 but we do get stylish double dotting, *appoggiatura* and ample extra decorations (though not as many as in Mackerras).

Immense vitality and musicianship are two qualities we might also expect to find in the *Dido* conducted by Sir Colin Davis. Expectations are this time fulfilled and this proves in many ways a comparable performance to that of Leppard. There is polished orchestral playing from the Academy of St Martin-in-the-Fields and especially polished singing from the John Alldis Choir, though how an entire string band in Purcell's day could have extemporized or even planned ornamentation with the mathematical precision and unanimity shown here is beyond me. John Constable provides a lively harpsichord continuo, but errs on the fidgety side.

Once again the cast is variable. Josephine Veasey makes no strong impression as Dido. She conveys nobility but ultimately seems wooden and impersonal. Her large voice lacks the flexibility for the recitatives and tends to spread uncomfortably (for example in the Lament). By contrast there are two fine characterizations from John Shirley-Quirk (Aeneas) and Helen Donath (Belinda). Donath is captivating, producing a delectable, clean, personal tone and showing a lively, positive response to her words. Elizabeth Bainbridge is a formidable Sorceress, backed up by two attendant witches clearly trained in the same coven.

Delia Wallis provides a pleasantly limpid 'Oft she visits' but Frank Patterson is a thin-voiced Sailor, and Thomas Allen is bizarrely cast as the False Spirit. Of all the options available this is the least appropriate, for the obvious reason that a baritone spirit removes any tonal contrast for the one scene in which he appears, the scene with Aeneas. Once again no conclusion is added for this scene. The edition approximates to Dart.

All in all this constitutes an unsatisfactory list of complete recordings despite individual achievements. One might have thought that music so vivid, and yet so comparatively simple from the technical viewpoint, would not prove an obstacle for the world's great musicians. Perhaps, however, therein lies the problem: too many conductors and singers are not prepared to allow the music to speak for itself.

The very nature of *Dido and Aeneas* precludes a substantial discography of excerpts. Of those that do exist, few have much to recommend them. In the orchestral field the Philadelphia Orchestra under Ormandy have left a 'Dido Suite' (arr. Caillet) on HMV DB 3975/6. This is at best interesting for its curiosity value; the arrangement makes Stokowski sound like the last word in authenticity. A more modern recording of orchestral music from *Dido* emanates from the English Chamber Orchestra under José-Luis Garcia (CBS 76719). The playing is crisp and elegant with the exception of a Triumphing Dance that neither sounds triumphant nor like a dance.

The only other excerpt apart from a collection of Laments seems to be the Sorceress's opening soliloquy sung by Edith Coates (HMV C 3447; HLM 7145), but this is taken from the complete recording conducted by Lambert.

Naturally, there have been several attempts at Dido's Lament, one or two of which will raise an eyebrow. The treble Michael Deacon Barrow (Abbey E 7612) gives a cultured reading remarkable for its bell-like clarity, but for obvious reasons this is an unsatisfactory piece for a boy soprano. It is more unsatisfactory for a tenor, though this fact seems to have escaped the notice of Kenneth McKellar (Decca SKL 5118); he adds insult to injury by maintaining throughout a stentorian *mezzo forte*, and by omitting the top E flat on 'may *my* wrongs create'. The prize for the strangest account goes to the Swingle Singers and The Modern Jazz Quartet (Contour 6870 516). Their sound is appealing in its way, but the original is to be preferred.

Practically all the more conventional recordings have been made by singers deeply rooted in the Grand Opera tradition. Maggie Teyte (BBC Artium REGL 369) gives a characteristic performance, but is fundamentally unsuited to repertory of this kind. Hilde Zadek (Philips A 00288) displays clarity of tone and a sustained line, but restraint is absent from the top notes. A distinctly fruity not to say unsteady contralto tone is a feature of Edna Thornton's recording (D 533; HLM 7145) transposed into F minor.

In E minor we have the contralto Karin Branzell (Rococo 5214) together with a Hollywood-style orchestral accompaniment including harp. Branzell's performance is very slow and luxuriantly upholstered. Another museum-piece comes from Marian Anderson (DB 6019) in E minor with piano accompaniment. She is probably not everyone's choice for Dido, but the voice itself is moving and she does convey well a profound, almost spiritual solemnity. By contrast Leila Megane (D 1567) in F minor is hard-edged and coarse; she phrases carelessly and pulls the rhythm around. The same faults, plus uncertain intonation, mar the recording of Blanche Marchesi (HMV JH 9).

A more recent artist, the Canadian Maureen Forrester (SXLP 20096), is altogether more successful. Despite the fact that she is a contralto, her singing of the Lament is light and her response to the words delicate. The preceding recitative has a good forward flow and the phrasing throughout is controlled and finely shaped. There is sympathetic accompaniment from the Vienna State Opera Orchestra conducted by Robert Zeller, and the closing chorus is provided by the Vienna Academy Chamber Choir.

The soprano Elsie Suddaby (E 354) indulges in rather too much *rubato* and *portamento*, but her small-scale pure voice is undeniably affecting. Olga Haley (Parlo. E 11121) is undistinguished. There is no steady rhythmic pulse either from her or the orchestra (a saccharine arrangement) resulting in lack of cohesion. The words and the vocal line are also altered – Haley goes down the octave at 'Remember me'. The music is barely recognizable as Purcell. Of substantially greater distinction is Kirsten Flagstad's performance (1C 14701492). This is an undeniably poignant interpretation matching her complete performance on World Records; it shows similar qualities of dignity and poise. Another fine artist unsuited to this music but who also gives a typically controlled, thoughtful account is Suzanne Danco (LXT 2557). Her tempo is very slow and she includes the preceding recitative. Among present day singers only Leontyne Price has recorded the aria separately (SER 5549). She also includes the recitative. Her performance is in the grand style and is encased in a rich cocoon of string sound; the great virtue of this record is the restraint Price shows at the climax to the aria, a restraint which adds immeasurably to the emotional effect.

I began with the recordings by Joel Cohen and Andrew Parrott, and have not often compared them to others since they do in a sense stand apart from the others. They are not perfect, but surely stimulating enough to inspire more performances from some of our other distinguished early music ensembles. Because of the nature of the piece, it is not a useful exercise to choose an ideal Dido cast, but it is worth observing that there cannot be many operas in which the leading roles can be sung by, in Dido's case, anyone from a contralto to a soprano, and in Aeneas's case, from a tenor to a bass-baritone. The decision for Aeneas's is not crucial, but Dido I am convinced is ideally a soprano role and yet all too few sopranos have been, or are, numbered among its exponents.

DIDO AND AENEAS

D Dido; *A* Aeneas; *B* Belinda; *AW* Attendant Woman; *S* Sorceress; *FW* First Witch; *SW* Second Witch; *Sp* Spirit; *Sa* Sailor

1936 N. Evans *D*; Henderson *A*; Hamlin *B*; Currie *AW*; *SW*; Jarred *S*; Catley *FW*; Dyer *Sp*; Northcote *Sa*/A Capella Singers, Boyd Neel String Orch./Raybould Decca X101–7*

1945 Hammond *D*; Noble *A*; Baillie *B*; Fullerton *AW*; Coates *S*; Hobson *FW*; Ripley *SW*; Patriss *Sp*; T. Jones *Sa*/chorus, Philharmonia/ Lambert HMV C3471–7*

1952 Flagstad *D*; Hemsley *A*; Schwarzkopf *B*; *Sp*; McNab *AW*; Mandikian *S*; Rex *FW*; Pollak *SW*; D. Lloyd *Sa*/Mermaid Singers and Orch./G. Jones World Records ⓜ SH117 Seraphim ⓜ M60346

1952 Houston *D*; Cummings *A*; Leigh

B; McKerrow *AW*; Cuthill *S*;
Harper *FW*; Clarke *SW*;
McCarthy *Sp*; *Sa*/Stuart Chorus
and CO/Gregory (actual name
John Bath)
Nixa-Period ⑩ PLP546

1961 Baker *D*; Herincx *A*; P. Clark *B*;
Poulter *AW;* M. Sinclair *S*; R.
James *FW*; Wilson *SW*; Dorow
Sp; Mitchinson *Sa*/St Anthony
Singers, ECO/Lewis
L'Oiseau-Lyre SOL60047

1964 M. Thomas *D*; Bevan *A*;
Sheppard *B*; *AW*; *FW*; Watts *S*;
Dales *SW*; Tear *Sp*; *Sa*/Oriana
Chorus and Orch./Deller
Vanguard (UK) HM46
(US) HM46 or S276

1965 De los Angeles *D*; Glossop *A*;
Harper *B*; Robson *AW*; Johnson
S; Walmesley *FW*; Michelow *SW*;
Sp; Tear *Sa*/Ambrosian Singers,
ECO/Barbirolli
HMV CFP40359 ④ TC-CFP40359
Angel S-36359

1967 Troyanos *D*; McDaniel *A*;
Armstrong *B*; Baker-Genovesi
AW; *FW*; Johnson *S*, Lensky *SW*;
Esswood *Sp*; Rogers *Sa*/Hamburg
Monteverdi Choir, Hamburg
Radio CO/Mackerras
DG 2547 032 ④ 3347 032

1970 Veasey *D*; Shirley-Quirk *A*;
Donath *B*; Wallis *AW*; *FW*;
Bainbridge *S*; Knight *SW*; Allen
Sp; Patterson *Sa*/Alldis Choir,

ASMF/Davis
Philips 6500 131

1975 Baker *D*; Pears *A*; Burrowes *B*;
Lott *AW*; Reynolds *S*; Palmer
FW; Hodgson *SW*; Everett *Sp*;
Tear *Sa*/London Opera Chorus,
Aldeburgh Festival Strings/
Bedford
Decca SET615 ④ KCET615
London OSA1170 ④ OSA5–1170

1977 Troyanos *D*; Stilwell *A*; Palmer *B*;
Gale *AW*; Hodgson *FW*; *Sp*; Kern
S; Maxwell *SW*; Langridge *Sa*/
English Chamber Choir and
Orch./Leppard
Erato STU71091
RCA (US) ARL1–3021

1978 (in Russian) Gorokhovskaya *D*;
Kaloshin *A*; Kozyreva *B*; Vainer
S/Leningrad Chamber Choir and
Orch.
Melodiya S10–09693–5 (3 sides)

1979 Fortunato *D*; M. Baker *A*; N.
Armstrong *B*; R. Anderson *AW*;
Fithian *S*; Gordon *FW*; Klebanow
SW; Fitch *Sp*; Cohen *Sa*/Boston
Camerata/Cohen
Harmonia Mundi HM10067

1980 Kirkby *D*; Thomas *A*; Nelson *B*;
Rees *AW*; Noorman *S*; Van Evera
FW; R. Bevan *SW*; *SA*; Bonner
SP/Taverner Choir and Players/A.
Parrott
Chandos ABRD1034 ④
ABTD1034

The Operas of Handel

STANLEY SADIE

Not so very long ago, Handel's operas were reckoned virtually unperform-able: because they were so long and so undramatic, and because no one dared attempt to sing them.

Since those days a great deal has changed. First, our ideas on musical drama have broadened to admit of the stylized nature of eighteenth-century *opera seria*; some writers have tended to laud Handel largely for his depar-tures from the patterns favoured in his times, but such an approach, based on historical hindsight and Romantic principles of music drama, overstresses particular kinds of originality and plays down what was central to Handel and his contemporaries – the capacity to write attractive, varied, dramatic music within the established framework. Second, our singers have extended their techniques. The *fioriture* demanded in *Giulio Cesare* or *Alcina* are actually no more difficult than some of those in *Messiah*, which singers of various levels of accomplishment have been managing without undue trouble for close on an unbroken 250 years. True, an opera singer is required to imbue such material with dramatic life, which is another question. And if he is to realize the music satisfactorily he should, in most arias, be able to embellish the music, especially in the repeated sections of da capo arias. Nowadays an increasing number of singers can cope with the technical aspects of Handel's vocal writing, and many are ready to add decoration themselves or to sing what a conductor or musicologist puts before them; that the results are not always happy, for technical or stylistic reasons, is only to be expected at this stage. After all, there were lapses of taste in Handel's time, too.

Until quite recently, the length of Handel's operas has been regarded as a problem. Record companies have been reluctant to allow them to spread over more than three discs; some have even confined recordings to two discs or just one, producing little more than series of excerpts. It may once have been true to suggest – for the arguments are usually presented this way rather than in terms of economics – that the operas, if given in full, are beyond the patience of a modern audience: so they are, at the sluggish tempi and with the ponderous recitatives once favoured. But livelier modern performances have begun to show otherwise. Most Handel operas play for between three and three and a quarter hours if given in full (*Giulio Cesare* is nearer three and a half, *Imeneo* only two and a half). None need take more than four discs, and for many seven sides would serve (the odd one could be used for alternative or rejected numbers). The recent five-disc *Admeto*, taken rather slowly, lasts barely more than three and a half hours.

The ways of cutting are various. Handel's own excisions are a dubious guide, as often they were made only for practical exigencies, like a singer's absence or inadequacy. One modern philosophy is that the plot must be left intact, so that cutting is restricted to the arias. The antithetic view is that, as we revive Handel's operas solely because of their musical quality, the recitatives should suffer the heaviest cutting; but clearly they must not be cut so much as to destroy the sense of the work. Most performances try for some sort of compromise: omitting inessential stretches of recitative and arias of less interest (though opinions may differ as to which are interesting). Sometimes Handelian precedent may be found for cuts, which makes the choice easier. Many recordings, especially earlier ones, make cuts within arias. Most of Handel's arias are in A-B-A (or da capo) form; some performers are content to drop the final A section, which is never justifiable because it leaves the singer in the wrong key and usually with the wrong sense in his final utterance; better to drop both B and A sections than that. Occasionally even the orchestral ritornello is omitted, so that the music stops, disconcertingly, in a foreign key. The desirability of keeping the whole of each aria should be stressed: da capo sections are of prime importance not only because they restore the original mood (or 'affect', as Handel's contemporaries would have said) but also because they give the singer a chance to display his virtuosity in the addition of ornamentation, to show how he could make the music more brilliant and more expressive. If it comes to that, no aria should be omitted either, in an ideal world, for the concept of characterization in this period, in so far as it existed at all, resides in the diversity of the music assigned to the character. But there is no denying that a Handel opera given in the theatre *in extenso* – granted our concentrated, attentive way of listening, which is far from how Handel's audiences listened – seems very long indeed. Such considerations do not of course apply to recordings, but equally troublesome economic ones, regrettably, do.

There is a further difficulty about performing Handel's operas that all but ruled them out for the last generation: the castrato parts. Virtually all the heroic roles in Handel's operas are intended for the high voice, occasionally for women in travesty but much more often for the high male voice – more for the alto-pitch singer Senesino than anyone else – though some in the later operas were nearer mezzo range, like those for Carestini or Caffarelli, or even at soprano pitch like those for Conti. In Germany, where the Handel opera revival began, in the 1920s, the 'solution' has nearly always been to transpose these parts down an octave and assign them to a man's voice, usually a baritone. This was a procedure that Handel himself never countenanced if a part was to be vocally reassigned (he would normally rewrite the music – though there are a few instances of a soprano-pitch aria being little

altered for a tenor) and it does such violence to the musical texture that
Handelians here have found it impossible to accept. Handel's style of writing
for the castrato voice is entirely different from his baritone writing, in its
melodic usage, its floridity, its relationship to the harmonic bass and so on.
The music thus transposed sounds at odds with itself, texturally confused,
limited in expressive potential and certainly never heroic. The German tradition finds it hard to accept a woman in a male role, or (for different reasons)
a counter-tenor; in Britain and, more recently, in the United States, this has
been the preferred solution. Arguments based on dramatic plausibility have
come to carry less weight as the understanding of, and sympathy with historical ideas of musical drama have developed. It is true that few women can
bring to this music the power and the weight that, for example, led Charles
Burney to talk of Senesino's 'thundering out' the divisions. But since we
revive Handel's operas above all for their music, it would seem sensible to
sing it at its proper pitch, not to distort it with downward transpositions.

What is a Handel opera? The definition strictly comprehends those works
written, in his youth in Germany and Italy and later exclusively in London,
for performance on the stage. These works make up the bulk of the material
considered in the following pages. But there are good reasons for extending
the definition for the purposes of the present chapter. Handel composed a
number of works in England which are essentially of a dramatic character
but were not actually designed for staging. Some of the oratorios fall into
that bracket (they have no place here, however) but there exist three fine
secular works that ought not to be excluded. One is a masque or a pastoral
drama (it has been described in numerous ways) – *Acis and Galatea*, which
may possibly have been given some kind of dramatic or semi-dramatic performance when it was first sung or at its early revivals. The others are *Semele*,
which was composed to a text headed 'An Opera' by its author, William
Congreve, and *Hercules*, a 'Musical Drama' according to its original libretto.
Accordingly these three works, all of which have been staged in modern
times, are discussed together with the Italian works.

Handel's Italian operas fall into three chronological groups. The first consists
of those operas he wrote before he came to London and the earliest London
works; the second is made up of the operas composed in the period 1720–28
for the London organization, the Royal Academy of Music; and the last
includes the operas that followed the collapse of the Academy in 1729 and
Handel's final disenchantment in 1741 with the promotion of opera in
London.

Most of the music of Handel's early German operas composed for the
opera house in Hamburg (where he played the violin or the harpsichord as
a youth) is lost. Only the earliest one, *Almira*, survives. Some of the dances
from this score, including music that in revised forms turns up in later Handel
works, are recorded on a disc 'Early German Opera from the Goosemarket'
(EMI/Electrola, 1C 037 45570); the Berlin Philharmonic under Wilhelm

Brückner-Rüggeberg play them solemnly and with some adjusted orchestration, including some sensuous harp continuo parts. Of Handel's earlier opera for Italy, *Rodrigo* (as it is generally called; its proper name is *Vincer se stesso è la maggior vittoria*), only the dance music has been recorded, by Anthony Lewis and the Philomusica on the very first stereo disc from L'Oiseau-Lyre (SOL 60001), sturdily done if not actually heavy-footed, then more vigorously by the Hallé and Barbirolli in a harsh-sounding Handel selection from Pye (CCL 30149). Neither quite respects Handel's orchestration (a complaint likely to become an *ostinato* in this survey, for conductors and arrangers seem to regard this most professional of composers as an unsatisfactory orchestrator: a commentary more on their own stylistic understanding than on Handel). More recently the *Rodrigo* dances have turned up on a Hungaroton record (HLX 90018), including for the first time the fine Passacaille, in performances by the Budapest Philharmonic under Miklos Erdelyi, more authentic in orchestration if not in general style.

Rodrigo was written for a Florentine academy in 1707; Handel's second opera for Italy, *Agrippina*, was written two years later, for Venice, and was his first great opera-house success. It has had several revivals this century, but awaits a recording; all we have on records is one side of an American Cambridge disc by Carole Bogard offering four of the arias for the title role (coupled with the cantata *Agrippina*, dealing with a quite different episode in the life of that deplorable Roman lady). Her singing is light, spirited and stylish, but here and there a shade insecure, and certainly not packing the dramatic punch needed for the big scene 'Pensieri, voi mi tormentate'; though the waltz-like final song is charmingly done. Miss Bogard includes another *Agrippina* aria, one from Poppaea's role, in her recital disc referred to below; Fischer-Dieskau offers an aria on his.

Handel's first London opera was *Rinaldo*. He had to write it in some haste and, understandably, he included in it several numbers from works he had written in Italy. This use of earlier music opens it up to criticism as musical drama, at least according to most present-day canons of taste and aesthetic propriety, but that need trouble the modern listener no more than it did the Londoners of 1711 – it could in fact be argued that it was the success of *Rinaldo* that laid the foundations for the continuance to our own day of foreign-language operas in London. Be that as it may, *Rinaldo* is full to overflowing with fine music; one effective number follows another in this lavish score. There has however been only a single complete recording, made by the French early music specialist Jean-Claude Malgoire with his group La Grande Ecurie et la Chambre du Roi. The first thing to say about this set is that, although it has many of the appurtenances of authenticity, it falls some way short in terms of sheer understanding of the style. Tempi are eccentric (usually on the fast side), phrasing is exaggeratedly detached, ornamentation is overdone and haphazard, and the ensemble and intonation of the orchestra would barely pass muster in ordinary professional circles. One senses Handel being frenchified, with mincing rhythms and inappropriate *notes inégales*.

There is nevertheless a lot to enjoy; Malgoire obviously relishes the music and directs with great spirit, and he does have a good cast. The title role is sung by Carolyn Watkinson, a strong mezzo, capable of conveying passion without transgressing the stylistic limits, and sure in the semiquaver divisions. Jeanette Scovotti, in the demanding role of Armida, is likewise precise and impassioned (regrettably, her aria at the end of Act 2 is shorn of its da capo). The other main soprano role, Almirena, is sung by Ileana Cotrubas, soft-toned and feminine, charming in the famous bird song, touching in the still more famous 'Lascia ch'io pianga', vivacious of manner, sweet of phrase. Paul Esswood draws a pure, clear line in the second castrato role, Goffredo, and as Argantes, the villainous King of Jerusalem, Ulrik Cold shows that Handel's big bass parts can sound fiery without bellowing or smudging of the line. The text followed is basically that of the 1711 version (Handel made many revisions for revivals) except for the small role of the Christian magician which is sung at bass pitch as in 1731.

The only other *Rinaldo* recording is an excerpt disc issued in the USA by RCA (ARL 1–0084), with the Vienna Volksoper Orchestra under the enthusiastic American Handelian Stephen Simon. These are sound performances of a selection of arresting numbers, distinguished by Rita Shane's dramatic Armida and Arleen Augér's graceful Almirena; but Beverly Wolff makes rather a meal of 'Cara sposa' and Raymond Michalski is a gruff Argantes.

Handel's second London opera, *Il pastor fido* (1712), is altogether a less grand affair – it belongs to the pastoral tradition, of course, and deals with the loves of nymphs and shepherds. The only 'complete' recording, by Cetra, is woefully incomplete. It includes the entire six-movement overture, which occupies almost a whole side; but in Act 1 three of the eight arias are omitted, in Act 2 four of the nine, and in Act 3 – unbelievably – six out of six and even the one duet (leaving only two brief sinfonias and a chorus besides the recitative). This is farcical: the overture could easily have been shortened and the recitative, though it is not badly done, could profitably have been speeded up. Better still, of course, to have let the set run to a third disc; there seems precious little point in reviving a Handel opera if more than half the arias are to be left out. Of the cast, drawn from I Commedianti in Musica della Cetra, I would mention the generally spirited if not specially characterful contributions of the three principals, Dora Gatta, Irma Bozzi Lucca and Cecilia Fusco, and the excellence of Anna Reynolds in the male role of Silvio. I was agreeably surprised to hear so many correct recitative *appoggiature* in a recording dating back to the late 1950s, less surprised to hear so much heavy 16-foot harpsichord tone. The conductor, Ennio Gerelli, favours slowish tempi and generous *rallentandi*, and must bear chief responsibility for the silliness of the cutting, not to mention the removal of two da capo sections. A few of the missing numbers (one aria in Act 2, three and the duet in Act 3) can be heard on a single-disc version from American Columbia, dating from the early 1950s, the days when one could still use piano continuo. The performances however are only just adequate to give an idea of the music; and, there is not a word on the sleeve to make clear that this is anything other than the entire work (it is about one-third of it).

Of Handel's other three pre-Royal Academy operas, nothing at all has been recorded from *Silla* or *Teseo*, the latter's overture apart, but excerpts from *Amadigi* are to be found on a EMI/Electrola disc (1C 037–45578) featuring music connected with Hanover ('Eine festliche soirée in Herren-hausen') – the connection is fairly slender, for *Amadigi* was not performed there. They consist of a short trumpet sinfonia, one aria for Dardano (Ursula Terhoeven) and three for Melissa (Teresa Zylis-Gara, in fine, brilliant voice). These are some of the strongest pieces from this admirable score, well and directly done under Fritz Lebhan (though one da capo is damagingly omitted).

One of my most curious experiences as a Handelian was in 1959, when I went to Halle, Handel's native city, to attend a congress and a series of performances to commemorate the bicentenary of his death. In the mornings, scholars discussed the correct historical ways of performing his music, the operas in particular; in the evenings, we heard the operas performed – in ways that violated almost every principle of authentic style. The morning sessions might as well not have happened for all the effect they had on the evenings. Two sets of discs originating from the stagings of Halle – which has naturally been one of the centres (in fact the main East German one) of the Handel opera revival – have been issued. In discussing Halle recordings it is, I think, important to understand the rather different context for per-formances in East Germany as compared with the West. Art in East Germany has to have a social purpose, and performances have to be directed at a wide audience; accordingly one finds strong emphasis on the plot, in particular on the opposition of good (young, progressive, freedom-loving) and evil (old, conservative, repressive). The operas are all given in German, and the recitative, which carries the story, is declaimed with much deliberation and weight, at a ponderous pace; and the characterization will seem exaggerated to a westerner, with much of ranting and of whispering and even actual speaking.

The two Halle sets give *Poro*, to be discussed below, and *Radamisto*, the first of Handel's Academy operas, dating from early 1720. Handel revised the opera late in 1720 for a partly different team of singers, writing many new arias and transposing others. The later version serves as a basis for the Eterna recording; but it is not as simple as that for, reluctant to omit some of the fine pieces Handel replaced, they throw them in too, in different contexts. And further they leave out some half-dozen items, mostly in the last act, although the set runs to four discs. There are several respects in which Handel's intentions are set aside to make what somebody in Halle regards as a more satisfactory piece of music drama. First, it is sung in

German. Second, all the high male roles are put down an octave. Radamisto was originally written for a female soprano, then adjusted for a male alto (Senesino, his first Handel role); here it is sung by a baritone, Hellmuth Kaphan. This is musically disastrous, for the music is conceived in terms that make it essential for the voice to ring out above the bass line, whereas here it constantly gets tangled with it. The heroic effect is altogether lost; and the duet with Zenobia, instead of the amorous, mellifluous ring of two high voices, has an ugly chasm between her soprano and his baritone (with the music interchanged compared with the original). Tigrane's part, written for a male at soprano pitch, is sung by a tenor – not badly, for Rolf Apreck does some of the role (notably his tender first aria, 'L'ingrato non amar') intelligently and musically, but the music is still misrepresented. Then Tiridate's part, written first for a tenor and then rewritten for a bass, is sung by a bass (the unsatisfactory Günther Leib); but some of the tenor music is included, duly transposed. Third, Handel's orchestration is subject to wholesale revision, with inner string parts constantly added to fill out the texture; one longs to get away from this warm bath of sound into the more spare world of harpsichord continuo accompaniment. Where Handel provides a single line for the violins, the editors, with misguided zeal, stuff in a second violin and viola accompaniment to flesh things out – and thereby destroy the clear and brilliant effect Handel sought. In one aria new horn parts are added. Finally, there is scarcely a note of added ornamentation throughout these four discs, even though the da capos are religiously included. The bright spots in the set are the two sopranos, Hanne-Lore Kuhse (Polissena) and Sigrid Kehl (Zenobia), both of whom sound well and cope ably with their music even if they do not excel in the expression of passion or anguish. The bass Farasmene is sung, a shade coarsely, by Reiner Süss; it is at least good to hear Handel's true bass textures for one of the three basses! Horst-Tanu Margraf, though he must be partly responsible for the vicissitudes this poor opera has to suffer, at least conducts with good discipline and in the main at well-judged speeds.

Handel's next three operas, *Floridante*, *Ottone* and *Flavio*, still await recordings; but then follows the most recorded of them all, *Giulio Cesare*, which owes its popularity – in Handel's time as well as today – partly to the familiarity of the story and partly to the sheer excellence of the music. There are two recordings dating back to the early days of LP, at the beginning of the 1950s: one from the Handel Society, an American organization, conducted by Walter Goehr, the other from Vienna, under Hans Swarowsky. Both occupy only two records, and so are heavily cut; in a sense these sets are merely large collections of excerpts. Both are in the original Italian; both use octave transpositions for the high male parts, which means a baritone Julius Caesar, a bass Ptolemy, and a tenor Sextus – Handel himself used a tenor Sextus at revivals, but he rewrote the music, and to have a tenor sing the music composed for soprano is to make the worst of the situation. All this means that the heroic air of Caesar's music is lost, and the craftiness implicit in the alto music for Ptolemy becomes something quite different – the kind of blunt, rough-edged evil that Handel gives his bass villains, who are usually military men or despots. The change for Sextus matters somewhat less, though Handel seems to have intended the soprano of the first version to be a youngster, perhaps in his mid-teens (he is the son of the dead Pompey), whereas the music composed for the tenor version implies a more mature character.

The big difference between these versions is that the Handel Society is a digest of the opera, with twenty items (many shorn of their middle sections and da capos), all connected by recitative, whereas the Vox makes no pretence at telling the opera's story and simply presents its lyrical items, twenty of them, independently. Almost all are done complete. But two are misplaced; perhaps someone got some tape tangled, for there seems to be no other reason. The choice of numbers is broadly the same; neither has much vocal distinction. The most stylish contribution comes from the tenor Herbert Handt, Sextus on the Vox, an elegant singer who adds a few discreet graces (which is more than anyone else does). The Caesar on the Handel Society set, Sandoz, however, sings musically, and so does the Cleopatra, Gähwiller, even if she is lightweight. The Vox Cleopatra, Elisabeth Roon, is also slender for the role, and her two deeply tragic arias, 'Per pietà' and 'Piangerò', are both done far too fast to carry real emotional weight; but in general both conductors do a fair job, considering the state of Handel performance in the early 1950s; the orchestral playing, inevitably, sounds too richly sustained by today's standards.

Three further recordings have stronger claims to completeness. The first of these, a 'private' version of a Rome performance in 1955, gives – as far as one can hear it – a fairly corrupt text, with cuts and interpolations from other Handel works, and all the high parts are down an octave. There is, however, a good deal to relish in Boris Christoff's grand and fiery Caesar, and Onelia Fineschi is not unimpressive as Cleopatra; but no Handelian will much enjoy Fedora Barbieri and Franco Corelli sobbing their way through the farewell duet for Cornelia and Sextus. The other two versions are the 1967 RCA set under Julius Rudel, based on the New York City Opera performances, and a DG set under Karl Richter, from Munich. These sets represent antithetic approaches. Richter is literal to a degree: he follows precisely the text in the Händel-Gesellschaft score (as good a basis as most), cutting nothing, decorating nothing, never making a conventional rhythmic adjustment of the kind Handel took for granted (like double-dotting in the overture); just occasionally the singers, as if by accident, introduce the odd *appoggiatura*. The recitatives are sung slowly and earnestly, irrespective of meaning or dramatic urgency, and are weighed down by a double bass. Except in the instrumental music, which Richter tends to push along, the tempi are mostly ponderous. All the high male parts are sung an octave down (even that for Cleopatra's eunuch!), which means that seventeen arias are at low pitch – the opera becomes a dark-toned, gloomy work instead of the brilliant one Handel composed. The dazzling *coloratura* writing turns into a dark brown baritonal mud-bath, with voice and instruments confusingly mingled; and once again the duets are changed in nature, the sweet-sounding thirds and sixths giving way to gaping tenths and thirteenths.

As far as the actual singers are concerned, this must be one of the most talented teams ever to have recorded a Handel opera, but the talents are woefully misapplied. Dietrich Fischer-Dieskau is cast in the title role, where he impresses in the two great accompanied recitatives, especially the apostrophe of Pompey at his tomb, but he over-characterizes, over-interprets several of the arias in a way that is at odds with their mode of expression, and he can do nothing to make the semiquaver divisions sound other than absurd. Franz Crass, as Ptolemy, fares still worse: dull, flat-toned, unsure in intonation, weak in Italian pronunciation. Peter Schreier makes an unheroic Sextus, lacking in youthful impetuosity. Best of the men – not surprisingly, as the only one singing at the right pitch – is Gerold Schramm as Achillas. Of the women, Julia Hamari sings cleanly but a shade blandly as Cornelia; Tatiana Troyanos does Cleopatra's two tragic scenes splendidly, but otherwise is a disappointment – assured singing, but an ice-cold characterization. Nothing of the joy or the sensuality comes through of a character whose sexuality and ambition are the principal motive forces of the opera.

The RCA has more life, of a sort, but the opera is terribly distorted. I object less to the cutting – although there is far too much of it, and it often damages the integral musical forms, which is hard to excuse – or even to the insertion of music from another work (*Il Parnasso in festa*, written ten years later), than to the re-ordering. For example, Cleopatra's magnificent lament when she thinks Caesar dead is inexplicably shifted to Act 1, when they first meet, where it makes no kind of sense; and their final love duet is moved to Act 2, so that they rejoice in their loving reunion before they have fallen in love or been separated – and when she is still disguised as a serving-maid, Lydia. Then again we have low voices in two castrato parts: Norman Treigle a ponderous, fuzzy Caesar, Spiro Malas clearer as Ptolemy. Sextus is done at the original pitch, by Beverly Wolff, ably but not in the least boyishly. The Cornelia is Maureen Forrester, a warm, romantic singer with a generous vibrato for Handel but a real sense of line. Opinions are divided over Beverly Sills's Cleopatra; I find it a compelling performance, clear and agile, with a certain frailty of line that is in its way alluring, and with a quiet intensity in the slow arias that makes them very touching. Rudel conducts the opera in romantic fashion, with slow tempi and generous *rallentandi*. He has also provided decoration, and that is one of the disasters, for he is not content to ornament the music but instead often rewrites the line – even to the extent that the orchestral music needs rewriting too, and here and there he 'improves' the scoring. It is hard to know whether Richter's piety or Rudel's liberties serve Handel worse. What is sure is that a new, more faithful recording of this masterpiece is needed.

There have been some excerpt discs of *Giulio Cesare*. On Deutsche Grammophon (SLPM 138 637), Irmgard Seefried and Fischer-Dieskau recorded some of the best music for Cleopatra and Caesar under Karl Böhm; she is accurate, clean and decidedly cool, he at his most controlled and sensitive. Lisa della Casa recorded five of Cleopatra's arias, regrettably in German, on Decca (LXT 5277); they are beautifully sung, with much warmth and a good deal of style, with the Vienna Philharmonic under Hollreiser. Finally, there is another Decca record (SDD 213), primarily of Joan Sutherland as Cleopatra – some marvellous singing, agile, a bit short of consonants, economical on vowels too. She does six arias, and the supporting artists (Elkins, Horne, Sinclair, Conrad) provide five more. But it should be added that the conducting (by Richard Bonynge) is flabby, that four of the eleven arias are much cut, and that there is a lot of heavy and inept ornamentation.

Giulio Cesare inaugurated, in 1723, a series of superb heroic operas, of which the next were *Tamerlano, Rodelinda* and *Scipione*. I wish there were a recording of *Giulio Cesare* half as stylish as the single one of *Tamerlano*. This one was made in Copenhagen, chiefly with American artists. *Tamerlano* deals with the fate of the Ottoman ruler Bajazet and his daughter Asteria in captivity at the court of the Tartar Tamerlane; it is unusual in that there is an important, semi-heroic tenor role – at this period tenors were generally assigned only parts for elderly men. Other features are the fine chain of short numbers that provide an Act 2 curtain of exceptional dramatic power, and the suicide scene for Bajazet at the end of the opera. These discs give a good, if not thrilling, account of it. John Moriarty directs soundly, if without quite the desirable dramatic vitality; unlike the conductor of any set mentioned so far, he has the cadence at the end of each line of recitative elided with the voice, which is correct performing practice and keeps the dialogue moving properly. There are some excellent singers, chief among them Alexander Young, who sings Bajazet's music with due style and character, nicely catching the captive king's inordinate pride and his nobility. As Asteria Carole Bogard sings lightly and brightly; the character – a young lady who is prepared to wed her father's conqueror in order to stab him – perhaps ideally demands a touch more steel in the voice. Sophia Steffan does well in the Senesino role of Andronico – a less heroic, more amorous one than usual. Tamerlane, the other castrato part, is taken by Gwendolyn Killebrew, a strong and agile singer (agility is pressed too far in some of her embellishment) but one with too feminine a sound, with more than a hint of plumminess, for a part like this. Joanna Simon (Irene) and Marius Rintzler (Leo) complete a capable cast. The libretto and notes are perhaps the best and most honest I have come across in the course of this survey.

Tamerlano is a long opera, a four-disc one – at least in this version, which includes music that Handel himself never performed. *Rodelinda* is shorter, fitting on to three well-filled discs with little of the music omitted. Although this opera, one of Handel's most consistent in musical quality, led with *Giulio Cesare* to the German revival of the 1920s (like *Cesare*, it was printed in a heavily cut and *bearbeitet* text at that time), it has had only one complete recording – and that, made in Vienna in 1964 by the American Westminster firm, was issued in Britain only on an excerpts disc (CSD 3555). This set, conducted by Brian Priestman, has a fair claim to be reckoned the best Handel opera recording ever made using traditional instruments. Priestman's sense of drama, his grasp of the broad rhythm of a movement and generally speaking his command of tempo mark him out as a true Handelian. That small reservation is necessary because, in two or three movements, he surprisingly chooses very slow tempi, quite out of keeping with Handel's expressive world. He has a strong cast, headed by Teresa Stich-Randall in the title role. She produces some gorgeous glittering sounds, a little tight in focus and narrow in vibrato (which means that the faintest divagation from true pitch shows up); it is not quite a comfortable performance, but there are lovely things in it, like the sombre, noble F minor aria in the third act. Some of her ornamentation is extravagant and over-strenuous. Alexander Young does splendidly in the tenor role, Grimoaldo, raging finely in 'Tuo drudo è mio rivale'. Maureen Forrester, in the Senesino role of Bertarido, makes much of one of Handel's richest parts – it includes the famous 'Dove sei?', a prison scene (which has been compared to Florestan's) and several brilliant pieces; the timbre is feminine at times, and occasionally there is a hint of oratorio hoot, but she sings expressively and in the main with a fine-drawn line. Helen Watts brings a touch of distinction to Unulfo's music, and Hilde Rössl-Majdan serves well in Edwige's; the bass, Garibaldo, is taken by John Boyden, who does it with a lightness and fluency anticipating the authenticists of today. The only other recording of music from *Rodelinda* is a single Period/Nixa disc, made in Stuttgart and dating back to the early LP days; Frederike Sailer sings Rodelinda's music quite impressively, but the castrato parts are put down an octave and with its generally pedestrian approach there is little else to enjoy on this record.

The only remaining Academy opera to have been recorded is *Admeto*, Handel's version of the story Gluck was to treat in *Alceste*. This five-record set from EMI/Electrola was made in Amsterdam under the direction of the American baroque specialist Alan Curtis, and, issued in 1979, it represents the first truly scholarly attempt to give a Handel opera in authentic style. In that, it is broadly successful; but the scholarship is not consistently matched by an equivalent level of musicianship. There is a generally polished and agile orchestra (though smaller than Handel's own); recitative endings are elided; ornamentation is done in the right places (though occasionally too generously done: ornamentation should never expose the singer's limitations, as sometimes happens). Tempi are on the slow side. Perhaps it is direction from the keyboard that leads to a certain shapelessness of the bass line, which is apt to plod; and that in turn leads to the music's sounding too 'samish', too little characterized. Best among the singers is Jill Gomez as Antigona, who does better in the light, delicate music than in the fiery numbers. This is one of Handel's operas with two prima donnas (the first was *Alessandro*, of 1726) – not surprising that the Academy was to dissolve after so unpropitious an idea – and the other, Alcestis, is sung here by Rachel Yakar, who is not sufficiently clean in attack or articulation, or dependable over pitch. Similarly, René Jacobs, the Belgian counter-tenor, singing Admetus, tends to slide and scoop too much and makes the character sound consistently weary and languid; his intonation too is patchy. Perhaps a counter-tenor cannot readily cope with the emotional range of such a part. However, James Bowman is in good voice in the second castrato role, Trasimedes; and the cast includes two first-rate lightweight basses, Max van Egmond and Ulrik Cold, both excellent stylists.

With three more operas (*Riccardo Primo, Siroe* and *Tolomeo*, all unrecorded), Handel's Academy period came to an end; the so-called 'second Academy', when the opera house was for a time run by Handel himself with a manager, began in winter 1729–30, with *Lotario* and *Partenope*. The latter is an opera unlike anything he had written before; in its vivacity, its charm and its gentle humour it is closer to *Agrippina* than to any of his more recent works. The textures are airy, there is more rapid music than usual, the phrase structure is simpler, the vocal colour gentler. *Partenope* is not one of Handel's greatest operas, yet the single recording of it (on German Harmonia Mundi), using authentic instruments, is certainly the most satisfying and stylistically the most accomplished of any I have heard, and is also absolutely complete in the version of the first performance (which has never been printed). Sigiswald Kuijken's direction of La Petite Bande has several of the traditional virtues that one had despaired of hearing from an authentic group: sparkling string playing, a firm and shapely bass, and a true rhythmic breadth and sense of purpose. The recitatives are properly quick and conversational, with elided cadences; indeed the only stylistic failing lies in the modest amount of ornamentation – many da capos are left unembellished, and even some cadences that cry for trills are . . . well, left crying. René Jacobs takes the main castrato role, Arsaces, and again is apt to swoon and swoop, but otherwise the singing is first-rate: Krisztina Laki makes a fluent, agile Partenope, with a happy glitter to her voice; Helga Müller Molinari is beautifully focused and controlled as Rosmira, infusing her passage-work with real vigour and passion (her C minor aria in Act 2 is a superb outburst); and the three English singers, John York Skinner, Martyn Hill and Stephen Varcoe all sing cleanly, lightly and accurately.

Partenope was followed by operas of a more heroic cast, the first of them being *Poro*, the middle one of Handel's three Metastasio settings. This tale of Alexander the Great and his Indian exploits has been recorded virtually in full in East Germany, by the Halle company. The recording's strengths and – more numerous – its failings are much as those in the *Radamisto* set already described: ponderous speeds; recitatives earnestly and urgently declaimed in expressionist German; the high male roles all sung an octave below pitch (including the one written for a female contralto, Bertolli, a specialist in male parts), and many numbers garnished with intrusive additional accompaniments. A diligent search through this set to find something kindly to say about the singing proved unavailing.

From 1732, the year after *Poro* (*Ezio* falls in between), comes *Sosarme* – a recording of which was among the earliest to be issued (1955). Dramatically it is feeble, a tale of dynastic rivalries in ancient Lydia, poorly motivated, with both *prima donna* and *primo uomo* marginal to the plot, and the most interesting character given no aria; but it is full of attractive music, especially Act 2, where number after number delights. This set has stood the test of time surprisingly well. Anthony Lewis conducts soundly and solidly; Thurston Dart's continuo accompaniments are the best to be heard anywhere, a model in their rhythmic life, their supportiveness, their discretion and their few but tasteful touches of elaboration. The singing is for the most part excellent. John Kentish, a high tenor put to an alto castrato role, is inevitably uncomfortable, and Nancy Evans does not make much of Erenice's music, but Margaret Ritchie gives a lot of pleasure with her sweet, bell-like tone and neatly placed detail in Elmira's music. So does Alfred Deller as Sosarmes – perhaps an unexpected casting, this, but it works remarkably well, even in the virile, heroic music, while the Act 2 love song 'In mille dolci modi' ravishes the senses. Then William Herbert provides smooth tone and shapely phrasing for Haliate's music, Helen Watts makes an attractive Melus and Ian Wallace, if taxed by the wide *tessitura* and expansive phrasing that Handel always supplied for his great bass Montagnana, does well as Altomaro. Three arias are omitted and seven given without middle section and da capo. There is a modest amount of embellishment.

The early-middle 1730s seem to have been just as outstanding a creative spell for Handel as the one ten years earlier that had produced *Giulio Cesare* and *Rodelinda*. For after *Sosarme* there came *Orlando* – and that was to be followed by *Arianna* (a relatively ordinary work) and then *Ariodante* and *Alcina*, both remarkable pieces. *Orlando*, arguably the most even in quality of all Handel's operas and the most consistently arresting, is another opera with dramatic shortcomings. Based, like *Ariodante* and *Alcina*, on Ariosto's *Orlando furioso*, it is a magical tale, and the situations in it are often allowed to reach impasses that nothing short of a wave of the wand from the magician Zoroaster will set right. I wish there had been a Zoroaster to conduct the recording, for its central failing lies in the less than potent baton of Stephen Simon – the rhythms plod, the recitative is static, and the judgement over cutting is so insensitive as to permit the removal of Orlando's wonderfully moving sleep song, justly reckoned one of the gems of the score. The title role is sung here by Sophia Steffan, rather over-round in tone for a castrato role (this was the last Handel composed for Senesino); but her attack is good, her rhythms vigorous, her intonation dependable. Unhappily her wild and ungainly 'ornamentation' seriously damages the da capo sections. The other high male part, Medoro, was originally written for a woman, and is excellently done here by the warm-toned and musicianly Bernadette Greevy. As Angelica, Graziella Sciutti brings a certain assurance to the music but cannot sing much of it in tune; neither is Carole Bogard as Dorinda perfect in this regard, and she too is apt to over-embellish, but she sings stylishly and offers a happy and charming characterization. Finally Marius Rintzler contributes an acceptable Zoroaster, though sometimes too woolly in tone. The continuo playing of Martin Isepp is too busy and distracting.

Much the same team made the first recording of *Ariodante* for RCA. It has the same shortcomings, though rather differently balanced. Again the cutting is curious: Dalinda's part, which Bogard sings charmingly, is much abbreviated, and Ariodante's chief triumph aria – the climax of his role, possibly of the whole opera – disappears. This part, higher in pitch than Orlando's (it was written for Carestini), is sung by Steffan, while Greevy is assigned the Duke Polinesso, to which she brings a warmth dubiously suited to one of the blackest villains of Handel's operatic output. As Ginevra, Sciutti is again assured and better in tune, if light in colour for this particular role, which has tragic elements; but how good it is to hear an Italian, treating the words as only an Italian can with feeling and understanding and appreciation of the sensuous quality of their sound. Italians are far too rare on the records I have been listening to, though the reasons for that are understandable. The cast here is completed by Ian Partridge, smooth, stylish, accurate, agile and characterless as Lurcanio, and Rintzler, gruff but sympathetic as the elderly King of Scotland. Simon has the dances moving on feet of lead.

The rival recording under Raymond Leppard, however, is not greatly to be preferred. It is much better conducted, in that it is tidier and more rhythmic, yet often the music is rendered in an oddly pernickety manner and the bass is allowed to plod. Tempi are studiously moderate, and that, combined with the low vitality of the recitative and the pauses between items, is seriously damaging to the drama. Indeed the set gives off little sense of an unfolding drama. Leppard has said that he does not believe Handel operas are dramatic enough to be staged, and, although there are indications that he no longer believes that, this recording serves as witness to such an attitude. The splendid music for Ariodante is sung here by Janet Baker, who has played the role in the opera house. She excels in the grand heroic arias, with their brilliant passage-work and virile rhythms, and also in the intense, emotional music – though I wish she had sung the opening arietta as gently as Handel intended (he often composed a piece of this sort to introduce a new artist, Carestini in this case) and that her other slow aria were not marred by over-prominent bassoons with grotesque trills added to their parts. Ginevra is Edith Mathis, a dependable and musical impersonation, modestly characterized; there is tenderness, but not the intensity the music calls for. Norma Burrowes is charming as Dalinda, though not very vivacious and a little insecure over pitch. As Polinesso, James Bowman has the measure of the character (he, too, has sung this role in the theatre) but the tone is out of focus and the verbal articulation is indifferent. David Rendall is a competent Lurcanio; Samuel Ramey as the King does better in the expressive music, which is warmly sung, than in the fiery. All the singers add ornamentation in the da capo sections; the opera is uncut and runs to four discs.

The last of this group is *Alcina*, one of the most spectacular of the operas, with its magical effects and its brilliant and testing vocal writing; it has enjoyed several modern revivals, not only because of the musical quality but also because of the attractiveness to sopranos of its title role. Both the recordings have Joan Sutherland cast as the evil sorceress. The earlier of them comes from a 1959 radio performance in Cologne; the later is a Decca set. Her performance on the Cologne version is on the whole superior: the vowels are better differentiated, the consonants are clearer, the phrasing more natural and less languid. On both the actual sound is beautiful and rich, with a silvery brilliance; the Decca recording serves that brilliance somewhat better than the other (though the sound there is as good as I have ever heard for a recording of this sort). Perhaps her tone is actually better focused in the later set, but there Bonynge's extreme tempi tend to force her into excessive languor or excessive rapidity, and in some ways the quality of her singing is better apprehended on the Melodram records. There the conductor is the solid, steady, highly professional Ferdinand Leitner. On both sets, incidentally, Sutherland takes the concluding aria of Act 1, which Handel originally intended to be sung not by Alcina, as some scores say, but by her sister Morgana (he later handed it over to Alcina). Sutherland also recorded this aria on the early stereo L'Oiseau-Lyre record I referred to above, where her singing of it is especially fine, with a slow tempo allowing her more time for detail.

The Ruggero on the Decca set is Teresa Berganza, both expressive and fiery, in this large role (written for Carestini); she does the famous 'Verdi, prati' movingly. On the other version this part is put down for a tenor, Fritz Wunderlich: a mistake in principle (though, as I have said, Handel just occasionally allowed himself this substitution, unlike a baritone for an alto), but Wunderlich does several of the arias with incomparable grace and sweetness and feeling for style – though not, unfortunately, 'Verdi, prati', which seems to lie awkwardly low. Monica Sinclair is persuasive, on the Decca, as Bradamante, who spends most of the opera in male guise; she shines in the big, energetic arias, which she attacks with real gusto. Norma Procter is relatively weak and oratorio-like in manner on the Melodram set. Luigi Alva, if not sounding a practised Handelian, acquits himself impressively as Oronte, much preferable to Nicola Monti, the decent but ordinary singer on the Cologne version. But Cologne has the admirable Thomas Hemsley to Decca's Ezio Flagello in the small part of Melisso. Graziella Sciutti (Decca) brings a touch of distinction to Morgana's music, if also a touch of unease over intonation; Jeannette van Dijck has good moments here but is not always secure. Cologne omit the episodes for the boy Oberto, who is sung on the Decca set in clean, musical style by Mirella Freni. The Decca version is heavily cut, with eleven arias shorn of their middle sections and da capos, while a group of dances originally composed for *Ariodante* is included (it is also done on the Leppard version of that opera noted above). Bonynge presses his singers hard, provides extravagant ornamentation, makes some damaging internal cuts and arbitrary rearrangements, and is not a good orchestral disciplinarian. Leitner is no stylist, but he is a better conductor, and the atmosphere of the earlier set is in some ways superior; and in the space made available by the omission of Oberto it gives several of the middle sections and da capos that Decca do without. Further, he correctly has recorders where Bonynge substitutes flutes.

Alcina is the last of the three mature operas in which Handel supplied extended ballet episodes, composed for the innovatory French dancer Marie Sallé; the others are *Ariodante* and the third version of *Il pastor fido* – Handel revised that early opera first in spring 1734, then further in autumn that year, adding a ballet prologue under the title *Terpsicore* and dances later in the work. Over the years Handel's ballet music has suffered a good deal of arrangement, at the hands of Beecham and others; recordings of it in more legitimate form include a disc by Neville Marriner and the Academy of St Martin-in-the-Fields (Argo ZRG 686) with all the ballet music from *Alcina* and *Ariodante* and a movement from *Il pastor fido*, played admirably with lively rhythms; more of the *Il pastor fido* ballet can be found on a French Musidisc record played by the Pasdeloup orchestra under Gérard Devos.

The latest of the operas to have achieved a complete recording is *Serse*, another work that has long been popular in Germany. Sometimes it is called a comic opera, but that is an exaggeration. *Serse* does however have one comic character, and, in tune with its early Venetian libretto, a good deal of ironic humour besides; the structure of the libretto also makes the opera different in shape from Handel's others, with shorter arias and more flexibility of music texture. And within the arias the music is lighter, moving more rapidly, more conversationally, in phrases of a more conventionally square and modern a cut. There are not many grand tragic or heroic arias here.

Serse has twice been recorded. The earlier version, made in Vienna under Brian Priestman, and issued in 1965 in the United States (only excerpts appeared in Britain), is much to be preferred. Priestman has an excellent feeling for the pacing and the character of the work; it moves with its proper fleetness and the singers catch the mixture of seriousness and gentle wit that informs the work. Maureen Forrester, who sings Xerxes and thus opens the opera with 'Ombra mai fù', the famous *larghetto* air that is universally known as 'Handel's Largo', is not ideal for a castrato role, but musical and dependable, while Lucia Popp makes a happy contribution as Romilda, bright and agile, Maureen Lehane sings firmly and purposefully as Arsamene, Thomas Hemsley supplies a well-sung Ariodates and Owen Brannigan an appropriately lusty, cheerful Elviro; the other roles are adequately done by Marilyn Tyler and Mildred Miller. The opera is given virtually uncut; the only flaw, once again, is the fussy, obtrusive harpsichord continuo playing of Martin

Isepp. The rival version, by Jean-Claude Malgoire and his ensemble, who aim at authenticity, was widely billed on its release in 1979 as the first complete recording; it is of course neither, coming second to the Westminster and being somewhat cut. There is some capable singing here, notably from Carolyn Watkinson, secure and vital in Xerxes's music, Barbara Hendricks, a lively Romilda with a good ring to her tone, and Anne-Marie Rodde, delicately witty in the coquettish music Handel supplied for Atalanta. I also liked Ortrun Wenkel's well-sustained Amastres, but the clumsy accents, the swellings on every held note, the choppy rhythms and the plodding basses make this set too unidiomatic to give much pleasure.

Of Handel's eight operas after *Alcina*, *Serse* is the only one to have been recorded 'complete'; and that is partly a commentary on the works themselves, for it has to be confessed that, once past the happy, lightweight *Atalanta* of 1736, Handel's operas do not quite maintain their earlier quality. The 1737 group, *Arminio, Giustino* and *Berenice*, have always had a bad press – worse than they merit – and *Faramondo* (1738) has done scarcely better. *Serse* itself, in Handel's time, had a mere five performances, *Imeneo* only two (and two more in revised concert form) and *Deidamia* just three. That, Handel's last opera, inaugurated the Handel Opera Society, but the days when a composer crowned his output with a *Parsifal* or a *Falstaff* were yet a long way off. Of all these, *Imeneo*, an opera with something of the light temper of *Serse*, has been the most often revived, in England and abroad. It is the only one with even a partial recording – an excerpt disc from Halle, with Margraf conducting and much the usual team of singers; it is sung in German, the accompaniments are heavily rewritten and heavily played, and the high male parts are put down an octave. But the disc is a generous one in terms of playing time, and Sylvia Geszty gives some pleasure in Rosmene's music.

The earliest of the English works to be considered is the pastoral, or masque, *Acis and Galatea*, composed in 1718 for performances – probably in some kind of stylized concert form, not on the stage – at the residence near Edgware of the Earl of Caernarvon (soon to become the Duke of Chandos). The musical establishment for which it was written was a modest one; Handel had, in all likelihood, no more than five singers, taking the solo parts and the choruses, and a tiny band of strings with a pair of oboes (doubling recorders) and a harpsichord. Many years later, he and others performed it on a larger scale, with additional items (in Italian) from his earlier Neapolitan serenata *Aci, Galatea e Polifemo*. The original text has an integrity that no later one can pretend to; but opinions may differ as to whether the very small-scale original performing conditions should be recreated in performances today. The earliest recordings (I leave out of the reckoning the 1949 abridged version on the rare Harvard label) tend to favour chamber orchestral proportions, with a separate chorus. The first, on the Handel Society label but presumably made in England (though never released here), is a complete performance, on three discs. Walter Goehr favours slow speeds on the whole, and some of the choruses in particular seem excessively heavy. Much of the solo singing has distinction, however: Margaret Ritchie is a clear, stylish Galatea, and William Herbert a charming Damon, and the young Richard Lewis sings most sweetly and gracefully in Acis's music. Trevor Anthony's public-school Polypheme is less happy and not always well in tune.

The 1960 recording under Sir Adrian Boult is also on a middling scale, with the Philomusica of London and a chorus. Not actually a very good chorus: some of their singing is decidedly rough at the edges. The great strength of this version is Peter Pears, whose singing of 'Love in her eyes sits playing' is an object lesson in style (in the fullest sense of that term) – beautifully phrased, perfectly articulated, and with a charming, almost sensuous lilt to its rhythms. He excels too in 'Love sounds th'alarm', especially its middle section. Then there is Joan Sutherland's Galatea, perhaps a shade artful in manner for a shepherdess but of course sung with exquisite tone; there is a good Damon in David Galliver and in Owen Brannigan a superb Polypheme, ripe and witty, every word and every note relished. There is however one serious blot on this performance: no fewer than eight of the arias are performed without their da capo sections, and in most cases the singers are left unhappily poised in the wrong key when the *ritornello* is played and the number brought to an uncertain, uncomfortable end.

The recording under Alfred Deller treats the work as chamber music: just five singers and six string players. It finds a vein of intimacy in the work that eludes the larger-scale performances, and the choruses benefit considerably from being sung one to a part in terms of clarity (though the crucial 'Wretched lovers' suffers from its excessive pace: the first part too rapid to be elegiac, the second downright hectic). But the solo singing is too decorous, too careful, to make much of the music; it is accurate and it is stylish, but that is not enough. And Deller's conducting is often plodding. In four arias the middle sections and da capos are omitted: a better cutting scheme in principle than on the Boult, but one is loath to forgo any music from this score. Both the 1978 recordings use solo singers in the choruses; Gardiner has the soloists themselves sing them, Marriner engages a different team. Both sing beautifully, and 'Wretched lovers' in particular greatly profits from the clarity of solo voices, gaining much in expressive force. Both versions use orchestras rather larger than those Handel had at Canons. There the resemblances end. Marriner's performance, with the Academy of St Martin-in-the-Fields, is a straightforward modern one; Gardiner's, with the English Baroque Soloists, uses authentic instruments. He does not always use them quite persuasively: some of his fast tempi gives them, and occasionally us, moments of discomfort, because they do not have time to articulate. Yet the advantages easily outweigh the drawbacks: the airiness of the phrasing, the cleanness of the sound and the vitality of the textures go a long way towards establishing a style that is of a piece with the words and the music and the pastoral convention to which they belong. That Gardiner's soloists are the more stylish is perhaps a commentary on the atmosphere of the two performances. Marriner's Galatea, Jill Gomez, is light and charming; Gardiner's Norma Burrowes adds to that a bewitching hint of pastoral sensuality. Marriner's Acis, Robert Tear, is sturdy, almost aggressive, so has the advantage in 'Love sounds th'alarm'; Gardiner's, Anthony Rolfe Johnson, is much gentler, and conveys in his singing the most exquisite longing, so pleases more in the sensuous music earlier in the work. Benjamin Luxon, for Marriner, provides an altogether more interesting, less inhibited Polypheme than Gardiner's Willard White; but the light, pleasant Damon supplied by Philip Langridge for Marriner cannot bring to the music the charm and elegance of Gardiner's Martyn Hill. Marriner's soloists provide more ornamentation, indeed too much, and his orchestral parts – quite improperly – are ornamented too. Neither version is cut; Gardiner sticks strictly to the 1718 text, while Marriner follows Handel's later emendations, notably the 'Happy we' chorus to follow the duet – understandable, but not really consistent with restoration of the original performing scale.

Semele (1744) was probably the most glorious of Handel's failures. He composed it when his Lenten oratorio seasons at Covent Garden were running, and made the curious mistake of including this highly secular tale in them. It was deplored by the oratorio enthusiasts and the opera lovers alike, had one tentative revival, and then lay unheard for the rest of Handel's life. It was never performed, or intended to be, as an opera, although Congreve's text had originally been so described and intended; concert performance does it limited justice, yet staging too can be problematic, as Covent Garden were the latest to prove with their 250th anniversary revival. *Semele* was first recorded back in 1955, under Sir Anthony Lewis, a recording which made some impression in its day and still has much to be said for it. Lewis, a fine Handelian, phrases the music broadly and with real feeling for the idiom. Yet the performance is in some respects dated, partly because of a certain decorousness – this comes less from Lewis's steady tempos than from the rather sustained style of playing and singing then favoured in Handel, from the hints of traditional oratorio style and diction, and from a general inclination to treat the work's sexual theme less as something to celebrate and relish than as something to be discreet and embarrassed about. For this, little blame attaches to the Semele herself, Jennifer Vyvyan, who though not greatly sensual sings with vitality and spirit, accurately in the quick passage-work and with a bright glitter to her voice. William Herbert is more obviously over-parted as Jupiter than a mortal might expect to be: there is clear diction, and some smooth, clean tone, but not much of grandeur or passion. Lewis makes it no easier by taking his sexually urgent 'Come to my arms' at an *andante religioso*. Handel originally had Ino, Semele's sister, and the goddess Juno sung by the same person, a sensible plan as Juno impersonates Ino for a time; here Anna Pollak is the goddess, Helen Watts the mortal. The Cadmus is a disaster, the Athamas a beautifully judged perform-ance by the counter-tenor John Whitworth – a fine singer, always underrated as outshone by the more spectacular Alfred Deller.

The recording under Johannes Somary is quicker-moving, on the whole, but not much more dramatic. Recitative is slowish, and so are several of the arias – including, again, Jupiter's urgent request for Semele's favours in Act 3, and now, too, Semele's response: no hint of the drama that belongs to this exchange. The touch of stickiness about Somary's rhythms tends to undermine the flow of Handel's phrases and the breadth of his structures. Listen for example to 'Where'er you walk', where the orchestra seems to think one chord at a time – and Robert Tear is allowed to over-elaborate the da capo. Yet the more detached articulation is on the whole to be preferred – the best available alternative, stylistically, if modern instruments are to be used. Tear's Jupiter has plenty of vigour and masculinity as well as a generally polished manner. The Semele here is Sheila Armstrong, in her happiest voice: a performance with a proper touch of sensuality and one that, if not as distinguished as Vyvyan's, gives real pleasure. Handel's original doublings are followed: Helen Watts sings both the mezzo roles, improving on her earlier Ino and improving still more, in diction and tonal appeal, on Anna Pollak's Juno, while Justino Diaz does admirably as both Somnus and Cad-mus. The cuts in the work are virtually the same in both versions, but Somary properly includes Juno's song of malicious triumph on Semele's death.

If the Lewis set is superior in general musicianship, and the Somary one generally to be preferred for its better singing, then the 1982 set by John Eliot Gardiner surpasses both on both scores. For a start, he has the benefit of an orchestra of period instruments, which permits a firm but light and airy manner of articulation; this, coupled with Gardiner's strong and well-sprung rhythms, produces a reading with a vitality and sense of drama that seem to propel the hapless Semele inexorably to her doom. The cast is on the whole admirable, though too numerous: Gardiner splits the roles of Juno and Ino, using Della Jones for the former (where she marvellously conveys jealousy in her spat-out consonants) and Catherine Denley for the latter. There is of course less reason to retain the Cadmus-Somnus doubling, and Robert Lloyd makes an appropriately anxious-sounding king of Thebes, while David Tho-mas provides quite a charming vignette of the god of sleep – not just comic, but graceful, even, in his amorous thoughts about the promised nymph Pasithea. And Patrizia Kwella's incisive Iris should be mentioned too. Jupiter is sung by Anthony Rolfe Johnson with real distinction. As 'the mighty thunderer' he would, perhaps, be no great shakes; but here Jupiter adopts the form of a mortal lover, and specifically one of the age of elegance, and that suits Rolfe Johnson's style to perfection – he is at once grateful and ardent. Norma Burrowes offers a lightweight, very sensual Semele, soft and warm in tone, perhaps a shade soubrettish: the high sexual quotient is right, but one might ask for a characterization of a little more fibre – falling in love with Jupiter ought to be something larger than naughty or frolicsome, as it sounds here. Further, there is a good deal of flat singing from her: top notes and leading notes are constantly allowed to slip below pitch, and the movements with demanding *fioritura*, particularly 'Myself I shall adore', often falter seriously: a real flaw in what is otherwise an excellent set. This version is also the most complete, though still omits several (admittedly inessential) numbers in the first act while including in the second a delicious little aria for Cupid which Handel himself cut out.

Lastly, to *Hercules*, the 'musical drama' Handel wrote in 1744 – not for stage performance, but, like *Semele*, at least in parts susceptible to it. For a work of its magnitude (Winton Dean has called it 'the highest peak of late baroque music drama'), *Hercules* has fared poorly on record until lately, with one official recording and one unofficial. The former, from the late sixties, was made in Vienna under Brian Priestman. Some of Priestman's opera recordings come from Vienna too; whatever the reasons may be for choosing Vienna, they would seem to be stronger for Italian opera than for English concert works with an important choral element. The Academy Chorus are competent, and blessed with a good tenor line; but they lack the definition and attack that Handel's magisterial counterpoint demands, and their words are elusive. In any case, Priestman takes several choruses too fast, notably the one after Hercules's death, 'Tyrants now no more shall fear', whose cheerfulness suggests that we are on the lucky tyrants' side rather than that of suffering humanity. Part of the famous 'Jealousy' chorus, too, lacks weight. Indeed the music is often curiously characterized, and the orchestral playing seems low in vitality. As in other Priestman recordings, Isepp's continuo playing is often distractingly busy; but at least the recitative moves pretty smoothly. Vocally too this set is patchy. The good patch is Alexander Young, attentive and accomplished as always in the music for Hyllus. Teresa Stich-Randall is miscast as Iole: the ideal here is a gentle, virginal voice, capable of warmth, and what is provided is firm, glittering tone, little phrasing, insecure divisions and a tendency to flatten. Louis Quilico gives a bland, respectable performance in the title role but with no real feeling for Handel's characterization of the hero with his bluffness and his swagger; and his pronunciation is frenchified. In a sense, however, the central character is Dejanira, Hercules's wife, whose jealousy (unwarranted in this version of the story) precipitates the tragedy. Maureen Forrester treats her music too much as if it belonged to the contralto part in *Messiah*; the final mad scene is not without drama, but there is little real attempt at characterization and the tone is plummy, the words unclear. The great aria 'Resign thy club', far from taunting him to abandon manly pursuits, sounds like her twitting of a tardy husband for dawdling at the Athenaeum of an evening.

The unofficial version, conducted with purposefulness and vigour by Lovro von Matačić, wants nothing in intensity or commitment. This is a 'private' recording, taken from a La Scala broadcast in 1958. In a way it is refreshing to turn to a performance that tries so frankly to put the work across, but the price is high. The sound is hazy, the work heavily reorchestrated (indeed in places rewritten), the language Italian, the cuts numerous and arbitrary, the audience and prompter noisy, and the singing unidiomatic. Franco Corelli, an improbable Hyllus, offends the worst; Fedora Barbieri supplies a Dejanira with plenty of bite and edge; Elisabeth Schwarzkopf sings with charm as Iole; and Jerome Hines makes a sterling Hercules.

Only with the new recording from John Eliot Gardiner, then, has the work received anything like its due. As with his *Acis* and *Semele*, Gardiner uses period instruments, though here and there one may have reservations about the way they are used, since they are sometimes played with modern ideas of expression. Yet there are, of course, all the usual advantages of an eighteenth-century orchestral sound: clear textures, and a style of articulation (by the strings especially) that is neither too heavy nor too light. The performance as a whole, however, is on the light side; Gardiner keeps it moving at a quickish pace, occasionally faster than the weighty nature of the issues of the work demand. Several arias move speedily along; as does the chorus about the tyrants, and so too does the chorus 'Wanton god', which is almost playfully treated as a huge *crescendo* (with a witty *diminuendo* in the closing *ritornello*). This is, in fact, something of a virtuoso performance by Gardiner, his Monteverdi Choir and his English Baroque Soloists, surely the most accomplished of the period groups. Less happily, there are a number of cuts, including internal ones, while Iole's role is severely curtailed notably by the damaging omission of her opening aria, 'Daughter of gods', which is important in the establishment of her character, like so many of the arias with which Handel has his principles introduce themselves. And the more so since the part is so attractively taken by Jennifer Smith, who happily captures Iole's blend of strength and innocence with her cool, firm singing. Hyllus is elegantly and appealingly sung by Anthony Rolfe Johnson, and Hercules is taken by John Tomlinson, who arguably overemphasizes the braggart element in the character of 'the world's hero' – if Hercules is too much lampooned in this way (and Tomlinson comes close to it) the powerful scene of his agony and death is inevitably undermined. Lichas is gracefully done by Catherine Denley, but the cuts leave her little to do. The central role of Dejanira falls to Sarah Walker, whose sure technique, dramatic intensity and expressive power provide a remarkable reading. Possibly her expressive approach is not entirely Handelian, showing a *Lied*-like feeling for detail rather than a true Baroque breadth; and certainly much of her ornamentation – far more florid and more abundant than that of others in the cast – is hopelessly un-baroque. That this is easily the best *Hercules* on records there is no doubt; but it is still heavily flawed.

The works discussed above have among them some thousand arias, and not surprisingly there have been countless recordings of many of them. Some, of course, have attracted numerous singers over the decades – 'Ombra mai fù' (*Serse*), 'Lascia ch'io pianga' (*Rinaldo*), 'Dove sei?' (*Rodelinda*), 'Verdi, prati' (*Alcina*), 'Care selve' (*Atalanta*), 'O ruddier than the cherry' (*Acis*), and 'Where'er you walk' (*Semele*), to name just a few. Here I confine myself to the more interesting recital discs, and in particular draw attention to those with music from some of the operas not represented above.

Some such discs are vitiated by having some or all of the arias sung in the wrong octave. A Gérard Souzay recital, half Handel and half French baroque opera, has five items, including one each from *Floridante*, *Tolomeo* and *Berenice*, but all are castrato songs put down an octave (Philips 9502 081). A Theo Adam record of arias mainly from German Baroque opera, includes two of Julius Caesar's arias down an octave, but Adam shows himself a fine Handelian bass when singing the real bass aria 'Gia risonar d'intorno', a brilliant piece from *Ezio* (Eterna 8 26 896). Fischer-Dieskau has a Handel recital which draws mainly on the oratorios but also gives 'Ombra mai fù' and arias from *Berenice* and *Ottone*, all three down an octave, and one short bass aria from *Agrippina* (DG 2542 187). Forbes Robinson includes one *Berenice* aria down an octave in a recital that also offers several oratorio songs and true bass arias from *Alcina*, *Ezio* and all three of the English works discussed above (ECS 738). A ten-inch disc from the Handel Opera Society gives mainly music from the oratorios, but also has Owen Brannigan giving characteristic accounts of 'O ruddier than the cherry' and, in English, one of the magician's arias from *Orlando* (ESD 7059). An impressive Bach-Handel recital by Ernst Häfliger includes 'Ombra mai fù', and one of Sextus's arias from *Giulio Cesare* (DG SLPEM 136 268).

Before moving on to female singers, I should pause at two counter-tenors. First, Alfred Deller, whose 'Neglected Handel Arias and Ensembles' record, drawn mainly from the late oratorios, also has 'Ombra mai fù', 'Lascia ch'io pianga' and two movements from *Orlando*, including the mad scene. This is quite a tour de force from Deller, though in the end the performances seem a shade sober and lacking in passion; perhaps this is one of those pieces beyond the scope of the counter-tenor voice (Vanguard VSL 11082; USA BGS 5029). Russell Oberlin has a much plainer style, and clear, true tone, almost of a high mezzo character; his Handel recital (DG LPM 18630) includes a powerful aria ('Ah dolce nome!') from *Muzio Scevola*, of which Handel composed just one act (1721), 'Ombre cara' from *Radamisto*, and two arias from *Rodelinda*, with generally restrained and musical ornamentation. Janet Baker has a fine Handel recital, nearly half of it drawn from the operas: it includes three popular items ('Ombra mai fù', 'Dove sei?' and 'Care selve'), but also an aria from *Ariodante* and Dejanira's mad scene from *Hercules* (Philips 6500 523). 'Dove sei?' is also included on a Marilyn Horne Bach-Handel recital, along with two more *Rodelinda* arias, sung very brilliantly and vigorously – a splendid voice for heroic castrato roles (SXL 6349). Bernadette Greevy's attractive, warmly sung Handel recital in English includes four of the most popular pieces (for once, not 'Ombra mai fù') and also arias from *Admeto, Partenope* and two from *Ottone* (Argo ZRG 501). A Mozart-Handel recital from Lucia Popp contains charming, beautifully formed performances of arias from *Ottone, Giulio Cesare* (Cleopatra's 'Piangerò'), *Rodelinda* and *Serse* (ASD 2334). An aria from *Alessandro* ('Lusinghe più care') is included on Judith Blegen's recital, half Handel, half Scarlatti, sung pleasantly if a shade shallow-toned (CBS 76636). Carole Bogard ranges wide through the operas in a recital disc (touched on above) – there is music from *Agrippina, Amadigi, Rinaldo, Radamisto, Orlando, Giustino* and *Imeneo* – all lightly and stylishly done, but with little strong feeling (Cambridge CRS 2712). And lastly, a reminder of the Joan Sutherland recital, referred to above (twice), with excerpts from *Alcina*, orchestral music from *Rodrigo* and oratorio excerpts (L'Oiseau-Lyre SOL 60001).

Handel on 78

ALAN BLYTH

In the days of 78 rpm discs, Handel's arias were much used as display pieces for leading singers, very often with scant regard for the singer's appropriateness for the pitch of the music in hand. The most extraordinary case of its kind is Gerhard Hüsch's account of Cleopatra's 'V'adoro pupille' (HMV EH 925; LV 76). But some performances became classics in their day and deserve mention here. Almirena's 'Lascia ch'io pianga' (*Rinaldo*) was a particular favourite with mezzos, who unfortunately tend to make the music too grief-laden, but Maria Olszewska (D 1465; LV 205) is worth hearing for all that. Claudia Muzio (Edison 82300; RS 310) is vocally nearer the mark and very affecting. *Il pastor fido* yields only John McCormack's delicate, idiosyncratic account of 'Caro amore' (DB 2867; COLH 123). 'Alma mia' from *Floridante* provoked performances by soprano Lily Pons (DA 1800 – backed by 'Lusinghe più care' from *Alessandro*, also recorded inimitably by Clara Butt and Isobel Baillie), tenor Richard Crooks (Vic. 2175) and bass Ezio Pinza (Vic. 17914; CDN 1021) variously anachronistic, but mementos of the singers concerned. From *Ottone* Kathleen Ferrier recorded 'Vieni, o figlio' and 'La speranza é giunto in porto' (DX 1194; HLM 7002), but in spurious English translations that ignore the original text's meaning and using a piano accompaniment. Still the skill and beauty of the singing as such is not to be denied.

Giulio Cesare finds Emmi Leisner a deal too fruity in Cornelia's 'Deh piangete' and 'Priva son d'ogni conforto' (Poly. 73019; LV 99); Hans Hotter, though an octave low, is not unimpressive in Caesar's 'Aure, deh per pietà' (LX 1538; 1C 147–01 633): the tone may appertain to nineteenth-century opera but the commitment is undeniable; Alfred Deller is his own inimitable self in Caesar's recitative 'Alma del gran Pompeo' (C 4222; HLM 7234);

Helene Cals offers a romantically inclined but characterfully sung 'Piangerò' (Parlo E 11115); and Victoria de los Angeles in the old *History of Music in Sound*, recently reissued on ASD 4193, sings a gently flowing 'V'adoro, pupille', including a brief interjection from Richard Lewis as a tenor Caesar and Arnold Goldsborough as a reasonably authentic conductor.

The lovely 'Dove sei?' from *Rodelinda* was often done, most notably by Ferrier (in English – K 1466; ACL 308), Isobel Baillie (DX 1022; RLS 714) and Leisner (Poly, 73023), but the expression of all three is that of the bad, old quasi-Victorian oratorio tradition. Likewise, 'Hear me ye winds and waves', always in English, from *Scipio* was popular with basses. Herbert Witherspoon – rhyming 'winds' with 'minds' is woolly (Victor 74513); Robert Radford (D 1300; HLM 7009) sings it with feeling and authority, though his voice is a little past its best; the New Zealand bass Oscar Natzke, who died tragically young, shows the quality of his fine voice (Parlo. E 11426), but is inclined to be lachrymose. Marian Anderson is miscast in 'Ch'io mai vi possa' from *Siroe* (with piano – DA 1480). Alexander Kipnis, on a typically impressive record (Am Col 7224; CBS 76021), sings the King's 'Al sen ti stringo' from *Ariodante* with suave beauty and deep eloquence coupling it with 'Si, tra, i ceppi' from *Berenice*, where his huge voice is nimbly effective.

From *Tolomeo*, Arthur Somervell adapted the aria 'Non lo dirò' into what became known as 'Silent worship' (again words with sentiments far from those being expressed in the opera). In that form it received performances of articulate grace from Heddle Nash (B 9719; HQM 1089) and Dennis Noble (Col. DB 1482). From *Partenope* the English bass Norman Allin sang the rollicking 'Furibondo spiro' (L 1612).

Sosarme finds no less a singer than Elisabeth Rethberg displaying her refined art in a touching account of the lovely 'Rend' il sereno al ciglio' (Brunswick 30119; LV 170) done in a lower key by Butt (AGSB 75, HLM 7025). *Alcina* is represented only by Marjorie Thomas's worthy account of 'Verdi prati' (C 3817).

Atalanta, by contrast, yields up a plethora of performances by sopranos, tenors and mezzos of the beautiful 'Care selve'. Some, such as Gigli's, are hopelessly unidiomatic (DA 1918; RLS 732). Others, such as those by the unforgettable Eidé Noréna (DB 5054; LV 193) and a little-known but fine north country soprano Ada Alsop (K 1164; ACL 323 – in English) would grace any performance today; so would that of the singularly pure-voiced Dutch singer Jo Vincent (Col. D 10038), the first soprano soloist in Britten's *Spring Symphony*. *Serse* brings forward the greatest number of aspirants – in all voice ranges – for Xerxes's opening recitative and aria, 'Ombra mai fù'. Reference to WERM will show its popularity in pre-war days from Caruso's overwhelming performance (DB 133; RL 11749) – powerful homage indeed to a plane tree – onwards. Tito Schipa's more delicate account, if one has to have it by a tenor (DB 1064; GEMM 151), is possibly less remote from Handel's intentions, and truth to say nearer them than the many fruity contraltos at the right pitch: Ferrier, Klose, Stignani, Olszewska, Maartje Offers, Leisner only the most famous among them.

From *Acis and Galatea*, there are beautiful but (of course) unadorned versions of 'As when the dove' from Elsie Suddaby (C 1742) and Isobel Baillie (DX 1158; RLS 7703). 'Love in her eyes' and 'Love sounds the alarm' were coupled by both Webster Booth (C 3796) and Walter Widdop (DB 1566; HQM 1164) of whom the latter is far preferable: Widdop sings the second air with a masculine ardour and metal in the tone that few if any Handel tenors aspire to nowadays. Heddle Nash, on the other hand, is to be preferred in 'Love in her eyes', which he sang with the most liquid and seductive tone on a briefly available 45rpm (7EG 8681), sadly without its da capo on its LP reissue (HQM 1089). Evan Williams's persuasive acoustic (4–2033; RLS 724) is worth seeking out. Polypheme's scena with its opportunities for bass *coloratura* was eagerly seized by the likes of Malcolm McEachern (Col. DB 1582), Norman Walker (DX 1909), Peter Dawson (C 1500; HQM 1217) – a performance of great character – and Norman Allin (Col. 747). The Belgian baritone Armand Crabbé, singing in French (DB 1213; 4C 051–23273), proves a much lighter, more athletic giant with nimble runs and the text relished – much more akin to today's ideas of interpreting Handel, his *rubato* apart.

From *Semele*, Suddaby recorded 'Endless pleasure' (B 2674), and 'O Sleep' (C 1437; HLM 7033), the latter a performance of great poise and feeling, as are those by Ada Alsop (K 1164; ACL 323), Alma Gluck (DB 278) and the diminutive American Dorothy Maynor (a little too fruity on DB 3989), all three to be preferred to the much-admired McCormack (Victor 66096; GEMM 159), in spite of his fabulous breath-control. He is also nasal and disappointing in 'Where'er you walk' (DB 2867; COLH 123), in which he is surpassed by the mellifluous Webster Booth (C 3305; HLM 7109) and Richard Lewis (K 2135).

ACIS AND GALATEA

G Galatea; *A* Acis; *D* Damon; *P* Polyphemus

1951 Ritchie *G*; R. Lewis *A*; Herbert *D*; Anthony *P*/Handel Society Choir and Orch/Goehr Handel Society
(US) Ⓜ HDL2 (3)

1959 (in German) Vulpius *G*; Rotzsch *A*; Czerny *D*; Rossler *P*/German Radio Chorus, Berlin CO/Koch Eterna Ⓜ 820095–6

1959 Sutherland *G*; Pears *A*; Galliver *D*; Brannigan *P*/St Anthony Singers, Philomusica of London/Boult L'Oiseau-Lyre SOL60011–2

1974 Sheppard *G*; Buttrey *A*; Jenkins *D*; Bevan *P*/Deller Consort; Stour Festival CO/A. Deller Harmonia Mundi HM833–4 RCA (US) VICS6040

1978 Burrowes *G*; Rolfe Johnson *A*; Hill *D*; White *P*/English Baroque Soloists/Gardiner DG 2708 038 ④ 3375 004

1978 Gomez *G*; Tear *A*; Langridge *D*; Luxon *P*/Vocal Ens, ASMF/ Marriner Argo ZRG886–7 ④ K114K22

1949 (excerpts) Willauer G; Perrin A; Tibbetts P/Lowell House Musical Society Chorus and Orch /Holmes Harvard ⓜ TR431/2

1960 (excerpts – recording uses Mozart orchestration, K566) Harvey G;

Vrooman A; Bruce P/Salzburg Mozarteum Choir and Orch/ Paumgartner
Fontana C875064Y
Epic (US) BC1095

ADMETO

1979 Jacobs Admetus; Yakar Alcestis; Cold Hercules; Apollo; Dams Orindus; Bowman Trasimedes; Gomez Antigona; Van Egmond

Meraspes/Il Complesso Barocco/ Curtis
EMI 1C 163 30808–12

ALCINA

A Alcina; R Ruggero; B Bradamante; O Oronte; M Morgana; Ob Oberto; Mel Melisso

1959 (broadcast performance) Sutherland A; Wunderlich R; Procter B; Monti O; Van Dijck M; Hemsley Mel/Cologne Radio Choir, Cologne Cappella Coloniensis/Leitner Melodram ⓜ MEL022

1962 Sutherland A; Berganza R; M. Sinclair B; Alva O; Sciutti M; Freni Ob; Flagello Mel/LSO and Chorus/Bonynge
Decca GOS509
London OSA1361

ARIODANTE

G Ginevra; D Dalinda; A Ariodante; P Polinesso; L Lurcanio; K King

1971 Sciutti G; Bogard D; Steffan A; Greevy P; Partridge L; Rintzler K/ Vienna Academy Choir, Vienna Volksoper Orch/Simon
RCA (US) LSC6200

1978 Mathis G; Burrowes D; Baker A; Bowman P, Rendall L; Ramey K/ London Voices, ECO/Leppard
Philips 6769 025 ④ 7699 112

GIULIO CESARE

GC Giulio Cesare; Cl Cleopatra; S Sesto; C Cornelia; P Ptolemy; A Achillas

1952 (heavily cut) Sandoz GC; Gähwiller Cl; F. Brückner-Rüggeberg S; Helbing C; Tappolet P; Kelch A/Handel Society Chorus and Orch/Goehr
Handel Society ⓜ HDL18
Musical Masterpiece Society ⓜ OP29

1952 Wiener GC; Roon Cl; Handt S; Kalin C; Curzon P; Poell A/ Vienna Academy Choir, Vienna Pro Musica CO/Swarowsky
Vox ⓔ 52011 (2)

1955 (live performance – Rome Opera, Milan) Christoff GC; Fineschi Cl; Corelli S; Barbieri C; Petri P; Cassinelli A/La Scala Chorus and Orch/Gavazzeni
Historical Recording Enterprises ⓜ HRE 318

1967 Treigle GC; Sills Cl; Wolff S; Forrester C; Malas P; Cossa A/ New York City Opera Chorus and Orch/Rudel
RCA (Germany) VL42527EX
(US) LSC6182

1969 Fischer-Dieskau *GC*; Troyanos *Cl*;
Schreier *S*; Hamari *C*; Crass *P*;
Schramm *A*/Munich Bach Choir
and Orch/Richter
DG (UK) 2720 023
(US) 2711 009
1960 (excerpts) Fischer-Dieskau *GC*;
Seefried *Cl*/Berlin Radio SO/

Böhm
DG 138637
1964 (excerpts) Elkins *GC*; Sutherland
Cl; Conrad *S*; Horne *C*; M.
Sinclair *P*/New SO of London/
Bonynge
Decca SDD574
London OS28576

HERCULES

H Hercules; *D* Dejanira; *I* Iole; *Hy* Hyllus; *L* Lichas; *P* Priest

1958 (live performances – Teatro alla
Scala, Milan) Hines *H*; Barbieri
D; Schwarzkopf *I*; Corelli *Hy*;
Bastianini *L*; Ferrin *P*/La Scala
Chorus and Orch/Matačić
Hope ⓜ 239 (3)
1967 Quilico *H*; Forrester *D*; Stich-
Randall *I*; Young *Hy*; Lerer *L*;
Grabowski *P*/Vienna Academy

Choir, Vienna Radio Orch/
Priestman
RCA (UK) SER5569–71
(US) LSC6181
1982 Tomlinson *S*; Walker *D*; J. Smith
I; Rolfe Johnson *Hy*; Denley *L*;
Savidge *P*/Monteverdi Choir,
English Baroque Soloists/Gardiner
DG 2742 004

IMENEO

1960 (excerpts) Leib *Imeneo*; Rotzsch
Tirinto; Geszty *Rosmene*;
Krahmer *Clomiri*; Vogel *Argenio*/

Leipzig Radio Choir, Handel
Festival Orch, Halle/Margraf
Eterna 820 648

ORLANDO

1970 Sciutti *Angelica*; Bogard *Dorinda*;
Steffan *Orlando*; Greevy *Medoro*;
Rintzler *Zoroaster*/Vienna
Academy Choir, Vienna

Volksoper Orch/Simon
RCA (UK) SRS3006
(US) LSC6197

PARTENOPE

1979 Laki *Partenope*; Jacobs *Arsace*;
York Skinner *Armindo*; Varcoe
Ormonte; Müller Molinari
Rosmira; Hill *Emilio*/La Petite

Bande/S. Kuijken
EMI/Harmonia Mundi 1C 157
99855–8

IL PASTOR FIDO – first version

M Mirtillo; *E* Eurillo; *A* Amarilli; *S* Silvio; *D* Dorinda; *T* Tirrenio

1953 (abridged) Warner *M*; Hunt *E*;
Rowe *A*; Brown *S*; Paris *D*;
Rogier *T*/Columbia SO/Engel
CBS (US) ⓜ CB17

1958 Gatta *M*; Bozzi Lucca *E*; Fusco
A; Reynolds *S*; Garazioti *D*;
Miville *T*/Milan Chamber Orch./
Gerelli
Cetra ⓒ LPS3265

PORO

1961 (in German) P. Fischer *Cleofide*;
    Herzberg *Erissena;* Enders
    Alexander; Leib *Porus*; Kaphahn
    Gandartes; Stumpfel *Timagenes*/

Handel Festival Orch, Halle/
Margraf
Eterna 820 048–50

RADAMISTO

1961 Kaphahn *Radamisto*; Kuhse
    Polissena; Leib *Tiridate*; Apreck
    Tigrane; Kehl *Zenobia*; Süss
    Farasmene/Leipzig Radio Chorus,
    Handel Festival Orch, Halle/

Margraf
Columbia (Germany) SMC91429–
32
Eterna 825 318–21

RINALDO

G Goffredo; *A* Almirena; *R* Rinaldo; *E* Eustazio; *Arg* Argante; *Arm* Armida

1977 Esswood *G*; Cotrubas *A*;
    Watkinson *R*; Brett *E*; Cold *Arg*;
    Scovotti *Arm*/La Grande Ecurie et
    la Chambre du Roi/Malgoire
    CBS (UK) 79308 ④ 40–79308

(US) M3–34592
1973 (excerpts) Augér *A*; Wolff *R*;
    Michalski *Arg*; Shane *Arm*/Vienna
    Volksoper Orch/Simon
    RCA (US) ARL1–0084

RODELINDA

R Rodelinda; *B* Bertarido; *G* Grimoaldo; *E* Edwige; *U* Unulfo; *Gar* Garibaldo

1964 Stich-Randall *R*; Forrester *B*;
    Young *G*; Rössl-Majdan *E*; Watts
    U; Boyden *Gar*/Vienna Radio
    Chorus and Orch/ Priestman
    Westminster WGS8205 (3)

1953 (abridged) Sailer *R*; Titze *B*;
    Fehringer *G*; H. Lipp *E*; Hagner
    U; Lips *Gar*/South German Radio
    Chorus and Orch/Müller-Kray
    Nixa-Period ⓜ PLP589
    Lyrichord ⓜ LL115

SEMELE

S Semele; *A* Athamas; *I* Ino. *J* Jupiter, *Jun* Juno; *Som* Somnus

1955 Vyvyan *S*; Whitworth *A*; Watts *I*;
    Herbert *J*; Pollak *Jun*; James *Som*/
    St Anthony Singers, New SO of
    London/ Lewis
    L'Oiseau-Lyre ⓔ OLS111–3
1973 Armstrong *S*; M. Deller *A*; Watts
    I; *Jun*; Tear *J*; Diaz *Som*/Amor
    Artis Chorus, ECO/Somary

Vanguard (UK) VSD71180–2
(US) VSD10127–9
1982 Burrowes *S*; Penrose *A*; Denley *I*;
    Rolfe Johnson *J*; D. Jones *Jun*;
    Thomas *Som*/Monteverdi Choir,
    English Baroque Soloists/Gardiner
    Erato STU71453

SERSE

S Serse; *R* Romilda; *A* Arasmenes; *E* Elviro; *Ar* Ariodante; *Am* Amastres; *At* Atalanta

1965 Forrester *S*; Popp *R*; Lehane *A*; Brannigan *E*; Hemsley *Ar*; Miller *Am*; Tyler *At*/Vienna Academy Choir, Vienna Radio Orch/ Priestman Westminster WST8202

1979 Watkinson *S*; Hendricks *R*; Esswood *A*; Studer *E*; Cold *Ar*; Wenkel *Am*; Rodde *At*/Bridier Vocal Ens, La Grande Ecurie et la Chambre du Roi/Malgoire CBS 79325

SOSARME

1955 Ritchie *Elmira*; N. Evans *Erenice*; Watts *Melo*; Deller *Sosarme*; Herbert *Haliate*; Kentish *Argone*; Wallace *Altomaro*/St Anthony Singers, St Cecilia Orch/Lewis L' Oiseau-Lyre © OLS124–6

TAMERLANO

1970 Bogard *Asteria*; Killebrew *Tamerlano*; Steffan *Andronico*; Rintzler *Leo*; Young *Bajazet*; Simon *Irene*/Copenhagen Chorus and CO/Moriarty Oryx 4XLC2

The Operas of Gluck

MAX LOPPERT

The new Grove *Dictionary of Music and Musicians* entry on Gluck lists forty-three authenticated operas; the scores of thirty-two are extant, and arias and other separate numbers are traceable from the remainder. The range of Gluck's experience as a theatre composer is perhaps still insufficiently recognized. He was trained in Milan, and steeped in the manners and modes of that city, and later London, Prague, and Naples; he travelled as conductor with the Mingotti troupe; in Vienna he became court composer; in Paris he made his mark as saviour and transformer of the moribund *tragédie-lyrique*. During the first two decades of a career in the theatre lasting more than forty years he produced Metastasian *opere serie*, *serenate* and *feste teatrali*, *opéras-comiques* (most of them for the French Theatre at Vienna), and much music for the dance outside the purview of this essay. The bulk of this activity was carried on before, alongside, and even after the creation of the first 'Reform' operas. (It is salutary to remember that Gluck's creative development draws a by no means unbroken or always unswerving line towards the innovative ideals of reform as expressed in the famous 1769 prologue to the first edition of *Alceste*. Three years after *Orfeo ed Euridice* of 1762, he was still able to collaborate on *La corona* with Metastasio, leader of the *ancien régime*.) A longer view of Gluck deserves promotion, if only because by such means the mist of ill-comprehended 'historical importance', which continues to limit popular appreciation of his true greatness, may yet be dispersed.

The gramophone could play an important part in promoting such a view. So far it has substantially failed to do this; to the long career – and, indeed, to any of the operas other than *Orfeo/Orphée* (discussed in *Opera on Record**) – records provide a mostly inadequate guide. Not wholly: treasures are there to be dug up in the Gluck discography. But these are largely long- and deep-buried treasures: general unavailability vies with exiguousness of existing material to frustrate even the most assiduous Gluck explorer. Of necessity, therefore, this survey deals cursorily with the early decades of Gluck's operatic career. The starting point must be *Le nozze d'Ercole e*

* Hutchinson, 1979

d'Ebe, the one-act festal *serenata* composed for a royal wedding at Pillnitz Castle (near Dresden) in 1747. The East German recording leaves little reason to dispute Grout's view (in his *Short History of Opera*) that the piece displays Gluck as 'an accomplished composer in a rather pretty, trifling Italian style'. Too little reason, I feel: while the conducting is unsleepy and the playing of a small orchestra sprightly (with harpsichord continuo properly functional in the balance), the singing moves minimally beyond tidy-minded dullness, 'correct' in aria and ponderous in recitative. This applies to Peter Schreier – as Jupiter, whose single aria reappears thirty years later, in revised form, as the *Armide* Act 2 duet of the heroine and Hidraot – quite as much as to the three less familiar female soloists (as in 1747, Hercules is taken by a woman). Graces are missing from the vocal line; da capo repeats are too often refused.

Of Gluck's Italian *opere serie* only two extracts have been recorded: the aria 'Vieni che poi sereno' from *Semiramide riconosciuta* (1748), a telling early instance of Gluck's powers as a melodist, in a spacious, distinguished, and passingly unsteady rendition by Povla Frijsh (with piano; Vic 2078); and the aria 'Se mai senti' from *La clemenza di Tito* of 1752 (see page 72). The *opéras-comiques* are slightly more numerous on disc. From the mid-1750s these increasingly occupied Gluck's attention, as the taste of the Viennese court grew for these samples of Parisian entertainment . He was initially required to produce only substitute *ariettes* alongside existing numbers, but was eventually moved to compose full new versions of previously set texts. The sixth of the series, *L'Ivrogne corrigé* after a La Fontaine fable, appeared in Paris in 1759; the libretto reached Gluck in Vienna the following year. The experience of compressing and reducing to essentials his musical techniques in the service of these quick-witted, plain-speaking theatrical trifles, with their rapid alternation of musical and spoken episodes, may not have made of Gluck one of the notable comic opera composers of musical history; yet it must be recognized as a factor of major importance in the refinement and concentration of his musical style. This one can appreciate while enjoying the roughly played but spirited Leibowitz record, from the early 1950s, of *L'Ivrogne corrigé*. As in *Le Cadi dupé* (1761) and the full-length *Recontre imprévue* (1764), last and most celebrated of Gluck's *opéras-comiques*, the serious humours of the plot are in danger of overburdening the comedy, because into these Gluck infuses an almost too intense directness of emotional expression, a 'speaking' pathos. In *The Drunkard Reformed*, Mathurin, bullying husband of the title, is cured of his taste for drink by being removed in a stupor to a nearby cave, there to be awakened to a supposed after-life in Hades. Not only in the latter scenes but also in the airs of the discontented wife Mathurine and ardent young lover Cléon can there be discerned a clear pre-echo of *Orfeo*. Jean Hoffman as Cléon is the only vocal weakness of a cast all deft at pointing the spoken dialogue in a way that seems to come naturally to French singers. No important voices here – though Bernard Demigny, also encountered in other Gluck records of the period, is of pleasing quality, and even at this early stage of his career Jean-Christophe Benoit's wit (in the title role) was readily flourished; his rustic accent is hilarious. But, in sum, a lively, communicative response to an unusually interesting piece.

The plot of *Le Cadi dupé* (a libretto set earlier by Monsigny) pivots – to late twentieth-century susceptibilities, distastefully – on a point of female ugliness, and therefore ineligibility for marriage, as a trap and punishment for the local Turkish tyrant. (In subject matter and in instrumental colouring this opera is a pointer to the contemporary vogue for *turquoiserie* that was to achieve its ultimate fulfilment in *Die Entführung*.) In 1878, the authentic full score being presumed lost, an arrangement of the vocal score was made by Johann Nepomuk Fuchs and Fritz Krastl (German translator); in this edition the work gained new currency. In consequence of the discovery, in the Hamburg State Opera archives, of an original full score, Electrola in 1975 added the work to its series of one-act German *Singspiele*. This performance declares an easy superiority over the earlier Paumgartner recording of the Fuchs/Krastl *Betrogene Kadi* – in musical character, in orchestral clarity and poise, and voice for voice. More important, the Electrola text declares its authenticity in details large and small, too numerous to be gone into here. Gluck's music is of sustained inspiration, meshing in each number Italianate melodic fluency and the simplified style of the French *ariettes*; there is limpid love music for the young couple Zelmira and Nuradin, a plaintive major-key air for the Cadi's rejected wife Fatima, and strangely evocative use of the minor key to depict the ugly Omega. One may have qualms about the exposed register changes and frayed timbre of the veteran Anneliese Rothenberger (Fatima) or the hefty vocalization of the mature Nicolai Gedda (Nuradin), yet the attractions of the record easily pacify them; and high among these is the broad but never blustery Cadi of Walter Berry. Nuradin's love song, in the Fuchs/Krastl version, is the single number to have been extracted from the work for independent recording – a fine-spun account, intelligently deploying limited resources, by the Romanian Petre Munteanu (Rococo 5391).

La Recontre imprévue, ou Les Pélerins de la Mecque was one of Gluck's most durable successes of the eighteenth century. It was given in many European cities, and as a German *Singspiel* maintained favour even in the face of the later *Entführung*, on which work (as on Haydn's *Incontro improvviso*) it was to exercise direct influence. As in earlier Gluck essays in the popular manner, comedy and seriousness of emotional expression fail to keep in scale; measured by standards less exalted than Mozart's opera both assumes and requires, it is a work emphatically deserving of modern revival (as was shown at the Barber Institute, Birmingham, in 1973). And deserving, no less than Haydn's *Incontro* (which has found a place in the Philips Haydn opera series) of a modern complete recording. Janet Baker's Gluck recital with Leppard and the ECO (Philips 9500 023) presents two delightful airs – 'Bel inconnu' (Act 1) of the lady-in-waiting Balkis and 'Je cherche à vous faire' of the slave Amina, both done with a buoyancy of accent that may surprise the listener without live experience of this singer's sense of fun.

Sadly, the most beautiful airs of the opera are so far unrecorded; these belong to the hero, Prince Ali (tenor), and belong to Gluck's finest vein of heartfelt simplicity – *La Recontre imprévue*, it should be recalled, came two years after *Orfeo*. But Vertigo, a *buffo* French painter (baritone), is provided with a linked sequence in Act 3, the second air of which, 'Un ruisselet bien clair' (in F) indicates both the calibre and the particular nature of Gluck's melodic inspiration in this opera. It became something of a concert piece, an *aria antica*, in the days when song recitals regularly commenced with a group of these. It is sung, in German, by Geraldine Farrar with orchestra (in G); by Lorri Lail with harpsichord (in E flat); and by Schwarzkopf with piano (in G). The music pictures, and in the onomatopoeic repetitions of 'cla-clé-cli-clo-clou' evokes, a murmuring stream. Ravishingly voiced, artful, and minutely nuanced, Schwarzkopf's *Lied*-like account lacks naturalness (RLS 763); Lail's, pleasant enough, lacks finesse (GSC 79); and the statuesque Farrar, in a translation that removes the onomatopoeia, lacks imagination (IRCC 67; Rococo 5216). What the music can be becomes dramatically – in all senses – clear in the delivery of two Frenchmen, both of whom precede the air with its predecessor, the bustling 'C'est un torrent impétueux' (in D). Lucien Fugère (in the original keys; with piano – D 15178; Rococo 5332) was a very old man at the time of recording. There remains no more than a fine thread of tone in his singing; and no more than he has seems at any point needed; three centuries of the most creative traditions of *opéra-comique* are caught and impressed in each wonderful syllable. Gérard Souzay, recorded in youth, is a 'straighter' singer – though not, it must be stressed, a more legato one. The line is elegant, forward, uncluttered, and clear (with orchestra; both pieces down a tone – Decca LX 3112). Both are prized pieces of Gluck singing.

ALCESTE

As in the case of *Orfeo/Orphée*, it needs to be made clear that more than one Gluck opera bears the title of *Alceste* – the *tragedia per musica* (Vienna, 1767) on an Italian libretto by Calzabigi, and the *tragédie-opéra* (Paris, 1776), to a French text of Du Roullet. The two are usually, but erroneously, thought of as the same work, the second simply an adaptation in translation, with minor revisions, of the first. In fact, while intimately related by common musical material – and, of course, by a common plot descended from Euripides – the two operas differ radically, in form, in style, and in important areas of musical and dramatic content. The Vienna *Alceste*, despite the famous prologue of 1769, can be seen as a more conservative, retrogressive work than *Orfeo*. Inessential minor characters are retained, and (notably in the second and third acts) the plentiful *secco* recitative tends to run dry of dramatic interest. In its first two acts the Paris *Alceste* speeds up, 'electrifies' the meshing of music and drama in a series of tremendous innovations, strokes of compression – the choral irruption into the final cadence of the overture, and the transfer of Alcestis's heroic B flat aria, itself thrillingly reshaped as 'Divinités du Styx', to a climactic position at the close of the first act, are only the most significant of many. The operas follow a different sequence of events in their third acts. In the first, Alcestis dies, to be returned to life on the intervention of Apollo; in the second, she is rescued at the gates of Hades by Hercules, who has made a sudden, wholly unmotivated first appearance earlier in the act.

Objections to what I believe is Gluck's grandest operatic conception – if not, in either form, his masterpiece – are several, and have often been stated. 'Cette lamentable jérémiade . . . larmoyer en chantant . . . une déplorable psalmodie, tout au plus bonne à exécuter à des enterrements', are among the gibes made by Gluck's Parisian opponents (and collected in Le Blond's *Memoirs*, 1871); these we may interpret as early formulations of distaste for the unrelieved gloom of the opera, whose plot was later described, by Ernest Newman, as 'pre-eminently (a drama) of one idea; the burden of the play is sorrow and lamentation, which simply shifts from Admetus at the beginning . . . to Alcestis in the subsequent acts'. In both operas, only the title role comes fully to life – and does so magnificently; Admetus, rendered in slightly sharper focus for Paris, remains even there an indistinct figure. In both operas, but crucially in the second, Act 3 is musically uneven. Gluck, as always, makes cruel demands on performers. Above all, he requires a heroic soprano, tireless (especially so for the Paris vocal line) at the top of the stave, noble in declamation, warm and clear of tone, chastely passionate in inflection; a tenor of stamina and distinct personality; and a conductor determined neither to rush nor to overweight vast movements in search of their natural grandeur. Given all these, and given the intrinsic difficulties outlined earlier, it is understandable that *Alceste* should be infrequently encountered in the theatre (in the 1767 original that is – 1981 and 1982 saw something of an international renaissance of the Paris *Alceste*) and that it should have fared none too well on the gramophone. Understandable but sad: Gluck was never again to strike to such sustained tragic depths as in Act 2, scene i of the Vienna opera or in the entire first act of the Paris. That snatch of conversation overheard and recorded at the Paris première – '*Alceste* has fallen'; 'Yes: from heaven!' – has the ring of truth.

As it happens, the Vienna *Alceste* is one of the few mature Gluck operas other than *Orfeo/Orphée* served with at least a basic competence on record. The 1956 Decca set, which later emerged in good early stereo, presents the work in full, in a sound edition; well-articulated orchestral playing and decent choral work show the care taken by the conductor, Geraint Jones. His is a worthy, somewhat oratorio-like reading: a want of dramatic energy in the statement of the large movements is underlined where we might have expected it to be contradicted, by Kirsten Flagstad in the title role. Not uniformly: in the scene from Act 2 mentioned earlier she rises to sovereign splendour. Elsewhere the ear supplies unhappy confirmation of John Culshaw's account (in *Ring Resounding*) of recording sessions attended by a great but now senior soprano in poor health. The tone is often opaque, slow to 'speak'; it regularly requires to be scooped into and along the phrases – the glorious, unstoppable flow of the prime Flagstad sound is missing. She enunciates Italian both imperfectly and unmeaningfully; great stretches of the recitative lag and drag (a weakness by no means peculiar to the prima donna alone). The Admetus of Raoul Jobin, another veteran, might have made a less dry, monotonously forceful effect in the Paris *Alceste*, and in his native tongue; his Italian is very ugly (r-sounds gruesomely gargled). An English supporting cast is supplied of immaculate and unruffled good manners; Thomas Hemsley, in youthful voice, gives us an Anglican curate assisting at Evensong, not a High Priest presiding in the temple of Apollo.

All these cavils notwithstanding, this remains a substantial item in the basic Gluck collection – especially as there seems no likelihood of its being repeated, let alone improved upon. And while repeated hearings over the years have tended to emphasize its weaknesses, it takes no more than a single encounter with the only complete recording* of the Paris *Alceste* to assert, by comparison, its strengths. Casting around for points in favour of the latter, it can be said that the work is given almost in full, minor cuts occurring in the dance suites of the second and third acts; that Demigny's High Priest exerts some assurance of style; that Leibowitz's conducting hints at convinced ideas about the score if incomplete control over their fulfilment (in the overture and in Alcestis's 'Non! ce n'est point un sacrifice!' Gluck's characteristic multiplicity of tempo markings is both sought and made sense of); and – the strongest point – that the heroine, Ethel Semser, albeit a soprano of uneven, frequently sour vocal disposition, sings with a verbal and musical sensitivity conveying a striking amount of commitment to the role. The Paris Philharmonic (a short-lived body, it seems) is the leak in the vessel: its trombones dropsical, its woodwind intonation aberrant, its strings mean and sandpapery. In the celebrations of Act 2 a woolly chorus and its wildly vaulting accompaniment keep out of step for bars on end. Enzo Seri finds a certain throaty Italianate sweetness in Admetus's arias – poor compensation, on the whole, for comically unstylish delivery of recitative and an all-pervading shortage of *squillo* in the tone.

The absence of an adequate Paris *Alceste* recording is, and has long been, one of the major gaps in the catalogue. (The failure of the record companies to preserve for posterity the partnership of Janet Baker and Charles Mackerras, both in incandescent form during the singer's 1981 farewell to Covent Garden, must be deemed an act of negligence for which the epithet 'criminal' is only a little too strong.) For a brief period the French EMI set of excerpts attempted to fill it; but the opera, though seemingly apt for presentation in excerpts, communicates its power far less readily thus than in long movements (especially when, in such a passage as the closing bars of the overture, EMI's failure to provide a chorus denies the listener such telling strokes of

* The complete Paris Baudo *Alceste*, with Jessye Norman, came too late for inclusion.

Gluck's dramatic genius as might even here be indicated). Even so, the record is valuable for the somewhat impersonal but very firmly sung Admetus of Nicolai Gedda, whose easy access to freely ringing high notes is especially well employed in 'Barbare! Non, sans toi'. René Bianco's High Priest, threadbare in places, commands authoritative declamation. The Alcestis is Consuelo Rubio, the Spanish soprano seen at Glyndebourne in the role during the 1950s. On record, an individual timbre, shedding dark lustre in the lower reaches, can be admired, likewise a warm responsiveness: Alcestis as grieving wife and stricken mother is poignantly rendered. Her noble, decisive heroism is here imposed upon by a tight, uncomfortable top; a sense of mounting strain in 'Divinités du Styx', pardonable enough, dims the climactic purpose of the final top B flat. The crudities of the Paris Opéra orchestra prove only a little less crippling than those of the Paris Philharmonic, and Prêtre's all-purpose stop-go approach discloses none of Leibowitz's gleams of interpretative perception.

In extracts, all from the Paris *Alceste*, Gluck has been rather more kindly treated. Of arias other than 'Divinités du Styx' there are few examples, yet all are, in differing degree, worth seeking out. Eileen Farrell, a dramatic soprano of exceptional vocal quality under-exploited in opera in her prime, made a delayed Metropolitan debut, in 1960, in *Alceste*. Her 'Grands dieux, du destin qui m'accable' (Act 1) has one important flaw: the opening instrumental melody, which belongs to and which indeed insists upon the plangent timbre of the oboe, is barbarously assigned to a solo flute. Farrell herself invokes softness and power, delicate accents, a tenderly drawn line (with a good trill); the voice is lightly but not flippantly used, the peculiarly Gluckian major-key pathos made explicit without over-emphasis (Odyssey Y31739). An American Alcestis of an earlier decade was Rose Bampton. On one side of Victor 18218 (CAL 293) she sings the magnificent recitatives enclosing 'Non! ce n'est point un sacrifice!' (Act 1), joining them with a shortened version of the aria itself; on the other, 'Ah! malgré moi', the 6/8 repeat shortened, and without chorus (Act 2). The manner is fiery, the utterance *con intenzione*; she grades the increasing determination of the first extract and the sudden onset of despair of the second with keen dramatic awareness; but the tone goes thin and shrill under pressure. For a better balanced, indeed a superbly eloquent, blend of stylistic comprehension and vocal application in the same first-act excerpt, Suzanne Balguérie's recording of 'Ou suis-je?' up to and including 'Non! ce n'est point un sacrifice!' comes aptly to hand – unfortunate only in that on the two sides of the original 78 there should not have been room for the recitative *after* the aria. Balguérie's noble soprano has at its command both grandeur and simplicity of utterance; in her spacious shaping of the phrases there is room for expression of heroic resolve and also (in the section of farewell to Alcestis's children) the most pained regret (Columbia LF 54).

Admetus's beautiful 'Bannis la crainte' (Act 2) is found in three versions. In Georges Thill's, apart from two over-driven climaxes, a frank, forthright, marvellously *clean* voice moves with classical decorum and exemplary verbal clarity through the wide musical compass – a masterly performance (LFX 39; 2C 061–12154). Ansseau precedes the aria with the recitative 'O moment délicieux' – altogether more headlong in delivery, less steady, perhaps even too unsparing of a vibrant, brilliant tenor (unpublished; 2C 051–11304). From our day there is Guy Chauvet, possessor of one of the very few genuinely trumpet-toned instruments to have come out of France since the war, artist of sadly immature though faintly decipherable musical instincts (Véga Polaris L80.007). A point worth noting is the proper observance in recitative, by both Ansseau and Chauvet, of *appoggiature*.

After Orpheus's lament, 'Divinités du Styx' is the Gluck aria most frequently encountered on record. Both Berlioz and Reynaldo Hahn wrote reproachfully of Gluck's faulty French word-setting; removed from context at the close of the first act, where it achieves, arguably, the most heroic climax in all eighteenth-century opera, it can seem square-cut, even drab, no more than a *cheval de bataille* for a singer intent on delivering herself of three big B flats. Or, given the requisite metal in the tone and an acute sense of how to maintain and increase dramatic tension, it can provide a tremendous thrill. Singers short of the requisite metal, for all their other qualities, are Janet Baker (unexpectedly weak in crucial low phrases), Josephine Barstow (with piano), Teresa Berganza (in soft-grained French), Inge Borkh (in German), Suzanne Danco, Leontyne Price (studio-bound in expression), Elisabeth Söderström (who decorates repeats and cadences), and, in Italian, a strained and unrhythmic Renata Tebaldi. Marilyn Horne (SET 309–10), trippingly accompanied, bangs out low notes and thins out on high. Unlike her *Orfeo* 'Che farò?', Edna Thornton's *Alceste* excerpt (down a minor third) is prim, the English translation too quaint for the comfort of these ears (D 864). Naděžhda Kniplová (SUA ST 50789) and Christel Goltz (PR 135005), both poor singers of French, both bumpy of tone and phrase, the former handicapped by Peter Maag's slow tempo, each engage stirringly with the music. Michael Scott (in the first volume of *The Record of Singing*) proclaims the stylistic virtues of Maria Gay's 1905 performance (down a minor third and missing the first 33½ bars – RLS 724). I sense only a vulgarly spotlit heart on sleeve, though the attractions of the voice occasionally breach the lachrymose atmosphere.

As this roll-call of names has demonstrated, mezzo-sopranos have often taken the aria, if not the role, into their repertory. Especially if downward transposition is resorted to, a heavier-voiced singer may usefully underline the dramatic impact of Gluck's significantly placed low phrases – the aria exudes fierce determination at both ends of a compass nearly two octaves wide. The complementary disadvantage of the heavier voice is that a matronly, oratorio-like quality may be substituted for urgency. Maria Olszewska (in German; down a minor third) brings impressive solidity to the line, at some cost to dramatic interest (Gram. 72777; LV 25). Stignani (in Italian; down a minor third), tender in the middle section, sounds uninvolved else-

where; one misses, in the rounded flow of tone, a spark of personality (Cetra
BB 25094; LV37). Even more magisterially than Olszewska's, Louise Homer's massive instrument (in Italian; down a minor third) sounds the music;
I find that her occluded vowels, all apparently aspiring to the condition of
'er', grow wearisome (Vic. 1519). In the original key, Irene Dalis (in German), not classically smooth of delivery, and flying at key points fractionally
sharp, rings out big, exciting phrases (Telef. GMA 42). Martha Mödl, caught
live (in German – Melodram MEL 075), is characteristically unsteady and
impure – but also characteristically grand and imperious, a genuine queen,
a believable heroine. No less exciting, and less effortful at climaxes (if more
so than Dalis), is the metal-tipped Rita Gorr: while her dramatic presence
is always well remembered, the unforced womanliness of her soft singing,
beautifully evinced at 'Mourir pour ce qu'on aime', should be no less insisted
upon (ASD 456). Of all these mezzos, however, it is Margarete Klose (in
German; down a tone) who seems to me to exploit to wisest purpose the
solidity of a full, evenly weighted mezzo-soprano. The spacious shaping of
her line betokens a natural Gluck singer; the voice bears the words with
unarguable conviction – hear Klose's unforced yet forceful enunciation of the
word 'Gattin' (DB 4532; LV 18).

Ideally, though, it is to the soprano timbre that I turn for complete fulfilment of the aria's possibilities. Not to Farrell, caught on recognizably less
good form than for the earlier aria (33CX 1596); and to Maria Jeritza less
for anything specifically penetrative or comprehending in the delivery than
for the example of a secure, shining top register in full sail (DB 355). A 1937
radio performance, conducted by Fritz Reiner, finds Elisabeth Rethberg
laboured in the slow section, shrill at the top, and generally uncomfortable
with the music and the classical style: a disappointment (Glendale Records
GL 8003). Helen Traubel boasts a splendidly well-placed middle voice, an
authentically regal manner, and good diction: this has native sweep (Victor
17268; VIC. 1228). Suzanne Balguérie (down a semitone) has this, and
something more: the natural nobility of a French soprano declaiming clearly
and forthrightly in her native tongue (Decca Poly. LY 6065; Club 99.114).
The great Wagnerian Helene Wildbrunn leaves an equivalent impression in
German (Rococo 5220). And, finally, Callas – hampered by Prêtre's soggy
beat, and unable, at this stage of her career, to avoid wild, precarious
wobbling on every note above the stave. Yet for me the genius of her artistry,
in the crucible of which are compounded legato smoothness and antique fire
(how defiantly those Cs below the stave bite into the words 'Ministres de la
mort!'), beams light through every vocal infirmity; indeed, her determination
to keep faith with a composer's intentions even at the cost of straining all
her resources amounts to the kind of truthfulness of interpretation on which
Gluck thrives (ASD 4306). That Callas, in addition to her other, more widely
celebrated talents, was a Gluck soprano of the very highest order is affirmed
by the recording of the 1954 La Scala production of *Alceste*, given in Italian
and conducted with fluency and commitment by Carlo Maria Giulini. In far

fuller vocal estate – if a relatively 'simpler' interpreter of 'Divinità infernal' – she answers almost every demand the role has to make. But be warned: the score is brutally hacked and snipped about, the male leads are painful, and sound quality and even pitch are apt to distort with sudden and maddening frequency.

PARIDE ED ELENA

Paride ed Elena (1770) was Gluck's last opera for Vienna, and his final collaboration with the librettist Calzabigi. It was not a success, being generally considered a work of 'strange and unequal taste', according to a contemporary observer; its reception may well have had the decisive effect of turning the composer's ambitions towards the Paris lyric stage. The libretto has been described by Einstein as 'shilly-shallying . . . prolonged over five acts'. It is remembered, if at all, for only one of its many beautiful arias. Yet the music, encountered in any larger quantity, casts a spell. Like the later *Armide*, it is a drama centrally concerned with sexual love; and Gluck's stripping to bareness of his musical means achieves a potently direct and economic depiction of such feelings. *Paris and Helen* and the much greater *Armide* are works peculiarly poised on the edge, as it were, of the eighteenth century – carefully composed of ceremonial, French-influenced tableaux; and, in their evocations of passionate romantic entanglement, extraordinarily intuitive of the Romantic era.

These are both operas long overdue for the full attention of the record companies. And yet *Paris and Helen* contains a number that has been much recorded. This is the first solo aria of Act 1, Paris's 'O, del mio dolce ardor'. The part was first taken by the castrato soprano Giuseppe Millico, who after his appearance in the 1769 *festa teatrale* version of *Orfeo* at Parma became a Gluck protégé. (All four principal parts – Paris, Helen, Cupid, Minerva – are for soprano voice.) The aria, in G minor, *moderato*, over gently murmuring strings, with a radiant central dialogue between voice and oboe, is the impassioned yet chaste outpouring of a young man's ardour. It has been recorded by soprano, mezzo, and contralto, by tenor and baritone (lower voices usually necessitating downward transposition), with orchestra, with piano, and in a variety of instrumental arrangements. In almost every combination, that is, except the original one of soprano, orchestra with oboe, and G minor. To my mind, the lower the vocal pitch, the less likely the dramatic depiction of a lovesick youth (the alternation of voice and oboe phrases in imitation at 'Cerco te' becomes less poignant when the voice sings an octave below the oboe).

This rule is not unbreakable, and in one of the most magical versions it is broken; for the aria is sung by a baritone, in E minor – and by a baritone sixty-seven years of age at the time of recording! Battistini (DB 737; GEMM 166) has left here a choice sample of his highly cultivated, infinitely imaginative art, touching in a kaleidoscopic display of vocal colourings the romantic centre of the aria and the character. (He clips two phrases, and avoids low notes.) At the opposite pole, albeit in the same key, is another baritone, Alexander Svéd, on an album of so-called *arie antiche* accompanied by 'period' instruments, one to a part – these contrast weirdly with the veteran Hungarian singer's juddering, notably impure emission (LPX 1289). In order of diminishing merit, Richard Tucker, Jan Peerce, Rudolf Schock, Louis Graveure, and David Hughes – all heard in arrangements that grotesquely re-orchestrate, re-harmonize, and even re-bar the aria – form a bunch of charmless tenors. Martinelli (in E minor; with piano – Top Rank 15/010), recorded in his seventies, does his reputation no service of any kind. Bonci (in G minor; with piano – Fono. 39241; Rubini RDA 002) demonstrates his freely lyrical style, though its appeal cannot, for me, quite outweigh the nagging effect of his ungrateful timbre. Another famous tenor voice here lacking the proper degree of romance in the tone is Hermann Jadlowker's (in G minor – Poly. 72761; Rococo 5227), though respect for period conventions – the ornaments are fleetly turned as ever – sets him apart from his fellows. The Russian Mikhail Alexandrovich – now, according to report, an elderly Israeli émigré – can be encountered in a bizarre version (in F minor; with organ – Melodiya 33S 0433/4) not unlike a Holy Week incantation, though an aged voice discloses an occasional moment of drawn-out sweetness. Gigli (in F minor – DB 2531; HQM 1170) should be heard even by those out of sympathy with his characteristic style; if aspirates are in abundance, and sobs only a hair's-breadth away from the final cadence, the light, translucent quality of the tone is not only irresistible in itself but even, in a way, a revelation of the music. I have not heard the Tagliavini version.

The aria was formerly a recitalist's standby, in which guise it was apt for delivery chiefly as an exercise in smoothly moulded vocalism. Performances of this sort, all with piano, all rather lifeless, include those by Suzanne Danco, Jennie Tourel, and Tebaldi (whose voice, in 1973, was badly showing its age). Tebaldi with orchestra (in E minor – SXL 6629), recorded at about the same time, sounds more strident, the registers ill-coordinated, yet at the same time a little less embalmed. Hedwig von Debitzka (in G minor; with piano – CA 8060) shows a crystalline soprano, and phrasing of lovely intimacy, though the slow tempo has begun to exert a languid air by the da capo. Also slow is Elena Gerhardt (in D minor – 043261; Club 99.506), who wins admiration for her earnest endeavour to make everything *tell*; the song emerges in a single impulse. Margarete Klose (in E minor – DB 4532) I admire even more, for spinning out a more alluring tone with spacious lyrical feeling; her duet with oboe is marvellously rapt. She is one of the few singers, incidentally, to join middle section to reprise, and to add ornaments and, at the final 'alfin', a cadential flourish. In Maureen Forrester's reading (in E minor – SXLP 20096), polite, well-prepared, and tonally buttoned-up, the avoidance of such necessary detail seems to leave the line particularly bare. Friedel Beckmann, singing in German (in E minor – DB 5627; LV 235), is *korrekt*, and uninteresting. Klose apart, none of these ladies fully persuades me of their 'dolce ardor'. Teresa Berganza (in E minor – SDD 193) does. This is not just a faultless piece of classical singing, pure and burnished of tone, the line finely drawn and full of the most delicate inflection: it responds miraculously to character and situation. (But how could her conductor, Alexander Gibson, have allowed the first violins *en masse* to supplant the solo oboe?)

Janet Baker's Gluck recital (Philips 9500 023) presents, each in a downward transposition, four of Paris's arias: 'O, del mio dolce ardor' and 'Spiagge amate' (closed off by a completed final cadence, not broken into by the Trojan messenger of the opera) from Act 1; 'Le belle immagini', the *Andante grazioso* that ends the second act; and the impassioned outburst in several tempi, 'Di te scordarmi' (Act 4). Even though the ECO under Leppard accompanies her with less than desirable tautness, Baker's assumption of this castrato role is marked, no less than were her Handel heroes and Idamantes in the opera house, by passionate intensity and candour of feeling given out in phrases serene, tender, and broadly carried. As Paris she approaches her best form; vocal discoloration at either extreme of her range is no more disguised here than elsewhere in the recital, yet her singing affords the 'moral' eloquence of the finest Gluck interpretation – above all in 'Spiagge amate', an invocation to nature made by Baker an apostrophe quite as directly affecting as 'Che puro ciel' in *Orfeo*. 'Spiagge amate' has also been recorded by Bonci (with piano – Fono. 39127; RLS 7706), by Muzio (with piano – Edison 82287; Rubini RS 310), and by Hulda Lashanska (Victor 964; RLS 743), all in the lingering, *rubato*-shaped style mostly disdained today. Bonci's tone strikes the ear here as a little more caressing than usual; the lovely Muzio spoils her line with a heavy overlay of emotional mannerisms (and her speed moves at about half what is currently understood by the *moderato* marking); Lashanska, vocally statuesque, attitudinizes. For a change, the most admired representatives of classical singing of our day – Berganza and Baker – hold their own with the past. Indeed, they emerge from such a comparison with flying colours.

IPHIGÉNIE EN AULIDE

The first of Gluck's operas for Paris (1774) is an elevated, varied, broadly effective, and colourful work. Unlike his others intended for the French lyric stage, all of them dependent for their impact on the performer of an exacting title role (to a certain extent this is true even of *Iphigénie en Tauride*), in their adaptation of Racine, Gluck and his librettist Du Roullet succeeded in sharing the dramatic focus more evenly among the principal roles – the titular heroine, Agamemnon and Clytemnestra have a similar weight and import-ance – as well as achieving a more consistently lively interaction of choral and solo scenes. It is not an opera that responds well to presentation in excerpts, for, with notable exceptions (which include Agamemnon's great monologues, Clytemnestra's hair-raising visionary *scena* and several exquisite airs for Iphigenia), interest resides less in the basic musical units than in their masterly combination. This, no doubt, is one cause of the work's scanty appearances on record, though surprises lie in wait for the explorer, both pleasant and unpleasant.

Heading the ranks of the latter, unfortunately, is the only complete set, in German, of the opera. This is, in fact, not Gluck, but Gluck-Wagner: the distinction is crucial. In 1847 Richard Wagner, 'for the sake of dramatic animation', revised the opera, rescoring *tutti*, making many cuts, adding accompanied recitatives and transitions of his own composition, radically reworking the third act, and (with the example of Euripides rather than Racine in mind) contriving a new ending – on the order of Artemis, Iphigenia is removed to Tauris. The Wagner *Iphigenia in Aulis* is not without historical interest; were there a recording of the original to throw its emendations and 'improvements' into relief, we might even welcome the existence of an issue which throws more light on Wagner's own attitude to Gluck than on Gluck himself. As the sole available recording of the opera, the RCA set will hardly suffice – especially as the Munich performers supply a full share of unhappy moments on their own account. The Clytemnestra and Achilles are inadequate, the latter intolerably so; Anna Moffo's Iphigenia, not entirely devoid of pathetic expression, produces few 'real' notes – and even in its best period, about fifteen years earlier, hers was surely never a true Gluck soprano; as Agamemnon, Fischer-Dieskau rants (in the smaller role of the priest Calchas, Thomas Stewart, despite spreading top notes, evinces a more apposite vocal authority). The pedestrian quality of the conducting declares itself from the start. One of the keenest strokes of drama in the opera is the connection without break of the overture and Agamemnon's 'Diane impitoyable'. Here, the overture plods, and the first vocal entry is flatly reached.

In the seventh volume of the HMV *History of Music in Sound* there can be found an excerpt from the first act – numbers 3 and 4 in the vocal score – conducted by Roger Désormière. Unglamorously but alertly performed, by Bernard Demigny (Agamemnon), Lucien Lovano (Calchas), the Farm Street Singers, and the New London Orchestra, it gives in one ten-minute track a more cogent demonstration of the opera's noble classicism than all of RCA's six sides put together. Agamemnon's solo, 'Peuvent-ils ordonner?', forming the centrepiece of the excerpt, is memorable for the phrase 'Le cri plaintif de la nature', with its accompanying oboe *appoggiature* rending that cry palpable (Berlioz was to absorb such essential features of the Gluckian expressive vocabulary into his bloodstream). It is most gracefully handled by Désormière; the extract is altogether worth reissuing in some more easily available format (HLP 17). Agamemnon's solos are those from the opera most frequently encountered. In 1951 Boris Christoff recorded a towering 'Diane impitoyable', each note impressed with his special majesty, the baleful blackness of the tone modulated, at 'Brilliant auteur de la lumière', into a heartrending *mezza voce* (in Italian; down a tone – RLS 735). In the same passage Emil Schipper (in German; down a minor third) is commanding but rough, a famous Wotan leaving upon Gluck-Wagner more than a trace of Bayreuth Bark (EJ 490; LV 95). Of 'Peuvent-ils ordonner?' we can hear an unusually thoughtful account, on the Prague Gluck recital conducted by Peter Maag (SUA ST 50789), by Lothar Ostenburg, whose French is Teutonic but clearly pronounced, and whose high baritone has presence and heft. Christoff again, recorded a decade later, deploys an even more varied armoury of vocal and verbal inflection for Agamemnon's tremendous Act 2 monologue. It is possible to imagine his bass not to every taste (in another context it was recently described, by one American writer, as 'shale-throated'), but impossible to imagine a dull response to such a blend of imperious melancholy and sudden choked tenderness (in Italian; down a tone – ASD 2559). In the same scene Imre Palló (in Hungarian – LPX 11569) is nasal, raw, hard on the ears at any but the lowest dynamic levels.

Samples of the other principal roles are few. Clytemnestra's *scena* ought to figure in the repertory of any major dramatic mezzo; I have heard only the Kirov singer Evgeniya Gorokhovskaya (in Russian; aria down a tone – Melodiya S10 09064) a robust, vibrant singer, strikingly firm in low phrases. The Wagner version of Achilles's 'Calchas, d'un trait mortel' (Act 3) was recorded by the *Heldentenor* Erik Schmedes, who blares it out above an oompah accompaniment in the style of a *Bauernfestlied*; the heroic symmetries of Gluck are miles removed (4–42098; LV 502). Three of the heroine's airs can be heard. The American Gwendolyn Walters sings with a darkly attractive soprano but lifeless words in the Act 1 *récit et air*, 'L'ai-je bien entendu?' (SUA ST 50789). In the Act 2 'Par la crainte' and its introductory *récit* Janet Baker is distinctively impassioned (down a semitone – Philips 9500 023). She and Christa Ludwig may be compared in Iphigenia's simply stated Act 3 Farewell, one of the few melodies of the opera to imprint itself instantly on the memory. Ludwig's lustre and evenness (in German – SCM 84) strike the senses as somehow impersonal (she cuts the repeat); Baker clouds over in high phrases, yet leaves an unforgettable souvenir of grief-laden dignity.

ARMIDE

It could fairly be said that the circumstances attendant upon the creation of this *drame lyrique* (Paris, 1777) are more familiar to many students of opera than is the work itself. It is well known that in commencing his setting of Quinault's *Armide* – produced nearly a century earlier for Lully – Gluck had previously abandoned the composition of *Roland* (another Quinault libretto) on learning that the Neapolitan Piccinni had been brought to Paris by the anti-Gluckists for the express purpose of being competitively engaged on the same task; this, at least, was Gluck's own account of the situation. The subsequent quarrel between the so-called Gluckists and the Piccinnists is one of the minor operatic controversies to which the textbooks unfailingly draw attention. Accepting – as a gesture of salute and challenge combined to the great tradition (now moribund) of the French *tragédie-lyrique* – such a libretto, loosely constructed and to some extent inconsequentially motivated, the celebrated exponent of Reform was inevitably laying himself open to charges of backsliding. The most frequent criticism made of *Armide* concerns, indeed, the fourth act, which, devoted entirely to the adventures of Ubaldo and the Danish Knight as they avoid the ensnarements of assorted demons and sirens, has been dismissed as dramatically superfluous. Even after such a criticism is accepted (which, after a recent live encounter with the opera, at Christ Church, Spitalfields in the summer of 1982, I find myself disinclined to do), I feel bound to mention that since a first hearing of the complete opera (in a 1974 BBC studio recording superbly conducted by Charles Mackerras) it has become my own favourite among all of Gluck's works. As an excursion into a world of courtly romance, it is quite different from, yet closely related to, the *tragédies-lyriques* of Lully and Rameau (which Gluck admitted to having studied before his first Paris initiative). Within a framework of chivalric-fantastic romance Gluck shapes scenes of a power, grandeur, and psychological penetration that threaten to rend the delicate fabric of poetry out of which the rest are woven. Threaten – yet they serve instead to heighten the unique atmosphere created in the music, surely, for all the moral force and dramatic succinctness of the other mature operas, the most sheerly and unstintingly beautiful that Gluck ever wrote.

The heroine is the most fully rounded and developed in his wonderful gallery of female portraits. The stages of her development are clearly marked; they show a proud enchantress gradually succumbing (in the closing scene of Act 2) to emotional temptation; later ecstatically partaking of the pleasures of her love with former mortal enemy Rinaldo (their love duet in the fifth act is peculiarly charged with sexual passion); and, at last abandoned by him, rising in the finale to heights of love-torn fury at the peak of which she razes to the ground her own enchanted domain. *Armide* is arguably the most original Gluck opera – a Janus-like whole, which adheres to the values of eighteenth-century dramaturgy and at the same time looks forward for long stretches to the ideal of 'continuous opera' that came in one form or another to dominate the nineteenth century, a work whose formal pattern of decorative divertissements and grand tableaux Gluck paradoxically uses to cleave to his central theme, the overwhelming power, sublime and destructive in equal measure, of sexual love. (Even the criticized Act 4 can be seen as essentially a variation on that theme.) The long neglect of the opera is not totally incomprehensible. Its uniqueness has almost always, in later periods, been misconstrued; and, on a practical level, the title role, an assignment for a Fremstad or a Litvinne, a Leider or a Destinn, is a monumental undertaking – Berlioz was exaggerating only a little when he said that 'to play Gluck heroines it is not enough to have genuine talent . . . nothing less than beauty and genius will do'. Perhaps the Spitalfields performances, with Felicity Palmer their heroine and Richard Hickox their conductor, will lead the way to a more reliable regularity of others; for if there was ever a work deserving of the title 'neglected masterpiece', it is surely *Armide*.

The knowledge that EMI has recorded the Spitalfields production (for intended release in 1983) will assuage the most passionate plaints of the Gluckians; for meanwhile we find a representation of the work on records that stretches no further than a single album of highlights and a handful of arias. The Angelicum Italian-language record of excerpts, made in 1958 in connection with Milan concert performances of the opera (and never, to my knowledge, much circulated outside that country), offers eight scenes. These make up a characteristic selection, subject in each case to internal snipping. The performance is a plain affair, undertaken with greater amounts of vitality than of accomplishment; yet is has given me pleasure – it is the sort of record that could stand reissue on an enterprising bargain label. In the same decade Gloria Davy was appearing at Covent Garden as Aida; Giuseppe Zampieri, the Rinaldo, was a Karajan tenor. She suggests a more certain understanding of the delivery of recitative and the traversal of Gluck's long melodic lines, at once sensuous and stripped of egregious ornament, than he does – the tenor solo of Act 2, the blissful 'Plus j'observe ces lieux' (in which Gluck's famous remark about having endeavoured to be 'more painter and poet than musician' in *Armide* is most vividly demonstrated), finds him respectful but inhibited, and choppy of line. Both, though, have warm, full-blooded voices; both have moments of touching ardour. Hate, the fury whose attempted exorcism of Armida's new-found love is one of the highlights of the third act, is taken by a bumpy, very lively Italian mezzo; other soloists, briefly heard, do no damage, and the Turin chorus sounds full of fresh young voices.

Single items, few in number, prove of high quality. The second-act duet of Armida and her father Idraote (baritone), mentioned earlier in connection with *Le nozze d'Ercole e d'Ebe*, is excitingly sustained, on the Prague Gluck record (SUA ST 50789) by Věra Soukupová and Lothar Ostenburg, he a suaver singer, less crude in French, than she. I have heard two tenors in 'Plus j'observe ces lieux', both of them singers of distinction. The leonine voice of Agustarello Affre, big, dark, of thrilling ring, is perhaps more honestly than poetically employed on Rinaldo's ravishing music, though there is no touch of insensitivity in his phrasing. He comes to an end several bars before the air itself properly does (Odeon 97011; GV 38). As an admirer of Joseph Rogatchewsky's art I have to confess a slight disappointment with his record: the timbre is individual but unvaried, and the delivery not ideally smooth. In this version, at least, there is a fuller account of Gluck's delicate orchestral writing (Col. LF 76; Club 99.44). With Frida Leider's 'Ah! si la liberté', the opening aria of Act 3, we come to one of the supreme pieces of Gluck singing on record – one that serves to demonstrate why Gluck is one of the most exacting but also one of the most rewarding of composers for the voice, and what the much mulled-over *bella simplicità* of style and content can mean when undertaken by a great artist. The long line is seamlessly unfolded; one thrills to a voice of extreme richness and beauty of tone selfless enough to avoid drawing attention to itself; words are carried caressingly on the breath. I love, too, the string *portamenti* under Barbirolli, almost as discreetly sensuous as Leider herself (D 1547; 1C 147–30 785/86M). In the face of such singing Suzanne Brohly's account of the same aria still merits high praise. There is strong character and distinction in her verbal delivery; a freely fluent manner of moulding the phrases is balanced by a forward, very impressive attack (W 441). The longest track on the Janet Baker Gluck recital (Philips 9500 023) contains, complete (and transposed down a semitone), Armida's *scène dernière*, from 'Le perfide Renaud' to the cataclysmic closing bars. The twice-uttered 'Mon lâche coeur le suit', rising and falling in perilous semitonal steps through the 'break' between middle and high registers, discovers the beat and also the cloudiness of tone to which this voice is prey when under pressure. Despite (perhaps even because of) this, emotional intensity is increased to an almost alarming pitch; for all the lacklustre articulation of the ECO violins, and the snail's pace at which Raymond Leppard chose to begin the number, the snowballing power of the scene is grandly set in motion.

IPHIGÉNIE EN TAURIDE

The penultimate opera (1779) – the last was the unsuccessful *Echo et Narcisse* – constituted Gluck's only undisputed Paris triumph; it remains the one Gluck opera generally admitted, even by his detractors, into the canon of sanctified operatic masterpieces. It can be seen and heard as the summation of his Paris operas, and of his creative output for the lyric stage as a whole. The music may not quite match (at their peak) the tragic depths of *Alceste*, the dramatic variety of the earlier *Iphigénie*, the charged atmosphere of *Armide*, or the lyrical warmth of *Orphée*; yet, at last, all these qualities are balanced, in a work that is intimate and also heroic, tragic without being oppressive, weighty yet unusually swift-moving in its succession of events. (Guillard's libretto lays the most tightly constructed ground plan of any Gluck opera.)

It is the work of a theatre craftsman of long experience, unfalteringly sure in every detail of his stylistic range and its application to chosen dramatic situations. In one particular, the gramophone can help to bear this out. Except where specially relevant, it has not been the business of this essay to trace and enumerate Gluck's continual recycling in later operas of earlier musical material; the habit is easily demonstrable, for it persisted throughout his career. Here, an example seems pertinent. On a German record (FSM Aulos 53517 AUL) of eighteenth-century arias performed by Kay Griffel (soprano) and Eckert Sellheim (fortepiano), we can hear the aria 'Se mai senti' from Gluck's *La clemenza di Tito* of 1752. Apart from minor differences in the underlay of the vocal line caused by the adaptation to the French language, the music is heard to be almost identical with that of 'O malheureuse Iphigénie!', the aria which provides the later opera's emotional centre-point, in Act 2. The fact that this self-borrowing, effected across a distance of nearly three decades, affords on its second usage one of the sublime moments of musico-dramatic fusion in all opera reveals Gluck's degree, by this stage in his career, of artistic self-awareness. 'Paradoxically,' Andrew Porter has written of the many passages of Gluck *opera seria* reconvened with absolute precision of purpose for *Iphigénie en Tauride*, '(his) most consistent opera is in some sense an anthology of his best ideas over nearly thirty years.'

The single complete recording of the opera was made with the forces of the 1952 Aix-en-Provence Festival production. It is 'complete' in the way of Giulini's *Alceste* at La Scala, two years later: that is to say, cuts disfigure almost every number, whether they be of no more than a few bars here and there, or whether they more extensively remove some treasured stretch of recitative, chorus, or dance music; repeats of any kind are a regular casualty. Since the construction of the opera has been expertly calculated, cutting of this sort throws out its balance; the effect is, in the longer term, actually to dull and disperse the dramatic impact. This is one of two major obstacles to involvement in the performance. The other, alas, is the singing of the title role. Patricia Neway, an artist of many fine, sentient, and lively ideas about the opera, shows herself unable to put them completely into practice because of a flawed, unreliable soprano. The flaws seem here not entirely predictable. Occasionally a notoriously taxing phrase will come off; more often a less troublesome one will go wrong, to the accompaniment of vocal effects variously unsupported, gratingly shrill, or 'stuck-in-the-throat'. She gets through the opera honourably, given all this; but more than honour is wanted.

The strengths of the performance, thus qualified, are none the less worth noting. Giulini, for all his apparent lack of confidence in Gluck the operatic architect, conducts his music with untrammelled warmth of feeling. He gives no hint of the formality or frigidity which sometimes affects conductors' attempts to be classical, yet the concern for shapely lyrical phrasing and sustained dramatic movement across each act never leads to hard driving (an alternative and no less serious hazard). Only true brilliance of timbre is missing in Léopold Simoneau's traversal of Pylades's third aria, the Beethovenian, 'Divinités des grandes âmes'; in most other respects he approaches an ideal – a deeply affecting performer, manly, dignified, and gentle (with what unforced sweetness he embodies the virtues of friendship in 'Unis de la plus tendre enfance', making the listener insist, at least temporarily, that this is Gluck's most beautiful aria). Some years before Robert Massard came to international attention as Orestes, he recorded this brave and largely successful account of Thoas's short but terrifyingly strenuous role (the voice itself, clear but callow, is only intermittently recognizable for qualities later justly admired). As Orestes we encounter Ansermet's first Pelléas, Pierre Mollet, a cultivated high baritone of Pelléas rather than Orestes dimensions; the uninhibited, hag-ridden power of expression is in short supply.

A complementary experience, so far as it goes, of the opera is provided by the EMI set of extracts. Prêtre's conducting, on more than one occasion palpably out of touch with the needs of his singers, whips up superficial shows of 'temperament'; Gedda's Pylades exhibits greater ring, much less tenderness, than Simoneau's; Ernest Blanc, a sterling-voiced, unsubtle Orestes, tends to roar out the high phrases of 'Dieux qui me poursuivez'; in Louis Quilico's energetic rendering of Thoas's 'Des noirs pressentiments' the notes are not always exactly in focus. The permanent value of the record is assured as a souvenir of Rita Gorr's Iphigenia. Here, we recall from the opera house and are able to reaffirm on the evidence of a limited number of appearances on record, was a singer of the front rank, of presence definite and delivery thrillingly bold. In classical roles the fire could be tempered, though happily never tamed, by the kind of soft, supplicating utterance so beautifully instanced here in 'D'une image, hélas!'. (In my mind's ear it is in Gorr's voice, its keen edge shaded by gently nostalgic melancholy, that such a phrase as 'Chassons une vaine chimère' is now indelibly carried.) Iphigenia is properly a role for a dramatic soprano; several passages cause the Belgian mezzo audible discomfort – the As of 'O malheureuse Iphigénie!' come dangerously close to shrieks. For the many marvellous things in her singing a few twinges of pain are uncomplainingly suffered.

Excerpts show us several distinguished Iphigenias. Régine Crespin was much admired in the 1965 Paris Opera production. (And on the Discoréale collection, *30 ans sur scène*, taken from live recordings, three long excerpts show us why, though the dragged, rhythmically invertebrate conducting of Georges Sébastian makes listening to them something of a trial – DR 10006/8.) For Decca Crespin recorded the long recitative 'Cette nuit j'ai revu', which leads directly (and here without choral and solo priestess interventions) into 'O toi qui prolongeas' (Act 1). While the large lovely voice, in less healthy form than on the live excerpts, may be flawed by hollow, uneasy top notes, its comprehension of the dreamy anguish of the recitative and suffering nobility of the aria insist that the singer has 'lived' the role, long and thoroughly, before bringing it into the recording studio. The sound of Crespin singing in French is a pleasure all its own (SET 520–1). Zinaida Yuryevskaya, whose soprano is no less lovely and whose control of it was in this instance rather more secure, offers the aria only, in a style of 'holds' and lingerings triumphantly justified by their musicianly intent (in German – P 1879; LV 89). From a 1937 radio broadcast, Elisabeth Rethberg's 'O toi qui prolongeas', if less disappointing than her *Alceste* aria from the same collection, still mixes radiant and strenuous phrases (Glendale GL 8003). By the time Maria Callas came to record 'O malheureuse Iphigénie!', for her second recital of French airs (33CX 1858), the parlous condition of the voice required adjustments of placement, attack, vowel formation etc., to almost every phrase in order to keep the line from possible collapse. On the 'private' issue of the 1957 La Scala *Iphigénie*, in Italian, the aria is much more freely voiced; yet in that strange way common to many Callas duplications, it is the later version, with all its disconcerting infirmities, but also with all its tokens of marvellously deepened perception, with its line even more subtly wrought and soulfully shaped, which remains to haunt the memory. (Like the Scala *Alceste*, mentioned earlier, this performance is weakened by feeble male casting, and damaged – perhaps less gravely – by cuts; but the sound quality is much better, and again Callas makes one wonder why her assumption of so difficult a role has not assumed the legendary stature of her Norma or Lucia.) Suzanne Balguérie, in the same aria, undertakes another kind of Gluck performance altogether. The line, not weighed with tragic implication, is heard to make its own effect by being traced with absolute straightforwardness; given Balguérie's wonderfully distinguished utterance of words and clear, noble tone, it cannot fail to do so (Poly. LY 6065). By comparison, Gwendolyn Walters sounds like a gifted student, with all the most important lessons of interpretation still to be learned (SUA ST 50789). None of these singers succeeds in disguising the strain of Gluck's high As; strain, nobly borne, must therefore be assumed to be an element of interpretation counted on by so canny an opera composer. Of the fiery 'Je t'implore et je tremble' (Act 4) and its preceding recitative Janet Baker (down a tone) gives a slightly muted account; I cannot quite feel, as I can while listening to Gorr in the same aria, that Iphigenia is at this point approaching the final 'crunch'.

In this opera, more than in any other of Gluck's, the memories of the two leading characters impinge on almost every action they undertake. We watch, and feel, the past clashing with the present, defining and influencing behaviour and response. It is Gluck's most psychologically profound human drama, and the long reach of his understanding of character motivation conscious and unconscious is what lends the scenes between unacknowledged brother and sister their painful intimacy. The player of Orestes, though by himself he cannot 'make' the opera (as at Covent Garden we have learnt, when the splendid Orestes of Robert Massard has had to play opposite a less suitably cast Iphigenia), is offered a role at once fearsomely difficult, in its sustained high *tessitura*, and enormously rewarding, in its broad spectrum of dark emotions. I think it a tragedy that no more of Massard's Orestes has been preserved than 'Dieux qui me poursuivez', a piece whose trumpet-and-drum D major, out of context, can seem curiously lightweight. Massard's high baritone, exemplary in definition, verbal clarity, and power of utterance, ensures that it does not (MSA 72A). So, to a lesser degree, does Håkan Hagegård, whose fresh, sensitive young voice goes a little stringy at the top. On the same recital record (CAP 1062) he sings the first part (including recitative) of Orestes's solo *scena*, stopping short of the Furies' incursion. Domgraf-Fassbaender couples the same two excerpts (in German – Gramm. 24323; LV 131); self-pitying in the first, he brings to 'Le calme rentre dans mon coeur' a *Winterreise* kind of deep weariness that is deeply moving. More even than Massard's, and far more than Hagegård's, his voice rides freely in high phrases – a wonderful sound. Lothar Ostenburg and conductor Peter Maag join 'Le calme rentre' to an almost complete account of the nightmare (a pity only that Iphigenia's dramatic intrusion, at its climax, should of necessity be replaced here by a perfect-cadence close). Singer, Czech chorus, and orchestra screw to a high pitch of tension a scene made out of deceptively plain materials (SUA ST 50789).

Pylades, noble personification of true, uncomplicated friendship, is the fixed point about which Iphigenia and Orestes move. When the role is woodenly played or sung with less than full measure of its peculiar musical grace, or both, we want to add him to the shortlist of tenor bores in opera. When strong, uncluttered feeling is enlisted by the performer on his behalf, the beauty of his music has to be recognized as one of the opera's supreme features. It would be hard to conceive of a more serene, manly statement of the first and most beautiful of the three arias, 'Unis de la plus tendre enfance', than Thill's; even Simoneau on the Giulini recording, fine as he is, cannot quite match Thill's radiant simplicity, his note-for-note thoroughness, which leaves for a later age an ideal of Gluck tenor singing (LFX 274; 2C153–11660/1). Other accounts of the aria include those by Charles Rousselière (with piano – 2-32808; SYO 5), insensitive in some details and rather too obviously concerned to put on show a fine voice; Guy Chauvet, who hews the line into chunks (Véga Polaris L80.007); the rather uncomfortable-sounding yet distinctively affecting Karl Erb, in German (Odeon 99775; 1C 147–30771/72); and, also in German, Fritz Wunderlich, whose addition of aspirates does not efface one's enjoyment of his manly, true style (DG 2700 709). The security and fluency of Wunderlich's technique is emphasized by the pleasant but in many ways somewhat stressful account of the same piece by his successor, Siegfried Jerusalem, who 'gets through' the aria rather than actually doing anything with it (in German – Eurodisc 200 089-366) On the above-mentioned Wunderlich record can also be found the third-act duet, 'Et tu prétends encore' (repeats removed), with Hermann Prey a lugubrious Orestes. Singing in German need not necessarily force the music into squareness of cut and impact (Gluck himself, after all, oversaw and partly translated the German version, first given at Vienna in 1781); but it does require a smoother, less blustery delivery than Prey's if squareness is to be fully avoided.

ALCESTE

A Alcestis; *Ad* Admetus; *HP* High Priest; *H* Hercules; *E* Evander

1951–2 (Paris edition – ed. Leibowitz) Semser *A*; Seri *Ad*; Demigny *HP*; Hoffman *H*; Mollien *E*/ Chorus, Paris PO / Leibowitz Olympic (US) ⓜ 9104 (3) Opera Society (UK) ⓜ OPS107–9

1956 (Vienna edition – in Italian) Flagstad *A*; Jobin *Ad*; Hemsley *HP*; *H*; Young *E* / chorus,

Geraint Jones Orch. / G. Jones Decca GOS574–6 Richmond SRS63512

1954 (live performance – Teatro alla Scala, Milan) (in Italian) Callas *A*; Gavarini *Ad*; Silveri *HP*; Panerai *H*; Zampieri *E* / La Scala Chorus and Orch. / Giulini Cetra ⓜ LO50 (2)

1960 (excerpts – in French) Rubio *A*;

Gedda *Ad*; Bianco *HP*; *H* / Paris   EMI ASD576
Opéra Orch. / Prêtre

ARMIDE

c. 1958 (excerpts – in Italian) Davy   Polyphonic Choir, Milan
    Armida; Zampieri *Rinaldo*;   Angelicum Orch./Cattini
    Mandalari *Hate*; Arena *Sidonia*;   Angelicum ⓜ LPA1009
    Cerutti *Lucinda*; Turin

LE CADI DUPE

F Fatima; *Z* Zelmire; *N* Nuradin; *O* Omar; *Om* Omega; *C* Le Cadi

1959 (in German – Fuchs and Krastl   Epic BC1062
    version) Von Welz *C*; Nixa *F*;   1975 (in German – original version)
    Djeri *Z*; Van Vrooman *N*; Smid-   Rothenberger *F*; Donath *Z*;
    Kowar *O*; Schönauer *Om* /   Gedda *N*; Hirte *O*; Marheineke
    Salzburg Mozarteum Orch. /   *Om*: Berry *C* / Bavarian State
    Paumgartner   Opera Chorus and Orch. / Suitner
    Musica et Litera MEL 9001   EMI 1C 065 28834Q

IPHIGENIE EN AULIDE

1973 (Wagner edition) Moffo   Weikl *Archas*/ Bavarian Radio
    Iphigénie; Fischer-Dieskau   Chorus, Munich Radio Orch./
    Agamemnon; Schmidt   Eichhorn
    Clytemnestra; Spiess *Achilles*;   RCA ARL2–0114
    Stewart *Calchas*; Augér *Artemis*;

IPHIGENIE EN TAURIDE

I Iphigénie; *O* Orestes; *P* Pylade; *T* Thoas

1952 Neway *I*; Mollet *O*; Simoneau *P*;   F. Albanese *P*; Colzani *T*; / La
    Massard *T* / Aix-en-Provence   Scala Chorus and Orch./ Sanzogno
    Festival Chorus, Paris   Cetra ⓜ LO54 (2)
    Conservatoire Orch. / Giulini   1961 (excerpts – in French) Gorr *I*;
    EMI ⓜ DTX130–2   Blanc *O*; Gedda *P*; Quilico *T* /
    Vox (US) ⓜ OPBX212   Paris Conservatoire Orch. / Prêtre
1957 (live performance – Teatro alla   EMI ASD465
    Scala, Milan) Callas *I*; Dondi *O*;   Angel S35632

L'IVROGNE CORRIGE

1952 Benoit *Mathurin*; Demigny *Lucas*;   PO / Leibowitz
    Collart *Colette*; Betti *Mathurine*;   Nixa ⓜ PLP238
    Hoffman *Cléon*; *Pluton* / Paris   Baroque ⓜ 2863

LE NOZZE D'ERCOLE E D'EBE

1967 (in German) Vulpius *Hercules*;   CO / Koch
     Rönisch *Hebe*; Prenzlow *Juno*;   Eterna 820677
     Schreier *Jupiter*; Berlin

Die Entführung aus dem Serail

WILLIAM MANN

Act 1

Act 2

Act 3

Until recent decades, when *Idomeneo* has won a new place in the canon, the earliest of the great Mozart operas was acknowledged to be *The Abduction from the Harem*, or *The Harem Snatch*, or *The Seraglio*, as English-speaking opera companies have variously rendered *Die Entführung aus dem Serail*. Mozart wrote this *komisches Singspiel* in 1781–82, shortly after he had removed from Salzburg to Vienna, to a text adapted for him by Gottlob Stephanie the Younger. It had been commissioned by the Austrian Emperor's short-lived German Opera in Vienna, and although that soon reverted to Italian opera, Mozart's *Entführung* continued to hold the German-speaking stage, with its exotic setting, dramatic mixture of comical and heroic elements, and charming, sometimes superb music.

Stephanie's libretto is less glorious in its diction, as reproduced in authoritative scores, and certain phrases have been sung to revised words at least since gramophone records first appeared. At that time (the earliest record I can trace dates from 1906) the quality of florid music attracted great singers to record the most famous numbers, and the discography of individual items is extensive. When complete, or near-complete Mozart opera recordings were launched by HMV's Mozart Society with the Glyndebourne Festival Opera in the 1930s, *Die Entführung* was not included, although it was performed there in three successive pre-war seasons: it is known that Fritz Busch was dissatisfied with some of the vocal casting. Perhaps HMV also feared that the international record-buying public would be less welcoming to an *Entführung* than to one of the Da Ponte Mozart operas.

At all events, the first nearly complete set of *Die Entführung* did not appear until after the war, when a Vienna State Opera cast, under its leading Mozart conductor, Josef Krips, recorded it for Decca. WERM I cites 78rpm numbers for it, but it was more widely known as the first LP opera, an impressive portent for the new type of gramophone record. Boldly, at a time when even Mozart recitatives were regularly suppressed in recorded versions, Decca included some spoken dialogue (in German) to separate the sung numbers – well spoken too, especially by the Pedrillo. There were some internal musical cuts, common in stage performances then, and Belmonte's 'Ich baue ganz' was replaced by his earlier 'Wenn der Freude Tränen fliessen', also quite customary (the former is exceptionally testing). The set was much admired at the time, and was later reissued. Today the acoustic sounds cramped, the singers closely miked, the orchestra backward (that was deprecated at the time). There is plenty of spirit and tenderness, and style as well, in Krips's reading, even if it is less than ideally reflected in the singing of the cast. Walther Ludwig sings a decently heroic Belmonte, his voice more grainy and robust than the average Mozart tenor of those days, though smooth and endearing enough in 'O wie ängstlich' and the duet with Konstanze just before the end. He had sung the part at Glyndebourne in 1935, when his Pedrillo was that paragon of English Mozart tenors, Heddle Nash. On this set the Pedrillo is Peter Klein, a rasping voice though an able singer; he was Covent Garden's standard Mime in the *Ring*, as well as Mozart's Don Basilio and Monostatos, but Pedrillo should sound a more cuddlesome suitor in his serenade 'Im Mohrenland'.

The two tenor voices are quite distinctive, as important in records of this opera as a contrast between the two sopranos – Belmonte and Konstanze more heroic, Pedrillo and Blonde more worldly and cheerful (the difference is acutely observed in the central section of the Act 2 Quartet, No. 16). That contrast is not clear in the casting of Wilma Lipp as Konstanze, pleasing, quite accurate in her virtuoso arias, but too close in vocal timbre to that of Emmy Loose, who effects the distinction by chirping and pecking at her notes too often, in the then common Viennese fashion. The Osmin, Endré Koreh, has the range for his music but not the accurate agile technique: his 3 is sketchy and careless, and he falls inappropriately into sentimentality in 2. For the most part his is a jolly performance, perhaps too harmless in 19 where sadistic relish is a *sine qua non*. The whole set is typical of Austrian Mozart in the late 1940s, a trough between earlier and later crests – witness the common resort to intrusive aspirates, the almost total non-observance of grammatical graces and flourishes, and low standard of accuracy in florid runs, as well as the soubrette pecking mentioned above, all common in individual records of the period, less so nowadays or in the gramophone's youth.

It was not until 1954 that another record company attempted a nearly complete *Entführung* and then DG went to Berlin and Ferenc Fricsay, who was to follow this set with *Figaro, Giovanni* and *Zauberflöte*, often with the members of this cast. Here the vocal characterizations are nicely distinctive. Maria Stader's soprano is not heroic in size, but there is a thread of gold in it that she uses, with a quick vibrato and musicianly insight, to indicate that the singer of 'Martern aller Arten' is a grander lady than the Blondchen of 'Durch Zärtlichkeit', neatly and prettily as that is done by Rita Streich. Ernst Häfliger sings a debonair, smooth but never spineless Belmonte, Martin Vantin an attractive Pedrillo, properly *sotto voce* in his serenade. Josef Greindl's voice was a noble, wide-ranging and quite steady bass in those days, with plenty of venom for Osmin's nursery sadism, and the joviality to remove it from real villainy, though aspirates in profusion soon outstay their welcome. Fricsay was a zestful, sensitive Mozartian, obtaining neatly balanced ensembles and vocal-orchestral rapport, rather speedy in the final Vaudeville. No. 15, as a matter of course, is resited in place of 17, and there is a small cut in 20. Some connecting dialogue was included, in several cases spoken by actors with voices obviously remote from their singing counterparts; this remained for some years a persistent bugbear of *Singspiel* records. The recorded sound is a distinct improvement on that of the previous set.

It is one of the tragedies of post-1945 musical history that Sir Thomas Beecham, supreme opera conductor and revered interpreter of Mozart, spent so little time during his maturest years in the opera house, and left so few records of complete operas. Apart from the *Zauberflöte* in 1938, his only recording of a Mozart opera was his *Entführung* of 1956, an eleventh-hour bicentennial tribute. A rehearsal record suggests his principal concern for *buffo* vivacity, achieved in the orchestral playing, in Gottlob Frick's brilliant portrayal of Osmin, and to some extent in Gerhard Unger's spirited and musically aware Pedrillo (13 is a good instance). Not, alas, in Ilse Hollweg's Blonde, able, silver-toned, but prim and static, too much like Konstanze, here less than heroically voiced by Lois Marshall, an admirable singer who persistently falls short of expectation. Leopold Simoneau contributes an expert, heroic Belmonte. There is some dialogue but, as in the Fricsay set, most of it is spoken by actors who sound nothing like their singing counterparts. The recorded balance favours voices more than orchestra, curious with Beecham in command. It is chiefly Beecham's insight which sustains affection for this set, even though he removes 'Martern aller Arten' to Act 3, before the duet, and replaces 'Ich baue ganz' with 'Wenn der Freude Tränen'.

From Dresden in 1962 came a set, produced by Philips, that suggested a sad decline in the prestigious standards of its State Opera. Otmar Suitner makes a heavy-handed job of the score, even of such jovial numbers as the trio, 'Marsch, marsch!' and the duet 'Ich gehe, doch rate ich dir'. Arnold van Mill's ripely sonorous Osmin is the most appreciable solo performance, as Jutta Vulpius's Konstanze is the least, the voice too heavy for the music – at least she is not an o'erparted Blonde. Rolf Apreck's grainy tenor might have sounded more agreeable if his arias were not made to plod so. Jürgen Förster and Rosemarie Rönisch contribute more enjoyably (though there is more base metal than true silver to her top E in 8). The Dresden orchestra accompanies with less than its famed precision. The dialogue was recorded in an unnaturally cramped, hollow acoustic, at odds with the spacious sound of the musical numbers.

More pleasure was to be expected from the Munich set conducted by Eugen Jochum for DG. His is a spirited, sensitive reading, with excellent orchestral playing (e.g. 11, with its *obbligato* concertante quartet). There is too a now-precious souvenir of Fritz Wunderlich's artistry in Mozart; if his vocalism is flawed in the taxing 17, his is a more than heroic attempt. Friedrich Lenz's Pedrillo, robust and earthy, falls down only in a breathless, dull Serenade. There is charm in Lotte Schädle's Blondchen, also some careless intonation, a fault, alas, shared by Kurt Böhme's vulgar and unsteady Osmin, by 1965 no longer his former delightful self. The Konstanze, Erika Köth, was a Blonde afflicted with ambition. At her best in 16 her voice sounds doll-like; in her heroic solos and the duet (20) she affects a fast vibrato and an edgy sound which, coupled with clumsy breath control and careless runs, contrast sadly with her earlier recordings from the opera (see below).

A year later, Josef Krips conducted his second recording of *Die Entführung*, for EMI this time. It was the most enjoyable of the sets to date, straightforward, musicianly, and skilfully cast. The Osmin, Frick, was in his vocal prime, alive to all the possibilities of the role, cheapening none, nor stealing limelight from colleagues, though every ensemble in which he takes part goes particularly well. Unger is in drier voice than before, as spirited and musical as ever. Lucia Popp's Blondchen is among the most reliable, and most endearing. Anneliese Rothenberger, another Blonde who has had

Konstanze thrust upon her, survives the transfer with success, expert and expressive in 6, touching with a semblance of grandeur in 10, vehement and triumphant in 11, noble if not quite tragic in 20. Nicolai Gedda is a romantic more than a heroic Belmonte, rather in the German tradition (see below under individual items), in less than full command of his florid divisions; he does not here attempt 17. The quartet and Vaudeville find these singers excellently matched and balanced. The dialogue is appreciably spoken and produced, the Bassa Selim uncommonly cogent in a role that, admittedly, seldom defeats an able speaking voice. One's only regret is that blunt ends in the vocal line were preferred to graceful *appoggiature*, but that was the fashion in 1966, and has seemingly remained so, alas.

The EMI/Krips set was not issued until 1970 in Britain and then on World Records: Beecham's recording was still in the catalogue, blessed by the magic of charisma, and EMI had other plans for this country, viz. an *Abduction from the Seraglio* sung and spoken in English. The forces derived from a production given by Phoenix Opera at the Bath Festival, whose artistic director was then Yehudi Menuhin. He conducted his Festival Orchestra, a group well known to record collectors at that time, in a production by Wendy Toye, responsible here for the dialogue, amenably delivered in Hugh Mills's free English version; the sung English text is by Joan Cross, *doyenne* of pre-war Sadler's Wells Opera, and her former colleague at the National Opera School in London, Anne Wood, Phoenix's founding director.

This was the first complete recording of a Mozart opera in English, helpful preparation for operagoers who do not understand German, and attractive too with a Konstanze and Belmonte internationally renowned. The voices are somewhat close-miked, but in a reverberant acoustic: words throughout are very clear, music sensibly paced and vivacious, with nice orchestral detail in, for example, 11 and 17. Mattiwilda Dobbs has sweetness and personality, a certain spiritual strength to differentiate her Konstanze from Jennifer Eddy's jolly Blondchen. Dobbs's American, and Gedda's Swedish accents are barely noticeable. Vocal imperfections are exaggerated by the microphone technique, not harmfully. Gedda's manful attempt on 17 earns respect, likewise Dobbs in 6, 10 and 11, keenly thought-out readings with strong characterization. John Fryatt, a star among comprimarios, portrays Pedrillo to a nicety and in 13 achieves the supposed impossibility of sustaining top A on both syllables of the word 'battle'. Noel Mangin, from New Zealand, popular also in Britain and Germany for some years, offers a strong, eccentric Osmin, immensely vital, brilliant with words, unwilling to attempt legato line or, in 9, even identifiable pitch, but inescapably a dominant comic personality (see also the Glyndebourne highlights below). To more or less serious effect, David Kelsey adopts a Laurence Olivier accent for the Bassa's words (how he recalls Peter Sellers in *A Hard Day's Night!*). For its necessarily limited market this is a successful version.

We come now to the 1970s, and contributions to two comprehensive

Mozart opera sets, conducted by Karl Böhm for DG, and by Colin Davis for Philips. Böhm conducted his set in Dresden, and therewith atoned for the crudity and carelessness of the earlier Philips/Suitner set discussed above. Here is the true Dresden, the Sächsische Staatskapelle that so inspired us on pre-war 78s, also conducted by Böhm, as it happens: silvery in the overture, full of incidental detail, possible at Böhm's sensible tempo, typical of his reading which is slow until a real *vivace* is required, and then he does not fail. He does not, for example, linger over 2, but makes the accompaniment truly incisive, while allowing Kurt Moll to sing it as a song, rather than as a pessimistic soul-parade.

The casting demonstrates the advance in Mozart singing since the late 1940s. Peter Schreier's Belmonte is robust, a man of action, no sentimental crooner, the tone keen and accurate, heroic but not thick, so that runs, even in 17, are tidily and expressively negotiated, and line in 15 is really legato – but here Böhm's steady pace does handicap the natural gait of the music. The quartet immediately afterwards should be the climax to date, a preparation for 20, which will trump everything. Here 16 plods, even if the vocal music is more tidily sung than in any other set, until the spirited, exhilarating coda. Schreier is never content to sing merely acceptably: he has to balance his weight of voice with the music's mood, and the orchestra's commentary, as in a superior account of 4, where every verbal and musical ingredient is on show.

His Konstanze is Arleen Augér, fine in rapid, high-flying music, moving in normal registers, golden-voiced for the heroine, though her top sounds like another, disembodied voice (one thinks of Calvé's 'third voice'). It has golden, heroic quality, warmth and intensity for 10, superb articulation in the rapid runs of 11, free of intrusive aspirates (an example to all). In 20, earlier hints of unsteadiness are confirmed, likewise the suspicion of shrillness.

The rest of the cast equals this serious musicianly level: Moll's stern vehemence comprehending legato and clean projection of notes, high, middle, and low, without hoodwinking for pseudo-expressive effect; an honest, remarkably complete Osmin; Harald Neukirch's rough, robust Pedrillo, too blatant in 18, but brave and firm in 13. 'Vivat Bacchus' is beguilingly shaped by Neukirch and Moll, jollity under true musical control, as nowhere else in these sets. Reri Grist, just as musical, sounds excessively shrill, more so than in the theatre. At last the gramophone offered a reasonably serious approach to *Die Entführung* without denying its frivolous elements. Sadly, the spoken dialogue again had other, different voices, even projected from the other side of the sonic stage.

So it was again, when in 1978 Colin Davis conducted the work for Philips. A major achievement of this set is the brilliant Osmin of Robert Lloyd, a match for every aspect of the role, including its rich bass resonance: but the speaker of Osmin's dialogue is no bass at all. The other parts are also split, and the opera is not experienced as an integer. The casting is respectable.

Stuart Burrows is an agile Belmonte, sensitive in his lovely solos, a good colleague in ensembles. Likewise his near-namesake – Norma Burrowes – as Blonde, and Christiane Eda-Pierre as a heroic Konstanze, not completely come to terms with a ferociously taxing part: some intonation raises eyebrows, top notes are less sung than punched out, the lovely soprano voice has to exert itself in the name of heroic status. Robert Tear brings nice humour to Pedrillo, though 'Frisch zum Kampfe' seems over-exaggerated: on records he must act for a blind audience. But Davis projects the music more percipiently than any other conductor, and his style is three-quarters correct, by the exigent standards of scholars. It has tremendous atmosphere all the time.

The Ariola set derives from collaboration with a Bavarian Radio studio broadcast of the opera, made in October 1979. A great asset, especially for German-speakers, is the quite full complement of spoken dialogue, mostly original Stephanie (the sung text is as much altered as usual). Alas, once again a separate cast of actors is employed for the spoken word and, once again, the speaking and singing voices do not match, in Blondchen's case to ridiculous effect, in Pedrillo's to near-slander. Edita Gruberova is a tireless Konstanze, vocally almost too rich and vibrant for the music, which, nevertheless, she sings with consummate expertise and telling intensity. Francisco Araiza has the manly voice, musical accomplishment, and sensibility for Belmonte, though his success in 'Ich baue ganz' is marred by heavily pulsed conducting which makes him appear to labour, and detracts from his natural charm as a singer. Norbert Orth, a pleasantly voiced tenor comprimario, and Ebel, whose pearly clarity of voice excels in 8, assist the vocal contrast. Roland Bracht's Osmin disdains charm and humour, and even the ripe *buffo* bass quality expected in the part. His singing is clean and dull. The reading as a whole achieves much in accuracy and opulence of sound, some spirit, and a measure of expressive tension. Yet, in comparison with the more admirable of the sets discussed above, this lacks Mozartian, Viennese classical virtues: it smacks of well-to-do suburbs, and supermarkets well stocked with the finest convenience foods, worlds away from Joseph II's Vienna of 1782.

In 1982 the Italian firm of Melodram issued what seems to have been the earliest recording of *Die Entführung*, one taken from a radio broadcast of 1945. The sound quality and musical balance leave something to be desired. Now and then Rudolf Moralt's tempi are too cautious for the spirit of the music, but there is some fine and eloquent orchestral playing. The dialogue is omitted, save for the exchange between Pedrillo and Osmin in 3, before 'Erst geköpft', but unusually long pauses separate the musical numbers. The interest of the set is Elisabeth Schwarzkopf's Konstanze. Her separate accounts of 10 and 11 are discussed elsewhere in this chapter; those in the set have the same heroic quality, and much of the musical insight associated with her later work, expressed through a voice of radiant youthfulness. The high *tessitura* of 11 is plainly not her favourite, but she flinches nothing; the runs are hardly to be faulted. The unexplained, surely technically motivated, omission of 'Ach, ich liebte' (a break in transmission, a vocal mishap?) is even more regrettable with a singer of this calibre, though there are compensations in her contributions to the quartet and duet (and the fill-ups on sides 5 and 6 include her only recording of Pamina's 'Ach, ich fühl's', a lovely one made in 1952). Belmonte is sung with real distinction by Dermota, including a brave attempt at 'Ich baue ganz', not quite complete. Herbert Alsen's Osmin is almost, not quite, worthy of praise.

Numerous records of highlights from *Die Entführung* exist, though only a few are independent of complete sets already discussed. The earliest of them commemorates a production at Berlin Staatsoper in 1942 when Robert Heger conducted a cast led by Erna Berger and Peter Anders. At the time they recorded the overture, and 1, 4, 10 and 15, presumably on 78s. In 1944 Karl Schmidt conducted recordings of 6, 11 and 20, in a less favourable acoustic, with some extra-musical stage noises in the duet. After the war these were all assembled on to a single twelve-inch LP which placed 6 after 10 and renders the overture, a spirited reading, in B major, a semitone lower than 1, which follows, after a long pause, at normal pitch. Berger's Konstanze is charming, efficient but not faultless, somewhat doll-like in timbre, though stronger, more heroic in 20. So, too, is Anders, whose 1942 solos, lightly sentimental in the accepted manner of time, with plenty of head-notes above the stave, are distinguished by the dapper, bright elegance of his voice at best, a little reminiscent of Heddle Nash in 15, (17 is omitted, as was then usual) though he tends to articulate his runs unevenly.

Berger was to improve on this account of 'Traurigkeit' in a later *Querschnitt* which does not, however, include 6 and 11. It also comes from the Berlin Staatsoper in 1953 with Wilhelm Schüchter as the spry, sympathetic conductor. Belmonte was now Rudolf Schock, burly of voice, yet dry: his rendering of 4, omitted here, occurs on a recital record of no special eloquence. Schock is heard at his best in 20, perhaps inspired by Berger, here and in 10 extremely fine, likewise in the Quartet No 16 where the four voices blend and contrast effectively. The Blonde, Lisa Otto, gives an effervescent, rather wiry account of 12. Unger over-aspirates 18 but characterizes it vividly, also the Bacchus duet (14) in which his partner is Frick – both were soon to record their roles complete with Beecham. Here Frick contributes 2, 3 and 19, less purposefully yet acceptably. They all combine in the Vaudeville (21) to conclude the record. The items are not ordered in sequence. 2 follows 15 and is succeeded by 12 which leads, with a sudden tape-join, into 14. Pedrillo's Serenade is precipitately interrupted by Osmin's Triumph Song. A rushed job, perhaps, but valuable for Berger's contributions.

Two further discs of highlights date from the 1950s. That from Berlin, conducted by Meinard von Zallinger, had Jutta Vulpius as Konstanze (see 1962 Philips set) and Unger as Pedrillo again. I have only been able to listen to excerpts from this, reissued on one twelve-inch side (Falcon L–ST 7068), beginning with John van Kesteren's dry but not insensitive singing of 1 (shorn of the preceding overture), then concentrating entirely on Blondchen and Osmin, i.e. 2, delivered as a song, without Belmonte's contributions, 9, 12 and 19. The Blonde, Ingeborg Wenglor, uses her pretty voice untidily. Gerhard Frei has the dark bass for Osmin, not a large voice, but inclined to spread. Intonation and note-values by both are questionable, as the close-miked recording emphasizes.

The *Querschnitt* from Cologne comes on two ten-inch discs, and consists of overture, 1–9, 12, 11, 13–16, and 18–21, in that order. The singing is low standard, careless and unstylish. Marilyn Tyler makes a brave attempt at Konstanze's virtuoso solos, for which the heroic quality of her soprano promised eventually to be well suited. August Griebel offers a bizarre Osmin, querulous in tone of voice, emotionally stiff and withdrawn, more like a Western cabinet minister than a middle-Eastern harem master.

The recorded quality of these anthologies now sounds quite antique, fuzzy, foggy, or unnaturally balanced. That of the Stuttgart excerpts conducted by Ferdinand Leitner in 1962, listed in the discography as an Ariola-Eurodisc, makes hardly more agreeable listening, though it is a matchbox, not a hazy sound, as a genial account of the overture suggests. There follows 1, with Josef Traxel, a smooth, grainy Belmonte, raw at the top but interesting. In No 2. Kurt Böhme (see DG/Jochum, already discussed) hams the music, mercilessly; subsequently he is heard only in 14, too close-miked, and the Vaudeville where he shouts. It is sad that his once famous, indeed irresistible Osmin is so unhappily captured on records. After 4 and 5, the selection jumps to 'Martern aller Arten', with lively orchestral playing thinly recorded, and with Ruth-Margret Pütz, an agile soprano with a tiresomely veiled quality above the stave (the omission of 6 and 10, and indeed 20, is regrettable unless it was diplomatic). Lieselotte Becker-Egner, a hard but alluring voice, very variable musically, then scampers through to 12, followed by 14 and 16, to both of which Unger contributes splendidly; 16 is given a pleasing performance on all hands, bar the gimcrack wooden recorded sound. The Vaudeville, clear words, neat balance, completes the selection.

Much the most enjoyable of all these *Entführung* 'cross-sections' is that on Classics for Pleasure deriving from Glyndebourne's 1972 performances, actually their second cast. At last a cross-sectic. with a clean, warm, natural acoustic, perhaps the Glyndebourne organ-room, where voices and orchestra are acceptably balanced. There is a curious jump from the end of the overture to 2, which Noel Mangin sings as a solo, without Belmonte's questions, and shorn of the duet. Mangin was already a fetching Osmin, generous with aspirates, and jolly rather than sadistic, but most distinctive of voice and personality. No. 4, with Ryland Davies, vocally still inexpert, but already a sensitive Mozartian, is followed by 6, a delectable account by Margaret Price, whose voice is almost perfectly placed for Konstanze's music, give or take a dubious note in high-soaring runs. Her interpretation of 10, with some restored *appoggiature* such as I hardly ever heard while listening to the records mentioned in this chapter, is exquisitely beautiful and moving. (For her recording of 11, see below.) Danièle Perriers gives a brisk, clipped, no-nonsense view of 12, followed by a jovial 14 in which Kimmo Lappalainen joins Mangin. In 15, Pritchard and the LPO steal the honours from Davies, not yet ready for so difficult an aria (let alone 17). No. 16 is well shaped, compounded, stylish, an agreeable performance but for the obtrusive voice of Blonde. Lappalainen's attractive voice, grain and oil adeptly mingled, makes a ready success of 18. After 19, Price and Davies sing 20 imperfectly but with real musical sensibility and admirable orchestral support.

Several solo recital discs include a number of items from *Die Entführung aus dem Serail*. A two-disc Mozart anthology, conducted by the late Istvan Kertesz (SET 548) must take precedence, with four items involving Manfred Jungwirth's vivacious, occasionally flawed Osmin, and with Werner Krenn doubling Belmonte and Pedrillo, both to nice purpose. The items are 4, 14, 18 and 19. Stuart Burrows includes all four of Belmonte's arias on his Oiseau-Lyre recital (DSLO 13), runs, nuances, legato all first-rate, 4 and 15 both outstanding, missing only the hero's incisive delivery, 17 a complete success until the last florid bout which strains this voice, as it does every tenor I have ever heard. Werner Hollweg (Philips 6500 042) offers the same four arias: he has the vibrant, robust heroic quality of voice denied Burrows; his intonation is virtually faultless, and a joy, until the last division in 17, which, however, has included a short but deplorable cut. Rightly, I am sure, Hollweg ignores Mozart's marking *adagio* for 15, and prefers a virile, emotionally fulfilled, more active tempo. Some aspirates in runs do not over-obtrude. The same four arias were recorded by the Hungarian tenor József Réti (Hungaroton SLPX 11679). His resinous, quite heroic tenor is well placed in all registers; only the top B flats in the agile last division of 17 give him trouble. No. 1 sounds well, 4 lacks poetry and a moment of brilliance, and reluctantly (since I admired his singing) the same may be said of 15 and 17. Schreier, Böhm's Belmonte, probably the most respected Mozartian tenor of the early 1980s, included the four arias in a Mozart recital (Telef. 6. 35 063 DX) with a pleasant, bright acoustic, good style and delivery, 4 slightly sentimental, 15 too hangdog, 17 not quite as neatly poised as in the DG set (the least flawed version of 17 on record that I have heard).

On a Telefunken record (6.42 232 AJ) Anders includes Belmonte's 1 and 4, coupled with Pedrillo's 18, the latter particularly sturdy yet confidential, 4 at once cheerful and sweet, inclined to linger. The three arias of Konstanze are included in a recital by Cristina Deutekom (CFP 164), a soprano with an exceptionally ugly voice, and exceptional powers of musical artistry, inasmuch as fair-minded listeners have been tempted to compare her singing with that of Maria Callas. Deutekom's articulation of scales in 6 and 11 is too eccentric to support the comparison: they are not exactly aspirated, but glottally stopped, as in true vocalization, so that legato is flawed. Her rasping, grainy soprano lends spirit and defiance to 6 and 11, both of them tense, and absolutely self-assured. No. 10 is taken slowly and heavily, but her breath-control is a match for the tempo, and it affords her a rarely touching interpretation, nobly poised, not querulous as might be expected. One can only wish that the vocal instrument were more alluring, like Elsa, not Ortrud, in Wagner's *Lohengrin*.

Gedda, Belmonte in two of the sets reviewed above, recorded 4, 15, and Pedrillo's 18 quite early in his career (33CX 1528). The Serenade, now reissued on RLS 5250, is the plum here, cheeky, insinuating, full of sensual humour, and delectably sung. No. 4 involves much winsome half-voice, high-class crooning. No. 15 begins as sentimentally, heroism deflected by tears, but Gedda's smooth line has to be admired, like his sensibility in nuance, though the rapid divisions are untidy. Nos. 1, 4 and 15 were coupled on a recital disc by Anton Dermota, a popular Viennese Mozart tenor of the 1940s and early 1950s (Preiser PR 135003). They are respectable, mellifluous performances, the runs cautious, too many intrusive aspirates, emotions veering into sentimentality, final consonants distorted (e.g. 'feuriss' for 'feurig'); the virtues outweigh the lapses. Erika Köth (see the DG/Jochum set above) also recorded Konstanze's arias separately. Nos. 10 and 11 (Ariola XA 25 276 R), conducted by Märzendorfer, to be avoided for technical faults too numerous to specify here, as well as a displeasing quality of voice. But 6, 10 and 11, with the Berlin Phil. and Schüchter (1C 147–30 607/8) should be heard by all who decry Köth's later recordings of this opera. The vocal quality is truly sympathetic, bright and incisive yet warm. The florid music and intonation are perfectly secure, the breath-control unexceptionable. 'Traurigkeit' is an interpretation of superior quality, 'Martern' very respectable indeed.

Here follows an alphabetically summarized *Entführung* discography of individual and coupled items, chiefly on 78s, beginning with Karola Agay (Hungaroton LPX 11432), a strong, crystalline soprano who should sing 11 admirably, but doesn't; the top of the voice is ugly, apt to crack by curdling. Callas had the same failing, but never sang as dully as this. Agay's version claims high priority in any list of the vilest singing on record. Norman Allin, splendid, ample English bass, recorded 2 in English ('When a maiden takes your fancy') tidily but with a morose tone of voice inapt to the music (Col. 9803). Webster Booth's version of 4 in English is decently sung, mercifully unsentimental, perhaps even too British to convey Belmonte's ardent, heart-racked longing (C 3402). A favourite Osmin of the 1950s was Owen Brannigan who recorded 2 and 19 (ESD 7059) genially, without villainous undertones, the runs in 19 sketchy, yet with so much individuality and personable artistry, including a respectable trill, that one does not tire of his interpretations. Another English singer of those days, Gwen Catley, recorded 6 in English, in 1947 (C 3696; HLM 7066). 'I was heedless' she begins: her runs and trills bear her words out, but there are lovely *cantabile* phrases to make up.

Two versions of 11 used to be ascribed to Maria Cebotari. It is now recognized that the second of these was in fact a performance by the young Elisabeth Schwarzkopf. Cebotari's account (1C 147–29118) has an abbreviated introduction and there are further cuts towards the end. The voice is golden and covered, forwardly projected, tempted to spread; some of Konstanze's runs lag behind the conductor's beat.

Schwarzkopf's interpretation, made in 1946 (RLS 763) includes the introduction complete, the concertante instruments well forward. As soon as Konstanze enters, we notice the verbal delivery of 'Ich verlache', the dipthongs characteristic of Schwarzkopf, likewise the pronunciation of 'Nichts . . . könnte sein'. There is a blazing, heroic quality here, arguably the most brilliant 'Martern' recorded.

Belmonte's 'Ich baue ganz' (17) was always omitted from performance until recently, being thought too difficult and taxing. Richard Conrad sings it on Decca SET 268, but with a soft-centred, unheroic tone of voice, tentative in style, that obliges one to prefer other tenors more fully attuned to the music's character (e.g. Schreier or Wunderlich). Ileana Cotrubas (CBS 76521) gives a highly expressive account of 6, appealing from the outset, tearful in admission of the *Kummer* in her breast, then bold, almost jaunty, in her florid runs which are irresistible if not flawless. She must be an outstanding candidate for the part of Konstanze in any forthcoming complete recording (she sang the role at Salzburg 1980/1). A superior performance of 19 comes from Franz Crass (1C 063–29073), the voice equal in all registers, poised and smooth, never plummy, words clear and appreciative, the music freshly approached with relish but not farcical conceit. The stereo recording makes him, at one point, run rapidly from prompt-side to O.P. and back again, an extra pleasantry.

The Russian soprano Goar Gasparian includes 6, sung in Italian, on a recital (Melodiya D 011745/6). Her runs are agile, her singing expressive and sensitive to nuance, the phrasing less stylish, and the voice itself too metallic, or shrill, for pleasure. Pavel Gerjikov, a Bulgarian basso, brings a dark, firm, typically Slavonic voice to 2 (Balkanton BOA 1227), with clear words but little attempt at *bel canto*, and primitive recorded sound. Sylvia Geszty, in 6 (London OS 26114), deploys her winsome, creamy soprano to touching effect in the opening section, and negotiates the florid music to admiration, though the very top of the voice involves an audible gear-change and sounds unlovely. Ria Ginster recorded 11, with piano accompaniment by Gerald Moore (DB 1832; LV 190), quite securely, and dully save for a magical echo effect just before the *più mosso* at 'Doch du bist entschlossen'. She ends the aria in the manner detailed below under Ivogün. Herbert Ernst Groh, a popular German tenor of the 1930s, recorded 4 (Parlo. E 11297; Rococo 5181) nicely in the Tauber manner but without a trace of sentimentality. The great Frieda Hempel left a recording of 11 (DB 331; Rococo R8), curiously sung in Italian (presumably because at the New York Metropolitan the opera was *Il ratto dal Seraglio*) and in a defensive tone of voice, inclined to hurry and clip note-values, in short vocally uncomfortable and unrepresentative of her best singing. The earliest recordings from this opera that I have heard are Wilhelm Hesch's 1906 fragment of 3, with piano, and 19 with orchestra

(3–42542, 3–42559; CO 300), dating from 1906, technically fallible, musically slipshod. Felicie Hüni-Mihacsek's version of 6 dates from 1923 (Poly. 65638; LV 93), and is both fervent and technically adroit, apart from awkward *gruppetti* towards the end, and a final gigantic application of brakes, well worth hearing.

Maria Ivogün, a superlative German light soprano, afterwards Schwarzkopf's chief singing teacher, recorded 11 three times (1917 Odeon unpublished; CO 380 and 1919 – Od. LXX 76812–3; LV 67 and 1924 Gramm. 85303; LV 69) and 20 once with her husband Karl Erb (1917 unpublished; CO 380). She was no overparted Blonde; the voice is elegant and heroic in character, at its strongest and most masterly in the 1924 version, but cogent already in 1917, though there she is swamped by the orchestra and recording engineers. Her articulation, intonation and agility, the clarity and force of her words, the nobility of her *portamento*, and the dramatic flair of her sustained *crescendo* top C should be studied closely by every aspiring Konstanze. In all three versions she makes a sudden, unnerving, downward *portamento*, almost a yowl, near the end of the aria at 'zuletzt befreit mich doch der Tod'. She sustains the penultimate G with a long trill and ends with a brilliant top C. This must have been admired, since Ria Ginster copies it all on her version. The duet with Erb finds him initially a trifle stiff, later an exemplary partner to his expressive, nobly musical consort; there is a small cut before the *allegro* conclusion. It is sad that Ivogün did not record 6 and 10: she must have been a non-pareil Konstanze. For a superior Blondchen of that generation we have but to hear Adele Kern in 'Durch Zärtlichkeit', gold as well as high-spirited determination in her voice (Poly. 66945; LV 57), a wooing legato delivery, and flawless runs, though again the cadences involve crude braking. Nor need one doubt, from his 2 (DA 1218; SH 280) that Alexander Kipnis was an ideal Osmin. The three verses (without Belmonte's interruptions or subsequent duet) are elegantly, alluringly unrolled, precisely the just quantity of malign granite in the voice, a seductive half-voice for the refrain, and a fetching *glissando* before the last refrain that later Osmins can only hope to approach.

René Kollo gets into this chapter for his account of 15, recorded in 1969 (CBS S 71076): the voice was still potentially Mozartian, though intrusive aspirates give no pleasure and his florid runs are no more than acceptable; there is also a reminiscence of the older-style, sentimental German Belmontes in his interpretation. Readers who remember the brassy glamour of Miliza Korjus, in her Hollywood successes of the late 1930s, may be surprised by the technical superiority and even the musical artistry which she brought to Konstanze's 11 in a recording from 1934 when she was working in Berlin as an opera singer (1C 147–30 819). The vocalism is masterly, the voice perfectly even in scale, the moods of the aria strongly suggested, but throughout there are small vulgarities of style which keep her version out of the top class. Konstanze's agonizing predicament is hardly suggested.

Selma Kurz must have been a splendid Konstanze, though her record of

6 (DB 779; CO 324) is poorly engineered, and involves an ugly cut. The finest 6 of all is that of Lilli Lehmann in her early 60s (Od. 80008; GV 66), strong and bright of voice, appreciatively alive to the place of *appoggiature* and other decoration in this music, real style, as we hear also in her 11, a minimally imperfect but most compelling version of this aria.

The young Anna Moffo (33C1063) recorded a likeable 6, fresh-voiced, alert and expressive, though sparing of legato, and subject to a minor, but harmful cut. Among modern Konstanzes the crown is earned by Edda Moser whose 11 (1C 063–29082) is nobly heroic, in style technically irreproachable (if you can accept a breath between 'Des Himmels' and 'Segen') and an invigorating musical experience, quite out of the common run. Oscar Natzke was a New Zealand bass who made a short but good career in Britain during the 1940s. His version in English of 2 (DX 1478) is delivered in the nicely confidential manner of a crony giving helpful advice; the voice is of glorious bass quality, firm and rich in all registers, though note-values and pitching sound unstylish.

No. 6 was recorded in 1929 by Maria Nemeth (EJ 498; LV 248); her first slow flourish is exquisite, but the *allegro* shows up the sketchy nature of her florid technique, as well as her gusty delivery, over-reliant on the attractive quick flutter of her vibrato. There are similar failings in her account of 11 (D 2023; LV 248); which has a complete orchestral introduction. Despite the sprightly runs, and some artistry in nuance, the total effect is rather senti-mental; the final cadence is taken in the old-fashioned way (see Ivogün). The Danish bass, Einar Nørby, recorded Osmin's 3 (Tono R 25097) and, with Edith Oldrup, 9 (Tono X 25097); their sense of humour is attractive, but the artistry of low standard. Julia Osváth brings an attractive soprano quality to 10 (Hungaroton SLPX 11818, sung in Hungarian), but the execution lacks artistic finish.

A coupling of Konstanze's 6 with Blonde's 12 may be thought dramatically inconsistent, if not mutually incompatible for the same voice. Nevertheless it has been done twice, each time sung in Italian. Lina Pagliughi (Parlo R 30028; GVC 20) brings a light, girlish voice with a good trill to them both. No. 12 suits her the better, though her orchestral accompaniment cannot have helped. The elaborate florid music of 6 is inaccurately negotiated, the quality of voice less than heroic. Koloman von Pataky, Glyndebourne's Don Ottavio in the pre-war Mozart Opera Society set, and a favourite in Vienna during those years, recorded 4 and 15 (Poly. 66810; LV 54) in a likeable lyrical tenor, with a fast vibrato that sweetens his tone. The style is endearing and romantic, but not truly heroic, and the low C in 15 hardly materializes; in the introduction to 4 he pronounces Konstanze's name as a tetrasyllable. The great stylist among Viennese Mozart tenors of that period was Julius Patzak, as may be heard in recordings of 4 (Poly. 15080; LV 31) and 15 (Poly. 35029; Top Classic 9041). He does not croon 'O wie ängstlich', but phrases it elegantly at a cheerful debonair tempo, not too fast for neatly articulated runs. Again in 15, Patzak's incisive tone and imaginative phrasing give solace to the ear; there is true manly ardour in his exclamation 'Ach Konstanze!' Belmonte's long division is not flawless but musically more substantial than Mozart's name of 'noodles' for such flights of virtuosity. The faster coda of this aria is unusually jaunty, yet firmly conclusive. James Pease, an admired Wotan and Sachs of the 1950s who died untimely, left a record of Mozart operatic excerpts, ranging easily from Papageno and Don Giovanni to Osmin (Pacific D 221). Nos 2 and (with Barbara Troxell) 9 disclose impressive virtues of voice and enunciation – both singers enjoy their competitive visits to nether regions in 9 – and it is sad that their Hamburg accompaniment is so heavy-handed. The Greek soprano Margherita Perras, who sang Konstanze at Glyndebourne in 1937, recorded 6 and 11 (DB 4439; LV 73). On stage she was considered a stiff actress, but her singing here is commendably expert; a golden, soprano quality, apt to the role since the upper register is perfectly secure, noble *portamenti*, brilliant athletic runs and a sense of grand composure even at *allegro* tempo. It is a pity that 11 had to be abbreviated to fit on to one side. Osmin was not among Ezio Pinza's famous Mozart roles, but during the mid-1940s he did record 19, in Italian as 'Ah! che voglio trionfare' (Am. Col. 71843D; Odyssey 32 16 0035), the voice keenly placed for legato and rapid patter, both of superior quality; he eschews the traditional *portamento* up two octaves, before the final reprise. Lily Pons, like Pagliughi, coupled Konstanze's 6 with Blonde's 12 singing the former in Italian, the latter in French, though Bruno Walter was her conductor (Col. L 20002; Odyssey Y 31152). In 1942 Pons's voice was in healthy condition, though her runs are aspirated, her trills and *gruppetti* careless, her *staccato* delivery of 12 unmusical. Neither item shows her best qualities as a singer. In 1940 she had recorded Blondchen's 8 in French (Victor 2110; VIC 1473), no more scrupulously; the top E is true but unlovely. The Glyndebourne Highlights record (see above) omits 11, but its Konstanze, Margaret Price, included it in a mixed Mozart record (SER 5675). There are small vocal imperfections, an ill-tuned top C, a momentary lag behind the beat, one questionable run; but it is a properly heroic, thoroughly musicianly performance, even to a bold flourish where Mozart indicated one (ignored by most modern Konstanzes). As usual in the records heard for this chapter, Price, like even the most enlightened modern singers, turns coy when faced with the unwritten-out *appoggiatura*.

In 1910 Thomas Beecham's operatic activities in London included a Mozart season which virtually introduced *Die Entführung* (and *Così fan tutte*) to a generation unfamiliar with them. His Osmin was the excellent British bass Robert Radford, who subsequently recorded No. 2 (D114) and 19 (D 114; HLM 7054), both in English. The voice is a bright, ripe forward *basso cantante*, cavernous down below, light and baritonal, though still robust, above the stave. The refrain of 2 is ineffectively reworded as simply 'Tra-la-la' without 'lera', and does not fit Mozart's music naturally. Radford's verbal enunciation is magnificent, with whirring rolled r's, e.g. 'pretty brace' in 19 which includes a rare and famous cadenza. This Osmin commands instant respect. Helge Rosvaenge, (DA 4417; Rococo 5247) gives an enter-prising account of 1, rather Tauberish in vocal quality but more forthright in manner.

The Parisian soprano Gabrielle Ritter-Ciampi, admired for her Mozart roles in the 1920s, recorded 11 in French, imperfectly but with so many virtues (including some basic graces, seldom observed by others) that her performance ranks high, even in the company discussed here. Runs, trill, declamation, pace, all repay attention. The end is treated in the Ivogün manner, though without the long trill on the penultimate G.

The Mozart records of Aksel Schiötz have been rightly admired. His coupling of Belmonte's 1 with Pedrillo's 18 (DA 5253; MOAK 2) conveys well the liquid beauty of his voice, though it sounds stiff, less enjoyable than the jolly account of 18, with plucked strings noisy enough to waken inebriated Osmin. Elisabeth Schumann's Blondchen, preserved in 1920 recordings of 8 and 12 (Poly. 65580; LV 186), does not survive technical scrutiny: the scoops, note-pecking, quaver-scamping, and faulty intonation, are as culpable as her detractors could wish. The verve and personality (more than mannerisms) triumph over them, and make 8, at least, treasurable. Elisabeth Schwarz-kopf's account of 11 has already been discussed above (under Cebotari). She also recorded 10, in the mid-forties. (LX 1249; RLS 763) with Josef Krips and the VPO, including its introductory recitative; here the young voice is beginning to mature, and the reliable musicianship, phrasing and nuance repay closest attention. It is an eloquent performance and includes a beautiful trill.

Beverly Sills, potentially an ideal Konstanze in her early vocal maturity, should have recorded more than 'Martern aller Arten', all I can find (ABC Audio Treasury ATS 20004). Her voice is perfectly steady, with neat, gleam-ing runs and a firm low register, the top slightly fluttery, least attractive in the coda, expressively done as it is; here is a short-breathed, but spirited account with excellent trills, not memorable in any particular musical respect. Beecham's Belmonte, Léopold Simoneau, made separate recordings of 4 and 17 (Ducretet-Thomson DTL 93091), 20 with his wife Pierrette Alarie (Pearl SHE 573) who also recorded 12 (DTL 93089). Her 'Welche Wonne' is animated and jolly, rather demure (perhaps the French accent). In the duet, very musical and ardently felt, her timbre may be thought too girlish, Blonde rather than Konstanze, though the top notes are splendid, as is Simoneau throughout. His arias are expertly done, heroic in tone, though too close-miked for comfort; they are poorly accompanied. Many Belmontes, in 1, have trouble with phrases above the stave (e.g. 'Und bringe mich ans Ziel'). An exception is Leo Slezak, heroic and elegant throughout, never an ugly note, appreciative in nuance too (3-42832; CO 332). Joan Sutherland re-corded 11 (SXL 2257), a clean, respectable account, short of grammatical *appoggiature* (how could that stylist, her husband, countenance it?), and eventually uninvolved emotionally, though the virtuosity cannot be ignored. I listened to Luise Szabo's 6 (Telef. E 759) but found nothing to recommend it. The Hungarian bass Mihály Székely, a well-known Osmin in his day, recorded 2 and 19 in Hungarian (LPX 1140, or HLP 117), with a ripe bottom register, poor but lively style, and some dubious intonation. 2 is treated to mock-pathos, as often and wrongly: sarcasm is a better idea.

The American soprano Eleanor Steber took Konstanze in an English-language production at the Metropolitan, New York, its baptism there in 1946, and thereafter recorded 11 (Victor 11–9773; VIC 1455) dully, quite neatly (the coda over-vibrant). Her 'Traurigkeit' had Bruno Walter as conductor, and was sung in German, more carefully and with stronger feeling for the situation and words, even some extra *appoggiature*, an enterprising, plausible reading, when not exaggerated (Odyssey 32 16 0363). The darling of pre-war Vienna, Richard Tauber, a marvellous Mozart tenor, recorded only 4 from *Entführung*, and that in hoarse voice (Parlo PXO 1024; 1C 047 28559), though the tone-quality is more robust than what I have elsewhere referred to as 'Tauberish', and the expressive treatment of words approaches the lofty standard of Patzak. Josef Traxel, a fine Mozartian tenor of the post-war years, never recorded Belmonte complete, but left evidence of special quality in 4 and 15, the words carefully enunciated, the voice ardent and flexible, elegant and smooth, some regrettable aspirates, the whole not quite verging on real greatness (1C 147–30774).

EMI's major project, the *History of Music in Sound*, undertaken in the 1950s, represents Mozart by the big quartet 16 (HLP 17) sung by Jennifer Vyvyan, Marion Studholme, Alexander Young, and Richard Lewis, a neatly balanced quartet of attractive voices. Vyvyan was by then a Konstanze of locally famed magnificence, and she leads a pleasant, though not extraordinary performance; perhaps it lacked the musical stimulus of an existing stage performance including them all together.

Richard Watson, an Osmin of Radford's generation, recorded 2 (Decca F 1652) unstylishly but with a sly vulgarity that, in English, fascinates the imagination, deplorable Mozart but good theatre. A great Osmin was Ludwig Weber, just after 1945. His versions of 2 and 19 (LB 96; 1C 177–00933) are full of life, pointfulness, and vocal colour, human, not thoroughly vile and sadistic, but not a clown either.

The recorded history of *Die Entführung aus dem Serail* is extensive, seldom dull, full of interest for students of musical style. Having listened to it all, I now want a complete set as vivid as Böhm or Davis, but more attentive to Mozartian style. At least the possibilities on record are far from exhausted.

DIE ENTFÜHRUNG AUS DEM SERAIL

K Konstanze; *Bl* Blondchen; *B* Belmonte; *P* Pedrillo; *Os* Osmin; *BS* Bassa Selim.

1945 (broadcast performance)
Schwarzkopf *K*; Loose *Bl*;
Dermota *B*;
Klein *P*; Alsen *Os*;
Vienna Radio Chorus,
Austrian Radio SO/Moralt
Melodramm ⓜ MEL 047

1950 Lipp *K*; Loose *Bl*; W. Ludwig *B*;
Klein *P*; Koréh *Os*; Woester BS/
Vienna State Opera Chorus,
Vienna PO/Krips
Decca ⓜ ECM730–1
Richmond ⓜ RS63015

1954 Stader *K*; Streich *Bl*; Häfliger *B*;
Vantin *P*; Greindl *Os*; Franck *BS*/
Berlin RIAS Chamber Choir and
SO/Fricsay
DG ⓜ 2700 010

1954 (concert version) Tyler *K*; Petrich
Bl; Van Kesteren *B*; Schiebener
P; Griebel *Os*/Cologne Opera
Chorus, Cologne Gürzenich
Orch./Ackermann
Musical Masterpiece Society (US)
ⓜ M13
Discophilia ⓜ KS20–21

1956 Marshall *K*; Hollweg *Bl*;
Simoneau *B*; Unger *P*; Frick *Os*;
H. Laubenthal *BS*/Beecham
Choral Society, RPO/Beecham
EMI SLS5153
Angel SB3555

1961 (live performance – Salzburg
Festival) Pütz *K*; Holm *Bl*;
Wunderlich *Bel*; Wohlfarth *P*;
Littasy *O*/Vienna State Opera
Chorus, Salzburg Mozarteum
Orch/Kertesz
Melodram ⓜ MEL702
(US) Period TE1102

1962 Vulpius *K*; Rönisch *Bl*; Apreck *B*;
Förster *P*; van Mill *Os*; Schütte
BS/Dresden State Opera Chorus,
Dresden State Orch./Suitner
Philips 6720 005
Turnabout (US); TV 34320-1S

1965 Köth *K*; Schädle *Bl*; Wunderlich
B; Lenz *P*; Böhme *Os*; Boysen

BS/Bavarian State Opera Chorus
and Orch./Jochum
DG 2726 051

1966 Rothenberger *K*; Popp *Bl*; Gedda
B; Unger *P*; Frick *Os*; Rudolf *BS*/
Vienna State Opera Chorus,
Vienna PO/Krips
EMI 1C 197 00070–1
Seraphim SIB 6025

1967 (in English) Dobbs *K*; Eddy *Bl*;
Gedda *B*; Fryatt *P*; Mangin *Os*;
Kelsey *BS*/Ambrosian Singers,
Bath Festival Orch./Menuhin
EMI SLS932

1974 Augér *K*; Grist *Bl*; Schreier *B*;
Neukirch *P*; Moll *Os*; Mellies *BS*/
Leipzig Radio Chorus, Dresden
State Orch./Böhm
DG 2709 051④ 3371 013

1978 Eda-Pierre *K*; Burrowes *Bl*;
Burrows *B*; Tear *P*; Lloyd *Os*; C.
Jürgens *BS*/Alldis Choir, ASMF/
Davis
Philips 6769 026 ④ 7699 111

1979 Gruberova *K*; Ebel *Bl*; Araiza *B*;
Orth *P*; Bracht *Os*; Leipnitz *BS*/
Bavarian Radio Chorus, Munich
Radio Orch./Wallberg
Ariola-Eurodisc 300 027–440 ④
500 027–441

1942 & 1944
(excerpts: live performance –
Berlin State Opera House) Berger
K; Anders *B*/Berlin State Orch./
Heger and Schmidt
Acanta ⓜ BB21495

1946 (names in brackets are the real
names) (excerpts) Camphausen
(Berger) *K*; Mehler (Wolf) *Bl*;
Horst (W. Ludwig) *B*; Ramms
(Herrmann) *Os*/Dresden State
Opera Chorus and Orch.
(Hamburg State Opera Chorus
and Orch./Schreiber (Schmidt-
Isserstedt)
Allegro ⓜ ALL3090

1953 (excerpts) Berger *K*; Otto *Bl*;
Schock *B*; Unger *P*; Frick *Os*/

German Opera Chorus, Berlin
SO/Schüchter
EMI ⓜ 1C 047 28569

1959 (excerpts) Vulpius *K*; Wenglor *Bl*;
Van Kesteren *B*; Unger *P*; Frei
Os/Berlin State Opera Chorus and
Orch./Von Zallinger
Eterna 820 039

1962 (excerpts) Pütz *K*; Becker-Egner

Bl; Traxel *B*; Unger *P*; Böhme *O*/
Württemberg State Opera Chorus
and Orch./Leitner
Ariola-Eurodisc S70168KR

1972 (excerpts) M. Price *K*; Perriers *Bl*;
R. Davies *B*; Lappalainen *P*;
Mangin *Os*/London PO/Pritchard
CfP CFP40032
Vanguard (US) VSD71203

La Cenerentola

HAROLD ROSENTHAL

The story of Cinderella goes back long before the birth of opera, and is almost certainly of Eastern origin. She was mentioned in German literature in the sixteenth century and popularized by the French writer Charles Perrault in his *Cendrillon, où La Petite Pantoufle* (1697), one of his *Contes de ma mère l'oye*. The glass-slipper part of the story, known to countless generations of English-speaking children, is a mistranslation from the French *pantoufle en vair*, the latter word being misread as *verre*. A *pantoufle en vair* was a fur or sable slipper; and as sable was only worn by kings, or princes, it was natural that the good fairy should give a pair of royal slippers to her favourite.

Charles Guillaume Etienne wrote a libretto, based on Perrault's story, for the composer Isouard, whose *Cendrillon* was produced with great success in Paris in February 1810; the same text was used later that year by Steibelt for his *Cendrillon* produced in Moscow. Etienne's text was also the basis of Felice Romani's libretto for Pavesi's *Agatina, o La virtù premiata*, which had its première at La Scala in 1814, and, of course, of Jacopo Ferretti's for Rossini. Ferretti was considered by many as second only to Romani as a librettist, and he provided texts not only for Rossini, but also for Donizetti, Mayr, Pacini, Mercadante, and many others.

The first performance of Rossini's *La Cenerentola* took place on 25 January 1817 at the Teatro Valle, Rome. Geltrude Righetti-Giorgi, who had created Rosina the previous year, sang Angelina, and the cast also included Giuseppe de Begnis as Dandini, and Andrea Verni as Don Magnifico. The work was enormously successful in Italy – at La Scala in its first season it received 44 performances. *Cenerentola* reached London in January 1820, when it was given at the King's Theatre in the Haymarket, with Teresa Belocchi as Angelina and Giuseppe Ambrogetti as Don Magnifico. It continued to be heard at the King's until the 1840s, and interpreters of Angelina included such famous singers as Laure Cinthie-Damoreau, Henrietta Sontag, Maria Malibran, and Pauline Viardot. Its first Covent Garden performance, in a much bowdlerized English (and musical) version, had taken place in 1830; it was first heard there in Italian in 1848 in the theatre's second season as the Royal Italian Opera, with Marietta Alboni as Angelina and Antonio Tamburini as Dandini. After that season it was not heard again there until the famous 1934 revival with Conchita Supervia, Dino Borgioli, Emilio Ghirardini, Ezio Pinza, and Carlo Scattola, and conducted by Gino Marinuzzi; it had, however, been briefly revived at the Shaftesbury Theatre in 1891, during Sgr Lago's season, with Guerrina Fabbri as Angelina.

In Italy too there was a long period of neglect – almost half a century – until the revival in 1921 at Pesaro, Rossini's birthplace, under the direction of the composer Amilcare Zanella, with the Mexican soprano, Fanny Anitua, in the title-role. It was not until the following year that Conchita Supervia first sang the part, in a series of performances conducted by Tullio Serafin, first in Ravenna for the Dante celebrations, then in Bologna, and finally in the spring of 1922, in Turin. By the late 1920s, what virtually amounted to Conchita Supervia's own company toured Italy and Europe, appearing not only in *Cenerentola*, but also in *L'Italiana in Algeri* and *Il barbiere di Siviglia*. This ensemble included Piesira Giri, Ebe Ticozzi, Laura Pasini, Dino Borgioli, Nino Ederle, Ernesto Badini, Vincenzo Bettoni, Carlo Scattola, and the conductor was generally Serafin.

The first Florence Festival in 1933 included performances of the work under Serafin with virtually the same cast that appeared the following year at Covent Garden under Marinuzzi. After Supervia's sudden death in 1936 *Cenerentola* found a new Italian protagonist in Gianna Pederzini, who appeared in the role at La Scala, the Teatro Colón, Buenos Aires, and elsewhere. During the war the young Fedora Barbieri sang the role, and she appeared in it during the first season at the rebuilt Scala, 1946–7. The Rossini revival under Gui at Glyndebourne was launched with this opera in 1952 and subsequently recorded with Marina de Gabarain in the title-role. She was followed in the 1950s by Teresa Berganza and Anna Maria Rota.

There had, in 1929, been a new German version of the opera by the Munich conductor Hugo Röhr, who rescored the title role for soprano, and rechristened the piece *Angelina*. It was heard under this title in Munich and other German cities with Fritzi Jokl, Adele Kern, and Lotte Schöne in the title-role. The Spanish coloratura soprano, Mercedes Capsir, sang what must have been an Italian soprano version of the role in Turin in 1937.

It is interesting that Spanish or Latin-American singers, be they mezzos, sopranos, or tenors, seem to have made a speciality of this opera from its very early days: Malibran, Viardot, Anitua, Supervia, Capsir, Berganza (and on records Los Angeles and Portuguese-born Eugenia Mantelli), Juan Oncina, and Luigi Alva. Yet of all the singers so far mentioned who were active since the invention of the gramophone, comparatively few recorded anything from *Cenerentola*; there is not a note of the opera on disc by Anitua, Pederzini, or Barbieri; I have only been able to find one recording (as distinct from extracts made from complete sets) of the tenor aria 'Pegno adorata e caro'; while such great baritones and basses as de Luca, Stabile, Baccaloni, Pinza, Didur to mention a few, either chose not to appear in the opera at all, or if they did, not to record anything from it. Surely the 'Segreto d'importanza' duet for Dandini and Don Magnifico is as worthy of recording as the Malatesta-Pasquale duet in Donizetti's *Don Pasquale*.

Of the six complete recordings, the oldest is the Cetra, made during Radio Italiana's 1949–50 Studio Opera season, and it was one of the first of Cetra's operatic list. It is perhaps not correct to call it a 'complete' recording, for not only does it lack the recitatives, but the Act 1 Quintet and the Act 2 Storm are omitted as well as the three numbers not written by Rossini but by Luca Agolini (who was also probably responsible for most of the recitatives); these are Alidoro's recitative and the aria 'Vasto teatro é il mondo' in Act 1; the chorus in A major, 'Ah della bella incognita', which opens Act 2; and an aria for Clorinda, in B flat major, 'Sventurata! Me credea' also in Act 2, following the Sextet. In addition, there are cuts in what is still left, including Ramiro's scene, which is a pity as Cesare Valletti makes an elegant and aristocratic-sounding Prince, and in the Sextet. In other words this performance is not really worth too much attention, though mention should be made of Giulietta Simionato's Angelina, in which she, not unnaturally, sounds much younger, less coarse, and so more convincing than in her 1963 recording. Saturno Meletti, never a great baritone, sings Dandini with style but little character, and Cristiano Dalamangas makes an exaggerated Don Magnifico. Mario Rossi conducts in a lively fashion.

The Glyndebourne 1953 recording omits the Alidoro aria and Don Magnifico's 'Sia qualunque delle figlie' in Act 2, which is a pity as Magnifico was one of Ian Wallace's best roles, and Gui should have allowed him his second aria. There are also some quite irrational small cuts in some of the numbers, including one in Don Ramiro's *scena*, in the Sextet, and even in the final Rondo; and the recitatives are considerably shortened, but that is hardly damaging.

The joy of this set is, of course, Vittorio Gui's superb conducting. This was the first of Gui's Rossini operas at Glyndebourne, and set a standard as far as Rossini style in England is concerned. Marina de Gabarain's Angelina is soft-grained, gentle, and lacks both sparkle and the vocal guns necessary to bring the opera to its scintillating conclusion. Juan Oncina, although inclined to indulge in falsetto singing more than one likes, is an elegant Ramiro and, like Sesto Bruscantini, phrases his music impeccably. Bruscantini's Dandini is a superb characterization – witty, all quicksilver, and wonderfully sung. I have referred to Ian Wallace's fine Magnifico above. Hervey Alan makes much of the small part of Alidoro, and Alda Noni and Fernanda Cadoni are a well-contrasted pair of sisters, bringing out in their singing all they had obviously learned from Ebert in the production.

The Russian Radio set (1951) provides more enjoyment than one might imagine. Rossini sounds better in Russian than in German, and in Zara Dolukhanova we have a most sympathetic and rich-sounding Cinderella, who is awarded an extra aria in Act 1, before the 'Zitto, zitto' duet, which I have been unable to place. There are the usual cuts, some odd musical liberties, including a generous contribution from the tenor, Orfenov, who obviously fancies himself as a Rossinian, in the final Rondo.

Decca's 1963 set, reissued in 1973, has Simionato for a second time as Angelina. But Simionato 1963-model is not a patch on Simionato 1949; she huffs and puffs in the coloratura, sprinkling it with a generous supply of intrusive 'h's. Still, her vivid personality comes through, even if one has the feeling that this Cinderella could round on all her family much as Amneris does on the priests in the last act of *Aida*. Ugo Benelli's Ramiro is sung with a fuller, more Italianate tone than Oncina's, and it sounds more beautiful too. Bruscantini's second Dandini is a trifle gruffer and less smoothly sung than in the Glyndebourne set; but it still remains a model of the *buffo* style. Paolo Montarsolo as Magnifico indulges in the over-exaggeration so loved by many Italian comic basses – Magnifico is pompous and funny, but not vulgar. As this set is virtually complete, Montarsolo has his second aria, and the Alidoro, Giovanni Foiani, is given Agolini's musically inferior 'Vasto teatro é il mondo', which is no great gain; in any case, Foiani hardly sounds like a worldly philosopher. The Misses Carral and Truccato Pace are no more than adequate as the sisters. Oliviero De Fabritiis, while not having Gui's grasp of the Rossinian style, none the less conducts with brio.

The 1971 set has five of the Scala cast who were heard at Covent Garden in 1976, and Claudio Abbado conducting the LSO; Alberto Zedda's edition of the score is used; it includes the aria for Alidoro, 'La del ciel nell'arcano' which Rossini wrote for the bass Gioacchino Moncada for the 1820 Rome performances, to replace Agolini's 'Vasto teatro'. It is out of style with the rest of the music, sounding as if it has strayed in from one of Rossini's *opere serie*. The really important feature of Zedda's edition is that it restores Rossini's original orchestration – we hear all kinds of charming instrumental detail, which makes it all the more regrettable that DG's acoustic has a dulling effect on the performance as a whole. Abbado is not a conductor to let things flag, and the performance certainly goes with a swing; the ensembles are crisp, and the recording, which followed the 1971 Edinburgh Festival performances with the same cast, is obviously well rehearsed. What one misses is a sense of fun, a warmth, and lightness of touch that both Gui and de Fabritiis brought to their performances.

Teresa Berganza's performance of the title role is vocally impeccable, full of charm and pathos and certainly the best on disc, but in the final resort lacking the piquancy of Supervia. Luigi Alva has not the vocal beauty of Benelli, but very nearly everything else to make him an ideal Ramiro. Renato Capecchi's dry tone and almost *parlando* style make his Dandini less satisfactory musically than it is as a characterization. Montarsolo has toned down those excesses that spoiled his Magnifico in the Decca set. Ugo Trama's somewhat leaden bass voice makes heavy weather of his role and his 1820 aria. The two sisters, Margherita Guglielmi and Laura Zannini, almost equal Noni and Cadoni on the old Glyndebourne set.

The most recent and far from complete recording was made to provide the sound track for a German Television performance in 1979, according to the date on the labels, but I suspect it was made a little earlier than that. It occupies six sides, but could easily have been got on to four. While I would not actually call it a 'highlights' performance, so much has been omitted that it cannot under any circumstances be called complete. Not only is there the expected omission of Alidoro's Act 1 aria, but also of the whole of Don Magnifico's wine-tasting scene with chorus as well as the scene preceding it between Dandini and Magnifico, which means that we leap from the end of the Quintet to the Act 1 finale, 'Zitto, zitto'. The opening scene of Act 2 including Magnifico's aria 'Sia qualunque' also goes by the board, and as Alfredo Mariotti is a good Don Magnifico he is hard done by. Strangely enough the often-cut aria for the Don Ramiro, with chorus, in Act 2, 'Pegno adorata e caro' is retained, which gives the excellent Benelli every chance to shine: his singing is stylish, and the voice sounds at times truly beautiful.

Bianca Maria Casoni made her debut nearly a quarter of a century ago and has always been a safe, reliable and rather dull singer. On the stage her performances as Rosina, Cenerentola etc. hardly sparkle, but one is always sure that she will give a musical performance – she does so here and is, as one would expect, more at home in the role's sadder moments than in the big party-scene and the final Rondo. Sesto Bruscantini's Dandini (his third recording of the role) remains a model of style, though naturally the voice no longer sounds as young as it did when he first sang the part under Gui at Glyndebourne in 1954. The two sisters are not very pleasant to listen to – perhaps they looked better on the TV screen than they sounded! Federico Davià does what he can with what is left of Alidoro's role.

Piero Bellugi does not seem to take naturally to Rossini; he is better known for his conducting of contemporary music; and the Berlin Radio Orchestra likewise sounds not at home in Rossinian climes.

Now to the individual discs. I will not comment on the many performances of the overture, which incidentally was originally composed by Rossini for his *La gazzetta* the previous year, except to say that they are varied in their style, as one would expect from such diverse conductors as Toscanini, Gui, De Sabata, Reiner, Giulini, Maag and their assorted orchestras. If you get Toscanini's Rossini overtures disc (RCA AT 108), you will not be disappointed.

Of the vocal numbers in the opera, I have only been able to find recordings of five: Don Magnifico's Cavatina, 'Miei rampolli femminini', in which he describes and interprets his dream; the duet between Angelina and Magnifico 'Signor, una parola'; Magnifico's 'Sia qualunque delle figlie' in Act 2, in which he describes life as he sees it after one of his two daughters has married the prince; Ramiro's 'Pegno adorata e caro'; and the famous final Rondo.

The earliest recording of Magnifico's 'Miei rampolli' was made by the bass Arcangelo Rossi in 1905 – in fact he recorded it twice that year, once on a Black and Silver Columbia (3117) and once on a Black Victor (4406). Rossi was obviously well-schooled in the *buffo* tradition, and appeared at both

Covent Garden (1905–6) and the Metropolitan (1903–7). He sang Yakuside, that odd character in *Madama Butterfly*, in the opera's first London and New York performances and he was also a well-known Bartolo (Mozart and Rossini), Dulcamara, Benoit and Alcindoro before his death at the early age of thirty-eight in 1907. Ernesto Badini, the famous Pasquale of the HMV plum-label set with Schipa, Toscanini's favourite Ford, and London's first Schicchi – indeed a baritone more than a bass and usually Dandini rather than Magnifico – also recorded it (Od. 605901); so did Pini-Corsi (Pathé 84542) and Conceto Paterna – he sang Pasquale to Badini's Malatesta at Covent Garden in 1920 – in more extended form (Fono. 92767–8). A recording by one J. Giuliani (P.29000) I have not heard.

Fernando Corena's performance (LXT 5307) is typical of that artist: full of chuckles, excellent diction, and the true *buffo* style allied to a very good voice. The American bass Ezio Flagello (Scope V0001-M) gives a straighter and more deliberate account. He has a good voice of the Pinza type, and demonstrates his range by taking a high G towards the end of his performance. More recently Jozsef Gregor (Hungaraton SLPX 12359) has recorded it nimbly, with splendid vigour and brio.

The duet 'Signor, una parola' is, in reality, the first part of the C major quintet; but even in the shortened form it is given by Conchita Supervia and Vincenzo Bettoni (Parlo. PXO 1021; OASI 643) shows these two artists, who had appeared so often together in this work, at their best.

The often-omitted Magnifico aria in Act 2, 'Sia qualunque', appears to have been only recorded three times, by Giuliani (P.29001), by Fernando Corena (LXT 5307) and by Gregor; and Ramiro's 'Pegno adorata e caro', only once, Nicola Monti giving a most elegant account on a 'private' issue.

So we come to the ten or so versions of the finale, ranging from Eugenia Mantelli's Erda-like performance (Zono. 12164–5; Club 99.79) made in 1906, via Marilyn Horne's 1965 performance (SXL 6149) in which she indulges her chest-like register to the full and produces a charmless impression, to the subdued Frederica von Stade (Philips 9500 098). The decorations and liberties taken by all the ladies vary from the acceptable (Berganza and Los Angeles) to the faintly ludicrous (Horne referred to above). Supervia (PXO 1018; HLM 7039) begins very slowly and deliberately; one notes the ease with which she sings the phrase 'Come un baleno rapido' with its runs and decorations; and then there is a lovely sense of mischief allied to her loving nature as she forgives father and sisters – throughout she is free with her *rubato*. Rose Bampton, the American soprano, but a mezzo in her earlier days, sings the scene almost straight (Victor 18217; CAL 293), and there is little characterization. On the other hand the Canadian-Russian mezzo, Jennie Tourel, gives what to me is the most satisfying performance musically and vocally (LX 1003; Odyssey Y2–32880); the phrasing and vocal shading are charming throughout, though some people might think what is lacking is the smile in the voice. Giulietta Simionato's account of the scene (LXT

5458) is not really satisfactory. She never could trill and, as in all her performances, is apt to sprinkle around those intrusive 'hs'.

Victoria de los Angeles's much-decorated version is sung with velvety tone (ALP 1284). Teresa Berganza's Rossini recital of 1959 under Alexander Gibson (SDD 224) includes a gentle performance of the scene, charmingly done. Finally there is an unlikely performance by Callas on a mixed recital disc (ASD 3984) which is effortful, the tone hollow. That she might have been an effective Cenerentola is proved by her performance on a 'private' recording of a Paris concert given in June 1963 in which she gives a truly beguiling performance, caressing the notes and bringing Angelina to life.

There is still room in the catalogue for additions to the *Cenerentola* entry. The last few years have seen the emergence of three outstanding Rossini mezzo-sopranos: the Italian Lucia Valentini Terrani, the Welsh Della Jones and the Irish Ann Murray, each one of whom has brought distinction to the role of Cenerentola in the theatre and any one of them would make an outstanding heroine in a new complete recording.

LA CENERENTOLA

C Cenerentola; *R* Ramiro; *D* Dandini; *A* Alidoro; *M* Magnifico

1949 (abridged) Simionato *C*; Valletti *R*; Meletti *D*; Susca *A*; Dalamangas *M* / Italian Radio Chorus and Orch., Turin / Rossi Cetra ⓜ LPO2017 ④ MPO2017 Everest ⓒ 432 (3)

1951 (in Russian) Dolukhanova *C*; Orfenov *R*; Belov *D*; Troitsky *A*; Polyaev *M* / Moscow Radio Chorus and Orch. / Bron Melodiya ⓜ M39275–80 Eclat (US) ⓜ ECL1003

1953 Gabarain *C*; Oncina *R*; Bruscantini *D*; Alan *A*; Wallace *M* / Glyndebourne Festival Chorus and Orch. / Gui EMI ⓜ RLS688 RCA (US) ⓜ LHMV600

1963 Simionato *C*; Benelli *R*; Bruscantini *D*; Foiani *A*; Montarsolo *M* / Florence Festival Chorus and Orch. / De Fabritiis Decca GOS631 London OSA1376

1971 Berganza *C*; Alva *R*; Capecchi *D*; Trama *A*; Montarsolo *M* / Scottish Opera Chorus, London SO / Abbado DG 2709 039

1977 (abridged – television soundtrack) Casoni *C*; Benelli *R*; Bruscantini *D*; Davià *A*; Mariotti *M* / German Opera Chorus, Berlin; Berlin Radio SO / Bellugi Acanta JB23271–3

L'Italiana in Algeri
and *Il Turco in Italia*

RICHARD OSBORNE

When he composed L'Italiana in Algeri *he was in the full flower of his youth and genius. He was not afraid to repeat himself: he felt no urge to create powerful music . . . this enchanting opera was not concerned to evoke the reality or the sadness of life; and most assuredly there was not a single head in all the audience which had the notion of submitting sensual delight to the test of critical judgement.* Stendhal

1813 is an *annus mirabilis* in the history of opera. In February *Tancredi* irradiated the Venetian winter season; on 22 May, the day of Wagner's birth, *L'Italiana in Algeri* confirmed the extent of Rossini's youthful genius; in October Verdi was born, the composer who was to be the principal beneficiary of the Italian operatic renaissance which Rossini's Venetian triumphs had effectively ushered in.

Like many of Rossini's major successes, neither *Tancredi* nor *L'Italiana* has had an easy passage down the years. 'Di tanti palpiti' apart, *Tancredi* has been poorly served by the gramophone and on the stage. Two extant complete recordings merely caricature with vocal ineptitude an opera which Giuseppe Carpani, a distinguished contemporary observer, had commended for its 'beautiful *cantilena*, its new *cantilena*, its magical *cantilena*, its rare *cantilena*'. Were it not for a distantly recorded 'off-the-air' set (Historical Recorded Enterprises 238) of a remarkable New York concert performance, given in 1978 by a cast which included Marilyn Horne, Katia Ricciarelli and Ernesto Palacio, the recorded chronicles of this elegant, chivalric work would be dim indeed.

L'ITALIANA IN ALGERI

L'Italiana has, on the whole, been better served, though its revival in the present century owes much to a single singer, Conchita Supervia. Radiciotti tells us that Supervia's 1925 Turin revival of the opera, conducted by Vittorio Gui, sent Richard Strauss 'mad with enthusiasm'; and a revival four years later, at the Théâtre des Champs-Elysées in Paris, set the seal on the opera's

renewed popularity for a generation and beyond. Happily, *L'Italiana*
accorded with the mood of the twenties. Rossini's special achievement had
itself consisted of a brilliant restyling and reordering of an existing tradition.
The libretto was second-hand – the composer, Luigi Mosca, had already set
it for a staging at La Scala, Milan in 1808 – and Rossini's act of reappro-
priation was a radical one. Pace and textural brilliance, a streamlining of
rhythm, gesture, and eighteenth-century vocal mannerism, and Rossini's own
individual delight in the power of words to energize music by alliteration and
onomatopoeia: these were some of the elements out of which the new comic
mechanism was made. Rognoni, in his book on Rossini, compares the
method with that of the silent films of the 1920s and the witty comic reduc-
tions of Sennett and Chaplin. If the analogy holds true (and I think it does)
then Supervia's success with *L'Italiana* is a case of personal genius being
felicitously matched to a particular historical moment.

Since the advent of LP there have been five recordings of *L'Italiana*. Two
date from the early 1950s and are in mono. They are a generally memorable
Russian performance led by the remarkable and heart-warming Zara Dolukhanova, and a rather traditional La Scala set with Simionato and Valletti,
conducted by Giulini. Of the three stereo sets, the newest, with Marilyn
Horne as Isabella, is by far the most significant since it is based on an entirely
revised text; one of several important Rossini revisions to have emerged in
recent years from the Fondazione Rossini in Pesaro. But let us begin, not
with the complete sets, but with Conchita Supervia; after which, old pre-
cedents and new scholarship can provide the proper context for discussion
of the rival claims of existing complete recordings.

To judge from the four items gathered together on the second side of the
Parlophone collection (PMA 1025), Supervia's Isabella was vibrant and vehement, an appropriately petulant creature capable of rare feats of nimble-
ness and wit. The selection begins with 'Ai capricci', Isabella's enraged and
careworn confrontation with her ageing *cicisbeo*, Taddeo. Nothing shows
more vividly than this Rossini's precocious comic mastery. Here raillery and
encircling doubt are marvellously juxtaposed in a duet which yet retains the
sense and shape of a beautifully turned musical number. Real emotion is
kept at bay, yet its surrogate, a wry comic pathos, is deployed by Rossini
with a detachment and a poise that calls to mind some of the more scabrous
pages of Evelyn Waugh. From first to last, Supervia attends to rhythm and
verbal accent with a fierce delight. Where Isabella advises Taddeo to think
no more of the present – 'Sarà quel che sarà' – rhythms skip and dance and
divisions take wing as they might in some spirited impromptu with Schnabel
at the keyboard. Especially remarkable is the pointing of the duet's central
section, Supervia distilling the pathos of the moment in a way unequalled by
any subsequent interpreter of the role on record. The Taddeo, Carlo Scattola,
also alone among recorded exponents of the part, sounds deliciously gaga,
the exchanges before the final movement a miracle of comic insinuation:
cackles and vituperative asides heard against wry chromatic whispers in the

orchestra itself. If any one item distils the comic genius of *L'Italiana*, it is this duet as Supervia and Scattola sing it.

'O che muso', Isabella's astonished response on first meeting the Algerian bey face to face, is again something which Supervia made peculiarly her own. Like Mae West's 'Peel me a grape' or Edith Evans's 'handbag', it is a moment Supervia pinpoints in a single declamatory gesture: a comic appropriation which renders all imitations null and void and most alternatives unthinkable. The selection also includes two of Isabella's solo numbers. What so distinguishes her rendering of 'Per lui che adoro' is its tremulous, love-lorn quality: tremulous yet with a gracious curve on the single word 'adoro' that is beguilingly simple, unutterably sincere. As for her account of 'Pensa all patria', the revolutionary showpiece in Act 2 which the Bourbon censors in Naples so promptly removed, here Supervia's rhythmic verve is the compelling, transforming factor. So often leaden in rival interpretations, here it leaps off the page with a mingled ardour and defiance that perfectly confirms the challenge of the quotation from the 'Marseillaise' which Rossini deftly insinuates into the preceding chorus.

How different from all this is the Isabella of the sensuous and sympathetic Russian mezzo-soprano, Dolukhanova. Of all Rossini mezzos in the pre- and post-war period none has a smoother, sweeter sound across the two and a half octaves from a remarkable low E flat to a perfectly luminous high C. The cavatina, 'Crude sorte!', rounded off with that beautifully taken high C, is full of guile and grace. By the time we reach 'Ai capricci' in the complete Melodiya recording, we are fully conscious of the fact that here is a wheedling, smiling, very feminine Isabella. And it is this feminine, gamesome quality which makes the famous confrontation with Mustafà so memorable. Dolukhanova's Isabella confronts the bey with a brilliant yet gracious gesture of comic disbelief, the one valid alternative I know to Supervia's 'O che muso' cited above. Abramov, the Mustafà, is just as warmly characterized. Being a Russian, he has at his disposal a plummeting low E flat, an octave below Dolukhanova's own and quite as ripe

Though it is sung in Russian, the Melodiya set is surprisingly rich in interest. The sound is smooth and clear, the conducting alert and thoroughly stylish, and the casting full of unexpected small treasures, including a lovely Russian soubrette, G. Sakharova, in the role of Elvira. Against this must be set piano-accompanied recitatives, some cuts, Slavonic horns, and a Slavonic tenor. But even in textual matters the recording is full of minor surprises. Lively wind-band flourishes before the *stretto* of 'Ai capricci', neglected on all but the two most recent sets, are included, and, curiously and most affectingly, 'Per lui che adoro' has its original preface for solo cello, something you can otherwise hear only in the addenda to Marilyn Horne's 1980 Erato recording.

Giulini's 1954 La Scala recording is conservative in style and disfiguringly cut; none the less it retains a distinction. 'The outstanding characteristic of this wonderful work,' wrote Stendhal, 'is its speed, its extreme economy, and its lack of turgidity.' At times, Giulini modifies all three categories. Conscious of the work's classic status, he treats the score seriously, like a picture-house pianist celebrating Chaplin's inspired comic symmetries with the music of Bach. Bertini (Acanta), Scimone (Erato), and the Russian, Samosud, are all gayer, less inclined to intellectualize the score. Yet, within the limits set by the La Scala/Ricordi edition, it must be said that Giulini conducts the opera with a blend of strength and zest which stabilizes the forms without necessarily inhibiting the wit. Arias and ensembles are carefully marshalled, structures symphonically built, before *stretti* which invariably move like quicksilver. Musically, and above all rhythmically, it is often compelling. The cast is memorable primarily for the Lindoro of Cesare Valletti. His ripe, sensual singing combines ease and eloquence with ringing, visceral high B flats in the (unhappily, edited) cavatina. Graziella Sciutti is a predictably charming Elvira, Mario Petri an imposing Mustafà. In the role of Taddeo, Marcello Cortis sounds genuinely elderly without managing to sound as fey or as foppish as Carlo Scattola, the wholly acted Taddeo of the Supervia recordings.

Like her conductor, Simionato is purposeful and predictable. In short, she catches Isabella's boldness but not her caprice. What is missing is the light and shade of the character, the mingled petulance and passion which makes Isabella as dangerous as gun cotton. 'Pensa alla patria' is particularly disappointing. The recitative is used as a short-cut to the aria and the cabaletta, high Bs vividly taken, is disfigured by a four-page cut. Throughout the set this cutting is persistent and damaging. Few major arias have cabalettas or *stretti* intact; recitatives disappear wholesale. Two popular ditties are omitted: Lindoro's 'Oh, come il cor di giubilo' and Haly's 'Aria del sorbetto' about the women of Italy, street songs, inconsistent with the lofty purpose and high seriousness of Giulini's reading. Mustafà's 'Già d'insolito', cited by Garcia as a classic test piece for the articulation of triplets, also vanishes. Yet, packaged as a two-disc bargain and published with a libretto in English and Italian (something omitted by Acanta and Erato), the set has merited its recent resuscitation.

The first stereo recording of *L'Italiana* appeared on the Decca label in 1964. Tricked out with a veneer of scholarship, plausibly conducted by Silvio Varviso, vividly recorded in warm, wrap-around sound and centred on Teresa Berganza, an enormously popular mezzo in the Mozart and Rossini repertory, it was quickly accepted as the standard recording, discouraging all intrusive rivalry for well over a decade. Unhappily, any faith in the 'classic' status of the set was, from the first, illusory. Though substantially complete, the musical text proved to be very much the mixture as before, with anachronistically blended late-nineteenth-century orchestration, such as we find on the consciously old-fashioned and rhythmically more stable Giulini set, robbing Rossini's score of much of its irony and wit. The downward transposition from E flat to D of Lindoro's cavatina proved to be no more than an experimental blind-side run, a piece of dubious scholarship that could not disguise from us the sketchy nature of Luigi Alva's singing of the role. Nor could Varviso's bright and breezy manner effectively conceal his failure to hold the larger ensembles unerringly on course, nor persuade the sharp-eared collector that the tuning of the Florentine woodwinds was anything other than dyspeptic (the oboe's preface to the tenor's Act 2 aria a typical problem). Central to the set's case, though, is the Isabella of Teresa Berganza, which is often static in rhythm and bland in accent. True, Berganza is not helped by her conductor, whose sense of rhythm seems as fallible as her own whenever anything other than metronomic regularity is called for. Most at home in the placid measures of 'Per lui che adoro', Berganza is most at sea in 'Ai capricci' (Rolando Panerai the encouragingly alert Taddeo) where even the scathing cry of 'al diavolo!' is sung *a tempo*, blandly, smoothly.

An antidote to the Decca set appeared late in 1979 in the form of an East German Acanta recording conducted with genuine lucidity and flair by Gary Bertini, with an experienced cast: Sesto Bruscantini, ever resourceful in the role of Mustafà; Enzo Dara, a sober, frock-coated Taddeo; Alfredo Mariotti a ripe-toned Haly, and Ugo Benelli a more gracious Lindoro than Decca's Alva. Textually, the set is unusually complete and unusually clean. The playing of the Dresden orchestra is elegant and expert, and it is clear from the outset that Bertini has looked afresh at Rossini's orchestration, returning to original source materials in order to cleanse, brighten and sharpen the sound. The Isabella is Lucia Valentini Terrani. Favouring a direct approach, in the Berganza style, she is generally fresher- and sweeter-sounding than her more celebrated rival. There is an expressive inwardness about her 'Per lui che adoro' and parts of 'Pensa alla patria', allied to an ease and buoyancy of rhythm which is apt to Bertini's purposes and winning in its own right. Valentini Terrani's characterization is not in any respect a strong one; but, then, neither is Berganza's; and of the two the younger singer is the more fluent vocalist.

The most significant complete recording yet to appear is undoubtedly the Erato set conducted by Claudio Scimone and recorded with an expert chamber orchestra, I Solisti Veneti, at Treviso, a stone's throw from the city in which the opera had its successful première in 1813. The performance is based on a new revision of the score by Azio Corghi. Apart from guaranteeing completeness, and adding on side six an important array of replacement arias written for Venice, Milan, and Naples between 1813 and 1815, the new edition principally affects orchestration.*

Nineteenth-century practice, as demonstrated in the Giulini and Varviso

---

* Four arias are included in the Erato addendum. Most straightforward is 'Per lui che adoro' given here with the original cello preface which Rossini deleted (replacing it with a solo flute) after the first performance. Most elaborate is Lindoro's 'Concedi, amor pietoso', an aria with clarinet *obbligato* written for the important Milanese première in the spring of 1814 and set in place of the more jauntily Venetian 'Oh, come il cor di giubilo'. Isabella's cavatina 'Cimentando i venti e l'onde', an unremarkable piece alongside 'Cruda sorte!' which it replaced at the second performance, was probably written at the insistence of the first Isabella, Maria Marcolini. More impressive is 'Sullo stil de' viaggiatori' which replaced the censored 'Pensa alla patria' in Naples in 1815. Censorship dogged *L'Italiana* in its early days. Not only 'Pensa alla patria', but the preceding reference to the 'Marseillaise' caused offence, whilst in Milan in 1814 the text of 'Cruda sorte!' was altered to render it less sexually suggestive.

recordings, rendered Rossini's orchestration smoother and more homogeneous than it originally was. From the first, there had been in Rossini's scoring a mischievous and fantastic element. Tonal volumes and differences of pitch were wittily exploited, textures laid bare, in a manner Stravinsky was later to reappropriate. We first hear this on the Scimone set (and in Bertini's recording) at the reprise of the overture's second theme (fig. 9 of the old Ricordi score) where, not flute, but piccolo and bassoon greet the world with all the comic incongruity of a pair of silent film comedians. There is exoticism, too, bordering on parody, in the Turkish percussion (drum, cymbals, triangle, glockenspiel, Turkish crescent) which, on slenderer evidence, Corghi has added to the overture: a tintambulatory jangle like the shaking of some outsize bracelet, intrusive until the ear adjusts. Though I Solisti Veneti do not use original instruments, their playing is finely geared to Rossini's mordant comic manner, with spry, forward woodwinds, elaborate and inventive keyboard and string contributions in the recitatives, and strings capable of pointed *al ponticello* effects, what the Italians call 'sliding on ice', which we hear in the overture, the Act 2 Quintet, and Taddeo's 'Ho un gran peso'. The set's only textual accommodation appears to be in Haly's ditty 'Le femmine d'Italia' which the veteran Nicola Zaccaria sings, less smoothly than Acanta's Alfredo Mariotti, a tone down in F.

The run of 'Ai capricci' suggests that Scimone has not completely mastered the elusive art of pacing larger operatic movements; the G minor interlude partially eludes him. But there is much to delight the ear. Domenico Trimarchi, like Acanta's Dara, makes a formal Taddeo but, alone among contemporary Isabellas, Marilyn Horne gives life to Rossini's dotted rhythms, sinuous chromaticism, scabrous consonantal clusters, and free-wheeling runs of repeated notes. 'Al diavolo!', so phlegmatically phrased by Berganza, becomes a dismissive vocal wave which even Supervia might have envied.

Where Supervia quelled Mustafà with derision and Dolukhanova resorts to charming incredulity, Horne is a good deal more forceful. 'O che muso' becomes an ominous confrontation with Samuel Ramey's black-browed bey. Later Horne yields to a happier kind of comic cajolery. Scimone misjudges the pace of the start of the *stretto*, reducing it to a gabble, but the rest of the finale, Rossini's earliest and possibly greatest Act 1 dénouement, is brilliantly done, better poised than the Varviso, better pitched than the Bertini, thanks to the shining high Cs of the winning Elvira, Kathleen Battle. In the solo numbers Horne is preferable to all the extant Isabella's, save Supervia and Dolukhanova. In lower *tessitura* she can sound a grimly stentorian note, the registers poorly matched around C and B flat; but for the most part Horne's virtuosity is exceptional. In 'Cruda sorte!' there are some honeyed *fioriture* woven around Lindoro's name and 'Già so per practica' has pace and poise. The Elektra-like laugh after 'A' presso a poco' is unsettling, though, after the perfectly witty timing of the cadence itself. Some may find Horne's 'Per lui che adoro' too marmoreal (I find her gentler and truer in the cello-led alternative version on side six), but there is a mesmeric seventeen-second bird's-wing trill at the reprise. Her 'Pensa alla patria' is very fine. Where Berganza is bland and Simionato bored, Horne is concerned for both dramatic verisimilitude and vocal dexterity: as fluent as Acanta's Valentini Terrani but more characterful.

The Lindoro is Ernesto Palacio, a supple and sensitive Argirio in the 1978 New York Horne/Ricciarelli *Tancredi*. He has both his arias, as well as the clarinet-wreathed 'Concedi amor' on side six. He is heard at his best in ensemble, in the Pappataci Trio, for instance, rather than in the cavatina, 'Languir per una bella', where the recording is temporarily unflattering and the accompaniment unhelpful. But though there is little of Valletti's ease and eloquence, the cabaletta is uncut, and there Palacio shows himself to be expert and inventive in the reprise. In sum, this is the most enterprising, and in many ways the most successful, recording of this joyous masterpiece now before the public; lively and literate not only in arias and ensembles but in the recitatives, too, where Venetian inventiveness shines out.

For the rest, there is a small but select catalogue of individual recordings from the score. The overture, whose start was once likened to a husband creeping stealthily in at dead of night and inadvertently knocking over a grandfather clock, has been recorded a good deal, with success by Davis, Giulini, Karajan, and Marriner; at speed by Toscanini in his New York Philharmonic days (DB 2943), and by Serafin, ever the affecting stylist (C 4012), in the early 1950s. In Lindoro's cavatina I would mention Benvenuto Finelli (MWL 300; GV 6); an Englishman by birth, Finelli's mastery of the high tenor arias of the school of Rossini, Donizetti, and Bellini was regarded at one time as something of an eccentric whim. (The recordings are with piano accompaniments, especially sensitive ones, by George Sas.) Yet in 'Languir per una bella' there is a beauty of tone and a skill with grace notes and trills which inclines one to think of Finelli as a graduate, with distinction, of the school of Schipa. Apart from a single recording of 'Le femmine d'Italia' by Fernando Corena there is nothing of further interest from male interpreters of the opera. On the female side there are recordings by Berganza, Dolukhanova (who is better heard on the complete set), Dominguez, Fabbri, Horne, and Tourel. Guerrina Fabbri's 'Pensa alla patria', shortened and spoiled by end-of-tunnel sound, is only of passing interest despite some fleet-voiced coloratura (G & T 053007). There is, too, a certain aerial buoyancy about Oralia Dominguez's version (SLPM 136025). Marilyn Horne's recital accounts of 'Cruda sorte!' (SXL 6149) and 'Pensa alla patria' (SET 310) are marred by an overbearing vocal manner. Teresa Berganza is more lissom, alert and feline in the quicker music, under the lithe direction of Alexander Gibson (SDD 224). Which leaves Jennie Tourel, to my ears quite the pick of the bunch, with limpid diction, expert passage work, and a natural sense of the character's wit and temporizing passion: vocal guile and feminine guile finely aligned. Her account of 'Cruda sorte!' (LX 1054; Odyssey Y2 32880) is well worth hunting down – a vocal trophy to set beside the Supervia.

IL TURCO IN ITALIA

Written between *L'Italiana in Algeri* and *Il Barbiere di Siviglia, Il Turco in Italia* is not one of Rossini's more ambitious works. More a painting on ivory than on canvas, it has few extended opportunities for the principal singers. Framed within a frame by a Pirandellian poet in search of a plot, the opera quietly reverses the story-line of *L'Italiana* by landing an exotic foreigner amid the jealous husbands, pining lovers, flirtatious wives, and coffee cups of *bella Italia*. It sits well on the stage and is flecked with a range of incidental delights – deft dabs of colour and brief numbers, including a haunting Act 1 Trio which Stravinsky might once have been tempted to purloin. Yet it does not commend itself to larger houses and larger expectations. (Glyndebourne is the ideal house for this elegant divertissement.) The Milanese audience thought little of it in 1814, and when Rossini returned to Milan in 1817 he gave them a much more substantial piece, *La gazza ladra*.

It was Maria Callas who, with Franco Zeffirelli's help, carried the work back to Milan in the mid-1950s after an earlier run in Rome's tiny Eliseo theatre. And it is Callas who carries the piece on the EMI recording. She, outstanding among the cast, has the flair and guile with which to shape and project Rossini's deceptively placid vocal lines in the recitatives, airs, and racy duologues. She also has the score's obvious comic highpoint when Fiorilla denounces her old husband (Franco Calabrese: who has quite the right hang-dog intonations) in terms which Norma herself could not improve upon, before the music begins to dance and spit with comic derision, motioning itself forward to the more emancipated world of Rosina and 'Una voce poco fa'. Otherwise Callas has no star numbers, though she handles the wry, laconic, minor-key ditty 'Se il zefiro si posa', a wheedling vaudeville number in the Neopolitan style, with consummate hidden art. The veteran Mariano Stabile, though dry of voice, has all the necessary presence required for the puppet-master poet, a nicely turned epilogue to a great career. Jolanda Gardino is the gipsy girl, the other cat in the basket, so to speak, with claws only a mite less sharp than Callas's. Gedda sings the typically slight cavatina with liquid, honeyed tone and the chorus caps it with a pulsing hymn to love. As the eponymous Turk, Nicola Rossi-Lemeni has presence, but Filippo Galli's divisions, in 1814, were probably quicker and smoother.

For the period, 1955, the recording is comparatively restricted, and the text is shortened. After a lugubrious start, Gavazzeni conducts a buoyant, often stylish reading. Horns and trumpets leave something to be desired, but the Scala woodwinds are wonderfully lithe and adept. For all its shortcomings, the set is one which followers of Rossini or Callas will not want to miss.

The HMV set, trimmed and foreshortened, sits neatly on two records; the 1982 CBS set runs to three. On the newer set the text, prepared for the Fondazione Rossini in Pesaro by Margaret Bent, is complete in every jot and tittle. Add to this Philip Gossett's notes, which identify for us stray passages thought not to be by Rossini as well as items which are quintessentially his, and the CBS set can be commended both for its authenticity and its completeness. Unfortunately, such scholarly completeness doesn't necessarily add to the listener's pleasure on the gramophone. There is one substantial gain – Fiorilla's letter scene and attendant 'Squallida veste' – but there are some less colourful additions as well as yards of jangling recitative. Where Callas gives us too little recitative, tantalizing us with what she does include, Montserrat Caballé, CBS's Fiorilla, leaves me longing for several swift acts of abbreviation. Elsewhere, Caballé's Fiorilla is no match for Callas's guileful, witty, ironically aware portraiture. With Caballé, 'Non si da follia maggiore' is turned back into a mere concert aria and Fiorilla's confrontation with her doting geriatric husband is here drained of colour and effect, where Callas gives us a vivid complex of feigned anger and simulated grief, guilefully mixed and wittily deployed.

The CBS set boasts a strong trio of bass and baritone voices: Enzo Dara, Leo Nucci and Samuel Ramey well able to match HMV's Calabrese, Stabile and Rossi-Lemeni. However, Ernesto Palacio is less suave of voice than HMV's young Nicolai Gedda. Riccardo Chailly's Rossini, like Abbado's, can seem efficient and unsmiling. The new Italian school of Rossini conductors seems not to know that easy turn of the wrist which was so characteristic a feature of the conducting of men like Serafin, Gavazzeni, and, above all, Gui.

L'ITALIANA IN ALGERI

I Isabella; *E* Elvira; *Z* Zulma; *L* Lindoro; *M* Mustafà; *H* Haly; *T* Taddeo

1951 (in Russian) Dolukhanova *I*; Sakharova *E*; Matiushina *Z*; Nikitin *L*; Abramov *M*; Tikhonov *H*; Zakharov *T*/USSR Radio Chorus, Moscow PO/Samosud Melodiya ⓜ D 03218–23

1954 Simionato *I*; Sciutti *E*; Masini *Z*; Valletti *L*; Petri *M*; Campi *H*; Cortis *T*/La Scala Chorus and Orch./Giulini EMI ⓜ RLS747 Seraphim ⓜ IB6119

1963 Berganza *I*; Tavolaccini *E*; Alva *L*; Truccato Pace *Z*; Montarsolo *M*; Corena *H*; Panerai *T*/Florence Festival Chorus and Orch./Varviso Decca SET262 London OSA1375

1978 Valentini Terrani *I*; Rossi *E*; Caputi *Z*; Benelli *L*; Bruscantini *M*; Mariotti *H*; Dara *T*/Dresden State Opera Chorus, Dresden State Orch./Bertini Acanta JB22308

1980 Horne *I*; Battle *E*; Foti *Z*; Palacio *L*; Ramey *M*; Zaccaria *H*; Trimarchi *T*/Prague Chorus, I Solisti Veneti/ Scimone Erato STU71394

IL TURCO IN ITALIA

DF Donna Fiorilla; *S* Selim; *DN* Don Narciso; *P* Prosdocimo; *DG* Don Geronio
Z Zaida

1954 Callas *DF*; Rossi-Lemeni *S*;
Gedda *DN*; Stabile *P*; Calabrese
DG; Gardino *Z*/La Scala Chorus
and Orch./Gavazzeni
EMI © SLS5148
Seraphim Ⓜ IC6095

1981 Caballé *DF*; Ramey *S*; Palacio
DN; Nucci *P*; Dara *DG*; Berbié
Z/Ambrosian Opera Chorus,
National PO/Chailly
CBS M–37859

La Sonnambula and I Puritani

RICHARD FAIRMAN

LA SONNAMBULA

In his own words Bellini has described the première of *La Sonnambula* in 1831 as an 'uproarious success'. Unlike today, producer and conductor get little credit for the triumph and even the merits of his beautiful score are modestly brushed aside, but for the singers there is nothing but praise. 'Pasta and Rubini are two angels,' he exclaimed, 'and they enraptured the whole audience to the verge of madness.' As the sleepwalker of the title, the celebrated Giuditta Pasta had caused something of a sensation, despite reports that she was far from a faultless vocalist. The English critic, Henry Chorley, has written that 'her voice was, originally, limited, husky and weak – without charm, without flexibility – a mediocre mezzo-soprano,' but she had the power to grip an audience and fascinate in a way known only to the greatest performers. If contemporary criticism is to be believed, this is the way Bellini should be done: vivid, compelling and powerfully expressive. Only in later generations did these roles fall to the throats of so-called coloratura sopranos, many of whom saw them just as fodder for an eager larynx. In comparing recordings from their time and ours, it is best to remember the advice of the librettist Felice Romani:

> The role of Amina, even though at first glance it may seem very easy to interpret, is perhaps more difficult than many others which are deemed more important. It requires an actress who is playful, ingenuous and innocent, and at the same time passionate, sensitive and amorous; who has a cry for joy and also a cry for sorrow, an accent for reproach and another for entreaty. . . . This was the role created by Bellini's poetic intellect.

It is sure proof of his words that even now commercial records offer only three singers who have recorded the role complete.

In the earliest set, released by Cetra in 1952, the first Amina is Lina Pagliughi, already well known in the role from her previous records of excerpts (E 11277; Rococo 5261, and E 11328). She gives an artless performance whose freshness of voice and open-air simplicity make her the touching country-girl to the life. Many eminent sopranos have worked harder for less,

and it is not difficult to see why so many enthusiasts have remained faithful
to these records. But we can, and should, demand more. Pagliughi has not
looked into the depths of the role or (sufficiently) into its difficulties. Many
passages of coloratura are scrappy (as, for example, the cabaletta 'Sovra il
sen'), and the difficult emotional crises of the role, such as the first-act finale,
are allowed to pass with little comment. Her best moments, and those of the
set as a whole, come in the charming duets with tenor Ferruccio Tagliavini,
a lyric and sensitive Elvino. He too had recorded excerpts on an earlier 78
(DB 21579; GVC 18) and, though the voice is no longer so fresh, brings to
the part an unusual plangency which is most affecting. Cesare Siepi is a
rich-toned Rodolfo, but the supporting parts and orchestra are no more than
satisfactory. Franco Capuana makes all the usual theatre cuts, and leads his
Turin forces in the rest with caution but also an authentic Italian feel. This
and a certain rustic charm will always assure the set a welcome.

Nothing could be a greater contrast than the challenging artistry of Maria
Callas. By good fortune a number of recordings exist of her portrayal from
the rather effortful and ill-tuned 1955 excerpts which she originally held back
from release (ASD 3535) to the complete HMV set and live accounts taped
in Milan and Cologne. Of these, it is the 1955 La Scala live recording under
Leónard Bernstein which best captures Callas's miraculously radiant and
involving Amina. It is as though she had banished every other operatic part
from her thoughts and even from her voice. The girl who sings to us sounds
a mere adolescent, all wide-eyed innocence and open vowels. What Pagliughi
and other light sopranos had by nature, Callas found by science; but she goes
far beyond them in the creation of a living creature, whose every line, both
as music and text, is expressive of truly felt emotion. If they give us the
musical skeleton in their singing, then Callas may be said to provide the
dramatic flesh. Here indeed is a cry for joy ('Sovra il sen') and a cry for
sorrow ('Oh! se una volta sola'), the personal accents of a voice with unusual
weight and colour. It is extraordinary how her Amina resembles descriptions
of the role's earliest exponents Pasta and Malibran (a favourite of Bellini),
whose performance was found by some to have a 'vehemence too nearly
trenched on frenzy to be true'. Not a description that could apply to many
interpreters since.

Recording quality apart, the Scala evening is a brilliant affair. Cesare
Valletti's Elvino is an interpretation to cherish, strongly intelligent and responsive, and Giuseppe Modesti is a sound Rodolfo. They receive crystal-
cut accompaniments from the Scala orchestra under Leonard Bernstein, who
deserves praise not only for his taut and concentrated direction (despite its
exaggerated tempi) but also for the opening of many traditional cuts. By
contrast, the HMV studio recording is a worthwhile set, but less far-sighted
in its vision of the work and its attitudes towards the printed score. Antonino
Votto is the sympathetic but routine conductor, well supported by Nicola
Monti as a sweet, if ineffectual, Elvino and Nicola Zaccaria as a warmly
paternal Rodolfo. In their company Callas seems less ambitious than before,

not so much in her aims as in their execution, which has become more ordinary. The live performance from Cologne offers a similar cast. A comparison of 'Ah! non giunge' in each shows why the designer Tosi remarked at Milan: 'It was more than *bel canto* brilliance, it was magic.'

When Callas failed to appear at a final performance of *Sonnambula* with the Scala company in Edinburgh in 1957, it was Renata Scotto who substituted and her accomplished, tightly controlled Amina can now also be heard in a private recording from Venice in 1961. Much of the style has clearly been absorbed from the earlier production, but Scotto's portrayal finds an individual personality in its harder tone and more restricted, but compelling, intelligence. If she misses the inner core of humanity which makes Callas's Amina so touching, so Alfredo Kraus as Elvino falls short of Valletti's achievement only in his lack of genuine charm. Both singers are equal to the demands of the score and Kraus at one point even inserts an unwritten high D. Ivo Vinco is an uninspiring Rodolfo despite his obvious popularity with the audience. A number of the usual cuts are sanctioned by Nello Santi in an otherwise neatly pointed and controlled performance. As a whole, this account misses the extremes of Bernstein's version but also its extensive depth and vision.

With the first of the two Decca recordings under Richard Bonynge we reach a set of academic importance, a version which has delved deep into the textual problems of the score but rarely scratches its emotional surface. Innumerable minor cuts are restored, a passage for two trumpets (not published by Ricordi) is added to the wood scene, and Lisa, the reliable Sylvia Stahlman, retrieves both the second verse of her opening cavatina and her whole scene in the second act. Allowances are made only for Nicola Monti, whose introspective Elvino – now in his second recording – is still shy of some top notes and uses the customary transpositions. (Bellini's written keys intended for Rubini are not even printed in the Ricordi score: most of the tenor sections are down a tone and 'Ah, perchè non posso' is down a third, from D to B flat.) Bonynge points the orchestral detail with inimitable care, but the music obstinately sounds more like the 'trite and faded themes' noted at its British première than under less assiduous conductors. A separate excerpt from the score (SXL 2256) had already raised hopes for Joan Sutherland's assumption of the title role. In the cabalettas she is brilliant, a nonpareil among present-day technicians. Elsewhere the tone is soft, themes become blurred in self-conscious phrasing, and the character remains wistfully faint. From her first entrance amid an acoustic haze, she has been a soft-focus Amina and little more.

Her later recording inevitably shows a decline in the beauty and steadiness of the voice. Even the passage work is not without a sense of strain. Nevertheless, the years of experience have brought with them a more straightforward manner which is welcome: the eloquent Bellini line, such as we hear in 'D'un pensiero', is now purposefully shaped in an unbroken span. If the result is only intermittently moving, it is because Sutherland rarely invests the music with the expressive power of her most creative predecessors. By this time she had, in any case, dismissed the role of Amina as 'just another cardboard character'. An earlier recording of 'Prendi l'anel' (SXL 6828), strangely cut, paired her with the Elvino of Luciano Pavarotti. At first his singing is notable for its fine legato and immaculate diction, but it soon degenerates into the insensitive forcefulness which mars all but the most lyrical sections of the complete recording. Nicolai Ghiaurov makes a grand and aristocratic Rodolfo, singing with less imagination than in his early days. A special interest in the set comes with the accomplished singing of Isobel Buchanan, a rather over-sympathetic Lisa. Bonynge now proves himself to be a truly understanding conductor of the score. There are signs too that he no longer worships at the altar of textual accuracy: brief cuts are made at the conclusions to both acts. On neither set was he able to persuade his principals to follow the original distribution of voices in 'Son geloso del zeffiro', a passage where Callas and Valletti, duetting in sixths as written, make such a fine effect.

By the turn of the century the role of Amina had long been appropriated by the sopranos. No better souvenir remains of their style from the late nineteenth century than the famous record of Adelina Patti (03084; RLS 711) in 'Ah! non credea' made in 1906, when the reigning prima donna was on the point of abdication. The record ungallantly lifts the veil from an old lady's weaknesses: unsure intonation, shaky breath control and failure in the cadenza, despite transposing down a tone. It is art, not accuracy that makes it valuable: our fascination is more than gratified by her individual eloquence and well-executed ornaments. Trills and graces are bound into the vocal line with the speed and dexterity of an instrumentalist. Comparison with other singers of the same period, such as the retired soprano Giulietta Wermez (Zono. 1596; Club 99.504) recorded in 1902, suggests a common inheritance of embellishments that could stretch back to Pasta herself. The cabaletta 'Ah! non giunge' sports certain leaps and turns still in use today. But for some reason singers in the gramophone era have slowly turned away from the same traditional decorations in the aria. Sopranos no longer want to indulge that affecting little chromatic run in the second verse, let alone the octave leap to a high C on the words 'novel vigore' (cautiously avoided by Patti). Even Sutherland's version is glorified by just one solitary trill.

Like Patti, the Russian-based soprano Olympia Boronat makes free with the timing of her line like a master-pianist improvising at the keyboard. She recorded 'Come per me sereno' (053188; DJA 100) in 1908 with piano accompaniment in the recitative, and it is one of her best records. She stops for a moment near the beginning and has to be urged on by well-wishers. Better still is Lucrezia Bori (82289; Rococo R 32) in 'Ah! non credea', recorded in 1913. Her singing breathes emotion. Everything here is sadness, pure and exquisite. Tempo, phrasing and vocal colour are subtly managed, but so slight are the means, the impact of her performance may take one by surprise. Once heard, Bori's Amina is not forgotten. Some fine, straightforward singing in a similar manner comes from Alma Gluck (DB 663; Club 99–30) in 'Ah! non credea', but the music simply does not mean so much. Rosina Storchio (92753; Rococo 5364) tries harder in the same piece but to no better effect. Here, in any case, a different style has begun to intrude. Some words are given a heavy and ungracious emphasis, warning signs of the encroaching influence of verismo.

Not all the singers of this period are aiming at docility or sweetness. Marcella Sembrich (DB 428; Sunday Opera MSC 1) sets off into 'Ah! non giunge' at a spanking pace and attacks the top notes with a sadistic relish. Her athletic singing is valuable for its brightness and clean leaps over wide intervals. More dazzling still is Luisa Tetrazzini (DB 533) in the same piece. This is a virtuoso display of sure tone, trills and volleys of *staccati*. The coloratura *par excellence*, she adds two vast cadenzas: one in the aria (2–053049) with a solo cello, and the other in the cabaletta with a solo flute. One side of a disappointing 78 (2–053070) recorded in 1912 finds her rushed and over-robust in the first-act scene. All Tetrazzini's records are reissued on GEMM 220–27. Four Spanish coloraturas belong in the same group: Maria Galvany in 'Come per me sereno' (53295; OASI 574), Maria Barrientos in 'Ah! non giunge' (Fono. 39011; GV 545), Elvira de Hidalgo (Fono. 92305) and the girlish Graziella Pareto in 'Ah! non credea' (053156; CO 376). All offer shallow accounts with simple legato and tightly executed ornaments. The listings are far from exhaustive.

Amelita Galli-Curci may well seem to be a species which belongs in the same aviary, but her recordings from *La Sonnambula* (DB 256 and DB 812; GV 578) demand separate treatment both for their quality and style. Dating from 1917–24, these solos are shy of any exhibitionist element, be it Patti's rubato or Tetrazzini's vocal fireworks. Some decorations do remain but they rarely intrude on that sweetness of tone and manner which makes Galli-Curci's singing – especially of 'Come per me sereno' (DB 256; RLS 743) – so satisfying. Two leading German sopranos recorded excerpts about this time: Selma Kurz (first heard on record as early as 1900) in the latest of her versions, warm and sympathetic in 'Ah! non credea' (DB 778; GEMM 121), and Maria Ivogün (Od. LXX 76971; LV 67) lighter of voice in 'Ah! non giunge'. Toti dal Monte (DB 1317; LV 184) offers clear Italianate tone and phrasing in 'Ah! non credea' but at the expense of expressive power. It is interesting to turn from this performance to the impassioned work of Claudia Muzio (LCX 27; 3C 053–00937) in the same piece. Made in 1934, when the singer was at the end of her career, the record offers throaty enunciation and melodramatic dynamics which show how far interpretation in this music could advance over three decades.

Apart from Callas and Sutherland, there are few in recent years whose voices clamour for inclusion. One exception is the gentle Margherita Carosio in 'Ah! non credea' (DB 6388), showing how an artist's hand can bind notes and consonants into a deeply expressive line. Another is Anna Moffo (Regal SREG 2064) limpid of voice and fluent in coloratura, but singing more intently on the words of 'Ah! non credea' as is the current fashion. Otherwise recordings offer little but disappointment. Time and again sleeve-notes promise the listener a 'natural coloratura' or an 'expert in Bellini', but their writers should know better in these days of the Trades Descriptions Act. Few can command an unbroken legato, and those that attempt the cabalettas offer clumsy and heavily aspirated coloratura. Into this category must fall Mado Robin (LW 5238) and Cristina Deutekom (SAL 3786) in 'Ah! non credea' with cabaletta, and Silvana Bocchino (LPO 2002), Virginia Zeani (LXT 5317) and the tremulous Mattiwilda Dobbs (CX 1305) in the aria alone. Bidu Sayao (Am Col. 71768D; Odyssey 32 16 0377) achieves a more touching effect with the words of 'Ah! non credea', and Halina Mickiewiczowna (Muza L 0171) though thin of voice offers unusual *staccato* decorations in the cabaletta. Lily Pons (LX 1259) deserves a mention, if only for the Hollywood re-orchestrations of her conductor André Kostelanetz. Beverly Sills (ASD 2578) is lavish in her decorations of 'Come per me sereno' but more parsimonious in matters of tone. Montserrat Caballé (SXLR 6690) deserves her position for sheer beauty of tone in the whole of the final scene, and Mirella Freni (CM 19) for a good central performance in the current style, although she omits the cabaletta. Nevertheless, as a general rule, it seems the values of the Golden Age have become tarnished.

Apart from Fernando de Lucia's strong performance of 'Ah! perche non posso odiarti' (52676; Rubini RS 305), tenors have restricted themselves to the duets, and usually the simple opening page of 'Prendi l'anel ti dono'. The vocal line moves gently stepwise and is not high or much embellished, but from it the singer must create sheer poetry. Almost alone of the few who try, de Lucia is a success. His singing in a duet recording with Maria Galvany (054217; RS 305) captures an ideal pastoral harmony, made from an even line and gentle top notes; both here and in their version of the second duet 'Son geloso del zeffiro' (054215; RS 305) he shows how to work the little flourishes into the melody, like some exquisite art of crochet that has now been lost. The best of the other duet versions come from Tito Schipa: in 'Prendi l'anel' with dal Monte (DA 1351) he sings notes rather than phrases, but his 'Son geloso' with Galli-Curci (DB 811; LV 219) is a beautifully liquid performance, its runs and melody flowing with an easy charm across the bar-lines. Such a natural appeal is all too rare, even though Bellini has instructed his singers in this duet to act 'sempre con crescente tenerezza'. In 'Prendi l'anel' Aristodemo Giorgini with Galvany (054112; Rococo 5339) is over-strong, Dino Borgioli with Surinach (D 1007; GV 537) sometimes hard of tone, and Nicolai Gedda with Freni in both duets (ASD 2473) is too unsmiling in accomplishment. Many of the same tenors – such as Giorgini (52194; ORL 223), Borgioli (D 1009; GV 537) and Schipa (Pathé 5591; GVC 10) – confirmed their characteristics in solo versions of 'Prendi l'anel', and to their number must be added the honey-voiced Beniamino Gigli (Harvest H 1001) and a competent account from Enzo de Muro Lomanto (D 1607). But though records such as these have their value as souvenirs of the great voices of the century, they rarely realize the full illustrative personality of Bellini's music.

There are a few miscellaneous items: the Scala chorus (B 2624) gives an accurate, but hardly chilling, performance of the ghostly chorus 'A fosco cielo'. Recordings exist of the ensemble 'D'un pensiero', one by Giorgini and Huguet (054250; Rococo 5339) and another by Borgioli and Surinach (D 1007; GV 537), in both of which the tenor outsings his soprano to great effect. A quintet of artists from English National Opera has recorded 'Lisa mendace anch'essa' with piano accompaniment (ENO 1001), a strange choice and not especially well sung.

Far more interesting are the basses and their recordings of 'Vi ravviso', that touchstone of *bel canto* style. Nationality is the key point here in evaluating the singer's efforts, not least when he is a bass with a Russian's granite strength and imposing spirit. Feodor Chaliapin recorded the aria three times in accounts which are said to reflect his admiration for a well-known recording by Antonio Scotti (052139; CO 363), but those who expect him to have donned an Italian mantle for this music will be disappointed. Though the earliest (052356; CO 390) does show some conscious refinements, the real Chaliapin – gulps, sobs and all – only comes through in the mature performances of 1922 (DA 101; GVC 5) and 1927 (DA 962; GEMM 152). Both his massive artistry and mannerisms have a direct descendant in a fascinating performance given by the young Nicolai Ghiaurov at Moscow Conservatory (USSR. D 013513/4), a more searching version than his later Supraphon EP (SUEC 811). Another impressive East European performance comes from Boris Christoff (ALP 1585), who brings a reflective stillness to the aria and makes a praiseworthy attempt at the cabaletta. By contrast, the Italians put emphasis not on the personal idiosyncracies of mood and character but on the straightforward tracing of an even vocal line: Francesco Navarini (62032; GV 14) recorded in 1907 has a correct musical approach and resonant tone, Tancredi Pasero (Parl. E 11357; LPC 55066) the same virtues and a strong account of the cabaletta. Further recordings include Oreste Luppi (Fono. 92530) and Andres De Segurola (2–52584) both comparatively plain in style, the latter with chorus. Raphael Arié (Decca K 2328; LX 3041) occasionally lifts into notes but has a sonorous warmth which compensates some strange rewriting in the orchestral accompaniment. Yet surpassing all of these is neither Russian nor Italian, but the French bass Pol Plançon (Vic. 85018; GV 76). In music that is at once simple and exceptionally taxing to sing well, he pours out a line with the liquid purity of the best Beaujolais and knows exactly when to relax or push ahead with *rubato*; here indeed is some of the best Bellini singing on record.

I PURITANI

As early as the London première of *La Sonnambula*, some voices had complained of a 'want of science' in Bellini's music. Whether consciously or not, the composer seems to have taken their comments to heart and with the première of *I Puritani* (his last opera) in 1835 offered his critics an opera with more complex musical substance. The orchestration showed progress, the score abounded with what Rossini chose to call 'German harmonies', and – most important of all – there was a new musical and dramatic unity. In this work, for all its length, it is difficult to make cuts that will not sever the artistic flow. Either the set pieces tend to become isolated sections, or the formal and harmonic equilibrium is upset. Yet, though it may be desirable to have a full version of the score, it is less easy to achieve one. Of the recent 'complete' recordings, no two offer the same text. Much of the confusion dates back to the emendations made by the composer himself: first, he added the brilliant showpiece 'Son vergin vezzosa' for his favourite, Maria Malibran; and then, finding the opera with its many encores was too long, he cut about thirty minutes of the original material. But still further rewriting and cuts are demanded nowadays by singers who have to follow the legendary Giovanni Battista Rubini in the role of Arturo, as the part contains stratospheric difficulties with its D flats and, at one point, high F. In the third act, Rubini was said to have 'carried every one to the seventh heaven', but present-day tenors have trouble reaching even the first.

The problems are exemplified in the first commercial recording, released by EMI in 1953, which has some thirty-three cuts removing about one seventh of the Ricordi vocal score (which is itself far from complete). Yet to what remains, Serafin gives his fullest devotion. It is a serious performance, almost romantic in the strength of feeling it can generate at an emotional crux such as the string introduction to 'Qui la voce'. The conductor always offers sound sense in his direction and is still the interpreter most central to the Italian tradition. As his Arturo, there is Giuseppe di Stefano, an impassioned hero but one with few vocal graces. A sound supporting cast includes the more than capable Riccardo of Rolando Panerai and an avuncular Giorgio in Nicola Rossi-Lemeni, but vocally the set is dominated by the tragic accents of its Elvira, Maria Callas. On an earlier Cetra disc (Parl. R 30043; GVC 16), the scena and aria 'Qui la voce' had already introduced the young Callas to an unsuspecting public. In an apparent break with tradition, she sang Bellini's music with a voice which was dark and guttural, an instrument born with an almost primeval intensity far removed from the cultivated sopranos of the first half of the century. The complete set confirms her characteristics: some ugly scoops and curdled notes, but a total performance of rare vehemence. When Bellini asks his soprano to sing *con tutta la disperazione del dolore*, it is Callas who plays Elvira to the life. The instinctive power of her portrayal can already be heard in the 1952 live relay from Mexico City, but there she was an artist among amateurs. While the baritone and bass fight an endless battle with the prompter, the conductor Guido Picco shows little haste in bringing the slaughter to a halt.

The hazards of live performance are far from Decca's 1963 recording with Joan Sutherland, but so too is the excitement. Tempi may be swift and rehearsal thorough, but Richard Bonynge's fastidious phrasing and dotting of rhythms end in a performance that cannot see the music for the notes. Wisely or not, Bellini has dissipated interest over a wide canvas, and a stronger lead is needed from the pit, if the opera is to maintain a keen dramatic focus. None of the cast provides a dominating personality. Pierre Duval as Arturo has most of the notes (except the F), but no presence. Reliable performances come from Ezio Flagello as Giorgio and Renato Capecchi as Riccardo, but the best reason for hearing the set remains the faceless beauty of Sutherland's Elvira. As they said of the creator of the role, Giulia Grisi: 'What a soprano voice was here! – rich, sweet – equal throughout its compass. . . Her shake was clear and rapid; her scales were certain. . . The clear penetrating beauty of her reduced tones was so unique, as to reconcile the ear to a certain shallowness of expression in her rendering of the words and the situation.' But as yet there are some odd inconsistencies (broken phrasing, missing notes) in Sutherland's coaching, which are matched by strange decisions regarding the text. Why, for instance, include the rare, unprinted cabaletta for Elvira at the end of the opera, but excise most of the first-act overture? The impression remains of an unformed, often vacuous, performance.

By and large the ghost of that set is exorcised with the re-recording of 1975. Above all, this is the fullest version to date: all the printed score is included, together with the final, joyful movement for Elvira (again) and the central *andante* of the duet she has with Arturo earlier in the act. This newly expansive opera is handled with far greater maturity by Bonynge, and Sutherland too seems to have recovered some of the spontaneity found in her 'Art of the Prima Donna' excerpts (SXL 2256). But the performer who steps into the spotlight now is the Arturo, Luciano Pavarotti. An earlier excerpt of 'A te, o cara' (SXL 6658) had already introduced his robust cavalier, brimming over with golden tone and impulsive spirit. He has the D flats, sung 'del petto' (from the chest), which would have surprised Bellini, and even makes a shot at the high F. His is best described as an arresting performance, more than well endowed with vocal muscle. Piero Cappuccilli offers a sturdy Riccardo, and Nicolai Ghiaurov a great-hearted Giorgio, who sings his aria 'Cinta di fiori' with exemplary finesse. The extravagance of casting from depth has proved a worthwhile investment. As a pendant to these two sets by Bonynge, a live recording from Italy in 1966 gives us Sutherland at her most effective, complete in her technical command and free from any self-conscious awareness of the microphone. Alfredo Kraus is a tensely concentrated Arturo and Nicola Ghiuselev an awkward Giorgio. Rolando Panerai as Riccardo loses most of his role in this abridged version of an already heavily cut performance.

With the American ABC version of 1973, we meet a conductor ready to command his forces. Julius Rudel leads a performance of martial discipline, the horns and trumpets of the Puritan army's reveillée calling us to an opera audibly set in times of civil strife. Whether at speeds faster or slower than usual, the direction is always just and demands from its actors a life-or-death involvement. The text offers the complete Ricordi vocal score enlarged only by Elvira's concluding song of joy, a necessary addition if the final key of D major is to establish its jubilant conclusion. (Extraordinary to recall that Serafin actually cuts material here.) So resolutely does Rudel dig at the emotional roots of the drama that one may not at first miss any vocal beauty. Beverly Sills is the most intense Elvira since Callas, but her strained tone and uneasy vibrato all too easily suggest a woman *in extremis*. As her lover Arturo, Nicolai Gedda has some of Rubini's renowned elegance, but none of his honey. Louis Quilico is an adequate Riccardo and Paul Plishka a strong, if prosaic, Giorgio. Solo scenes and arias are the least satisfactory, but in concerted passages (such as the first-act finale) the confrontations are between characters with drama coursing through their veins. Largely thanks to Rudel, the set has added up to more than the sum of its parts.

If that performance is judged too fraught with tension, the listener may well find his ideal in the 1980 HMV set conducted by Riccardo Muti. With the exception of a brief orchestral introduction to the baritone's cabaletta found also in Rudel and both versions by Bonynge, Muti uses the text of the Ricordi vocal score. Singers and orchestra alike are held to its every detail: cadenzas are exactly as written, all top notes and decorations are eschewed (even in second verses of cabalettas) and, at worst, the composer's smallest directions are observed with pedantic obviousness. Yet, dogma apart, Muti's direction offers many rewards. With some passages among the nimblest on record there is no lack of excitement, but the special moments of the set are those with a rare, almost serene sensitivity. This performance has more than is usual of lyric grace and draws its singers on towards the most intimate cooperation with conductor and orchestra. One such example is 'Qui la voce' sung with a radiance and almost unspeakable poignancy that make Montserrat Caballé the most sublime Elvira of recent years, falling from grace only in the most awkward sections of passage work. Her Royalist lover is Alfredo Kraus, not always ingratiating in tone but technically secure and now aiming to phrase with real sensitivity. Matteo Manuguerra as a dark, dangerous Riccardo and Agostino Ferrin as a lacklustre Giorgio head a mostly strong supporting cast to make up a set whose insight reveals much of the musical richness of the opera.

In excerpts from the opera, tenors have been understandably cautious. They rarely venture beyond the solo verses of their entrance aria, 'A te, o cara'. Rubini's singing of this number was said to be among the wonders of those early performances, a display of 'every resource of consummate vocal art and emotion, which converted the most incredulous'. Recorded tenors are unlikely to win over many unbelievers. Even when the piece is transposed down (to avoid the C sharp at the beginning of the second verse), it sits high in the voice and tends to provoke singing whose aim is to get the notes, no matter how. Both Aristodemo Giorgini (2–52423; ORL 223) and Hipolito Lazaro (Col. 48783; Rococo 5279) were respected in the role and recorded the aria with sound technique, but their solid efforts would hardly enrapture the soprano, or the audience. Imaginative grace in this music is a rarity to be cherished. The best example is Alessandro Bonci's famous version (Fono. 39084; CO 343): the piece may be transposed, but in any key Bonci phrases like a vocal wizard and conjures a magical C sharp (or whatever) out of thin air. Fernando de Lucia has a similar poetry. Yet his records of the aria and the third-act duet 'Vieni fra queste braccia' with Angela de Angelis (Phonotype M1764), also transposed, show in addition the strength which made him a sought-after artist in verismo roles. Some unexpected breaths apart, these are remarkable performances. The way he can play with a note, extending it or shaping it for expressive effect, suggests a genuine creative force and recalls an earlier age of vocal liberation.

In this he is not entirely alone. Robert D'Alessio (D 12259; Rococo 5317) treats the ornaments of the aria like extemporization and Francesco Marconi in the third-act duet with Maria Galvany (VB 4; Rococo R 22) hardly takes two phrases at the same tempo. Of later exponents, only Giacomo Lauri-Volpi exhibits the same kind of insight. An early recording of 'A te, o cara' (Parlo. E11939; ORX 104) is relatively plain, but his well-known 1928 electrical version (DB 1438) goes far towards realizing the full potential of this simple writing. Five years earlier, Miguel Fleta's recording (DA 445; LV 96) is more ordinary, but not unaffecting. From this period tenors have increasing difficulty in controlling an even, unbroken line. They seem to regard expression as meaning various degrees of force and duly cap their efforts with every decibel at their disposal. Aureliano Pertile (DA 1183; LV 279) is clumsy, despite transposing down to C. Eugene Conley (LM 4534) is clearly taxed. Gianni Raimondi (AL 3442) sings the notes loudly, and Franco Corelli (ASD 529) louder still. The extent of present exasperation can be heard in the case of Benvenuto Finelli (GV 6). Armed with an Italian pseudonym, this English tenor manages the top notes with a specially trained head voice, but is unseated by the simplest demands of Bellinian *cantilena*. 'A te, o cara' is best. In the other items his intonation is unreliable.

Some interesting recordings exist of the baritone's aria. Most complex is the 1911 record by Mattia Battistini (DB 195; CO 327), the only version under discussion to include both 'Ah per sempre' and the second section 'Bel sogno beato'. Like Patti, Battistini treats the music with unusual freedom. Nothing is merely proper or stuffy here. This is living music, full of spontaneous and kaleidoscopic detail. Nor is a sure technical foundation overlooked. In 'Bel sogno' the smooth, floating vocal line is incomparable, an object lesson in the use of *portamento*. The other essential performance comes from Giuseppe de Luca (DB 220; LV 173), made in 1922 and already less flamboyant in manner. Secure in tone and phrasing, more strictly in tempo, his singing is the very best of the plainer style, as favoured by Galli-Curci and others in this period. Both singers have their admirers. Umberto Urbano (ES 387; LV 278) tries to emulate Battistini and Paolo Silveri (LX 1509) does the same for de Luca, but neither is quite a match for his predecessor. In general, singers after the war are less adept at giving Bellini's vocal line an even flow of motion. They tend to bump or aspirate along individual notes. Carlo Tagliabue (DB 11303; LV 270) has lost just this sense of forward movement. And Giuseppe Taddei (PR 9832), though supported by no less than Serafin, is still more choppy and heavily aspirated. One of the best is Gabriel Bacquier (Mondiophonie MSA 71 A), outstanding for his lean tone and flexible moulding of phrases. Sherrill Milnes (SXL 6609) does, at least, try to phrase with feeling. But after the voices listed above, he sounds not so much gentle as ill-focused in tone.

Among the basses, Andres de Segurola (052204; SJG 130) gives a straight-forward solo version of 'Sorgea la notte', part of the first-act duet with Elvira. Ezio Pinza (DB 828; GEMM 162/3), recorded in 1924, offers unlachrymose singing of the lovely aria 'Cinta di fiori'. Oreste Luppi (Fono. 92530; T 312) is less distinguished in the same piece, clean and outgoing in manner. An early favourite was 'Suoni la tromba', the second-act military 'duet for two basses' (sic) which entranced the town at its first London performance. Competent accounts were made by Mario Ancona and Marcel Journet (054135; GV 562) and, with more swagger, by Journet and Pasquale Amato (DK 110; Cantilena 6201). Amato paired with Luppi (Fono. 92529; CO 346) is poor in intonation, while Titta Ruffo and de Segurola (VA 16; CO 322) seem not to have agreed in advance what cuts they will be using. Tancredi Pasero and Gino Vanelli (GQX 10248; LV 34) start generously at 'Il rival salvar tu dei'. Robert Radford and Peter Dawson (D 967) offer a slower, bluff and hearty version in English.

It is entirely thanks to the exuberant Maria Malibran that sopranos have two solo scenes to record. Bellini wrote 'Son vergin vezzosa' specifically for her and also transposed 'Ah, rendetemi la speme' down a minor third. (Malibran, like Pasta, was described as a mezzo-soprano.) He wrote that he regretted she would not be able to end the first act, but added that during the final chorus she could 'fill the stage with her insane, emotional cries – she can be admirable at this kind of expression, which is new to the stage'. Sadly, no records exist of a singer trying anything so outrageous. In the first decade of this century Olympia Boronat is more tender than extravagant. Her 1904 piano-accompanied recording of 'Qui la voce' (VA 11; H111) contains broken phrasing and, to our ears, some very ungainly lunges. But four years later with orchestra (053282; HMB 20) she finds a more refined, personal manner, far from the sort of impassioned response that could be expected later in the century. Regina Pacini (Fono. 39238; Club 99. 84) has a similar style, though the preparatory sounding of notes is more pronounced. A shallow frailty comes from Lucienne Tragin (LF 66) singing the whole scene in French; and, with deeper affection, from Selma Kurz (053277–8; GV 89). Though she avoids the most troublesome scales in the cabaletta (as did so many at this time), Kurz offers lovely sotto voce coloratura tinged with the most delicate side of madness, just as Bellini's numerous markings in the score seem to suggest.

Most of the sopranos may have read his instructions, but not all act on them. Luisa Tetrazzini (2–053072; GEMM 220–27) recorded only the cabaletta and rushes past directions and *fioriture* alike with energetic abandon. With unrelenting severity Marcella Sembrich (2–053160; Rococo 23), singing the whole scene, purges the piece of sentiment and even *portamento*, but her iron tone and constructive phrasing hold the mark of a positive musician. Others see the music as a pin from which to hang their coloratura baubles. As far as the distant recording allows us to hear, Maria Barrientos (Fono. 39010) sings a playful, light-hearted 'Son vergin vezzosa'. And after an admirable 1914 recording of 'Qui la voce' (DA 248), Frieda Hempel goes on to a performance of the cabaletta (DB 296) which is as empty of sense as it is full of notes. Consuela Escobar de Castro (82177), recorded in 1919, decorates the second verse of 'Vien diletto' with many *staccati*. The most satisfying artist in this period is, again, Amelita Galli-Curci. Her 1917 recording of the scena (Vic 74558; GV 22) has all the sweetness and smooth emission of tone for which she is renowned, together with a technician's grasp of rhythmic import. The scrupulous phrasing of semiquavers in the opening theme of 'Son vergin vezzosa' is a sparkling bonus (DB 641; GV 584). It has been said that singers' accuracy had deteriorated in this music by the 1920s. We would, however, often be glad of their standards after the war.

Recent decades hold not a few curiosities. What are we to say of Lily Pons's 1949 recording of 'Son vergin vezzosa' (LX 1514; Odyssey 32 16 0270), starting off all aspiration and muddied coloratura only to change key in mid course so that she can take the most tricky section in D flat? Or of Mado Robin in the same piece (LW 5238), aspirated again and strikingly uninteresting until she suddenly lets off an A in alt. during the last few bars? One might hardly credit such performances. But here they are, preserved in wax like some museum of vocal horrors for future generations. Other singers are at a higher level, but there are few who can be recommended for serious study. These recent versions do, at least, usually offer both 'Qui la voce' and 'Vien diletto'. Virginia Zeani (LXT 5317) and Maria Chiara (SXL 6548) are two sopranos who have forfeited total control over their sizable voices in slow *cantilena*. Lina Pagliughi (Parlo. E 11335) and Teresa Stich-Randall (WST 17130) lack the precision of coloratura. Among the best is Margherita Carosio (DB 6858) who offers only the aria, but is at once masterly and beguiling. Both Mirella Freni (ASD 622) and Renata Scotto (ASD 4022), sharper in tone, have the measure of the whole scene, and Anna Moffo (SREG 2064) has in her voice the most aching sadness of any in the last few years. They all sing in the current style: slower tempi, more intrusive words, and an even emission of sound less of a priority. This is certainly music which sorts out the true artist from the amateur. In his refined nineteenth-century prose Henry Chorley once remarked:

> That the singer of an opera-tale ought to predominate in the opera . . .
> is in fact no more to be disputed than the platitude that a ball is not a

walking-party, or that a chamber quartet of stringed instruments is not a sonnet by Wordsworth.

In *La Sonnambula* or *I Puritani* the singer is still the star, even now.

LA SONNAMBULA

A Amina; *E* Elvino; *R* Rodolfo; *L* Lisa

1952 Pagliughi *A*; Tagliavini *E*; Siepi *R*; Ruggeri *L*/Italian Radio Chorus and Orch., Turin/Capuana
Cetra © LPS3240
Everest © 435 (3)

1955 (live performance – Teatro alla Scala, Milan) Callas *A*; Valletti *E*; Modesti *R*; Ratti *L* / La Scala Chorus and Orch. / Bernstein
Cetra ⓜ LO32

1957 (live performance – Cologne Opera House) Callas *A*; Monti *E*; Zaccaria *R*; Angioletti *L* / La Scala Chorus and Orch. / Votto
Foyer ⓜ FO1005

1957 Callas *A*; Monti *E*; Zaccaria *R*; Ratti *L* / La Scala Chorus and Orch. / Votto
EMI © SLS5134 ④ TC-SLS5134
Seraphim ⓜ IB6018 ④ 4X2G6018

1961 (live performance – Teatro La Fenice, Venice) Scotto *A*; Kraus *E*; Vinco *R*; Zotti *L* / La Fenice Chorus and Orch./Santi
HRE ⓜ HRE337

1962 Sutherland *A*; Monti *E*; Corena *R*; Stahlman *L* / Florence Festival Chorus and Orch. / Bonynge
Decca SET239
London OSA1365

1980 Sutherland *A*; Pavarotti *E*; Ghiaurov *R*; Buchanan *L* / London Opera Chorus, National PO/Bonynge
Decca D230D3 ④ K230K33
London LDR73004

I PURITANI

E Elvira; *A* Arturo; *R* Riccardo; *G* Giorgio

1952 (live performance – Palacio de Bellas Artes, Mexico City) Callas *E*; Di Stefano *A*; Campolonghi *R*; Ruffino *G*/Bellas Artes Chorus and Orch. / Picco
Cetra ⓜ LO52 (3)

1953 Callas *E*; Di Stefano *A*; Panerai *R*; Rossi-Lemeni *G*/La Scala Chorus and Orch./Serafin
EMI © SLS5140 ④ TC-SLS5140
Angel ⓜ 3502CL

1963 Sutherland *E*; Duval *A*; Capecchi *R*; Flagello *G* / Florence Festival Chorus and Orch./Bonynge
Decca SET259
London OSA1373

1973 Sills *E*; Gedda *A*; Quilico *R*; Plishka *G* / Ambrosian Opera Chorus, London PO/Rudel
ABC ATS20016
Ariola-Eurodisc XG27988R

1975 Sutherland *E*; Pavarotti *A*; Cappuccilli *R*; Ghiaurov *G*/Royal Opera House Chorus, LSO/ Bonynge
Decca SET587 ④ K25K32
London OSA13111 ④ OSA5–13111

1979 Caballé *E*; Kraus *A*; Manuguerra *R*; Ferrin *G*/Ambrosian Opera Chorus, Philharmonia/Muti
EMI SLS5201 ④ TC-SLS 5201
Angel SCLX3881

Luisa Miller

HAROLD ROSENTHAL

Luisa Miller was Verdi's fifteenth opera (fourteenth if you count *Jérusalem* and *I Lombardi* as one and the same): it was also the third of the four operas based on plays by Schiller – *Giovanna d'Arco, I Masnadieri* and *Don Carlos* are the others. Verdi's librettist for this opera was Salvatore Cammarano whose first libretto was for *Alzira*, produced at the San Carlo, Naples in 1845; he had also provided the text for *La battaglia di Legnano*, produced in Rome in January 1849, the same year which was to see the première of *Luisa Miller* in Naples.

In a letter from Paris to his librettist dated 24 September 1848 Verdi asks Cammarano to bear in mind that he needed a short drama 'very interesting, very lively, and very passionate, so that I can set it to music more easily'. There then followed some correspondence about an opera to be called *The Siege of Florence*, a project soon forbidden by the Naples censor. So Cammarano, on 14 April 1848, wrote to Verdi saying: 'I can do no better than return to your alternative proposition, Schiller's *Love and Intrigue*; and while waiting for your answer, I shall draw up a synopsis to save time.' During May there followed a typical Verdi correspondence between composer and librettist, and as Andrew Porter pointed out in an essay in *Opera Annual No. 3* (1956): 'If we compare Cammarano's original schedule with the opera in its final form, we find that he adopted all of Verdi's proposals.'

From the musical point of view *Luisa Miller* is quite different from Verdi's previous works: it is his first really 'intimate' opera, and clearly anticipates *La traviata*, especially in the way Verdi arouses our sympathies for the heroine. It has been until recently both an underrated and a neglected work.

The opera's première was at the San Carlo, Naples, on 8 December 1849; Marietta Gazzaniga sang the title role, Achille de Bassini that of Miller, Settimio Malvezzi was Rodolfo, Teresa Salandri Federica, Marco Arati Wurm, and Antonio Selva Count Walter. Press reviews of the actual event are missing, but the work was apparently a success and there were the usual productions at the other leading Italian houses during the next few seasons. Trieste staged it for five seasons during the 1850s.

The first London production was at Sadler's Wells Theatre on 3 June 1858, when it was sung in an English translation by Charles Jefferys; the part of

Miller was sung by one Edmund Rosenthal – no relation to the present writer as far as I can ascertain! Five days later the work was staged at Her Majesty's Theatre with a cast that included Piccolomini, Alboni, Giuglini, Beneventano, Vialetti, and Castelli. The Rev. J. E. Cox, in his 'Musical Recollections of the Last Half Century' commented, 'Mdme Alboni made nothing of the small part of the Duchess Federica, although she evidently tried to do so by substituting a cavatina for the original duet of the opera.' This, according to Julian Budden, was Leonora's aria from *Oberto*; at the same performance, again according to Budden, Giuglini substituted Carlos's aria 'All'argilla maledetta' from *I Masnadieri* for 'L'ara o l'avel' and also omitted part of the Act 1 finale, which ended with the concertato!

The work's only Covent Garden production until 1978 was in 1874, when it was sung by a cast that included Patti, Nicolini, Graziani and Bagagiolo. Famous productions this century included those at the Metropolitan, New York in 1929 with Ponselle, Lauri-Volpi, De Luca, and Pasero, conducted by Serafin, and in 1968 with Caballé, Tucker, Milnes, Flagello and Tozzi; at the Florence Festival in 1937 with Caniglia, Lauri-Volpi, Basiola, and Pasero, under Gui, and again there in 1966 with Suliotis, Tei, MacNeil, and Cava, conducted by Sanzogno; and at the San Carlo, Naples, 1963, with Roberti, Cioni, Guelfi, and Ventriglia, conducted by Erede – this was the production that came to the Edinburgh Festival the same year but with Cappuccilli replacing Guelfi as Miller. Several of the singers mentioned in this paragraph have taken part in one or other of the complete performance on disc or have recorded extracts from the opera. However, except for the famous tenor aria 'Quando le sere al placido,' *Luisa Miller* was not an opera favoured by singers in the days of 78s, and indeed even in the LP era extracts on recital discs are few and far between.

The first complete performance was made from a German radio tape of a studio performance in 1943; perhaps 'complete' is not the correct word, for there are the traditional theatre cuts that have remained current in Italy and some of which were observed at the Metropolitan in 1968. It is a very German performance of Verdi, with only Maria Cebotari and Josef Herrmann as Luisa and her father making any real effect, though Cebotari's voice had, by that time, lost some of its freshness and had also become heavy because of her singing such roles as Turandot and Salome. Herrmann, always an effective actor on stage, approached Verdi via Wagner, while Hans Hopf treated him as a cross between Weber and Lortzing. The playing of the Dresden State Orchestra under Karl Elmendorff is dramatic but lacks poetry.

The Cetra recording is likewise based on a radio studio performance, dating from the Verdi year (1951) when Radio Italiana gave a complete Verdi cycle. Here too the customary Italian theatre cuts are observed; thus we are deprived of the second scene in Act 1 which includes the duet for Federica and Rodolfo, the latter's aria 'Deh! la parola', and the Duchess's invitation to Rodolfo to plunge his sword into her bosom, which caused so much amusement at Sadler's Wells in 1953. Lucy Kelston in the title role goes hell-for-leather at Verdi's music, which often suffers as a result; Lauri-Volpi, then in his late fifties, was still able to sound exciting, and his characteristic enunciation is much in evidence; but line and intonation suffer at times. Colombo is a musical Miller; Giacomo Vaghi an off-pitch Walter, Baronti an adequate Wurm. Mario Rossi conducts in routine style.

After several rehearings of the RCA recording, I find that my reactions to it are far warmer than they were when I first reviewed it. This applies especially to Anna Moffo's performance in the title role, which I originally thought too slight. Although I still feel that ideally a more dramatic voice is needed in the part, I now find her performance wholly convincing: enchanting in the early parts of the opera, moving in the drama's latter stages. Bergonzi is not quite at his best, but I still prefer him to any other Verdi tenor of the post-war period. It is true that when one begins to compare his performance of 'Quando le sere' with those by Schipa, Pertile or Anselmi, one has reservations; but then, how many members of an audience in an opera house consciously do that? That, in a way, is one of the drawbacks of being a critic.

Cornell MacNeil sings the part of Miller with a beautifully rounded tone, and Flagello is well cast as Wurm. On the other hand Giorgio Tozzi and Shirley Verrett both sound too light for their respective roles, and Fausto Cleva, in a Toscanini-like mood, though without that great conductor's genius, opts for fast tempi. He scrupulously observes the composer's markings (there are no cuts), but one is never carried away, except perhaps in the soprano-baritone duet in the last act; but then nothing can destroy Verdi's genius here.

The 1976 Decca recording under Peter Maag has a high-powered cast: Caballé, Pavarotti and Milnes in the leading roles. Although the sound is better than in the RCA, Maag a more committed conductor than Cleva, and Milnes a more involved Miller than MacNeil, I prefer, of these two, the RCA set. By comparison with Caballé, who incidentally and surprisingly baulks at most of the trills marked in the score and scrambles some other passages, Moffo is by far the more convincing and unaffected Luisa. In a word, Caballé is the prima donna, while Moffo is Luisa.

Pavarotti is a warm-voiced Rodolfo, but Bergonzi more the stylist. Bonaldo Giaiotti is a solid and unsubtle Count Walter who takes liberties with the composer's markings at the end of his Act 1 aria. Richard Van Allan, however, as Wurm, displays a nice line in villainy, and Anna Reynolds is an imperious-sounding Duchess, less obviously the *grande dame* than was Verrett.

The most recent complete recording was based on the 1979 series of performances at Covent Garden. The idea of basing a recording on an actual series of performances in the theatre is, in theory, ideal; but when a recording schedule has to be arranged to fit in with six live performances in the opera house, it is hardly surprising if the principal singers are not at their best. Still, there is a great deal to admire in the performances of Katia Ricciarelli,

Renato Bruson and Placido Domingo, and the Luisa-Miller and Luisa-Rodolfo duets and the final trio capture the magic of their performances in the theatre. Ricciarelli is ideally suited to the role of Luisa, singing with lyric or dramatic tones as the mood of the moment requires and displaying her exquisite soft high notes both for her and our delight. Bruson's Miller confirms, if confirmation were necessary, that he has developed into the finest Verdi baritone of the day; and Domingo gives a committed account of the role of Rodolfo, his singing of 'Quando le sere' equals the best that are discussed below. Verdi would have been pleased.

Gwynne Howell offers some beautiful singing as Count Walter, but the casting of Vladimiro Ganzarolli as Wurm can hardly be called a success; he did not sing it at Covent Garden – there it was Van Allan – but obviously because Van Allan had recorded the role for Decca it was impossible for him to do so again. Another miscalculation in the casting was the engagement of the Russian mezzo-soprano Elena Obraztsova to sing the role of the Duchess Federica. She gives a blowzy and unidiomatic account of the part which Elizabeth Connell had sung so successfully in the Covent Garden production.

Although the Covent Garden Orchestra's contribution to this recording is a major one, it would have been even finer under a conductor other than Lorin Maazel who seems to brutalize the score. He is inclined to over-emphasize the composer's band-master effects and play down the work's lyrical section. And just because this opera is a 'domestic' piece rather than 'grand opera', I would still opt for the RCA recording.

As I have already mentioned, except for the famous tenor aria, this is not an opera that has been favoured by singers, and so there are few excerpts to discuss. The overture, as several writers have pointed out, is unlike any previous Verdi overture. Based on one theme only and in one movement, it is probably, as Budden suggests, Verdi's 'most striking *musical* achievement in this field'; and he goes on to paraphrase Churchill: 'In no other of his overtures is so much musical thought concentrated in so few notes'. Of the several versions on disc, those by the New Philharmonia under Muti (ASD 3366) and the NBC Symphony Orchestra under Toscanini (ALP 1452) are the best – the former from the point of view of performance and recording, the latter because of its authenticity, remembering Toscanini's close connection with Verdi and his world.

There are four excerpts from Act 1 that have been recorded: Luisa's opening aria, 'Lo vidi e il primo palpito'; Miller's 'Sacra la scelta'; Count Walter's 'Il mio sangue'; and the duet between Federica and Rodolfo.

The Luisa aria is included in one of the several 'off-the-air' discs sung by Elena Suliotis; this I have not heard.

The great confrontation between Miller and Wurm, which includes Miller's aria 'Sacra la scelta' and its ensuing cabaletta 'Ah, fu giusto il mio sospetto', receives an impressive performance from Sherrill Milnes and Paul Hudson on Milnes's recital disc (ARL1 0851) with Santi and the NPO providing a somewhat *sotto-voce* accompaniment. The aria, accompanied on the piano, is also included in an odd recital disc by Theodor Uppman, on a label called Internos Records (INT 0001). Uppman, who was Covent Garden's first Billy Budd and a well-known Papageno, is hardly a Verdi dramatic baritone.

Count Walter's 'Il mio sangue' has been recorded by Tancredi Pasero (DB 5440; LV 261) and Luciano Neroni (Cetra BB 25254). Pasero's lovely, rich, round voice, Pinza-like in quality, was at its best in Verdi. He, like Giaiotti in the complete Decca recording, believes he knows better than the composer and takes several liberties at the end of the aria, including a top note Verdi never even hinted at. The Neroni disc I have not been able to hear.

The Federica-Rodolfo duet, 'Dall'aule raggianti', the one that is often omitted in stage performances, appears on another 'off-the-air' disc; as it is sung by Anna Maria Rota and Renato Cioni it obviously comes from either the Bologna, Naples or Edinburgh performances of 1963, all of which featured those singers.

From Act 2 there are two extracts: Luisa's recitative and aria 'Lo spemi invano . . . Tu puniscimi' and the famous tenor aria, 'Quando le sere'. Sutherland included the first in a two-disc recital entitled 'Command Performance' (SET 247–8); it was subsequently transferred to a 'Joan Sutherland Sings Verdi' disc (SXL 6190). For reasons best known to herself and Mr Bonynge, she takes unwarranted liberties with the cadenza, interpolating several unwritten top notes and ending way up in the stratosphere. Suliotis (SXL 6306) does not sing the recitative, but begins with the aria proper, 'Tu puniscimi, O Signore', and includes the exciting cabaletta 'A brani, a brani', with of course the pages for Wurm omitted. There is also a 'private' performance of the aria and cabaletta by Caballé.

And now to the tenor's, or rather the discography-compiler's, marathon. There are more than forty versions of 'Quando le sere', some with recitative some not; some with piano accompaniment, some with orchestra; and not a few in which the ending differs from the printed score. I think it would perhaps be best to list the singers in alphabetical order; those marked with an asterisk I have not heard.

Mikhail Alexandrovich* (Melodiya D2219)
Giuseppe Anselmi (Fono. 62159 – recit., 62166-aria; GV 64)
Giacomo Aragall (Acanta DC 29391)
Romeo Berti (Black & Silver Col. 10572)*
Carlo Bergonzi (2) (SDD 391; Philips 6599 924)
Alessandro Bonci (Fono. 39691–2; Col. D 8084; Edison cylinder)
Franco Bonisolli* (Acanta DC 21723)
Gabor Carelli (Qualiton LPX 1061)
José Carreras (Philips 9500 203)
(Caruso recorded the aria in 1910, Matrix no. C8725; it was never published)
Fernando de Lucia (3) (052239; RS 305 and Phonotype M1754 and C2529)
Mario del Monaco (SXL 6429)
Anton Dermota (Acanta DE 23120–1)
Giuseppe di Stefano (SLPM 138827)
Placido Domingo (SB 6795)
Aristodemo Giorgini (2–52422)
Fiorello Giraud (052070)
Ernst Kozub (Philips 837047GY)
Sergei Lemeshev (Melodiya D 029717/8)
Giacomo Lauri-Volpi (DB 5449; QBLP 5057)
Giuseppe Lugo (DB 5093)

Giovanni Martinelli (Celebrity CLT
   1001)
Wieslaw Ochman (DG 2536 002)
Giuseppe Oxilia (52356)*
Luciano Pavarotti (SXL 6377)
Jan Peerce (2) (RCA 26. 35015; Philips
   SGL 5853)
Aureliano Pertile (DB 1111; LV 245)
Gianni Poggi (Decca LX 3172)
Giancinto Prandelli (LX 1320)
Gianni Raimondi (Philips AL 3442)

Antonio Salvarezza (Cetra BB 21512)
Tito Schipa (DB 1372; GEMM 151)
Leopoldo Signoretti (Zono. 1170)*
Donald Smith (OAST 7584)
Cristy Solari (CQ 352)
Ludovic Spiess (Intercord 120582)
Ferrucio Tagliavini (Cetra BB 25230)
Richard Tucker (2) (Philips GBL 5585;
   CBS SBRG 72336)
Emilio Venturini (Black & Silver Col.
   10116)*

It is intriguing that so many of these tenors never sang the role of Rodolfo
on the stage, obviously because of the comparatively few performances that
the opera has received this century until the period after the Second World
War and others, like Schipa, would have been too light to sustain the role
on stage had they been asked to sing it. As for the performances themselves,
such fine artists as Pertile, Schipa, Peerce, and others pointedly ignore the
composer's markings and even the actual notes as printed at the end of the
aria in order to make an effect with interpolated top notes, sobs and the rest.
Lauri-Volpi's performance is even justified on the sleeve of the LP reissue,
which informs us that: 'This romance is sung in a unique way' [an understatement if ever there was one] by alternating gorgeously the gentle phrases,
such as "t'amo, amo te sol dicea" and the vigorous ones where we can hear
the harmonic wealth and the natural power of the sound track.'

This seemingly cavalier treatment of one of Verdi's loveliest arias – 'this
divine cantilena' as Boito called it – may perhaps be explained by Abbiati's
observations on it. According to him there exists a sketch of the aria in which
the Andante appears to have been jotted down straight away in its final form
though a tone higher, while the cabaletta was drafted in more than one
version. Perhaps some Verdi scholar, singer or conductor can throw some
more light on this for us? In any case, repeated hearings of the aria have
convinced me that the more one observes the markings in the Ricordi score
(I am referring to the 1966 Italian edition which was 'in the care' of Mario
Parenti), the more effective the aria sounds.

From the above list I would choose four as standing head and shoulders
– if that is the right phrase to use about a vocal performance – above all
others: Anselmi's classic performance; Schipa's elegiac one; Pertile's committed and passionate account; and of the present-day tenors, Wieslaw Ochman's beautifully sung, and musically meticulous performance – indeed not
even Anselmi manages that sudden transition from ff to pp on the final 'Ah!
mi tradia' as effectively as Ochman does.

To return to Anselmi I can do no better than quote Desmond Shawe-
Taylor's description of his performance which appeared in a 'Gallery of
Great Singers' article in *Opera* in March 1966: 'The *Luisa Miller*, generally
reckoned as Anselmi's masterpiece, is notable for the passionate indignation
of the long recitative, the honeyed opening of the aria, the subtle *rubato*

introduced into the second verse, and the finely managed concluding cadence'. There is also 'passionate indignation' in the treatment of the recitative in both the versions by Bergonzi and in that by di Stefano. Bergonzi, like Anselmi and Ochman, really begins the aria proper *appassionatissimo*, as directed in the score; Tagliavini in his honeyed, Schipa-like performance almost achieves that final *pp*, but his disc lacks the recitative. There is also a very sweet-toned performance from Giorgini; an exhibition of exquisite legato singing from Bonci, though the actual sound of his voice has never appealed to me; and I like even less de Lucia's, though I know he has many admirers.

Toscanini's two tenors, Pertile and Peerce, have much in common, though the latter, once away from the great conductor's surveillance in his second recording made in Vienna in 1965, shows that he was not above taking liberties with the music. Martinelli recorded his performance in 1958 when he was over seventy; he should never have sanctioned its release. Neither of the Tucker versions has much to commend it, though there is no denying the beauty of the voice; and the less said about del Monaco in this kind of music the better. If you do not mind hearing the piece sung in Russian, Lemeshev's performance is enjoyable without being subtle. There is little to commend the performances by Salvarezza, Prandelli or Poggi; even less those by Kozub, Carelli and Spiess. Lugo had lost some of the beauty of voice he had in the early 1930s when he came to record the aria in 1939; Solari's white, open tone is more suited to Rossini than Verdi; and the Australian Donald Smith is hardly audible through the mush of the presumably 'off-the-air' recording made in Tasmania!

The two Spanish tenors, Aragall and Carreras, both give respectable but not inspired performances, and Raimondi, a much underrated singer, is almost in the first league. Notable absentees, unless some unknown recordings of them in this aria exist, are Gigli and Corelli; and such German or German-singing tenors as Tauber, Rosvaenge, Piccaver, Wunderlich, etc. Nor could I trace a performance by a single French-speaking tenor.

Let me conclude (for there are no single extracts from Act 3, and that soprano-baritone duet surely cries out for recording on its own) by quoting in full what Boito wrote about that 'divine cantilena'. 'Ah if you knew the kind of echo and ecstasy that this divine *cantilena* awakes in the soul of an Italian, especially in the soul of one who has sung it from his earliest youth! If you only knew.'

LUISA MILLER

LM Luisa Miller; *R* Rodolfo; *M* Miller; *F* Federica; *CW* Count Walter; *W* Wurm

1944 (in German) Cebotari *LM*; Hopf *R*; Herrmann *M*; Rott *F*; Böhme *CW*; Hann *W*/Dresden State Opera Chorus, Saxon State Orch./ Elmendorff Preiser ⓜ LM11 Acanta ⓜ BB21805

1951 Kelston *LM*; Lauri-Volpi *R*;

Colombo *M*; Truccato Pace *F*;
Vaghi *CW*; Baronti *W*/Italian
Radio Chorus and Orch., Rome/
Rossi
Cetra ④ LPO2022 ④ MPO2022
Everest © S456 (3)

1965 Moffo *LM*; Bergonzi *R*; MacNeil
M; Verrett *F*; Tozzi *CW*; Flagello
W/RCA Italiana Chorus and
Orch./Cleva
RCA (UK) SER5713–5
(US) LSC6168

1975 Caballé *LM*; Pavarotti *R*; Milnes
M; Reynolds *F*; Giaiotti *CW*; Van
Allan *W*/London Opera Chorus,
National PO/Maag
Decca SET606 ④ K2L25
London OSA13114 ④ OSA5–
13114

1979 Ricciarelli *LM*; Domingo *R*;
Bruson *M*; Obraztsova *F*; Howell
CW; Ganzarolli *W*/Royal Opera
House Chorus and Orch./Maazel
DG 2709 096 ④ 3370 035

Les Huguenots

VIVIAN LIFF

After spending ten years in Italy learning his craft, Meyerbeer settled in Paris in 1824. It was here that he found his ideal collaborator in Eugène Scribe, a highly successful playwright of the day. Their first work for the Paris Opéra, *Robert le Diable*, was presented to the public in 1831 and proved the greatest success in its history, establishing Meyerbeer immediately as one of the most celebrated composers in Europe. Combining spectacle, novel instrumentation, striking dramatic effects, unbounded romanticism and memorable melodic inspiration, it arrived at precisely the right moment to meet the needs of an audience already captivated by such operas as *Masaniello, Zampa* and *Guillaume Tell*.

With his characteristic and obsessive fear of failure, Meyerbeer took his time over his next offering. Scribe chose as the basis for its libretto a story by Prosper Merimée *Chronicles of the Time of Charles IX* and five years after the sensational first night of *Robert le Diable* the Opéra again witnessed the success of another work from Meyerbeer's pen – *Les Huguenots*. Oddly enough, despite the brilliant cast and settings, the work initially proved only moderately successful compared with the furore which had greeted its predecessor. Subsequent performances confirmed its great superiority and it soon became one of the most performed operas in all the principal opera houses of the world. In the age of the prima donna it established itself as the perfect vehicle not just to display the talents of two or three great singers of the day, but also to provide stellar roles for no less than seven. The public got its money's worth in no uncertain fashion.

More than any other composer before him, Meyerbeer was meticulous in the notation of his scores. Every member of the cast, from chorus to orchestral player, was given precise instructions concerning phrasing, the use of *portamento*, dynamic levels and so forth, leaving little to chance or the personal idiosyncrasies of wilful opera stars. Thus the study of a Meyerbeer score, while not providing the complete answer to the performing style of his day, does allow us to form a far better idea of it than is possible from perusing the scores of his predecessors.

It is a sad fact that the slow but steady decline in Meyerbeer's once formidable reputation had already started by the final quarter of the last century. Many famous musicians including Wagner and Schumann were not slow in criticizing a composer whose meteoric and unabated success must have proved somewhat galling. As Michael Scott perceptively wrote in his brief monograph on the composer: 'The trouble with these attacks was not that they were not true but that they were not relevant. None of Meyerbeer's critics sympathized with his methods or appreciated his objectives. Even now we are still living in the wake of their prejudices. The German ideal, in the music of Wagner, has triumphed; taking its cue from Bayreuth, the opera house has ceased to be principally a place of entertainment and instead become a temple of enlightenment, with the composer as high priest where formerly the prima donna had been mistress of ceremonies. It is hardly surprising therefore, that Grand Opera, epitomized in the works of Meyerbeer and his librettist Scribe, has become a pejorative term; a catch-all cliché used to damn a brilliantly successful type of music drama which did not, as modern taste would have it, put depth of characterization or psychological consistency before sheer entertainment value. Its aim may not have been elevating but its achievements within its chosen terms of reference – which are the only ones by which any work of art should be judged – were considerable.' Although most of Meyerbeer's works were still in the repertories of the major opera companies up to the turn of the century, thereafter they were gradually dropped until by the 1920s it was only pre-Hitler Germany and Austria that staged them with any degree of regularity.

This decline is exactly mirrored in the recording history of his operas and it is therefore scarcely surprising that by far the largest group of recordings from *Les Huguenots* was made in the early years of the gramophone at the beginning of this century. This in itself has a value. It is true that the gramophone cannot be said to have preserved Meyerbeer's own performing style in the way that it has captured that of such composers as Richard Strauss, Stravinsky, Falla, Britten, Poulenc, Vaughan Williams etc. However it is probably fair to claim that it has preserved a Meyerbeer tradition almost in the same way as it has preserved that of Verdi. Problems of performing style are most acute when the operas of a composer are revived after being absent from the repertory for many years. In the case of the operas of Meyerbeer and Verdi it can at least be said that all the singers of the first quarter of this century were part of a continuous performing tradition. Although the stage works of Meyerbeer belong to an earlier generation than those of Verdi, it is nevertheless likely that in the most classically correct of the early recordings we can hear something that is close to the performing style of Meyerbeer's own time.

Inevitably it would seem that the passage of years results in a gradual corruption of the original performing style and thus the basis taken for criticism and evaluation of the performances which follow has been the score – and in particular the dynamic markings of the composer. The experience of listening to more than sixty versions of 'Plus blanche que la blanche ermine' and between thirty and forty of 'Nobles Seigneurs' and 'O beau pays' has convincingly demonstrated that when the composer's own markings are strictly observed (particularly the *piano* markings on top notes) the maximum dramatic effect is achieved, as well as a natural increase in delicacy. Moreover, although it may be currently fashionable to dismiss Meyerbeer's *fioriture* as merely meretricious or empty pyrotechnics, there is a noticeable increase in expressive feeling when a singer is able to encompass these effortlessly.

The possibility of reviewing every single recording made from *Les Huguenots* is remote. In the fourteen years that have elapsed since this task was attempted in association with Richard Bebb in *Opera* (and upon which this present survey is based) much new material has been traced so that it is to be hoped that there are now few major omissions from this discography. Understandably the greater portion of the recordings are on the old 78 rpm format, and it has thus seemed sensible to review these first, leaving the smaller group recorded since the advent of the long-playing disc to the end of this survey.

Raoul's entrance 'Sous le beau ciel' is the first aria in the opera. Of the eight versions heard (Enrico Caruso: Pathé 84006; HLM 7030; Leo Slezak: G&T 3–43202; GV 47; Marius Corpait; Od. 97348; GV 82: Agustarello Affre: Pathé 3509; (Club 99–59) Pierre Cornubert: Od. 56047; Ignacy Dygas: Syrena 837; Ottokar Mařak: GC 4–42074; Hermann Jadlowker: Od. 99926) the finest is undoubtedly the Jadlowker while those by Corpait, Dygas, Affre and Cornubert run it a close second. Jadlowker deals with every technical aspect of the air superbly, producing exemplary singing which immediately conveys the importance and breeding of the character entirely through the music. Corpait displays an attractive voice with a fast, controlled vibrato and sings with great finish. His recording is further enhanced by the singing of Dinh Gilly as Nevers. Affre sings with fine style, observes the score meticulously and sounds important – as indeed do Dygas and Cornubert in their equally commanding versions. In comparison Caruso's version, which dates from his very first recording session in 1900 or 1901, is both clumsy and unidiomatic (although there are moments when the young Caruso's magnificent voice carries all before it), while the Slezak and Mařak versions sound slightly coarse and lacking in poetry. However, the power of Mařak's high notes is most exciting.

One of the deservedly most frequently recorded excerpts from the opera is Raoul's 'Plus blanche que la blanche ermine' – in fact Slezak recorded this no less than eight times! The four so far heard (G&T 2–42501; G&T 3–42922: CO 309; Od. 5497; Col. D 536) are all typically virile performances, but as in so many of Slezak's operatic recordings there is little nuance – this Raoul is not quite the gentleman. Other versions that can be speedily dismissed are those by Nicolai Figner, the idol of Tchaikovsky (G&T 22594 and G&T 02200) both effortful and eccentric performances although forgivable since made perforce in his declining years; Léon Lafitte (Zono 2177; Rubini; RS 304) sings in an unremitting *forte* with no light or shade; Lev Klementieff

(Amour 022130; USSR D 014921/2) has a few rather fine touches but he is tonally unsteady; Carlo Albani (Pathé 4904; Club 99.113) sings with some sensitivity but sounds generally depressed. He also simplifies the cadenza in a most unstylish fashion; Florencio Constantino (Columbia A 5204) is beset with intonation problems, choppy phrasing and the lack of legato; Enzo Leliva (Fono. 39926; Muza XL 0109) is below form and singularly lacking in distinction; Jose Mojica (Edison 82347; Club 99.23) is pleasant but far too lightweight; Georges Thill (LFX 111; C 061–12154) starts well, but tires badly before the end of the aria; Paul Franz (HMV 032268) sings beautifully but stolidly; Helge Rosvaenge (Decca Poly. LY 6027 and Telef. SK 1272; Top Classic TC 9042) has great intensity but is unable to disguise the effort involved – of his two versions, the Decca Polydor, which is without the recitative, is much the better; César Vezzani (Disque W 1087; Rococo 5234) starts with attractive ardour but coarsens progressively until the cadenza is really painful; Antonio Paoli (DB 470; Club 99.1) also begins sensitively but later lacks charm and nuance; Hipolito Lazaro (Col. D 18008; GV 506) displays a ludicrously lachrymose style liberally sprinkled with intrusive 'h's; Louis Morrison (HMV AT 11; C 051–23276) brings unlovely tone and short phrasing but does manage a reasonably accurate cadenza. He also sounds over-parted although his repertoire included many dramatic roles; Werner Alberti (Od. 50271) sings with ugly constricted tone and is totally unstylish; Andreas Dippel (IRCC 136) like Alberti, seems to combine all the least attractive qualities of the German *Heldentenor* of his time and has a most unpleasant vocal quality; Ivan Gritchenko (Extrafon 24302) the leading tenor of the Odessa opera in the early years of this century, displays an attractive lyric voice, here over-parted; Basil Sevastianov (Syrena 10348), his contemporary, has an excellent and powerful voice producing clean, stylish singing but is not really in the top class; Mario Gilion (Fono. 92685; GV 96) offers unattractive constricted tone which severely restricts his interpretative possibilities – a drastically curtailed cadenza is also a debit; Costa Milona's version (Vox H 010218; Sunday Opera SYO 2) suffers this last fault also, although his attractive voice, which so resembles that of Caruso, makes much of the opening measures. Unfortunately he later becomes plaintive and loses momentum; Koloman von Pataky (Poly. 95375; LV 54) has to resort to much faking to guide his light lyric voice through the aria but at least produces attractive tone and clean singing in the Patzak mould, though his more famous contemporary is unlikely to have abridged the cadenza. Visually Johannes Sembach (Gramm. 3–42968; CO 404) must have been one of the most convincing Wagnerian heroes ever to have graced the lyric stage but his rendition is totally prosaic, lacking poetry , minus cadenza and surprises with a totally unexpected choral conclusion. In a class of his own is John O'Sullivan (Col. 12459; Club 99.6). He was James Joyce's favourite tenor (and also the Raoul of the notorious 1927 performance at Covent Garden) but he sings so appallingly that he would have shattered the reputation of a greater composer than Meyerbeer!

Recommendable versions include Giovanni Zenatello (Fono. 92779; CO 357) who gives a generally sensitive rendering marred only by one or two lachrymose moments and an abridged cadenza; Sirotini (Zono. 092000; OASI 615), thought by some to be a pseudonymous Gerson Sirota but here revealing a far lighter vocal timbre than heard on any of the famous cantor's other recordings, demonstrates a mastery of legato and the florid style even if this latter quality must be assessed from a slightly abridged cadenza; Andrei Labinsky (Amour GC 2–22775) cleverly disguises the fact that his voice is insufficiently heroic and sings with style even though he simplifies the final cadenza, offering an almost endless high note in compensation; Karl Jörn (G&T 2–42546 and G&T 3–42779) sings attractively in fine style and gives much pleasure despite a basically lyric tenor voice; André d'Arkor (Col. RFX 22; 1A 153–52641) is impressive with a fine sense of line but he ultimately lacks finesse; Rudolf Gerlach-Rusnak (HMV EG 2698; LV 71) has a most attractive voice and his singing is very much in the Wittrisch mould. This is a sensitive and enjoyable version lacking perhaps the ultimate distinction; Fritz Krauss (Od. 0–11058; LV 158) sings with great fervour and is remarkably sound throughout. Only the final note of a well-executed cadenza takes him to the limit of his capabilities, and it is not a pleasant sound; Jacques Urlus (Musica H 22008; GV 67) sings with great authority, but of all the European languages surely the most damaging, at least to foreign ears, must be the Dutch; Tino Pattiera (Od. 80808; RLS 743, LV61) again sounding curiously like Caruso, sings sensitively, but his highest notes are not without effort; Marius Corpait (Od. 97660) again sings attractively and gives a stylish performance which is only marred by a simplified cadenza. For a less than immaculate attempt at this same cadenza Ivan Erschov (G&T 022011; RLS 7706) must be excluded from the very finest renderings; Agustarello Affre (Zono. 2026, G&T 2–32685, Od. 36413; Club 99.90 and Pathé 3496) also forfeits inclusion in this category for, although his versions have much to recommend them, there is a significant lack of light and shade in most of them. The Odeon perhaps catches him at his finest – an impressive and important sounding Raoul; Pierre Cornubert (Fono 39275; IRCC L7023) reveals a ringing voice with tremendous top notes, but though he observes most of the dynamic markings this version is not quite in the top class; Serge Lemeshev (USSR 21311; GV 36) produces some fine touches but his basically appealing voice has become unsteady in its middle range. Interpretatively it is in the Labinsky manner but he does attempt a full cadenza; Giacomo Lauri-Volpi (HMV AGSB 57; OASI 549, Discophilia DIS 258) gives one of his finest performances on record. It must remain a mystery as to why this recording was not issued at the same time as his other excellent discs of the early thirties. It is a fine, heroic performance acutely sensitive to all the dynamic markings; had he not drastically curtailed the cadenza it would have qualified for the highest class. It has to be admitted that the two Caruso versions are oddly disappointing. The first and more admired attempt made in 1905 (G&T 052088; ORL 303) finds him in really luscious voice, but it is an unidiomatic essay, not because it is sung in Italian, but because he sounds both lachrymose and depressed. The 1909 recording (HMV 2–052008; RL 13373) is in better style but unfortunately the tenor is in much poorer voice. Neither version, however, can be lightly dismissed – both have the stamp of Caruso's immense authority upon them.

Three tenors are in a category apart. Fernando de Lucia (Phonotype M 1812), even though at the very end of his career when he made this recording, displays a complete mastery of the style – perhaps better than any other tenor he observes Meyerbeer's direction to open the aria *con delicatezza* and the cadenza holds no terrors for this master of the florid style. His virtues are emulated by Jadlowker in his two recordings (Gramm. 032295; CO388 in French; and Od. JXX 81007 in German). Some may find the actual vocal timbre of de Lucia and Jadlowker displeasing but they undoubtedly possessed techniques that place them among the very greatest singing artists. Their attention to dynamic markings is scrupulous, their *piano* top notes are ravishing and the general elegance of their versions is most striking. Additionally Jadlowker concludes with a cadenza of great brilliance containing a long trill on a high G sharp from which he rises to the final A in one breath. It should be emphasized that it is primarily the elegance and finish of these performances which makes them outdistance so many rivals, not just the pyrotechnics. These superb versions are perhaps surpassed by those of Dmitri Smirnov (HMV 022338, 2681c and 2688c) all sung in Russian. Smirnov's voice is arguably a more attractive instrument and his versions include all the others' virtues (though without Jadlowker's interpolated trill) and even elaborate on the cadenza to thrilling effect. Of the three attempts, that on 2688c (GV 74) seems marginally the finest, being slightly more relaxed and poetic than the issued one while that on 2681c is marred slightly by faulty playing from the viola d'amore. All these versions seem little short of ideal. It should be mentioned in passing that none of the recordings of this aria includes the second written verse which contains a cadenza requiring incredible virtuosity. One may speculate whether this is indicative of a decline in the technical proficiency of tenors by the turn of the century or simply the inability of the old records to accommodate the extra music.

The basses take charge for the next two arias and it must be confessed that as a group they do much better than their tenor colleagues. The first aria 'Seigneur, rampart et seul soutien' is well sung by Ivar Andrésen (HMV EH 227 and Col. LX 13; LV 45) but he does not sound involved. This same criticism can be levelled at Armand Narçon (Col. RFX 7; Club 99.115) whose soft-grained voice encounters problems with the lowest tones. Adam Didur (Fono. 92003; CO 360) and Paul Aumonier (Pathé P 0302; Club 99.107) and Paul Knüpfer (Gramm. 4–42567; CO 304) display their magnificent voices to fine effect and are excellent by any standards. Wilhelm Hesch (G&T 3–42397 and Od. 38019) is similarly imposing, but the G&T version is to be preferred for the Odeon reveals a quite uncharacteristic sense of strain on his lowest notes. Lev Sibiriakov (RAOG 8291), the Italian-trained Russian bass, has no trouble at all in the lower register but his bland version is short-phrased and lacking in momentum as is that by Walter Soomer (Vox 03038; CO 400) though marginally less bland. Finer versions are provided by Andreas de Segurola (G&T 52634 and PD 2–32634) in Italian and Alexander Kipnis (Homocord B8276; Club 99.55) in German, in which both singers obey the dynamic markings perfectly so that the second strophe is sung with an interior, hushed quality which is most moving and conveys the religious quality of the music. However it is the Russians again who have the last word and Vladimir Kastorsky (G&T 3–22860) and Kapitan Zaporozhetz (Syrena 10021) provide versions which are well nigh perfect. Kastorsky's opening is absolutely electrifying and his singing throughout is exemplary while the Zaporozhetz, possibly the finest version on record, reveals an enormous voice of stunning quality. He sings with varied nuance and has the impressive ability to colour his voice as required by the music. The lowest notes are taken with staggering ease. One curious feature of all these versions is that none of the basses attempt the marked trills. This is strange when it is known that the technique of several of them, Hesch and Zaporozhetz for instance, included this vocal grace.

Versions of Marcel's second aria 'Piff, paff, pouff' that can be speedily passed over include those by Luciano Neroni (Parlo. R 30026), which is dull and unsteady singing; Armand Narçon (Col. RFX 7; Club 99.115), which lacks attack; José Mardones (Col. A5192; GV 44) which is ruined by a very ugly final note; Virgilio Lazzari (a 'private' disc), which is quite eccentric and only sketchily conforms to the written notes; David Ney (Favorite 1–29503; Hungaroton LPX 11310) whose voice is of provincial quality (he turns the aria into something resembling a Hungarian folk song); Lev Sibiriakov (RAOG 8290) who sings only one verse and treats the score in cavalier fashion and Marius Chambon (Zonofono 2088; Rococo 5347) which has nothing to recommend it save rarity.

Acceptable renderings include those by Paul Payan (HMV P 529 and Od. 123657) of which the Odeon is marginally to be preferred, although both provide fine examples of his attractive and well-schooled voice; Léon Rothier (Col. A5876), which is also good, straightforward singing; Léon Rains (Od. 99527; IRCC L7023), which includes the written trills and is exemplary singing from a bass who lacks a really first-class voice; Marcel Journet (DB 307; Discophilia DIS 371), which is marvellously expressive but kept from the highest class by a slight loss of quality on the lowest notes and less than perfect runs; Vladimir Kastorsky (G&T 3–22826) also reveals some uneasiness on the low notes but his is nevertheless a fine interpetation of great authority and the trills, though sketchy, are attempted. Finally Knüpfer (Gramm. 4–42568; CO 304) provides reliable, firm-voiced singing in an interpretation which misses greatness by a hair's breadth and Ivar Andrésen (Nordisk Polyphon SX 42184; 1C 153 35350) also impresses with vigorous, venomous, large-scale singing.

Ten versions are particularly fine. Paul Aumonier (Pathé 0120 and Pathé

P 0302; Club 99.107) is both vigorous and agile, displaying a rich, black, velvet voice but of his two recordings, the earlier is much to be preferred. Paul Seebach (Edison cylinder 26123) also impresses by the sheer size and range of the voice which, like Aumonier's, responds easily to all the demands made upon it. Sibiriakov's second version (Syrena 12855; Club 99.504) is possibly still a little cavalier in style, but expressively it is magnificent. His perfect vocal control makes it unkind to fault him for certain rhythmical liberties. Adam Didur (Fono. 39489; CO 360) is also impressive with even tone throughout and all the awkward intervals and runs managed with consummate ease in an intense performance. Journet's Victor recording (V. 74156; RS 320) is without the faults of his HMV version and he gives a compelling and venomous account in which the low notes are firm and the runs exemplary. Hesch (Od. 38005; CO 300) astonishes by the sheer weight of solid bass tone produced yet, despite the size of the voice, vocalizes the aria with skill and precision. Dmitri Buchtoyarov (Zonophone X 2–62552), like Hesch, surprises with the voluminous majesty of his voice. He provides a vigorous and spirited rendition calculated to make the listener quail. As a frequent member of the Metropolitan's 'Seven Star' casts, Pol Plançon's records (Zono. X 2061 and G&T 2–2661; GV 76) are of special interest. His singing is superb in almost every respect, from the vocal agility in the florid sections to the ease of the low Es and Fs. Only a low emotional temperature (especially in the Zonophone version) vitiates against the perfection which may perhaps be claimed for the recording by Zaporozhetz (Syrena 10021; USSR D 02627), which is positively thrilling. His voice has a richness, weight and solidity rare even among Russian basses and it encompasses all the florid music in a virtuoso performance of real venom. Whereas some of the above singers attempt the written trills, Zaporozhetz is one of the few to accomplish them with any ease.

Urbain's first aria 'Nobles Seigneurs, salut' is something of a puzzle. Despite the really tremendous technical accomplishment of many of the versions, it must be confessed that only two approach the ideal. None of the ladies, whether singing in the soprano or contralto key, really brings off the aria with the lightness of touch and the smile in the voice that it needs – would that either Yvonne Printemps or Conchita Supervia had recorded it.

Disappointing versions are those by Frieda Hempel (unpublished HMV) which is curiously uncertain for her; Marion Beeley (Col. 694) sounds infantile and lacks the necessary technique; Armida Parsi-Pettinella (Fono. 39645; Club 99.106) is gusty with such inferior coloratura that she omits both the cadenza and trill; Xenia Belmas (Poly. 66715; LV 79) is rushed and unstylish; Hedwig Jungkurth (Decca Poly. LY 6027) displays an unattractive voice and poor technique; Hermine Bosetti (Od. XX 76348) obviously hit a bad day, most of her recorded output is far finer than this perfunctory offering; Jane Laval (Col. LFX 4) is bright in timbre but lacks finish; Lucette Korsoff (Disque W 224) provides a correctly sung and reasonably accurate rendering totally devoid of charm or brio; Claudine Armeliny (G&T 33634) offers more in the way of charm but, astonishingly for the period, is without a trill and her technical accomplishment is tame in the extreme; the great Selma Kurz (Zono. X 23014) reveals intonation problems, and in this version omits the entire central section and cadenza – doubtless due to the exigencies of the available recording time at this early date, but how it must have pained her to lose such a chance for display; Mabel Garrison (HMV AGSB 70; Club 99.48) is musicianly and quite stylish but lacks any memorable quality; Alice Williams (Zono. X 83166) offers an uncharacteristically poor effort from a leading soprano at the Nice Opera House; Eugenia Mantelli (Zono. 12590; Club 99.71), who sang Urbain in performances that included Nordica, Sembrich, Jean and Edouard de Reszke, Plançon and Maurel, is a particular disappointment. The voice is even-scaled and attractive, her technique is serviceable if not brilliant, but she phrases poorly and sounds totally uninvolved; Adelaide Andrejewa von Skilondz (Parlo. P. 1384) astonishes with the agility and fleetness of her scale passages but her conclusion is tame; Antoinette Laute-Brun (Apollon 2078) sings clumsily and without charm, a verdict which must also be registered against Lise Landouzy (Od. 56110); finally Berthe Kiurina (Zono. X 23321; LV91) produces her only really poor recorded performance – totally lacklustre, indifferent singing. Among the contralto versions, Margarete Matzenauer (Vic. 6471) is a good deal too rushed even though the technical excellence of the singing is remarkable; Louise Homer (DB 665) is matronly; Zara Dolukhanova (USSR D 3265; GV 9) opens the air with enormous authority, but aspirated runs and lack of tonal variety bring eventual disappointment; Carolina Lazzari (Edison 82567) is dull, while even the mighty Sigrid Onegin (DB 1290; LV 7) sounds staid – though her cadenza and trill in the central section are to be wondered at: this version, whatever its faults, should be in every collection.

Among the finest of the soprano versions is another by Kurz (HMV 043 Z32; CO 324), who offers graceful highly decorated singing – possibly over-decorated for some tastes. Her version includes a cadenza with two superb trills and a staggering *glissando* which is great even by her own standards (her third recording of the aria on Polydor 72847 is much inferior to the HMV); Katherine Arkandy (Poly. 65698), the successor to Maria Ivogün in Munich, has nearly all her predecessor's virtues including a voice of singularly attractive timbre. Her decorations are both accomplished and tasteful including a well-judged series of rising trills in the final cadenza; Aurélie Revy (G&T 43824) displays the voice of a typical soubrette but it could be that of a mischievous boy, so is not entirely inappropriate. She later surprises with a virtuoso cadenza and caps the air with a Kurz-type trill; Minnie Nast (GC 2–43285; CO 405), the original Sophie in *Der Rosenkavalier*, provides a sensitive, responsive account which she finishes with a fine flourish. The lovely, even quality of her voice is an added bonus. Much the same can be said of the version by Grete Forst (G&T 43362) who displays a first-rate florid technique and a particularly well-knit trill; Lotte Schöne (Vox 176A) offers a wonderfully judged central section in which the *rubato* is cunningly applied, but unfortunately the aria as a whole lacks brio, confirming the view that this exquisite singer is at her best in tragic roles; José Grayville (Col. 30114) has a bright voice, an even scale, considerable charm and sings with much accomplishment; Maria Ivogün (Poly. 85312; LV 69 and Od. LXX 76997; LV 68) contributes lovely singing of great finish and elegance – especially on the Odeon disc; Elise Elizza (G&T 043001) contributes a most satisfying attempt, the voice even and of warm quality, the tempi well judged and the whole aria crowned by an elaborate yet totally stylish cadenza; Adelaide Andrejewa von Skilondz (Gramm. 043233) improves markedly upon her Parlophon effort; Gabrielle Ritter-Ciampi (Pathé 0404; Club 99.9 and Pathé X7193) provides what is probably the most correctly sung of all the versions – the later, electrical recording, is marginally to be preferred; Emmy Bettendorf (Od. XXB 6772) surprises with fleet, alert singing from a normally lethargic singer – this is a most charming record with the smooth and attractive vocal quality also in its favour. Adele Kern (Poly. 66946; LV 57) and Fritzi Jokl (Parlo. E 10362; LV 138) come near to being ideal. Both combine technical excellence and a real sense of style with considerable charm and Jokl includes a most elaborate cadenza. Of all the recordings in the contralto key, the two most pleasing are those by Eleanora de Cisneros (Col. A. 5626) and Homer (Vic. 15–1011, Vic. 1519; Rococo 5258). The former is in the best style while Homer improves remarkably on her HMV version: although still slightly lacking in sparkle, she introduces delightfully imaginative *rubato* touches.

The Queen's aria which opens the second act is cast in the form of a slow first section 'O beau pays', a middle section with Urbain and female chorus and a cabaletta 'A ce mot tout s'anime'. None of the versions on 78s contain the complete music and several singers only recorded the first section. Among these there is, surprisingly, only one poor version, namely that by Maria Galvany (PD 053164) who sings without style and with a disturbing lack of repose. Better efforts include those by Antonia Nezhdanova (HMV 2–23317; CO 366), which is most artistic if a little white in tone; the great Lilli Lehmann (Od. 50394; CO 385), who provides finely graded, authoritative singing, but the timbre is, alas, rather sour; Hempel (HMV AGSB 59; CO 302) is stylish but not particularly accurate, with a characteristic white top D inserted in the cadenza; Hedwig Francillo-Kaufmann (Gramm. 2–43210; CO 356) exhibits a particularly fine trill, and she sings the air with great refinement lacking only the ultimate in distinction; Irene Abendroth (G&T 43249; Rococo 5297) demonstrates the suitability of a Lamperti-based technique for this music and includes stylish ornaments. Unfortunately the primitive recording does her a grave disservice, playing havoc with the pitching. A prevailing impression of flatting also mars the pleasure in a limpid rendering by Emilie Herzog (G&T 43863; CO 418) due, possibly, to the loss of natural overtones in the voice through the acoustic recording process. Claire Clairbert (Poly. 66920), the pre-war star of La Monnaie, supplies good clean singing in the slightly steely inter-war Gallic style, but her version is highly accomplished with a noteworthy trill; Alexandra Dobrovolskaya (Mus Trest 06005), on a rare electrical recording with piano accompaniment, fascinates in a performance of great character and charm. The voice has lost some of the freshness and beauty evident on her G&T recordings, but this remains a lovable version – as indeed is that by Giuseppina Huguet (G&T 053072; GV 68) whose poised, clean singing demonstrates all the virtues of the old Italian school.

Two of the finest versions are contrasted in style. For sheer classical musicianship allied to great tonal beauty, all three of the records made by Alice Verlet, the great star of the Paris Opéra, are recommended (Pathé 4861, Edison 82090 and HMV 33678; GV 18) though the HMV is marginally the finest. Kurz's version (G&T 43886; Rococo R37) is wayward in the extreme but such is the fascination and authority of the singer that one is charmed into submission, whilst the lazy ease of her coloratura suits the dreamy, reminiscent mood of the music to perfection.

Four versions manage to contain both aria and cabaletta on one side and three of these, alas, must be speedily dismissed. In Luisa Tetrazzini's case (HMV VB 41; CO 344) the attempt to cram the music, heavily cut of course, onto a single side results in a rushed tempo that totally destroys the atmosphere of the slow section. Although Eidé Norena (Od. 123636; LV 193) avoids this fault and manages a lovely opening, she ruins the cabaletta with strings of intrusive 'h's. Conversely Lucette Korsoff (Edison FS 889) redeems an opening beset by intonation problems with a fleet and dazzling finale. Only Gabrielle Ritter-Ciampi`(Pathé 0405) succeeds in offering a poised and suitably languid opening in conjunction with a sparkling cabaletta – albeit severely reduced in length. Double-sided versions include Marie Michailova (G&T 23468, PD 2–43070 the aria, Berliner 23093 the cabaletta) whose 'pre-dog' version of the aria (reissued on GV 26) is to be preferred to the piano-accompanied early version although both are excellent and display a lovely quality of voice. Her cabaletta is highly accomplished too if lacking true brilliance. Esperanza Clasenti (Fono. 39499/500) has a typically bright Spanish voice of attractive timbre but lacks a first-class trill; Giuseppina Finzi-Magrini (Fono. 39677/8) sounds a fine singer of the second rank; Yvonne Brothier (HMV W 1086), is, alas, quite out of voice. Lily Dupré (HMV 033158/9) is interesting for her inclusion of more of the score than any other; she sings well throughout and offers a particularly thrilling cabaletta – only the lack of a truly sensuous tone keeps this out of the highest grade; Deborah Pantofel-Nechetskaya (USSR 15792/3) has a white, very small voice strongly reminiscent of that of Miliza Korjus but her technique and musicianship are exemplary (she manages the *staccati* more accurately perhaps than anyone else) – ultimately, however charming, she lacks the authority required for this part.

There are three versions of outstanding merit. Hempel (Od. RO 524; CO 302) improves immeasurably on her HMV effort. Of all the sopranos she decorates most elaborately but always with fine taste and in the correct style.

Since all Meyerbeer's other requirements are met, it is difficult to imagine that he would have objected to decorations as elegant as these. This is poetic and beautifully contained singing. Olimpia Boronat (HMV S/P 1516c and PD 053187; Club 99.3) is wayward, even eccentric, but what character is conveyed – the whole performance has a command that only the truly great singers possess. Finest of all, perhaps, is Margarete Siems, the original Marschallin (Parlo. P 246; Rococo R20) whose version is easily the most elaborate but who sings with indolent grace and effortless bravura. When this is allied to a musicianly attention to dynamic markings, it has a largeness and grandeur of style that this music requires.

Before leaving this aria, mention must be made of a Mapleson cylinder (IRCC 5002; VRL 50365) taken at a performance of the opera on 11 March 1901 at the Metropolitan Opera House. Nellie Melba, the Marguérite de Valois on that occasion, can be heard singing with the greatest possible brilliance almost the entire cabaletta before the audience erupts into an enormous and well-deserved ovation. None of this famed soprano's commercial recordings approach the abandon and brio, transcending the primitive recording medium, here demonstrated.

The Page's second aria 'Non, non, non, vous n'avez jamais' was written for Marietta Alboni and has rarely been recorded. There is a four-square version by Dolukhanova (USSR 21859). The only other heard is by Parsi-Pettinella (Fono. 39646; Club 99.106) which is both expressive and accurate with a moderate measure of charm.

The fine duet for Raoul and the Queen has been recorded in both single-sided (invariably cut) and double-sided versions, but Leo Slezak (G&T 3–42375; CO 309) manages to fill a 10-inch side with Raoul's opening solo. The leisurely tempo he is able to adopt allows him to produce some of his finest singing in this role and demonstrates forcibly how careful one should be in judging singers only from these early recordings. When the tenor is joined by Elise Elizza (G&T 044024; Rococo 52) the necessary increase in tempo results in unlovely tone and little nuance, although it must be admitted that the soprano manages to provide singing of great beauty and elegance. The heavily cut version by Alexander Davidov and Marie Michailova (G&T 24395; GV 26), despite one or two delightful touches from Michailova, allows neither singer to show to advantage. Urlus and Cato Engelen-Sewing (Pathé 30235) sing well, though again the performance is rushed and not exactly helped by the Dutch translation. Affre and Landouzy (Od. 56161; GV 38) combine in an idiomatic and stylish rendering, the tenor, particularly, sounding both heroic and important. Two normally excellent singers – Andrejewa von Skilondz and Mařak (Gramm. 3–44098/9) are in indifferent voice and produce a thoroughly perfunctory version. However Siems paired with Desider Aranyi (G&T 044034; Rococo R41) sings superbly with scintillating brilliance while her partner provides sensitive support of a more heroic nature than expected. The voices blend particularly well in a virtuoso performance. The only version found in Italian is that by Giuseppina Huguet and José

Maristany, both Spaniards (G&T 54029). The tenor is adequate and of provincial calibre but the duet is cut so as to remove most of his contribution and one may thus enjoy the stylish, graceful, cultivated singing provided by his accomplished partner. It is perhaps fitting that the fullest version of the duet is also the finest – that by Jadlowker and Hempel (Od. 76902/3; CO 395). Apart from some whiteness of tone from Hempel, this version approaches the ideal for all the dynamic markings are scrupulously observed and the performance has the utmost delicacy and elegance.

Thirteen versions of the duet for Valentine and Marcel 'Derrière ce pilier' have been located. Three of them feature the fine bass Andreas de Segurola who sings with Isabel Grassot (G&T 54030/1), Maria Grisi (G&T 54331) and Cecilia David (PD 054184). He is wonderfully expressive in all three and it is to be regretted that Grisi, who easily steals the soprano laurels, has to be content with the most heavily cut version. It is the unsteady tone of the soprano which ruins the otherwise excellent version by Juste Nivette and Amelia Talexis (Od. 60644/651) for the bass, as always, is magnificent. Likewise it is a lack of authority on the soprano's part which lets down an otherwise more than adequately sung version by Leon Rains and Riza Eibenschüz (Gramm. 2–44436; CO 402). André Gresse and Maria Lafargue (Gramm. 034183/4; IRCC L7038) sing acceptably in the correct style but, although both possess fine voices, the final result is unmemorable. Like De Segurola, Hesch made early recordings of the duet with three different sopranos. Sophie Sedlmair (G&T 044028; Rococo 5377), Elsa Bland (G&T 044070; CO 317) and Frl. Schubert (Od. 38083). Amazingly it is the unknown Frl. Schubert who makes the greatest impression with firm, even-scaled, authoritative singing and a superb trill. Bland sings with finer style than Sedlmair whose uncharacteristically poor attack on certain notes reduces what is otherwise a commanding performance. Needless to say Hesch sings superbly on all three versions but sounds especially solid and impressive on the Odeon disc. Two little-known singers, M. Ticci and Alfredo Brondi (Od. 37759/60) sing with fine style and conform strictly to the score, even to the extent of a well-executed trill from the bass. Only the acidulous vocal quality of the soprano makes this version less than ideal. Perhaps this accolade might have gone to that heard in the Metropolitan Opera House in January 1903 when the voices of Johanna Gadski and Edouard de Reszke were caught on four Mapleson cylinders (re-recorded onto IRCC 168) in sections of the duet including the final *allegro moderato* unrecorded elsewhere. Despite the primitive recording, which must render it *hors de combat*, it is possible to appreciate the superlative singing offered by both artists.

It is left to the Germans, Paul Knüpfer and Barbara Kemp (Poly. 65268; LV 13) to provide the most complete as well as the finest version in acceptable sound. They sing with rich authority and complete command – all the dynamic markings are observed; it is a real joy to hear two singers blending such firmness of attack with so much finesse. Knüpfer also recorded this duet with Helene Offenberg (Gramm. 044159/60; CO 352) who has a soft-grained, pleasant enough voice. Although she sings well throughout, the concluding bars stretch her resources and she nowhere sounds really authoritative or important.

The exciting 'duel' septet which follows almost immediately receives a thrilling performance by the clarion-voiced tenor Léon Escalaïs, ably supported by a cast including Antonio Magini-Coletti, Ferruccio Corradetti and Oreste Luppi (Fono. 39370; Rococo 5278). In equally vigorous, though less idiomatic fashion, Slezak leads a starry team of Viennese singers including Richard Mayr, Arthur Preuss and Gerhard Stehmann (G&T 2–44427). That neither version can be accounted ideal is due solely to the limitations of the acoustical recording process in coping with concerted voices.

A single recording of Nevers's brief solo at the end of this scene was made by Mario Ancona on an Edison cylinder dating from 1906. Its neglect by baritones is hardly surprising since it is not one of Meyerbeer's happiest inspirations. Ancona displays his magnificent velvet-like voice to fine effect, but unfortunately his singing in this instance is singularly lacking in subtlety and he exhibits an alarming disregard for note values.

Act 4 opens with the famous concerted scene known principally for the melody of the rousing solo allotted to St Bris in the 'Conjuration' section, which lingered in the repertory of many 'Palm Court' orchestras throughout this country. In the following section, which really comprises the 'Bénédiction des Poignards', St Bris only sings a few phrases so that complete versions of the whole scene are relatively few. André Pernet (DB 5004; FJLP 5062), Pierre d'Assy (HMV 034032/032108; Discophilia DIS 376) and Anton Baumann (HMV EH 365; Top Classic H670) provide three-virtually complete renderings. Pernet's well-recorded version displays good, solid singing without much polish; d'Assy reveals a voice of fine quality and sings with exemplary style; Baumann is an adequate if dull German baritone whose recording is only noteworthy for the magnificent playing and singing of the Berlin State Opera Orchestra and Chorus under their conductor Leo Blech. Jean-François Delmas (Fono. 39027, Od. 56178 and 56181) sings a slightly abridged 'Conjuration' and a complete finale on three sides although he can scarcely be heard on the two final discs. The great merit of his performance is that he really sounds as though he hates the Huguenots, but he does ride rough-shod over the dynamic markings.

Versions of the 'Conjuration' alone are fairly numerous and most have something to commend them. Delmas (Zono. 2021 and Edison cylinder 2495) is again impressive but less well served by these earlier recordings – although the cylinder, in particular, clearly indicates the sheer size of the voice; Gaston Dulière (Edison cylinder 27105) exudes authority although his timbre is slightly coarse; René Fournets (Edison cylinder 17203; Rococo 5347) has a fine, dark voice but is clumsy; Alexander Haydter (Favorite 1–25097) is also vocally well endowed and sings with great accomplishment; Journet (DB 307; GV 503) spoils what is otherwise an excellent straightforward rendering by a poor final note; Sibiriakov's (PD 4–22021) Italian training shows to advantage but despite his magnificent voice the performance is short phrased and inexpansive; Maximilian Maksakov ('Monsieur Max') (G&T 22866) provides superb legato singing revealing a voice of superior quality with an attractive fast vibrato; Kastorsky (Amour 3–22564) possessor of one of the loveliest bass voices of his time also sings with a refined legato line and a wonderfully even scale; equally impressive in its way is the version by Friedrich Schorr (Poly. 65673; LV 241), a perfect synthesis of authority and grandeur; Aumonier (Zono. 2083 and G&T 32103) again shows off his fine voice and sings stylishly on both recordings although the G&T is far too rushed. This fault is avoided by Payan (Aerophone 920) on his impressive rendering, which leaves one marvelling yet again at the wealth of superb bass voices available in the early years of this century.

Two final excerpts from this scene deserve brief mention. On Amour 3–22872 Kastorsky sings the linking passage for St Bris 'Et vous qui repondez au Dieu' without chorus, making it sound remarkably fine even though he imparts an unexpectedly Russian flavour to the music – it could have come from *Boris Godunov*! The voluminous voice of Nazzareno de Angelis (Fono. 74127/8) can be heard in a few interjections to the 'Benediction' on a disc which is mostly choral.

The musical climax to the opera, without question, is the great duet for Raoul and Valentine 'O ciel! Ou courez vous?' which even Wagner admired. Easily the fullest version on discs is that by Laute-Brun and Affre (Od. 97512/3/4; ORX 117). Neither of them has a particularly beautiful voice, yet they sing with great ease and considerable artistry – altogether they have the right style. Affre also recorded the 'Tu l'as dit' section with Mathilde Comés (Pathé P. 2501) and Marcelle Demougeot (G&T 34036; GV 38) and these are also highly recommendable versions. Destinn and Jörn recorded the opening section twice (PD 2–44365 and 044079; GV 581) when both singers were at their very best – thrilling top notes from the soprano and sensitive expression from the tenor. The completion (PD 044080; GV 581) alas, is not so happy with some clumsy singing from the soprano and unfortunate intonation lapses from the tenor. Gino Martinez-Patti and Ida Giacomelli (G&T 054075) perform with insensitivity. Other poor versions include those by Cecilia David and Augusto Scampini (G&T 054179; Rococo 5263); Maria Llacer and John O'Sullivan (Col. D 4968; Club 99.6) and Albertini and José Palet (DB 713). Indeed O'Sullivan and Palet are grotesque. Almost in this class is the version by Geneviève Moizan and Henri Legay (HMV HMS 93; HLP 23) in which both singers are comically over-parted. Natalya Yuzhina and David Yuzhin (G&T 2–24024; GV 63) provide the only version in Russian. The tenor is not exactly the most refined artist and additionally lacks the range required but his wife's exciting vocal quality (Lord Harewood once aptly described her as 'a Russian Frida Leider') makes their disc of more than passing interest. Maria Labia and Valentine Jaume (Edison 316B; GV 92) are chiefly remarkable for the splendour of their upper notes. Jaume sings with a fine legato style but his actual vocal quality is not entirely pleasing while the middle register of Labia's voice also falls unhappily upon the ears. Nevertheless this must be accounted a winning version in many ways.

The 'Tu l'as dit' section (Phonotype M1816; GV 502) could justly be described as a *tour de force* by de Lucia. He is accompanied by the white-voiced Angela de Angelis. Although it must be admitted that he indulges in considerable liberties with tempo, it is difficult to disapprove of a performance combining such irresistible *élan* and effortless technique. Slezak and Bland (G&T 2–44050; CO 309) combine to thrilling effect in this same section, which contains some of the finest singing committed to disc by these occasionally variable artists. They complete the duet in equally brilliant style on G&T 2–44033. This concluding section is exactly duplicated on G&T 044009 where Slezak is partnered by Sedlmair. He again sings with sincerity and vigour while Sedlmair, with her first phrase, reveals the command and stature of a great singer.

This leaves the celebrated version of the duet by Margarete Teschemacher and Marcel Wittrisch (HMV EH 734; HLM 7004 and LV 63). The music is considerably condensed, but both artists sing very well indeed with scrupulous attention to dynamic markings. Yet, fine though this record undoubtedly is, it is hardly ideal – this is one of those rare cases when artistry and fine vocalism are not quite sufficient. Wittrisch, despite his great skill and accuracy, simply lacks the grandeur of style that, for instance, Affre possesses.

Before investigating the LP recordings, a final 78rpm curiosity is worth consideration. On G&T 3–32722 Jean Vallier sings Marcel's contribution to the 'Interrogatoire' in the final scene. He displays a lightweight voice of good quality and makes as much of this passage as is possible when deprived of the tenor and soprano responses.

The only absolutely complete recording of the opera is from Decca (1970). The cast is virtually the same as that for a concert performance mounted by the London Opera Society at the Albert Hall some time before this recording. Sadly in the interval between, the tenor Anastasios Vrenios had apparently suffered a form of vocal breakdown. Whereas his voice in the Albert Hall had easily covered Joan Sutherland's loudest outpourings, there remains on these LPs only a pale shadow. His sound is like a light lyric tenor's, incapable of tackling any of the heroic music other than in falsetto or an unsupported head voice. To be fair to Vrenios he does sing the notes with accuracy and is clearly quite stylish but vocally he does not even begin to fill the role of Raoul. His French is also indifferent – a charge which certainly cannot be levelled against the Urbain of Huguette Tourangeau. She provides stylish, accurate singing throughout and her second aria is especially charming, easily qualifying as the finest version on record. As Marcel, Nicola Ghiuselev sounds important, but all the vital low notes are weak and he sings without finesse. However, despite certain technical deficiencies, it is an imposing assumption. Sutherland is in fine voice and displays incredible virtuosity in her solo which opens Act 2. Here she is given two verses of 'O beau pays'

– a bonus it has not been possible to trace in any score so far, and fine though her singing is, it has to be admitted that her early version (SXL 2257) is much to be preferred. The Valentine, Martina Arroyo, has a voice of some quality and provides several exciting moments, but far greater refinement of style is ideally required. She is also found wanting on some of the purely technical aspects of the role. The unfocused voice of Dominic Cossa makes nothing of the role of Nevers. Gabriel Bacquier's stringy tone and lack of a true legato makes nonsense of most of the music allotted to St Bris. On the positive side both the orchestral playing and choral work is of a high standard and Richard Bonynge's conducting is responsive and sympathetic.

Three further more-or-less 'complete' versions require consideration. On an 'off-the-air' set may be heard the performance which took place at La Scala in June 1962. Quite extensive cuts were made but at least time was found to include an abridged version of Act 5 rather than ending the opera with Act 4 as had been standard practice for some years. Franco Corelli as Raoul possessed one of the most beautiful tenor voices of his day, but he does not come within hailing distance of the role. Dynamic markings are ignored entirely and in some cases also the written notes. Giulietta Simionato, normally an excellent artist, apparently found this catching, for as Marguérite she commits these same sins and additionally omits all the written cadenzas – it has been suggested that this was at the behest of the conductor. Fiorenza Cossotto as the Page does not appear to advantage and everywhere betrays her lack of a true florid technique. Even Sutherland is below her best form. Nicolai Ghiaurov is a rough and forceful Marcel and the St Bris of Giorgio Tozzi is colourless. Only Vladimiro Ganzarolli's Nevers emerges with any distinction – good, clean singing and more than a nodding acquaintance with the score. Gianandrea Gavazzeni's conducting is generally competent although never inspired. The Act 4 duet for Raoul and Valentine generates a certain animal excitement, but this recording is not for those seeking style or elegance.

These will be found in greater measure in the version conducted by Ernst Märzendorfer in February 1971 in Vienna. It is available in fine stereo sound on a 'private' issue and also in an abridged version. The conductor favours brisk tempi, but he is generally stylish and especially sensitive to his soloists. He is fortunate in having as his Raoul one of the most musicianly and technically accomplished tenors of our day, Nicolai Gedda. There can hardly be another tenor living capable of singing the role with anything approaching the accomplishment that Gedda brought to the task. It is possible to fault him perhaps for a certain lack of charm in his duet with the Queen, and even his most fervent admirers would scarcely claim that he possesses a voice of sensuous quality, yet in every other way his assumption is masterly and one can only regret that Decca were unable to secure his services for their recording. Likewise one would have wished his Valentine, Enriqueta Tarres, on the commercial label. This is easily the most accomplished singing she has put on record and in the final duet with Gedda both singers rise to great heights, producing what must certainly be the finest account of this music on a modern recording.

Jeanette Scovotti as Urbain supplies some breathy coloratura and a poorly resolved trill yet the voice is bright, efficient and attractive so that the final impression is a winning one. Rita Shane, Marguérite de Valois, is too similar in vocal quality to Scovotti and lacks repose in 'O beau pays'. However hers is a basically pleasing voice and even if her interpolated notes *in alt* are a mistake, she does attempt a cadenza requiring great virtuosity and brings some character to the role. Justino Diaz as Marcel has problems at the lower end of the scale and his voice is dry and hollow-sounding. Nevertheless he offers musicianly singing – a verdict which cannot be applied to the wild and woolly St Bris of Dimiter Petkov or the characterless Nevers of Pedro Farres.

Another 'off-the-air' version, taken from an Italian radio broadcast in 1956, features the veteran tenor Giacomo Lauri-Volpi and others in the cast include Anna de Cavalieri, Antonietta Pastori, Giuseppe Taddei, Jolanda Gardino, Nicola Zaccaria and Giorgio Tozzi. Only Taddei and Zaccaria emerge honourably from the travesty of the score here presented. Some idea of the quality of this performance can be sampled from the excerpts issued in the fifties by Cetra. On EP 0344 Lauri-Volpi can be heard singing 'Plus blanche' and the Raoul/Marguerite duet with Pastori. It is a sorry memento of a once-great voice, for the solo is without style and the once attractive vocal quality and fine breath control have vanished. The soprano is merely adequate and both this record and the complete recording are best forgotten. Even in this age of low vocal standards it is astonishing that any company should have considered this performance worthy of reissue.

In the fifties a two-disc, abridged version of the opera was issued in France. Originally on Pléiade P 3085/6, it later appeared on Vega 80–018. It featured Renée Doria, Jean Rinella, Simone Couderc, Guy Fouché, Adrien Legros, Henri Medus, Charles Cambon and the Orchestre de l'Association des Concerts Pasdeloup, conducted by Jean Allain. It is puzzling indeed to know why this set was issued for it merely provides an example of the low standard of French singing in that period. The tenor's 'Plus blanche' has been excerpted onto Vega 16.243 enabling one to experience his unsteady voice, which comes to grief in the cadenza, without enduring the whole work. The only member of the cast to attain an acceptable standard is Doria, who, possessing a generally pleasing voice, alone appears to have a feeling for the correct style.

Single excerpts on LP are confined to the tenor romance, Urbain's solo, the two arias for Marcel and the Act 4 duet. Five versions of 'Plus blanche' have been heard and of these only that by Alfredo Kraus (Carillon CAL 1) comes near to the required style. He commences most sensitively and sings generally with understanding and elegance but towards the end of the aria his lack of a true *mezza voce* and florid technique bring disappointment. Franco Corelli (ASD 541) offers a marginal improvement on his stage performance but it remains inelegant singing. Tony Poncet (Philips 837065GY),

Alberto da Costa (Concord 3004) and Mario Filippeschi (Col. QC 5029) display enormous lung power but virtually no regard for the score. In fact da Costa sings the entire aria in an unremitting *forte* that is positively painful.

Marcel's 'Chorale' has been recorded by Cesare Siepi (Decca LW 5169) who follows it with 'Piff, paff, pouff'. He sings both excerpts in French with strict adherence to the score. Unfortunately his actual vocal timbre, as recorded here, is not entirely pleasing and the tone becomes unsteady in the *forte* passages. Jerome Hines (Epic LC 3934) also betrays signs of unsteadiness in his version of 'Piff, paff, pouff', but it is an impressive rendering which the slightly hollow quality of his voice and aspirated runs do not entirely negate. Ghiaurov (SXL 6147) again provides good, unremarkable singing and poor attempts at the trills.

Of the four versions heard of the Page's first aria, Janine Micheau (Col. SAXF 221), Marilyn Horne (SXL 6149). Frederica von Stade (CBS 76522) and Rita Streich (DG 19137), that by Micheau is the most characterful. It has to be admitted, alas, that her tone is sour, her trill less than perfect and the aria is taken faster than the score's *cantabile, con grazia* would suggest. However she exhibits the exact teasing quality required, and one is left wishing that she had been asked to record the aria earlier in her career when the voice was in its prime. Streich sings sweetly and correctly but with no attempt at characterization. Von Stade displays the most attractive vocal timbre, and moreover has a good idea of how the music should go, but is let down by a tentative central section, an embryonic trill and a lack of real authority, while, conversely, Horne's superbly accurate and technically accomplished rendering is singularly lacking in sparkle.

Only one modern recording of the famous Act 4 duet, Montserrat Caballé and Bernabé Martí (ASD 2723), prompts speculation as to why other famous teams of our time have ignored this truly splendid *scena*. Is it possible to imagine how it might have sounded in the care of Callas and di Stefano, Tebaldi and del Monaco, Milanov and Björling? Caballé and her husband bring their own individual accents to the music but even allowing for the dry, unheroic quality of Martí's voice, his lack of any useful range of dynamic or nuance and his most imperfect French, this performance would still be totally destroyed by the unidiomatic and lifeless conducting. There is no forward pulse or cohesion and the music emerges as a series of unconnected episodes. Caballé is in fine voice and at moments sings like an angel but, as so often with this soprano, the impression is given that she is sight-reading the music and has no real idea of the import of the scene as a whole.

Perhaps it would not be inappropriate to end this survey by admitting that the experience of listening to so many versions of the various set pieces from *Les Huguenots* has resulted in an increased admiration for Meyerbeer's talent, even if exposure to complete recordings has raised nagging doubts about the true musical value of the work as a whole. Certainly when the music is sung with a scrupulous attention to dynamic markings and with the correct blend of delicacy and power, it can be extraordinarily atmospheric.

If these elements are lacking, however, as they are in nearly all the recordings made in the LP era, then the effect that the music is capable of making is almost completely nullified. It may possibly be accounted a basic weakness in Meyerbeer's music that it should be so dependent on a correct performing style. Whereas the operas of Mozart, Beethoven, Verdi, Wagner and Puccini can, and still do, survive successfully many rough-and-ready performances, those of Meyerbeer will not, and additionally they must have great singers, not just great voices. When this rare but happy conjunction occurs, as it does on the finest of the records reviewed above, Meyerbeer is revealed as a very considerable musical dramatist.

LES HUGUENOTS

M Marguérite de Valois; *V* Valentine; *U* Urbain; *R* Raoul de Nangis; *Mar* Marcel; *N* Nevers; *SB* Saint-Bris

1956 (broadcast performance – in Italian) De Cavalieri *M*; Pastori *V*; Gardino *U*; Lauri-Volpi *R*; Tozzi *M*; Zaccaria *N*; Taddei *SB*/ Italian Radio Chorus and Orch. Milan/Serafin
Replica ⓜ RPL2401–3

1970 Sutherland *M*; Arroyo *V*; Tourangeau *U*; Vrenios *R*; Ghiuselev *Mar*; Cossa *N*; Bacquier *SB*/Ambrosian Opera Chorus, M New Philharmonia/Bonynge
Decca SET460
London OSA1437

c. 1953 (abridged) Doria *M*; Rinella *V*; Couderc *U*; Fouché *R*; Medus *Mar*; Cambon *N*; Legros *SB*/ Pasdeloup Orch./Allain
Pleiade P3085–6
Westminster OPW1204

The Operas of Berlioz

DAVID CAIRNS

In his masterly book *Man and his Music* Wilfrid Mellers groups Berlioz with Verdi and Wagner as one of 'the three greatest operatic composers of the nineteenth century'. Even in 1962, when the book was published, that must have raised a good many eyebrows, and it will still strike most people as a highly eccentric judgement. But a generation or two earlier the statement would have been totally unthinkable. What had made it possible was the production of *Les Troyens* at Covent Garden in 1957 under Rafael Kubelik. It was the shock of that event that set in motion the whole modern Berlioz revival, creating a new awareness of his music and establishing overnight an enthusiasm for the work that was to have many consequences, foreseen and unforeseen.

The Covent Garden revelation did not, of course, come straight out of a clear sky. It was the culmination of a gradual process of recognition. Erik Chisholm had conducted a semi-amateur production in Glasgow in 1935 which caused a startled Tovey to describe *Les Troyens* as 'one of the most gigantic and convincing masterpieces of music-drama'. The work was on the prospectus of Beecham's 1939–40 Covent Garden season, before the war put a stop to the company's activity. In June 1947 Beecham conducted a studio performance, relayed on the Third Programme. The Oxford University Opera Group staged a cut version under Jack Westrup in 1950, and in 1952 Ducretet-Thomson issued a recording of Part 2, *Les Troyens à Carthage*, conducted by Hermann Scherchen. But these were isolated events, without sustained impact. It was characteristic of the whole strange history of the opera that the full score had never been published (and was not published until 1969, a hundred years after the composer's death); it was available only on hire from the Paris firm of Choudens, in a corrupt text whose physical dilapidation (pages glued together, orchestration altered, etc.) only added to the obstacles the work seemed destined perpetually to encounter. *Les Troyens* remained an opera more talked about than known; as Edward Dent, who had translated the libretto into English, remarked, it was like some buried city of the ancient world waiting to be discovered.

Berlioz's operatic output as a whole still languished in general obscurity. It is symptomatic of the then state of affairs that nearly all the Berlioz vocal recordings on 78s come from *La Damnation de Faust*, a work not conceived for the stage but frequently regarded as an opera in all but name and, until the last twenty-five years, staged more often than all the operas put together. Gramophone Fausts, Marguerites, Mephistos abounded. French mezzos and sopranos immortalized their 'D'amour l'ardente flamme'; every French baritone or bass, and quite a few Italians, had to record his 'Serenade' or his 'Voici des roses'. In sharp contrast, recorded Didos and Aeneases were rare birds, and Cassandras, Teresas and Beatrices unknown.

LES TROYENS

LP recordings have played a major part in the dissemination and acceptance of Berlioz's music in the last ten or fifteen years. Here again the influence of *Les Troyens* has been decisive. The complete Philips recording of 1969 caused a worldwide stir, won more international awards than any other except the Decca *Ring*, and – against the expectations of Philips themselves – made a profit. Yet until the last minute it was in doubt. Gramophone companies are very conservative institutions, and the idea that a complete recording might be a feasible and commercially viable proposition was slow to penetrate. Despite the evidence of the Covent Garden production, the old myth of the opera's immense and impractical length persisted (it had recently been stated as eight hours by *Opernwelt*), and attempts to interest the major companies were invariably met by the objection that the project would need at least twelve sides and was simply not on. In 1965 the appearance of a shredded and potted two-disc *Troyens*, with Régine Crespin singing what was left of the roles of Cassandra and Dido and various other singers adding a phrase here and there, made a complete recording both more necessary than ever and, it seemed, less likely. The identification of Madame Crespin with such a travesty was, I think, one reason why she was not actively considered for the role of Cassandra in the complete recording which eventually came about in the Berlioz centenary year, 1969. The recording, based on the new Covent Garden production conducted by Colin Davis, was originally scheduled by EMI, and Davis was ready to ignore his exclusive contract with Philips in order to make it. Not till very late in the proceedings did Philips take the plunge and finally agree to produce it themselves.

The last-minute character of the enterprise, plus the fact that the recording was tied to an existing production and made not after but during the run of the opera, meant that wholesale changes to Covent Garden's almost exclusively British cast were out of the question. Pierre Thau was brought in to sing Priam, Mercury and the Soldier in scene 1, and Roger Soyer for the Ghost of Hector and Narbal (he came within an ace of missing the crucial final session when the Paris police mislaid his passport). Berit Lindholm replaced Anja Silja as Cassandra.

One may regret that Corebus, Anna, or Hylas are not sung by the top-line French singers who in different circumstances could no doubt have been found for them. Peter Glossop's Corebus is solid and vigorous but a little unimaginative; Ryland Davies's attractive Hylas is marred by flatness on the F at the top of the stave; Heather Begg's tone, as Anna, is not ingratiating. But the advantages of a recording based on an ensemble currently performing in the theatre triumphantly outweigh the disadvantages. Listening to it again after many years – and, I hope, long enough after the event for my first-hand involvement in it to have yielded to a reasonable degree of objectivity – I find it every bit as exciting as I remembered. From the first page it is alive, rhythmically exact, richly coloured, ardently phrased. The whole thing radiates an intense conviction. Under Colin Davis the orchestra of the Royal Opera House, Covent Garden, play with extraordinary fire and eloquence, and the Chorus, if not the most youthful-sounding in the world, know the notes and understand the drama. They are uncharacteristically tentative in the Andromache scene, and that is one of a handful of numbers where Davis, in striving for expressiveness instead of letting it happen, sets too deliberate a tempo and checks the natural flow of the music. Sometimes, too, he allows his soloists to labour the recitatives – a function, perhaps, of their not being native French singers (Soyer's singing of the recitative at the beginning of Act 4, a model of classical French declamation, makes an instructive contrast). But over most of the opera's five acts and fifty-two separate numbers Davis's authority is scarcely to be faulted.

Of the principals, Josephine Veasey came near to being a great singer with her tragic, passionate Dido. Vocally a little off colour at the beginning of Act 3 (Dido's first appearance), she produces a fine glowing line in the quintet and is consistently grand and fiery in the great scenes of Act 5. Berit Lindholm's Cassandra can be criticized for several faults, which boil down to her unfamiliarity with French and the absence of that hard gemlike core to the voice that many of the best French singers have. She constantly breaks up vowel sounds into diphthongs or triphthongs, with an unidiomatic and clumsy effect. But her heroic soprano has what many mezzos lack in the part: a cutting edge to penetrate orchestra and chorus and dominate the big ensembles; and to my mind, despite stylistic shortcomings, she imposes herself by sheer vocal energy and dramatic involvement.

As to Jon Vickers's Aeneas, each time I have listened to it I have been staggered afresh by the epic scale, the *élan*, and the sheer voltage of it. All objections are swept aside as by a force of nature. True, he strains and gasps a bit in the love duet and makes a quite unnecessary meal of the recitative before the septet, 'Mais bannissons ces tristes souvenirs'. Certainly, his French is wayward and at times bizarre; a Paris critic has referred to his '*nasales insupportables*'. I respect the criticism, but when Vickers sings 'En un dernier naufrage', 'Ma tâche jusqu'au bout, grands dieux, sera remplie', 'A toi, mon âme' – and not only the big exalted paragraphs, for his outburst to the Ghost of Hector is equally fine in its sense of awe and pity – or when he throws off his disguise in Act 3 with that spine-tingling 'Reine, je suis Enée', it is the tragic hero incarnate, the authentic voice of the ancient world in all its grandeur and melancholy. The high B flats and the one top C, though they ring out bravely, are more constricted than they would have been ten years earlier; but the performance as a whole has the unique charge of Vickers at his most formidable. No one else, not even Georges Thill, comes near him in the part.

The other complete or fairly complete *Troyens* is the 'private' issue of Beecham's live broadcast performance. As the work was given in two parts, on successive evenings (3 and 4 June 1947), it is hard to see why there should have been so many cuts – some large, others small and niggling, all damaging – unless it is that they reflect the condition of the Choudens orchestral parts that were used. There is some evidence of insufficient rehearsal, especially in voice-orchestra ensemble in recitatives, and Beecham at times seems to be feeling his way through a relatively unfamiliar score (for example, the vital distinction between *andante* and *moderato* in Dido's 'Je vais mourir' is ignored). But there are many moments of characteristic orchestral electricity, and some of it is powerfully atmospheric and beautiful, with vivid detail. The BBC Theatre Chorus makes a well-rehearsed and lively contribution. Both Cassandra and Dido are sung by the French soprano Marisa Ferrer – very well, with full, incisive tone and shapely phrasing. Her Cassandra is a bit phlegmatic and lacking in dramatic commitment, her Dido more positive, and culminating in a finely sung 'Adieu, fière cité'. The Aeneas, Jean Giraudeau, was a lyric, not a dramatic, tenor, and he makes a particularly feeble impression in Act 1 and again in Act 3, where his languid 'Je suis Enée' makes me want to reply, like Tennyson when Oscar Browning presented himself to the poet with 'Hello, I'm Browning': 'No, you're not'. But though nowhere near the trumpet tones and heroic style required ('A toi, mon âme' is absurdly lachrymose), his Aeneas warms up considerably in Acts 4 and 5. Yvonne Corke is a fresh and vital Anna, if lacking in elegance, and Charles Cambon a firm-voiced Corebus. The Hylas (Colin Cunningham) clearly hadn't learnt his part: he goes wrong twice. Thanks to this, however, we hear the voice of Tommy chiming in for him, an unexpected bonus. Altogether, the set inspires poignant feelings of might-have-been. Beecham became increasingly interested in the work during his final years. He was due to conduct the 1960 revival at Covent Garden, but ill-health prevented him. During his convalescence from his first stroke he was planning to make his comeback with a series of concert performances of Berlioz's dramatic works at the Albert Hall, including *Les Troyens*, when a further stroke killed him.

Scherchen's *Les Troyens à Carthage* – Acts 3–5 of the complete opera – is almost equally frustrating. An interpretation that is often exciting, hardly ever dull, at times perverse and occasionally magnificent is largely set at naught by the wretchedly inadequate recording, which is so thin and shallow as to give the impression of a mere handful of musicians. Not that the playing of the Conservatoire Orchestra is exactly vintage stuff: the wind's intonation is uncertain and the oboe's tone is like a harmonica. Some instruments are missing from the offstage Trojan March in No. 44. Scherchen, as was his wont, has moments of bewildering eccentricity – the wonderful A minor 'Va, ma soeur, l'implorer' is taken crazily fast, and in general his tempi are very much on the quick side (though 'Dieux de l'oubli' is dragged unbearably). But with all his wilfulness he was capable of genius; and sometimes the music's intensity of feeling kindles in him an answering fire which illuminates it with a fierce, incandescent light. The brilliant Chasse Royale, very fast but convincing, is one example. Jean Giraudeau's Aeneas has gained in robustness since the Beecham broadcast. Bernard Gallet is a shaky Iopas (Ian Partridge on the Philips set gives the most idiomatic performance on disc) and hardly better as Hylas, Janine Collard a pleasant and assured, if slightly plummy, Anna. The star of the cast is Arda Mandikian, the Dido. Her voice lacks opulence: the timbre is lean and not in itself remarkable for beauty; but even at her vocally least impressive she declaims the text and phrases the music vividly, and both instinctively and as an artist she understands the idiom of the part, its raptures and agonies. This Dido conveys, at her very grandest, a frightening vulnerability. She is like a wildcat in the final confrontation with Aeneas, and her 'Je maudis et tes dieux et toi-même' strikes like an avenging fury; and there is a harrowing reality in the self-abandonment of her 'Plûton me semble' and the despair of the last prophetic utterance.

In comparison, Janet Baker, on the HMV disc (SXLP 30248) of the final scenes of Act 5 (unfortunately all that exists on record of a memorable Dido), is domesticated. Or, to put it more positively, her interpretation keeps within her limitations, exploiting her strengths, her pathos, fine-drawn phrasing, keen response to words, and vital declamation. It might have acquired greater power if Alexander Gibson's efficient, well-pointed conducting had been less detached and 'classical' in feeling, more in the grand style. He fails to observe the distinction between the two tempi in 'Je vais mourir' (on disc only Davis, Scherchen and Kubelik do so). But his brisk, incisive handling of the dramatic recitative 'Dieux immortels, il part' is very effective. 'Adieu, fière cité' is beautifully sung – still, quiet, a very private statement.

On stage, too, Baker has been finest in the scenes of Dido's private delights and torments. If Veasey's Dido, by contrast, is always the queen ('Je suis reine et j'ordonne'), Régine Crespin on the two-disc set of 'Scenes from *Les Troyens*' is never less than a *grande dame* and hardly ever anything more. She has moments of great energy, especially in the scene of the Wooden Horse and in 'Dieux immortels'; and to hear even a savagely truncated version of the two roles sung by a first-rate French soprano with a commanding, well-controlled voice and good diction is an experience not to be despised. What is lacking is any sense of dramatic involvement. Crespin toys majestically with the music. Her massive unconcern makes the garden scene – the largest single extract, performed uncut from the quintet to the end of the act – sound almost perfunctory. The effect of pathos in 'Je vais mourir' is wholly contrived, without a grain of feeling. It could scarcely be otherwise, given the anti-artistic atmosphere of the enterprise. This is mayhem in the great French tradition of vandalism against their own masterpieces. The set represents not a selection of coherent highlights but a 'version' of the score slashed and stitched together to satisfy the voracious demands of the prima donna, with changes to the verbal text and the orchestration and indiscriminate cuts made within the musical numbers – the hallowed impresario's formula of 'ma femme et cinq poupées'. The *poupées* include Guy Chauvet, Marie-Luce Bellary and Gérard Dunan; but it is Madame Crespin's show. The Paris Opéra Orchestra has just enough moments of eloquence to make one wish heartily that the whole thing had been a little more serious; a good French orchestra playing Berlioz with whole-hearted commitment adds an authentic savour to the music, as the Orchestre de Paris – reflecting a new attitude in France – has demonstrated lately under Barenboim. But this sad affair belongs body and soul to the Dark Ages.

It is a matter for regret, too, that Guy Chauvet was brought up in the same complacent, careless environment. He has the notes and the clarion ring for Aeneas's *scena*, as he shows again on a Polaris disc of famous tenor arias (L 80.007), but the feeling and style are resoundingly absent. Chauvet sings as if he had learnt the part by rote and had no glimmer of an idea what it means. There is no intensity, no drive. The conductor, Jésus Etcheverry, seems equally powerless to supply it. Curiously enough Mario del Monaco, singing in Italian (Levon ML 1003), raises more sparks than Chauvet; but this is a live performance, as the barking voice of the prompter and the applause for the stentorian and prolonged high B flat at the end make very clear. Del Monaco sings without much line but sounds quite heroic in his rough and ready way. He is, however, worlds away from Vickers – or from Georges Thill.

Thill's 1934 recording of Aeneas's *scena* (plus most of the following two numbers) deserves its fame. His manner may be a little stiff, suggesting a Third Republic cavalry commander rather than an epic hero, but the voice is gloriously firm, even and open-toned, the rhythm exact and the diction exemplary. A pity we are not allowed to hear more of him: nearly half of 'En un dernier naufrage' is cut (LX 395; 2C 061–12154).

Of the sopranos and mezzo-sopranos who have recorded extracts from Dido's music, the earliest two are Marie Delna and Félia Litvinne. Not a great deal can be divined from the resulting discs. Litvinne sings 'Adieu, fière cité' on a Pathé cylinder (1903) later transferred to disc (IRCC 200; Rococo R38). Only a ghost of an impression survives from these thin and scratchy sounds. The 'flame-like' voice that contemporaries praised has faded beyond recall; a certain plangency is all that comes across. The tempo is all over the place, though the anonymous and ineffective pianist may be partly to blame. Delna, whom Massenet thought 'music itself', was an admired Dido. According to her official date of birth, if it can be believed, she was only fifteen when she sang both Dido and Cassandra at Karlsruhe under Mottl in 1890 – the first staged performance of *Les Troyens*, though in two parts. Gide heard her Dido in 1906, and it moved him to 'rapture'. In 1903 she recorded 'Chers Tyriens' from Act 3, (Pathé 3513; Club 99.59, RLS 7705). It is very slow, somewhat cavalier in rhythm, and accompanied by a jangling pub-like piano. However, a plummy but well-focused voice can be clearly heard. The sleeve calls her a contralto, but she goes easily and smoothly up to the high B flat, with even tone over the whole compass.

A French singer of a later generation who recorded 'Chers Tyriens' with orchestra in the 1920s was Frozier-Marrot (Disque W 1032). She sings it even more slowly than Delna, but the voice is striking – firm and velvety but with an attractive rapid vibrato and a hint of sharpness that merely adds to its piquancy. On the same disc is her 'Adieu, fière cité': again too slow to be convincing, but with some singing of touching tenderness and a lovely controlled *crescendo* and *diminuendo* from *pp* to *pp* on the final sustained E flat.

Rita Gorr's 'Je vais mourir/Adieu, fière cité' (HLP 23) is less good than I remembered. The recitative, partly because the conductor Lawrance Collingwood fails to observe the distinction between the two tempi, lacks passion, though the long descending phrase from F to low E natural, 'Esclave, elle l'emporte en l'éternelle nuit', is beautifully gauged. The aria, though on the slow side, comes off better; 'ma carrière est finie', sung in one breath, is phrased and coloured movingly. Beecham had wanted Gorr to sing Dido for him at Covent Garden in 1960, and with her sumptuous voice and generous temperament she would surely have been impressive. Josephine Veasey recorded the same scene in 1968 for Decca's Covent Garden Anniversary Album (SET 392–3), a year before the complete recording. With fewer vocal resources than Gorr she makes 'Je vais mourir' much more vital (helped by Kubelik's idiomatic conducting), and the aria also flows at a more convincing tempo.

If *Les Troyens* remains a problematic work, this is not so much because of its length as because of the rarity of the classical heroic tenor. Since Vickers stopped singing Aeneas, no one has come forward (at the time of writing) to replace him. Barenboim's plan to perform the work with the Orchestre de Paris and then record it as part of the DG Berlioz Cycle has, it seems, been shelved pending the appearance of a successor.

BENVENUTO CELLINI

To some extent the same problem faces *Benvenuto Cellini*, Berlioz's third completed opera*. The title role is not so heavy as Aeneas, but it is longer. Much of it lies high, and the singer must combine robust tone and energetic declamation (sextet, final scene) with lightness and delicacy (trio) and lyrical warmth and sustained legato ('Sur les monts'). The original Cellini, Gilbert Duprez, seems to have been deficient in the latter qualities; when conceiving

---

* The first two were *Estelle et Némorin* (a prentice work, subsequently destroyed) and the original *opéra-comique* version of *Les Francs-Juges*, which survives only fragmentarily.

the part Berlioz probably had in mind the more flexible heroic style of
Adolphe Nourrit, reigning tenor at the Opéra in the 1820s, whom he saw in
Orphée and *Guillaume Tell*. Such tenors are uncommon; and it is fortunate
that Nicolai Gedda should have had Cellini in his repertory and have been,
if no longer in the first flush of youth, still very much equal to the role when
Philips – committed to a complete Berlioz Cycle after the success of *Les
Troyens* – turned their attention to the work in 1972.

Ten years earlier, in 1962, Gedda recorded 'La gloire était ma seule idole'
and 'Sur les monts' (the latter with a large cut in the middle) as part of a
recital disc, 'Gedda à Paris', with the French Radio Orchestra under Georges
Prêtre (SLS 5250). The voice is noticeably younger and fresher than on the
complete recording. By that time, however, Gedda had performed the role
in the more serious atmosphere of Covent Garden, and there is a more than
compensating gain in artistic understanding. Even so, there are moments –
as happens occasionally with this fine singer – when he seems to lose intel-
lectual concentration and purposefulness, and then he sounds a bit of a
ninny. But if the characterization is somewhat lacking in force, it would be
hard to imagine this varied and exacting role better sung.

Gedda is the centre round which Philips grouped a strong cast. This time
it was assembled specially for the recording (though a performance at the
Proms followed a few days after the final session), and apart from Gedda
himself, whose French is good, all the main roles are taken by French-
speaking singers – Jules Bastin (the pompous Papal treasurer Balducci) is
Belgian and Christiane Eda-Pierre (his daughter Teresa) from Martinique.

Not only is the title role very demanding, but both the orchestral and the
choral writing are of unusual technical difficulty. *Benvenuto Cellini* is still,
after nearly a hundred and fifty years, one of the hardest of all operatic
scores, because of its mercurial changes of metre (often to be executed at
rapid speed and with light-fingered delicacy), its frequent displaced accents,
and its endlessly varied orchestration, forming a further element in the
music's already considerable rhythmical complexity. When these problems
are not solved the work sounds, not surprisingly, chaotic (as it did at the
Holland Festival in 1961 and in Geneva in 1964), but when they are, the
result is exhilarating. On the Philips set Colin Davis's interpretation relishes
both the virtuosity and the humour and tenderness, and the BBC Symphony
Orchestra cope admirably with its demands, the Chorus adequately. Eda-
Pierre is a spirited Teresa (after some trouble with her intonation at the start
of the cavatina) and Bastin a splendidly portentous, irascible Balducci. Jane
Berbié, as Cellini's apprentice Ascanio, sings incisively, with full, tangy tone
– though the high B in 'Cette somme t'est dûe par le Pape Clément' is a
squawk – and characterizes the part with relish. Robert Massard is an amusing Fieramosca and his firm, well-placed baritone is a pleasure to listen to,
but he is inclined to overdo the farce. Roger Soyer's Pope, on the other
hand, though nobly sung, is too bland; he misses not only the richness of the

lower notes – for which a true bass is needed – but also the glint of cynicism that is such a distinctive feature of this half-majestic, half-mocking portrait.

The recording is based on the original two-act Paris *Cellini* of 1838, not on the more familiar and shorter three-act 'Weimar version' of 1852–3. Quite apart from the fact that it makes greater sense of the stage action, the Paris version contains music that it would be a pity to lose, such as the fizzing *buffo* finale to the sextet and the quiet, mysterious ensemble in F minor, 'A l'atelier', later in the same act. In preparing the score for Weimar, at Liszt's request, Berlioz reduced it to the shorter length customary in Germany at the time and also toned down the *buffo* element, and later agreed to further extensive cutting. In its original conception *Benvenuto Cellini* was an *opéra-comique*, with spoken dialogue and a systematic juxtaposition of the comic and the dramatic, the passionate and the picturesque. The mixture of genres was retained when the work was upgraded for the Opéra, but dialogue, being forbidden there, was replaced by recitative. Covent Garden, basing its production on the researches of Hugh Macdonald, Maurits Sillem and Arthur Hammond, not only restored a good deal of musical material buried in the Opéra's archives but also reintroduced dialogue; and in this, as in much else, the recording followed it. The result, as so often, is less than satisfactory. The conversation outside Teresa's bedroom in Act 1 goes with a swing, with Bastin sounding like a character in *Les Enfants du Paradis*, but most of the later exchanges lack pace and conviction. Philips's recording, made in Wembley Town Hall, is less spacious and warm than *Les Troyens* (made in larger Walthamstow). Offstage effects, of which the work is full, are generally well managed, but the cannon of Sant'Angelo, in the Carnival Scene, makes a very muffled pop. All in all, however, a notable success.

BÉATRICE ET BÉNÉDICT

Another six years passed before Philips recorded Berlioz's last stage work, the *opéra-comique Béatrice et Bénédict*.* Till then the field had belonged to the Oiseau-Lyre version (1962), also conducted by Colin Davis. In so far as the two interpretations differ, the differences do not indicate any significant change of view. If the Oiseau-Lyre Beatrice-Benedick duet has a more 'youthful' freshness and wit, the overture is still more vital on the Philips set – a performance of terrific verve. Indeed, Davis's reading has lost none of its flair. What can be said is that the incidental numbers – the opening chorus, the Sicilienne, the drinking scene, the *Choeur lointain* for sopranos, altos and tenors with guitar accompaniment – are done with even greater conviction than on the Oiseau-Lyre set (partly because the excellent John Alldis Choir surpasses the perfectly adequate St Anthony Singers). The Philips set includes the second verse of Somarone's Epithalamium, cut by Oiseau-Lyre, and here enlivened by Bastin's memorably fatuous spoken interjections, and

* The usual French form of Shakespeare's Benedick.

also a ration of dialogue: a pretty meagre ration, and lamely delivered, but a bonus none the less.

Against this, the generally cleaner sound of the Oiseau-Lyre recording allows more of the exquisite orchestral detail to emerge. There is little to choose between the playing of the LSO on the two sets. On balance, the Philips cast is the stronger. Eric Shilling's Somarone is no match for Bastin's, and John Mitchinson's Benedick is less assured and pointed than Robert Tear's. Thomas Allen makes more of the small part of Claudio than John Cameron (Oiseau-Lyre). There is a much narrower margin between the sensitive and stylish Hero of April Cantelo and that of Eda-Pierre (Philips), but the latter's French diction and more focused voice (despite an occasional sharpness of pitch) give her the edge. Helen Watts is the dependable, sympathetic Ursula on both sets. As to the two Beatrices, Josephine Veasey (Oiseau-Lyre) and Janet Baker (Philips), they differ in much the same way as these two singers' Didos: Veasey grander, more exalted, Baker generally more vivacious, more varied in expression and subtler in her use of words. Baker's subtlety, as sometimes happens with this highly sophisticated artist, lures her into some self-conscious vocalism in the *Andante* of Beatrice's *scena*, where her legato singing is so carefully contrived that calculation seems to take the place of feeling; but as a whole hers is a fine performance. To sum up, for all the virtues of the Oiseau-Lyre *Béatrice*, the Philips version is to be preferred.

On paper, the recent Barenboim version (DG) should be at least its equal; but despite its considerable virtues – excellent female soloists, lively, affectionate playing by the Orchestre de Paris – it isn't quite that. The cast, though, is potentially the strongest on disc, and in the case of both the sweet-voiced Hero of Ileana Cotrubas and the Beatrice of Yvonne Minton, the promise is fulfilled. Minton is at her most keen-voiced and animated; her big scene in Act 2 is admirably done. Nadine Denize contributes a fine Ursula, and the women's trio is sung beautifully. The men's trio is less successful, chiefly because it is here that the lack of piquancy and vivacity in Placido Domingo's Benedick is most apparent. Needless to say Domingo makes some glorious sounds, and he is more on top of the part than he is that of Faust (see below). Fischer-Dieskau, so interesting a choice for Mephistopheles (in the Barenboim *Damnation de Faust*), sounds rather less at home in Somarone's drinking song, and gets no chance to show what he can do with the Epithalamium, since its spoken commentary is cut out. The chorus, here and elsewhere, is only moderately good. Barenboim conducts with warmth and verve. Occasionally, there is a want of tautness and lightness of touch, and the direction becomes a little too relaxed; but this is a minor flaw on a generally enjoyable performance. More questionable is the decision to replace the spoken dialogue with a narration, delivered at some length by an actress (Geneviève Page) between the musical numbers. Dialogue, I know, is a problem; but this is not a satisfactory solution.

Beatrice's *scena* appears on a disc of French arias sung by the American mezzo Frederica von Stade, with the LPO under John Pritchard (CBS 76522). Her beautiful voice suits the music, but the reflective *Andante* comes off better than the exuberant *Allegro* (corresponding to Shakespeare's 'Benedick. love on, I will requite thee!'), and I find the whole thing unvaryingly elegiac in mood and lacking in high spirits. Clarity of diction is not a strong point of the artist's singing; but it is the sameness of vocal colour that is most responsible for the want of dramatic vitality.

An operatic recital (Supraphon SUA 10539) by the Czech baritone Ladislav Mráz, with the Czech Radio SO and Choir under František Dyk, includes the drinking scene from *Béatrice et Bénédict*, sung in Czech. This is a curious affair. The tempo is exceedingly slow, the trumpets and the cornet play flat, and the guitar part appears to be taken by a harp. In the circumstances, the singer's firm, clear voice is not heard to much effect.

LA DAMNATION DE FAUST

La Damnation de Faust remains the most recorded of Berlioz's dramatic works. There are eight complete versions, as well as two sets of extracts and a host of recordings of single numbers. Yet ironically, whereas a first-rate version exists of all three operas, there is no satisfactory *Damnation* on disc. One contributory factor is that so many of them use non-French singers. Not that the presence of French singers is by itself a guarantee of excellence, of course. But in no other Berlioz work, not even *Les nuits d'été*, is it so important that the sung text be delivered by singers capable of pointing and stressing and colouring the words in an idiomatic and characteristic way. It is not enough to be able to get by in French: one must be thoroughly at home in it. Yet of the five most recent recordings two have no French-speaking singers at all in the principal roles and the other three have only one each. The 'decline of French singing' seems to be accepted unquestioningly by most of the recording companies as a fact; no one bothers to find out if it is really true, and as a result good French singers are ignored: Pierre Thau, for example, an admirable Mephistopheles, appears only as Brander (on the Prêtre recording).

Another reason why the perfect *Damnation* is so elusive is simply the enormously demanding orchestral score, its exceptional range, concision, and mercurial changes of mood, style and texture. The musicians have to know 'the intention of every orchestral touch', as Shaw observed when reviewing a performance under Hallé in which the music 'came to life in the hands of players who understand every bar of it'. Successful Berlioz performances, Shaw goes on, are 'soldiers' victories, not generals'. He overstates the case: the soldiers' understanding derives ultimately from their general, and without a sagacious and far-sighted general no amount of prowess on their part will win the day. But the reverse is no less true: the most perceptive view of the work will remain earthbound if the conductor fails to communicate to his players 'the intention of every orchestral touch'. Add that the large part for male chorus demands, ideally, to be sung by professional tenors and basses but is nearly always entrusted to amateurs.

None of the recordings gets everything right, though one or two come close to doing so. The earliest, issued in 1948 by Columbia on fifteen 78s and transferred to LP by American Columbia, is in fact not strictly a complete version; as in the Markevitch recording, there are several sizeable cuts in Parts 3 and 4. The conductor, Jean Fournet, begins promisingly, with a fine lyrical flow in the opening Pastoral Symphony. But the Hungarian March is destroyed by a blatant acceleration three-quarters of the way through. Thereafter, good things – a stealthy, atmospheric opening to Part 2, a crisp and glittering Minuet – alternate with others that show less insight. The French Radio Orchestra and the Emile Passani Chorus, however, are generally punctilious and lively. All the singers are French, though none is particularly distinguished. Paul Cabanel's Mephistopheles has a strong, bright voice (with rapid vibrato), clear diction and a commanding manner, but not a great deal to say for himself. Mona Laurena, the Marguerite, is sloppy in 'Le roi de Thulé' and, though better in the Romance, is inclined to sing flat. The best of the soloists is Georges Jouatte as Faust. His 'Le vieil hiver', sung with a keen sense of line and phrase, is a powerful lyric statement. Jouatte also catches the hushed rapture of 'Merci, doux crépuscule'. He avoids the high C sharps in the duet, and in the trio is not entirely comfortable even on A. None the less his 'Nature immense' comes as a disappointment: inaccurate in note-values and peppered with intrusive aspirates (a fault noticeable earlier) but worse still, constantly anticipating the beat, so that what begins as a tempo of unhurried grandeur, appropriate to this hymn to vast, indifferent Nature, finishes by being rushed off its feet.

Charles Münch recorded *Damnation* in 1954 with the Boston Symphony, his own orchestra, with whom he frequently performed the work. Though ritually invoked by French critics as the last word in Berlioz interpretation, Münch had a wilful streak that could lead him wildly astray, but this is one of his most authoritative and convincing performances. From the very first phrase on the violas, played quietly but with a decisive spring, the score comes vividly alive. The miscalculations and errors are few: a hurried and accelerating March, an over-quick Minuet, an earthbound 'Ciel', some painfully strident cornet and trumpet tone. Again and again Münch finds the touch and colour and dynamic to characterize the music: the yearning melodic lines in the Easter Hymn, the sizzling *strettissimo* of violins and violas at Mephistopheles's first appearance, the plangent tone of the solo cornet in 'Voici des roses', the magical drifting fall of the choral harmonies at the end of the Sylphs' scene, the glee of the scampering will o' the wisps in answer to their master's summons, the sense of a monstrous, clattering guitar in the *pizzicato* accompaniment to the Serenade.

Münch has perhaps the best of the Fausts in David Poleri – not a French tenor, but at home in the language and the style and, if not the subtlest interpreter of the music, a refreshingly forceful one, with a feeling for its large melodic line and ardent lyrical utterance ('Adieu donc, belle nuit' in the finale to Part 3 is gloriously sung). The Marguerite of Suzanne Danco, too, is unusually fine. Berlioz specified a mezzo (having at first thought of it as a soprano role); and it is true that Danco's voice is not quite weighty enough for the climax of the Romance. But her gem-like concentration of tone, musical phrasing, sensitive use of words and general intelligence give continual pleasure. The weakness of the set is Martial Singher's prosaic Mephisto, stolid as a policeman, and devoid of humour or menace. One would hardly know he was French, so unidiomatic is his performance. But for this, I should be tempted to overlook the substitution of trombones for tubas in the Drinking and Amen choruses (an error of the old Breitkopf edition) and call it the most authentic of the recorded versions.

The version by Georges Prêtre, the other French conductor to record the work (1969), is authentic only in its conformity to the worst traditions of perfunctoriness and routine. Some of the ensemble is all over the place, notably in 'Le vieil hiver' (where, in addition, flute and clarinet miss an entry altogether), the Peasants' Chorus, and Marguerite's apotheosis ('Remonte au ciel'). At other times a sleepy competence settles over the proceedings. Yet there are enough flashes of vitality and insight to show what it could have been if some trouble had been taken. The Paris Opéra Chorus of that epoch was in a bad way but the orchestra knew the score backwards, and here and there they cannot prevent themselves from playing it really well.

Nicolai Gedda is not the artist to thrive in this sort of atmosphere. His Faust keeps threatening to become interesting but in the end it founders in a thoroughly undisciplined 'Nature immense'. Gabriel Bacquier's Mephistopheles is more effective. His first entry, with Prêtre and the strings rousing themselves briefly to a crackling accompaniment, is excellent – amused, taunting, yet frighteningly menacing. It is clear what a fine Mephisto he could be; thereafter his performance declines into mediocrity. By far the best is Janet Baker. True, her voice lacks power in the duet and trio, and her opening phrases ('Que l'air est étouffant', etc.) are sung in a 'little girl' tone that sounds self-conscious. But she is the only Marguerite to hit exactly the right manner for the 'Roi de Thulé', that of a song sung with only half the singer's mind on it, while she is doing something else (in this case, braiding her hair). Her Romance has an air of heartbreak that is equalled by few other singers, and inspires the cor anglais player to richly expressive tone and phrasing. The enumeration of Faust's qualities ('sa marche que j'admire', etc.) is beautifully done. At the climax she observes the *crescendo* at 'retenir' and links the note to the next phrase, 'O caresses de flamme', with telling effect; and her final 'Hélas' breathes a sense of quiet but extreme desolation. She alone, in this shoddy performance, is able to create an artistic ambience.

After Prêtre, to listen to Markevitch (1960) is a tonic. The vital, singing line of the strings of the Lamoureux Orchestra in 'Le vieil hiver' gives the performance a lively start, and the sweet tone and natural phrasing of the French-Canadian tenor Richard Verreau confirm the good impression.

Verreau's singing is not very varied and at times, gliding too easily over the notes, suggests an abstracted, thoughtless Faust; but he achieves a ringing climax to 'Nature immense'. By that time, however, Markevitch has thrown away his advantage. It's not only that, presumably to fit the work onto four sides, he countenances a number of cuts (some large, like the first half of the Easter Hymn and a big chunk of the Minuet, others small and fiddly). The interpretation as a whole acquires a slightly hysterical sense of haste from the accumulation of fast tempi: the March (recalling Shaw's remark apropos of an electrifying performance under Hallé, 'taken at about half the speed at which Lamoureux vainly tries to make it "go" '), the double chorus, the Minuet (what is left of it), the duet. Verreau, though not ideal, is the best of the soloists. Consuelo Rubio's Marguerite, never very convincing, becomes blowzy in the duet and the Romance; her rich, dark voice spreads badly under pressure in the higher register. Michel Roux, the Mephistopheles, does his best to turn his vocal limitations to account, and at first his slightly camp, ageing manservant is not ineffective; but it soon palls. He is weakest in the Evocation, the Serenade and the climax of the Ride to the Abyss (where he loses his place), at his most appealing and suggestive in the final recitative 'A la voûte azurée'; a pity that Markevitch chose to make a large cut in it.

The second Deutsche Grammophon recording is conducted by Ozawa and dates from 1974. It has a dream orchestra, the Boston Symphony. This is the best playing of the score on disc. The 'soldiers', in fact, are magnificent. It is their 'general' I have doubts about. Ozawa secures a brilliant performance from the orchestra, and good work from the Tanglewood Festival Chorus; and in music in which precision, perfectly balanced textures and a just tempo lead by themselves to the right expression he is admirable. The final numbers, where personal feeling is not present, are superlatively well done. There is a prodigious climax to the Ride to the Abyss, a Pandemonium of awesome power, and an Apotheosis irradiated with a luminous serenity, such as none of the other versions come near equalling. Elsewhere, however, Ozawa sounds uninvolved. His interpretation moves with superb assurance over the surface of the score, getting the details in place but seemingly ignoring the human emotions which animate it. A stronger cast might have kindled his interest. But Stuart Burrows, over-parted as Faust even on a recording, makes a feeble impression (though it is to his credit that unlike most tenors he doesn't speed up during 'Nature immense'); and Donald McIntyre, the Mephistopheles, though he works hard and has moments of power and authority, is handicapped by a language and style relatively unfamiliar to him. Edith Mathis comes out the best of the three. Her rather light soprano voice cannot command the sustained tone or the strong lower notes required in the Romance, nor does she manage much of a high B flat in the trio, but her singing from the first is responsive to the music's dramatic character. The long opening recitative sounds a note both of timidity and of exaltation, and the Romance, especially the latter half, has a keen sense of pathos.

It might have been expected that the Colin Davis recording (1973), following his masterly *Troyens* and *Benvenuto Cellini*, would give us something like a definitive version of this familiar but elusive work. It has Gedda, Veasey, Bastin and the London Symphony Orchestra and Chorus: if not ideal participants, on paper at least unusually strong ones. But the performance is uncharacteristically laboured. Davis's interpretation exhibits many fine intentions. He sets some unusually broad tempi, in principle very welcome, as the movements concerned – 'Sans regrets', the double chorus, the duet, 'Nature immense' – often glide by too glibly. But in practice they don't quite take off, because the playing has insufficient life and 'lift'. 'Le vieil hiver', the opening number, is symptomatic: a grand conception, but weighed down by pedestrian phrasing. The strings of the LSO sound – for them – in unresponsive, lacklustre form, the violins especially. The same is true of the LSO Chorus; their tone lacks body and warmth, and the tenors are particularly weak. As Faust, Gedda gives a far more considered and artistic performance than on the Prêtre recording, but there is a sense of effort and a lack of bloom that are evidence of advancing years, though 'Merci, doux crépuscule' is elegantly done, and his *pianissimo* high C sharp in the duet still leaves all other recorded Fausts far behind. Like many Marguerites, Veasey finds the 'Roi de Thulé' harder to bring off than the Romance. The former lacks natural flow and suffers from slight flatness of pitch (and from an undistinguished viola *obbligato*). In the Romance, inspired by sensitive cor anglais playing, she gains in eloquence as the music proceeds, rising to a wild grief in the *più mosso* section and a sense of passionate abandonment in 'voir s'exhaler mon âme dans ses baisers d'amour'.

The best of the soloists, however, is Jules Bastin, the Mephistopheles. No other Mephisto declaims the text as powerfully and subtly, none finds so much nuance and colour in it or rolls it round his tongue with such sardonic relish or quiet meaningfulness. There are certainly more beautiful 'Voici des roses'. But his headlong, brilliant 'Flea' is a tour de force, at once whimsical and brutal, and 'A la voûte azurée' is a masterpiece of chilling irony. Indeed, there are passages that go just as one would wish. The whole scene in Auerbach's cellar, where orchestral finesse is much less important and the chorus is safely doubled by brass and woodwind, has great panache. Here Richard Van Allan (Brander) makes a strong contribution; it is good, too, to hear the tubas booming away in the accompaniment to the choruses, leaving the trombones to Mephistopheles, whose instruments they are.

Daniel Barenboim's performance – Deutsche Grammophon's third and most recent *Damnation* (1978) – comes tantalizingly close to answering the need for a first-rate version. It has, in the Orchestre de Paris, a group of French musicians who respond to Berlioz's music as to their natural heritage. The chorus, the Choeurs de l'Orchestre de Paris, is the best on record, trained to a near-professional sonority and exactitude by Arthur Oldham (who was so much less successful with the LSO Chorus). Barenboim understands the score, and knows that, to make it spark, it is not necessary to set fast tempi. The opening, taken at an almost ambling pace, is intensely springlike in feeling; the double chorus moves unhurriedly but with a powerful swagger; the *moderato* pace of the Minuet brings out the ritual element in this witty, disturbing piece. The quicker speed adopted in the reprise of the duet is a rare example of Barenboim not giving the music time to register. It is the casting that lets the performance down. Placido Domingo is an imaginative choice for Faust, and, tenors capable of singing Berlioz being in short supply, a valuable recruit; but it must be said that here he is still feeling his way. The enunciation of the French text causes him some problems, for example in the Easter Hymn ('Sur l'aîle de ces chants vas-tu voler aux cieux?' is a gabble), and in 'Le vieil hiver' the unfamiliarity of the score betrays him into some rhythmically imprecise singing, to the detriment of the ensemble. But there are thrilling sounds in the duet and in 'Nature immense'. With more experience of the part and some hard work on his French he could be a very impressive Faust. If Domingo is unstylish but exciting, Yvonne Minton's Marguerite is disappointingly dull – characterless in 'Le roi de Thulé', more impressive yet curiously unmoving in the Romance. Bastin makes a predictably pungent Brander. The surprise star of the cast is the Mephistopheles of Fischer-Dieskau. The very sophistication that can occasionally make his lieder-singing sound contrived is an asset in the part of the prince of illusionists and master of calculation. Fischer-Dieskau holds sway over the role from his first entry. His sinister joviality as the cynical 'Spirit of Life' is spine-chilling. There is no 'Voici des roses' more atmospheric than his, and in the trio he achieves a truly demonic energy. Only his 'Flea' lacks savour.

It is hard to say exactly why the Solti recording (Decca) disappoints. Up to a certain point it is remarkably good. It has a magnificent orchestra (Chicago Symphony), an adequate choir (Chicago Symphony Orchestra Chorus) and a better-than-average cast. The American tenor Kenneth Riegel sounds slightly constricted in tone, and in the duet he adopts a jerky, overemphatic style which breaks up the vocal line; but this is untypical. Elsewhere his singing is both virile and musical, with arrestingly bright timbre, wellshaped phrasing and keen dramatic involvement; and he rises to the challenge of 'Nature immense', responding to the grandeur and to the desperation of the music. Frederica von Stade, the Marguerite, sings with much more understanding, variety and passion than her earlier recital recording of the Romance (see below) would suggest, and the beauty of her voice is a constant pleasure. marred only by her oddly genteel way of pronouncing the vowel sound 'ou'. The Mephisto of the Belgian bass-baritone José van Dam is one of the most convincing and finely sung on disc. 'Voici des roses' is a model of suavity and quiet power, and his domination over Faust in Part 4 is conveyed with impressive force and authority.

Solti paces the score well: there are few tempi that do not seem right. His reading abounds in telling dramatic detail: jagged, violent double-bass phrases at the end of the duet, piquant, debonair violins in the 'Flea'; the exquisite lament of the cor anglais in the Romance, the menacing cornet solo in 'Voici des roses', the prodigious string *crescendi* in 'Nature immense' and the rumbling, rolling bass lines in the same piece, the wild, distracted oboe in the Ride to the Abyss – such examples could be multiplied. The Chicago players (apart from an occasional imprecision of ensemble and one very strange trombone chord in 'Voici des roses') make the most of their opportunities. Yet in comparison with their Boston rivals or the Orchestre de Paris they do not yet have the music in their bloodstream. Their splendid playing sounds like the product of skill and application but not of instinctive understanding – the sense of 'the intention of every orchestral touch'. With all its formidable qualities the performance, to my mind, lacks the vital spark.

The ten-disc set issued in 1933 under Piero Coppola comes somewhere between the complete (or near-complete) versions and the highlights and single numbers. This was the first recorded *Damnation*, and it has some good points. Coppola brings out many nice touches in the orchestra (the Orchestre des Concerts Pasdeloup) that modern recordings often manage to obscure. The choral singing (Chorus Saint Gervais) is well drilled and sensitive; the Sylphs' Chorus, with its gently flowing tempo and transparent textures, is just about the best version on record. José de Trevi is a competent Faust. Mireille Berthon, the Marguerite, has one of those neat, no-nonsense French soprano voices, bright and hard as a new pin. 'Tout s'efface', sings Marguerite at the moment of her seduction; but this one remains thoroughly in control, not a stocking rumpled or a hair out of place. Charles Panzéra's Mephistopheles begins with some polite if well-articulated singing in Auerbach's Cellar (the first encounter with Faust is cut), then produces a 'Voici des roses' as fine as any on disc. This is a model of *bel canto* used in the service of dramatic expression: velvet tone and phrasing, with the hint of an iron hand. 'Où glissera sur toi plus d'un baiser vermeil' is sung in a beautifully veiled, mysterious *pianissimo*, the high Ds at 'Ecoute' with a masterly resort to head voice. The whole aria becomes a thing of magical deception, with an undercurrent of immortal longings.

A few of the delicate touches of the Coppola recording would not have come amiss in the disc of highlights issued in 1960 under André Cluytens. The Paris Opéra Orchestra is at an even lower ebb than on the Prêtre recording, and the Chorus lamentable. The soloists promise good things but achieve them only intermittently. Gérard Souzay brings to the 'Flea' and the Serenade his usual care for diction and inflexion, but try as he will it goes against the grain: this is Mephistopheles in a frock-coat, ineluctably respectable. Gedda is sluggish in 'Le vieil hiver' (this is at least partly the conductor's fault), better in 'Merci, doux crépuscule', and better still in 'Nature immense': his voice is in its prime, and the interpretation grand and spacious; for once, Cluytens and the orchestra rise to the occasion. After a heavy accompaniment to the 'Roi de Thulé' they also rouse themselves in the Romance, where the dark, glowing tone of the cor anglais matches the beauty of Rita Gorr's tone and her passionately sensuous phrasing. Gorr's voice, inappropriately sumptuous in the 'Roi de Thulé', is heard to fine effect here, except for some ominously strained notes above the stave.

There is nothing much to say about the half-LP of highlights sung by Raoul Jobin and the Greek mezzo Irma Kolassi with the LSO under Fistoulari (LXT 5034, coupled with extracts from *Werther*). I find Kolassi's voice an attractive mixture of dark and bright, but here she does little with it. Her detached manner achieves a merely negative effect in 'Le roi de Thulé' and is out of place in the Romance. Jobin is an uninteresting Faust, his singing characterless, his voice lacking in timbre. 'Sans regrets' is cautiously sung, and the only virtue of his 'Nature immense' is that he keeps to the tempo. The duet is taken meaninglessly fast; and the whole thing is singularly devoid of dramatic feeling. One further excerpt deserves special mention: a recording of the Elbe scene, taken from the broadcast of a Toscanini concert with the NBC Symphony Orchestra, and Mack Harrell as Mephistopheles, on 16 February 1947 (ATS 1058). The interpretation is leisurely, lyrical, strongly and beautifully shaped, and gives a glimpse of the fine things that might be expected of a Toscanini performance of the whole work. But there is no suggestion in Harvey Sachs's authoritative biography that he ever conducted the complete *Damnation* in America.

The single-number recordings offer a rich choice of Marguerites and Mephistos, and only slightly fewer Fausts. I have unearthed fifteen. None of them is ideal. Desmond Shawe-Taylor remembers a performance of the *Damnation* at the Opéra in which Georges Thill sang the opening number, 'Le vieil hiver', with overwhelming splendour. Unfortunately Thill doesn't seem to have recorded it. 'Le vieil hiver' is sung by another French tenor in the same mould, Léon Beyle (Disque 032134 5, made in about 1910 when he was forty). The voice is firm and even, with a heroic gleam and an admirably steady line; the high A on 'éclatants' rings out grandly. But the quieter tones of Faust's paean to awakening Nature find him lacking in suavity, and 'Sans regrets' on the other side betrays the same deficiency: it is just strong, well-drilled, rhythmical singing, without nuances.

Beyle made many recordings, but I have not come across a 'Nature immense'. He may well have sung it more accurately than Thill does on a Columbia disc made in about 1929 (L 2064; LV 224) which is marred by some imprecise rhythm and wrong note-values. At its best, however, it is magnificent – the effortless opening out of tone at 'fière', the grandeur of 'je retrouve ma force'. Unfortunately the engineer loses his nerve in the final stretch and turns down the volume just as Thill is moving to the climax of the piece with the stride of an Olympic athlete.

Fernand Ansseau's performance (DB 487; LV 116) shows an ever-greater disregard of the printed notes. The dragging out of the final bars is clearly designed to draw attention to his voice, but though quite heroic it is hardly in the Thill class. A much more formidable rival is Paul Franz, a great French *Heldentenor* of the generation before Thill. His 'Nature immense', from the early 1920s (Pathé 0258; Cantilena 6243) is rock-steady – amid considerable discouragement from the orchestra's wrong notes, altered pitches and sloppy rhythm – and full of presence and authority. The voice, to judge by the recording, does not quite have the glow and force of Thill's, but it was clearly a fine instrument, used here with taste and skill. By contrast, Albert Vaguet's 'Nature immense' (Pathé 107), recorded a few years before Franz's, suggests a forced-up baritone. Though the monologue does not go above A and the *tessitura* is not particularly high, he almost kills himself getting there; this, however, lends the performance a certain undeniable tension. Charles Rousselière's bright, strong voice sounds much more naturally suited to the lie of the music, but his 1907 version (Pathé 4710; Club 99.95) is carelessly sung, and there is a big cut in the middle.

The version by René Maison (Od. 123 502), a Paris Opéra tenor of the interwar years later heard at the Met., has been reissued on CBS 76691 as part of 'Les très riches heures de l'Opéra de Paris', unfortunately transferred a good half a tone sharp, which accentuates the singer's somewhat bleating quality. The rapid vibrato and thin, penetrating timbre may not be to all tastes; but he delivers the music with conviction. That cannot be said for Théo Beets (Poly. 516682, from the early 1930s). His voice has nowhere near the necessary power, and he seems to acknowledge the fact by getting appreciably faster at 'Oui, soufflez, ouragans'. The timpani player loses his place. Only in Beets's final bars does the music come momentarily to life.

In 'Merci, doux crépuscule' on the other side, Beets, after an uncertain start, sounds more at home, and there are some long-breathed phrases; but he does not have much to say. A more assured account of the aria is the one by Henri Saint-Cricq (Pathé X 7236), a lyric tenor with attractively suave, bright, forward tone. There are two versions in Italian – 'A te grazie, o crepuscolo' – one by Giuseppe Krismer (Fono. 92577; GV 69) which despite an insufficiently smooth, over-emphatic style and a rather reedy timbre achieves a sense of atmosphere. The other, by Giovanni Malipiero, is much superior, alive to the poetry of the aria and very sensitively sung (DB 5445; Tima 14). Malipiero was clearly an artist, and he has the benefit of first-rate orchestral accompaniment under an anonymous conductor (possibly Antonio Guarnieri who was active in Italy at the time the recording was made, about 1942). 'Natura immensa', on the other side, is a little less good: to make up for a certain lack of power in his essentially lyric voice the singer occasionally resorts to bluster. Once again the accompaniment is excellent.

There is an impressively large coven of Mephistos. Several of them are Italian. *Damnation* has had periods of popularity in Italy; Toscanini, for example, gave twenty-six performances at La Scala in the 1902–3 season.* The Mephistopheles in that production was Giuseppe de Luca, who a couple of years later recorded all three solos with piano accompaniment (Fono. 39165/68170 transferred to LP on Rococo R 24 and also – minus the Serenade

* Toscanini's Faust was Zenatello. All that survives on disc is a version with piano of the brief lyrical interlude ('Adieu donc belle nuit' – 'Addio notte soave'), taken at so funereal a pace as to be meaningless. This *cannot* have been Toscanini's tempo.

– on CO 391). The Serenade is vigorously but not very imaginatively sung, but the other two pieces make a powerful impression. If in the 'Song of the Flea' (C'era una volta'), with its 'devilish' laughs after verses 1 and 3, its emphatic declamation and its very deliberate preceding recitative, Mephistopheles's rapier becomes a bludgeon, the result is none the less effective – a dark, imposing portrayal. 'Voici des roses' ('Su queste rose') is beautifully sung: sensuous, virile yet delicate, with a memorable *diminuendo*, to a *piano* of extraordinary intensity, at 'di parole divine tu sentirai l'incanto', and a haunting *pianissimo* at the second 'ascolta', taken at the higher octave. Only the too-loud cadential bars impair the magical effect.

In comparison Battistini's 'Su queste rose' (DB 189; GV 79), fine though it is, sounds like an exercise in *bel canto* – if one excepts the surprising intrusive 'h' at 'notte'. Despite some flatness of pitch in the first few bars, Eugenio Giraldoni's caressing-menacing account of the aria is more authentic and alive (Fono. 92423; Club 99.58).

The other two pieces lend themselves less well than 'Voici des roses' to the Italian language. Indeed, the coarse-grained effect of de Luca's 'Flea' may well be due partly to translation. Tito Gobbi's pungently declaimed performance (on a previously unpublished recording of 1955, HLM 7166) goes much further in the same direction, with a fantastic repertoire of stage laughs paraded at every conceivable and inconceivable opportunity and a general air of sweaty conviviality, as if he were not Mephisto mocking the tavern drunks but Leporello joining them at their own level. But I must admit the result is irresistible.

Titta Ruffo's Serenade (DA 164; Rococo 5361) goes all out for force, not wit. Sparing with the dotted notes, relentlessly unsubtle in character, it nevertheless has a certain brutal power. Quite apart from being sung in French, Riccardo Stracciari's Serenade, which he recorded in 1925 when he was fifty, could hardly be more contrasted. The manner is aristocratic, the singing marked by admirable legato; but I find it flavourless (Col. X324; GV 501). Emilio de Gogorza's Serenade, also sung in French (DB 184; Cantilena 6203) is much livelier – insinuating, with a nice light sneer to it, but a trifle unrhythmical.

To complete the non-French (or non-Belgian) Mephistos, neither Jerome Hines (CBS 4379) nor George London (Columbia P 14179), both singing in French, makes much of the Serenade, though London's performance has a nice leisurely swing, and the sound of his dark, ominous voice raises hopes. There is also a version in English by Robert Radford (E 388), complete with the preceding recitative ('To this *lewt* I sing a serenade'). Despite the virtuoso demonic laughs in the final bar of the recitative, this is an intensely genteel interpretation. The Russian-born bass Georges Baklanov sings 'Voici des roses' with attractively virile, incisive tone but is inclined to overdo the *rubato* (7–32020; LV 118).

The dozen or so French Mephistos make a curiously disappointing lot. Few of them can boast a 'Flea' to approach the panache of Bastin's on the

Philips complete recording or a 'Voici des roses' to equal Panzéra's on the ten-disc 1933 set. Of those who recorded all three solos, two are also heard on complete recordings or highlights, Martial Singher and Gérard Souzay. Souzay gives a more convincing account of the role on a disc of 'French Operatic Arias' (LXT 5269) than on the Cluytens record of extracts. The Serenade is nicely done, but the 'Flea' again suggests, incongruously, a Mephistopheles with no iron in his nature and without much sense of humour. Singher's 'Flea' has more life and more light and shade than on the Münch complete recording, but 'Voici des roses' is prosaic and the Serenade merely vigorous (Am. Col. 71679). Jean Segani's cheerful but quite unmenacing 'Flea' (Alpha SP 6014) and Tilkin Servais's self-consciously *bel canto* account of the same piece (Disque P 618, coupled with an excellent performance of Brander's 'Rat Song' by Willy Tubiana) may also be passed over quickly.

Better are Roger Bourdin (Od. 188 534) and José Beckmans (Poly. 561010), each of whom recorded two of the three pieces. Bourdin's 'Voici des roses', though not very seductive and sung with a kind of grave formality, is not to be dismissed. His 'Flea', for which he changes to a quite different, much lighter timbre, is notable for its exact, well-pointed rhythm. Beckmans labours the start of 'Voici des roses' and in doing so falls behind the conductor, but he improves and ends by generating a considerable sense of power. His Serenade shows keen attention to diction and conveys here and there a feeling of menace, without catching the essential note of debonair, faintly sneering mockery combined with a sense of diabolical power in reserve. Etienne Billot, a baritone active at the Opéra-Comique between the wars, comes much nearer it in his lightly teasing performance, preceded by a scathing recitative, and showing its claws in a ferocious final 'Que fais-tu?' But his 'Flea' – reissued half a tone up, in F sharp – has little dramatic character, though the diction is excellent. Both these are on CBS's 'Très riches heures de l'Opéra de Paris' (76691). Billot's 'Voici des roses' (Od. 188 731) is not very interesting. Two other French Mephistos may be briefly mentioned – Léon Rothier, whose very early 'Voici des roses', with piano accompaniment, is quite strong if prosaic, and Jean Claverie, who gives a disciplined, rhythmical account of the Serenade (Brunswick 29560; Cantilena 6203).

That leaves the four most distinguished names, Plançon, Journet, Renaud and Vanni Marcoux. Strangely, though an amalgam of their best would produce a princely Mephistopheles, none of them is consistently satisfactory. This may seem unfair to Vanni Marcoux, who didn't record a 'Voici des roses' (or if he did, I haven't managed to discover it); but his Serenade, after a wonderfully leering recitative, is not quite as characterful as his vivid, commanding 'Flea' led me to expect. The 'Flea', well conducted by the lively Coppola, was recorded uncomfortably close to the microphone, but the power of personality that leaps from Vanni Marcoux's performance is independent of artificial aids (DA 1158; Rococo 5358). The great Pol Plançon recorded all three pieces. In two of them, the 'Flea' and 'Voici des roses', he tends to sing sharp. 'Voici des roses' (DB 659; GV 76) remains, for all that, a magisterial piece of velvet-smooth legato singing. But best, to my mind, is his suavely sinister 1906 Serenade on another disc (DA 340; GV 39): it reconciles *bel canto* with vivid diction and potent characterization. The Serenade of 1903 with piano accompaniment is uneventfully bland (3–32179; GV 76).

There are also two recordings of the Serenade by Marcel Journet, one with piano (3–32687) and the other with orchestra (DA 759; LV 55, strings playing *arco*, not *pizzicato*!), neither especially memorable. Journet is heard to much greater advantage in the Evocation, 'Esprits de flammes inconstantes', where Mephistopheles summons his creatures, the will o' the wisps (Disque P 349). This is regal singing, at once masterfully declaimed and rich-toned, melodious.

Maurice Renaud's Serenade (D 858; GV 52, 1902) with piano accompaniment is much more impressive than Journet's, but its jocularity sounds slightly forced. There is also the feeling of a 'performance' about his 1908 'Voici des roses' on the same disc; but it is noble singing, with both the long-spanned phrases and the hint of aching regret for lost bliss that mark a great performance of this music. Even better, if anything, is Journet's 'Voici des roses' with piano accompaniment (3–32686; RS 304). Unfortunately the transfer suffers from fluctuations of pitch.

Apart from the Serenade, Marguerite's Romance 'D'amour l'ardente flamme' is the most recorded of all the solo numbers in *Damnation*. There has been, understandably, less competition for the ballad 'Le roi de Thulé', which gives the singer far fewer opportunities and is also much harder to bring off. It should sound at once offhand and exotic, monotonous and touched with a hint of the wonderful. Marguerite is singing, humming almost, idly to herself while she plaits her hair; but – as the tritone in the melodic line suggests – she is, without knowing it, in the power of Mephistopheles. The problem is to find the narrow path between too much expression and too little – to sound neither laboured nor facile. Some mezzo-sopranos (e.g. Gorr, Veasey) have difficulty in lightening their voices so that the angular phrases move easily, without an inappropriate sense of effort. Others, like Solange Michel (Pathé DTX 137), are simply dull – monotonous in the wrong sense.

Suzanne Juyol's muscular rendering conjures up a brisk, efficient Marguerite who would stand no nonsense from Faust or Mephistopheles (DB 11188). Nor can I summon much enthusiasm for the version that Ninon Vallin recorded – together with the Romance and (with Guy Fouché) the duet – in 1955 when the singer was fifty-nine (P 3082). The voice sounds admirably clear, firm and focused, but the interpretation is quite unremarkable.

Happily the remaining three recordings are much nearer the mark. The earliest, by Auguez de Montalant, made in 1909 (33775; Club 99.112), achieves the expressive inexpressivity that eludes so many singers. Her tempo is slow, but the music has the right dreamlike flow. It is a pity that verse two is omitted and the epilogue replaced by a version of the orchestral refrain. The splendid Germaine Martinelli, without overloading the song, evokes a mood of telling melancholy simply by means of line and timbre. I find her more remarkable in the Romance, but this is a good performance (Poly. 566040). In some ways the most striking recording is Conchita Supervia's (HMB 11; OASI 533). It has the slightly unearthly tang which is so rare but which, when you hear it, you recognize as essential to the music. This quality is independent of the Mediterranean flavour of her accent (or of a slight flatness of pitch here and there); it comes from the vibrant sound of her voice and from the subtle emphasis she gives, for example, to the melody's poignantly flattened sixth.

I have heard fourteen versions of the Romance, fifteen if you count the aged Geraldine Farrar singing the tune while accompanying herself at the piano with a random succession of chords (IRCC L 7001). American singers are well represented, beginning with Auguez de Montalant who, though she made her home in France, was born in Baltimore. Her 1911 recording (033 103/4; Club 99.112) sounds its age, and as a piece of characterization is therefore hard to assess, but the beauty of her finely focused tone and the grace of her singing are unmistakable. (She can also be heard singing the trio with Beyle and Journet on Disque GC 34234.) Rose Bampton's account of the Romance is very much a recital performance, correct but lifeless (Victor 12–0015; CSLP 504). The other four recordings by American-born singers have considerable virtues. Those of Leontyne Price's version are more vocal than interpretative. The music is grandly though also feelingly sung, with a strongly drawn melodic line but without much variety of expression (ARL1 2529). Frederica von Stade's Romance (CBS 76522) is movingly desolate; the naturally plaintive quality of her voice fits the music, and the phrases are sensitively turned. All that is needed to make it memorable is a greater sense of urgency; this Marguerite sounds a little too resigned to her loss. How intense an utterance of grief it is we are instantly reminded by the passionate singing of Shirley Verrett (SB 6790). The tone-quality is glorious, but never an end in itself or a medium for generalized emotion. She varies its colour in response to the moods of the music, lightening it with the gleam of a smile at 'sourire', finding a sharper expression of pain under the goad of memory. Only Callas conveys a sense of wilder longing (IC 053 00578). The very first phrase establishes an atmosphere of utter forlornness, and she shapes the performance from that point, with supreme intelligence and musicianship and with an understanding of Berliozian phrasing and dramatic style that make it a truly tragic oversight that she never sang Cassandra or Dido. There are few Marguerites who would not wither in the flame of her genius.

One of them is Germaine Martinelli (Poly. 566040). Perhaps she suggests too mature a woman; but what an artist she was. The expressiveness of her *rubato*, her subtle, wonderfully apt and vital colouring of the words are unequalled on disc or – in my experience – off it. There is also a good performance by Jeanne-Marié de l'Isle, recorded in 1905 (Zono. X 83162); the voice is touchingly pure and girlish, the words tellingly vivid. Unfortunately she recorded only as far as bar 50, omitting more than half the piece.

The rest of the French contingent is disappointing. Ninon Vallin I have already mentioned. I like Yvonne Gall's clear, rather childlike voice (LFX 5; Club 99.118) but not the unimaginative use she makes of it. (Like nearly all the earlier generation of recorded Marguerites she replaces 'd'une amoureuse flamme' in bars 67–69 with the less improper 'd'amour l'ardente flamme'.) Suzanne Juyol (DB 11188) is a trifle less unconvincing than in her 'Roi de Thulé', but the animation of the final verses comes too late to save her. Régine Crespin (SET 520) is her usual authoritative self, but in a manner – grand and placid – quite at variance with the dramatic content of the music; and, though a soprano, she finds the piece uncomfortably high for her. Nor is she in rapport with the conductor, Alain Lombard, to judge by some poor ensemble. As for Lyne Dourian (Philips 835 791 LY), she has really nothing to say. Joan Hammond's performance (BLP 1073), though handicapped by the English language as well as by a fundamental lack of sensuality, puts these phlegmatic ladies to shame by its energy and enthusiasm.

The ideal cast? A disciplined Thill, Franz, or Poleri; Vanni Marcoux, Bastin, Van Dam, perhaps Bacquier under a conductor who realized his potential; Callas, Martinelli, Baker, de Montalant or Verrett; the choir of the Orchestre de Paris or the present-day rejuvenated Opéra Chorus; the Boston Symphony, under an amalgam of Münch, Davis, Solti and Barenboim, with Ozawa for the final scene. One day we may get a complete *Damnation* which leaves nothing to be desired. Or may be that is a will o' the wisp – as Mephistopheles would say, *sancta simplicitas*!

BÉATRICE ET BÉNÉDICT

B Béatrice; *H* Héro; *U* Ursule; *Bén* Bénédict; *C* Claudio; *DP* Don Pedro; *S* Somarone

1962 Veasey *B*; Cantelo *H*; Watts *U*; Mitchinson *Bén*; Cameron *C*; Shirley-Quirk *DP*; Shilling *S* / St Anthony Singers, LSO / C. Davis L'Oiseau-Lyre SOL 256–7

1977 Baker *B*; Eda-Pierre *H*; Watts *U*; Tear *Bén*; Allen *C*; Lloyd *DP*; Bastin *S* / Alldis Choir, LSO /
C. Davis
Philips 6700 121

1981 Minton *B*; Cotrubas *H*; Denize *U*; Domingo *Bén*; Soyer *C*; Macurdy *DP* Fischer-Dieskau *S* / Paris Opéra Chorus and Orch. / Barenboim
DG 2707 130

BENVENUTO CELLINI

1972 Gedda *Cellini*; Bastin *Balducci*; Massard *Fieramosca*; Soyer *Pope*; Herincx *Pompeo*; Eda-Pierre *Teresa*; Berbié *Ascanio* / Royal
Opera House Chorus, BBC SO / C. Davis
Philips 6707 019 ④ 7675 002

LA DAMNATION DE FAUST

F Faust; *M* Mephistopheles; *Mar* Marguerite; *B* Brander

1948 Jouatte *F*; Cabanel *M*; Laurena
Mar; Pactat *B* / Passani Chorus,
Radio Paris Orch. / Fournet
Columbia ⓜ FHX 5003–5
Columbia (US) ⓜ SL 110

1954 Poleri *F*; Singher *M*; Danco *Mar*;
Gramm *B* / Harvard Glee Club,
Radcliffe Choral Society, Boston
SO / Münch
RCA (UK) ⓒ VICS 6019
(US) ⓜ AVL2 0679

1960 Verreau *F*; Roux *M*; Rubio *Mar*;
Mollet *B* / Brasseur Choir, French
National Radio Choir, Lamoureux
Orch. / Markevitch
DG 2705 026
US 2700 112

1969 Gedda *F*; Bacquier *M*; Baker
Mar; Thau *B* / Paris Opéra
Chorus, Orch. de Paris / Prêtre
EMI 2C 167 02019–20
Angel SCL 3758

1973 Gedda *F*; Bastin *M*; Veasey *Mar*;
Van Allan *B* / Ambrosian Singers,
Wandsworth School Boys' Choir,
LSO / C. Davis
Philips 6703 042

1974 Burrows *F*; McIntyre *M*; Mathis
Mar; Paul *B* / Tanglewood

Festival Chorus, Boston Boychoir,
Boston SO / Ozawa
DG 2709 048

1978 Domingo *F*; Fischer-Dieskau *M*;
Minton *Mar*; Bastin *B* / Orch. de
Paris and Chorus / Barenboim
DG 2709 087

1980 Riegel *F*; Van Dam *M*; Von Stade
Mar; King *Br* / Chicago SO and
Chorus / Solti
London LDR 73007
Decca D259D3 K259K33

1933 (abridged) de Trevi *F*; Panzéra *M*;
Berthon *Mar*; Morturier *B* / St
Gervais Chorus, Pasdeloup Orch.
/ Coppola
HMV C 2399–2408

1952 (excerpts) Fouché *F*; Vallin *Mar*; /
Pasdeloup Orch. / Cruchon
Vega ⓜ L35PO367

1954 (excerpts) Jobin *F*; Kolassi *Mar* /
LSO / Fistoulari
Decca ⓜ LXT 5034

1961 (excerpts) Gedda *F*; Souzay *M*;
Gorr *Mar* / Paris Opéra Chorus
and Orch. / Cluytens
EMI 2C 061 11684
CFP CFP40039

LES TROYENS

D Dido; *A* Aeneas; *C* Cassandra; *Cor* Corebus; *An* Anna; *N* Narbal; *As* Ascanius;
I Iopas; *P* Priam; *M* Mercury; *H* Hecuba; *Hy* Hylas

1969 Veasey *D*; Vickers *A*; Lindholm
C; Glossop *Cor*; Begg *An*; Soyer
N; Howells *As*; Partridge *I*; Thau
P; *M*; Bainbridge *H*; Davies *Hy* /
Wandsworth School Boys' Choir,
Royal Opera House Chorus and
Orch./ Davis
Philips 6709 002

1947 (broadcast performance) Ferrer *D*;
C; Giraudeau *A*; Cambon *Cor*; *N*;
Corke *An*; *H*; Braneze *As*;
Vroons *I*; Joynt *P*; Frank *M*;
Cunningham *Hy*/BBC Theatre
Chorus, RPO / Beecham
Melodram ⓜ MEL 303

1952 (Part 2 – 'Les Troyens à

Carthage') Mandikian *D*;
Giraudeau *A*; Collard *An*; Depraz
N; Rolle *As*; Gallet *I*; *H* / Paris
Vocal Ensemble, Paris
Conservatoire Orch. / Scherchen
Ducretet-Thomson (UK) ⓜ DTL
93001–3
(France) ⓜ 300C117–9

1965 (excerpts) Crespin *D*; *C*; Chauvet
A; Béllary *As*; Vernet *N*; Dunan
I; Hurteau *M* / Paris Opéra
Fanfare, Chorus and Orch. /
Prêtre
EMI 2C 181 16395–6
Angel SBL 3670

Les Pêcheurs de perles

LORD HAREWOOD

Les Pêcheurs de perles, written when Bizet was twenty-four, is no masterpiece of music drama to set beside *Carmen*, yet it tops the poll whenever a
magazine asks its readers which operas they would like to see join the
repertory. Dramatic drawbacks, such as the too casual election of Zurga as
chief, the inept treatment of his debt to Leila for saving his life and the
necklace which symbolizes it, the unconvincing denouement, are as nothing
when set against the tremendous 'plus' of Bizet's melodic invention and the
skill with which he manipulates it. The score is packed with memorable
tunes, each beautifully turned, apposite to the not always plausibly told
drama, more than just a vehicle for fine singing.

Most performances, and all but one of the complete recordings, have until
recently perpetuated the unauthorized changes to Bizet's original, contained
in posthumously published vocal scores. For nearly a century these
superseded the 1863 score and in them the great duet in Act 1, 'Au fond du
temple saint', is rewritten to exclude its contrasted F major final section and
substitute a return to the main theme; some unnecessary cuts are made in
the scene between Leila and Zurga; and there is extensive tampering with
the finale, involving a new trio 'O lumière sainte' (written by Benjamin
Godard and set to the words Bizet used for a shorter duet for the two lovers),
a repeat of a chorus from earlier in the scene, and a different ending. Since
no full score survives, Bizet's orchestral intentions for these scenes have to
be reconstructed from the 1863 vocal score. For Act 3, recent moves towards
accuracy result in pure gain, but I must admit that repeated hearings in
theatre and on record leave me with much sympathy for the anonymous
musician who cut the second half of the Act 1 duet and allowed us to hear
the main theme again.

All but one of the complete recordings use the 'corrupt' version as described above, some with additional cuts traditionally sanctioned at the
Opéra-Comique. The earliest, originally issued by Nixa, has reappeared
under the Everest-Cetra label. It is technically rather dim, but capably conducted by Leibowitz, a 'modern' musician responsible for several enjoyable
recordings of 'traditional' operatic music. There is a charming Leila from the
lirico-coloratura Mattiwilda Dobbs, a one-time pupil of Pierre Bernac's and

able to float a top note with the best of Leilas, and some strong dramatic singing from Jean Borthayre as Zurga. Enzo Seri's voice rings out at the top, but he often sounds ill at ease as Nadir and is one of two tenors in complete sets to transpose the aria.

A year later, Philips took advantage of their contract with Léopold Simoneau to make a recording with him, and I would unhesitatingly class his Nadir as the finest on record. There are sounds of uncommon beauty in, for instance, the recitative before the Act 1 duet, his performance of the aria is beautifully sustained and the allure he brings to soft passages, his strength in recitative, are never obtained at the expense of a natural approach to singing. A major artist at the top of his form. Pierrette Alarie, Simoneau's wife, sounds a little taxed by the heavier sections of Leila's role, but there is sweetness at the top of her voice. René Bianco's Zurga is adequate rather than distinguished, but Xavier Depraz is the only recorded Nourabad to make his assignment sound other than a chore. The stodgy conducting of Jean Fournet seems to incommode his cast strangely little.

Columbia's conductor André Cluytens proves the score's finest advocate on record, with a well-placed performance which avoids the temptation to whip up excitement and provides an object lesson in the classical French nineteenth-century manner. The cast is stylish rather than vocally outstanding. Michel Dens is a sterling singer with a natural delivery of the text, once the staple of French singers, rarer perhaps today when to ape the Italians is more important than to maintain a native style. The names of neither Angelici nor Legay will be written in letters of gold in the annals of French singing, but they manipulate their slightly undernourished voices with style and knowledge, welcome qualities but requiring a little more backing if they are to sustain gramophone interest.

A curiosity of the 1950s is the Russian recording, which shortens the finale, favours voices at the expense of orchestra, and is conducted without insight. The cast, not otherwise distinguished, contains Sergei Lemeshev, a tenor whose sympathetic, individual timbre suits the role of Nadir very well indeed. He transposes the aria down a tone and sings it disappointingly but this apart, his voice is perfect for the role: a mixture of bold attack and soft vocal colouring. His share of the duet in Act 2 is governed by the expressive *rubato* of which he was always a master.

EMI's 1961 casting at first suggests something approaching the ideal, yet I wish I could enthuse over so renowned an exponent of the French style as Nicolai Gedda, whose singing, richer of sound than that of most French tenors, is less consistent than I had expected. There is much to admire in the resonant voice of Ernest Blanc, at the time of the recording one of the finest baritones before the public, but the Act 3 aria sounds disjointed, perhaps because of insensitive tape splicing; Janine Micheau, a dominant factor in French opera for a whole generation, fails as usual to do herself justice on records.

Unusual in its way is a performance in French with Italo-Spanish singers and conductor (though Adriana Maliponte pursued her early career in France). Cillario is, with Cluytens, perhaps the most stylish conductor to tackle *Les Pêcheurs* for the gramophone, and the set is memorable for Alfredo Kraus's long, expressive singing line and the individual and beautiful quality of his voice, Italianate rather than French, but never for a moment all-purpose 'international'. He sings a clear, *mezza voce*, interpolated high C in the cadence of the aria, and no complete recording by so stylish a singer can be lightly set to one side, least of all when he numbers among his colleagues the forthright, honest singing of Sesto Bruscantini as Zurga and the often attractive, limpid voice of Maliponte.

The only 'correct' *Pêcheurs de perles* is EMI's 1977 set with no cuts, the proper finale to Act 3 and the tenor-baritone duet as Bizet wrote it. Georges Prêtre conducts portentously, and most of the singing is on an expansive scale. Alain Vanzo tackled the complete role of Nadir rather late in his career, twenty-five years after he had won a prize in a competition at Cannes, and his strict control of effects involves, for instance, a certain monotony in the unremitting *mezza voce* in the aria and cannot prevent an element of explosiveness in recitative. The Mexican baritone Guillermo Sarabia, none too idiomatic in French, sings powerfully if with some unnecessary 'international' fat on the voice. Ileana Cotrubas, a hint of unsteadiness apart, makes a touchingly vulnerable vocal figure of Leila.

Les Pêcheurs, an ideal opera you might think for highlights, does not come off too well on the four discs I have heard. Three excerpts from Act 1 were poorly recorded 'privately' in The Hague in 1940 with Luigi Fort, Scipio Colombo and Diana Micelli. Only the tenor contrives to shine; in spite of transposing the aria down a tone, he reveals in life as in the studio a genuine sweetness of tone. Even eight years before she undertook the complete recording, Janine Micheau, short of breath and fluency, fails on record to make the powerful impression she produced in the theatre, the Swiss Libero de Luca is an unsubtle Nadir, and the admirable Jean Borthayre is already adequately represented in the Nixa-Everest recording. Less interesting still, in spite of powerful studio recording, is the Dutch-based affair but, a dull soprano apart, there is much to be said for the 1961 double-sided selection from Orphée. Vanzo's poised, golden tone is rare among French tenors and he was in fresher voice than on the complete set of sixteen years later – on this evidence, Simoneau's closest recorded LP rival as a French tenor stylist. Robert Massard is one of the most appreciable of post-war French baritones, and his clear, incisive singing demonstrates the virtues of the school.

Of the five most extensively recorded excerpts, three (the duet for tenor and baritone, the tenor aria and the love duet) are concerned with a kind of erotic hypnosis, gentle and compelling, musically elusive and yet here omnipresent, with which Bizet ensnares his young lovers and impregnates his score – hence I believe one of the secrets of its attraction.

This element is strongly suggested in the score's third number, the duet

'Au fond du temple saint', which was too long to fit uncut on to 78s, so that some omit recitative or the middle section, others from the two-voice refrain cut straight into the reprise. Some Italian recorded performances end after the tenor's start of the middle section with an E flat cadence which is effective enough but in context unknown to Bizet (this must once have been standard Italian performance practice since Fort and Colombo sing it like that on their excerpts disc). So did the masterful Giorgini with Rasponi in support (Pathé 86263), Alessandro Bonci and Antonio Magini-Coletti for Fonotipia, persuasively but with Italian rather than French overtones, the mellifluous Fort and the rough Piccioli (CQ 1393), and, I believe better than either, Dino Borgioli and Benvenuto Franci (Col. D 5127; GV 537; be warned, here it is transferred nearly a semitone too high). The best recordings of this Italian version are the several involving Beniamino Gigli, whose limpid tones would melt a heart harder than that of any baritone Zurga. He recorded it first in 1919 with Pacini (DB 269; HQM 1194); twice in 1927 with Giuseppe de Luca, first for Vitaphone in a rather full version, then for Victor (DB 1150; GEMM 165), a justly famous disc which shows the tenor's glorious voice sitting to perfection on the music and in which the stylish de Luca gives him ideal support; last, (BC 153 54010/7) with a certain Vagnozzi in Rio in 1953, a real curiosity with piano accompaniment in a drawing-room acoustic but with the tenor still the immaculate vocalist of thirty-four years earlier.

The duet was additionally sung 'straight' in Italian by Acerbi and Minolfi (054118; at 74 rpm) in a good performance by McCormack and Mario Sammarco in ten-inch and twelve-inch versions (Vic. 87082; GEMM 156 twelve-inch version) which exactly catch the mood of other-worldly obsession; and in 1907 by Caruso and Mario Ancona (DK 116; GV 542). Caruso's *legato* is nothing short of perfection and immediately induces the state of near-hypnosis which I believe Bizet was after.

The vocally gifted Hermann Jadlowker and Joseph Schwarz (Gramm. 044315; LV 86) at a very slow tempo seem to have been the earliest (1916) to record the duet in German, but they were soon followed by Robert Hutt and Heinrich Schlusnus (Gramm. 72753; LV 187), more flexible of line than most German singers. There is less to be said for the hefty 1934 performance of Marcel Wittrisch and Gerhard Hüsch (DB 4430; LV 98), which sounds to me (and is indeed transferred) transposed down a semitone, or the uninteresting singing of Walther Ludwig and Karl Schmitt-Walter (Acanta 21489–3). Peter Schreier and Theo Adam are more stylish, though not much more Gallic, on DG 2536 031. There is only one recorded performance in English, rather self-consciously enunciated at a public concert in 1946 by Richard Tucker and Robert Weede, confidently sung although apparently transposed down a semitone. Two very enjoyable performances exist in Danish, by Nissen and the talented Vilhelm Herold, whose smooth, classical singing adorns the grateful line (084013), and by Stefan Islandi and Skjaer (DB 5268; BLPC 4), Islandi the possessor of so fine a tenor voice that I should not willingly be without any of his records.

'Au fond du temple saint' was always a favourite with French recording artists, whether the vigorous Léon Beyle and Hector Dufranne (34169), the elegant Charles Fontaine and Jean Noté (Pathé 2547), the fluent, well-schooled Capitaine and Lestelly (Disque W 326), or the strenuous César Vezzani and Louis Musy (DB 4862; Rococo 5234). Louis Dister, for years a stalwart of la Monnaie, Brussels, sings well in a slow but atmospheric performance (D 14255) with the powerful baritone Louis Richard, who was heard at the Paris Opéra in the 1920s, a period during which Victor Pujol, an attractive light tenor, and Julien Lafont were intensely active at the Opéra-Comique; their performance is on both sides of Odeon 188637. I enjoyed the confident singing of Villabella and Lantéri on a double-sided Pathé (X 7160), but found the same tenor disappointing in what I take it is a later performance for the same company with André Baugé. Disappointing too is the prosaic Franz Kaisin even with the smooth Robert Couzinou in support (Poly. 516589), but the American Richard van Vrooman and the Canadian Norman Mittelmann sing pleasantly enough with piano (HMS 30 804 recorded in 1965). Clarity of diction, accuracy of intonation, precise vocal colouring are features of the double-sided performance by Vergnès and Arthur Endrèze (Od. 123803), which is surpassed vocally though perhaps not stylistically by Jussi Björling and Robert Merrill in a performance of the late 1940s (DB 21426; RCA RL 43243), where the ardour of the tenor's tone and approach produce an effect impossible to resist. Just as persuasive are Domingo and Milnes (SER 5593), who modulate their great Italianate voices to fit the French music in (for records) a relatively rare complete performance of the 'usual' revised version. If I had to pick a single performance in French it would, in spite of cuts, be that of Edmond Clément and Marcel Journet (DK 105; Rococo R 40) in which the delicacy of Clément's art combines with his very positive phrasing to provide, given solid support from Journet, a sample of French singing which is a joy to listen to.

One of Bizet's finest melodic inspirations comes with 'Je crois entendre encore' ('Mi par d'udir ancor' in Italian), a shapely tune which epitomizes the mood of intoxicated surrender with which the composer drugs his lovers as with an opiate. Written in A minor, it is tailored precisely to the strengths of the lighter French lyric tenor, marked *piano* throughout, and rises in the repeated refrain twice to a sustained high B natural. It is often, and by Italians mostly, transposed down a tone to G minor, sometimes only by a semitone, which enables the singer to take an easier high B (or high B flat in G minor) in an interpolated cadence at the end of the aria. Occasionally this effect is duplicated even in the original key, which gives the singer the possibility of a soft top C. To avoid constant repetition of the keys in which the various recordings are sung (though an element of judgement is often involved, where there is doubt, I have tried to indicate what governed my choice), the discs are divided into groups by keys.

In acoustic days, the tendency seems to have been to transpose down, and I can only find two early tenors who certainly sang in the original A minor.

The Spaniard Florencio Constantino sounds curiously short of breath on Victor 74067 (Italian), but Carlo Dani's 1906 record (Fono. 39964) is the epitome of the *tenore di grazia* and demonstrates a *voce mista* nothing short of perfection (not least in an interpolated C). Disappointing are electricals by David Devriès, Enrico di Mazzei (RO 20045), Herbert Ernst Groh (in German; Od. O–25110), and Tony Poncet, but a Ukrainian, Miro Skala-Staryckyj, sings capably in French (Arka ARC 806), and there is some controlled singing in German by the top-note specialist Rudolf Gerlach-Rusnak (EG 2910; LV 71) and by the unusually high-lying German tenor of the 1950s, Josef Traxel (DGG 32030). Traxel includes a top C before the end, so does the Pole Wieslaw Ochman (Muza XL 0465), who sings the aria beautifully in French, as does of course Villabella (Pathé X 90026) who sounds right at 80 rpm. He sings a beautiful top C in head tone and confirms his high reputation at the Opéra-Comique. So too does Marcel Claudel (Poly. 566064), who sings the written text with considerable assurance.

A little on the robust side perhaps is Alfredo Kraus on one of his earliest records (CAL 1); he sings in Italian, like the Portuguese Tommaso Alcaide (LX 108; Rococo 5206), whose brilliant timbre yet allows for an exquisitely modulated C before the end. Even with unidiomatic French diction, Richard Lewis's early recording (Decca K 2291) is fluent and stylish (eschewing unwritten high notes), and a strong rival to the exquisitely poised version by Mallabréra (Vega 16244; to be played a little slower than $33^1/_3$ rpm).

Only three original-key performances seem preferable to these. Placido Domingo's solidity of tone and dark vocal colouring, more like Caruso's than Clément's, might be expected to lie uneasily on the music in its original key, but the performance is perfectly judged and Domingo (with Giulini's accompaniment; DG 2532 009) maintains a seamless line as he soars easily to high B natural and down again and then rises to an interpolated C at the end. It is a remarkable technical feat coming from the leading Otello of his day and the performance is far more beautiful than his earlier version (ARLI 0048), which is strangely subdued as well as being transposed a whole tone. Quite different is the singing of Alain Vanzo (Mode CMDINT 9487), made at the height of his career when smoothness in no way impeded an ardent approach and when the mixed-voice high B naturals preceded a C dying slowly away in the manner of the Golden Age. Only Nicolai Gedda's performance of the aria seems to me in some ways superior (33CX 1130); with its confident, poised line and golden tone, to say nothing of the perfect C before the close, it is as nearly ideal as you are likely to hear.

To my surprise, when I counted up I found more versions in A flat minor than in the original A minor, almost all of them soaring to an unwritten B before the end. Discounting Vezzani (Disque P 733), peremptory of tone and perfunctory in effect, of little more than souvenir value are versions by Aristodemo Giorgini (Pathé 30032; GV 700), the overpowering Gaston Micheletti (Od. 188898), the beefy Richard Tucker (MS 6831), the competent Russian Nicolai Sereda (Eurodisc 913074), and the less than imaginative

Nino Ederle (OASI 629). Carlos Mejia sings charmingly in Italian on a late acoustic Blue Victor, Alfred Piccaver (Od. O–8097) is rerecorded in Bel Canto Club 3 half a tone down (which sounds right to me) and reveals assured but uninvolved singing, and John McCormack (DA 502; GEMM 156) sings immaculately in Italian and with just the right weight for the music. More interesting perhaps are three admirable Russians: Davidov (G&T 22813 recorded in 1900–1) who floats the line ideally above the piano accompaniment; Slovtsov (ARSC 0569/70), whose beautiful high voice adorned the Bolshoi before and after the Revolution but whose B flats are undeniably taken falsetto; and Konstantin Ognevoi (Col. D 16216), a post-Revolution singer who uses a plangent tone in expressive long phrases and finishes with a B natural of unusual beauty. Bonci sang Nadir with Tetrazzini at Covent Garden in 1908, and his recording (Fono. 39686; Rubini RDA 002), played at 75.5 rpm, with piano, shows clean singing and an impressive approach to the music, but no more so than his compatriot Dino Borgioli, whose aristocratic manner and ideal control of his material, to say nothing of an interpolated B natural of real quality, are revealed hardly less convincingly on an acoustic Regal than on his better-known Columbia electrical (Col. D 1002; GV 537), the latter transferred at too high a pitch if the neighbouring tracks and the evidence of one's own ears are to be believed. If anything even more preferable is the performance of Badridze (USSR 15393), slow in tempo but a wonderfully dreamy, evocative piece of singing, with perfect control of the soft ending.

Fortunately you do not *have* to choose between Leonid Sobinov, Dimitri Smirnov, Caruso and Gigli, who seem to me the pick of those who transpose by a semitone. Caruso's 1903 performance (VB 44; HLM 7030) in Italian feels right to me played at 73 rpm when it sounds in A flat and reveals the great voice rather full-bodied for the music but so smooth and controlled as to silence doubts. Sobinov (in Russian on DB 896; CO 353) sings powerfully but with the control of an instrumentalist, very 'correct' and very beautiful in effect; there is also a 1904 version, which I have not heard. His compatriot Smirnov has perhaps a more individual timbre, but even his command of colour, dynamics and *rubato* hardly prepare the listener for the extraordinary beauty and imaginative colouring of his soft B flats and the B natural before the aria's end (recorded in 1913 in Italian; 052417; COLH 129). Gigli's performance was recorded at least five times, in 1929 and 1931 commercially, in 1947, 1951 and 1952 on 'private' discs. Whether at thirty-nine, forty-one, fifty-seven, sixty-one or sixty-two, he seems able to maintain the same flow of full, round, golden *mezza voce* tone, the same ornaments, the same control which in a less communicative singer one would think of as impersonal but which with Gigli risks nothing so dull. Repeated hearings suggest to me and to those with whom I was listening that the 1929 Victor (issued years later as AGSB 56; GEMM 204) was recorded in G minor at 74 rpm which means it would, misleadingly but by design, sound a semitone higher when played at 78; the same 'trick' was perpetrated a dozen years later when he recorded 'Di quella pira'! The 1931 HMV (DA 1216; ALP 1681) is, in contrast, certainly in A flat. If there is a touch of sentimentality in the phrasing, it quickly comes to seem unimportant in face of such liquid tone and seamless phrasing. The three 'private' versions are sung down a tone in G minor and in public performances, that in London in 1952 with orchestra, the others with piano.

I have heard well over thirty versions transposed to G minor. Discounting the stentorian Lazaro, the undistinguished Bruno Landi (Italian: Halo 50236) and Thomas Hayward, the unidiomatic Walther Ludwig, Marcel Wittrisch, Jean Löhe, and Koloman von Pataky, there are recordings of the American Richard van Vrooman, the Italians Romeo Berti and Primo Vitti, the Hungarian Udvardy Tibor, the Mexican José Mojica, and the Russian Dimiter Onofrei (once active in the USA), which are of no more than souvenir value. More curious because he sings in Hebrew is Cantor Josef Shlisky (Vocalion K 05096), because they attempted to sing it at all are Jussi Björling (RLS 715), whom it did not suit, Lauri-Volpi (Victor 84033; OASI 575), whose performance is beset with pitch problems, and Tino Rossi (Col. DB 1765), who floats his falsetto top notes well but bends note values to make a popular song of the aria. An odder case of a less than satisfactory version is that by Giuseppe Lugo, whose reputation as Nadir brought him the 100th performance at the Opéra-Comique in 1936 and took him to La Scala in the same role in 1938 (Decca Poly. CA 8158; LV 161), but to my ears demonstrates no imagination or beauty of tone whatsoever.

Much more interesting is the Romanian Ion Piso, whose attractive vocal timbre and control throughout his compass is heard on ECE 0149 and on a later Russian recording, D 011473/4. The same description applies to the Dane Otte Svendsen (Tono X 25110). Vladimir Pikok (Zono X 62775) sings in Russian with a fine command of a strong masculine voice, Lenghi-Cellini, best known as a ballad singer but heard at Covent Garden in 1911, demonstrates charm and control (Beka-Meister), Nino Martini sings agreeably with piano, Richard Crooks's performance (Victor 15544) is one of his most attractive discs, Miguel Fleta's (DB 1071; LV 96) characteristic in its pursuit of effects, though the transposition seems with him as with the stylist Joseph Rogatchewsky (Col. D 12527; LV 239; 1929) to rob the aria of the 'brilliant' quality Bizet undoubtedly attached to it.

Giuseppe Anselmi tackled it twice, with recitative on a double-sided Fonotipia (62270/71; GV 64), where the tone is very bright and Italianate, the singing full-blooded, but the whole so well shaped as to captivate the listener, more so I found than in his previously unpublished Edison version (GV 64). Lemeshev, pre-war I think, gives a gentler, more evocative performance on Melodiya 06941 than in the post-war set; Luigi Fort caresses the phrases with true elegance (DCX 49; OASI 567); di Stefano early in his career with hardly less distinction and an even more attractive voice (RLS 756; 1944 with piano); Heddle Nash is cultivated and convincing in English (C 3409; HQM 1089); and Nicolai Gedda, if heavier roles have removed some beauty from the voice, sounds in a public performance some fifteen years later than his original Columbia, just as sure of execution. When I heard him sing Nadir in London, Ferruccio Tagliavini transposed freely as he does in his recordings of the aria, but he imbues them with such charm as to remove any idea that the music is thereby robbed of brilliance. There are two separate recordings; on Cetra (BB 25237, August 1948) he sings, not without strain at the top, in A flat minor, but at a public performance of (I surmise) the 1960s preserved on Mizar Records, wisely adopts G minor to fine effect.

There remains Caruso's second recording (DB 136; various reissues) made in 1916, the year of the successful revival at the Metropolitan which he shared with Hempel and de Luca. If the transposition by a tone in other hands risks removing an essential quality from the music, Caruso's dark tone at this stage of his career somehow legitimizes the lower key, and his superb control of the mighty voice makes an effect as of a cellist in full flight. In its way, the recording is beyond competition – but this would be to reckon without Fernando de Lucia, who in his 1906 recording (2–52520; Rubini RS 305) sings it expressively, with much beauty and poise. On Phonotype (M 1758; GV 575) around 1920 when he was about sixty he is no less successful but in F sharp minor.

The finale to Act 1 contains Leila's first significant solo utterance, 'O dieu Brahma', a chant with slightly Eastern overtones. Jeanne Mérey, who made her Opéra-Comique début in 1897, sings it confidently and with brilliance (Pathé 1993; ORX 503), Lucette Korsoff in 1907 (G&T 33644) makes the aria's second half sound more like a slow waltz than a chant but vocalizes admirably, as did Linda Brambilla in the same year but in Italian (053105); it plays at 74 rpm. The best performance as you might expect comes (in 1908) from Tetrazzini (2–053012; GEMM 221), who sang the role at Covent Garden in 1908 and here exhibits a fullness of tone and brilliance of execution without serious rival, not even from the charming, accurate Toti dal Monte (DB 1316; LV 184) not at all from a best-forgotten, 1974 attempt on the music by Anna Moffo (RCA ARL1.0844).

Leila's great opportunity comes with her extended aria early in Act 2, a piece contoured not unlike Micaela's a dozen years later, even to horn colouring in the introduction. There are fine early versions from Georgette Bréjean-Silver (Od. 56006), who (in 1905) sang the second half only with full, rounded tone, Korsoff (033167), and Teresa Arkel (Fono. 39361) stylish, with great clarity of articulation, in Italian. Of early recordings, I liked best Tetrazzini's uncharacteristically gentle singing, as if Leila were already under the spell of Nadir's obsessive love (053228; GEMM 221), and Olimpia Boronat's (1904 St Petersburg 53353; Rococo 28), which contains some explosive attack and exhibits a taste in *rubato* belonging to another age but shows too a glorious richness and beauty of tone and a personal alertness of approach which I found magical.

Late acoustics have been by Galli-Curci (DB 255; CDN 1004), full of charm and with lovely soft high notes as well as unbelievably sloppy diction;

Ada Sari, a Polish soprano who sang at La Scala; and Graziella Pareto (2–053178; CO 376), whose vocal allure and skill explain why she was a favourite of Beecham's, with whom she sang the opera at Covent Garden in 1920. Nezhdanova had the ideal mixture of forward sound and flexibility when she sang the aria in Russian (2–23074; Club 99.5), but nobody floated the melody more exquisitely than Claire Dux in 1921 (DLV 84); her soft vocal quality and command of legato fit the music to perfection; she sings in German, as does Grete Stückgold (Gramm. 19238), with scarcely less beauty of voice and style.

Elizaveta Shumskaya shows commitment in Russian (Melodiya D. 012721–22), Erna Berger, who sang in the 1934 Berlin revival, is clear and clean in German (Poly. 10285; LV 234). Rina Gigli (DB 11316), Carteri (Cetra LPC 55009), Scotto (LPC 55050) have recorded the aria in Italian with varying success, but perhaps only the plaintive singing of dal Monte (DB 1316; LV 184) and Lina Pagliughi (E 11406), not unlike it in approach, produce Italian performances of lasting appeal.

As one might expect French singers have not left the aria alone, and there are recordings by the confident Georgette Mathieu, active at the Opéra-Comique in the 1930s, Germaine Féraldy (LFX 25; FCX 50001), rather shallow of tone; the brittle Lucienne Jourfier and lightweight Thérèse Schmidt (Véga); Mady Mesplé (EMI); and Janine Micheau (LXT 2528), limpid of tone and brilliant in the cadenza though apparently unable to carry through phrases with full weight. The best of this batch are by the capable Jeanne Guyla, endowed with a voice of particularly attractive timbre (DB 4872), and Ninon Vallin (RO 20178; CBS 78314), urgent in the recitative, full of authority and the right kind of edge in the aria.

In the end, non-French singers come well out of the comparison. Pilar Lorengar (SXL 6267) is short on personality but strong of voice and technique. Joan Sutherland chooses a rather dark, veiled tone and her diction is at its least distinct (though not to rival Galli-Curci's), which robs the singing of colour, but even when she is not at her most committed, she is a glorious vocalist (SET 454). By 1963, it is arguable that Callas was well past her vocal prime but here her imagination is engaged, she lightens the tone to suit the music, and this soft, contained singing with a good C in the cadenza puts her version (1C 053 00578) in a high category.

Nadir re-enters immediately following Leila's aria and with him the mood of gentle eroticism Bizet has already been at pains to establish. His serenade, 'De mon amie fleur endormie' ('Della mia vita'), introduced by cor anglais and accompanied by harp, suggests the longing felt by both lovers and cannot often have been more insinuatingly sung than by Fernando de Lucia, who with piano accompaniment executes the turns and decorations with such delicacy that anyone would forgive him for transposing the music down a semitone (2–52474; Rubini RS 305). Most others maintain the original D minor, and Caruso's 1916 Victor shows the mighty voice under perfect control (DA 114; Rococo 5275). Fine, clean singing comes from Aristodemo Giorgini

(Pathé 86250; GV 91), and other tenors who sing it in Italian are Manuritta, appealing of voice but rather sentimental of manner (Col. DQ 1069), Roberto d'Alessio, with unyielding vocal quality, and Dino Borgioli (Col. D 12580), transferred sharp on to Rubini GV 537, is as stylish as you would expect. Lugo is confident in French (Poly. 561083; LV 161), and Rogatchewsky sings with intensity on a 1928 Columbia (D 13041; LV 239). Nobody catches the mood of dreamy ecstasy more perfectly than Reynaldo Hahn (4–32078: R 5322), but he has piano accompaniment and at 78 rpm (when the voice sounds right) sings the music a tone lower than it is written – but to what insidious effect!

If de Lucia relies less than usual on *rubato* for his 1906 performance of the serenade, he gives a complete demonstration of its expressive possibilities the same year in the duet which immediately follows – or rather, in the beguiling climactic section beginning 'Ton coeur n'as pas compris le mien' ('Non hai compreso'), all that was recorded in acoustic days (054082; RS 305). I find the effect extraordinarily beautiful, but after de Lucia's expansive singing, there is room for little from Huguet on her own before they cut to the unison section. In 1920, de Lucia recorded the duet again on Phonotype, this time with Tina de Angelis, down a semitone – at least, I think so; at 78 rpm, the voices sound human, the decorations and *rubato* similar to de Lucia's of fourteen years before (Phonotype M1820; GV 575).

The duet found little favour in acoustic days, though the Italians Piccoletti and Zaccari sang it satisfactorily on G&T 054064 (1906), Korsoff and Beyle over-robustly (34190; at 74 rpm), and the Russians Nezhdanova and Sobinov (DB 896; CO 353) with such beauty of tone and distinction of manner as to provide the best all-round performance on disc, not surprising since it is the only one with two great singers combining at the height of their careers. Pareto is her usual elegant self in this music (CO 376) but she has an uningratiating partner in Ciniselli. Gigli recorded the duet in Italian late in his career (1951) with his daughter Rina (DB 11347; 3C 153-03480/6); some of the old beauty of tone is apparent but Leila's solo music is cut and the performance generally perfunctory. A complete version (ALP 1353), starting with the serenade, comes in Italian (in 1956) from Carlo Zampighi and Margherita Carosio, the tenor well able to support a partner whose breathless, over-anxious vocalism too seldom suggests the charmer whose singing gave much pleasure at La Scala and in London immediately post-war. Also complete and in Italian is a version by Carteri and di Stefano (3C 053–17658), each singer still in good voice but stretched by music and style alike. Gedda tends to overwhelm Mady Mesplé's thin-voiced Leila (2C 063–14010), but his performance is in itself appreciable. The roles are very much reversed in the 1975 performance (in French of a sort) from Caballé and di Stefano (Alhambra SCE 974). He is coarse and loud throughout, but she sings with ravishing beauty of tone and line so as to suggest that with another colleague this must have been the definitive version.

Act 2 ends with what is dramatically a well-focused finale, but the third act starts with a fine prelude and one of Bizet's most effective baritone arias, as lyrical and grateful as if he were writing for tenor. It fitted badly on to acoustic discs, needing the orchestral prelude to fill two sides, but too long for a single. However Francesco Bonini demonstrates his splendid Italian voice in it on Fonotipia 92561 (it plays at 74 rpm), and Louis Lestelly is a hardly less impressive French baritone in a precise and yet attractively impulsive performance (Disque W 326). Two German baritones have tackled the aria, Mathieu Ahlersmeyer in his native tongue without much subtlety (1936), Fischer-Dieskau in 1961 (SLPM 138700). Fricsay and the RIAS Orchestra here give a fiery account of the prelude and it is followed by an outstandingly well-shaped performance from Fischer-Dieskau, the voice fitting the music well and the singer finding musical nuance to which most are deaf.

Soon after 1945, two leading Italian baritones sang the music for record to good effect, Carlo Tagliabue in 1946, powerfully and correctly (DB 5359; LV 270), Paolo Silveri a couple of years later, stylishly and with sympathetic vocal colour (LB 107).

One would have thought of this as music pre-eminently for French voices, but there is little to be said for a leaden pre-war performance by Pierre Dupré (even the transfer on to CBS 78314 is poor), but Michel Dens is solid and reliable on Pathé DTX 315. Reynaldo Hahn's penchant for this music can be heard on his late, self-accompanied recording (D 2021); it is in key, words and music are articulated with exemplary clarity if without ordinary operatic weight, but the composer fills the music with a tenderness so rare as to impel the listener to an immediate encore. On LXT 5269 Gérard Souzay sounds not unlike Fischer-Dieskau, but this is a somewhat light-weight performance by a singer little associated with opera. IRCC issued a performance by one of the most distinguished of modern French baritones Martial Singher (L 7019). If by the 1950s, when I judge the recording to have been made, some smoothness had gone from the voice, there remains a consistently expressive singing line, and the performance is, with Fischer-Dieskau's, probably the nearest in achievement to that of Arthur Endrèze, the American baritone who represents a high point in French singing style between the wars. Here Endrèze's diction is as immaculate as his tone, and his shaping of the aria makes the record (Od. 123022; Club 99.117) one to prize.

Recordings of *Les Pêcheurs de perles*, like perhaps the opera itself, end on something of a down beat. From later in Act 3, comes a powerful Italian performance by Rina Corsi of part of the scene for Leila and Zurga ('Pour moi, je ne crains rien'), and there is a spirited rendering also in Italian recorded in 1907, by Brambilla, Acerbi, Cigada (05124; plays at 74 rpm) of the less than spirited trio by Benjamin Godard which has for so long disfigured Bizet's score. I prefer to remember the glories of French, Italian and Russian tenors in their successful attempts at recreating the rapt atmosphere of obsessive love which the young Bizet has so unerringly and to such innovatory effect built up in the earlier parts of the opera. That is something the gramophone recaptures to perfection.

LES PÊCHEURS DE PERLES

L Leila; *N* Nadir; *Z* Zurga; *Nour* Nourabad

c.1950 (in Russian) Kazantseva *L*;
Lemeshev *N*; Zakharov *Z*;
Antonenko *Nour*/ Bolshoi
Theatre Chorus and Orch/Bron
MK ⓜ D 02133–8

1952 Dobbs *L*; Seri *N*; Borthayre *Z*;
Mans *Nour*/chorus, Paris PO/
Leibowitz
Musidisc-Festival ⓜ 262
Everest ⓒ 422 (2)

1953 Alarie *L*; Simoneau *N*; Bianco
Z; Depraz *Nour*/Brasseur
Chorale, Lamoureux/Fournet
Philips ⓜ 6747 404
Philips (US) ⓜ PHC 2–016

1954 Angelici *L*; Legay *N*; Dens *Z*;
Noguera *Nour*/Paris Opéra-
Comique Chorus and Orch/
Cluytens
EMI ⓜ 2C 153 12057–8

1961 Micheau *L*; Gedda *N*; Blanc *Z*;
Mars *Nour*/Paris Opéra-Comique
Chorus and Orch/Dervaux
EMI SLS 877
Angel SBL 3603

1970 Maliponte *L*; Kraus *N*;
Bruscantini *Z*; Campó *Nour*/
Barcelona Gran Liceo Chorus
and Orch./Cillario
Bongiovanni GB 503–4
Carillon SCAL 16–17

1977 Cotrubas *L*; Vanzo *N*; Sarabia
Z; Soyer *Nour*/Paris Opéra
Chorus and Orch./Prêtre
EMI SLS 5113 ④ TC–SLS 5113
Angel SXBL 3856 ④ 4X2X–3856

1953 (excerpts) Micheau *L*;
L. de Luca *N*; Borthayre *Z*/Paris
Conservatoire Orch./Erede
Decca ⓜ ACL 276
London ⓜ LL 939

1961 (excerpts) Doria *L*; Vanzo *N*;
Massard *Z*; Scellier *Nour*/chorus
and orch/Etcheverry
Orphée STO E 61016

1978 (excerpts) Madden *L*; Holland
N; Bakker *Z*; Holl *Nour*/
Rotterdam Opera Chorus, Frysk
Orch./Pešek
EMI 5C 053 24595

Roméo et Juliette

RICHARD LAW

Roméo et Juliette was composed for the Théâtre Lyrique, predecessor of what is now the Théâtre de la Ville, at the invitation of that astute impresario Léon Carvalho. By the time of its première in 1867 Meyerbeer was dead and Berlioz a spent force, while Bizet's short career as an opera composer had hardly begun. As Ravel said, French music would have cut a poor figure under the Second Empire had it not been for Gounod.

The popularity of *Roméo* has always run second to that of *Faust* (1859), and the verdict may be just. In many ways, however, it represents for Gounod as great an advance on *Faust* as does, for example, *Don Carlos* in the case of Verdi on *Un ballo in maschera*. At first hearing, *Roméo* was criticized for its lack of tunefulness and for being excessively influenced by Meyerbeer and Wagner, an accusation common enough in those days and as commonly chalked up to a composer's credit in these. As to lack of tunefulness, certainly it has fewer seductive 'numbers' than *Faust*, though both score and libretto are much more succinct. Nor is there anything to tickle the fancy of the groundlings comparable to the frisson of seeing the Devil being hammed up on Walpurgis night by some *monstre sacré* like Chaliapin. Indeed the weakest music of *Roméo* is that written for the bass voices. Frère Laurent fully justifies the celebrated strictures uttered in a different context by Nancy Mitford's Uncle Matthew, while Capulet's constipated exhortations to jollity would have put a damper on Mafeking night.

Fortunately the musical foundation of *Roméo* rests on the four beautiful duets for the two lovers, exemplifying respectively burgeoning love (the Madrigal), passionate declaration (the balcony scene), ecstatic fulfilment (Juliet's bedroom), and despairing farewell (the tomb scene). For delicacy and originality the well-known numbers like Romeo's cavatina and Juliet's waltz song must take second place to the ensembles and to Mercutio's 'Ballad of Queen Mab', a late example of a patter song transformed not for comic but for poetic effect to express a genuinely Shakespearian *fantaisie*, and correspondingly difficult for the singer to bring off.

After a *succès d'estime* at the Théâtre Lyrique, *Roméo* was taken into the repertory of the Opéra-Comique in 1873 and in the next fifteen years achieved close to four hundred performances. But what really put it on the map was its transfer to the Paris Opéra in 1888 in a celebrated production conducted by Gounod himself, for which Patti was persuaded to relearn Juliet in French (she had created the part in London, but in Italian), and in which the de Reszke brothers made their débuts as Romeo and Frère Laurent. The de Reszkes appeared the next season at Covent Garden with the almost unknown Melba as Juliet, a performance which constituted the real springboard of that singer's career.

Textually Gounod made a few alterations for the Paris Opéra, mainly to the finale of Act 3 (the scene of the duels). He also composed some ballet music, which is reprehensibly omitted from most modern scores. Also, Juliet's waltz song, originally written for Mme Miolan-Carvalho in G, was in 1888 rewritten for Patti in F, in which key it is still generally printed. Patti's presumable reluctance at the age of forty-five to tackle it in the higher key is interesting in view of her reputation for bravura. A few sopranos, and several on record, still sing it in the higher key.

No successful opera has been more closely associated with its early protagonists. Patti, Melba, and the de Reszkes were succeeded in London before 1914 by a group of great singers who were able to keep *Roméo* warm in public affection: Emma Eames, Suzanne Adams, Mary Garden, John McCormack, Charles Dalmorès, Paul Franz, Pol Plançon, Marcel Journet and Vanni Marcoux among them. It then slowly faded from the repertory in London, making two final appearances at Covent Garden under Barbirolli in 1930 until its revival at the English National Opera in the 1980s. Outside France it has survived more tenaciously in Soviet Russia and in New York, no doubt because the Metropolitan continued regularly to cast it with singers like Eidé Noréna, Bidu Sayão, Björling, de Luca, and Pinza.

This brief performance history explains the wealth of early recorded material and the relatively scurvy treatment the opera has received on LP. The 'complete' recordings – all actually embody the traditional cuts – can be dealt with pretty shortly.

The date of the second Bolshoi recording, sung in Russian, is 1947. Its sole redeeming feature is the Romeo of Sergei Lemeshev. The voice is attractive in the throaty Russian manner, and he sings the cavatina with style but not much character. The vile recording, at the same time cavernous and violent, encourages one to draw a veil over the shrill and inaccurate Juliet, a Laurent who is ponderous without being impressive, and a brutally charmless Mercutio.

At least the 1953 Decca version has a French-speaking cast, always a great plus in French opera. Unfortunately there is not a single first-class voice among them. Nor is the conducting better than competent, which is a pity since Decca, uniquely, include the ballet music, played here immediately after Frère Laurent gives Juliet the fatal potion. Heinz Rehfuss, an excellent singer but a high baritone, was a perverse choice for Laurent, for his frequent low Gs are inaudible. Claudine Collart is neat and charming in the page's song 'Que fais-tu, blanche tourterelle?', with its Dvořákian turns of phrase

and harmony; but her soubrettish tones cannot remotely suggest the dangerous young blade who draws his sword on Tybalt. Pierre Mollet has none of
the thrust required for a convincing Mercutio, while Raoul Jobin's violent
and inflated singing as Romeo is an abuse of modest but not unattractive
resources. Janine Micheau, who sings her waltz song in G, sounds, alas,
shrill and *passée*. The recording betrays its age, and can only be recommended to those willing to pay a heavy price for the ballet music and for
hearing the text idiomatically declaimed. The other cuts are standard and
include Juliet's 'Amour, ranime mon courage' and the so-called
Epithalamium.

The 1968 EMI set is better, though far from good. We do not get the
ballet music or Juliet's second aria in Act 4, but at least the opening prologue
and Capulet's ball are complete. The recording is heavy and reverberant,
which reflects Alain Lombard's overall view of the piece: grandiose and
unexpectedly spacious. The playing is generally good, and Gounod's imaginative, if not original, effects like the strings and harp music in Juliet's scented
garden in Act 2 or her slumber music in Act 5, are well managed by the
conductor. These passages are genuine inspirations and are unmatched by
anything in *Faust*. But this is not really a conductor's opera, and the set is
in its way as badly cast as the Decca. The Mercutio and Laurent are both
musical and French, which is something, though over-modest in manner.
Mirella Freni's Juliet has a certain charm, but she abbreviates her *fioriture*
and her French is only so-so. 'Je veux vivre', so easily made to sound vapid,
she sings slowly and without the brilliance written into it for Mmes Carvalho
and Patti, but she catches the shy debutante prettily enough. Franco Corelli's
bronze-toned Romeo, inaccurate and in vile French, is the decisive drawback
of these records. Pulling about the slow tempo of 'Salut, tombeau!' as he
does makes it sound like recitative, gracelessly sung.

The 1964 disc of highlights is better all round than this. Michel Dens is
easily the best Mercutio on LP; the voice is light and reflects the quizzical
better than the formidable side of the character. Rosanna Carteri is, like
Freni, an undisciplined Juliet, but she manages the *poco meno allegro* section
of her aria with variety and sensibility. She has the big voice of the true
verismo singer, but one is thankful for a Juliet who is not just a dizzy girl.
Nicolai Gedda plays about with the tempo in the middle section of 'Ah!
Lève-toi, soleil' and the voice is less than superlative; but his declamation is
easy and natural, and he finishes the aria with a firm and confident *piano*
high B flat.

The 1912 Pathé recording was originally made on twenty-seven hill-and-
dale discs, one of the gramophone's earliest complete recordings, and evidence of the opera's early popularity. Its transfer to LP is backward and it
is dully conducted. The recording is especially unkind to Yvonne Gall, the
admirable Juliet. But Agustarello Affre has plenty of 'ping' in his high notes,
and Marcel Journet is a majestic Friar. A valuable sample, then, of a not

quite top-notch performance such as one might have heard in Paris before 1914.

Two 'private' records of Metropolitan performances are better than any yet discussed. The first, dating from 1935, gives us Giuseppe de Luca as a Mercutio full of juice and spirit, despite approximate French; the Juliet is Noréna, just starting to sound her age (over fifty), and there is a small lapse at the end of her waltz song, but it is a lovely performance in every way that matters; there is an artistic and dramatic Romeo in Charles Hackett, though he is taxed by his cavatina; Léon Rothier is a sonorous Laurent; Gladys Swarthout a splendid page, who rounds off her song with an excellent trill and a fine cadenza taking her up to C. Another record, made in early 1947, gives us Björling in magnificent voice – quite outclassing Hackett; John Brownlee singing his Mab ballad with taste and poise; Nicola Moscona, steady and resonant; and the excellent Bidu Sayão, whose beautiful commercial recording is faded in at the waltz song. Her timbre as recorded is occasionally sour but she was clearly a superb performer. The whole is conducted with taste and authority by the Russian Emil Cooper.

It will be clear from what has already been said that the material on 78 is extensive, and often of fine quality. A link with the composer is provided by Léon Melchissedec (Rococo 5262), who was born in 1843 and sang Mercutio under Gounod in 1888. Earlier he had been the Opéra-Comique's original Capulet. The vitality and high spirits of his 'Allons, jeunes gens' leap from the ancient recording. Even more festive and extravert is Delmas, the actual Capulet of 1888, on an Odeon of 1906/7 (56180; IRCC L7014), a startlingly forward recording. Plançon's 1902 (G&T 2660; GV 39) is, as expected, a model: all the rapid triplets and the high F are perfectly in place, and anyone who grows impatient at one's complaints about non-French singers in this music should study the perfection and naturalness of the singer's declamation. Willy Tubiana, another Opéra-Comique stalwart, gives us more expert singing, light and rapid, in the old style (Disque P 505), though he is less smooth than the excellent Arthur Endrèze (E 11129; GV 512). Endrèze was *né* Krackman in Chicago but trained in France with Jean de Reszke, and it shows.

An Odeon LP (ORX 135) is worth finding, since it contains a number of the best early electric 78s: not only Endrèze's Capulet but also his Queen Mab ballad in a performance that is staid but makes every word tell. (It is now reissued on Rubini GV 512.) Parlo. E 11129 couples his Queen Mab with what the label calls 'Air de Capulet', and is in fact part of the Act 4 quartet in which he prepares Juliet (vainly) to marry the County Paris. More elegant singing here; Juliet, Gertrude, and the Friar are omitted. Unlike Endrèze, Dinh Gilly had a big career in London and died there in 1940, having retired before he was fifty; his Queen Mab (Od. 97308; GV 82) reveals a typical French lyric baritone of the period but no special merits. Tibbett's voice (Rococo 5266) is too heavy, though impeccably managed, and his French is mediocre so as to deprive Mercutio of all his charm and high spirits. Other foreign Mercutios only to be mentioned in passing are William Samuel in English (D 274) and Sven Herdenberg in Swedish (7C 153 35351). Robert Couzinou, like Gilly popular in London, shows us exactly how this difficult piece should be done (Poly. 516593; Club 99.76): much flexibility at a moderate tempo, exemplary clarity, and splendid pointing of the text. An outstanding record. Martial Singher (AmC 71697D; Odyssey 32 16 0304) is forthright and dangerous, a fine actor, and sings with taste and the right voice, if not with ideally seductive tone. Jean van Gorp (Alpha SP 6013) of the Opéra de Wallonie is prosaic despite a good voice and recording, while Gabriel Bacquier (Mondiophonie MSA 11–A) presents Mercutio as the formidable young duellist. In an interesting performance, Bacquier's *marcato* singing is noteworthy and he is one of the few who does not slow up at the words '. . . dont la mèche blanche/Est prise au rayon' – rightly, for the marking *poco rit.* actually comes later. Gérard Souzay has included the ballad in two recitals. The first, made in 1957 (LXT 5269), is delicious: rapid, quirky, and delicate. At the opposite extreme from Bacquier, Souzay gives us Mercutio as poet rather than swashbuckler, making every word tell at a hot pace, and with all the *fantaisie* lacking in singers like Tibbett and Gilly. His 1966 recital (Philips SAL 3574) shows him in fuller voice, naturally less youthful and lyrical, but good all the same and notably well accompanied by Serge Baudo.

And so to Juliet's waltz song, the opera's *pons asinorum*, and recorded so often that only the outstanding versions can be noted. If the opera 'made' Melba in 1889, one can tell why from her 1904 record (DB 367; RLS 719): the marvellous voice, the vigorous attack, the brio and panache are stunning. She studied with Gounod and this performance carries complete conviction. Among those who shared the part with Melba in London were Emma Eames (Victor 88011; Rococo R29) who had a heavier voice – she also sang Aida and Sieglinde, and the American Suzanne Adams (Col 1197; CBS BRG 72145), an expert performer with a bright unvaried voice who ended up running a laundry in London, where she died in 1953. Tetrazzini's seven-inch Zonophone of 1903 (10003; GEMM 220/27) is cut, though the vitality comes over all the same; but she is less imaginative than Regina Pinkert (Fono. 39482) recorded in G with piano. Pinkert's singing is flexible, varied, and wholly convincing. Nezhdanova's legendary Hill-and-Dale (Pathé 21852; GV 42) made in St Petersburg in 1904 is dim and noisy, but cannot conceal the vigour of the singing and the superlative quality of the voice. Georgette Bréjean-Silver's two records are both good (Fono. 39224 and Od. 56908), with polished *fioriture* and a good trill. The Odeon disc is especially relaxed and charming, and the middle section 'Loin de l'hiver morose', which sounds so tame in the mouth of the average coloratura, is here brought imaginatively to life. This is a private rather than public expression of pleasure. Geraldine Farrar also recorded the piece more than once; her 1906 G&T (33618; CO 315) reminds one of Melba, though the high notes are not effortless, and it is no surprise that in 1911 (IRCC 114) she leaves them out. Her slow, dreamy approach to the music in the latter is attractive and quite different from the 1906 version. Virtuosity gets the upper hand again with the Russian Eugenie Bronskaya (Amour 023127), but despite her remorseless facility in *staccato* this 1911 disc has a girlish quality missing from the later Columbia (A 5211), which is sung in Italian with a lavishly un-Gounodesque cadenza. Her greater near-contemporary, Maria Kouznetzova, singing in French, fills the notes out with little graces (Pathé 0123; SJG 003) in a cultivated and charming performance.

For virtuosity, however, Frieda Hempel (Od. XX 76952) singing in German and the higher key of G takes the palm, with all that that implies about a certain chill efficiency. At the other extreme is Galli-Curci (DB 264; GEMM 189) singing in weird French, but this is the real *voix d'or*; the phrases are exquisitely linked with that true legato which is imaginatively as well as physically realized, and the voice at that date is still properly supported. Lucrezia Bori's performance (DA 129) recorded in 1922 is not quite up to this, though poised and elegant. Blanche Arral (Victor 74151; Club 99. 69), who avoids the top D in the cadenza by cheating, and Alice Verlet (Apga 1072), remembered for having been Beecham's Konstanze in 1910 at His Majesty's, are nothing special.

Florence Macbeth (Col. A 6163), Ada Sari (Poly. 73009), Hjördis Schymberg (Swedish HMV X 4776) in Swedish, Elizabeth Newbold (Zono. GO 25), Gertrude Johnson (Col. 9193) and Joan Taylor (Decca K 1201) in English have nothing remarkable to offer. But Evelyn Scotney, an underrated Australian, is elegant and musical. Her later electric (D 1435), lively and lightly decorated, is better than her earlier acoustic (Vocalion 0213), which is capable but dull. Luella Paikin (Vocalion A 0251) is also dull and often flat, but Miriam Licette (L 1665) with Harty's sensitive conducting is accomplished, if less brilliant than the great names. Her acoustic HMV (D 113) with Percy Pitt is equally good.

This short look at singers who did not sing the part in major theatres ends with Gwen Catley (C 3902; HLM 7066), whose cool, pretty singing with Eric Robinson as conductor sounds careful, as though it were a concert piece. At least it is not a mere curiosity like the thirteen-year old Julie Andrews (Col. DB 2470), whose childish, pretty singing, in French, has Mum at the piano. Jeanette Macdonald did at least attempt the part in the theatre, even though her fame sprang from Hollywood. Here we have a small, delicate voice (DB 3940) well schooled and with a good trill. She is over-careful about the florid bits and tends to swallow the (French) words; also there are odd pauses here and there as though she were not sure what came next. Patrice Munsel's record (BLP 1023) comes from the soundtrack of the film in which she played Melba, and includes the short prior exchanges with Mercutio and the Nurse. She is not unmusical, just boring, not always in tune, and the coloratura is laboured; it lends strength to the suspicion that her short career at the Met. was due to looks as much as to talent.

With Noréna it is a relief to be back with great singing (Parlo. R. 20162;

ORX 135), a magnificent voice and perfect identification with the part. At the opposite pole from the wayward fascination of Galli-Curci, this is my favourite electric of the piece. Her HMV (DB 4922) is only just less exquisite and is backed by a melting performance of Micaela's aria from *Carmen*. Sayão is quite different from this, and almost as good (Am C 17301-D; Odyssey Y31151): the unaffected simplicity and the delicate musicianship reflect de Reszke's teaching. Jourfier (Pathé PD 73) belies her Opéra-Comique reputation with a performance that is lightweight but merely efficient, as is Lily Pons on a disappointing disc (LX 1067) sung straight in G, but with a notable tremolo.

It is contrary to expectation that a Norwegian and a Brazilian should be so pre-eminent in this part. The delightful Leila ben Sedira, though an Algerian, is a sharp reminder of the authentic French high soprano (R 1323). She sings in G and is brilliant and fluent. Fanny Heldy's resources (DB 1304; LV 223) are altogether larger, reminding us that she was Toscanini's choice for Louise and Mélisande at La Scala. Here is expert vocalism and the real French *voix blanche*. She has no trill, but she manages a rapid tempo with aplomb; this is an impulsive Juliet, full of character, who actually sounds as though she were enjoying the party. Barsova in Russian (E 11186), recorded in Berlin about 1930, rounds off this group of pre-war electrics, and very well too. She makes it a virtuoso piece with ready coloratura and *staccato*, but plenty of infectious enthusiasm as well.

Janine Micheau's career links pre- and post-war performances. On her 78 of the waltz song (K 2158) she is in fresher voice than in the LP set and substantially justifies her reputation. She sings in G, is musical and convincing, and especially well accompanied by the Paris Conservatoire orchestra under Roger Désormière.

This brings us to LP recitals, increasingly dominated by non-French singers. Joan Sutherland, singing in G, includes the piece on an early LP (SXL 2457). She is notably accurate and the voice was at its remembered zenith, but alas the singing is tame and characterless, with neither the animal high spirits of Melba nor the sensual charm of Galli-Curci. Crisply accompanied by Molinari-Pradelli, it is among the better modern versions, for all that that is faint praise. The Hungarian Sylvia Geszty reveals a darkish voice for a noted coloratura (SLT 43117), but the singing is delicate, even tentative, and the whole effect over-polite. Maria Stader, another Hungarian (DGM 19157), is too po-faced, and spoils her reputation for scrupulousness by virtually ignoring the grace notes attached to Juliet's opening crotchets. The less said about Miliza Korjus's late mono LP (Venus) the better. Caballé's effort (DG 2530 073) is a disappointment: girlishness is not Caballé's line, but there is no reason why a big-voiced singer should not be successful in this music (*cf* Patti and Noréna, or Callas); she tends to fade out phrase ends, e.g. at 'Loin de l'hiver morose', and is altogether over-careful. Of course, Callas (ASD 4306) shows everyone how to do it with this weight of voice. Her delicate slight hesitations and pressings-on, the pellucid declamation, all perfectly judged, are combined with the simplicity proper to Juliet. She is accompanied with exemplary punctilio by Georges Prêtre. Is some beat audible in those clotted high notes? Well, I ought to feel critical but just can't.

No recent French singers come up to this, but Mady Mesplé (2C 063–10411) is certainly good. She sounds young, and sings in G. The voice is a little vinegary and not too smoothly produced, but this is a sensitive and touching performance. Mado Robin (2C 061–11691) singing in F, makes no impression for good or ill: a neutral performance.

One turns with some relief (in my case) from these soprano cavortings to the beautiful so-called Madrigal, the duet 'Ange adorable'. The recording by Kozlovsky and Nezhdanova (USSR 08952/3) sung to a flowery piano accompaniment embodies very beautiful singing, although Kozlovzky's orien-tal timbre and cavalier attitude to note values will shake the purists. This is believed to be a unique copy. Much more traditional is the 1913 record of Edmond Clément and Geraldine Farrar (DB 172; Discophilia DIS 215), with Farrar full of character at 'Ah! Je n'ai pu m'en défendre' (molto determinato, orders Gounod). Clément is Romeo as poet rather than hero, and a bit bleaty in timbre, but is otherwise delicate, charming, and altogether right. Alice Verlet, with her bright, forward voice, recorded this duet with Ralph Errolle (Edison 82211), whose elegant tenor earned him this sort of part at the Met. in 1924–26. Lastly Gaston Micheletti, the Corsican tenor with a plangent voice and the kind of rapid vibrato much disliked fifty years ago but now much admired, together with the excellent Noréna, puts it all together in a satisfying disc (Od. 123.064; Club 99.32).

Act 2 brings us to Romeo's cavatina 'Ah, lève-toi, soleil!', a harder piece to bring off than appears at first sight because of its exposed voice part. Jean de Reszke recorded it for Fonotipia in 1905 (69000), but appears to have vetoed its issue, which thus remains the greatest and most tantalizing non-event of gramophone history. Emile Scaremberg recorded it for the same company in the same year (39172; Rococo R 18); he is hardly the young man in love and makes the aria sound like a concert piece, but the brilliance and attack suggest what heroic singing can do for a part now usually given to lightweights. Albert Alvarez in the same mould (Pathé 1625) is slow and leisurely, with fine high notes and great panache. Charles Dalmorès (Victor 85121; CO 392), originally a horn-player and later the 1908 Lohengrin at Bayreuth, brings clarion high notes but also good legato and cultivated musicianship, enough finally to convince one of the rightness of this kind of voice in this music. Edmond Clément exemplifies the other school (Od. 56000), but high B flat was his limit and he jibs at attacking it from the D at the end, lending an increased sense of fragility to his singing, charming though it is.

Nicolai Figner (3–22707; GV 15), in Russian, phrases squarely, often chops off phrase ends, and sounds elderly, but it is clear the voice had once been fine. Of this school too are Leonid Sobinov and Dimitri Smirnov. The former's red G&T of 1904 in Russian (022077; D Melodiya 025209/12), with its characteristic open voice production, has the high spirits of youth, but also a tendency to hog the high notes; it exemplifies the truth that in this music a lovely voice is not enough. Smirnov's 1909 record in Russian (VB 38; CO 379) is 'straighter' than his later one (DB 595) sung in French. The languid phrasing of the latter, the caressing *morendo* effects, and the thin but well supported tone are all *echt* Smirnov – the characteristic *diminuendo* on the high B flat may be an affectation, but what an affectation!

Other non-French tenors have also made successful attempts in their own language. Vilhelm Herold's record in Danish (Danish HMV M 50; GV 73) is imaginatively and beautifully sung with no straining at the high notes. A black G&T of Leo Slezak (42930; CO 309), in German, stuns with its sumptuous tone and youthful exuberance despite cruel abbreviation of the music. Equally unmistakable is Fernando de Lucia's pre-dog (2–52660; RS 305) with its rapid whinny and timbre whitening under pressure. But even this is more to my taste than Florencio Constantino (Col. A 5110), recorded in shocking French and neither musical nor in tune.

This is perhaps the place to mention a delightful 'off-the-air' LP of Gigli containing most of Act 2, sung in Italian, recorded in 1934 at La Scala under Santini with Mafalda Favero as Juliet. He was a famous Romeo. The elegant use of *portamento*, the easy high notes, the marvellous soft singing – all recreate to perfection not only the legend of the great tenor on stage but also the atmosphere of Juliet's garden on a hot summer night.

With Lucien Muratore (Pathé 4884; RS 304) we are back to 'singles'. Like Florence Macbeth he was a celebrity in Chicago, and it is easy to see why; gifted with a big voice, he gives a poetic and warm performance and crowns it beautifully with a *piano* high B flat. Every bit as good is the Belgian tenor, Fernand Ansseau (DB 486; Club 99.4 and DB 951; LV 116), also in the heroic manner. He was a good actor and a handsome man, and one delights in the marvellous solid tone of the voice on these two discs. The acoustic is not perhaps ideally rhythmical; the electric is in every way magnificent.

Micheletti (E 10881) sings in forthright – too forthright – style, often sounding effortful as he pushes hard at his high notes, which sharpen. His cavatina leads into the balcony duet 'O nuit divine' (Od. 123,605; Club 99.32) in which matters are as usual given a lift by the appearance of Noréna. This record carries on, after a brief cut, to the *andante* section beginning with Romeo's 'Va, repose en paix!'. Micheletti, I must add, is hereabouts heard at his best as an ensemble singer, being unusually scrupulous about such details as the full value of sustained notes. The whole scene is conducted with care and flair by the excellent Gustave Cloëz.

Francisco Nuibo (Victor 74013), lyric in timbre but unimaginative, is a more obscure figure than these, as is Obein whose throaty and awkward singing can be heard on Pathé H.&D. 0622. Razavet (P 0373), though described on the label as 'du Théâtre de la Monnaie', had a good career at the Opéra-Comique in the 1920s, but he is loud and monotonous, if less prone than Obein to give one a sympathetic sore throat.

César Vezzani, Georges Thill and José Luccioni all made excellent records in the thirties. Vezzani (DB 4931; FALP 50037) gives us both 'Ah! Lève-toi, soleil' and 'Salut, tombeau' in athletic and uncomplicated style, with clear declamation of the text. He was a real *tenor de force* and still singing well at sixty. There is little nuance here, but the voice is healthy and brilliant, somehow typically Corsican. This, one feels, is what Corelli ought to be! Thill (L 1985; 2C 061–12094) is satisfying as usual, though somehow anonymous despite the fine voice and sure taste. Luccioni, also a Corsican, gives us clean, vigorous singing in the grand style (DB 1115; 2C 053–11655). There is not much subtlety and the phrasing is a bit narrow, but one can see how the big voice and free, clear vocalism made him a successful Calaf and Otello in London. For this group of Frenchmen Alain Vanzo must bring up the rear (Vega L 80 009). We are back with the lyric style, but unsuccessfully, I fear. Vanzo gives us plain, careful singing, but too plain and too careful to succeed in his particular style.

Lastly, a small group of foreign tenors. Hermann Jadlowker (2–032006; Rococo 5227) sings with his characteristically brilliant, throaty, cantorial timbre, but I don't like his poor French and habit of cutting notes off abruptly. Piccaver in German (LV 26) produces a lovely *diminuendo* on the B flat. but sings with an air of almost offensive detachment; it might be a vocalize. The attempt of the American Richard Crooks (Victor 15542; VIC. 1464), though he was a noted Romeo, is remarkably dull, despite the fine voice; the timbre is nasal, the style heavy. Sydney Rayner's record (K 677; GV 596) is sung, as one would expect, in good French, steadily and capably; the voice rather glottal. Many readers will remember Ken Neate's singing in London and Paris after the war, but his 1955 record with piano (Rococo 5387) was made too late. There is a genuine voice audible but also a wide beat, and the phrasing is puddingy and laboured. William Heseltine's version (Col. 9276), in clear English, sounds charmless and elderly – of curiosity value only. A late Heddle Nash recording (C 3492) has the high notes sounding peaky and is not really a satisfying memorial. Libero de Luca's effort (DG EPL 30339), with the Berlin RIAS orchestra under Dohnányi, is disconcertingly uneven: a fine voice with oddly bare patches and a wide beat, but he pleases with a poised final phrase not sung flat out for effect.

With Jussi Björling we come to the only great recent Romeo. His 1930 record in Swedish (X 3628; HLM 7115) has the lovely lyrical ease of the very young singer, though the phrasing is too confined and the whole approach over-modest. In the 1948 record (DB 6249; IC 147–00947) sung in French, the mature Björling gives us the best: the easy high notes, the sure taste, the magnificent voice. The effect may be a little antiseptic compared with the live performance noticed earlier, but even by this singer's standards the record is a marvel. Domingo (ARL1 0048) is not quite in this class: the voice is inclined to subside awkwardly on leaving high notes, and in this music it shows. But the singing is thoroughly honest, musical, clean and in fair French. One would be lucky to hear better today.

Romeo's powerful exhortation, not surprisingly, brings Juliet out on to her balcony, and my favourite record of the ensuing duet – even better than Noréna and Micheletti – is an acoustic of Gigli and Bori (DA 381; GEMM 202–6) who sang this opera together often. They begin at 'Ah, ne fuis pas encore!', and the voices blend to perfection. I play this little disc to my friends who complain of Gigli's vulgarity. Also charming is Kozlovsky singing in Russian with Shumskaya (USSR 5289–56), presumably from their complete set, which I haven't heard. He is more disciplined than in his madrigal duet, but some of the gilt is taken off the gingerbread by his partner's shrillness. The LP of the Canadian Léopold Simoneau and his wife Pierrette Alarie (DTL 93018) is attractive for those who prefer the lyric to the heroic in this opera. Even so, Alarie sounds over-parted, but Simoneau is excellent and the voices blend well. The reverse has the bedroom scene from Act 4, which is well enough sung, but too cool for what is after all Gounod's answer to Act 2 of *Tristan*. The interlocking phrases at 'O volupté de vivre' sound merely polite. The excerpt extends as far as the *allegro* section beginning at 'Roméo, qu'as-tu donc?'.

But we must go back to Act 3 and the arrival of that prosy old interferer, Frère Laurent. Marius Chambon (Zono. 2182), recorded in 1902, impresses one with a huge black voice with a big vibrato, but he does little else for the music. Etienne Billot's record (Od. 56159), followed by the quartet, is better: here is a fine firm voice, and his colleagues are so good that I regret having been unable to hear the companion record of the Act 4 quartet (56135). Laurent's Act 4 scene, while we are on the subject, has also been recorded by Willy Tubiana (W 932) with a vitality that cannot conceal that he is miscast as the Friar; and also by Robert Radford (Zono. GO 24) whose singing is lugubrious enough to threaten a long corpse-like sleep for Juliet without need of the fatal potion.

But the high spot of Act 3 is really the little song for the page Stephano: 'Que fais-tu, blanche tourterelle?', a delicious and original trifle which has an almost Slavonic freshness of melody and harmony. Elisaveta Petrenko in Russian, recorded about 1910 (2–23522; RLS 743), is inaccurate and makes no attempt to sing the little flourish at the end, but she is a neat and charming singer all the same. Nina Friede (Am Col 35088; RLS 7706) is a capable singer, but the voice sounds worn and the flourish at the end is rewritten. Better is Rita Fornia (Victor 74211) with lots of *espiéglerie* and a lovely trill. Best of all is Germaine Corney (Col. D 12048). She was another Opéra-Comique star of the twenties and sounds an absolute 'natural': plenty of *élan*, charmingly varied in tone and tempo. Technically she is admirable, fleet and expert with an excellent trill, and she is well accompanied. Gladys Swarthout's record (Victor 11–8280; VIC 1490) reveals more heavyweight resources but is not up to her 1935 live performance: her French is vague and she makes no attempt at the trill. Frederica von Stade included the song in a 1975 recital (CBS 76522), but I found this item distressingly lacking in *diablerie*, or indeed any pronounced character at all. This is in spite of much beautiful singing, including a good trill and a finely managed cadenza. She is however vivid compared with Marie Laurence (Alpha SP 6013), whose French is excellent but whose singing is flavourless and uncertain.

Act 4 opens with the bedroom duet, which struck early audiences as erotic to a Wagnerian degree. Since the good Friar has pronounced a form of marriage, the lovers' night of passion was presumably permissible. True, they had no parental consent, to put it mildly, and were under age, but let's not quibble! The G&T of Affre and Agussol (34004), a placid performance mistily recorded, would not have disturbed even Victorian audiences, though what one can hear of Affre makes me regret not having heard more of his several records from the opera. Noréna and Micheletti are again excellent (Od. 123.066; ORX 135), and begin at 'Va, je t'ai pardonné'. Noréna's recitative is a joy, and how beautifully she pronounces 'C'est le doux rossignol, confident de l'amour!' Micheletti, though reliable as ever, lacks tingle at his high notes and avoids the high C so often sung (though not written) at 'cette ardente ivresse'.

An interesting LP giving the scene complete (CTL 7034) is that by Jean Fenn and Raymond Manton with the Los Angeles Orchestra conducted by Franz Waxman, who is better known as a composer of film music. Manton's is a small voice, but of good quality, a sort of mini-Björling. Fenn is paler than this but adequate. The orchestra is first class and Waxman clearly a conductor to be reckoned with. Scotto and Domingo also begin at 'Va, je t'ai pardonné', and the National Philharmonic Orchestra is conducted by Kurt Herbert Adler, long the moving spirit behind the San Francisco opera (CBS 76732). The orchestral sound is rich and well recorded. Scotto sounds matronly and pulls the tempo about, mostly within acceptable bounds. 'Non, non ce n'est pas le jour' is dragged as though it were verismo, and her words start a bit woolly, but this improves and the whole thing warms up nicely after the first pages. Aided by the vigorous and musical Romeo of Domingo, this is an impressive record of the scene.

After pausing to note briefly Arthur Endrèze's distinguished singing of Capulet's 'Que l'hymne nuptiale' (Od. 123 720; ORX 135), we come to Act 5, to the tomb scene and to the finest of all 78s from this opera: Paul Franz's 'Salut, tombeau' (03227; Club 99.10). Franz worked as a navvy on the railways before his voice was discovered, but his singing is a model of sensibility and poetry. Note the tender colouring of the voice at 'O ma femme', and the distinction of the phrasing; this is married to some superb heroic singing and put across with a magnificent voice. A record about which it is hard to speak with moderation!

After this anything would be a let-down. Miguel Villabella was a Spaniard who made his career in France. His typically 'open' production makes him sound like a verismo singer, though his career details refute this notion. His cavatina (Od. 123.639; ORX 135), where the music's regular metre helps him, is better than the tomb scene (Od. 123 573; ORX 143), which is neither elegant nor stirring. Nor is the voice of the best quality, despite a certain vitality and coarse charm. Probably these records do not do him justice. The same may be true of René Maison who had a long and honourable career, first in Paris and after 1935 in the USA, in a repertory that embraced Florestan and Wagner. In this music the papery timbre and rapid vibrato are disconcerting (Od. 188.600; ORX 135), but the voice is evidently large and he is an excellent singer, sensitive and musical.

Vezzani's virtues (DB 4931; FALP 50037) I have mentioned already, also Heseltine's failings (Col. 9276). So here are Georges Thill and Germaine Féraldy (LFX 1–2; COLC 115) to complete the tale with a final scene, whole, and beautifully done. Thill manages the *larghetto* ('Console-toi, pauvre âme') as well as anyone else on records: he makes it sound at once tragic and natural. Féraldy has a typically shallow French lyric soprano, but uses it with intelligence and character: the sort of singer one must teach oneself to admire if one is to do French opera justice. They are well recorded for the date and their accompanying orchestra is directed with notable thrust by J. F. Szyfer. It is a pleasure to be able to end this survey with such a characteristic and admirable product of the maligned thirties.

As for my ideal cast, I would settle for the singers who actually appeared together in the piece at Covent Garden in 1893 in a performance staged to celebrate the marriage of, as they afterwards became, King George V and Queen Mary: namely Melba, Jean and Edouard de Reszke, and Plançon. To whom I would add Couzinou as Mercutio, Corney as Stephano, and Cooper or Désormière to conduct. If the de Reszkes are barred by the absence of recorded evidence, I would substitute Franz and Journet.

ROMEO ET JULIETTE

R Roméo; *J* Juliette; *M* Mercutio; *S* Stéphano; *L* Laurent

1912 Affre *R*; Gall *J*; Boyer *M*; Champel *S*; Journet *L* / Paris Opéra-Comique Chorus and Orch. / Ruhlmann
Rococo ⓜ 1002

1947 (in Russian) Kozlovsky *R*; Shumskaya *J*; Burlak *M*; Sokolova *S*; Mikhailov *L* / Bolshoi Theatre Chorus and Orch. / Orlov
Melodiya ⓜ D 0 32563–8

1947 (in Russian) Lemeshev *R*; Maslennikova *J*; Burlak *M*; Sokolova *S*; Mikhailov *L* / Bolshoi Theatre Chorus and Orch. / Nebolsin
Melodiya ⓜ D 01336–41

1953 Jobin *R*; Micheau *J*; Mollet *M*; Collart *S*; Rehfuss *L* / Paris Opéra Chorus and Orch. / Erede
IPG ⓜ 115.027–9
London ⓜ A4310

1968 Corelli *R*; Freni *J*; Gui *M*; Lublin *S*; Depraz *L* / Paris Opéra Chorus and Orch. / Lombard
EMI SAN 235–7
Angel SCL 3734

1964 (excerpts) Gedda *R*; Carteri *J*; Dens *M*; Rouleau *L* / Paris Opéra Orch. / Lombard
EMI 2C 061 11688
Angel S36287

Samson et Dalila

ALAN BLYTH

Surviving the shafts of Shaw, bans by the Lord Chamberlain, cries of 'oratorio' from New York pundits, Saint-Saëns's *Samson et Dalila* continues to win popular acclaim whenever it is performed. There may be some truth in the dictum that it is a cross between Mendelssohn's *Elijah* and a Meyerbeer opera, even more in the claim by Alfred Einstein that the piece was written according to the conventions of Grand Opera, but Saint-Saëns's musical sensibilities ranged far wider than either of those statements would imply. Indeed any close study of the piece shows the debt he owes to Handel, Gluck, Berlioz, Verdi (*Aida*'s influence paramount), and Wagner, while at the same time he subtly formed an individual style. Martin Cooper has compared the piece to *Oedipus Rex* where 'the perennial and the archaic, the "modern" and the trivial are amalgamated into a convincing unity'.

What cannot be in doubt is that the composer created a work in which authority, compassion, tragedy and sensuality are unerringly brought into focus by his writing for his three principals. Delilah's overpowering sexuality and her dark soul are magnificently portrayed in her three main solos and her long duet with Samson, who in turn is a tragic figure of proud defiance brought to the ground through his erotic appetite. The High Priest is forcefully delineated as a frustrated, vengeful, overweening figure (one wonders if he would like to bed Delilah, did his religious scruples permit it). All this is depicted succinctly by Saint-Saëns against the background of the suffering Jews, the superstitious and wild Philistines.

It follows that there are three *sine qua non* for its successful performance. They are a mezzo with a sensuous, smooth, seductive timbre, a heroic tenor with plangency in the tone, and a superb chorus. The most recent recording fulfils at least two of these requirements and has a conductor, Daniel Barenboim, aware of the work's stature, as he was when he directed it at the Orange Theatre in 1978, a performance from which this set derives. Shaw's comment that the opera 'requires *entrain*, even at its quietest; and from this normal activity it has to be worked up to the utmost vivacity and impetuosity' has been noted, consciously or unconsciously, by Barenboim and his Paris forces. He realizes the sensitive proportions of the prelude and Dance of the Priestesses. He makes no excuses for the more obvious pages – the Delilah–

High Priest duet and the Bacchanale. He paces the central scene of seduction in a single span of gradually increasing eroticism.

In support he has Domingo's fully involved Samson. His delivery is notable for its keen edge and defiant heroism, its dignity in misery; it is one of his most successful assumptions on disc in French opera. Elena Obraztsova shows that Delilah has the heart of a devil inside her nubile body – she seems almost willing Samson to betray himself and his people – but there is a harshness in her voice that accords ill with this music, a bumpy line in the big solos, taken slowly by Barenboim, and no feeling for the nuances of the French language. She gains a point, however, for singing the phrase 'Ah réponds ma tendresse' as Saint-Saëns wrote it, that is without a repeat of the word 'reponds' made by all other mezzos in the complete sets. Renato Bruson hectors to strong but rather unfocused effect as the High Priest, Pierre Thau is an average Abimelech, Robert Lloyd a truly French-sounding Old Hebrew. The Paris Chorus cleverly differentiates between suffering Israelites and complacent Philistines in its fresh, well-projected singing.

If you find Barenboim's approach almost too grandiloquent for this piece, you may prefer the Patanè set of five years earlier. While not neglecting the work's dramatic impetus, particularly in the mob glorification of Dagon in the final scene, he brings out the sensuous quality of Saint-Saëns's scoring even more successfully than Barenboim, and his yielding direction of passages such as the A major trio 'Je viens célébrer' in Act 1, with its subtle chromaticisms, and the delicacy of the Priestesses' Dance, are commendable. Christa Ludwig is in agreement with this approach. She is longing personified in 'Printemps qui commence' and in the inward questioning and scheming of 'Se pourrait-il', but she lacks that element of *diablerie* called for in 'Amour! viens aider' and she does not ravish the senses as she should at 'Ah, réponds'. Perhaps, as in the case with her Carmen, the impersonation is a little too polite and withdrawn for the music in hand.

James King gives a well-sung, honourable performance as Samson, but it lacks the degree of ardour, conviction and in the end tragedy and desolation of the noblest Samsons. Good intentions and a good voice are simply not enough here. Much the same applies to Bernd Weikl's purposeful High Priest; he suggests some but not enough of his peeky malevolence. In the end, all three are wanting in knowledge of how to treat the French language.

That fault applies doubly to the Romanian set of 1972, where Elena Cernei is an accomplished Delilah in a generalized way: secure in tone, suitably seductive in manner, but missing the detail that can bring her role alive. Ludovic Spiess is stentorian enough of voice for Samson – more sensitive than expected when he joins Cernei's fruity tone at the repeat of 'Ah, réponds', but elsewhere the power and presence of his singing are vitiated by a failure to phrase with meaning and by a propensity to bleat. Kurt Adler handles the score with some aplomb and, like Patanè, has an excellent choir at his command. You might be pleased to hear such a performance on a holiday evening in Bucharest, but as a permanent view of the work it is not worthy of consideration.

By contrast, the 1962 EMI set has been spoken of as the central interpretation in modern times, and it has indeed much to commend it. Prêtre, as conductor, may go to extremes, with tempi either on the slow or fast side. Vickers, of all the tenors on the complete sets, declaims with the most individuality, with the greatest dignity of expression, rising to agonized heights at 'Prends ma vie en sacrifice' in the third act. His involvement, as we know from all his interpretations, sometimes leads him to over-emphasis and to approaching notes from below. I must say I find a sentimentality in his singing here that is foreign to the role's true nature: the performance, for all its power, is not quite idiomatic.

Without any special insights to her interpretation, Rita Gorr's Delilah is sung with full, rich tone, but with something less than the voluptuousness of mezzos more limited in their resources. A degree of restraint is not what one wants in 'Amour! viens aider', but as a whole Gorr's performance fulfils most of the role's demands. Ernest Blanc is a properly preening High Priest but his demands on Delilah in Act 2 need to be delivered with rather more bite. Anton Diakov is weak as both Abimelech and the Old Hebrew. The René Duclos Choir and the Opéra Orchestra are more than adequate, but they are sometimes clumsily directed by Prêtre.

Something much closer to a *vrai* Saint-Saëns style is to be found in the 1946 set directed by Louis Fourestier who, without resorting to the over-emphasis of Barenboim and Prêtre, most easily captures the mood of the piece. Obviously he, his cast and orchestra had worked closely together on the stage of the Opéra, and as always that experience tells in the studio. Besides, one seems to be hearing here the tail-end of a tradition, now lost, in the art of enunciating and singing French opera. We hear this most arrestingly in Hélène Bouvier, who made her Opéra debut in the part of Delilah in 1939, and sang it there regularly afterwards. The voice (largish yet warm and compact), phrasing and diction are instinctively correct for the music. Such passages as 'garde à son retour' and 'Samson soit enchaîné demain' are delivered with real meaning, the words forward and on the breath, then at 'et tremble de mon bras', she sounds at once commanding and irresistibly desirable. Later when she declares 'J'ai preparé mes armes' we know this Delilah means what she says. Then in the *allegro moderato* of the duet with the High Priest both she and Paul Cabanel spit out their words with real vengeance in their souls. 'Mon coeur s'ouvre à ta voix' is seductive and smooth, yet sung as part of the scene not as a 'big' solo. José Luccioni, though often wooden as to phrasing, proves himself one of the last in a previously generous line of heroic French Samsons.

As I have implied, Cabanel is a superb High Priest, easily the best in any set, in spite of a second-division voice. Every time he sings, the listener has to sit up and take note, such is the conviction of his delivery, perhaps at its most potent when he riles Samson in Act 3, but never less than compelling.

Charles Cambon, an erstwhile High Priest, is a splendidly taunting Abime-lech, keen words again the key to the force of his performance, Henri Médus a more than adequate Old Hebrew.

Such authenticity does not extend to the two commercial discs of highlights, both with Risë Stevens as Delilah. Stokowski milks the score unmercifully, killing it with kindness, and cuts gratuitously even the sections he plays. In 'Printemps qui commence', Stevens is too obviously the vamp and the tone has no sure centre, but the touch of evil and determination in her voice when calling love to her aid is appropriate, and 'Se pourrait-il' is full of expectancy so that one can hear why she was admired in the role at the Metropolitan, and hereabouts Stokowski etches in the wonderful wind *obbligato* with a deft hand. 'Mon coeur' is matter-of-fact with an awkward, extra breath in 'Ah, réponds', corrected by the time the later disc was made. Jan Peerce is a coarse, over-emphatic Samson, somewhat better in his *misère* than in his night of love.

On the Cleva record, Mario del Monaco is predictably forceful and virile (as in the 1959 'live' performance on Melodram, not recommended), but also too stentorian in his phrasing, brutal in his treatment of French. Stevens's voice has deteriorated noticeably, the vibrato much looser, giving the impres-sion of a madame rather than a *poule de luxe*. Abimelech's music is included and Ezio Flagello sings it strongly.

On their 1964 record, 'Duets of Love and Passion' (SXL 6144), Sandra Warfield and James McCracken sing most of scene iii of Act 2, starting at 'Un Dieu plus puissant' and give an object-lesson in how *not* to sing French opera: both offer rough, overbearing performances of no specific interest. By contract the EJS highlights, rudely culled from a matinée at the Metro-politan on 26 December 1936, can be cited as a model (in most respects) for a performance of Saint-Saëns's work. You can sense the electricity of a live performance in Maurice Abravanel's inspiriting direction. René Maison is a Samson of profound musicality with a richly heroic tenor to carry out his good intentions. His call to arms in Act 1 is at once commanding and noble. He precisely catches Samson's agony of mind in the duet with Delilah, imparting to such phrases as 'Ah, cesse d'affliger mon coeur' a real sense of reproach, ideally voiced. His *misère* is a little too tearful, forgiveable in a stage portrayal; then he rises to tragic stature in his urgent demands to God for help in the finale.

Gertrud Wettergren's Delilah is not on this peak of interpretative great-ness, but her light, airy delivery is often very much to the point, particularly in Act 2, where in both duets her intelligent use of the text matches that of her partners. 'Mon coeur', in spite of an inclination to too many breaths, is natural in its phrasing and increasingly voluptuous as the solo develops. Ezio Pinza's High Priest is simply the best I have heard, suggesting the man's religious bigotry and his ferocious, overbearing personality. The singing from this king of basses is predictably superb in diction and tone. All the important scenes are included on this record, though you have to be on your toes to spot the sudden elisions from one to another. Happily 'J'ai gravi la montagne' from this performance has recently been included in the Pearl/Pinza album (GEMM 162/3).

And so to Delilah's much-recorded solos. Irving Kolodin once said that an ideal Delilah must have 'a voluptuous voice in an irresistible body'. Without the help of the latter we are left requiring on record the former, allied to a delivery of the text with real meaning. Practically all the performances listed below exhibit the characteristics of the mezzo's country of origin, and (sadly) it is surprising how few are by native French singers. Any in the list (and there must be many more I have not found) not mentioned afterwards can be taken merely as souvenirs of the artist concerned, little more.

1. Printemps qui commence
2. Amour, viens aider ma faiblesse
3. Mon coeur s'ouvre à ta voix

Rosette Anday (unpubl., EG 2340; LV 15) 1, 2, 3 (2, 3 *Ger*)
Marian Anderson (Belvox 505B, C 3047; GEMM 193) 2, 3 (*Eng*)
Margarete Arndt-Ober (P 423/4) 2, 3 (*Ger*)
Francine Arrauzau (Readers Digest 6323) 3
Larisa Avdeyeva (Melodiya) 2, 3 (*Russ*)
Ljuba Baricova (Opus 9112 0414) 2, 3
Maria von Basilides (Od. 0–7625; Hungaroton LPX 11310/1) 1, 3 (*Ger*)
Gabriella Besanzoni (7–53039; Accord 150002), 1, 3 (*Ital*)
Bette Björling (ALPC 1) 2
Irina Bogacheva (Melodiya) 3
Hélène Bouvier (PDT 188) 1, 2
Karin Branzell (Brunswick 50158; LV 182; Gramm 66689; LV 47) 1, 2, 3 (2, 3 *Ger*)
Suzanne Brohly (D 196, Disque W 431/2) 1, 2, 3
Elisa Bruno (53241/2) 2, 3 (*Ital*)
Muriel Brunskill (Col. 3328) 3 (*Eng*)
Grace Bumbry (DG 138826) 3
Clara Butt (Col. 74004; GEMM 168) 3
Maria Callas (ASD 4306) 1, 2, 3
Gabriella Carturan (ALP 1720) 3 (*Ital*)
Bruna Castagna (Am Col 71058, 71390; OASI 605) 1, 2, 3
Germaine Cernay (LFX 262, LX 385; 2C 153–16211/4) 1, 3 (3 with Thill)
Elena Cernei (Electrecord) 1, 3
Maria Charbonnel (Od. 111228) 2

Florica Cristoforeanu (E 11178, 11282; Electrecord) 1, 3 (*Ital*)
Alice Cuccini (053121/2) 1, 2
Julia Culp (DA 152) 3
Biserka Cvejic (Jugoton) 2, 3
Irene Dalis (Telef. GMA 42) 1, 3 (*Ger*)
Marguerite D'Alvarez (DA 1000, Vic. 6590, DB 1353; Cl. 99–73) 1, 3
Marie Delna (Pathé 4877; Cl. 99–59) 1
Blanche Deschamps-Jéhin (Od. 97028; RS 304) 3
Emmy Destinn (Od. 118501; CO 307) 3
Zara Dolukhanova (Melodiya) 1, 2, 3 (*Russ*)
Marie Duchesne (VA 28; Rococo 5234) 3 (with Vezzani)
Frozier-Marrot (Pathé X 26) 3
Maria Gay (Col A 4280) 1, 3 (*Ital*)
Jeanne Gerville-Réache (Vic. 88184, 88244, Col. 36875; Rococo R 14) 1, 2, 3
Alma Gluck (7–33026; Cl. 99–30) 3
Maria Goetze (43848/83) 2, 3 (*Ger*)
Jeanne Gordon (Rococo 5254) 2
Rita Gorr (ASDF 141) 1, 2
Louise Homer (DA 1080; Roc. 5268) 3
Louise Homer (DB 299; Vic. 1519) 2, 3
Elisabeth Höngen (Preiser 1111 165) 1, 3 (*Ger*)
Marilyn Horne (SXL 6345) 1, 3
Kathleen Howard (Pathé 5365; RS 300) 3
Janet Howe (K 1200) 2, 3 (*Eng*)
Maria von Ilosvay (Philips 45 SBF 214) 2, 3
Sabine Kalter (Od. 80710, unpubl.; LV 231) 1, 2, 3
Louise Kirkby Lunn (DB 509; CO 374) 1, 3
Marta Krásová (Supraphon) 2 (*Czech*)

Emmi Leisner (Od. AA 79412, Poly. 65614, 66734; LV 99, LV 189) 1, 2, 3 (*Ger*)

Félia Litvinne (Od. 562181; Roc. R 38) 3

Maria Maksakova (Melodiya) 1, 2, 3 (*Russ*)

Margarete Matzenauer (Vic. 6531; CO 313) 3

Ottilie Metzger (2–43235; CO 310) 1 (*Ger*)

Kerstin Meyer (7C 061–35593) 3

Solange Michel (Pathé DTX 137) 1

Alexandrina Milcheva (Balkanton) 2, 3

Mildred Miller (JH–100)

Irene Minghini-Cattaneo (DB 1303, 1332; Cl. 99–54) 1, 2, 3 (*Ital*)

Jeanne Montfort (Poly. 566041) 1, 3 (with Franz Kaisin)

Elena Nicolai (R 30049; Balkanton) 2

Elena Obraztsova (Melodiya) 1, 2, 3

Nadezhda Obukhova (Melodiya) 1, 2, 3 (*Russ*)

Maartje Offers (DB 912/3; LV 263) 1, 2, 3

Maria Olszewska (DB 1386, 1465; LV 205) 1, 3

Rose Olitzka (Col. 30825/6; Cl. 99–86) 1, 3

Sigrid Onegin (043323/27) 1, 3 (*Ger*)

Sigrid Onegin (Brunswick 50018, 50028; GV 508) 2, 3

Sigrid Onegin (DB 1420; LV 82) 1, 3

Zenaida Pally (Electrecord) 1, 3

Rosa Ponselle (Private) 1, 2, 3

Marianna Radev (Jugoton) 1, 2, 3

Alice Raveau (Pathé X 7222; Cl. 99–18) 1, 3

Regina Resnik (LXT 5668) 3

Gladys Ripley (C 3404, DX 1709) 1, 2, 3 (*Eng*)

Eliette Schenneberg (LFX 642) 1, 3

Ernestine Schumann-Heink (Col. 1380; CBS BRG 72145) 3 (*Ger*)

Ernestine Schumann-Heink (Vic. 88190; Roc. 5271) 3

Clara Serena (DX 245) 1, 3 (*Eng*)

Dolores de Silvera (Col. D 12043) 3

Giulietta Simionato (LXT 5458, LXT 5326) 1, 3 (3 in *Ital*)

Věra Soukupová (Supraphon) 2

Risë Stevens (Am. Col. 71974D) 3

Ebe Stignani (DA 5383; QALP 10144) 1 (*Ital*)

Ebe Stignani (DPX 23; LV 237) 1, 2, (*Ital*)

Ebe Stignani (LX 976; 3C 065–17659) 3 (*Ital*)

Ebe Stignani (GQX 11376; 3C 065–17659) 2 (*Ital*)

Conchita Supervia (R 20192; Cl. 99–74) 1 (*Ital*)

Gladys Swarthout (LM 1156; VIC 1490) 1, 2, 3

Gladys Swarthout (DB 2992) 2, 3

Laura Tessandra (Od. 123014) 2, 3

Kerstin Thorborg (Od. D. 6022, X 2749; Roc. 5367) 2, 3, (*Swedish*)

Kerstin Thorborg (Od. 11971; LV 209) 3 (*Ger*)

Jennie Tourel (LX 1555) 1, 3

Cyrena Van Gordon (Col. 60000D) 1

Shirley Verrett (SB 6790) 3

Luise Willer (HMV EH 50; LV 104) 1, 3 (*Ger*)

Constance Willis (Vocalion K 05166, Broadcast 5144) 1, 3 (*Eng*) 1

Of the East Europeans, I would mention first Maksakova and Obukhova, both singing in their native tongue, both notable Bolshoi Delilahs, both notable for their forward production, even delivery and the feeling of a real presence. Maksakova's uttering of 'lublyu' in 2 and the smile in Obukhova's tone in 1 are worth noting. Obraztsova, in the original, is much more commendable than in her complete set. Though still too harsh to be ideal, the sexy, sappy sound is hard to deny. Far better than either of these three, indeed near perfection, is Dolukhanova, luminous and gentle in 1, insinuating and finely accented in 2, particularly in the *dolce* passage, a most lovely quality of tone to support a seductive 3. Of the others, only the Czech Krásová deserves a word for her glorious voice and her sense of longing in 2.

Across the seas and continents to the numerous American or American-based contraltos. Of early interpreters, Schumann-Heink is unforgettable for the refulgence of her voice and what John Steane calls (in *The Grand Tradition*) her 'exquisite care for the score in every line'. This is the old-fashioned style heard at its best, beside which Homer sounds phlegmatic, even hooty, Swarthout boring, Anderson oratorio-like (though always accurate and pleasing to the ear), Matzenauer unilluminating, D'Alvarez wayward (but shading her tone finely on DA 1000, with piano). Gluck and Destinn both transpose 3 *up* a semitone and sound out of their element. Tourel and Thebom are simply dull. In more recent times Grace Bumbry's version of 3 is bewitching in vocal quality, but like so many others she is uncommunicative with her words. Horne, hampered by ludicrously slow speeds, is stodgy. Resnik, though the tone is too fruity, shows a welcome attention to her diction, even if it is not idiomatic. The young Verrett is better than these, building the hackneyed 3 to an urgent climax and, like all the best Delilahs, sounding as if she really believed in her amorous effusions. The absence of idiosyncracies here seems a positive advantage. Until you hear a true French interpreter, you feel this is just how the music should go. Ponselle is best overlooked.

The British ladies present stark contrasts. Butt is grand, chesty, but surprisingly sensuous. Brunskill is bosomy, oratorio-like, Kirkby Lunn stately, uninvolved, Thornton lighter, a little genteel: she, like many others, takes unto herself Samson's words at the end of 3, a curious and silly close. Clara Serena floats her tone easily on the text in 1, but is unresponsive in 2. I am much more inclined to the two 1940s interpreters. Ripley, a much underrated artist, burns with love in 1, is vividly commanding in 2, caressing in 3, and her diction is irreproachable. The voice itself, poised between mezzo and contralto, is apt for the part. Janet Howe, with Boyd Neel as unlikely conductor, is even better. Her dark, menacing tone, perhaps a little head-mistressy in character, makes 2 severe and poisonous. In 3, she is at once pressing and intense, her *rubato* just right.

Most Italian mezzos almost inevitably suggest Amneris in another context. Besanzoni's suave, insinuating 3 of 1921 accords with her reputation. Minghini-Cattaneo is the slinky schemer personified: the tone bites, the glottal stop works overtime in her biting versions of all three pieces, but she remembers to be *dolce* at 'contro l'amor' in 2. Stignani is at her formidable best in the 1936 version of 2 conducted by Gui, imparting urgency to her wily plans. The wartime version of 1 on HMV is sonorous; she manages to be gentle despite the opulence of tone. Simionato is more sultry and sings excellent French in 1 so it is odd to find her in Italian for her stodgy 3 (Solti conducting).

Of the older school of German-based interpreters, Arndt-Ober is, as usual, urgent and lovely, her quick vibrato adding colour to her accounts of 2 and 3. Metzger recalls Schumann-Heink but is less imaginative. In the next generation, Branzell and Onegin, not surprisingly, stand out. Branzell's version of 1, happily in French, is delicate and caressing, a sound to which any Samson might capitulate. Everything about her 2 and 3, though now in German, is deeply felt and controlled, the tone velvet and seductive. One-gin's voice is, if possible, even more suave, particularly in her early, German versions, a long-treasured disc of mine. In French the sculpted phrasing may be a little studied, concert-like, but control of line and dynamics is faultless and 'Ah, réponds' is done as written without the unwritten repeat of 're-ponds'. Leisner, in her three similar versions of 1 and 3, is earth-mother rather than Eastern vamp. Culp, in 3, is a wooing, gentle seductress, very plausible. Thorborg, as expected, is a much more vibrant, positive Delilah than any of these, the Swedish versions slightly preferable to the German. Kalter marries *bel canto* to sensuality in a remarkable way in 1 (no wonder she was referred to as Schumann-Heink's successor), brings a touch of steel to 2, a true though somewhat maternal *cantabile* to 3, where Olszewska is simply maternal. Offers, with Sargent as conductor, sounds appealing but too likeable. Willer is firm, linear, almost eloquent.

Turning to the best French interpreters is like sipping a *café filtre* after too many cups of powdered coffee, and the memory of the real thing similarly lingers long. Starting with the legendary Litvinne, one discovers how the composer must have intended the music to sound in word and music; even at forty-seven, she maintains an ideal line and suggests the delights of the couch. By contrast Delna seems a bit mature for courtesan duties. Deschamps-Jéhin (an early interpreter) is light and lacking in colour, while Gerville-Réache is as hooty and static as Max Loppert found her in *Orphée* (see *Opera on Record*), the kind of singing that gets her era of singers a bad name. Charbonnel, in 2, is properly menacing, with a fiery chest register.

The next generation sports hardly anything but winners. Alice Raveau, though not tonally one of nature's Delilahs, charms us with her 'douce ivresse' and *dolcissmo e cantabile* 'Mon coeur'. Duchesne, in her version of 3 with Vezzani, offers a rich, poised mezzo, though her style is a little anonymous. The versions of 3 by two little-known inter-war mezzos are both ravishing. That by Dolores de Silvera is the kind of forgotten disc that has to have another hearing once played: 3 is sung off the words in an utterly captivating, Supervia-like way, the single word 'tendresse' sending shivers up the spine. Schenneberg, a mezzo of the late thirties at the Opéra, is less personal but appreciable for the mellow quality of her voice, 1 more suited to her than 3. Her contemporary Frozier-Marrot is a more positive, rich-toned Delilah, perhaps a little too formidable, a bit like Janet Howe, while Montfort only confirms the strength of the Opéra's mezzos in this era with her smooth, poised, firm singing. She gains credit for taking 'Ah, réponds' as written. Delilah was her début role in 1921. Kaisin, her Samson, is awful.

Bouvier is even more plausible than on her set. What a sensual sound she produces in 1! *The Record Year* was lavish in its praise of Cernay's 1, classically poised, unaffected, round in tone. She is even better in her famous version of 3, which with Thill as a virile, open-throated Samson rises to erotic heights not attained elsewhere, lest it be with Wettergren and Maison in the second verse. How one longs for a complete version of the opera with these two principals. Arrauzau, among modern interpreters, is attractive of voice, intense of manner, to be preferred to Gorr, who fails to charm us by her rich but casual approach: she is better in her set. By contrast Solange Michel comes near a modern ideal in 1, her tone *dolce* and smiling, her expression becoming increasingly sensual in the *poco animato* passage. She might animate any Samson.

Hors concours are Supervia and Callas in 1. Supervia's reading, as you would expect, is highly idiosyncratic and utterly captivating, the growing emotional involvement at the *poco animato* precisely caught but, be warned, she is free with the written notes and tempo. For comment on Callas I can do no better than quote Ronald Crichton in an issue of Covent Garden's *About the House* ('Sacred and Profane'): 'Callas, in her matchlessly intelligent and instinctive record, is like an elegant young tigress stretching her limbs in the spring sunshine.' Her 3, issued for the first time, is almost as special.

When we turn to the tenors, we find too few performances of Samson's wonderful solos, but almost every one of them rewarding. With the French interpreters, one is amazed by the high standard of voice and enunciation and regretful that this kind of tone and style has become as uncommon as the sight of certain butterflies. Charles Dalmorès, one of Covent Garden's first Samsons, sings his first solo 'Arrêtez, o mes frères' (A), where Samson urges the despondent Israelites to trust in God and rise against their Philistine masters, with the right fervour and abandon (Vic. 87087; RLS 7705) confirming contemporary opinion that he was 'in stature, style and voice all that can be desired', except that when we hear Paul Franz, his successor in the part, in the same music (DA 442; GV 548), we encounter an even more thrilling sound and declamation with the top of the voice fuller and more confidently placed than is the case with Dalmorès. In B, 'Vois ma misère' (Pathé 0259; GV 548), one can only echo Michael Scott's words (and he is no easy listener to please) on Franz that his singing is 'trenchant and noble, uttered with the dignity of a tragedian'. His clarion voice and expressive French evoke the pity due to the stricken suppliant.

Fernand Ansseau comes very little behind Franz. His A (DB 1263; LV 291) is thrilling in its firm, rounded beauty of tone even when he presses a little hard on it. Both his 1925, acoustic version of B (DB 623) and the 1928 electric remake (DB 1268; LV 291) catch the pitiable state of the wounded warrior, 'et je proclame ta justice' urgently exclaimed. Vezzani's version of A (Disque W 1069; Cantilena 6244) and B (Disque W 1075; Rococo 5234) are freer with the music and, in the case of B, sentimentalized but the voice is so vibrant and vital that a former-day Vickers is conjured up. Léon Beyle (4–32283–4) is his reliable, articulate, self in B. Georges Thill in B (LFX 430; 2C 061–12094) sings the passage simply, movingly with an innate rightness to his phrasing. René Verdière in A (Od. 123012) and B (Od. 123035) shows insight into the text, but his light, tremulous tone is not quite what is wanted for Samson. Similar in vocal quality is Maurice Dutreix (Disque P 524; Accord 150002) in B only, but his intensity of expression and enunciation at 'Dieu! prends ma vie', so beseeching, suggests a more heroic Friant. Léon Escalaïs's version of A (Fono. 39371; OASI 597) exhibits, as usual, a brilliant voice and a provincial style. He alters the last line to show off his high notes.

I was surprised to find that eminent Italian interpreter of the part, Martinelli, doing the same thing (VB 42; CDN 1016). In any case, singing in French he is not as communicative as is his wont in Italian. In 1950 he was caught at a recital singing various passages with Claramae Turner. An EJS issue of these is best avoided: the great man is well past his best. Caruso's famous version of B, recorded in 1916 (DB 136; various reissues) is one of the most elegiac of his later discs. The sympathetic ease of his singing, full of Samson's woe, is most affecting even when he takes liberties with note values. Zenatello's A in Italian (Fono. 92211; GV 77) is suitably heroic in voice but ignoble in expression. Tamagno in the same piece (56281; GEMM 208/9), also in Italian, is magisterial in declamation but slow and self-indulgent in the context of the part. Antonio Paoli (052169; Club 99.1) simply makes a big noise. The *allegro* 'Israel! romps ta chaine' was sometimes recorded alone. Erik Schmedes in German (3–42890) is more like Tannhäuser, and an unattractive one at that. Paoli neighs. David Yuzhin, by contrast, catches the inspirational vigour of the passage, singing in Russian (3–22781; GV 63). B was recorded with some feeling but in oratorio style by Morgan Kingston (Col. 532).

What might be termed the High Priest's Curse, or perhaps his Credo 'Maudite à jamais', needs really to be heard in context. Versions that catch the character's vengeful crudity are those by M. Nucelly (4–32364), Paul Lantéri (Pathé X 0709), with his tremendous brio and exciting top Fs, Cesare Formichi (Col. D 1491; LV 229) – what an imposing voice – and Charles. Cambon (Poly. 522391). Henri Albers (Pathé 798; SJG 123) has a voluminous baritone but proves a weak interpreter. Arthur Endrèze (Pathé PD 18) lacks authority. More recently, Michel Dens (2C 065–12541) has uttered the curses more pointedly than Ernest Blanc (Pathé ASTX 1259).

The trio 'Je viens célébrer' has a marvellously sonorous performance from Homer, Caruso and Journet (DM 126; various reissues), a less assured one from Brohly, Georges Granal and Armand Narçon (034086), though the mezzo sounds suitably plausible. Two French basses, Jean Vallier (032069) and Willy Tubiana (W 590), recorded the scene of the Old Hebrew with chorus 'Hymne de joie', the former more characterfully than the wooden Tubiana. Charbonnel and Dutreix recorded the Delilah/Samson duet 'En ces lieux' on both Odeon and Disque, passable but not particularly illuminating. Duchesne and Vezzani did the same (DA 4819/20; Cantilena 6244), part of which has already been mentioned as VA 28; both sing true to form.

The duet for the High Priest and Delilah has not received much attention but performances in English by Homer and De Gogorza (Vic. 87501), in

Italian by Panerai and Ribacchi (Parlo. R 30033) and (of the last part, beginning 'Il faut pour assouvir') in German by Ottilie Metzger and Eduard Erhard (2–44499; CO 310) have been heard and enjoyed more for the singers taking part than for any special insights into the music.

I would propose an ideal cast of Cernay or Bouvier, Franz (with Thill in reserve), and Cambon as the High Priest, with Abravanel to conduct. In a heavenly seat, though, I would try to persuade Callas to team up with Vezzani; that would certainly generate some heat on the celestial clouds.

SAMSON ET DALILA

S Samson; *D* Dalila; *HP* High Priest; *A* Abimelech; *OH* Old Hebrew

1946 Luccioni *S*; Bouvier *D*; Cabanel *HP*; Cambon *A*; Médus *OH* / Paris Opéra Chorus and Orch. / Fourestier
EMI ⓜ 2C 153 1061M–9
CBS (US) ⓜ SL107

1959 (live performance – Teatro San Carlo, Naples) Del Monaco *S*; Madeira *D*; Puglisi *HP*; Clabassi *A*; Riccò *OH* / San Carlo Opera Chorus and Orch. / Molinari-Pradelli
Melodram ⓜ MEL30

1962 Vickers *S*; Gorr *D*; Blanc *HP*; Diakov *A*; *OH* / Paris Opéra Chorus and Orch. / Prêtre
EMI 2C 167 12837–9
Angel SCL3639

1972 Spiess *S*; Cernei *D*; Iordăchescu *HP*; Dumitri *A*; Florei *OH* / Romanian Radio and TV Chorus and Orch. / Adler
Electrecord ECE0428–30

1973 King *S*; Ludwig *D*; Weikl *HP*; A. Malta *A*; Kogel *OH* / Bavarian Radio Chorus and Orch. / Patané
RCA (UK) LRL3 5017
(US) ARL3 0662

1978 Domingo *S*; Obraztsova *D*; Bruson *HP*; Thau *A*; Lloyd *OH* / Orchestre de Paris and Chorus / Barenboim
DG 2709 095 ④ 3371 050

1954 (excerpts) Peerce *S*; Stevens *D*; Merrill *HP* / Shaw Chorale, NBC SO / Stokowski
HMV ⓜ ALP1308
RCA (US) ⓜ LM1848

1958 (excerpts) Del Monaco *S*; Stevens *D*; Harvuot *HP*; Flagello *A* / Metropolitan Opera Chorus and Orch. / Cleva
RCA (UK) SB2052
(US) LSC2309

Les Contes d'Hoffmann

ROBERT HENDERSON

The only thing that can be said with certainty about *Les Contes d'Hoffmann* is that there now seems to be little that can be said with absolute certainty about what Offenbach's own final conception of his opera might have been. It may be possible, on the basis of freshly discovered evidence, to eradicate some of the more obvious distortions and anomalies that encrust the traditionally accepted scores to restore other critical and usually omitted passages, yet there is almost as much in any attempted reconstruction of a 'definitive' version that must inevitably remain speculative.

If Offenbach had lived to complete it, or more importantly, if he had been able to revise and alter it in performance (as was his normal habit) would he have finally decided in favour of sung recitative, as seems to have been his original intention, or spoken dialogue? Who was responsible for the musical setting of the greater part of the recitative as we know it today, Guiraud, as we have always assumed, or Offenbach himself? How much of the music did he actually complete, and how much is the work of other hands; or did he, as has recently been suggested, leave simply a brilliant idea and a bundle of tunes? Though composed in 1875 for the operetta *Le Voyage dans la lune*, and inserted into *Hoffmann* only in 1907, is it reasonable at this late stage to omit as familiar an aria as Dapertutto's 'Scintille, diamant'? And what about the famous, though spurious Septet that was interpolated into the opera at the same time; why indeed is it always called a Septet when there are only six solo voices joined later by a four-part chorus? What shape would be eventually have given to the problematic 'Giulietta' act? What indeed is the most satisfying order in the theatre of the three central acts? The logical sequence as indicated in the libretto, and the surviving material, is Olympia, Antonia, Giulietta, yet many musicians are still convinced that it is the Antonia act which, on purely musical grounds, provides the most satisfactory climax to the three stories.

For over thirty years, these and many other similarly daunting problems have taxed the ingenuity of conductors, producers and scholars, in an effort to recapture the spirit, if not the letter, of Offenbach's original intentions. Mostly, however, their proposed solutions have raised just as many new questions as those they have attempted to settle, and the more deeply one probes the musicological background the more confused the picture becomes.*

Though increasingly acknowledged in the theatre, recordings of *Hoffmann* have so far shown little interest in the restoration work that has been going on since the 1940s, in the radically revised versions of Arthur Hammond, Felsenstein in Berlin, or more recently of Antonio de Almeida and Fritz Oeser. Of the nine more-or-less complete versions that I have heard (I have not been able to trace a copy of the 1951 Royale performance), all but one remain faithful to the corrupt 1907 Choudens score. With so much already in doubt about this notoriously unreliable source it seems improper, even impertinent, to demand from singers a scrupulous fidelity to the printed text, to comment on their occasional deviations from the written dynamics, rhythms and decorative figurations.

The three heroines (four if you include the normally omitted Stella) should ideally, as separate incarnations of a single, unattainable beloved, of perhaps the eternal feminine, be taken by the same singer, a practice followed in only two of the nine recordings. The four villains, as manifestations of the evil spirit that consistently thwarts Hoffmann's desires, are more commonly assigned to the same performer, while the four servants Andrès, Cochenille, Pitichinaccio and Frantz, are variously distributed between one, two and sometimes three buffo tenors.

Generally speaking the pre-war recordings of individual numbers from the opera mainly belong to one or another of two distinctive performing traditions, the German and the French, which are neatly and instructively contrasted in the sets deriving from Berlin and Paris that appeared in the 1940s.

Easily dominating the abridged German version, recorded in a draughty, rain-swept air-raid shelter in the dark days of 1946, is the elegant Hoffmann of Peter Anders. If the tone does thin a little as his voice moves into its highest register, or begins to run out of breath at the end of phrases, a smoothly flowing, eloquently grained lyricism, an impulsive, though finely contained virility and a restrained fervour mesh subtly in his singing to make him an authentically romantic, Hoffmannesque figure, creating a feeling of ardent, yet almost trance-like reverie in the central section of 'Kleinzach', of rapt, self-communing wonder as he catches his first glimpse of the sleeping Olympia, reticent in 'Ah, vivre deux', vivid and energetic in the 'Couplets bachiques'. The young Rita Streich also seems to me a near-ideal Olympia, fresh and youthful, the coloratura of her moderately paced 'Doll Song' not only flawless in rhythm, intonation and its bell-like clarity, but revealing a personality of a natural, unforced charm. The casting of her famous teacher Erna Berger as Antonia is not quite so plausible, her singing precise and

---

* For a more detailed discussion of the complex historical and musicological background to Offenbach's opera see Antonio de Almeida 'Hoffmann: The Original(?) Version in Opera, December 1980, Hugh Macdonald Hoffmann's Melancholy Tale in The Musical Times, October 1980. Richard Bonynge's introductory essay to his 1972 Decca recording, and Alexander Faris's Jacques Offenbach (Faber, 1980).

scrupulously attentive but a little too light and sweetly toned. Annelies Müller, whom Furtwängler described as his ideal of what a contralto of our modern times should be, makes an excellent Nicklausse, Margarete Klose is richly expressive as the voice of Antonia's mother, Jaro Prohaska a disappointing Dapertutto, but more persuasive as a darkly menacing Dr Miracle. Though severely cut, the distinguished cast assembled by the conductor Artur Rother for what was called at the time this 'air-raid shelter' *Hoffmann* was a deliberate act of faith in an opera that had long been prohibited in Nazi Germany, the enthusiasm and effervescent spirit that his singers and players brought to the music trenchantly underlining its considerable historical interest.

If there are certain facets of that performance which seem to belong more to the pre-war than post-war years, memorably enshrined in the 1948 recording conducted by André Cluytens is another very different, but also apparently soon to be forgotten tradition, that of the Opéra-Comique. Within the generally brisk tempi there is a marvellously spontaneous sense of inner movement, the points made easily and naturally and without the slightest trace of mannerism. Whether in the swiftly flowing narrative of the story of Kleinzach, the steadily growing animation of its central section, or the suavely contoured lyricism of 'Ah! vivre deux' or 'O Dieu de quelle ivresse', Raoul Jobin's Hoffmann has a seemingly effortless mobility of phrase that amply compensates for its occasionally impersonal character. The discreet touches of irony in the delightfully realistic Nicklausse of Fanély Revoil, perhaps the perfect performance of the role on record, the impeccably tuned and moulded coloratura of Renée Doria, the more dramatically voiced Giulietta of Vina Bovy, the exemplary clarity of André Pernet's Coppélius and gravity of Charles Soix's Dapertutto, are each in their own way object lessons in the French *opéra-comique* style at its most instinctive and idiomatic. Nor once heard is it possible to erase from the memory the idiosyncratic, strangely wistful accents of the comedian Bourvil, whose account of Frantz's little song in the Antonia act is again a model of its kind. But more than any individual contribution, it is its conversational intimacy, the way in which the music flows gracefully and wittily through the words, its identity of sound and sense, that gives to the performance as a whole its very special flavour; as it clearly demonstrates Offenbach's, or Guiraud's, recitatives need never sound dull or prosaic.

A nice (and authentic) touch in the Rother set, but one not taken up in other performances, is a brief recapitulation in the Epilogue of a verse of Hoffmann's story of Kleinzach, revealing the opera as an expansive and explanatory gloss on that single aria. Cluytens, in what is virtually a complete account of the Choudens score, also chooses, wisely, the longer, alternative ending in which the Muse of Poetry finally appears to Hoffmann as his one true guide and inspiration. Neither are particularly imaginative conductors, but their performances have a style and consistency which none of the later recordings, in spite of their technical advantages and various incidental merits, quite manages to recapture.

In Cluytens's second recording of *Hoffmann* of 1964 there is already an unmistakeable coarsening of tone and accent. All three heroines are unconvincing, the Olympia plain and graceless, Elisabeth Schwarzkopf uncomfortably out of place as the Venetian courtesan, Victoria de los Angeles (Antonia) at her most tense, nervous and insecure. Nicolai Gedda is as observant and perceptive as ever, but the expression begins to sound forced and studied, imposed on the music from outside rather than growing naturally out of an instinctive feel for the words. The unusual casting of a baritone Nicklausse tends to create more problems than it is worth, the only saving grace being the stylishly idiomatic Spalanzani of Michel Sénéchal.

Apart from a few individual performances, the three versions dating from the 1950s have little to recommend them, apparently confirming the view that *Hoffmann* is not a work that has fared particularly well on record. As one would expect, it is the presence of Sir Thomas Beecham, in the set derived from the sound track of the famous film of Michael Powell and Emeric Pressburger, that provides the main interest, for no other conductor can quite match the inimitable lilt and sparkle, the aristocratic finesse with which he invests the music. The clean, open Hoffmann of Robert Rounseville begins promisingly, but remains too candid, too unvaried in nuance to hold the attention for very long, suggesting more a Jamesian innocent abroad in corrupt old Europe than Hoffmann's or Offenbach's ardently romantic poet. Dorothy Bond is a fragile, but precise, Olympia, Monica Sinclair an astutely personable Nicklausse. Otherwise the singing is undistinguished, Grahame Clifford's exaggerated Oxbridge accents sounding ludicrous in this particular context, Bruce Dargavel's delivery (as the villains) of the English translation scrupulously clear in a richly voiced, but slightly blustering and lugubrious manner. The score has also been extensively cut and altered to fit in with the scenic demands of the film.

Nor probably is full justice done to the conducting of Pierre Monteux in the Cetra set, which possesses more of the disadvantages than the advantages of a performance recorded live at the Metropolitan in 1955, the music interrupted at every conceivable moment by enthusiastic applause, the sound often rough, boxy and impenetrable. Some arias are limited to a single verse, and there are all the usual theatrical cuts. Lucine Amara is a shrill Antonia, Risë Stevens a squally Giulietta, Roberta Peters a bright, silvery toned Olympia, though sometimes a little rushed and uncertain in rhythm, while Richard Tucker's coarsely sung Hoffmann has all the bald exuberance, the forthright energy and machismo of an American football player. Much more persuasive is the subtly contained, smoothly flowing style of Martial Singher as the four sharply and deftly characterized villains, his singing showing just a touch of strain in 'Scintille, diamant' though transposed down from its original key of E major to E flat. The one other notable performance here is the Nicklausse of Mildred Miller, firm, teasing and securely focused.

There could hardly be a stronger contrast to the coarseness of Richard Tucker than the illuminating restraint, the elegantly mellifluous phrasing and impeccable, yet instinctively relaxed savouring of the text of Léopold Simoneau in the one remaining version from the 1950s, which is briskly and competently conducted by Pierre Michel Le Conte. There is also an impressive authority in Heinz Rehfuss's portrayal of the four clearly differentiated villains, Lindorf sinister and sneering, Dapertutto darkly, mysterious, the long-breathed phrases of his leisurely paced 'Scintille, diamant' (in E flat and including one curiously misread note) eloquently moulded. Apart from these echoes of an older and fading tradition, and a likeable Nicklausse from Nata Tuescher, the singing is in general disappointing, the music extensively cut, the arias and duets mostly reduced to a single verse.

It was only with the Sutherland/Bonynge version of 1972 that the four heroines, Olympia, Giulietta, Antonia and Stella were taken for the first time on record by the same singer. Nor is this its only departure from all previous versions. Even more radical is its rejection of sung recitative in favour of spoken dialogue, a controversial decision of sometimes doubtful merit. Following hints contained in the original libretto, Giulietta dies by accidentally drinking the poison intended for Hoffmann instead of gliding away into the night with the deformed Pitichinaccio, and the spurious Septet is rearranged to replace the lost quartet of the Epilogue. Dapertutto's 'Scintille, diamant' is retained, and so too, for exclusively musical reasons, is the traditional, if incorrect, order of the three central acts. It thus secures both an intelligent and manageable compromise between established practice and modern research.

As perhaps could be predicted, Joan Sutherland is at her most effective as Olympia, the coloratura brilliant and incisive, if not always faultless in pitch and rhythm at slightly too fast a pace. Giulietta is never a particularly rewarding role and here she sounds a little ill at ease. Nor as Antonia does she show much feeling for the smoothly moulded legato that the music properly demands, the tone finely tempered but too mature for the young girl of the story. Placido Domingo catches more of an authentically French elegance and discretion than one might have thought possible, but though Richard Bonynge conducts with an admirable thrust, litheness of spirit and sensitivity, it is the malevolence of Gabriel Bacquier and the succinct little portrait sketches of Hugues Cuénod, who could well have been listening to and remembering some of Bourvil's inimitable inflections, that leave the most indelible imprint.

In an introductory essay to his recording Bonynge makes out a strong case in favour of his editorial changes and emendations. The two latest studio recordings of *Hoffmann* have remained unmoved, however, by all the scholarly activity to which the opera has been subjected during the past three or four decades, preferring the comfortingly familiar, if now largely discredited Choudens score. The Oeser edition does find representation on disc in the live recording of Antonio de Almeida's 1980 Dallas production, itself of little merit.

The trills, runs, and rapid decorative figurations of Sills's Olympia in the 1973 HMV set have a bright, hard-edged precision, the coloratura expertly calculated. Her fussy Giulietta, and an Antonia in which there is little pathos or tenderness, little suggestion of a young girl singing to herself of joy mixed with doubt and apprehension, illustrate even more clearly than in the Sutherland version the enormous problems involved when a single soprano attempts all three roles. With the exception of the attractively uncomplicated, young-sounding and carefully nurtured Hoffmann of Stuart Burrows, the casting is rarely more than adequate, the dull conducting of Julius Rudel, sluggish and stagnant in the Barcarolle, never establishing any clearly defined centre, or consistent stylistic focus.

Whereas that performance remains throughout stylistically uncertain and anonymous, the newest studio version, conducted by Heinz Wallberg and issued in Germany in 1979, is conceived on the grandest scale, in a spaciously Germanic mould. The boldness and virile thrust of Siegfried Jerusalem's Hoffmann almost makes something of a Wagnerian hero out of Offenbach's yearningly romantic poet, with little variation of light and shade in the vocal inflection. In keeping with the ambitious, almost epic style of the performance, Jeanette Scovotti's Doll Song is deliberate and resolute, and technically faultless, formidable rather than enticing; Norma Sharp's Giulietta is rich and dramatic, Julia Varady's Antonia plaintive, full of vocal interest but rather too knowing. Whereas Fischer-Dieskau tends to exaggerate the differing personalities implied in the four villainous roles, the excellent Munich-based character tenor Friedrich Lenz maintains a skilfully disciplined reserve that is no less telling or effective, his singing of Frantz's little couplets intriguingly slow and serious. Every note of the Choudens score is there, including the longer, alternative ending, but so expansive and indulgent has it become, so far removed in scale and spirit, and in the delivery of its German text, from the versions issued in the 1940s that it is sometimes difficult to believe that one is listening to the same work.

One inescapable conclusion suggested by the more-or-less complete recordings of *Hoffmann* is that, however the parts are distributed, it is a peculiarly difficult opera to cast consistently and with equal success through all its various roles. This is largely confirmed by the highlight discs which range from the reasonable and competent, with some striking individual performances, to the purely eccentric.

Though the complete Royale set of 1951 has so far eluded me, I have been able to hear a selection of highlights from the same source (Royale 1213), and recorded in the same year, with Herbert Guthan conducting the Berlin Opera Orchestra. It is a curious compilation, beginning with a glutinous Barcarolle sung (in Italian) by Maria Corelli and Diana Eustrati. Then follows Dapertutto's 'Scintille, diamant', delivered in a modest, easy-going manner by Hans Wocke, and a swaggering account by Rudolf Schock of

Hoffmann's 'Couplets bachiques' (both in German), the rest being devoted to a lengthy orchestral synopsis of the work's main tunes, nostalgically reminiscent of the operatic selections played in the town squares of Italy or Sicily by the local band on Sunday afternoons.

Equally novel in its choice of material is the anthology sung in English by members of the Metropolitan Opera and poorly conducted by Jean Morel, no more than a sketchy précis of the Prologue, the Olympia and Antonia acts (there is only one verse each of 'Kleinzach', the Doll Song and Antonia's 'Elle a fui'), framing a far more substantial portion of the Giulietta scene. Linking the musical items is a spoken narration of an immediately recognizable type ('There I was in this Munich beer cellar waiting for my girl when . . .'), its slightly incongruous tone combining with the coy, Hollywoodish Olympia of Laurel Hurley, the sour Antonia of Lucine Amara, the good, clean, all-American boy suggested by Jon Crain's Hoffmann and the naive choral singing to give the entire production an almost *Wizard of Oz* flavour.

Most entertaining of the oddities, however, and for all the wrong reasons, is the selection of highlights, conducted by Wolfgang Martin with the Berlin State Opera Orchestra. Neither soprano nor mezzo-soprano can manage much more than the merest approximation of the notes, Dapertutto's aria is ludicrously sung by Keith Engen, and the Hoffmann of Heinz Hoppe is well meaning though clearly out of his depth. As if cruelly to emphasize the almost comic inadequacy of the singing, the music has been decked out in a brand-new orchestral dress, with swooning harps in virtually every bar, crooning, Mantovani-like strings, newly composed linking passages, and a full, technicolor chorus to fill in the background, for instance, to 'Scintille, diamant'.

The other highlight discs that I have heard are all more sober and predictable, both in their obvious choice of music and in the way in which it is presented. Of the versions in German, that conducted by Berislav Klobučar has a forceful, energetic, vigorously masculine-sounding, if sometimes tight-throated Hoffmann in Rudolf Schock. Ruth-Margret Pütz is an attractive Olympia, her coloratura clean and flexible, though not always perfectly tuned, Pilar Lorengar's sensitive phrasing of Antonia's music is constantly undermined by an irritating flutter in her voice, and the baritone Marcel Cordes in the villainous roles is coarse and sluggish. If occasionally a little overwrought, Sándor Kónya's heroically toned Hoffmann stands out from some otherwise no more than average singing on the DG record conducted by Richard Kraus. Nor does Waldemar Kmentt show much patience with the more reflective side of Hoffmann's nature in his urgent and stirring portrayal of Hoffmann in the Eurodisc excerpts conducted by Franz Bauer-Theussl, the most notable feature of which is the leisurely, maturely expressive Dapertutto and Dr Miracle of Walter Berry.

On another DG record of excerpts conducted by Richard Kraus, this time in French, the only performance of any real note is the pleasingly unaffected, straightforward Hoffmann of William McAlpine (who once sang the part at the London Coliseum). Rita Streich's Olympia is now more strained, more self-conscious and rhythmically inexact than in the Berlin set of the 1940s. Though the women are again disappointing, something of the inwardly suf-fused lyricism and natural ardour of the authentic French style is vividly recalled both in the generously voiced singing of Tony Poncet and in the incisively characterized, but smoothly moulded, long-breathed phrases of the fine baritone René Bianco on the 1963 Philips disc, and also in the conducting of Robert Wagner, who invests the Barcarolle with a voluptuously romantic atmosphere, its two solo voices properly distanced. Albert Lance, the Hoff-mann in the Mondiophonie extracts conducted by Jésus Etcheverry, belongs to the same tradition, but with little variation of tone, character or dynamic nuance, the notable performances here being those of Robert Massard, more dramatic than most in 'Scintille, diamant' but without any loss of phrase or flowing line, and of Andréa Guiot, an intense, tenderly confidential Antonia. There is also a nice touch of cheeky, but graceful and stylish comedy in Jean Giraudeau's delivery of Frantz's little couplets.

Taking the individually recorded arias in the order in which they appear in the opera we have first, from the Prologue, Hoffmann's ballad of Kleinzach 'Il était une fois'. Neatly crystallized by Marcel Claudel (Poly. 522700) and Emile Marcelin (Disque Y 72) are the essential features of the older French style, its lightness, flexibility and narrative ease. Both are pleasing, neither particularly distinguished. After a single verse Claudel cuts straight into the central reverie and there is no chorus. The Marcelin version is complete, including the choral interjections, his singing in the central section pushing fervently on as Hoffmann gradually loses the thread of his story and becomes increasingly obsessed by the vision of his beloved. Gaston Micheletti's dis-tinctive timbre is appealingly straightforward in the narrative verses (Od. 188533; ORX 119), but then loses face by omitting altogether the crucial central episode. Also singing in French, Giacomo Lauri-Volpi (DA 108; LV 36) allows himself a slightly greater freedom of expression, a more heroic tinge: the tone and accent are Italianate, yet sensitive to the demands of French style. As immaculate as that of any French tenor is the exemplary diction, in English, of Tudor Davies (D 1142; GV 529); his ardently Hoff-mannesque response to the emotional curve of the music placing it firmly within its proper operatic context. Similar in quality, in its attractively lithe, open delivery of both words and music is the version recorded in 1910 by another fine British tenor Walter Hyde (D 106) with Beecham conducting.

In German, Richard Tauber (Parlo. R 20089; GEMM 153–4), at the peak of his career in June 1928, floats the lyricism of the central reverie with a refined and effortless legato, words and music inflected with a telling subtlety. Just as impressive in its seamless lyricism and ardour is the first of the two versions of that famous Viennese Hoffmann, Julius Patzak (Poly. 66985; LV 191), the phrases as Hoffmann slowly begins to emerge from his reverie permeated with a marvellously rapt sense of inner wonder. By the time of his second recording in 1950 (Decca BR 3062) the expression had become even more direct, the essence of the narrative style distilled with an artistry that absorbs all hint of artifice. Marcel Wittrisch (HMV EG 2457; LV 98) allows himself a few more touches of exaggerated expression within the same lyrical mould, while Rudolf Schock (DB 11500; 1C 147–29 140–41) still retains in 1947 memories of the older tradition, though the details have coarsened. And from a much earlier age, the very individual timbre of Hermann Jadlowker (042492; CO 388) sounds far from natural in this particular music, too forced and forthright.

On the reverse side of the same disc recorded in 1916, Jadlowker seems much more comfortable in Hoffmann's first-act romance 'Ah! vivre deux', his singing luminous and relaxed as he first sets eyes on the sleeping Olympia, and then slowly increasing in emotional intensity. Here again, however, it is Patzak (BR 3062) who comes closest to the ideal performance, both in his suavity of line and the rapturous glow that suffuses his singing as he invokes the sun whose ardour has united two loving hearts in eternal bliss. Villabella is vivid and stylish, if too idiosyncratic in tone for my liking (Od. 188603; ORX 119), Charles Dalmorès (HMV AGSA 7; and there is a second version, both on CO 392) clear and open, and scrupulous in his response to both words and music in a quite swiftly paced *parlando* manner.

In Coppélius's solo 'Je me nomme Coppélius' and its continuation in 'J'ai des yeux', it is that same natural clarity in the singing of the baritone André Pernet (Od. 188715; ORX 146), the way in which the words flow instinctively through the melody to delineate the character, that sets a reliable standard against which to measure other interpretations. Etienne Billot (Od. 188529; ORX 119), another Opéra-Comique singer of the inter-war generation, has a greater tendency to twist and turn the music to fill out the character, whereas José Beckmans (Poly. 524062) takes far fewer liberties while being less surely in control of the musical phrase. The Polish-born Adam Didur, also singing in French, invests the phrases of 'J'ai des yeux' with an apt, and menacingly dark satanic edge (Perfect 11521; GV 45). Coming closer to our own time, we can hear the richly, never indulgently dramatized, slightly mocking version recorded in 1956 by Gérard Souzay (LXT 5269), though he occasionally reveals a momentary difficulty in holding the pitch, and that of Norman Treigle (Westminster WST 17145), the character strongly and succinctly projected.

Apart from a modicum of charm, all that is basically required by Olympia's decorative couplets 'Les oiseaux dans la charmille' is a true, freshly burnished sound, resilient yet flexible technique, intrepid coloratura and infallible rhythm, conditions easier to enumerate than to fulfil. A notable early interpreter of all three Offenbach heroines in the opera house was Hedwig Francillo-Kaufmann, whose Olympia has been described as one of a cold virtuosity. In her 1909 recording (2–43177X; CO 356) she sings just one verse in German; her coloratura is cleanly and brightly toned, her rhythm, phrasing and articulation sometimes disconcertingly idiosyncratic, with the final trill prolonged far beyond the terms of its natural life. Another of the earliest versions is also one of the most interesting, sung in English, at a slowish pace, and with a small, but delightful-sounding, securely trained voice by the little-known soprano Caroline Hatchard (HMV 03193; SHB 100). It was recorded in 1910 with Beecham conducting, the same year in which he directed his famous Covent Garden performances. 'As at the Shaftesbury Theatre, London' is the note attached to the attractive, technically assured 1915 record of the Doll Song by the New Zealand singer Nora D'Argel (D 208), neatly defining its perhaps slightly unusual, but not altogether inappropriate musical-comedy flavour. Also well schooled, in spite of a few snatched notes, bright and neat if a little characterless, is the 1916 version in French by the American soprano Mabel Garrison (DB 501; Club 99.98). From the same year, and in German, Melitta Heim (Od. Rxx 76579; CO 342) begins by falsely lulling one into a feeling of security and then suddenly shoots off at a tangent, pitch and rhythm, with her own additional decorations, becoming increasingly, almost comically eccentric. Marion Talley (DB 1142) in 1927 is no more than competent, possessing little elegance or finesse: Thérèse Gauley (Od. 188533) is lazy.

Much more enticing (in German) are Hedwig von Debitzka (Poly. 66922; LV 65), smooth, accurate and graceful, with a nice waltz lilt in the accompaniment, Miliza Korjus (HMV C 2770; 1C 147 30819–20), the voice small and thin but both the light, pure tone and the rhythm steady as a rock, and Adele Kern (Parlo. P 9226: LV 195) whose fresh, mellifluous, meticulously precise singing is only spoilt by the fact that she performs just one verse. Isobel Baillie in one of her earliest records is attractively cool, bright and compact, the coloratura impeccably controlled (Col. DX 165). Gwen Catley, also in English and recorded in 1949, is just as clean and polished, the decorative figurations possessing an irresistible charm at a moderate, beautifully judged tempo (C 3902; HLM 7066). In their refusal to worry the music, to impose on it any inappropriately self-conscious interpretation, both offer an instructive contrast to the irritating fluctuations of speed and vulgar mannerisms of Lily Pons with André Kostelanetz conducting (LX 1122). As in his complete set, the excessively fast pace adopted by Richard Bonynge for Joan Sutherland's 1970 performance (SET 454–5) inevitably produces a few smudged details, whereas Sylvia Geszty (Telefunken SAT 22503) is seriously hampered by a dangerously slow speed, making heavy weather of the music in spite of some exciting sounds, Janine Micheau (LXT 2528) is tidy, but hard and metallic, Erika Köth (Eurodisc S70777KR) warm and decisive in personality but unsteady in her runs, trills and decorations.

Almost as frequently recorded as Olympia's Doll Song is Dapertutto's 'Scintille, diamant' from the Giulietta act. As we know, it was not inserted into the opera until 1907, the same year in which it was committed to record by Marcel Journet (DB 882; GV 503) in a mellow, fluid, smoothly grained performance without a trace of mannerism or self-indulgence. Again representing at its most authentic the typically French identity of word and phrase is Pernet (Od. 188715; ORX 146), warm, elegant and naturally expressive,

Billot (Od. 188529), a more convincing Dapertutto than Coppélius, and Beckmans (Poly. 524062) who, though bigger in voice than Pernet and not as well controlled at about the same pace, keeps the expression sensitively contained within itself. Whereas most of the early versions transpose the music down to E flat, Louis Richard (Col. RFX 10) sings it in its original E major. A Monnaie baritone, more familiar at the Opéra than the Opéra-Comique, his voice is much darker and heavier, reliable rather than particularly memorable, the character more suited to Verdi than Offenbach. Two modern French versions worth noting are those of Michel Dens (2C 065 12541) his singing, in E major, pliable and free-flowing at a quickish tempo, and of Gabriel Bacquier (Mondiophonie MSA 11–A), more dramatic and menacing, in E flat, and in the same naturally unhurried style.

Of the versions in German, that recorded in 1916 (in E major) by Joseph Schwarz (042496; LV 14) is pervaded with an imposingly aristocratic spirit, his lovely, beautifully focused voice and impeccably disciplined line finely attuned to the sentiments expressed in the music. A famous Wotan, Rudolf Bockelmann (C 1680), gives an impressively weighty, though hardly idiomatic, Wagnerian patina to Offenbach's simple aria. There is no question, however, about the authority of his singing, nor of that of Heinrich Schlusnus (Poly. 67190; LV 108). In their company Mathieu Ahlersmeyer (Acanta DE 21388) sounds disconcertingly tough and raw, Josef Metternich (1C 047–28 598) a little colourless, though with a far greater nobility in his carefully tempered lyricism. Thomas Tipton (RBM 3031) also singing in German (in E flat) is honest and unfussy with not much body or richness in his voice, Hans Braun (C 3982) maturely sympathetic, his long, expressively contained phrases (in E flat) building easily, and at a fluid, unhurried pace, to the aria's central climax. The strong, firm voice of William Samuel (D 274) turns Dapertutto into something of a clubbable English gentleman. An oddity from the 1940s is the performance in Swedish by Hugo Hasslo (Danish HMV Z 309), big, heroic and exciting, but totally out of character Leonard Warren (RCA 26.41410AG) and Sherrill Milnes (SER 5584), both in French and in the original E major, are resourceful and attentive, but curiously anonymous.

In the first of Hoffmann's two second-act solos, the 'Couplets bachiques', Walter Hyde (D 106), in English and again superbly accompanied by Beecham, and Jadlowker in German (042535; Scala 839), respond to the music's almost desperately flamboyant spirit with an exhilarating thrust, physical energy and vocal prowess.

Jadlowker (4–52589; CO 388) and Wittrisch (HMV EG 2457; LV 98) in Hoffmann's other second-act aria 'O Dieu! de quelle ivresse' show much the same virtues and weaknesses as in their performances of 'Ah vivre deux'. Tauber (Parlo R 20089; GEMM 153–4) again offers a flawless example of German lyrical singing at its most cultivated and refined, with a superbly sustained *pianissimo* in its second half. If anything even more inimitable are the long, arching phrases of Patzak (Poly. 66985; LV 191), his faultless breath control and the ecstatic lift that he gives to the final bars. In comparison the more recent performance of the East German tenor Eberhard Büchner (Eterna 8.26.665) can provide no more than a pale, though well-intentioned reflection of a lost tradition. Even Villabella (Od. 188598; ORX 119) and Dalmorès (HMV AGSA 7; CO 392) representing the classic French style in its most authentic form cannot quite match Patzak here, and certainly not Michel Cadiou (Versailles STDX 8025) in its modern and dull incarnation. Nor can the Monnaie tenor M. Razavet (Pathé 0373), excellent in diction but musically uninteresting.

In the one other separately recorded aria, Antonia's 'Elle a fui, la tourterelle', the ideal performance could well have been set down as long ago as 1915 by Lucrezia Bori (DB 153; Rococo 5321), the plasticity and tenderly plaintive accents of her long-drawn legato phrases, and the subtle fusion of urgency, confidence and uneasy apprehension with which she invests the words 'Mon bien aimé, ma voix t'implore' as affecting now as they must have been when she sang the role at the opera's Metropolitan première two years earlier. Frances Alda (DB 365; Club 99.91) is just as tender and reflective, without the sentiments being quite as delicately or as movingly charged, and Geneviève Vix (Pathé 0315), another lovely singer of the same period, projects words and music with a touching, yet ardent reticence. Neither shake faith in Bori. But then one turns to Féraldy (LF 122; FCX 50001) who, fractionally quicker though without the faintest trace of pressure or haste, probes an even deeper vein of fragile emotion, conveying with a poignant freshness and veracity the feelings of a young girl experiencing simultaneously the thrill of love, ineffable yearning and the always present fear of imminent loss. Equally haunting is Eidé Norena (DA 4840; Rococo 5359), rapt yet strangely ageless, vulnerable yet supported by an unquenchable inner strength, and unforgettably wistful, creating a supple mood of indefinable magic. Nor must one overlook Claudia Muzio (Edison 82324–R; OASI 571), sensitively employing the again distinctive character of her voice to evoke a telling simplicity of expression.

With such performances lingering indelibly in the memory, Janine Micheau (Col. SAXF 221) sounds no more than competent, the phrasing awkward, the intonation questionable. In addition to Meta Seinemeyer (Parlo P 2235; LV 276), whose voice in her 1926 recording is a little too matronly, but who holds the atmosphere with near perfection, there are two other German versions which, however far removed they may be from any recognizably operatic context, are as ravishing in their own way as the finest French performances. In that of Lotte Lehmann (Parlo. RO 20263; HQM 1121) just one verse of Antonia's Romance is presented as an object of a pure and moving beauty; an earlier, acoustic version (Gramm. 76489; LV 180) has similar virtues.

At a hypnotically slow pace, the soft enthralling spun line of Emmy Bettendorf (Parlo. 1272; LV 251) weaves a subtle web of almost indescribable loveliness, its dreamy, trance-like mood sustained in the Antonia–Hoffmann duet 'C'est une chanson d'amour' both with Eugen Transky on the other side of the same record, and in a second version with the tenor Herbert Ernst Groh (Parlo. R 1757). As an important historical memento of an earlier age is the record made in 1902 on a black G&T by two singers of Mahler's Vienna Opera, Marie Gutheil-Schoder and Franz Naval (44067; CO 394).

Closer to the idiomatic spirit of the opera in its mobility and elegant distillation of joy, sadness and the transience of love is a French version of the duet by Emma Luart and Gaston Micheletti (Od. 188574; GV 525) which may well have never been surpassed. Similarly, in the trio 'Tu ne chanteras plus?' Louis Guénot, Feraldy and Abby Richardson (RFX 28) embody the lighter, though still fervently dramatic French style. Margarete Tesche-macher, Margarete Klose, and Willi Domgraf-Fassbaender (DB 4410), the weightier German tradition.

On that same record Teschemacher and Klose bring a wonderfully smooth, creamy sound to the Barcarolle, the baritone voice of Domgraf-Fassbaender with Felicie Hüni-Mihacsek (Poly. 66862) adding just that extra touch of richness to the texture. Féraldy and Cernay (LF 122) and Luart and Cernay (Od. 123678; ORX 119), the latter with chorus, are fluid and graceful, subtly evoking the gentle lapping of the waters, Bori and Lawrence Tibbett (DA 912) sensuous and seductive, the lovely voices of these two great stars of the Metropolitan (singing in English) perfectly matched. Also in English and finely blended are Isobel Baillie and Nellie Walker (Col. 9654), Lucy Marsh and Marguerite Dunlop at a relaxed, lilting tempo in their 1913 recording (2–4169), and the soprano and contralto of Jeanne Dusseau and Nancy Evans (C 3126), their voices at once clearly differentiated and pleasingly balanced. The Barcarolle of Lore Wissmann and Hetty Plumacher, in German and with Leitner conducting (Poly. 68397), is a bit too rich and fruity. That with Jennie Tourel singing both parts (Col. LB 80; ABE 10082) is only of interest as a stunt recording, as is that of Elisabeth Schumann (DB 361; HQM 1187) lovely as it is. The more modern manner is suitably represented by Mont-serrat Caballé and Shirley Verrett (SER 5590).

LES CONTES D'HOFFMANN

H Hoffmann; *O* Olympia; *G* Giulietta; *A* Antonia; *L* Lindorf; *C* Coppélius; *D* Dapertutto; *M* Miracle; *N* Nicklausse

1946 (in German) Anders *H*; Streich *O*; Langhammer-Klein *G*; Berger *A*; Prohaska *C; L; D; M;* Müller *N*/Berlin Radio Chorus and Orch./Rother Acanta ⓜ DE21804 (2)	M. Sinclair *N*/Sadler's Wells Opera Chorus, RPO/Beecham Decca ⓜ ACL177–8 Turnabout (US) ⓜ THS650123–4
1947 (in English – film soundtrack) Rounseville *H*; Bond *O*; Grandi *G*; Ayars *A*; Dargavel *C; D; M;*	1948 Jobin *H*; Doria *O*; Bovy *G*; Boué *A*; Pernet *C*; Soix *D*; Bourdin *M*; Musy *L*; Revoil *N*/ Paris Opéra-Comique Chorus and Orch./Cluytens

EMI ⓜ 2C 153 14151–3
CBS (US) ⓜ SL106

c.1951   (pseudonyms used on record
sleeves – artists could be as in
1946 Acanta version) Wilhelm;
Kovatsky; Camphausen, Schenk/
Dresden State Opera Chorus
and Orch./Rubahn
Royale ⓜ 1269–71

1955   (live performance –
Metropolitan Opera House, New
York) Tucker H; Peters O;
Stevens G; Amara A; Singher L;
C; D; M; Miller N/Metropolitan
Opera Chorus and Orch/
Monteux
Cetra ⓜ LO45 (3)

1958   Simoneau H; Dobbs O; A; Graf
G; Rehfuss L; C; D; M;
Tuescher N/Concerts de Paris
Chorus and Orch/Le Conte
French version Epic BSC 101
Festival CFC 60016
Concert Hall SMS 2108
German version Concert Hall
SMS 2107

1964   Gedda H; D'Angelo O;
Schwarzkopf G; De los Angeles
A; Ghiuselev L; London C; M;
Blanc D; Benoît N/René Duclos
Choir, Paris Conservatoire
Orch./Cluytens
EMI 1C 165 00045–7
Angel SCLX 3667

1972   Domingo H; Sutherland O; G;
A; Bacquier L; C; D; M;
Tourangeau N/Swiss Radio,
Lausanne Pro Arte and Du
Brassus choruses, Suisse
Romande Orch./Bonynge
Decca SET 545 ④ K 109K32
London OSA 13106 ④ OSA 5–
13106

1973   Burrows H; Sills O; C; A;
Treigle L; C; D; M; Marsee N/
Alldis Choir, London SO/Rudel
HMV SLS 858
MCA (US) ATS 20014

1979   (in German) Jerusalem H;
Scovotti O; Sharp G; Varady A;
Fischer-Dieskau L; C; D; M;
Gramatzki N/Bavarian Radio
Chorus, Munich Radio Orch./
Wallberg

EMI 1C 157 45351–3 ④ 1C 289
45351–3

1980   (live performance – Dallas
Opera) Gedda H; Welting O;
Elias G; Putnam A; Van Dam
L; C; D; M; Forst N/Dallas
Opera Chorus and Orch./
Almeida
HRE HRE 33OS

1932–3   (excerpts – in German)
Rosvaenge H; Von Debitzka A;
Ruziczka D; Neumann N/Berlin
State Opera Chorus and Orch./
Melichar
Decca PO 5079–81*
Polydor 24969–71*

c.1950   (excerpts – in German) Schock
H; Streich G; O; Metternich L;
C; D; M; Wagner N/Berlin
Municipal Opera Chorus, Berlin
SO /Schüchter
EMI ⓜ 1C 147 28577

1952   (excerpts – in German) Hoppe
H; Owen G; A.; Schwaiger O;
Engen D; M; Freudenberg N/
chorus, Berlin Municipal Opera
Orch./Martin
Telefunken ⓜ NT 207
Telefunken (US) ⓜ TC 8028

1955   (excerpts – in German) Ludwig
H; Nentwig O; Schlemm G; A;
Wiener D; M; Hoffman N/
Württemberg State Opera
Chorus, Bavarian Radio Chorus,
orchs/Leitner and Hollreiser
DG ⓜ LPE 17049

1956–7   (excerpts) Crain H; Hurley O;
Elias G; Amara A; Singher C;
D; M; Vanni N/New York
Metropolitan Opera Chorus and
Orch./Morel
RCA (US) ⓜ LM 2310

1960   (excerpts – in German) Schock
H; Pütz O; Hillebrecht G;
Lorengar A; Cordes C; D; M;
Wagner N/Berlin Municipal
Opera Chorus, Berlin SO/
Klobučar
EMI STE80636

1960   (excerpts – in German) Kozub
H; Vivarelli O; Lorand A; G;
Crass L; C; D; M/chorus and
orch./Wagner
Philips 837 016 GY

1961 (excerpts – in German) Kónya
H; Dobbs O; Kuchta G; Klug
A; Stewart L; C; D; M; Ahlin
N/Berlin RIAS Chamber Choir,
German Opera Orch./R. Kraus
DG 2537 009

1961 (excerpts – in German) Kmentt
H; Lüttgen O; Zimmermann G;
Sorell A; Berry D; M; Draksler
N/Vienna Volksoper Chorus and
Orch/Bauer-Theussl
Ariola-Eurodisc K 86814R

1961 (excerpts) McAlpine H; Streich
O; H. Ludwig G; Klug A;
Symonette L; C; D; M; Gust N/
Berlin RIAS Chamber Chorus,
Berlin Radio SO/R. Kraus
DG SLPEM 136230

1963 (excerpts) Poncet H; Vivarelli
O; Lorand G; A; Bianco C; D;
M; E. Rehfuss N/chorus and
orch/Wagner
Philips 837 024GY

1965 (excerpts) Lance H; Mesplé O;
Sarroca G; Guiot A; Serkoyan
L; Giovannetti G; Massard D;
Bacquier M/chorus and orch/
Etcheverry
Mondiophonie MSA7002
Adès ④ C8002

Thaïs and Don Quichotte

RODNEY MILNES

THAÏS

Thaïs is an opera with an undeserved reputation as hokum, a reputation that dies hard. The basic situation – tart meets repressed puritan – became stock Hollywood material (Somerset Maugham's *Rain* and all that) and thus something not really to be taken seriously. Too many productions have emphasized the pseudo-hokum content for obvious commercial reasons; one in the United States saw opera's first full-frontal nude (Carol Neblett), which perpetuated the aura of 'sexploitation' and tawdry naughtiness that has hovered round the piece since Sybil Sanderson accidentally (I wonder?) exposed her bust at the première in 1894. The fact that none of the complete recordings made since the work lapsed from the repertory of the Paris Opéra in 1956 is entirely satisfactory has been no help in dispelling that aura. Having practically lived with the score and the twin protagonists for some years now, I remain more than ever convinced that it is a serious work of art with as much to say to audiences today as it ever has in the past.

Anatole France's novella is set in and around Alexandria in the fourth century AD, a Hellenic world far removed from the Egypt of the Pharaohs, designers please note. It is a bitter, mercilessly ironic attack on one kind of religious fanaticism. France has no sympathy with the monk Paphnuce (the name changed to Athanaël in the opera, lest ribald rhymes should spring to mind), mocks his repression, gloats over the mental and physical degradation that come with the growing self-awareness resulting from his conversion of the courtesan Thaïs, whom he has loved, or rather with whom he has been unhealthily obsessed, for a matter of years. Louis Gallet's libretto, one of the earlier unrhymed texts written for music, perforce simplifies the action and, by removing the Symposium-like philosophical discussion *chez* Nicias, concentrates on the personalities of Thaïs and Athanaël. Massenet's music adds one important element: compassion. The last words of the novel, as the nuns mistake Athanaël for a vampire and run screaming into the desert, are: 'He had become so repulsive that, passing his hand over his face, he recognized his own repulsiveness.' The last word of Massenet's opera is simply: 'Pitié!' There but for the grace of God, he seems to be saying, go so many of us. Yet Massenet's setting of the novel is not without an irony of its own, albeit gentler than France's.

Massenet's musical characterization is as searching here as anywhere in his operas: there is much for singers to interpret. The score is littered with . . . are they instructions or recommendations? Although one should perhaps beware of taking the markings in a score, even in a score by a composer as successful in his day as Massenet, who always corrected his own proofs, as gospel (any more than one should take stage directions as gospel), it does emerge after listening to so many singers in these roles that those who follow the composer's own suggestions as to phrasing, dynamic, breathing, etc., probe the characters more deeply. A word about these characters: Thaïs herself is a woman at the very top of her profession, and thus has no need to try and sound sexy: she is a very *grande horizontale* indeed, not a saloon-bar vamp. Her public utterances in the first part of the opera have humour, style, and a certain class. She is no longer young, a point stressed in the novel, and she knows it. Perhaps, in Alan Bennett's memorable phrase, there is also 'the menopause just shoving its nose above the horizon'; there is not a little of Hofmannsthal's Feldmarschallin about her. She is approaching retirement, and like so many of her calling – Liane de Pougy and Hortense Schneider to name but two – she will spend that retirement in religious devotion.

The famous or, in innumerable souped-up renderings, infamous 'Méditation', a marvellous, self-generating, endless melody, ironically drawn from the music accompanying the erotic visions that torment Athanaël's sleeping hours in the desert is, as no less a critic than Ernest Newman has pointed out, perfectly apt to the situation. There is a radiant calm and purity to the music for Thaïs after her conversion, in ironic contrast to the evermore fevered utterances of Athanaël as he comes to recognize his true self, too late. He is a Jochanaan drawn in depth, much younger than Thaïs, having first approached her at the age of fifteen but been turned away from the threshold of her place of work through a combination of shyness and poverty. Having mulled this over for about ten years in the desert, mortifying his flesh in the company of, we may hope, less emotionally stunted anchorites, he returns to Alexandria to re-encounter and convert Thaïs, and the situation can only be, to say the very least, explosive. He too is converted, to another kind of truth, a kind denied as often as the religious variety.

Of the four more or less complete recordings, two may be dismissed briefly. That on HMV (1976) seems to lack seriousness of intent. Lorin Maazel skates over the emotional depths of the score in a depressingly superficial reading. Beverly Sills's voice was, at this stage of her career, too unsteady to sustain Massenet's line, and her taste for unwritten *tenuti* impedes the music's flow. Her lightly teasing tone in the first act, however, has its moments. Sherrill Milnes gives a smoothly sung but too generalized account of Athanaël – the character eludes him almost entirely. Nicolai Gedda sounds old and effortful as Nicias. The only recommendable feature of this set is the excellent essay in the booklet by Andrew Porter, who seems to have undergone an almost Athanaël-like conversion to the work. The booklet also contains a photograph of Maazel and Sills grinning admiringly at each other as the former plays the violin solo in the Méditation.

The 1952 Nixa version has the husband-and-wife team of Roger Bourdin and Géori Boué, both experienced in the roles on stage. The soprano is in very acid and thin voice here, a drawback emphasized by a recording shallow even for its day, and she is unable to cope with anything *piano* above the stave – and there is plenty in the score. She also ducks the high Ds in the finale; no one else does that. Bourdin, late in his career, sounds tonally undernourished but the words, as always with this baritone, are vividly projected. Jean Giraudeau is an ideally elegant and stylish Nicias. I would very much like to have seen Géori Boué – a beautiful woman – on stage, but there is little pleasure to be derived from listening to this recording. (I have been unable to hear the Italian-language broadcast version of 1954 on Cetra.)

If the best of the Decca (1962) and RCA (1974) sets could be combined by some electronic wizard, we would have an almost ideal version of the opera. The Decca cuts the penultimate scene, a pity, since without a further dose of torment in the desert for Athanaël (during which he gets precious little support from his fellow monks) the overwhelming power of the finale is lessened. Robert Massard brings a certain nobility to his Athanaël and is capable of tenderness in the early scenes, but he is unyielding in his delivery and there is little of the self-doubt lurking in the music. He tends to hector in the conversion duet, and seems embarrassed by the sudden flood of emotion at the oasis. His finale is disappointingly bland. While his is the most smoothly sung of the post-war Athanaëls, there is much in the character that he misses. Renée Doria, though, is by far the most satisfying Thaïs of her day. In a word, she has class. Her tone in the leave-taking duet with Nicias (Michel Sénéchal, well cast) is perfect: most winsomely phrased, full of lazy regret and kitten-like charm. Here, and in her gentle teasing of Athanaël ('Qui te fait si sevère') with some suggestive *portamenti*, she manages to be hugely sexy without for a moment setting out to be. Only a Frenchwoman, surely, can manage this. In her 'Air du Miroir', the feeling of emptiness in the recitative is followed by just the right amount of panic in the first section, panic very properly intensified in the repeat when her mirror has not given her the answers she requires. Doria is meticulous in her attention to Massenet's markings, and the aria emerges as it should – the expression of an emotional crisis as intense as Violetta's scena in the first act of *La traviata*. Her touchingly serene contributions to the oasis and final duets are slightly compromised by lack of response from Massard and the routine conductor, Jésus Etcheverry.

In the RCA set, the boot is on quite the other foot. Anna Moffo, virtually voiceless at the time of the sessions, croons her way through the role in would-be sexy, would-be religiose fashion. The result, apart from being pure Hollywood, is simply grotesque, and one can only admire Miss Moffo for allowing it to be released. And be grateful to her as well, for Gabriel Bacquier's Athanaël is a marvellous recorded performance. To be sure, at this comparatively late stage in his career, he finds the high *tessitura* of the earlier part of the role extremely testing, but covers his difficulties with characteristic professionalism. His penetration to the very heart of this tragic character, the way he lays bare the enormity of the man's self-deception, both make for uncomfortable listening. The change of tone from the sadistic hectoring of Thaïs on the march across the desert to *douceur ineffable* when he sees the blood on her milk-white feet (a truly *fin-de-siècle* concept), and the supreme tenderness of his singing in 'Baigne d'eau' are impressive enough, but the moment of enlightenment itself at 'Elle va lentement' as Athanaël delivers the penitent to *les blanches filles* is heart-stopping; at his tormented cry of 'Je ne la verrai plus' the recording engineers add a touch of echo, and it is as though the man, alone in the agony of the moment, turns to let his voice resound through the vast emptiness of the desert. Add to this the way that the conductor, Julius Rudel, follows the compassionate Massenet's hint and delays the resolution ('sans presser le groupe') at the semiquaver triplet for a brief eternity, and you have one of those rare occasions on records where musicians and technicians combine to achieve a unique effect. In the finale, Bacquier manages with vocal inflection alone to suggest the physical degeneration described by Anatole France, and his frenzied renunciation of faith followed by 'je t'aime' (marked *dolce* by Massenet, the brute) make for another string of unforgettable moments. His searing 'Pitié' sets the seal on a classic reading. One thing is missing, I admit: youthfulness. But that is soon forgotten. I must add that, quite unfairly, I find it hard to believe in José Carreras as the hedonist philosopher Nicias, and that Rudel, although plumbing the depths of emotion in the score, just misses some of its theatrical excitement.

There is theatrical excitement in plenty in the French EMI highlights disc of 1964. Jacqueline Brumaire and Michel Dens both have soft-grained, warm voices that perhaps lack edge for the more hectic passages; Mlle Brumaire, contemplative, placid almost in the 'Air du Miroir', is much better suited to the later scenes, which she phrases very sweetly. Dens's account of 'Voilà donc la terrible cité', very attentive to the markings, is one of the best, but here as elsewhere it is the contribution of Pierre Dervaux, that sorely underestimated French conductor, and the Paris Opéra Orchestra that makes this record well worth hearing. On no other recording is the effect of the beating of the wings of the angels that Athanaël summons in the last part of the first aria so graphically suggested, and in no other version is there quite so much danger in the conversion duet; the suppressed desire lurking beneath Athanaël's posture of saintliness is there in the music, and Dervaux finds it. Sadly the scene is broken off halfway through, and in the oasis duet, played in full with a chorus of *blanches filles*, Dervaux adopts too jaunty a tempo for 'Baigne d'eau', as if embarrassed by it. Otherwise, his conducting is aware and exciting.

A steady flow of 78s bears witness to *Thaïs*'s popularity until the post-war period. One of the most frequently recorded extracts is Athanaël's first-act aria 'Voilà donc la terrible cité' – understandably, since it is one of Massenet's comparatively rare showpieces for baritone and repays careful interpretation. In the first part Athanaël, returning to Alexandria from the desert, greets the city of his birth with both verbal and musical rapture, in a wash of strings and harp; with a sour little chord on woodwind he seems to remember himself, and launches into a diatribe against the beauty and knowledge to be found in the city; and in part three he summons angels to purify its corruptions. One of the most satisfying versions is that by Louis Guénot (Col. D 14220), who has a voice round in tone, penetrating and ideally free at the top, who finds just the right vocal colour for each section, and who uses the words with vigour and point. Arthur Endrèze (Parlo. E 11110; ORX 120) has a lighter, less colourful voice and is slightly less obedient to the markings, but his treatment of the text is equally vivid. Among earlier baritones are Hector Dufranne (Col. A 5558; RLS 743), who spins a fine legato line despite sounding short of breath and finds the last section most congenial; Robert Couzinou (Poly. 566021; Club 99.76), who sang Athanaël for Beecham at Covent Garden but whose top sounds unreliable here; and Louis Lestelly (032320), who is hampered by a ludicrously slow accompaniment. Edouard Rouard (Od. XXP 6851) is one of those light, open French baritones and brings great verbal urgency to the aria, especially in the last part, but his top too sounds unsupported. Yves Noël (Cantoria AR 504) has a rounder, almost woofy voice, brings little variety of colour to the three parts, and is pretty free with note values. The heroic tones of Charles Cambon (DB 11238) are allied to lively diction, so a certain uniformity of delivery is all the more disappointing. There is no lack of verbal nuance in the version of Gérard Souzay (Philips SAL 3574), but the rapture with which he greets his birth-place is not matched by much violence in the curse. In another of the few modern versions, José Van Dam (Erato NUM 75023) sings with beautifully rounded tone and phrases smoothly, but sounds too calm at the opening, too half-hearted in the curse, and brings insufficient sense of urgency to his summoning of the angels. The accompaniment under Claudio Scimone is washy.

There is a version by Marcel Journet (DB 1196; Club 99.34) of Athanaël's arioso earlier in the act, 'Hélas, enfant encore', in which he tells the monks of his fruitless original visit to Thaïs (the seventh, interval of desire, much in evidence) and his determination to lead her to God; on the other side we have 'Honte! Horreur!' as he awakens from the first of his graphic dreams, and the C major hymn as he sets off on his fatal journey of discovery. Although lack of a chorus makes the first extract distinctly disjointed, Journet sounds properly *troublé*, phrases the first part lovingly, and suggests the latent hysteria under the hymn: marvellous singing throughout.

In the second scene of the first act we have the first confrontation between Thaïs and Athanaël, which the former wins game, set and match with 'Qui te fait si sévère', a wonderfully sly piece of mocking sensuality. Marie-Louise Edvina, the first London Thaïs (1911) prefaces her 1919 recording (VA 48; Rococo 5254) with a wicked chuckle and from then on the tone is light and mischievous – just right. Georgette Bréjean-Silver (Od. 56063; Rococo 5255), with piano accompaniment, makes rather heavy weather of the piece, with much supposedly sexy *portamento*. Mireille Berthon (Disque P 738) on the other hand adopts a tone of roguish mock-solemnity, which is wittily effective; there are forty-three markings in the three pages of vocal score and two of them are *bien chanté* and *avec charme, avec séduction*. Mlle Berthon follows both to the letter in a classic account.

The soprano's big showpiece is the 'Air du Miroir', where there is as much scope for interpretative nuance as in the baritone's first-act aria. In the recitative she must express disillusion with her way of life and the emptiness of her soul, and in the da capo aria that follows she seeks reassurance from her mirror with more than a hint of panic in her questions. In the B section she hears less than reassuring answers: she will grow old and Thaïs will cease to exist. In the da capo, intensity of delivery, the sense of growing panic, take the place of vocal decoration, and the character ends up in an emotional crisis that makes her easy prey for whatever Athanaël can offer her in the ensuing duet. Ninon Vallin (Pathé X 7229; Rococo 5354) gives by far the best all-round account of this number. The quality of her voice is beautifully rounded, full of colour throughout the range. Through subtle inflection she suggests the impatience in the recitative, is just sufficiently nervous in the A section, and then breaks into a vocal cold sweat as she hears the *voix impitoyable*, intensifying the terror in the repeat to tingling effect. Throughout she follows Massenet's markings, not just slavishly but constructively; here is an example of a creative artist working with a composer rather than through, or indeed roughshod over him. Particularly effective are the difficult *diminuendo* from B flat through A and D to G on the word 'belle', and the false but telling emphases on '*les* roses de *mes* lèvres'. And she has a good trill. At first hearing many will find, as I did, Fanny Heldy's soprano too steely and unyielding (though it is of honey compared to Géori Boué), but her account of the aria (DB 1129; LV 223) has a classic grandeur to it that may not in every respect be fitting to the situation but is undeniably impressive. She is a grand Thaïs, not a pathetic one: there is defiance in her interrogation of the mirror. Her use of words, too, is in the manner of a great French actress. The only real drawback is lack of dynamic variety.

Of post-war interpreters, two can be dealt with summarily: Montserrat Caballé (DG 2530 073) takes the Air slowly and makes it sound sentimental, and Leontyne Price (SER 5589) is dull. On the other hand Joan Hammond (DA 1997; HQM 1186) is among the most eloquent. The quality of her voice is bright and full and she colours the words well in, admittedly, very individual French. The sense of wonder, of nervousness almost, in her questioning is most touching, and she too follows the composer's markings in constructive fashion. Stanford Robinson's idiomatic conducting is an added bonus.

There are disappointingly few versions of the following duet: I have heard only one. Emma Luart and Roger Bourdin (Od. 123 652/3) sing off the words in true French fashion and catch the shifting stances of the characters as they circle warily around each other. Bourdin, in fuller voice than on the post-war recording, starts in a calm, matter-of-fact manner that makes his literal and metaphorical disrobing all the more effective. He also makes the most of his muttered prayers for protection. Had Luart just sung the 'Air du Miroir', then one could admire the way she snaps out of her mood and back into her professional manner. The slightly sick-humorous misunderstanding, where he offers her an unknown love and she replies that he comes too late – 'Je connais tous les ivresses' – comes off well. Luart's collapse into nervous hysterics is very convincingly managed, which is saying a lot: the musico-dramatic dialogue here is dangerously compressed. Gustave Cloëz plays the big A major tune for all it is worth, but cannot quite match Dervaux's dramatic intensity on the post-war highlights record.

Thaïs's post-Méditation solo, the asymmetrical arioso 'L'amour est un vertu rare', in which she seeks to save a statue of Eros from the holocaust, is one of Massenet's most elusive pieces in its utter simplicity – a simplicity that sounds meaningless if unadorned by the subtlest vocal art. Maria Jeritza (DA 972; LV 122) makes nothing of it in a mechanical, rather shrill reading. Edvina (VA 48; Rococo 5254) brings pure tone but little in the way of phrasing. Mary Garden, a protégée of Sybil Sanderson and one of the most admired exponents of the role, recorded it twice. In the first version (IRCC 3055) she audibly fights a metronomically inflexible accompaniment, and the sound is primitive. The second (Col. A 5440; Odyssey 32 16 0079) is a beguiling example of the art that conceals art: refinement of phrasing, purity of line and tone, all are unanalysable yet indisputably represent great singing. A passing moment of flatness would have been an occasion for a retake today, but presumably there were no such things in 1912. Nevertheless, until hearing Garden I had no idea of what this passage could yield.

The Oasis duet is no less tricky, not least at 'Baigne d'eau' – too slow and it sounds gluey ('sans lenteur' says Massenet), too fast and it carries no emotional weight. I have heard five versions. That by Jane Lindsay and Henri Danges (Od. 34064) is put out of court by the soprano singing flat throughout. Mattia Battistini and Attilia Janni (DB 215; CO 327) sing in Italian and the baritone makes the running: the soprano supplies a mere thread of tone. His legato is most persuasive. There is a big *rallentando* at the end – tempting, I know, and it often happens – where the composer specifically forbids one. Yvonne Gall and Arthur Endrèze (Pathé X 90072; Club 99.118) perform the scene in full from 'L'ardent soleil'. She phrases very sweetly with white tone, and he brings disappointingly little variety of tone between the sadism of the opening and the tenderness of the post-blood passage. Perhaps because they were running out of time, 'Baigne d'eau' is very fast and very loud; luckily, at least, there is no time for a *rallentando* at the end.

In the version by Heldy and Journet (DA 940; LV 223) the soprano sounds anything but exhausted at 'O messager de Dieu', which is where this version starts: this, as in her 'Air du Miroir', is big, grand singing by a lady who is not going to be inconvenienced by anything so trifling as a route march across the desert. Journet is nicely concerned and tender, but 'Baigne d'eau' sounds churchy and religiose, which it shouldn't. The most completely effective account is by Mireille Berthon and John Brownlee (Disque P 719), though the label attribution to the Australian baritone has been disputed. Whoever it is, he is marvellous, but this is Berthon's record. The beauty of her phrasing and the colour of her verbal nuance throughout 'O messager de Dieu' gives just the right impression of radiant transfiguration, and the grace with which she moves from the G flat of 'front brûlant' to the G natural of 'Plus fraîche', with Massenet's comma and *subito pianissimo* perfectly poised, is stunning. The speed for 'Baigne d'eau' is perfectly judged. Both singers get the most out of the exchange 'O divine bonté' and 'O douceur ineffable', and eschew a *rallentando* at the end. This is one of the most winning of all recordings from the opera.

Of the versions of the finale, the oddest is that by Geraldine Farrar (DB 247; GV 530). Her voice is as pure and radiant as ever, but she does without a baritone altogether. Still, this record provides hours of innocent fun for amateur Athanaëls to sing along with the great soprano (I have done so frequently). The account by Luart and Bourdin (Od. 123562; Rubini CC 2) is first-rate. Her tone may perhaps be too white, her vibrato too restless for this serene music, but his steadily increasing derangement and breathless 'je t'aime' are properly hair-raising. Although one shouldn't be surprised, it is difficult not to be by the wholly idiomatic account in unexceptionable French by Dorothy Kirsten and Robert Merrill (DB 21184; VIC 1394), very dramatically conducted by Jean-Paul Morel. Kirsten's phrasing is exquisitely moulded, and Merrill's portrait of a broken, desperate man is quite as shattering as those by Bacquier and Bourdin.

My desert-island cast would be Berthon or Vallin, with Doria covering, Bacquier twenty years ago, and conducted by Dervaux.

DON QUICHOTTE

Don Quichotte, a more readily recognizable masterpiece, and one now secure in the European repertory, is also about a professional lady and her ill-suited admirer, but there the resemblance ends. *La belle Dulcinée*, an invention of Jacques le Lorrain, on whose play (1904) the opera is based, is a small-town tart, but one as aware as her Alexandrian *consoeur* of the passing of time – a conceit understandably favoured by the male sex. *Don Quichotte* is as much, if not more, an autobiographical sketch of the eccentric playwright as of Cervantes's doleful knight, and one also senses a strong autobiographical streak in the opera. Lucy Arbell, creator of Dulcinée and a tough little madam from all accounts, one who took Massenet for all she could get, was the object of the last of the composer's *amitiés amoureuses*; the courtly and rheumaticky composer was now in his late sixties. Quichotte and Dulcinée inhabit different worlds, worlds that scarcely recognize the other's existence and worlds with different languages; the moment when those worlds meet briefly with the wraps off in the fourth-act duet is the most moving in the opera. What one seeks from interpreters of the title role is that sense of innocence, of other-worldliness, and the naive belief that all other people live by his traditional, long-gone values. Once the veil has been lifted, there is nothing left for Quichotte but, like one of Wagner's strong-minded heroines, to sit down and die.

I approach the recorded legacy of *Don Quichotte* from the beginning since the first interpreters of the title role (Fyodor Chaliapin at the Monte Carlo première in 1910, and Vanni Marcoux in Paris later the same year) both committed extracts to disc. Their approaches could scarcely be more dissimilar, and from the evidence of Massenet's memoirs there can be no doubt as to which he preferred: Chaliapin is casually dismissed in a parenthesis, and Vanni Marcoux is praised extravagantly. I am on Massenet's side. In Chaliapin's autobiography, the Russian bass describes how he was so moved by the fourth act at a play-through with the composer at the piano that he broke down in uncontrollable sobs. 'Calme-toi,' ordered Massenet, asking him to leave the room and compose himself. 'Wait until the end, and *then* you can cry.' Chaliapin had the last word, however, with his recording of Sancho's fourth-act aria (previously unpublished; RLS 710), a massive, pulsating travesty of what the composer wrote, generously larded with characteristic sobs (notably at the mention of the name 'Jésus') and with a speed for the C major tune so slow that all sense of melody is destroyed. Nor are the notes when they are discernible especially distinguished: both E naturals sharpen horribly. This is a monstrosity. Chaliapin's Death Scene, recorded in 1927 (DB 1096; GEMM 152), is more worthy of serious consideration. He takes the roles of both Quichotte and Sancho (one imagines that only an exceptionally strong-willed producer prevented him from essaying Dulcinée as well – the role is taken by Olive Kline), thus establishing an unfortunate tradition. There are some lovely passages that he actually sings – 'Tu n'est qu'un homme enfin' and 'Prends cette île' among them – but he spoils the latter by lavishing too much self-conscious 'art' on the final words: 'C'est l'île des rêves'. Otherwise, any old notes, much *parlando*, an intrusive 'er' before too many words like a Shakespearean actor of the Victorian school, copious sobs, and a Boris-like approach to the death with a real comic-book 'Aaaarrrgh!' at the end, capped by yet more sobbing from Sancho. As ham it may be magnificent, but Massenet – here at least – was not in the hammarket.

Vanni Marcoux's vocal art defies verbal description. At a first hearing he can sound cool and uninvolved; he is not. His legato is instrumental in its purity; it is tempting to write of his use of *portamento*, but that word suggests a conscious effect, whereas with Vanni Marcoux it is a way of joining notes together, and the French word *liant* is nearer. His control of his instrument is faultless. His words grow out of the notes and vice versa. He recorded the first-act Serenade twice, and his slightly detached delivery suggests the other-worldliness of the character perfectly. On the first record (DA 631) he sounds like a light baritone (the bottom A flat at the end is almost growled) but the line is seamless. In the second version (DA 934; Club 99.101) the voice is recorded nearer and is fuller in tone, more like a real bass, and the legato even more pronounced. In both versions he uses the words to maximum yet unforced effect – his moulding of 'son oeuil calân' is most affecting. Both records cut from the first verse to the reprise at the end of the act.

His line is ideally suited to the third-act Prayer, when, captured by the bandits, he prepares himself for death and then quells his captors with his curriculum vitae (DA 936; Club 99.101). His haughty delivery of the second part is finely calculated. There are three versions of the Death. The first (DA 631; Club 99.104) starts at 'Je meurs' and, as in the Serenade on the other side, he sounds like a baritone. He sings all the notes as written, and there is no mezzo. There is neither Dulcinée nor Sancho on the second recording (DA 934/5; Rococo 5358), but it starts at the beginning of the scene. There is an infinitely touching impression of regretful melancholy to his portrayal of the disillusioned knight, and much visionary eloquence to his description of the 'île des rêves'. Here is a shining example of the power of understatement and of Vanni Marcoux at his best. In the third version (DA 4857; Club 99.101) he has both a well-positioned Dulcinée (Odette Ricquier) and a Sancho (Michael Cozette), who is in even smoother voice than before, and also sounds horribly like a dying man. He is slightly freer with note values than before, but never with notes themselves – save for one unpitched choking sound after summoning his last strength for 'Je fus le chef', permissible surely. Although, since there are supporting artists and the bass achieves greater dramatic verisimilitude, this version is the most theatrically valid, Vanni Marcoux just out-sings himself in the earlier recording. I could not possibly do without both.

Perhaps this is the place to dispose of the other Death scenes. There is a remarkably powerful one from Jean Acquistapace (Pathé X7177), singing both roles from the beginning of the scene. The voice is full and round (he is described on the label as a baritone, but is surely a bass) and he keeps sentiment at bay by sticking to the written notes (just). He has the requisite tone colour at his command. Roger Bourdin (Od. 123518; ORX 147), with Germaine Cernay (lovely) and Julien Lafont (very poor), is in much rounder voice than in his later *Thaïs* recordings. The emotion is possibly a little too contained in the earlier part of the scene, but the 'île des rêves' is spot-on. The conductor keeps Dulcinée and the solo violin on the move – many do not. There are three post-war versions. George London (Am. Col. ML 4489) sings Sancho as well, with Rosalind Nadell as Dulcinée, and Jean Morel sets an impossibly slow speed for the opening: the effect is glutinous. London's singing is certainly deeply felt, but he resorts to too much *parlando* for all tastes. Norman Treigle also sings both roles, with Ellen Klein (WST 17145); his version is very straight, very attentive to the markings, and sensitively conducted by Jussi Jalas. Ruggero Raimondi's account (Erato STU 71434) is ponderously conducted by Emil Tchakarov – his speed for the 'île des rêves' is ludicrous, destroying all sense of flow – but the Italian bass eschews sobs and sings carefully and musically in good, if not quite perfect French. He is all but upstaged by his sensitive Sancho, Jean-Marie Frémeau. The distant Dulcinée is Michèle Le Bris.

To go back to the beginning, there are two further records of the Serenade worth noting. Bourdin (Od. 188805; ORX 147) is cool, elegant and serious, and Cernay phrases the counter melody in the second verse with much allure (the standard cut in bass/mezzo versions is followed). Paul Payan (32493; GV 14) has a beautifully black, inky voice – few French basses have – but does disappointingly little with it: the Serenade lacks poetry and is on the loud side. Suzanne Brohly is his excellent Dulcinée.

André Pernet, an inter-war Boris and another real bass, gives an entrancingly witty account of Quichotte's 'C'est vers ton amour' at the opening of Act 2 (Od. 188783; ORX 147), with a delicious whistle of triumph as he finds his final rhyme – sheer joy. By way of contrast, on the other side he is grave and powerful in the second part of the Prayer ('Je suis le chevalier'): few bandits could resist such dignity. Pierre Dupré, a baritone Sancho, is as comic as his master, flip almost, in 'Comment peut-on penser', his diatribe against women (Od. 188802; ORX 147). Perhaps he is too comic in the context: a little edge does not come amiss here. But his enunciation is full of relish. He then joins Bourdin in a lively account of the Windmill duet (Od. 188802; ORX 147). Willy Tubiana sings the Prayer complete on Disque 4–32730; he too has a dark, round voice, more baritone than bass, and is more successful in the second part than in the Prayer proper, where his intonation is insecure.

Dulcinée is sadly under-represented on 78s, and even Germaine Cernay's 'J'ai bien assez . . . Lorsque le temps d'amour a fui' (Od. 188805; ORX 147) is a slight disappointment; this is Dulcinée's one moment of reflection, and Cernay sounds cross rather than *troublée*. Her voice is of course lovely in quality, and her enunciation in the classic French style. In the song with guitar with which the lady breaks her introspective mood, one of those amiable pieces where French composers give their idea of what Spanish music should really sound like, Suzanne Brohly (33862) keeps her high spirits more or less under control, and places the scales neatly. The guitar playing is so frightful that one suspects Brohly of following the lead of Arbell and accompanying herself.

I have heard only one version of the climactic fourth-act duet, by Bourdin and Cernay (Od. 123755; ORX 147). The baritone again tends to be cool, too much so for a proposal of marriage, but both he and Cernay are admirably faithful to Massenet's markings and the first part of the excerpt (starting at 'Marchez dans mon chemin') goes well. The duet itself ('Oui, je souffre votre tristesse') is taken fast; I know it can sound saccharine if lingered over, but this is too cool for so fraught an emotional situation.

The Air de Sancho, in which the faithful squire rounds on those mocking his crestfallen master and the passage that so moved Chaliapin and was subsequently massacred by him, is taken very slowly by Jean Claverie (Parlo 29538; ORX 147) in a serious, dignified interpretation. He is a bass Sancho, and one who comes off the notes to upbraid the tormentors – fair enough in the heat of a stage performance, perhaps less so on record. Dupré (Od. 188804) is more baritonal in timbre and by contrast underplays the scorn and sings the notes carefully and musically. This is a very difficult number to bring off, and we shall come later to a baritone who succeeds magnificently, but meanwhile José Van Dam's modern version (NUM 75023), beautifully phrased, just sufficiently contemptuous, full of warmth, loyalty and affection in the final lines, should not be overlooked.

For many years the only complete recording available was the one with Miroslav Changalovich and Belgrade forces under Oscar Danon, sung in fair French. The Yugoslav bass's voice is sumptuous indeed, but he takes too sentimental and tearful a view of the role and scoops up into the note at the the start of virtually every phrase. This soon becomes more than wearisome. Dulcinée (after a clumsy start) and Sancho (a baritone and straight) are acceptable. Danon's approach is heavy-handed: he overplays the *ritardandi* and adds not a few of his own. There are harmful cuts: a chunk of the fourth act and all the dialogue for the bandits. The opera doesn't flow, and sounds too much like second-rate Puccini. The same is true of the 'private' recording sung in Italian, taken off the air from Milan in 1958, and conducted by Alfredo Simonetto. In the title role, Boris Christoff is very much school-of-Chaliapin – powerful, and in no sense vulnerable. He makes a meal of the Death, with any number of Boris-like spasms. Perhaps Teresa Berganza sees the role of Dulcinée, like that of Carmen, as a slight on Spanish womanhood: hers is a hearty young lass who might as well be wielding a hockey stick as idly plucking at a guitar. The quality of her voice is beautifully firm and dark, and if the big duet sounds, again, more like Puccini than Massenet, at least its first-rate Puccini.

Happily, and unusually in a book of this kind, we can end with a thoroughly recommendable modern version. The 1979 Decca recording may not be in every respect ideal – what recording is? – but it puts the competition well and truly in the shade. Nicolai Ghiaurov's Quichotte is for me one of his finest interpretations on record. He sings in good French, sings the notes, takes the lead from the markings, phrases with gentle eloquence and humour as appropriate, and his grainy but well-rounded tone is ideally suited to the role. He also gives the impression of being somewhere else, of not being on quite the same planet as the rest of the cast, and I find this extremely moving. Not that he is detached from the character: the reprise of the Serenade at the end of the first act is a real tear-jerker, and he creates a quietly comic mood for the second act. The only worry is his failure to make the most of

Massenet's dotting: the line is occasionally ironed out and the emotional power compromised – as in 'Je suis le chevalier' and the Death scene.

Similarly, Régine Crespin has done little on record to surpass her Dulcinée. Of course there are some purely vocal problems – squally singing at the top of the range and an insufficiently secure legato for 'Lorsque le temps' – but they pale beside her delightful delineation of the character. Taste, teasing allure, sharp wit (her enunciation of the word 'intact' when Quichotte returns from the bandits is deliciously naughty), overwhelming sexiness – all are combined to build an interpretation quintessentially and indefinably French. In Crespin's and Ghiaurov's hands, the fourth-act scene leaves not a dry eye in the listening room, yet the dampness is in no sense self-indulgent or facile, and that is what Massenet is all about.

Gabriel Bacquier's Sancho is another classic. Maybe he is rumbustious rather than sly in his second-act scene, but it is hard to resist the pungency of his delivery. More important, he catches just the right balance of tone in the fourth-act finale; while his rebuking of the mockers is duly biting, it is Sancho's over-riding and protective love for his dotty old master that comes welling out of that broad C major melody. And the balance is right in the Death scene too. So powerful is Bacquier's projection that he seems almost to be upstaging the withdrawn Quichotte, but he is not. It is through Sancho's reactions that the listener draws the sense of tragedy at the departure of so much that might once have been good, honourable and gloriously impractical from a world now left to tawdriness.

The one aspect of the score that Kazimierz Kord just misses is its pawky humour: all else is sensitively realized. The smaller roles are well cast, particularly the lively actors as the bandits: their scene is expertly controlled in Christopher Raeburn's skilful production. In all, a very satisfying issue. Maybe in a better, Quixotic world there will be a recording with the middle-period Vanni Marcoux, the young Crespin, and Bacquier, and – why not? – conducted by the composer himself.

THAÏS

T Thaïs; *A* Athanaël; *P* Palémon; *N* Nicias

1952 Boué *T*; Bourdin *A*; Roux *P*; Giraudeau *N* / Paris Opéra-Comique Chorus and Orch. / Sebastian
Nixa ⓜ ULP 9227
Urania ⓒ S 227

1954 (live performance – Teatro Verdi, Trieste) Forti *T*; Bastianini *A*; Massaria *P*; Scarlini *N* / Teatro Verdi Chorus and Orch. / Toffolo
Cetra ⓜ LO57 (3)

1962 Doria *T*; Massard *A*; Serkoyan *P*;

Sénéchal *N* / chorus and orch. / Etcheverry
Decca GOS 639–41
Westminster WST 8203

1974 Moffo *T*; Bacquier *A*; Diaz *P*; Carreras *T* / Ambrosian Opera Chorus, New Philharmonia / Rudel
RCA ARL3 0842

1976 Sills *T*; Milnes *A*; Van Allan *P*; Gedda *N* / Alldis Choir, New Philharmonia / Maazel

EMI SLS993
Angel SCLX3832Q ④ 4Z3X3832
1964 (excerpts) Brumaire *T*; Dens *A* /

René Duclos Chorus, Paris Opéra
Orch. / Dervaux
EMI 2C 061 12105

DON QUICHOTTE

DQ Don Quichotte; *SP* Sancho Panza; *D* Dulcinée

1958 (in Italian – broadcast
performance) Christoff *DQ*;
Badioli *SP*; Berganza *D* / Italian
Radio Chorus and Orch. Milan /
Simonetto
Cetra ⓜ LSR 13
1966 Changalovich *DQ*; Koroshetz *SP*;
Kalef *D* / Belgrade National
Opera Chorus and Orch. / Danon

Everest S440–2
1978 Ghiaurov *DQ*; Bacquier *SP*;
Crespin *D* / Suisse Romande
Radio Chorus, Suisse Romande
Orch. / Kord
Decca D156D3 ④ K156K32
London OSA13134 ④ OSA
5–13134

The Bartered Bride and Dalibor

PETER TANNER

THE BARTERED BRIDE (Prodaná nevěsta)

Overture

Act 1

1 Chorus (with Mařenka, Jeník): Proč bychom se netěšili
2 Aria (Mařenka): Kdybych se co takového
3a Duet (Mařenka, Jeník) part 1: Jako matka požehnáním
3b Duet (Mařenka, Jeník) part 2: Věrné milování
4 Trio (Ludmila, Krušina, Kecal): Jak vám pravím, pane kmotře
5 Trio (Ludmila, Krušina, Kecal): Mladík slušný
6 Quartet (Mařenka, Ludmila, Krušina, Kecal): Tu ji máme
  Polka

Act 2

7 Chorus (with Jeník, Kecal): To pivečko
  Furiant
8 Aria (Vašek): Ma-Ma-Ma-Matička
9 Duet (Mařenka, Vašek): Známť já jednu dívčinu
10a Duet (Jeník, Kecal); part 1: Nuže, milý chasníku
10b Duet (Jeník, Kecal) part 2: Každý jen tu svou (Kecal solo)
10c Duet (Jeník, Kecal) part 3: Znám jednu dívku
11 Aria (Jeník): Až uzříš . . . Jak možna věřit
12 Finale: Pojďte, lidičky

Act 3

13 Aria (Vašek): To-to mi v hlavě le-leží
   March of the Comedians
   Skočná (Dance of the Comedians)
14 Duet (Esmeralda, Principál): Milostné zvířátko
15 Quartet (Háta, Vašek, Mícha, Kecal): Aj! Jakže? jakže?
16 Sextet (Mařenka, Ludmila, Háta, Krušina, Mícha, Kecal): Ne, ne, tomu nevěřím
17 Sextet (Mařenka, Ludmila, Háta, Krušina, Mícha, Kecal): Rozmysli si, Mařenka

18   Aria (Mařenka): Och, jaký žal! . . . Ten lásky sen
19   Duet (Mařenka, Jeník): Mařenko má! . . . tak tvrdošíjna, dívko, jsi?
20   Trio (Mařenka, Jeník, Kecal): Utiš se, dívko
21   Finale: Jak jsi se, Mařenko, rozmyslila?

The Bartered Bride was for many years the only Czech opera in the international repertory. Then the exploration by opera houses of the operas of Janáček and of operas by Martinů and Dvořák, as well as others by Smetana, led to an eclipse of *The Bartered Bride*; but in Britain, at least, the eclipse seems to have been temporary: there has been a minor flood of productions in recent years.

Smetana's operas are the musical expression of the resurgence of the Czechs' awareness of national identity in the mid-nineteenth century. Before Smetana there was no significant Czech opera; and it took an external stimulus to get Smetana's first opera written. In 1861, a Count Harrach announced a competition to encourage the composition of Czech National Opera and *The Brandenburgers in Bohemia (Braniboři v Čechách)*, completed two years later to a libretto by Karel Sabina, was Smetana's entry, eventually judged the winning work. Nothing could be more nationalistic than the plot, set in the late thirteenth century, dealing in fictional terms with the factual episode when the occupying Brandenburg forces were driven out of the country.

This weighty, heroic work was still awaiting performance when Smetana began setting a second Sabina libretto, at the time untitled because Sabina could not think what to call it. It was the composer who gave it the name *Prodaná nevěsta* (literally *Sold Bride*). It offered a strong contrast to *The Brandenburgers*: here was a work no less nationalistic in character, but one that portrayed an episode from an idealized village life of the country. At this early stage in its career it was more of an *opéra-comique*, with musical numbers separated by spoken dialogue. Only after four revisions did it emerge in the definitive form which we know today.

Perhaps it is not surprising that *The Bartered Bride* was not an instant success when we consider that in its first version it lacked the three popular dance movements – the Polka, the Furiant and the Skočná (known as the Dance of the Comedians) – and most of Mařenka's third-act aria. The recitatives were only written for the last version of the work, in 1869, when there was the prospect of a production at St Petersburg. The Prague audience was slow to take to *The Bartered Bride* – probably the picture of village life was too rustic for the sophisticated city dwellers – but in 1882, two years before the composer's death, the hundredth performance took place; it was the first Czech opera to achieve that distinction.

As far as recording *The Bartered Bride* (or any Czech opera) is concerned, the record companies face a problem over language. Do they try to assemble a Czech-speaking cast or do they record it in translation, thereby inhibiting international sales? A good many of them do not record it at all, which is one way out of the dilemma. Of the eleven complete or near-complete recordings that have been made of the work, five are in Czech, five in German, and one in Russian.

Four of the Czech language recordings use native forces. The earliest set was conducted by Otakar Ostrčil, Director of the Prague National Theatre from 1920 until his death in 1935. He is said to have been unhappy about the technical quality of the recording: as the available copy of the 78s had poor surfaces, I would not presume to comment on this save to say that the dry acoustic of the National Theatre seems highly appropriate for so outdoor a work. Ostrčil secures excellent playing from his orchestra: the overture has tremendous vitality and a rewarding, if indefinable, feeling of tradition about it. In the long introduction to 1 the first clarinet is outstanding, but this seems to be true of all the Prague recordings. It is only when the singing starts that things begin to go wrong. There are no psychological depths of character to be explored in *The Bartered Bride*; but surely the youthful lovers ought to sound youthful. Ada Nordenová, the Mařenka here, was in her early forties when the records were made but her tremulous emission puts years on the character. Likewise, the Jeník of Vladimír Tomš, with his slightly nasal tone and heavy vibrato, seems to be approaching middle age. (Alas, the poor fellow never reached middle age: he died two years later, when he was still only thirty-five.) Of the two tenors it is actually Jaroslav Gleich as Vašek who displays the steadier, more ringing, more conventionally heroic voice; it is not surprising that Gleich went on to to give many performances as Jeník at the National Theatre after Tomš's death. Unfortunately his Vašek is wooden and unconvincing: the stammering is accurate in its observance of Smetana's notation, but it fails to come alive, possibly because Gleich gives too much tone to his stammered syllables.

The Kecal in this set is Emil Pollert, who by the time of recording had already enjoyed a career of thirty-five years, for twenty-nine of which he had been singing this role at the National Theatre. He relishes every word of the text but throughout is cavalier with note values, thus undermining the rhythmic vitality which is so fundamental an element of the score. Furthermore, he is no less approximate with regard to pitch. Pollert was a much-loved and honoured artist in Prague, and I regret that I have not been able to hear any of the records he made in the first decade of the century; in view of the esteem in which he was held, I assume that this inadequate performance, recorded in his mid-fifties, shows him when he was a long way past his best.

The next Prague recording of *The Bartered Bride* is a vast improvement on the first. The conductor, Jaroslav Vogel, went into print stating his view of the pre-eminent importance of rhythm in this work: 'One of our guiding principles was to do justice to the dance and march character of the music, strictly preserving the rhythms, and to lighten the dynamics at the same time.' Certainly his conducting is as good as his word. One could not hope to hear a more faithful rendering of Smetana's *vivacissimo*, two-in-a-bar marking for the overture; he takes it at breakneck speed, but the orchestra nevertheless manages to play it with the utmost precision. Indeed his faithfulness to the score is exemplary throughout the whole opera. For instance, in 1 every one of the composer's many accents is observed. The singing in this set is full of good things. As Mařenka, Milada Musilová has a bright, light voice, tending slightly to shrillness above the stave, but generally free of what we in the West refer to as 'Slavic wobble'. She is responsive to words and to phrasing and is absolutely enchanting in 9: one would not need to be a simple fellow like Vašek to fall for *this* Mařenka. The low notes of the recitative in 18 cause her some problems, but in the aria proper she finds just the right mixture of wistfulness, grief and disbelief.

Her Jeník was the young Ivo Žídek – he was still only in his mid-twenties at the time of recording. His caressing of the line in 3b (marked *dolce amoroso*) is irresistible; early on there is a tendency for his voice to spread under pressure, but he has it under control by 11, which he sings with an abundance of warmth and passion. Oldřich Kovář as Vašek follows Vogel's lead in finding the spirit of the score through the observance of its letter; though every stammer is given exactly as written, there is not a hint of woodenness in the performance. Kovář specialized in character roles. He did not have a particularly large voice, but there was sufficient to get him through, and he strikes just the right note of self-pity in 13. Karel Kalaš brings to Kecal the steadiness of voice that was so lacking in Pollert; he, too, relishes every word, but also manages to keep time and, what's more, he can trot out a trill when it is required. Among the smaller parts Marie Veselá is a splendid old battle-axe of a Háta; and mention must be made of Karel Hruška as the Principal Comedian, a part he made very much his own. He sang it on the 1933 recording as well, and performed it on stage over a thousand times.

The booklet accompanying the first stereo recording of *The Bartered Bride* carries a smiling picture of the conductor, Zdeněk Chalabala, radiating the Czech equivalent of *Gemütlichkeit* and this is not contradicted by the interpretation on the discs: the work is well performed in many respects but lacks the near-manic singlemindedness of the Vogel. It is an affectionate reading. The cast is good in places: Žídek's upper notes were not his strongest point on his earlier recording, and sometimes here he is decidedly strained; but if his voice is not as fresh as it was and he has lost a little of his youthful exuberance, he makes up for that with even greater tenderness. His Mařenka, Drahomíra Tikalová, displays a certain amount of wobble but it is within acceptable limits and her voice is much more telling in its lower register than Musilová's. Her performance of 18 is marred by Chalabala's shambling accompaniment, which does not seem to know where it is going. Eduard Haken, like Kalaš, conveys the cynical, self-important marriage-broker to the life, but without Kalaš's steadiness. Haken's trill is barely distinguishable from his normal vibrato. Vašek is again sung by Kovář, by this time nearing the end of his career. He had been singing the part in Prague for over twenty years and had perfected every detail of his treasurable portrayal.

The most recent version was recorded digitally in 1980/81, though the sound is some way short of ideal. There is an aggressive immediacy to the voices which verges on the strident, and the overall acoustic is unpleasantly reverberant. However, it is a fine performance. Zdeněk Košler has the knack, not shared by all opera conductors, of following his singers while still remaining firmly in charge of proceedings. Here he is conducting the Czech Philharmonic and, though it may sound churlish to complain at the presence of so distinguished an orchestra, the result is over-lush for the opera's rustic charms. The Jeník is the Italian-trained Petr Dvorský: he has an admirable command of legato and, unlike Žídek, finds the top Bs no problem; but he does not bring the same degree of warmth as Žídek to such passages as 3b. As Mařenka, Gabriela Beňačková is unusual in that vibrato is a device in her expressive armoury rather than an affliction. This, allied to the attractive slight edge to the voice, is reminiscent of that other Bratislavan, Lucia Popp, though there is a wholly individual, plaintive element in Beňačková's timbre that is dominant in her performance, crowned with a superb account of 18. Certainly, this is the finest complete Mařenka to date on disc. Later in 1981, Beňačková recorded the aria again for a recital disc (Supraphon 1116 2843), when she refined her interpretation still further; and the analog recording of the recital is kinder to her voice. Richard Novák (Kecal) is splendid: a rich sense of character is evident, without his ever overstating it, and his voice not only has all the notes but can produce them in tune and in time. If one had not heard Kalaš, Novák would seem even better. The Vašek of Miroslav Kopp appeals less: he is rather too forthright, *gleich* Gleich. The mums and dads are all well in the picture and combine for an excellent 17.

The only other Czech language complete recording was made in Yugoslavia at Ljubljana. The orchestral playing under Dimitri Gebré is feeble; the all-important first clarinet is out of tune for much of the time and the piccolo is wretched. The Mařenka (Vilma Bukovec) has a pleasing voice, bright without shrillness and with an effective lower register, but she tends to push and go sharp on high notes; hers is a faceless performance. The tremulous Kecal (Latko Koroshetz) fails to establish the self-important hustler at his first entrance and, though he finds more character later on, it is by then too late. Miro Brajnik as Jeník displays a free, pleasant tone, but beside either of Žídek's performances it wants life. The two mums are trying; and such minor delights as Vekoslav Yanko's telling Krušina and the slightly steely Esmeralda of Sonia Khochevar cannot outweigh the shortcomings of this set.

The first of the German-language recordings is the Berlin Städtische Oper version, conducted by Hans Lenzer is a pretty dismal affair. The ponderous performance of 1 makes it hard to believe that this chorus ends with an invitation to dance! The comic roles are crudely done: Kurt Böhme's Kecal is conceived in broad strokes and coarsely sung, and Ralph Peters's Vašek is so grotesquely overplayed as to suggest that the character is certifiable.

The Principal Comedian speaks most of his *Spiel* (a German tradition). When at last he started to sing, I was thankful that he had not done so sooner. Rita Streich's Esmeralda is nicely enough sung, but her one number (14) is sabotaged by sluggish conducting and a partner who seems to care little for either the pitches or the durations of the notes. The Jeník (Sebastian Hauser) gives a colourless performance and does not sound comfortable in the higher reaches of his part. Traute Richter's Mařenka is more impressive in anger (19) than in sorrow (18), though her account of 18 is well shaped, marred only by her tendency to edge her way on to notes that are marked with accents or *sforzandi* and by the fact that the ludicrously over-reverberant recording here, as in many other places, reduces the woodwind and strings to a generalized mush. No. 20 is omitted from this set; it is just as well for by that stage one is longing for the end.

The Walter Goehr recording is much more heavily cut, presumably to accommodate what remains on two discs. For the most part the cuts are quite sensible, apart from the excision of the greater part of 3b, thereby making little sense of Smetana's quotation of the music later in the opera. This Frankfurt performance represents a considerable improvement in certain respects over the Berlin one. The conductor is obviously in close sympathy with the music (though he is hampered by an atrocious orchestra among whom ensemble both of rhythm and pitch is at a premium), and the three principals are all acceptable, one of them substantially more than that. Elfriede Trötschel's Mařenka does not evoke superlatives, but rather brings to mind such adjectives as 'serviceable', 'intelligent', 'musical'. She is particularly effective in 2 – heartfelt, but without exaggeration – though the top Cs in 19 are just outside her grasp.

As Jeník, Kurt Wolinski displays an agreeable, light, open voice, with little sense of strain at the top, save in 11 where the high *tessitura* does put him rather under pressure. However, he copes well with this aria, with some excellent legato singing. Some of his intonation in 10a is questionable, but other than that, his is a most enjoyable performance. The outstanding singing on this set comes from Heinz Rehfuss. Unlike most German singers of Kecal – Rehfuss, of course, is Swiss – he realizes that the notes Smetana wrote can be a help rather than a hindrance in creating the character. It is an intense musical performance, but one which nevertheless gives due weight to the words of the Kalbeck translation. The smaller parts are in general taken by small singers. The Principal Comedian is none other than Carl Ebert, whose accomplishments did not apparently run to vocal prowess. In 14 he sings those notes which do not lie too high for him, but surely a singer would have done much better. The chorus is sluggish, and its members cannot be depended on either to begin or to end a phrase together.

The HMV set of 1962 is on an altogether higher level of achievement. Kempe was in charge and his hard-driven but buoyant conducting of the overture arouses eager anticipation for the rest of the performance. The chorus in 1 sounds small in number but spirited and responsive. In 2 Lorengar and Kempe collaborate to give the aria a wonderful flexibility of tempo without ever pulling the music out of shape. The elegiac tone of 3a is caught to perfection and in 3b Smetana might have invented the marking *dolce amoroso* with Wunderlich in mind. That Wunderlich sings well can be taken for granted; but there is also a wealth of character in his Jeník. This carefree lad sounds fully a match for Kecal's machinations. You can almost see him out-scheming the broker as he dictates the terms of the contract in 10. Lorengar's Mařenka is a shade on the cool side, the sort of performance one might perhaps expect from a singer who excels in the classical repertory; but she rises to a superb 18, fluctuating between passionate resentment and grief-stricken incomprehension. The role of Kecal calls for a very wide range, more than two octaves. Gottlob Frick is not at all comfortable at the upper end of the part. He was in his mid-fifties at the time of recording, and seems unwilling to trust his voice for much really soft singing: he becomes monotonous and noisy. The main drawback of this recording is the supposed humour applied to the Comedians' scenes at the beginning of Act 3. The March is almost drowned by rent-a-crowd's 'rhubarb'-ing; again the Principal speaks his *Spiel*; when he starts to sing, one wishes he had not bothered; and we have the bonus of the pathetically unfunny, deliberately-bad-trumpet-playing joke, doubly unfortunate in that it seems that these daft antics tempt Karl-Ernst Mercker, whose Vašek has in earlier scenes been admirably retained and credible, to go way over the top. Nevertheless, as a whole this set is eminently desirable for Wunderlich, for Lorengar and, above all, for Kempe. Ostrčil, Vogel, Chalabala and Košler all display different facets of the authentic *Bartered Bride* tradition. It takes a conductor of true genius to come to the work from right outside that tradition and to establish convincingly his own authenticity. Such a conductor was Kempe.

A fifth conductor from within the Prague tradition is Jaroslav Krombholc, but he conducts a German-language performance, recorded in 1975 as the soundtrack for a film, starring Teresa Stratas, René Kollo and Walter Berry. The voices are forwardly balanced, presumably to match lots of close-up shots on the screen; this came as a particular shock directly after listening to the Kempe recording where the voices are backward, forming an integrated element in the overall texture. Stratas is a tough, steely Mařenka; everything is a bit overstated, as though she were forgetting that she was in a recording studio and was concentrating on projecting every syllable to the back of some 3000-seat auditorium. In 9 Mařenka should both scare the wits out of poor Vašek and charm him; Stratas is more convincing in the former than in the latter capacity. In 18 she achieves an apt feeling of wistfulness, but she does not really get to the heart of the matter. With Kollo it is as though he has an 'acting' voice, light and natural, for recitative passages and a 'singing' voice, rather Siegfried-like, for the arias and ensembles. He is musical, but his voice is, or has been trained to be, essentially heroic. His forceful – one might say forced – upper register sorts ill with such lyrical music as much of 11. Berry is a bass-baritone rather than a bass proper, and he only just gets the bottom notes of Kecal's part. However, the rest of the role is uncommonly well sung. The characterization is a trifle bland and understated, particularly when compared to Kalaš or Frick. Of course he takes higher options which Böhme and Frick avoid. The excellent Vašek is Heinz Zednik who, as a leading Mime, is thoroughly experienced at being downtrodden! As in the other two German sets, here also there is a scarcely singing Principal Comedian (the veteran Karl Dönch), which means that 14, the only item Esmeralda sings, is sabotaged by her partner's lack of vocal prowess. Here Dönch adjusts his line down an octave in places to suit his depleted resources. This is the more regrettable in that Esmeralda is sung by the sparkling Janet Perry. Krombholc's conducting inclines to the Vogel view of the work without being so hard-driven; among several felicitous touches I noticed especially the lovely lumbering dance movement with which he invests the end of 1, and the way in which he manages to set what feels like the perfect tempo for the Furiant, so that the two-against-three rhythm makes its maximum effect.

The set conducted by Otmar Suitner has eluded me so we pass on to the final near-complete recording emanating from the Bolshoi Theatre, conducted by Kyril Kondrashin in a brisk, if charmless manner. The overture is well-regimented: every *sforzando* is in place and the typically strident Russian trumpets make their presence felt. When the opera was first performed in Russia, 1 was encored; Kondrashin redresses the balance here by chopping 172 bars (including the music for Jeník and Mařenka) out of it. In 2 he is rather unyielding, though Shumilova manages to convey well the hesitancy of Mařenka's questioning of Jeník. No. 3a is dispatched at a furious pace and 3b is helped on its way by the simple expedient of cutting 16 bars. Shumilova has an acidic element in her voice and approaches too many notes from too far underneath. The reflective aspect is lacking in 18, giving a suggestion that Mařenka's anger at Jeník is present here rather than being provoked by the ensuing recitative. She makes her entry for her scene with Vašek in Act 2 laughing as though she were auditioning for Klytämnestra. As Jeník, Nelepp displays a hard edge to his voice which, combined with his vibrato, becomes very wearing after a while.

The most surprising bit of casting is of Shchegolkov as Kecal: why the Bolshoi of all companies should field a baritone rather than a bass is mystifying. I cannot report on whether the low-lying passages give him any problems, because he transposes them up an octave when it suits him. Achieving absolute precision at Kondrashin's relentless tempo seems to preoccupy him at the beginning of 4, but when later the tempo lets up, he is the only one of the principals to establish anything like a character. This recording has a particularly agreeable touch in the March of the Comedians: after several repeats of the *Repete ad libitum* section, the whole thing shambles to a halt in mid-phrase, rather than stopping crisply at the double bar. A pleasant surprise from Kondrashin who, on the whole, spends too much of the recording giving the listener unpleasant surprises!

In between the first two Prague recordings of the complete *Bartered Bride* the Czechs made two substantial batches of excerpts on 78s; of these I have managed to hear most of those conducted by Vašata and Charvát, less of those conducted by Jeremíaš. In the former, the bulk of the conducting falls to Rudolf Vašata, who favours brisk tempi throughout: he directs efficiently and not unmusically, but the playing lacks something in detailed pointing. As the discography at the end of this chapter shows, not only the conducting but several of the singing parts are shared. Miluše Dvořáková is Mařenka in 2 and 3b: she has a rather 'white' voice, true and musical, but she shares with the conductor the tendency to let finer detail pass unheeded. For 18 the singer is Ota Horáková who, unlike Dvořáková, is not ideally steady, but her singing is so much more alive in its use of words that purely vocal shortcomings – and they are not excessive anyway – pale into insignificance. She is, in turn, succeeded in 19 by Marie Budíková, who is splendid; she manages her slightly unwieldy voice brilliantly, so one hardly notices that of all the pieces for Mařenka in the opera this is probably the one least suited to her.

She is partnered by Jindřich Blažíček whose voice is a little under strain at the top of its compass but who displays plenty of humour. However, most of Jeník's plums (3b, 10 and 11) are sung by Jaroslav Gleich. I suggested above that Nature had intended Gleich for a Jeník rather than a Vašek and here the point is proved. In 11 particularly his singing is steady and tender, maintaining a secure line, though his experience in the character part means that he makes the most of his words.

The young Eduard Haken is Kecal in the more important places (4 and 10) and he is free of the unfortunate wobble which afflicted his voice by the time he came to record the role complete under Chalabala. At his best he was, on this showing, in the Kalaš class. Vašata's brisk tempo for 4 pays dividends, vividly conjuring up the picture of the broker bulldozing any doubts Krušina and Ludmila may have about his schemes.

I have heard only one disc of the Jeremíaš set, but it is a crucial one containing 10c and 11 along with the passage of recitative which joins them. Though I would not want to be without either of Žídek's performance as Jeník, it is nevertheless a shame that Beno Blachut never recorded the complete role for certainly in terms of international reputation he was the leading National Theatre singer of the post-war era. On this disc his voice is steadier than those who know his singing only from LP might expect. The recitative passage was well worth including here. The two singers (and the conductor) had obviously played together in the theatre often, so that the drama of the sparring between Kecal and Jeník comes leaping out of the groove. In Blachut's freely voiced performance of 11 all Smetana's marks of expression are scrupulously observed, catching to perfection both the tenderness and the certitude of the aria.

The disc of excerpts conducted by Wilhelm Schüchter significantly is not banded (at least, not in the incarnation in which I heard it). It attempts a medley of the hit tunes from the opera; only one number is given complete and the order of the items differs strikingly from Smetana's order. Erna Berger and Rudolf Schock are an ill-assorted pair of lovers: she is lightweight, steady and easy at the top of the voice, while not telling strongly enough in the lower reaches; he is the precise opposite. Frick's Kecal is coarse, unsubtle and uniformly loud. The aural evidence suggests that there was a lack of discussion on matters of tempo between the conductor and the singers. Schüchter is good at following, but the result is flabby and spineless.

The sleeve of Wilhelm Loibner's excerpts disc has a photograph of about half a dozen characters from the Ljubljana production, also on the Philips label, ironic that the disc itself seems to have been cheaply done, presenting as much music as is possible with only three characters and with no chorus. The orchestral contributions are well played, but with too much care and too little abandon. Hilde Zadek, unwieldy and tremulous, and Hans Hopf, baritonal, stolid and passionless, manage skilfully those feats for which nature did not intend them. After criticizing Kecals, who sacrifice accuracy in trying too hard to be 'characters', it may seem ungrateful to complain that Edelmann does not try hard enough. Maybe he is too busy thinking about the problems that the role's wide *tessitura* cause him to be worried about acting, but whatever the reason, it is a singularly unsmiling performance.

Perhaps I was doing the artists involved an injustice, but I was surprised how enjoyable I found the excerpts on DG, conducted by Fritz Lehmann. (I heard only the two EPs issued in Britain on which Josef Greindl's Kecal goes unrepresented.) The performers obviously regarded 3 as a moment of stillness between the merrymaking and the plotting, and it is given a very dreamy performance, well sustained by Anny Schlemm and Walther Ludwig. In 9 Schlemm displays spirit and humour in abundance and Paul Kuen is an endearingly eager-but-hesitant Vašek. 18 is taken very steadily; Schlemm gives a deeply felt performance, conveying the aria's regretfulness admirably. Her voice is also well suited to 19 and she is superb in anger. Poor Ludwig's Jeník hasn't a hope of presenting his explanation for their misunderstanding. More than in any other performance I got the impression here that Mařenka is angry with Jeník not because she loves him no longer, but precisely because she *does* still love him.

I described Zadek's voice as 'unwieldy'; I am not quite sure what epithet that leaves to describe Melitta Muszely's, but it is certainly far from wieldy and in tone reminiscent of a vinegar milkshake and you will gather that the pleasures of the Hollreiser excerpts are decidely mixed. Schock is a musical Jeník, but is no more vocally suited to the role than he was on the Schüchter medley disc; he is tested to his limits by the top B flats in 3b, and beyond them by the B at the end of 10a; 11 is nicely managed and he gets a good cocky smile into his voice for 19, which, incidentally, is followed by the Polka to end the disc. As Kecal, Böhme either cannot or will not sing quietly and is careless about pitch.

The HMV disc derived from a Sadler's Wells Opera production is sung in the translation by Eric Crozier and Joan Cross which may, in its day, have done good service but to the modern listener offers moments of unintentional hilarity, chief among them the immortal line: 'If there is any hanky-panky from your naughty daughter . . .' The selection of excerpts is unusual; the enterprise was very much a company effort, and the extracts were obviously designed to give as many people as possible a fair hearing. Only one of the arias (18) is included. James Lockhart was the conductor, and there is a lack of incisiveness in the orchestral playing, or rather in its subdued recording. Without a score it would be hard to tell that the introductions to the first two items on the disc start *fortissimo* with lashings of accents. Perhaps the recessed orchestra is the price one has to pay for the admirable clarity of the chorus – a good, strong, sinewy sound. After such Kecals as Böhme and Frick, it is a relief to hear a performance of the role which is understated (if a bit too much so) by the slightly dry-voiced John Holmes. Donald Smith seems on scant evidence to be a splendidly ringing, forthright Jeník, but he is the chief loser from the unusual selection of excerpts. There is intelligence and sensitivity in Ava June's singing of 18, though here and elsewhere she lacks the ability to make the listener feel a lump in the throat. Kevin Miller contributes a Vašek full of gentle humour.

John R. Bennett's book *Smetana on 3000 Records* lists a quite terrifyingly large number of performances of individual excerpts from *The Bartered Bride*. Many of the singers involved, by reason of linguistic and political barriers, have enjoyed little or no reputation in the West, and as a result it has been possible to trace only a small proportion of the discs concerned. One Czech singer whose records were well known in the West was Emmy Destinn; her performance of 2 (Odeon 50026; CO 307), in German, is forthright and rather lacking in subtlety, but she maintains a wonderful legato. Kamila Ungrová's voice was much lighter, but quite expressively used without achieving a true *sotto voce*; unfortunately she was rather too free with rhythm in this aria (HMV 273013; Supraphon DV 6206).

With 3 we come to the first of the few records of this opera to be sung in French. Germaine Féraldy and Marcel Claudel give a very delicate account of the duet, conveying well the tenderness of 3b missing from many a more robust performance (Col. D 15120). In Czech Rudolf Vašata conducts a performance (Supraphon B 22580) so fast that Horáková's and Blažíček's singing is reduced to a meaningless gabble. Ottokar Mařak is loud and sometimes flat in 3a. If he had been making less noise, he might have learned a few things about phrasing from the sweet-toned Ungrová. In 3b Mařák sings more musically, but tends to push the already brisk tempo (G&T 074003; CO 367). Both Margarete Teschemacher and Marcel Wittrisch (DB 4538; LV 63) draw a fine line of sound, marred only by slack intonation from the tenor, particularly in his upper register. The cadential top B flat caused both him and me considerable discomfort. The same is most emphatically *not* true of Richard Tauber's performance with Elisabeth Rethberg (Od. RXX 80749; GEMM 153). This is a wonderful performance (of 3b only), the music caressed with the utmost gentleness. The words go for little, but with this sort of phrasing, seconded by the swaying sixths in the clarinets, we understand Mařenka's and Jeník's feelings well enough. Fears that a belted B flat at the end would shatter the atmosphere, as it does in so many performances, proved groundless: the old magician croons it in head voice. Admittedly it is not the *forte* which Smetana wrote, but it is a practical solution to an impractical piece of writing.

Passing with haste over Jiři Huml's performance of 4 (Od. 51607/8; Supraphon DV 6206), we come to the record of 5 by Pavel Ludikar-Vyskočil (as Kecal) with Marie Budíková and Zdeněk Otava (Ultraphon F 12298). Ludikar was a bass-baritone, not a true bass, and by the time he made this and the other records mentioned below, the voice was unsteady at the top and lacking body in its lower register. It is still possible to hear what a marvellous instrument it had been, and it was still in fairly good shape and expertly managed. Overriding purely vocal considerations is the fact that his performance has such 'face'. In this trio the unctuous salesman, trying to convince Mařenka's parents that Vašek is an ideal son-in-law, is so vivid he is almost visible. In 10b Ludikar assumes the gravity of the philosopher, holding forth on the subject of wedded bliss, and in 10c he becomes the fast-talking hustler, wanting to convince Jeník that he has just the right bride in mind for the young man as an alternative to Mařenka. There is a tendency to bludgeon rather than persuade; Smetana's *leggiero* markings go for nothing. There is a fine contribution from Blažíček here: his lightness of touch and the way in which he makes his grace notes sound like chuckles tell us that he is quite unconvinced (Ultraphon B 12296; GV 87). Blachut, in addition to his recording of this duet with Kalaš mentioned above, also recorded it with Haken (Supraphon LPV 473). Every phrase from the tenor makes its mark, though in this excerpt it is Kecal who makes most of the running. Haken was not in his best voice – he is unsteady in the middle and coarse at the top – but nevertheless it is a lively, convincing performance. On Electrola EH 1036 there is in this duet a younger, fresher-voiced Walther Ludwig than is to be found on the DG excerpts; he sounds full of bouncy self-confidence. Wilhelm Strienz, the Kecal here, not only sings well, but shapes his singing with great subtlety. Unlike Ludikar, Strienz conveys to the listener the fact that Kecal is persuading rather than bludgeoning Jeník. There is much lightness in his singing and much imagination in the colouring of his vowels. Michael Bohnen, partnered by Joseph Schmidt (Telef. F 626; TS 3183), would have seemed better had I not heard him directly after Strienz. He phrases and articulates his words intelligently, though his intonation is not rock solid; and he blots his copy-book by interpolating a vulgar and gratuitous top F sharp. Schmidt seems to rely on his excellent, bright voice to see him through, rather than on any subtlety of interpretation. Charles Kullman and Eugen Fuchs (LX 316; BASF 98 22177–6), in German, sing well but are unilluminating. Fritz Schrödter and Vilém Heš (G&T 44167; LV 501) are faceless and coarse respectively.

Of the recordings of 11 the earliest heard is that by Ottokar Mařak, made in 1909 (072015; CO 367). His is an essentially lyrical performance, with a good line, though not pulling any punches at the end. Having missed out on this aria in the excerpts conducted by Vašata, Blažíček recorded it as a separate issue with the same conductor (Supraphon B 22580). It is good, strong singing, though clearly his feelings for Mařenka elicit more passion than tenderness. Of German accounts, Patzak (Poly. 95268; LV 191) gets real scorn into the recitative: 'Arrrrrmer Narrrrr'. Another roller of 'r's' is Tauber (Odeon JXX 81030; GEMM 153); his is a very fine performance. Much of the aria is written to be sung loudly, but how much more subtle it sounds when phrased like this. Rather naughtily he adds a cadential top G, which at least is not going as far as the Swedish tenor Conny Söderström (7C 153–35356) who adds an A as well. However, Söderström's performance is not just a vehicle for vocal display; he starts with the utmost tenderness and at no point degenerates into mere 'can belto'. Siegfried Jerusalem, a splendid fresh voice (CBS 76829), Anton Dermota, slightly strained at the top (Acanta DE 23120–1), both in German, and James Johnston (Col. DB 2217), in English, give forthright, if rather unsubtle performances.

When it came to 18, the first record off the pile proved one of the most strikingly individual: it is by Hilde Konetzni (LX 1074; RLS 764), Beecham's Mařenka at Covent Garden in 1939. The aria, sung in German, is spread over two 12-inch sides; it is taken very slowly, and she is obviously intent on wringing every last ounce of pathos from the music and allowing the glorious depth of tone of the Vienna Philharmonic strings, under von Karajan, to make its full effect. Konetzni is well able to sustain the long phrases and, though the performance is totally unidiomatic, one has to admire the way in which she achieves what she sets out to do. The only blot is that she approaches the last top A flat from its nether side. Ada Nordenová's record of the aria (HMV AN 319) probably pre-dates her performance in the complete recording under Ostrčil; certainly she is here in fresher, less matronly voice. Věra Manšingerová (HMV AN 318) tends to sing flat and pulls the tempo about mercilessly, Ada Sari (HMV AN 679; Muza L 0388) sounds hurried until she gets to her top A flat which she seems to hold for ever. The Hungarian Erzsébet Házy (Qualiton LPX 11410) breathes noisily as she sings, but otherwise gives a most sensitive performance with her light, young-sounding voice. In Beňačková's first recording of the aria (Supraphon 1 12 2194) she is already something special, and the National Theatre Orchestra play beautifully for Vašata, who seems with advancing years to have got rid of his tendency to rush everything. Drahomira Tikalová (Supraphon LPV 473) is audibly younger in this lovely performance than when she recorded the role complete with Chalabala. Libuše Dománinská (Supraphon 0 12 1810) has more weight of voice than Tikalová – and more wobble too. Hers is a musical performance but not a very special one. There is much to admire in Lucia Popp's performance (Acanta 40.23.326). The impassioned declamation of the opening recitative sets the tone for the whole number;

she plays down the wistful reflectiveness, portraying Mařenka as almost aggressively resentful of her plight. The recording catches too prominently her characteristic quick vibrato, allowing it to obtrude in Smetana's long-breathed lines.

Elisabeth Lindermeier's recording in German with the Berlin Philharmonic under Kempe (Electrola WCLP 548) is deeply felt and superbly played, but it is irredeemably marred by her shaky intonation. Both Joan Cross (RLS 707) and Joan Hammond (SXLP 30205), in English, lack youthfulness, and both have difficulty at the top of their voices. Cross manages her resources better; Hammond becomes squally. Elisabeth Schwarzkopf (SXDW 3049) brings the Lieder singer's art to the aria. There is infinite attention to the articulation of every syllable; but all those little verbal nuances which distract attention from the vocal line, rather than enriching it, are counter-productive. That said, on its own terms it is a brilliantly realized performance with Schwarzkopf in full, radiant voice. I have deliberately left the best till last in this aria – Sena Jurinac (DB 21136; HQM 1024). Though precisely why Jurinac's recording (in German) stands head and shoulders above all others is hard to say. There are the absolute evenness of tone on the *arpeggio* at the end of the recitative, her colouring of the first line of the aria, 'Wie fremd und tod ist alles umher', and the countless other things none of which would explain why this is a performance of sheer perfection. The vocalization is flawless, but beyond that there is a total identification of singer and character which, aided by an unerring musical judgement, leads to an absolutely truthful emotional weight behind every note and every phrase.

In addition, Jurinac also recorded 19 with Peter Anders (HQM 1024) in German. The virtuosity of her ire is awe-inspiring; her *staccato* passages are among the most accurate and are certainly the fastest of any I have heard. Anders is a superb foil: the listener can hear the smile in Jeník's voice which serves only to make Mařenka more furious. The whole effect is irresistible. Destinn and Mařak recorded 19 in 1909 (074005; CO 367). Even in the early days of recording, when standards were less perfectionist than they are today, I am surprised that they did not have another take of this item. Dreadful ensemble throughout culminates in Destinn's omitting a bar and so ending that much ahead of Mařák and the orchestra. Both singers hurl themselves into the duet with tremendous verve and to hell with the notes – a comical way in which to end this survey.

DALIBOR

Both *The Brandenburgers in Bohemia* and *The Bartered Bride* were unperformed when Smetana began work on his third opera, *Dalibor*. (In fact, he was still working on the scoring of *The Bartered Bride* at the time.) The libretto of *Dalibor*, by Josef Wenzig, was originally written in German and was translated into Czech by Ervín Špindler before Smetana set it to music. The work was first performed on 16 May 1868 in the evening of the day which had seen the laying of the foundation stone of the Prague National Theatre building. *Dalibor* never achieved popularity, even in Czechoslovakia, during the composer's lifetime. It was not until 1886, two years after his death, that it was received with much warmth by press and public. Since then it has become one of Smetana's most frequently performed works at home, but it has never gained a firm foothold in the international repertory.

This is reflected in the number of recordings it has enjoyed, far fewer than *The Bartered Bride*: there are just three studio-made sets, all on Supraphon, and a 'private' recording of a performance given in New York.

The first of the Czech recordings was originally issued – at any rate domestically – on eighteen 78s, which may account for a few alarming changes in pitch in the LP issue. But whatever its shortcomings in this and other respects, it is on the whole a magnificent performance. Krombholc's sense of pace and of the relationship between the tempi of succeeding passages is unerring. His grasp on the shape of Act 1 (the only one of the three acts to be cast as a single scene) is particularly impressive, as is the passionate playing of the orchestral part in the duet for Milada and Dalibor at the end of the second act.

Among the singers the weak links are the two sopranos. Petrová is capable of some fine, delicate singing, as in her opening passage in Act 1, but her voice spreads alarmingly above the stave. Maria Podvalová's voice has built-in wobble in all registers. At times the ear can accustom itself to the sound and admire the dramatic declamation; her account of the narrative indicting Dalibor is a case in point, but her death scene is distressing for the wrong reasons. Both ladies come unstuck when duetting with their respective tenor partners. Antonín Votava's Vítek makes it plain why he was first engaged by Talich for such roles as Don Ottavio and Almaviva, so smooth is the tone. The title role demands of the singer both heroism and lyricism. Beno Blachut's voice at the time of recording lay ideally between these two contrasting elements and he had no difficulty in encompassing both. Dalibor is rather a passive hero and can seem dull, but, particularly in the more reflective sections, Blachut's intelligence, his subtlety in inflecting a phrase, a word or a single syllable, make sure that the listener never loses interest. The gaoler Beneš is rather sketchily characterized, but he hardly seems so in Karel Kalaš's richly sung, eloquent performance. As the King, Václav Bednář seizes his more limited opportunities effectively. The chorus of judges sounds tentative and under-nourished.

This is certainly not the case on the second Supraphon recording, again conducted by Krombholc. His view of the work seems to have undergone few changes in the intervening years; but in the 1967 set his strings seem to have more body to their tone and greater assurance, not wholly attributable to advances in recording technique. The women on the stereo discs are a considerable improvement over their predecessors. The Jitka is Hana Svobodová-Janků, a larger, steadier voice than Petrová's, with rather an edge to it enabling her to ride the chorus and orchestra with ease where necessary. Naděžda Kniplová's voice is an instrument of utterly individual timbre, with some rough edges. She can keep it under control when gentleness is what is needed – her death scene is affecting for the *right* reasons – but in the dramatic music, she shows she is absolutely inside the part; every word tells and she is not afraid to make a few ugly sounds in projecting text and music. I find it a thrilling performance along the same lines as the earlier of her recordings of Kostelnička in *Jenůfa*; others will not be able to close their ears to the vocal inelegancies.

In the title role Vilém Přibyl tends to the side of heroism and seems unwilling or unable to bestow any really quiet singing on the more lyrical passages. His performance of the apostrophe to the dead Zdeněk in Act 2 has been praised for avoiding sentimentality; it also avoids all of Smetana's *piano* markings. However, it is a good strong sound and, when that is what is needed, Přibyl rises to the occasion splendidly. Jaroslav Horáček (Beneš) sings well without ever inviting comparison with Kalaš. Jindřich Jindrák's King is powerful in Act 1 but is too unsteady to sustain the Act 3 solo satisfactorily. As a whole the achievement of this recording is more even than that of its predecessor, but it does not equal the best (Blachut and Kalaš) of the earlier set.

Přibyl and Horáček repeat their roles on the 1979 Brno recording. Přibyl's singing betrays a few more vocal rough edges – by this time he was fifty-four – but these are not serious when set against the increased commitment and insight he brings to the part. The years have dealt less kindly with Horáček who here sounds hoarse, effortful and unsteady. The King of Václav Zítek is splendid: it is a fine, solid voice, conveying the right degree of authority without resort to hectoring. As Milada, Eva Děpoltová offers a similar dramatic intensity to Kniplová without so much of her predecessor's reckless abandon of vocalization; her death scene is extremely delicate and affecting. Naďa Šormová's voice is a smaller instrument than Janků's and some may find it relentlessly over-bright, but her timbre contrasts effectively with Děpoltová's and she manages comfortably to hold her own when the two are heard in duet. Under Václav Smetáček the orchestral playing lacks the crisp incisiveness that Krombholc achieves and the unhelpful, muddy acoustic does not improve matters. Also, there is some decidedly insecure ensemble and Smetáček's performance as a whole fails to find the dramatic thrust of the two Krombholc versions.

The Supraphon recordings are absolutely complete, but the fourth 'complete' recording (of a concert performance in Carnegie Hall on 9 January 1977) lacks 207 bars. This was obviously recorded for devotees of Nicolai Gedda, for it sounds as though the microphone was pointing at him and the other singers had to take their chance! I am not sure that this was the kindest direction in which to point it, since if Gedda once had the vocal weight to qualify as one of Nature's Dalibors, by 1977 he had it no longer and there is considerable forcing of the tone in the more strenuous passages. Whether or not Czech is one of the innumerable languages in which Gedda is fluent, he certainly sounds convincing (at any rate, to a non-Czech), much more so than some of his American colleagues. Teresa Kubiak sings Milada's Act 2 solo with great urgency, but elsewhere she often disappears into the murk of the recording, which cannot completely submerge Paul Plishka's telling bass as Beneš, audible down to his bottom E. The only Czech in the cast, Nad'a Šormová (as Jitka), comes over on this occasion uncomfortably shrilly.

As with the complete recordings, the majority of excerpts from *Dalibor* on disc are by Czech singers, singing in Czech.

Emil Burian recorded the King's solos from both Act 1 (Od. 123018) and Act 3 (HMV AN 34). The voice was a light one, but rock steady and suitably majestic. The Act 1 solo is spoiled by too many blunt instruments growling away grotesquely in the bass.

The hero's solos in Act 1 ('Když Zdeněk' and 'Slyšel's to, příteli') are well represented. Jindřich Blažíček (Ultraphon G 12581) and Richard Kubla (HMV AM 797) sing both sections; each singer has a good bright voice and Kubla offers some distinguished phrasing, but they are both let down by poor intonation. Kubla made another record of 'Když Zdeněk (Supraphon DV 6206) where the pitch is much more secure, but the rhythm is slack and he comes adrift from the solo violin in several places.

Ottokar Mařak recorded this excerpt late in his career (Ultraphon B 10717). His tone is threadbare, and the higher passages are very effortful. He is heard in far finer vocal state in his performance of 'Slyšel's to, příteli' (HMV 2–72090; RLS 743), a splendid ringing sound, but like Vilém Přibyl (Supraphon 1 12 2194), he offers no quiet singing. The same is true of Karel Burian in 'Když Zdeněk' (Supraphon 0 12 1579). Hermann Winkelmann (3–42299; RLS 7706) was fifty-six when he came to record 'Slyšel's to, příteli' (in German) in 1905. His breath control was no longer good and there is considerable sense of strain, but the timbre of the voice is still remarkable. However, the record is more interesting as a document of Winkelmann, than for any illumination it sheds on Smetana. For such illumination we should turn to Beno Blachut (Esta M 5169) who understands the meaning of such instructions as *piano* and *dolce e con anima* and sings 'Když Zdeněk' with a superb legato. He trusts the composer's markings and immediately character and situation come to life. These excerpts on Esta find him in even more eloquent voice than in the 1950 complete recording.

The same set of excerpts offers the best performance of the duet for Jitka and Vítek in Act 2, 'Ta duše, ta touha' (M 5172). The singers are Marie Budíková and Bronislav Chorovič and there is real spring in their rhythm and meaning in their words. This is not an easy piece to bring to life out of context: Štěpánka Jélinková and Jindřich Blažíček (Ultraphon G 12852), Ada Nordenová and Miloslav Jeník (HMV AM 2169) and Karla Tichá also with Jeník (HMV AM 2924) all fail to do so.

Emil Pollert recorded the solos for Beneš in Acts 2 and 3 (both Supraphon 0 12 2193). He catches well the *con duolo* marking (Act 2): the voice sounds really careworn. But something a little more robust is needed in Act 3 and he fails to provide it. By this late stage in his career, the low notes were quite inadequate. Vilém Heš recorded the Act 2 solo (3–42628; CO 300). He had a fine, rich voice, but too many of his top notes are flat.

Milada's solo in Act 2, 'Jak je mi?', has fared well on disc. An early Děpoltová version (Supraphon 1 12 2194) is weak in the lower register and lacking the fire of her own later effort and of Alena Míková (Panton 11 0689). Míková has a bright, if not perfectly controlled voice. Wholeheartedly seconded by Krombholc's conducting, she conveys well Milada's excitement of anticipation at the thought of meeting Dalibor. Joan Hammond (SXLP 30205) also gives a most distinguished performance (in English), spoiled only by Susskind's sluggish accompaniment to the recitative section and by the singer's tentative approach to the climactic top B (marked *sff*). Destinn (73309; RLS 7706) approaches the top B and, indeed, the whole piece with fearless attack. Her pungent lower register lends her performance tremendous authority: a thrilling record.

In Dalibor's Act 2 solo, 'Ó, Zdeňku', Karel Burian (Supraphon 0 12 1579) is approximate in both rhythm and pitch. Franz Völker (Poly. 67603; Top Classic TC 9043), singing in German, is accomplished and sensitive and he ends quietly as marked. So, as by now you would expect, does Beno Blachut (Esta M 5169). He really caresses the vocal line with more of that superb legato remarked in his Act 1 excerpt. But when vigour is what's needed, as it is in Dalibor's Act 3 solo, 'Ha, kým to kouzlem', Blachut provides it in plenty (Esta M 5172). He brings the same fearlessness of attack to bear as Destinn did in 'Jak je mi?': two great singers at their most commanding.

THE BARTERED BRIDE

J Jeník; *M* Mařenka; *K* Kecal; *V* Vašek; *Kr* Krušina; *L* Ludmila; *Míc* Mícha; *H* Háta; *R* Ringmaster; *E* Esmeralda; *I* Indian

1933   Tomš *J*; Nordenová *M*; Pollert *K*; Gleich *V*; Konstantin *Kr*; Pixová *L*; Otava *Míc*; Krašová *H*; Hruška *R*; Horáková *E*; Marek *I*/ Prague National Theatre Chorus and Orch./Ostrčil
HMV AN 801–15*
RCA (US) set M 193*

c.1949 (in Russian) Nelepp *J*; Shumilova *M*; Shchegolkov *K*; Orfenov *V*; Skazin *Kr*; Ostrumova *L*; Soloviev *Míc*; Verbitskaya *H*; Yakushenko *R*; Firsova *E*; Korokov *I*/Bolshoi Theatre Chorus and Orch./ Kondrashin
Melodiya ⓜ D 035493–7
Concert Hall (US) ⓜ CHS 1318

1951   (in German) Hauser *J*; Richter *M*; Böhme *K*; Peters *V*; Koffmane *Kr*; Blatter *L*; Lang *Míc*; Hagemann *H*; Streich *E*; Heyer *R*; Lang *I*/Berlin Municipal Opera Chorus and Orch./Lenzer
Vox (US) ⓜ OPX148 (2)

1952   Žídek *J*; Musilová *M*; Kalaš *K*; Kovář *V*; Bednář *Kr*; Štěpánová *L*; Otava *Míc*; Veselá-Kabeláčová *H*; Hruška *R*; Pechová *E*; Mráz *I*/Prague National Theatre Chorus and Orch./Vogel
Rediffusion ⓜ HCNL8009–10
Urania ⓜ B231

1954   (in German) Wolinski *J*;

Trötschel *M*; Rehfuss *K*; Müller
V; Kümmel *Kr*; Bindhart *L*;
Heimpel *Míc*; Schlosshauer *H*;
Ebert *R*; Rosenthal *E*; Altmann
I/Frankfurt Opera Chorus,
Frankfurt Opera House and
Museum Orch./Goehr
Musical Masterpiece Society ⓜ
MMS2109

1956　Brajnik *J*; Bukoveć *M*; Korošeć
K; Lipušček *V*; Yanko *Kr*;
Stritar *L*; Dolničar *Míc*;
Karlovač *H*; Štrukel *R*;
Khočevar *E*; Čerhigoi *I*/
Slovenian National Opera
Chorus and Orch./Gebré
Philips ⓜ ABL 3179–81
CBS (US) ⓜ SC 6020

1961　Žídek J; Tikalová *M*; Haken *K*;
Kovář *V*; Bednář *Kr*; Dobrá *L*;
Horáček *Míc*; Štěpánová *H*;
Vonásek *R*; Pechová *E*; Joran *I*/
Prague National Theatre Chorus
and Orch./Chalabala
Supraphon 50397–8 ④ KSUP
50397–8
Artia (US) ALP 0825

1962　(in German) Wunderlich *J*;
Lorengar *M*; Frick *K*; Mercker
V; Cordes *Kr*; Puttar *L*; Sardi
Míc; Wagner *H*; Krukowski *R*;
Freedman *E*; Stoll *I*/Berlin
RIAS Chamber Choir, Bamberg
SO/Kempe
EMI 1C 153 28922–3
Angel SCL 3642

c.1964　(in German) Apreck *J*; Schlemm
M; Adam *K*; Neukirch *V*; Leib
Kr; Burmeister *L*/Dresden State
Opera Chorus and Orch./Suitner
Eterna 820326–8

1976　(in German) Kollo *J*; Stratas *M*;
Berry *K*; Zednik *V;* Wilsing *Kr*;
Bence *L*; A. Malta *Míc*;
Wewezow *H*; Dönch *R*; Perry *E*;
Nicolai *I*/Bavarian Radio Chorus
and SO/Krombholc
Ariola-Eurodisc XG 89036R ④
SK 57460R

1981　Dvorský *J*; Beňačková *M*;
Novák *K*; Kopp *V*; Jindrák *Kr*;
Veselá *L*; Horáček *Mic*;
Mrázová *H*; Hampel *R*;

Jonášová *E*; Hanuš *I*/Czech
Philharmonic Chorus and Orch./
Košler
Supraphon 1116 3511–3

1940s　(excerpts) Gleich, Blažíček *J*; M.
Dvořáková, Horáková,
Jirásková, Budíková *M*; Haken,
Mandaus *K*; Kovář *V*; Muž *Kr*;
Veselá *L*; Otava *Míc*;
Štěpánová *H*; Hruška R;
Dvořáková *E*/chorus, Prague
National Theatre Orch./Vašata,
Folprecht and Charvát
Ultraphone G 14301–8*

1940s　(excerpts) Blachut *J*; Budíková
M; Kalaš *K*; Šrubař *Kr*;
Štěpánová *L*/Prague National
Opera Chorus and Orch./
Jeremiáš
Esta H 5082–8, 5090, 5093*

1951–2　(excerpts – in German) Ludwig
J; Schlemm *M*; Kuen *V*; Greindl
K/Bavarian Radio Chorus and
Orch./Lehmann
DG ⓜ LPEM 19014

1954–5　(excerpts – in German) Schock
J; Berger *M*; C. Ludwig *L*; Frick
K; Nissen *Kr*; Höffgen *H*;
Schlott *Míc*/Hanover
Landestheater Chorus, North-
West German PO/Schüchter
EMI ⓜ 1C 047 28568M

1955　(excerpts – in German) Hopf *J*;
Zadek *M*; Edelmann *K*/Vienna
SO/Loibner
Philips ⓜ GL 5695
Epic ⓜ LC 3181

1962　(excerpts – in English) D. Smith
J; June *M*; Holmes *K*; K. Miller
V; Drake *Kr*; Robson *L*;
Stannard *Míc*; Rex *H*/Sadler's
Wells Chorus and Orch./
Lockhart
HMV CSD 1473

1963　(excerpts – in German) Schock
J; Muszely *M*; McDaniel *Kr*;
Ahlin *L*; Talvela *Míc*; Hesse *H*;
Böhme *K*/Berlin State Opera
Chorus and Orch./ Hollreiser
World Record Club SOH 103
Ariola/Eurodisc 201 025–250 ④
401 025–251

DALIBOR

D Dalibor; *V* Vítek; *Vl* Vladislav; *B* Budivoj; *Ben* Beneš; *M* Milada; *J* Jitka

1950   Blachut *D*; Votava *V*; Bednář *Vl*; Šrubař *B*; Kalaš *Ben*; Podvalová *M*; Petrová *J*/Prague National Theatre Chorus and Orch./Krombholc
Supraphon Ⓜ SUA 10220–2

1967   Přibyl *D*; Švehla *V*; Jindrák *Vl*; Svorč *B*; Horáček *Ben*; Kniplová *M*; Svobodová-Janků *J*/Prague National Chorus and Orch./Krombholc
Supraphon 112 0241–3
Genesis (US) GS 1040–2

1981   Přibyl *D*; Ježil *V*; Zítek *Vl*; Maršík *B*; Horáček *Ben*; Děpoltová *M*; Šormová *J*/Brno Janáček Opera Chorus, Brno State PO/ Smetáček
Supraphon 1416 2921–3

1944   (excerpts) Blachut *D*; Chorovič *V*; Haken *Ben*; Červinková *M*; Budíková *J*/Prague National Opera Chorus and Orch./Charvát
Esta H 5169–72*

1940s (excerpts) Masák *D*; Blažíček *V*; Muž *Vl*; Munclinger, Višegonov *Ben*; Podvalová *M*/Prague National Opera Chorus and Orch./Vašata and Folprecht
Ultraphon G 14351–6*

The Queen of Spades

JOHN STEANE

'The Queen of Spades stands for secret enmity.' This dark saying taken from what my translator calls *The Latest Book of Dreams* stands at the head of Pushkin's story, and I fancy that its sentiment may have been echoed by many who have had to do with Tchaikovsky's opera. Despite the intensely dramatic character of the story and the individual scenes, it is a notoriously difficult opera to bring off with complete success in the theatre. Nor does it suit all tastes. The Russians took it to their hearts straight away and have cherished it ever since, but in the West it has only very slowly gained a hold. The first Italian performance at La Scala in 1906 with Zenatello in the leading role gave it a good start but that was all. In New York the eminent cast included Slezak, Destinn, Didur and Forsell. Alma Gluck sang in the Interlude; Mahler conducted; the production was lavish. But, 'The subject is dark', said *The New York Times*, and 'the general course of the action makes little appeal'. That was in 1910, and not till the final season of the old Metropolitan in 1965 did the opera reappear. In England, Vladimir Rosing opened his season of French and Russian opera with it in 1915: 'a grave mistake', said *Musical Opinion*. And in France, despite the French title by which it is still widely known, the opera had to wait till 1957, when it was seen not in Paris, but in Strasbourg. The 'dark' subject-matter is no doubt one reason for the lack of popular interest up to comparatively recent times. Another may be a feeling like that expressed by Lord Harewood (*Opera* February 1951) that 'Tchaikovsky never really tackled the basic problems of opera and particularly those of shape and design'. It may be the simple fact that the leading role needs a tenor of exceptional ability as singer and actor to do it full justice. At any rate, for one reason or another, complete success has proved elusive, and the maleficent lady of the cards has probably been a chilling presence in the latest book of many an opera-ridden nightmare.

Her secret enmity extends, it would appear, to the gramophone. There are six complete recordings that come under review here, none of which entirely suffices. They are good enough in part, and individual extracts from the opera have been sufficiently well done *in toto* to induce a wistful sense of what might be, but a wholehearted recommendation would be hard to give.

The two most recently issued in Britain are conducted, respectively, by Boris Khaikin (1967) and Mstislav Rostropovich (1976). Khaikin's is by the Bolshoi Company; Rostropovich's was made in France, with French orchestra and chorus, and an international cast. Not surprisingly, the later recording has clearer detail, greater spaciousness, truer perspective and finer exposure of orchestral texture. In the earlier one the soloists are further forward and the choruses vividly produced; it is all rather more compact, not objectionably so, but the listener is likely to *notice* more in the other. This is due as much to the conducting as to the recording. One feels that Khaikin conducts a business-like performance of an opera he knows inside-out, but that Rostropovich is conducting *from* the inside. Thus in the Prelude he begins very softly and inwardly, shaping and taking time, where Khaikin makes a relatively prosaic statement. When the brass enters with its three-cards motif, Rostropovich gives it a more aggressive edge, a more sinister thrust. And then with the theme of Hermann's yearning, that mounting, ever-expectant sequence of phrases that have so much of Tchaikovsky in them, where Khaikin simply allows the *crescendo* and the interplay of strings and brass to speak for themselves, Rostropovich brings an altogether more personal touch, a greater deliberation. He introduces the theme almost diffidently, with a little *rubato*, and then builds up both strings and brass to a more impassioned, fierce climax. This typifies Rostropovich's handling of the score throughout. Some listeners might find it over-pointed and turn with a sense of renewed comfort to Khaikin's more generalized but still idiomatic account. But I fancy that judging from this Prelude more would prefer the intense individuality of Rostropovich, along with the technically more sophisticated recording.

As the curtain rises, the Bolshoi recording becomes more competitive. The different groups of the chorus achieve stronger differentiation than with Rostropovich, and the boys' brigade, as well as having a more formidable commander, sing with brighter voices and greater gusto. Then if one starts sampling the soloists it becomes clear that Khaikin's cast has positive strengths, Rostropovich's definite weaknesses, and that neither is by any means ideal. The role of Hermann demands so much that almost inevitably something will be lacking, and indeed both of the singers in these sets cope well up to a point. Zurab Andzhaparidzye is said to have made an impression of outstanding dramatic power in the role when he sang it with the Bolshoi Company at La Scala in 1964, and certainly his voice impresses on the records. There is something of a baritonal quality about the middle range, strong and solid around the F and F sharp, and often ringing out excitingly on top. But dramatic quality in any subtle sense is precisely what he fails to impart here. The first solo for example ('Ya imeni' – 'I do not know her name') is all outgoing and loud, with hardly any of the shading that the music requires and the inward-looking romanticism that is part of the character. Later, in Hermann's room, with the vision of the Countess, a tenor Boris Godunov is wanted, and though Andzhaparidzye sings cleanly and with good tone he brings little imaginative intensity to it. Nor in the last scene do we have any sense through a bitterness in the voice that the man's horror has suicidal depth. In this respect, Rostropovich's Hermann, Peter Gougaloff, does better. In that first solo, too, there is some sensitive shading. But his voice is a curious one, often unsympathetic in timbre, sometimes throaty or husky until it comes to the splendidly ringing high notes. Still, it is not Hermann who spoils the Rostropovich set. Vishnevskaya, who sings Lisa, comes perilously near to doing so. The gramophone has never been kind to her voice, but some recordings – notably song recitals – have caught her great distinction as an artist. Opera elicits a squally quality, a beat that (especially in loud passages) makes her singing a doubtful pleasure. She brings her customary imaginativeness to the role, for she is a master-colourist and sings from a full heart. But this Lisa is too much the mature opera-singer; the tone is inappropriately overripe. Tamara Milashkina, with Khaikin, is much more aptly cast. Hers too is a strong, distinctly operatic voice, but under better control. There is a Slavonic glitter in the timbre, with plenty of character if not exactly subtlety. In the two leading parts, then, the balance inclines towards the Khaikin recording.

Where Khaikin gains most, however, is in the stiffening of his cast with particularly fine singing in two of the supporting roles: Irina Arkhipova as Paulina and Yuri Mazurok as Prince Yeletsky. Both have solos which are beautifully done, and in the Prince's aria Mazurok provides a piece of singing to cherish: the precise definition of his voice, the fresh beauty of tone and evenness of line place him in a special tradition of lyric baritones, the kind of voice for which this song (apart from its low-lying start) is ideally suited. Their counterparts in the Rostropovich set are less distinguished: Hanna Schwarz, ample but too matronly-sounding for Paulina, and Bernd Weikl, individual rather than beautiful in tone though impressive in the climax of his song. There remain the important roles of Count Tomsky and the aged Countess Anna, possessor of the secret of the three winning cards. Tomsky is, perhaps, a 'character' part, but he has two solos that want real singing (de Luca and Didur, for example, have sung them). Khaikin's Mikhail Kiselev lacks polish; Rostropovich's Dan Iordăchescu's performance, as recorded, is beyond redemption, wobbling and mouthing, and in his solo in the final scene hardly to be endured. The Countess, on the other hand, strengthens both recordings. With Khaikin it is Valentina Levko, a firm, dark-toned contralto, fine in the big scene in Act 2, as is Regina Resnik with Rostropovich. Resnik's deep, mellow voice murmurs the phrases of the Grétry aria hauntingly, and she has from Rostropovich, throughout this scene, far more sensitive accompaniment than Levko has from Khaikin, who never suggests the hush and mystery.

This, too, is lacking in another Bolshoi recording, dating from 1975 and conducted by Mark Ermler (issued in America but with only limited circulation in the United Kingdom as an import). Here, in the bedchamber scene the orchestral playing is more careful, but still unhushed – with no hints of the germinating darkness, the rustling of old silks and the whispering of still older secrets. Nor is the atmosphere right in other scenes, especially those that should take place out-of-doors but which echo like a great empty opera house. Milashkina again sings Lisa, but now with a voice that has lost its firmness and which, like Vishnevskaya's, is too mature for the Countess's granddaughter: even so, her performance, too, is thoroughly committed and at times moving. The Hermann, Vladimir Atlantov, has the voice but not the finesse. The marking *dolce* means nothing to him; he grades his tone hardly at all and brings little grace to his phrasing. Later, his fervour impresses as does the sheer volume, and he avoids over-dramatizing in scenes which tempt others to excesses. Occasionally a phrase emerges with dramatic power matching the strength of voice: as in the chilled tone of his exclamation that after the Countess's death the secret is buried for ever. But the character of Hermann (that is, the character of his music) has much more refinement and poetry than Atlantov's portrayal of it. As for the others, the Countess and Paulina are fine; Yeletsky gives an admirable account of his song; and the Tomsky is strong in tone and dramatic quality. Ermler brings a fresh touch to the score, the orchestral playing is well disciplined and, apart from some almost statutory Slavonic wobbling among the women, the chorus work is good. It is a pity the two principal singers leave one dissatisfied, for otherwise the recording has much in its favour.

The three earlier complete recordings suffer, more than they might with most operas, from the almost inevitable lack of atmosphere. Philip Hope-Wallace reviewing one of them in *The Gramophone* (June 1956) put it well, as he always did. The music could, he said, have spine-chilling effect: 'But it really does need footlights and the large shadows cast by a guttering candle to point it up.' Modern recordings are produced, in the sense in which a stage performance is produced; and certainly the Rostropovich set is the only one in which the flickering shadows softly come and go. These others, from the early days of LP, have no footlights, no sense of stage perspective. Nevertheless they are not without their attractions – except possibly in the case of the one Hope-Wallace was reviewing.

In this, Kreshimir Baranovich conducts the Belgrade Opera in a recording that reached England in 1956 and was reissued in 1969. Good brass and woodwind are offset by teashop strings. The *crescendi* build up well, the *rubato* allows some personal feeling without sentimentality. That is in the Prelude; later, comparison with Ermler shows up all too readily the lack of attack and of spring in the rhythms. The chorus women wobble here too, and the lads could well do with the Bolshoi malchiks to smarten up their drill. We begin to sample the soloists, without much confidence. The Hermann, Alexander Marinkovich, bright-toned but sometimes nasal, sometimes constricted, never graceful in his first solo, shows himself capable of tenderness in the appeal to Lisa; he acts vividly in the ghost scene and with effectively ruthless energy in the finale. One always listens 'through' the quintet in the first scene to catch the first sound of the Lisa (I still remember the disappointment of finding that Ljuba Welitsch's once glittering voice now shone as no more than a dim glimmering over the ensemble at Covent Garden in 1953). In this Belgrade recording, Valerie Heybalova gives little assurance of good things to come, and indeed there are precious few of them: she feels the music, but lifts up to notes and produces thin, uneven tone. The Countess, Melanie Bugarinovich, is better (though PH-W said her lullaby 'might be Amneris having a snooze in her dressing room in *Aida* Act 3'). The Yeletsky, Dushan Popovich, is worse: his round, ample voice crudely used, and his aria (out of tune at the end) overlaid with pathos and emphasis.

Duller in the technical quality of recording, the early Bolshoi performance under Samosud is only marginally more pleasing as a performance. The Prelude surges and lingers effectively, chorus work is strong and so is the first of the main soloists, the Tomsky. Alexander Baturin impresses as possibly the best singer of this role in the complete recordings. The voice has depth (and the role needs it), the high Fs and F sharps are good too; he also sings with character and a sense of style. The Hermann, Khanaev, varies: at worst he pushes, loses focus and sometimes the intonation slips, yet he does take note of expression marks and makes some striking contrasts. Panteleimon Nortsov as Yeletsky, a clear, high baritone, enjoying his high G if not his low B flat, comes near but doesn't join the front rank of his line. And of the ladies, Lisa (K. G. Djerzhinskaya) is tonally under-nourished and stylistically provincial, while the Paulina sings and acts as she should and there is a formidable Countess. But the labels of the English issue bear the legend 'Only great Art endures' and thus ring their own knell.

By contrast, Alexander Melik-Pashayev's Bolshoi recording of the fifties should survive. One may not think so at the start. The violins swoop around in the big tune, the recording is in a box, the boy commandant is not merely formidable but terrifying, and it would be optimistic to detect promise from the first solo voices. But Hermann does command attention right from the start, and when Prince Yeletsky enters we sit up, for here is a singer. He is Pavel Lisitsian, and one of the best singers of his time. Not, one would assume, a particularly loud voice, it is none the less an unusually beautiful one, and so evenly produced as to fall like a blessing on ears which throughout this survey have not had all that much that can be called beautiful singing come their way. The Prince has some fine phrases in this first scene, perfectly written to suit this kind of high lyric baritone. When we hear him later, in the solo aria, the impression is confirmed and supplemented, for his broad, imaginative phrasing shows him a polished artist just as the wide range of the song exploits his individual timbre and free, even resonance. The Hermann, too, is worth hearing: Georgy Nelepp, a much more flexible, imaginative artist than most. The first solo has something of the poet about it, a well-modulated soft tone as well as a good ringing top A. Later in the act he is not tempted by the declamatory phrases to shout or leave the written notes, and in the scene with Lisa his plea ('Prosti, prelestnoye sozdanye' – 'Forgive me, loveliest of creatures') is most tender and 'inner': in the tradition of the best of the earlier singers who recorded it. Then, in the scenes with Countess, ghost of Countess, and the three cards, Nelepp is convincingly dramatic without overplaying – in short a remarkably good performance in this most demanding role. The women are less interesting but by no means bad: Smolenskaya as Lisa has a bright-toned voice, not always in focus, and she catches the excitement of her first big aria. Paulina and Countess do well, and, in sum, one is left feeling that the generation that grew up learning the opera from this recording could have done a lot worse.

I suppose the 'worse' might have included a two-record abridged version in German on the Urania label. The prime attraction of this is that it has for its Lisa the lovely and under-recorded artist, Elisabeth Grümmer. Nor is the rest of the cast negligible: Rudolf Schock makes a surprisingly effective Hermann and Margarete Klose's deep, velvety tone distinguishes the Countess. Hans Heinz Nissen, Jaro Prohaska and Karl Reimann sing the other male roles – decent performances, though Yeletsky's aria shorn of its top G will not quite do, and Tomsky's solos, for all their hearty humour, gain from having a little more style brought to them. Schock, passionately involved in his part, nevertheless fails to convey the feverish, obsessive side of the character and, throwing himself wholeheartedly into the final solo, comes near to disaster with some of the high notes – reminding us again what a tough singing role it is. Klose's Countess has such presence in her first two appearances that one expects great things of the bedchamber scene. But here, in spite of the sumptuous tone, there is no magic, for not until the very end, as the old woman nods off to sleep in her chair, does it begin to sound as though she is singing to herself; instead of a dreamy nostalgia, we have a woman with a glorious voice enjoying herself exercising it. Grümmer's Lisa shares something of this limitation. As pure singing, her performance gives a pleasure that none of the Russians have provided: at times the beauty of tone calls Tiana Lemnitz to mind, and there are refinements such as a trill at the end of the duet with Paulina (written in the score and, as far as I remember, otherwise observed by none). Yet her style remains curiously square, unimaginative, unauthentic. And no doubt this is partly the fault of the conductor, Artur Rother, who presides over an unreflective, extrovert performance. Or perhaps the trouble really lies with the notion that even a cut version (quintet, Governess, ballroom chorus and Interlude all gone) can be squeezed on to two records: it's an opera that does not like being hurried.

I don't think it particularly likes being sung in German, either. A single side of 'highlights' (coupled with excerpts from *Eugene Onegin*) may excite some interest if only because the Hermann is Fritz Wunderlich. But no, what emerges has all the stamp of the old lady's 'secret enmity' upon it. Wunderlich, whose beautiful voice, free production and feeling for pathos combine to give a fine account of the Act 2 aria, inclines towards a Germanic dramatization that is subtly wrong. It might conceivably be argued that Hermann is, after all, 'Hermann, a Teuton' as they say in the story and that therefore a Germanic touch should be in order, but musically I think it is not so. In any event the point cannot be extended to Prince Yeletsky who in this record is another Hermann – Prey – and whose style is 'Germanized' greatly to the detriment of his aria. At first Prey sings gracefully enough, but soon the guttural consonants, the underlinings, the overt self-pitying tearfulness take over and inflict an alien style on an aria for which Prey certainly has the voice, and which, as we shall see, other of his countrymen have sung well. The soprano in these excerpts, Melitta Muszely, has little tension in her singing, best when quiet and often unsteady otherwise. The Bavarian State Orchestra conducted by Meinard von Zallinger keeps its distance; interest centres on the voices, as in days of old.

And to those days we now must turn, finding sometimes, though by no means reliably, the kind of distinction lacking in much of the singing heard in the complete sets. Lisa's first aria ('Zachem zhe eti slyozy?' – 'Why am I crying?') was generally passed over in favour of the famous 'midnight' solo in Act 4. In this, the 'creator' of the role in 1890, Medea Mei-Figner, sets a standard which in some ways still lies beyond the achievements of her successors. Her voice, recorded with marvellous clarity in 1901 (G&T 23135; Rubini RS 301), has the kind of fresh beauty that, of itself, suits the part to perfection. Her style derives much from the exercise of a well-judged freedom in shading and *rubato*: there are many refinements here. What I cannot regard as a refinement is the low ending over which the singer herself took such pride. The Rubini Mei-Figner album (a magnificent achievement in all respects) ends with the recording of an interview which a Danish critic had with the ninety-year-old singer in her Paris home in 1949. In this she tells how she spoke to Tchaikovsky about his original ending of the aria, staying on the low E: 'Maestro, I think it doesn't work that way, but I could finish it thus, which I think would be better'. 'Thus' meant descending to the key-note, the A below the stave. Tchaikovsky replied that he could not write the low A in 'because it would be very difficult for an ordinary soprano to take that low note', but Mei-Figner had his permission to sing it – which she does, both in the interview and in the St Petersburg recording. The whole thing is really a nonsense. There is nothing very remarkable about the low A: several later sopranos follow suit and offer it without apparent difficulty (Yermolenko Yuzhina, Xenia Belmas, and Tcherkasskaya for instance). And of course it weakens the effect first by sounding common, second by losing the point of the dull, hopeless monotone. One cannot help wishing that the interviewer could have reported a different kind of conversation between singer and composer, one that went like this for instance: 'Maestro, I observe that on the last syllable of the aria you write a short note, a quaver. I would like to be sure I understand the point of this . . .' Or: 'Maestro, at the climax of the aria I see you ask for the high note, the top B, to come in off the beat, on the half-beat in the manner of a syncopation. Will you listen to me and make sure that I achieve the effect you want here.' The 'creator' record shows no signs of Mei-Figner having paid attention to such matters or to the really accurate rendering of the dotted notes with a pair of demi-semi-quavers following. And this is one reason why I remain generally unconvinced by the claims commonly made for the 'authenticity' of such 'creators' records'. Certain kinds of authenticity are to be found here. The voice-type, for instance, is surely ideal in that it has power and glamour and yet remains maidenly and fresh (a vocal score I have been using has somebody else's pencil markings, including a repeated caution in the loud passages 'No Brünnhilde!', and surely this is right). There is authenticity too in the light and shade, the held notes, the *portamento* and so forth. But another type of authenticity should also be present – that which works on the assumption that a composer means what he has written (a tied note going across the beat, or a single quaver for a short final syllable) and that it is the artist's business to understand why he has written so and not otherwise, and to fulfil his intentions.

Mei-Figner's successor was the excellent Natalia Yermolenko-Yuzhina, who has also been the subject of an album in the enterprising Rubini series. She sings the 'midnight' aria sensitively and with ideally firm, shining tone (G&T 2–23313; GV 63). Among the next generation, outstanding are Nina Koshetz and Xenia Belmas. Belmas (Poly. 66883; LV 79) has not quite the 'inner' quality or subtlety of shading to be found in the Mei-Figner, but she does convey the tension of the music as well as its sadness, and her voice has a quite special beauty in the middle register. Accuracy in note-values and an effective *stringendo* contribute to a powerful climax. The Koshetz recording (Brunswick X 8959–2; Club 99.36) is, I think, the loveliest of all. The youthful, limpid sound of the voice with its gentle unobtrusive vibrato combines with a beautifully lingering style to give the music its most appealing expression. The performance is very personal yet properly attentive to the details of the score (and, also very properly, does not attempt to include the Mei-Figner low A). Less interesting Andreeva (Zono 2–62672) has a clear voice but is rhythmically lax and unvaried in expression. On a Vocalion disc (A 01015) a soprano called Rosovsky displays infirm tone and a low A. A. Tikhanova (USSR 7–307), recording in the thirties, gives a sympathetic and accurate performance, showing a good, clear voice. Djerzhinskaya (USSR 16621) from the same period, shallow-toned and somewhat unsteady, has the usual inaccuracies, and the Lithuanian V. Grigaitiene (GMX 301) spoils the effect of her quite beautiful middle voice with some tight upper notes and wobbly low ones.

Radmila Bakočević (STV 213322) shows real feeling for the music, and tone that is sometimes lovely, sometimes tremulous. She takes us into recent times, where there is also a powerful recording by Teresa Kubiak (Muza SX 1144). She made her Metropolitan début in this role in 1972, and is particularly exciting on the high notes of the climax-phrase. Contrasting with most of these, and in some ways more likeable than all except Koshetz, is a version by Netania Davrath (Vanguard VSL 11046). Hers is a light voice but she makes best use of her resources and is unique, as far as I know, in feeling in a positive way the effectiveness of the ending as Tchaikovsky wrote it.

Both of Lisa's principal solos recorded by Vishnevskaya in 1964 are included in a Tchaikovsky recital of 1969 (ASD 2451): a touch of distinction is never far off, but even at that date the uneven emission of tone, so much more noticeable in the complete set, combines with the too mature, imperious voice-character to lessen pleasure. Milashkina's solos, from her earlier recording, are included in a recital on Melodiya D 01385/6, and these are well worth having on their own, for the voice is beautiful, the inflections are subtle, and there is much expressiveness, deep in its yearning melancholy.

There exist several notable recordings in other languages, starting with Emmy Destinn's in German. I have not managed to hear her first version made about the time of the first Berlin performance in 1907 (043134; CO 364). The second was made in America, along with two duets from the opera with the mezzo-soprano Marie Duchesne, in 1915 (2–043019). Its first attraction is the irreplaceable individual timbre of a great singer; the second is its tense, urgent dramatization. There are inaccuracies, for instance, the dotted-quaver-plus-demi-semis is turned, both times, into something nearer a triplet. An impressive memento of her performance even so. A magnificent version is the post-war Decca recording by Ljuba Welitsch (X 523; ECS 812). It is coupled with the Act 2 aria, glorious in the clarity and personal quality of the voice, though relatively unsubtle in expression. The 'midnight' aria is more vividly characterized, has some beautifully softened phrases and reaches a thrilling climax. A version in Italian by Irene Jessner (Vic. 17559) is hardly worth seeking out: an unattractive tone, not quite steady, drily recorded. Joan Hammond's two recordings in English (DB 21451, conducted by Tausky, and SXLP 30205, with Susskind) have much more character, the earlier being the warmer and ampler in voice. I wish that another English recording could be added: perhaps it is an accident of taste or experience, but the voice in which I still hear Lisa's music is that of Marie Collier who sang the role at Covent Garden. She brought a wealth of feeling to it, as well as a voice that at its best was one of the most exciting I have heard.

Hermann's solos have also attracted a large number of singers, most of whom offer the plea in Act 2 ('Prosti'). In early days the standard was set by Alexander Davidov and Dmitri Smirnov. Smirnov's is the more interesting (DA 569). He pleads as from weakness, appeals with gentler but ever-intensifying importunity until the last high note is almost an animal cry for help. It all implies a very well defined concept of the character, confirmed in the Act 4 aria ('Chto nasha zhizn?' – 'What is our life?') on the reverse side of the record: this is a reflective man whose philosophy of *carpe diem* is as sad in its origins as it is twisted in its application. Davidov presents a more straightforward character. In the Act 2 aria he pleads but without an intense sense of need, and in the Act 4 he questions but without brooding. 'What is our life?' is on G&T 3–22550 (GV 90); the other exists in several versions, of which Zono. X3–62014 (matrix 2922) is probably best (there is another Zonophone matrix, 4975, and also a more commonly found HMV recording on EK 45). Davidov, if less subtle and individual than Smirnov, still strikes one as a fine stylist, fastidiously lyrical and admirably clean-cut in his tone. Vladimir Damaev, expressive and spacious in style, often silky-voiced though slightly tight on the highest notes, finishes his recording (4–22248; GV 30), made around 1910, with an adapted ending. Vladimir Rosing (2–022000) shows a strong sense of the rhythmic 'build' of the aria: his voice is less finely focused than the others and his warmth of feeling, though not exaggerated, lacks comparable refinement (the Act 4 aria on 2–022001, which I have not been able to hear, may be more suited to his style). These are four of the best early tenors heard in excerpts. From the inter-war years two are outstanding, one singing in French, the other in Lithuanian. Joseph Rogatchewsky, the Russian-born favourite of the Opéra-Comique and La Monnaie, was essentially a lyric tenor, and he sings the two principal arias (LF 114; LV 239) with lyrical grace and a velvety beauty of tone; but in addition he provides one of the most commanding and moving of recorded performances, presenting a face as well as a voice. Best of all, perhaps, is the Lithuanian, Kipras Petrauskas (Col. LM 2003; Lithuanian Arts Club SLX 329). He also sings the Act 1 solo ('I have not learnt your name'); both are exquisite. There is power as well as beauty in the voice (his finest achievement was reckoned to be his Otello), and the great marvel is the way in which the purest *bel canto* method also forms the basis for such an expressive interpretation. An elegiac, vulnerable kind of intensity, a skilful and sparing use of *portamento*, a delicate feeling for the shading of phrases and a sure grasp of structure: these too are features of what are indeed classic performances.

No post-war recordings I have heard match up to these. Beno Blachut (SUA 10469) recorded the Act 2 aria with the scene following in 1962, too late in his career: there is concentration and intelligence, but the vibrations have begun to loosen, the voice is ageing. Nicolai Gedda included the second and fourth-act arias in a Russian recital (1C 063–28 070), and here the voice itself has sweetness and a healthy ring; the weakness is that the feeling is over-explicit, the neurosis too overt, the musical beauty too subject to emotional disturbance. Gedda might well have been the tenor who in our times could have continued the line from such singers as Smirnov and Petrauskas, but as heard here his methods are crude in comparison with their refinement.

A similar point emerges if one compares recent recordings of Prince Yeletsky's aria with the best of earlier times. Yeletsky's role in the opera offers limited opportunities to the baritone, but by way of compensation he has probably the most rewarding of the solos. Prey's over-emphatic and overt performance has been mentioned in a discussion of the 'highlights' recordings (ALP 2016), but it exemplifies one trend in modern singing. Håkan Hagegård (Caprice CAP 1062) shares it, though to a lesser degree. Sherrill Milnes (SER 5584), singing in Russian, also favours a commanding, impetuous reading rather than an affectionate one: a strong conviction, and a fine sturdy voice, but no suavity, no real beauty in the performance. Contrast these, now, with two recordings made in earlier times by two German baritones, the more recent being Hans Braun on C 3982, the other Schlusnus (Poly. 67050; LV 110) in 1932. Braun sings with an affectionate style and phrases with genuine artistry, better indeed than Schlusnus in that last respect. But Schlusnus is a model in the texture of his tone, the poise and freedom of his voice in the upper-middle range where much of the aria lies, and in his way of conveying passion without resorting to Germanic emphasis. Rather surprisingly, too, he does not sound in this record to be much troubled by the low-lying start – it was not Tchaikovsky's most considerate stroke to start an aria for a high lyric baritone on a low B flat. The first German Yeletsky of all, Leopold Demuth, was not bothered by that – his troubles came later. In his 1903 recording (042036; CO 303) he begins admirably, but the *tessitura* is all wrong for him: the climax on the high G is rewritten and the last phrases are omitted entirely.

Returning now to the Russians, one notes of course that modern times have brought some fine performances of the aria, notably by Mazurok, and before him by Lisitsian, whose unsurpassed recording can also be heard on Melodiya D4316 and in an album M10–35905. Otherwise the best version I know is by the Estonian, Georg Ots (Melodiya D7001). It is sung smilingly, as a love-song, marvellously free in voice and sensitive in phrasing and nuance. Like Petrauskas he is a singer whose relatively few records deserve to be much better known here in the West. Sergei Mikhail (a pupil of Battistini) also does well with the aria, conveying a rather inspired feeling of suppressed excitement in the last pages (recorded around 1937, Melodiya M10–38793). Among earlier versions, Adolf Katkin (EV 15) hectors stiffly and Bohumil Benoni (2–72115), the creator of the role in the first Czech performance, is more interesting in the timbre of his voice than the quality of his interpretation. Kamionsky (2–22756; Rococo 5258) and Karakash (D 014923–4), both with voices of the high, well-pointed type, give performances that are nearly models of their kind, the first being marred by some over-emphasis and the second by some obtrusive breathing.

These singers are part of a clear line of Russian lyric baritones, with Battistini as their nearest Italian counterpart (Yeletsky was one of the roles he sang in Russia) and Schlusnus the nearest German. In this, Yeletsky's part contrasts with the other baritone role, that of Hermann's friend Tomsky. He tells the story of the three cards in a vigorous solo in Act 1 and has another important semi-humorous song with chorus in the gambling scene of Act 4. The latter is the one most commonly recorded as a separate excerpt, sometimes by basses despite its several exposed high Fs. It comes as something of a surprise then to find Giuseppe de Luca including it, both in his early Fonotipia series (39936; CO 391) and in a recital made towards the very end of his life in 1949 (Continental CON 100, also on T304). Beautifully bound phrases, a graceful *rubato* and plenty of zest characterize both. In the latter we know of course that it is the voice of an old man, but it retains the roundness of tone and with it an endearingly benevolent, half-playful smile. Still, how one wishes he had chosen to record the Yeletsky aria instead!

Among the early Russians I have heard, Vladimir Kastorsky (3–22554; GV 2) is particularly strong, with depth to the voice and a vivid personality (born in 1871, he made his last appearance, in this very role, in 1943). The chorus sound like men who enjoy their vodka. Still more raucous appreciation greets P. Z. Andreyev (USSR 16370; OASI 598) at the end of his performance; he deserves the bravos for his fine legato, sympathetic tone and authoritative style. Yuri Modestov (Zono. 2–62492) deserves something else: a ponderous, graceless affair. A little disappointing too I found the record by the mighty Lev Sibiriakov, somewhat lacking in grace and animation and not as rock-solid in tone as usual. But these and other versions all pale before the magnificence of Adam Didur, the great Polish bass who recorded both solos in Italian on Fonotipia. The 'three-cards' ballad (39512) is superb in the quality and resonance of the voice throughout the wide range and in the wedding of a vigorous narrative style with a scrupulously musical use of the voice. The other solo (39811) is again a marvellous piece of singing and both have been well transferred in a selection of Didur's recordings on the Rubini label (GV 45).

There remain now the two mezzo or contralto roles, those of Paulina and the Countess. Paulina's song, which she herself accompanies at the harpsichord, requires a rich voice and a two-octave range, preferably without breaks between registers (they tend to show up in this). Fine versions by Nadezhda Obukhova (USSR M10–39667–8) and Zara Dolukhanova (Chant du Monde LDM 8134) are matched if not surpassed by a particularly lovely recording from 1912 by Rose Olitzka (Col. 38439; Club 99.86). I prefer these to Eugenia Zbruyeva's recording of 1906 (2–23174; GV 20) which conveys little personal feeling fine though it is in tone-quality. A rare early recording by Olga Valovskaya in Czech (1904, Odeon 58661) lacks firmness and evenness. A plummy, rich contralto called Ernestine Färber-Strasser singing in German (Poly. 24025) uses a lot of *portamento* for pathos and has a break between registers. Gladys Swarthout, the American mezzo, sings in English with a sturdy voice in a 1936 recording unissued till the days of LP (VIC. 1490). Anne Ayer (Famous FAM 501) hasn't the voice for it, nor for the Countess's Grétry solo also included in her recital made in 1970.

That solo is one of the most haunting in the opera. The old Countess murmurs a melody that recalls her great days in the French court, and the simple, nostalgic air of Laurette from Grétry's *Richard Coeur de Lion* was an inspired choice (the original air, incidentally, can be heard in a recording by Christiane Eda-Pierre on Philips 9500 609). Apart from Anne Ayer, there is a version in Czech by Věra Krilová (SUA 10469) which shows some feeling for the drama, and the recording made around 1905 by Klavdila Tugarinova, selected for inclusion in Volume 2 of *The Record of Singing* (33533; RLS 743). She takes too many breaths (many of these early Russian singers did), but there are lovely moments – the little catch in the voice at 'malgré moi', the vivid phrases of recitative and the sleepy return to Grétry's melody.

Tugarinova is also heard in duets with Marie Michailova. They sing in exemplary style the Mozartian Pastoral from the Interlude in Act 2 (24377) and the duet for Lisa and Paulina at the harpsichord in Act 1 (24376). The voices are beautiful in themselves, and beautifully matched; but most lovely are the delicate touches of light and shade, the lingering, the lively play of affection and imagination throughout. Michailova has another partner in these duets in a mezzo named Nosilova (Amour 24309, 24505), heavier, less sensitive, though the soprano is fresh and charming as ever. I have not been able to hear a version of the Pastoral by Koralenko and Zbruyeva (Amour 2–24129; OR 403), or of the Act 1 duet by Destinn and Marie Duchesne (Vic. 88520). Their recording of the Pastoral (DK 105) I find something of a disappointment, plodding, lacking in lightness. Cherkasskaya and Panina (EK 45; D 014921/4) are unremarkable, as are not Eugenie Safonova and Finaida Erchova (DX 440) for they are labelled 'Chauvesourris' and have some unbelievable fiddlers to accompany them. Also remarkable but not therefore to be recommended is Miliza Korjus in duets with herself (Venus SK 3083). The record is entitled 'The Viking Nightingale' and *The Queen of Spades* is described as 'one of Tchaikovsky's pearls'. And perhaps while among the curios one should mention highlights from the film *Tchaikovsky* (Philips 6499 130) where Dmitri Tiomkin incorporates some excerpts from the opera, while Laurence Harvey narrates ('He lost himself in composing *The Queen of Spades*. In his despair he saw himself as Hermann and identified the old Countess with his estranged benefactress'). Well, as the chorus murmurs piously at the end of the opera, 'Lord forgive him'.

THE QUEEN OF SPADES

H Hermann; *T* Tomsky; *Y* Yeletsky; *C* Countess; *P* Paulina; *L* Lisa

1940s Khanaev *H*; Baturin *T*; Nortsov *Y*; Zlatogorova *C*; Maksakova *P*; Djerzhinskaya *L* / Bolshoi Theatre Chorus and Orch. / Samosud
Ultraphon ⓜ ULP 141–3

1949 (abridged – in German) Schock *H*; Prohaska *T*; Nissen *Y*; Klose *C*; A. Müller *P*; Grümmer *L* / Berlin Municipal Opera Chorus, Berlin Radio SO / Rother
Classics Club ⓜ X135–6
Urania ⓜ URLP 207

1955 Marinkovich *H*; Gligor *T*; Popovich *Y*; Bugarinovich *C*; B. Cvejic *P*; Heybalova *L* / Yugoslav Army Chorus, Belgrade Radio Children's Chorus, Belgrade National Opera Orch. / Baranovich
Decca GOS 568–70

Richmond SRS 63516

1957 Nelepp *H*; Ivanov *T*; Lisitsian *Y*; Verbitskaya *C*; Borisenko *P*; Smolenskaya *L* / Bolshoi Theatre Chorus and Orch. / Melik-Pashayev
Melodiya ⓜ D05158–63
Artia ⓜ MK207C (3)

1967 Andzhaparidzye *H*; Kiselev *T*; Mazurok *Y*; Levko *C*; Arkhipova *P*; Milashkina *L* / Bolshoi Theatre Chorus and Orch. / Khaikin
HMV SLS5005
Musical Heritage Society MHS 3865–8

1975 Atlantov *H*; Fedoseyev *T*; Valaitis *Y*; Levko *C*; Borisova *P*; Milashkina *L* / Bolshoi Theatre Chorus and Orch. / Ermler
CBS (US) M33828 (3)
Melodiya S10–05801–6

1976 Gougaloff *H*; Iordăchescu *T*;
Weikl *Y*; Resnik *C*; Schwarz *P*;
Vishnevskaya *L* / Tchaikovsky
Chorus, French Radio Women's
Chorus, French National Orch. /
Rostropovich
DG 2740 176

(US) 2711 019
1962 (excerpts – in German)
Wunderlich *H*; Prey *Y*; Muszely *L*
/ Bavarian State Orch. / Von
Zallinger
EMI 1C 063 29011
Seraphim S60023

Hänsel und Gretel

ALAN BLYTH

One encounters perfection of performance too seldom when working on these surveys. Therefore its appearance deserves to be loudly acclaimed. As I listened to Erna Berger's interpretation of Gretel on the Urania set of 1943, I found myself constantly astonished and delighted as passage after passage was given an ideal reading – ideal in tone, accent and phraseology. At once one is struck by the girlish innocence of Berger's voice, then by her sense of rhythm (surely supported by Artur Rother's conducting) as she launches the 'Brüderlein' duet, then by the open naturalness, as crisp as morning, of 'Ein Männlein', that wonderfully imagined start to Act 2. And so it continues. She catches Gretel's sense of amazement as she awakes in the forest, delivers the sometimes embarrassing 'Ti-re-li-re-lis' with keen buoyancy of attack, announces her dream as though it were a single paragraph of music (as it is), then with her gift for enlightening words, is appropriately astounded – 'Bleib still' – when catching sight of the gingerbread house.

Happily Berger's performance has excellent support. Even if nobody else quite approaches her superb achievement, the rest of the cast gives the performance a sense of unity of purpose as though the singers had been working for long as an ensemble – as indeed they may have been. Marie Luise Schilp's tone suggests more an Octavian than a Hansel, but she is convincingly boyish and, like her partner, gives meaning to her enunciation. Elisabeth Waldenau projects the picture of an old-fashioned German 'Mutti' in her equally old-fashioned contralto security. Hans Heinz Nissen, as Peter, is just as solid and steady as his Gertrud. Like everyone else he sings off the text, witness his relishing of 'zum schmausen gibt', as he proudly presents his basket of goodies to his wife, and his rolled 'rs' help him to bring to life his six-eight description of the witches. The veteran Margarete Arndt-Ober, whose gramophone career stretched back to acoustic days, shows no vocal decline: her Witch may be a little too Wagnerian, but she happily avoids caricature and the 'hocus-pocus' is characterized not guyed. She is greatly helped by Rother's forward-moving direction of her music. I don't think that the high spirits of her galop or the Witch's Waltz are captured more successfully elsewhere. Altogether Rother's account of the score has a heady, incandescent quality that is irresistible. That, taken in conjunction with the warmly eloquent playing of the Berlin Radio Symphony Orchestra of the day, give to the Dream Pantomime, and much else (say, the Witch's Ride) an intensity almost its own: Humperdinck is treated with high seriousness and repays the attention. Speeds are fast and that only helps to give the score a dramatic bite that quite dismisses any charge of a soft centre.

Humperdinck is often thought to have derived most of his skill and ideas from folk-song and Wagner. Rother, as a few of the other conductors, help us to realize that he is steeped in an older tradition. Weber and Mendelssohn are just as often present as Wagner in the feeling of fairies, woods and forest hobgoblins that suffuse the piece – and perhaps Marschner in the homespun quality of the domestic scenes. It was Humperdinck's gift to bring them all together in his unique and succinct score, and it is not surprising to find those conductors who understand the German tradition as being the most successful in catching this late flowering of German Romanticism.

After Rother, the most significant among them is Fritz Lehmann who has another orchestra brought up in the right tradition to help him give a reading that is almost as vivid as Rother's and, like his predecessor, he also favoured faster speeds than we have become accustomed to today. Even more than Rother, Lehmann reminds us of the similarities between the Witch's Ride and the Ride of the Valkyries and of how Weber-ish is the forest music. Still another resemblance between the two sets comes in the Gretel of Rita Streich. A pupil of Berger, Streich obviously learnt her beautiful phrasing from her teacher and mirrors Berger in many places. If that is possible, Streich surpasses her mentor in the 'Ein Männlein' solo, mainly because she is allowed both verses (Rother unaccountably cuts the second). Streich proves beyond doubt the benefit of singing Gretel absolutely 'straight' – that is the way to sound truly child-like. By her side, her Hansel, Gisela Litz, is a trifle matronly in tone and too monochrome, but the two voices blend sensitively both in the Evening Prayer and in the duet before the Witch's house, which is also conducted with subtlety and sensitivity. Res Fischer is one of the most telling of Witches. She relishes the role and her words – what joy she puts into 'Das ist nett'. Her tone is that of a fruity Wagnerian but she does not allow it to spread. Maybe the touch of Clytemnestra in her portrayal is not wholly inappropriate. Marianne Schech is an uninteresting Gertrud, Horst Günter an honest Peter, a simple man who lives properly in awe of the dark deeds at Ilsenstein as his six-eight description of the doings there tells us. Elisabeth Lindermeier is a neat Sandman; the Dew Fairy is sung by a breathy boy.

A more recent set, also emanating from Bavaria, is further evidence of the advantages of having a German orchestra playing this music, also the benefit of quickish tempi. This is the one conducted by Kurt Eichhorn. It has other advantages but also several disadvantages. Helen Donath makes one of the freshest, most uninhibited of Gretels: this is a properly ingenuous, artless reading of the role, properly girlish too. It only serves to show up the unsuitability of Anna Moffo as Hansel: her vocal character is definitely that of a woman. On the other hand, one can hardly imagine two other roles being better done. Much more affectionate and fatherly than most Peters, Fischer-Dieskau adorns his role with many perceptive touches, not least the sure imitation of the market-call 'Kauf Besen' and 'the legend of the cannibal witch' (as Lionel Salter so vividly described it in his *Gramophone* review of December 1974) given an appropriate feeling of melodramatic horror.

The Witch, who is almost as difficult to characterize correctly as Hansel, is here done to perfection by Christa Ludwig with marvellous relishing of key words and phrases ('Wie schlau' and 'rudeln' come immediately to mind). There is a full-scale Wagnerian range, with no shirked high notes, in her singing but at the same time a sense of glee and malice achieved without undue exaggeration. All prospective occupiers of the Ilsenstein hideout should listen to Ludwig first, as sopranos should hear Lucia Popp as the Dew Fairy – one cannot imagine a more delightful prospect than being awakened by her fresh, keen tones. By her side, Arleen Augér is a po-voiced Sandman. Charlotte Berthold is too much of an unsteady scold as Gertrud. The more serious drawback to this set is the gimmicky over-reverberant recording, which calls attention to itself in the wrong way. The worst of several effects is the echo-chamber given to the Witch's spell: Ludwig is quite able to suggest its magic without extraneous help.

The classic Karajan set of 1953 wears its years lightly, and must remain a general recommendation for all those wanting to add this work to their collection (how seldom one can say that in discussing sets of a given opera). It has an overall unity of approach, many delights, few if any weaknesses. As a pair, I do not think the two Elisabeths, Schwarzkopf and Grümmer have been surpassed (though Cotrubas and von Stade come close to rivalling them – see below). The sheer loveliness of both sopranos' tone and their steadiness would, in any case, be hard to match; yet the contrast between the two children's voices is quite clear, the girl's sweet and bright, the boy's darker, more grainy. On the other hand they blend to perfection in the 'Abendsegen'. Grümmer's eager, forward, smiling Hansel is beyond praise, another ideal for which to be thankful. Schwarzkopf, always phrasing with subtlety and much thought, does not avoid a suggestion of archness and sophistication, however slight, from which Berger is quite free: a small criticism but one that has to be made. Josef Metternich is very much the rough rural father, admirably secure, not particularly revealing in his phrasing. Maria von Ilosvay, Covent Garden's Fricka, Bayreuth's Waltraute at the time this set was recorded, is a suitably steady and concerned Gertrud. Anny Felbermayer nicely doubles Sandman and Dew Fairy, clearly differentiating between the two and managing Karajan's slow tempo for the former (followed by an equally slow and rapt Evening Prayer) easily. Else Schürhoff, the Witch, lapses too often into overdone speech-song, but there is no doubting the voracious appetite of this joyful ogress, even if a higher voice would have avoided lower alternatives, some written, some not.

The Philharmonia, in its prime, plays with beauty and refinement for Karajan, whose tempi are sure and steady, spacious but not slow. Ravishing sounds, finely paced, are to be heard in the Prelude and Dream pantomime, full-blooded Wagnerian attack in the Witch's Ride (prelude to Act 2). From first to last one is conscious of Walter Legge's careful preparation and guiding hand. About the whole interpretation, there is a sense of stage performance unfolding before our eyes with subtle perspectives (for instance, the distancing of Gretel for 'Bleib still' as though she was backstage looking at the Witch's house) and imaginative, unobtrusive effects, such as the echoing voices (single ones, as Humperdinck asks for).

What a pity Legge's successors have paid so little attention to his disciplines and standards. None of the true stereo sets of more recent times reach his high plane of achievement. Nor, by and large, are the performances so attractive. That dating from the 1960s conducted by André Cluytens, suffers from his slack, anonymous conducting and the too-distant placing of the orchestra. There is not enough differentiation between the voices of the two children. In any case Anneliese Rothenberger's Gretel sounds much as any of her other, many portrayals on record – accurate but uninteresting. Irmgard Seefried's Hansel is, by contrast, full of character, tomboyish in the right way, but recorded just a little too late in the singer's career (compare those two treasurable 78s with Schwarzkopf made in the late forties – see below). Walter Berry makes a thoughtful, sensible Father, but does still better in the Solti set. Elisabeth Höngen, a Witch in the Res Fischer vein, has a high, old time, delivers the text with real bite, but her voice is just too worn for her performance to be wholly admired. Grace Hoffman is also too edgy as the Mother.

The version directed by Otmar Suitner, emanating from East Germany, is a stronger contender, not least because it has the Dresden Staatskapelle (beautifully recorded) in attendance and again we appreciate the *echt* string sound that not even the Philharmonia can quite emulate. It is at once evident in the overture, one of the most atmospheric performances of that richly wrought piece in any recording. Throughout Suitner favours fastish speeds, giving a lighter mien to the score than is customary. The local cast includes a sound, middle-of-the-road not very characterful pair of children in Renate Hoff and Ingeborg Springer, the former much like Margaret Neville in timbre, the latter a lightish mezzo. Gisela Schröter for once a young, un-Wagnerian Gertrud, is not helped by the hurried tempo for her sad tale, Theo Adam makes a model Peter, in a different way from Fischer-Dieskau. His theatrical sense and faultless enunciation allow him to build up a real sense of terror in his description of the gobbling ogress. The big surprise here is the tenor Witch, Dresden's own son Peter Schreier. His is an intelligent, fairly straight performance, with a superb account of the Ride, but nothing he can do prevents him seeming like Mime unaccountably transported from Nibelheim to Ilsenstein (not such an impossible jump if one comes to think about it particularly when this Witch talks about Gretel's 'last sleep').

A similar novelty is attempted in the Heinz Wallberg version of four years later, where a teenage boy and girl portray Hansel and Gretel. The first reaction is how delightful and natural Eugen Hug and Brigitte Lindner sound, but one is not far into the Dance Duet before one realizes that the tone of both young artists is too thin and insubstantial for the task in hand. Of course, the casting has its advantages: Hug-Hansel sounds really frightened when he finds he has lost his way in the forest, and there is genuine feeling of relief when the Witch has been dispatched. Hermann Prey is too swaggering and gluey as Peter, but Ilse Gramatzki makes a properly young Mother for her children. Edda Moser, a soprano Witch, is screechy and indulges in unwanted histrionics, but she undoubtedly brings verve to her task. Wallberg is a plain, pedestrian conductor and the orchestra not more than average.

That brings me to the two 1978 entrants who attempted to challenge the hegemony of the EMI-Karajan set. Solti's appeared first. The overture, fast and hard-driven, sets the tone for the performance, one full of post-Wagnerian touches. Unlike its predecessors it places conductor and orchestra very much (too much) in the forefront, the voices on the stage behind and above the players (the excellent members of the VPO). The producer Christopher Raeburn has added generous effects, a rather too mechanical cuckoo instrument, echo for 'hocus-pocus', a loudly breaking milk-jug, a spectacular oven collapse: all this is in the best(?) Decca tradition.

Lucia Popp is, predictably, a charming, lovable Gretel, only a touch below Berger and Streich in naturalness, a little less rounded in tone than Schwarzkopf. Brigitte Fassbaender, a definitely mezzo Hansel, is a shade hearty in the first scene, but develops her portrayal carefully, showing real high spirits in the awakening scene, but those who know her Octavian may mistake the one character for the other and that cannot be right. Berry is here a nonpareil of a Father: his entrance song is poetic almost, the words subtly coloured and later 'sie werden gefressen' strikes a real note of folk-terror. All in all, he finds the happy medium between the Fischer-Dieskau and the Adam approach. By his side, Julia Hamari's Mother is dull with a plum-in-the-mouth delivery.

Norma Burrowes makes an almost cheeky Sandman, a fresh, unfettered account of this glorious solo, beautifully supported by Solti and the VPO. She, more than any other, manages to make the 'sh's' sound genuine. Edita Gruberova's Dew Fairy is conversely stodgy, too deliberate. Anny Schlemm's Witch is truly malevolent with exaggerated chest-notes, broad *portamenti*, and distorted vowels – the full treatment, you might say, and thus a little wearying.

In the rival, John Pritchard, version the Witch is taken, controversially, by Elisabeth Söderström. Her portrayal is an acquired taste that I have not yet acquired. Her assumed voices sound too contrived; she often seems like a participant in Rossini's cat duet, not like the evil, old ogress and Pritchard's slow tempi only allow her to indulge herself too fully. That is a pity because otherwise this set (backward recording of the orchestra apart) has so much to commend it. Ileana Cotrubas and Frederica von Stade, as I have already said, make a pair of children to rival Schwarzkopf and Grümmer. Cotrubas, apart from a tendency to compensate for a slightly too mature tone by emphasizing girlishness, is a delightful and charming Gretel, full of unforced fun at first, then true vulnerability in the woods. All through, her individual timbre cajoles the ear. Her voice blends ideally with her partner's in the Evening Hymn. Von Stade makes a lovely, full-hearted and full-throated Hansel, not quite attentive enough to her consonants. Siegmund Nimsgern is another youthful-sounding Father but not one with any special insights into his part. Sadly Christa Ludwig sounds out of sorts with herself as the Mother and definitely shrill at times. Kiri Te Kanawa is a creamy-voiced but unimaginative Sandman, Ruth Welting an unsuitably soubrettish Dew Fairy. Pritchard casts a loving eye over the piece, but sometimes dawdles when he should move the music along, here making the utmost contrast with the more impulsive Solti. Karajan and Lehmann seem to strike a more balanced view.

Two versions in English remain to be considered. British readers will surely be familiar on stage or record with the notable Sadler's Wells cast of the 1960s. Margaret Neville, as on stage, makes a wonderfully wide-eyed Gretel, truly girlish, never coy, diction precise. Patricia Kern's tone, rich for Hansel, is used with such smoothness that one forgives her the occasional touch of a principal boy in pantomime, and with Neville she suggests the sense of a stage performance. In 1964 Rita Hunter had to be content with roles such as Gertrud, but some of us already thought of her in Wagnerian guise and her full top B here tells us why. She is also the most musical and steady Mother on disc. Raimund Herincx makes a bluff, articulate Peter. Ann Howard is among the very best of Witches, keeping the amusing and menacing aspects of her part in the right proportion and really *singing* the role – but the producer perpetrates a real horror in the echo-laughter of the Ride. Both Sandman and Dew Fairy are excellent. Mario Bernardi draws full-blooded not always sensuous enough playing from the Sadler's Wells Orchestra of his day, which was all too short (he soon moved back to his native Canada).

The 1947 Max Rudolf set, originally issued on 78s, need not detain anyone long. Nadine Conner is a Neville-like Gretel and therefore to be admired, but her 'Männlein' is prosaic. Risë Stevens makes a mature Hansel, with awkward pronunciation ('Gray-tell'). Claramae Turner, Gertrud, sounds as though she had strayed out of an all-American opera. On the other hand, John Brownlee's entrance as Peter sounds like Vaughan Williams's Vagabond Song: he makes an upright Father, singing with a commendable *legato*, but his very precise diction, transports the six-eight legend into *Ruddigore*-land. Thelma Votipka has a clear top B but is a tame Witch. This is the only version that does not rise to a separate children's choir. (There is a high standard of these choirs in every other version.) This is virtually a replica of performances at the Metropolitan so it is surprising it has little taste of the stage.

Votipka turns up, more suitably cast, as Mother in a Metropolitan Opera Record Club disc of highlights made some time in the fifties and also conducted by Rudolf. A new, a much more American-sounding, translation is used. ('Don't be snooty, Hans'.) Laurel Hurley is very much the outdoor-all-American girl as Gretel, but Mildred Miller, as her reputation might lead you to expect, is a joyful and forthright Hansel. Calvin Marsh sings Peter's song with *brio* and sounds a youngish father. An abridged Act 1 is followed by an even briefer Act 2. In Act 3, most of the Witch's music is preserved, a sensible choice as Regina Resnik ('Rosina sugartooth' indeed!), in mid-career, had just the right voice for the part, relishing the text ('Now eat this then, and shut up') and singing with welcome accuracy, hardly exaggerating at all.

What is inevitably known as the 'Fink and Funk' record of highlights conducted by Miltiades Caridis and made with second-rate Vienna forces has an abridged overture, opening duet, the 'Männlein' solo and duet, then cuts to 'O Gretel' and the Evening Prayer followed by Act 3, scene ii, slightly cut. Rose Fink is a more-than-adequate Gretel, Ursula Schirrmacher a too feminine Hansel. Emmy Funk is a standard soprano Witch, her music unduly rushed by the conductor. A member of the Vienna Boys Choir sings the Sandman nicely. On a single side of Telefunken LGX 66067, we hear an abridged overture, the Dance Duet; Peter's Legend; 'Ein Männlein'; Sandman and Evening Prayer; Dew Fairy; 'Wie duftet's von dorten; Witch's dance; Gingerbread Waltz; and the finale – a fair selection. Sonja Schöner's Gretel is fresh and keen-eyed, Renate Laude's Hansel too mature. Mimi Aarden is to be noted as a full-voiced Sandman. Robert Koffmane (Peter) and Edeltraud-Maria Michels (Dew Fairy) complete the cast. Wolfgang Martin conducts the chorus and orchestra of the Berlin City Opera.

The abridged set from 1929 on four 78 rpm records conforms to the pattern of all the Polydor highlights of the time in being a shortened version edited and arranged by the conductor Hermann Weigert. Tilly de Garmo is a grown-up Gretel, Else Ruziczka an Octavian-like Hansel. Indeed the pair might have been happier in *Rosenkavalier*: the Evening Prayer, though sung with inward feeling, sounds more like an excerpt from that opera. Eduard Kandl is a Berry-like Father and so excellent. The Witch, sung by whom?, is full of the right sort of high spirits. Weigert conducts the first-class Berlin State Opera Orchestra of the day with such warmth and feeling for the innate romanticism of the piece that one wishes the work was being given complete.

The 78 rpm era did not treat the opera very well. There are a few ancient discs of not much consequence, apart from the duetting of Alma Gluck and Louise Homer (DB 576; VIC 1519). Despite the hurried tempi and some intrusive high jinks, the security of the evenly matched voices is welcome in the 'Brüderlein' duet. Homer then sings a lovely Sandman, and to avoid her immediately turning back into Hansel the two singers exchange phrases before the Evening Prayer, where the ethereal purity of the singing is admirable. Homer also made a record of the Witch's waltz (Victor 87131; VIC 1519) which John Steane, in *The Grand Tradition* said showed her as a 'fearsome witch': she certainly has a high old time of it. On the sleeve of the Victor reissue, one of Homer's daughters commented that 'Mother enjoyed the role of the Witch and took delight in thinking up new ways of turning herself into the terrifying creature that she became'. Elisabeth van Endert, either with Käthe Herwig or Birgit Engell as her Hansel, recorded the various duets without any special distinction on early Polydor discs. Emmy Bettendorf and Emma Bassth, and a nice cuckoo, recorded 'Ein Männlein' with a delicate use of *portamento* and offered eager singing in 'Bleib still' (Parlo. E 10092). Then, in the most unusual disc in this survey, Medea Mei-Figner sang 'Ein Männlein' in Russian in 1902 (Pathé 24085 with piano), the voice sounding rich and beautiful though hardly Gretel-like; she repeated the feat in 1930 to her daughter's accompaniment (Rubini RS 501), with hardly any degeneration in the timbre.

Elisabeth Schumann, the Gretel voice par excellence, recorded from 'Wo bin ich?' with a real sense of wonder back in 1920 (Gramm. 65613; LV 186); a touch of fun adds pleasure to the bright, fresh voice. Later, for HMV, she recorded the 'Männlein' solo, the Sandman's Song, and the Evening Prayer (both voices!) with Ernest Lush at the piano (DA 1439).

Conchita Supervia, utterly *hors concours* as Hansel, was joined by Ines Ferraris for the opening scene sung in Italian (Parlo. R 20111; Club 99–74), a disc on which the fun of the interpretations comes leaping out of the groove. Supervia points the text in her own individual, inimitable way and sounds suitably boyish. A very different impression is made by Meta Seinemeyer and Helene Jung in the 'Abendsegen'; in contrast to their Spanish contemporaries these are more staid, well-behaved children with rounder, fuller voices. Like so many German singers, they call to mind Octavian and Sophie, but the actual sound is quite lovely in its warmth and richness. They can also be heard in the 'Knusperwalzer' on the reverse of Parlo. E 10870 (reissued on LV 115) – the elation here is almost palpable. I have already referred to our final pair, Schwarzkopf and Seefried, on a treasurable pair of late 78s (LX 1036–7; RLS 763), the voices ideally matched in the Dance Duet, taken deliberately by Josef Krips. Next we hear Schwarzkopf sing the most secure, ethereal Sandman on record: what a heavenly voice to send one to sleep. Seefried then sings both the phrases before the equally wonderful Evening Prayer, rapt and *innig*. From 1949 we have an extract from a Hamburg performance: the charming Gretel of Lore Hoffmann partnered by the unlikely but amazingly nimble Hansel of Martha Mödl (Melodram 075).

On a record called 'Besenbinderlied', Gerhard Hüsch sings Peter's entrance song (HMV EH 1024; LV 76), then jumps straight on to his description of the witches and their ill deeds. The singing is forthright and clean, as one would expect from this artist, but he does not improve on several interpretations on the complete sets. And I must not overlook that enormously popular disc of the 'Brüderlein' duet (Col. DB 9909; SEG 7705) by Manchester children in the early thirties; it has real élan.

For an ideal cast I would choose Berger or Schumann as Gretel (with a fond glance towards Schwarzkopf in certain places), Grümmer as Hansel, von Ilosvay as Gertrud, Berry as Peter, Ludwig as the Witch, Burrowes as the Sandman, Popp as the Dew Fairy, conductor: Fritz Lehmann or Artur Rother with a German orchestra.

HÄNSEL UND GRETEL

H Hänsel; *G* Gretel; *P* Peter; *Ge* Gertrud; *W* Witch; *S* Sandman; *DF* Dew Fairy

1943 Schilp *H*; Berger *G*; Nissen *P*; Waldenau *Ge*; Arndt-Ober *W*; Erdmann *S*; *DF* / Berlin Mozart Children's Choir, Berlin Radio SO / Rother
Urania ⓜ 5212

1947 (in English) Stevens *H*; Conner *G*; Brownlee *P*; Turner *Ge*; Votipka *W*; *S*; Raymondi *DF* / Metropolitan Opera Chorus and Orch. / Rudolf
CBS (US) ⓜ Y2–32546

1953 Anonymous soloists/Dresden State Opera Chorus and Orch. / Schreiber
Royale ⓜ 1518–9

1953 Grümmer *H*; Schwarzkopf *G*; Metternich *P*; von Ilosvay *Ge*; Schürhoff *W*; Felbermayer *S*; *DF* / Choirs of Leighton High School for Girls and Bancroft's School, Philharmonia / Karajan
EMI ⓒ SLS 5145 ④ TC–SLS 5145
Angel ⓜ 3506BL

1954 Litz *H*; Streich *G*; Günter *P*; Schech *Ge*; R. Fischer *W*; Lindermeier *S*; Brückmann *DF* / Bavarian Radio Women's Chorus, Wittelsbach Gymnasium Boys' Choir, Munich PO/Lehmann
DG ⓜ 2700 008

1964 Seefried *H*; Rothenberger *G*; Berry *P*; Hoffman *Ge*; Höngen *W*; Maikl *S*; *DF* / Vienna Boys' Choir, Vienna PO / Cluytens
EMI 1C 063 00792–3
Angel SBL 3648

1964 (in English) Kern *H*; Neville *G*; Herincx *P*; Hunter *Ge*; Howard *W*; Robinson *S*; Eddy *DF* / London Boys' Singers, Sadler's Wells Orch. / Bernardi
EMI SXDW 3023
Capitol (US) SCB07256

1970 Springer *H*; Hoff *G*; Adam *P*; Schröter *Ge*; Schreier *W*; Krahmer *S*; *DF* / Dresden Cross Choir, Dresden State Orch./Suitner
Telefunken AN6.35074

1971 Moffo *H*; Donath *G*; Fischer-Dieskau *P*; Berthold *Ge*; Ludwig *W*; Augér *S*; Popp *DF* / Tölz Boys' Choir, Bavarian Radio SO/ Eichhorn
RCA ARL2 0637

1974 Hug *H*; Lindner *G*; Prey *P*; Gramatzki *Ge*; Moser *W*; Roleff *S*; Frohn *DF*/Cologne Children's Choir, Cologne Gürzenich Orch./ Wallberg
EMI 1C 197 28972–3Q

1978 Fassbaender *H*; Popp *G*; Berry *P*; Hamari *Ge*; Schlemm *W*; Burrowes *S*; Gruberová *DF*/ Vienna Boys' Choir, Vienna PO/ Solti
Decca D131D2 ④ K131K2
London OSA 12112

1978 Von Stade *H*; Cotrubas *G*; Nimsgern *P*; Ludwig *Ge*; Söderström *W*; Te Kanawa *S*; Welting *DF*/Cologne Opera Children's Choir, Cologne Gürzenich Orch./Pritchard
CBS (UK) 79217 ④ 40–79217
(US) M2–35898

1929 (abridged – arr. Weigert and Maeder) Ruziczka *H*; de Garmo *G*; Kandl *P*; Bassth *Ge*; Wagenar *S*; *DF*/Berlin State Opera Chorus

and Orch./Weigert
Decca CA8000–3

1946 (abridged – in English: adapted
Rose) Saxon *H*; Powell *G*;
Donaldson *S*; *DF*/orch./Dragon
Columbia (US) ⓜ ML2055

1954 (excerpts – in English) Miller *H*;
Hurley *G*; Marsh *P*; Votipka *Ge*;
Resnik *W*; Cundari *DF*/

Metropolitan Opera Chorus and
Orch./Rudolf
RCA (US) ⓜ LM 2437

1961 (excerpts) Schirrmacher *H*; Fink
G; Krause *P*; Sjöstedt *Ge*; Funk
W/Vienna Boys' Choir, Vienna
Volksoper Orch./Caridis
Ariola-Eurodisc 201 024–250 ④
401 024–251

Adriana Lecouvreur

DAVID HAMILTON

For most of its history, *Adriana Lecouvreur* has been an essentially Italian phenomenon. After a brief flurry of international attention – London in 1904 and 1906, New York in 1907 (withdrawn after only two performances, despite the presence of Caruso in the cast) – it soon retreated to its homeland. The recorded literature reflects that localization; although vocal scores containing translations were issued (mine has a German text), I have encountered no recording from *Adriana* in any but the original language, and few indeed that were made outside Italy or by singers independent of the Italian tradition. The opera's somewhat wider vogue during the past twenty-five years reflects, one supposes, the advocacy of sopranos rather than a groundswell of public demand. At minimal vocal risk, the protagonist enjoys gratifying opportunities to play at being a great actress – much easier than really acting, yet equally rewarding, with the supporting cast commenting frequently and admiringly on her dramatic ability.

To non-sopranos, *Adriana* may appear a less satisfactory work. Clumsy to begin with, Arturo Colautti's adaptation of the Scribe/Legouvé play was made even less coherent by Cilèa's subsequent tampering. What we hear today as *Adriana Lecouvreur* is both shorter and more obscure than what was presented on the first night, 6 November 1902, at Milan's Teatro Lirico. For example, in Act 3, just before the party guests arrive, the current vocal score crams rehearsal numbers 7–18 onto a single page – a certain trace of cutting. In what appears to be the first published vocal score, a 1903 edition of 311 pages, we find at this point: first, a scene among the Prince de Bouillon, the Princesse, and the Abbé de Chazeuil, in which it is revealed that the Prince is an amateur chemist and owns a notorious poison, so potent that the merest whiff entails certain death; second, a conversation between Princesse and Abbé, speculating about the identity of Maurizio's beloved. In a subsequent edition (1905, 306 pages), the second of these episodes has vanished – no great loss – while the first remains. However, it too has disappeared in Cilèa's *Fassung letzter Hand*; the Prince's hobby, the nature of the poison, and the Princesse's potential access to such an arcane means of long-distance murder are all withheld from the audience, to obviously confusing effect. (In the Rullman libretto published for the first New York performance in 1907, lines of text are found that are set in none of the scores I have seen – even some additional material for Michonnet's well-known monologue in the first act.)

Nor is Cilèa's score so strong as to sweep away reservations about the faulty stagecraft. His melodic gift, though genuine, is short-winded, and his resources of thematic development are limited indeed. The modulatory freedom of the then-prevalent harmonic style he uses only to local and often arbitrary effect; without any evident theoretical foundation for his use of chromatic harmony, he fails to make anything of its potential for long-range characterization and articulation – in short, he has heard *Tristan* but not really understood it. As a result, he falls back on merciless 'plugging' of his tunes and motives; the two principal melodies (Adriana's 'Io son l'umile ancella' and Maurizio's 'La dolcissima effigie') return again and again, in contexts both obvious and obscure; the ominous three-note motive that stands for the Princesse's jealousy can hardly sustain the unstinting, unvaried exposure to which it is subjected. Even one of Cilèa's more notable technical achievements – the rapid-fire ensemble of the players, the Prince, and the Abbé in Act 1 – is at the same time a dramatic miscalculation, obscuring most of the information the audience needs in order to comprehend the intrigues of Act 2. And the touches of 'exotic' modality are not used with enough security to convey a clear expressive intent: the plagality of 'Poveri fiori' (surely inspired by Manon Lescaut's 'Sola, perduta, abbandonata'), the tentative Lydian beginning of 'No, la mia fronte' end up sounding merely odd, even accidental.

Cilèa's continual tamperings may have made the opera shorter, but probably did not make it better. Traces of that tampering can be detected in *Adriana*'s recorded history. One of the very first discs, from the year of the première, sung by the bass Giulio Rossi (Pathé 84079), bears the mysterious title 'Candida lieve' – which turns out to be the Prince's description of his poison, from the later-omitted episode described above; unfortunately, I haven't located a copy. At some point in the history of his opera, Cilèa added a counterpoint to the melody of his most famous aria, Adriana's 'Io son l'umile ancella'; in all the acoustic recordings that have come my way, its opening bars are accompanied by mere bare chords, but the familiar counter-melody turns up with the first electric and generally prevails thereafter (the exceptions – for example, versions by Hammond, Callas, and Scotto recorded in London – suggest that unrevised orchestral material remained in circulation outside of Italy, never having been replaced during the years of the work's neglect). At the same time, evidently, Cilèa also shifted the metrical position of the first word of the aria's second part, 'Mite', so that it now begins on a downbeat instead of an upbeat!

As the opera treads an uncertain stylistic path between Puccini's emotionalism and Massenet's elegance, so has the performance tradition, as tracked, for example, by recordings of that entrance aria. The first Adriana, Angelica Pandolfini, recorded it in 1904 (G&T 53340; IRCC L 7013, MCK 502), but she seems ill at ease in the studio and her interpretation is neutral; like several other early Adrianas, she declines the option of ascending an octave on 'novo' in the final phrase. Emma Carelli, in 1906 (Fono. 39734; Club 99.100) is more businesslike, giving the aria shape and point if no great glamour; her firmer but whiter voice turns pinched in the upper register. A subsequent Fonotipia version (92045; Rococo 5364), by Maria de Macchi, is stiffly phrased and uncertainly pitched. Yet another Fonotipia is the first to project real personal warmth and tonal magnetism: that of Salomea Krusceniski (Fono. 92088; Rococo 5211); her voice has spin and colour, and she phrases with the authority of a great theatrical personage, despite an awkward moment at the end.

The verismo impulse is represented by Eugenia Burzio's 1908 version (Fono. 92161; dubbed flat on Club 99.87/88), full of chesty emphases; I have not come across her later version (Columbia D 11355). Claudia Muzio's Edison (82247; RLS 743, GV 92, Odyssey Y–32676) is the first recording to include Adriana's recitation (and also four additional bars of orchestral introduction, which later fell to Cilèa's revisionary scissors); her emphases are less crude than Burzio's, but the stylistic background and the fervour are similar. Among a host of other more-or-less 'black-label' versions from the acoustical period, I have heard only the undistinguished ones of Elda Cavalieri (Victor 64059; OASI 639) presumably Victor's 'cover' version for the 1907 Met performance featuring the more glamorous and unrelated Lina Cavalieri) and Giuseppina Baldassare-Tedeschi (reissued on OASI 541, from an unidentified original).

By the 1930s, the verismo approach was prevalent; I have not heard versions by Zamboni (DQ 1076), Caniglia (DB 6356; QALP 10210), or Tassinari (Cetra BB 25325; LPC 50033), but I would expect them to fall into this tradition, as certainly do Adelaide Saraceni (S 10243; OASI 613), Gina Cigna (GQ 7176; LV 137, Rococo 5251), and Augusta Oltrabella (DA 1479; OASI 569), none of whom sings at all well. One arrives with relief at Magda Olivero's slender tones, cleanly weighted words, and straightforward shaping of the aria (Cetra CB 20149; LPC 55015). From 1949, Joan Hammond (HMV C 3901; HQM 1186) sings better than any of her earlier Italian colleagues, but the neat result is unidiomatic and under-committed.

Since Rosa Ponselle reportedly retired from the Metropolitan Opera because Edward Johnson refused to revive *Adriana* for her, a certain melancholy interest attaches to her 1950 home recording with piano: sloppy and self-indulgent, it remains, alas, only a curiosity. Another survivor of the Italian tradition of the thirties is Licia Albanese; I have not heard her first recording (DB 5383), but the second one, from the 1940s (Victor 12–0658), has the urgency of the verismo performances without their vocal excesses; not subtle, this is a performance of real authority. A still later version, published in 1959 (RCA LM 2286), discloses a pronounced beat in the middle of the voice, and the urgency now amounts to stridency.

The happiest result of the postwar shift towards greater refinement is found in a 'private' recording that has circulated in several forms: Renata Tebaldi singing at a 1950 San Francisco concert, with radiantly creamy voice, easily consistent from bottom to top, from softest *fil di voce* to richest climax; the straightforward, sunny manner is both apt and winning. In Tebaldi's studio recording of a decade later (SXL 6030) we can hear a loss of focus and warmth on top, of steadiness in soft singing, and consequently of smoothness and consistency of line – trends still more pronounced in her complete recording. (A curiosity, to be heard at New York's Rodgers and Hammerstein Archives of Recorded Sound, is the unpublished 1913 Edison by Carmen Melis, Tebaldi's teacher; her slightly pinched top notes detract little from an interpretation that shares some of Tebaldi's directness and line.)

Few other postwar versions are as successful as Tebaldi's, though their shortcomings are at the opposite pole from those of the thirties. Maria Callas (ALP 3824) is so inward and restrained as to be uncharacteristically ineffective; Montserrat Caballé, with an exceptionally clumsy orchestra, is lackadaisical and adipose, though creamy of sound (SXL 6690); Leontyne Price (RCA ARL1 2529) is fervent but unidiomatic; Raina Kabaivanska (Cime Ars Nova ANC 25004), recorded at a 1977 concert in Verona, gives us more tremolo than note; the pretty but bland Maria Chiara (SXL 6864) suffers from a dragged and pretentious accompaniment; Inge Borkh (Decca CEP 645) is quavery and hasty; and Renata Scotto's solo version (CBS 76407) is rhythmically wayward by comparison with her vocally less firm performance in the complete recording. The versions by Mary Curtis Verna (Cetra LPC 55005), Felicia Weathers (Decca AG6 41947), and Mirella Freni (ASD 2457) have not come to hand.

Many of these ladies can be heard as well in Adriana's last-act aria, 'Poveri fiori' – a more awkward piece to sing, with its exposed octave leaps to that hard-to-keep-in-tune patch around the upper break. (Where no numbers are given, this aria is coupled with the preceding one.) Carelli (Fono. 39735; Club 99.100) muddles her words and does not project much of anything; Krusceniski (Fono. 92089; dubbed flat on Rococo 5211) is disappointing, due to pitch problems; Burzio (Col. D 9290; Club 99.87/88, another flat dubbing) and Bianca Lenzi (Pathé 10304; Bongiovanni GB–1013) tear into the piece with ample chest tones and frequent sobs, the former achieving a vivid if extravagant effect; Baldassare-Tedeschi (Fono. 69300; OASI 541) sings smoothly but uninterestingly.

Though Muzio's version of 'Io son' is on the emotional side by comparison with many of her early contemporaries, her 'Poveri fiori', recorded at her final sessions in 1935 (Col. LC 20; 3C 053–00932), is restrained for the thirties – an eloquent performance, easier to listen to by far than Saraceni, Cigna, the quavery Rosetta Pampanini (GQ 7212; 3C 065–17052), or, after the war, the undisciplined Ponselle and the edgy Adriana Guerrini (DX 1577; OASI 618, a flat dubbing).

Apart from their vocal deficiencies, many of these singers misjudge the scale of the aria. It is very short, and its musical substance does not accumulate enough weight or tension to justify a climax of the order of 'Un bel dì' or Isolde's 'Liebestod'. Magda Olivero (Cetra CB 20149; LPC 55070) is one who wisely and successfully matches the piece to her resources, relying on a firmly drawn line and forward verbal projection to create tension; though she abandons the words in the climactic phrase, hers is an eloquent performance. Callas achieves a similar effect with more vocal substance (ALP 3824), and Freni is very good indeed (ASD 2457), with the charm and colour that Chiara lacks. Despite beauties of detail, Tebaldi's studio version forces the climax too hard, as does Scotto's. Albanese, though singing in the fifties (Victor DM 1420; LM 111, LM 1839), recalls the thirties with her sobby inflections, driving the upper register hard to keep it firm and in tune. Price is another over-scaler (RCA ARL1 2529), making so much of the first cadence that one feels the piece must already be finished; in this performance, she sounds more effortful than in 'Io son'. Antonietta Stella's DG version (SLPEM 136290) shows a voice in trouble, the thin white tone cautiously manoeuvring around the tricky intervals. I have not heard the recordings by Caniglia, Hammond (ALP 1076), and Marcella Pobbé (LPV 45010).

A similar discrepancy between musical scale and emotional weight can be observed in the performances of Maurizio's second-act arioso, 'L'anima ho stanca'. Here, the model for striking the right balance is one of the earliest recordings, Fernando de Lucia's 1904 G&T, with the composer at the piano (52083; Rubini RS 305, dubbed – correctly, I am sure – a semitone below score pitch). De Lucia observes the *mezza voce* indication at the beginning and builds the piece slowly, as indicated, to the climactic phrase 'ma se amor', still leaving himself enough room to swell on the high A flat. The climax is achieved, and the tension created, by the voice's control and ability to sustain, rather than by simple dynamic impact. From the same year, we can also hear Aristodemo Giorgini (G&T 52174; Rococo 5339), who has the same general conception of the piece but lacks either the technique or the imagination (or both) to bring it off so well. I have not heard some other acoustics (including a second de Lucia on Phonotype, and two by Garbin), or the electrics by Stefan Islandi, Alessandro Granda, or Galliano Masini, but the only modern tenor to aspire to an interpretation along de Lucia's lines is Carlo Bergonzi (SDD 391), an earnest, but rather dry-toned performance.

Without such technical control, a singer might choose to narrow the dynamic range to be covered in these fourteen slim bars. By choice or necessity, most tenors opt for the loud end of the range, turning Maurizio's lament into a proclamation. Aureliano Pertile (Col. GQ 7178; GV 598) cannot move around in the middle register smoothly enough to sustain a line, and his tremolo is fearsomely evident. Mario del Monaco (DA 11349; 3C 147–18226/7) is firmer and louder – much louder – but does not connect his notes. Franco Corelli (ALP 1978), despite one spectacular *diminuendo*, is clearly a belter too, though his tone is sweeter and more flexible than del Monaco's. The most convincing exponent of the larger-scale performance is Placido

Domingo (RCA ARL1 0048), achieving some dynamic variety and intimacy, while Luciano Pavarotti, who could do better, sounds as if he is sight-reading, with noisy, clumsy releases (SXDL 7504).

Maurizio's properly more declamatory first-act aria, 'La dolcissima effigie', attracted few exponents in the acoustic era, but has been more popular since (again, numbers are given only when not coupled with the preceding aria). One of the best is Pertile's HMV version (DA 1185; LV 46), grandly phrased and built to a fervent climax; this is one of the recordings that shows why Pertile was so much admired despite the unpleasant sound he made. (A Columbia version, GQ 7178; GV 598, is less poised musically, rougher vocally.) Pertile cannot sing the high-lying phrase 'Bella tu sei' softly as marked, but then neither does anyone else – least of all Galliano Masini (Parlo. AT 0106; Cetra LPC 50034), who turns this declaration of love into a call to arms. Del Monaco, with his hard, 'fixed' tone, is particularly unlovely in this piece, and Bergonzi seems swamped by it. Both Giacomo Aragall (London OS 26499) and Pavarotti are technically clumsy. I have not heard Giuseppe di Stefano (DG SLPEM 138827) or Domingo (SXL 6451). An intriguing disc offers this aria and the subsequent duet from a 1940 Rome performance with Gigli and Olivero, singing with much *slancio* and conviction (3C 153 54010/17).

Other excerpts have been scantily recorded. Of three recordings of the Act 1 monologue made by Giuseppe de Luca, the original Michonnet, I have heard only the first, made in 1902 with the composer at the piano (G&T 52420; Rococo R 24). I have always found it disappointing, in large part because the musical substance – orchestral reprises of earlier material, requiring sustained tone – simply does not go well on the piano. What is clear, at least, is that de Luca did not treat this as a 'heavy' baritone part, avoiding the exaggerated emotionalism of Mario Sammarco, London's first Michonnet (Fono. 39121; Tap T 326). From much later, we find two restrained and characterful versions by Tito Gobbi: 1955, conducted by de Fabritiis (HLM 7018), and 1964, conducted by Erede (ASD 606/7) – very similar, with the earlier one perhaps more subtle dynamically. Giuseppe Taddei's more overtly emotional performance (Preiser PR 9832) benefits from Tullio Serafin's firm and varied tempi.

The Princesse de Bouillon has one excerptable solo, at the beginning of the second act. Louise Homer recorded this in the wake of the first Metropolitan performance (which she, however, did not sing); the tone is rich, but the words are not vivid and the voice tends to flat (Vic. 85110; Rococo 5268). Far superior is Cloe Elmo's splendidly dramatic version (R 30003; OASI 628), in which the Big Tune ('O vagabonda stella') is uttered with a warmth that Elena Obraztsova's brassier tone cannot match, nor are her words projected as compellingly as Elmo's (ASD 3459); Fiorenza Cossotto's Ricordi disc (AL 3443, Everest 3224) has not come my way. Elmo is at her best, too, in the scene with Adriana from the end of this act, but we listen to this performance with a queer reversal of sympathy, for the Adriana is Gina

Cigna, of quaver-ridden and unlovely voice, and Elmo as the Princesse sounds so much more attractive a person (BB 25029; OASI 628).

Two early recordings of the fourth-act scene between Adriana and Michonnet ('Bambina, non ti crucciar') have eluded me, as has Franco Ghione's disc, with the Scala orchestra, of the Act 2 Intermezzo and the Act 4 Prelude (HMV HN 795), but the latter can hardly have matched the sables-and-diamonds splendour of Karajan's 1967 Berlin Philharmonic in the Intermezzo (DG 139031). The Adriana/Maurizio duets from Acts 2 and 4 have also had little attention since the acoustic days. In a late-sixties version of 'Tu sei la mia vittoria' (SXL 6585), both Tebaldi and Corelli are past their best, while a thirties version of the final duet by Saraceni and Piero Pauli (DB 2012; OASI 613) is clumsy and ineffective. More flavourful, if occasionally hard to listen to, are the 'private' versions of these two passages from a 1940 performance by Gigli and Caniglia. And, to conclude the survey of *Adriana* excerpts back at the beginning, there is, of course, a creator's record of Maurizio's solo 'No, più nobile' from the final duet, sung by Caruso with the composer at the piano (G&T 52419; HLM 7030); the curious ornaments are sung truly, the line is well sustained, but the effectiveness of the whole is compromised after Caruso finishes by the shapeless playing of Cilèa, who finally breaks off in mid-phrase!

Much of what is to be said about the complete recordings is prefigured in the single discs. The earliest sets, from the beginning of the fifties, have little to offer. Alfredo Simonetto leads briskly for Cetra, but his cast of second-rank voices makes a weak case for the work: Carla Gavazzi's vibrato-ridden tone is used monotonously, Giacinto Prandelli's occasional good intentions are compromised by his inability to pitch his high notes reliably, Saturno Meletti is a sympathetic Michonnet in Act 1 but turns lachrymose later, and Truccato Pace (Princesse de Bouillon) is a nonentity. Del Cupolo's version, even less well recorded, also moves along at a good clip, and boasts one performance of real distinction and historical interest: the Adriana of Mafalda Favero, conceived more on the delicate scale of Olivero than in the opulent style of Tebaldi, her successor in the role at the Scala; Favero's tone is still firm and attractive, her delivery of text direct and lively (although she is not comfortable in the spoken recitations), and only in 'Poveri fiori' does she succumb to verismo stresses. Her colleagues are not on the same level, although Elena Nicolai is at least a respectable rival.

Olivero, who resumed her operatic career as Adriana at the request of Cilèa, never recorded the opera commercially, but a 1959 Naples performance led by Mario Rossi has appeared in several 'underground' guises: an uneven affair, with Corelli operating mostly at full tilt (and not always in tune), Ettore Bastianini a free, clumsy Michonnet, and Giulietta Simionato a strong and vivid Princesse. Olivero's performance is *sui generis*, a curious combination of latter-day vocal refinement and the dramatic style of an earlier generation; no doubt it had to be seen as well as heard. (I have not tracked down several other 'private' versions, including several with Caballé and José Carreras.)

As suggested earlier, Tebaldi was no longer at her best by the time Decca produced a complete *Adriana*. Franco Capuana leads a fairly rough-and-ready performance, with strong work from Simionato and Giulio Fioravanti, a good 'character-baritone' view of Michonnet. Del Monaco is past his prime, too; much of his work is a sort of *fortissimo* whine, not always securely pitched; a serviceable version, no doubt – and probably corresponding fairly closely to the kind of performance the opera was getting in Italy around 1960.

That more might be done with the piece, hardly anyone imagined (or, perhaps, cared) but in 1977 came James Levine to show what was possible; one imagines that Toscanini's performances of minor Italian operas around the turn of the century must have had a similar effect. Instead of simply barging through the piece and making the singers comfortable in their mannerisms, Levine takes the trouble to shape and point each episode, clarifying rhythm and phrase structure so that the music makes at least the kind of rudimentary sense that Cilèa could manage, while still leaving the singers ample latitude to make *their* effects, save in the *moto perpetuo* passages that obviously imply metrical regularity. The New Philharmonia produces for him a bright, light, Italianate brass tone, and their execution in the second-act Intermezzo is fully the equal of Karajan's Berlin band, with some welcome *slancio* as well. It may not make Cilèa a great composer to show, say, that he took the trouble to add a busily bouncing violin line to the later part of the first-act ensemble, but it does at least give him his due, and surely makes for more consistently interesting listening, while the brio that Domingo and Levine bring to Maurizio's battle narrative, 'Il russo Mèncikoff', almost distracts our attention from the clumsy declamation that assaults the ears so forcibly in every other performance (and that probably explains why this piece – so obviously intended as an applause-getter – has never been recorded separately).

The cast may not be ideal, but it boasts four genuine first-class voices. Scotto's sound is fraying at the top, but her prima-donna mannerisms are entirely at home in this part: her instincts and her intense involvement are very 'Adrianatic'. Obraztsova as the Princesse gives her a run for her money vocally, if not verbally and emotionally (one does miss Simionato here). Domingo is in splendid voice; one wishes that he had studied that de Lucia recording, but no other modern Maurizio has been so apt or attractive (a limited encomium, I fear; as noted, most of them are barely listenable). And Sherrill Milnes is, most of the time, a luxury as Michonnet, only rarely making too much of a meal, vocally, of relatively trivial material. We are, I think, unlikely ever to hear *Adriana* to better advantage than this – although perhaps the next recording will have a look into the possibility of restoring the passages omitted from the 1903 edition.

ADRIANA LECOUVREUR

AL Adriana Lecouvreur; *M* Maurizio; *Mich* Michonnet; *P* Princesse

1950 Favero *AL*; Filacuridi *M*;
Borgonovo *Mich*; Nicolai *P* / La
Scala Chorus and Orch. / Del
Cupolo
RCA (Italy) ⓜ VLS 32628
Colosseum (US) ⓜ CRLP 1018–20

1951 Gavazzi *AL*; Prandelli *M*; Meletti
Mich; Truccato Pace *P* / Italian
Radio Chorus and Orch., Turin /
Simonetto
Cetra © LPS 3218
Everest © 457 (3)

1959 (live performance – Teatro San
Carlo, Naples) Olivero *AL*;
Corelli *M*; Bastianini *Mich*;
Simionato P / San Carlo Opera
Chorus and Orch. / Rossi
Cetra / Documents ⓜ DOC 19

1961 Tebaldi *AL*; Del Monaco *M*;
Fioravanti *Mich*; Simionato *P* /
Santa Cecilia Academy Chorus
and Orch. / Capuana
Decca SET 221
London OSA 13126

1977 Scotto *AL*; Domingo *M*; Milnes
Mich; Obraztsova *P* / Ambrosian
Opera Chorus, New Philharmonia
/ Levine
CBS (UK) 79310
(US) M3–34588

The Merry Widow

ANDREW LAMB

Act 1

1   Introduction: 'Verehrteste Damen und Herren'
1½ Ballroom music
2   Duet (Valencienne, Camille): 'So kommen Sie'/'Ich bin eine anständ'ge Frau'
3   Entrance song (Hanna) & ensemble: 'Bitte, meine Herren'
3½ Ballroom music
4   Entrance song (Danilo): 'O Vaterland'/'Da geh' ich zu Maxim'
5   Duet (Valencienne, Camille): 'Ja was – ein trautes Zimmerlein' ('Zauber der Häuslichkeit')
6   Finale: 'Damenwahl!'/'O kommet doch, o kommt, Ihr Ballsirenen'

Act 2

7   Introduction, dance and Vilja-song (Hanna, chorus)
8   Duet (Hanna, Danilo): 'Heia, Mädel, aufgeschaut'/'Dummer, dummer Reitersmann'
9   March-septet: 'Wie die Weiber man behandelt'
10 Play-scene and dance duet (Hanna, Danilo)
11 Duet and Romance (Valencienne, Camille): 'Mein Freund, Vernunft'/'Wie eine Rosenknospe'
12 Finale: 'Ha! Ha! Wir fragen'/'Es waren zwei Königskinder'

Act 3

13a Entr'acte (Vilja-song)
13b Maxim's music
13c Dance scene (Cake-walk)
14 Chanson (Valencienne, grisettes): 'Ja, wir sind es, die Grisetten'
14½ Reminiscence (Danilo, grisettes): 'Da geh' ich zu Maxim'
15 Duet (Hanna, Danilo): 'Lippen schweigen'
16 Finale: 'Ja, das Studium der Weiber ist schwer'

Additional numbers

Act 3

Overture (composed 1940)
Dance and chorus (Grisettes): 'Butterflies'
Song (Njegus): 'I was born, by cruel fate'   composed for London, 1907

Attitudes towards Lehár's *Die lustige Witwe* have changed enormously during the LP era. A quarter of a century ago the work was widely dismissed as just a musical comedy, fit mainly for the attentions of amateur theatrical companies. Today, fortunately, a more realistic attitude prevails. *The Merry Widow* is recognized as not just a collection of melodies that appealed in days gone by to the man in the street, but a work of irrepressible individuality and freshness, full of refined vocal and harmonic writing, and superbly orchestrated – worthy material, in fact, for the attentions of the very finest singers, conductors and producers. Here, at least, popular appeal and quality go hand in hand.

The different levels on which the work has been – and still is – appreciated are well exemplified by the recorded heritage. Of 78 rpm recordings only a relatively small proportion were by international opera singers. By contrast, the LP era has produced an increasing number of full-scale German-language recordings of the work with international stars, though at the same time there have continued to be unashamedly 'popular' interpretations. Anyone who judges the significance of a work by the number of 'complete' recordings may well be amazed at just how vast the *Merry Widow* recorded legacy is, for the norm has tended much less to be complete versions with extended stretches of dialogue than single LPs of excerpts which, by omitting dialogue altogether, can offer almost as much music as some of the supposedly complete versions.

Moreover, in operetta far more than in opera, performances in the vernacular have great advantages, and this too is reflected in the number of recordings in a variety of languages. To attempt to seek out and mention all such versions here would have been an endless, thankless task, and to keep this survey within reasonable bounds it seemed appropriate to limit it to recordings in German and English – though that rule has been bent in one or two instances.

The reassessment of this operetta during the 1950s owed much to the first LP recording, the earlier of two produced for EMI by Walter Legge. At once the standards for the LP recording of operetta were set, with singing and orchestral playing of the highest order and just enough dialogue to create atmosphere and ensure continuity. Elisabeth Schwarzkopf is a vivacious widow, individual of voice and producing beautifully poised singing, especially in the rather slow 'Vilja-Lied'. Unfortunately, her Danilo, Erich Kunz, is badly miscast. He is a fine artist who thinks the role through and produces some charming inflections; but the part lies too high for him, so that it turns out a too-mature sounding, literally low-key interpretation. He freely adjusts the vocal line and sings 'Da geh' ich zu Maxim' a major third down, so that, coming at the start of a side, it sounds for all the world as though the record is running slow. The young Gedda makes a captivatingly lyrical Camille, and Emmy Loose is agreeably sweet-toned, if a somewhat apologetic grisette in Act 3. Otto Ackermann's is a leisurely interpretation, full of subtle inflection and drawing beautiful playing from the Philharmonia. Alone of 'complete' recordings it includes the slick overture that Lehár composed in 1940; but otherwise it is in fact far from complete, omitting numbers 5, 10, 13a–c and 14½.

By comparison, the 1958 recording from Decca sounds hard-driven in the hands of the highly experienced but less imaginative Robert Stolz. Hilde Gueden is a characterful widow, if inevitably lacking a little of Schwarzkopf's sheer magic. Loose is again the Valencienne, perhaps a shade less well-poised than for EMI, and Kmentt is a hard-toned Camille. Karl Dönch makes a convincing Baron, and the Danilo certainly is a great improvement on EMI's. Per Grundén perhaps reconciles as well as anyone on disc the requirements of a tenor voice and a raffish character. The recording remains the most complete available, falling short only when, ten bars from the end, Stolz spoils everything with an appalling transition into a reprise of the 'Merry Widow' waltz. He also begins the recording with a brash orchestral potpourri of his own. In terms of production the recording cannot match the achievement of Legge, and there are one or two noticeable tape-joins.

With the benefit of stereo Legge set out in 1962 to match the high standards of 1953 and succeeded magnificently. Schwarzkopf recaptures the spontaneity and gaiety of her earlier assumption and dominates proceedings irresistibly. Waechter sustains EMI's penchant for a baritone Danilo, but he at least has no difficulty with the vocal range. Indeed he is a close rival for Grundén, the major question mark hanging over his tendency towards sing-speak and towards blustering, as in the Maxim's reminiscence in the Act 2 finale. Gedda is now a much more confident Camille, but still able to produce the refinement of tone that enables him to surpass other interpreters of the role. Hanny Steffek is a lovely, creamy-voiced Valencienne, with a touch of Gueden about her, and she makes an absolutely irresistible grisette. Lovro von Matačić does not quite have Ackermann's feel for the Viennese lilt, and the opening of Act 1 especially sounds rushed; but he keeps up the high spirits superbly, and the more vigorous numbers (the march septet and the grisettes' chanson) come off incomparably well. And how well the Philharmonia plays, enhancing the effect of such numbers as the Act 2 dance scene (omitted in the 1953 recording) in which Hanna and Danilo first show their feelings for each other. It is the sheer rightness of such points that gives this set a magic missing elsewhere. The 'Zauber der Häuslichkeit' duet and the cake-walk are, alas, omitted.

That the 1965 Eurodisc recording was less successful than any of its predecessors is due again to the plodding direction of Stolz (then nearing eighty-five), to the longer than usual dialogue, and to Margit Schramm's thin, piercing vibrato in the title role. Listening to her is at times a painful experience. Rudolf Schock, seasoned operetta artist that he is, does well enough by Danilo, though he tends to pull the tempo around. Dorothea Chryst is a somewhat breathless but credible Valencienne and Jerry J. Jennings an agreeably uncomplicated Camille, both giving more life to the characters than is often the case. Benno Kusche gives the first of his unmatched performances as a loveable, fruity-voiced Baron. Though not quite complete, the recording does include all the vocal numbers of the German score.

Perhaps the biggest disappointment among the complete versions is the 1973 set from DG. Karajan sets off at a cracking tempo in the orchestral prelude; but when the voices enter the tempo drops sharply. Thus it goes on, with Karajan taking unusually slow speeds and apparently caring far more for the orchestral sound – which is absolutely superb – than for the operetta spirit. Elizabeth Harwood as Hanna sings beautifully, with a gorgeous vocal sheen; but the effect of her entrance number is spoilt when taken so slowly. René Kollo has the advantage of being a tenor Danilo, but he is a thin-voiced one. If Kunz sounded too elderly, then Kollo is almost school-boyish. Werner Hollweg and Teresa Stratas sing idyllically as Camille and Valencienne, but their pavilion duet is more evocative of Valhalla than the Pontevedrin Embassy in Paris. Still, nowhere else can one hear such things as the rippling accompaniment to 'Ich bin eine anständ'ge Frau' so beautifully brought out or discover points of unexpected lyrical beauty in such numbers as 'Es waren zwei Königskinder'. The 'Zauber der Häuslichkeit' duet is again omitted.

The most recent version appeared from EMI in 1980, just in time for the operetta's seventy-fifth anniversary. The widow is Edda Moser, who sings intelligently and enjoyably; but she lacks the personality and individuality really needed for the role. Hermann Prey perpetuates EMI's incomprehensible preference for a baritone Danilo, and though he copes far better than Kunz he sounds less comfortable than Waechter. He sings with his usual command, and his taste for the girls of Maxim's is evident; but the familiar touch of arrogance in his voice is disturbing. The vocal honours go instead to the second couple, Siegfried Jerusalem and Helen Donath, to whom EMI for once give the full quota of three duets. Outstanding, too, is Benno Kusche, repeating his rich characterization of the ambassador. The choral and orchestral support is excellent and Heinz Wallberg directs with sympathy and fluency. The entr'acte before Act 3 is omitted, and Hanna's party has what sounds like a cimbalom rather than tamburizzas.

Recordings of excerpts in German began with eight 78 sides made by Mizzi Günther and Louis Treumann, the first Hanna and Danilo, in 1906 (Gramm. 2–44073–5, 3–42524/529/785, 43769/70; Rococo 4012). They sing not only their own numbers but also 'Ich bin eine anständ'ge Frau' and 'Zauber der

Häuslichkeit'. The recorded sound is faint; but the impression given is of Günther making an honest attempt at the music with sweet, appealing voice while Treumann acts the fool, interjecting in a silly, high-pitched voice. Can this possibly bear any resemblance to what went on on stage? 'Zauber der Häuslichkeit', incidentally, is sung with the slow section ('Ja, wenn man es so recht betrachtet') as coda rather than as middle section between the two verses. Did Lehár have second thoughts? I wonder.

There are also various souvenirs of another famous production – the Erich Charell revue version produced at the Metropol Theatre, Berlin in 1928. Fritzi Massary was the star, and the score was much rewritten for her. The recorded numbers (HMV EG 1170, EG 1185, EH 249–50; many reissues) include 'Ich bin eine anständ'ge Frau' (with Walter Jahnkuhn), the 'Weiber-Marsch' (as a solo), the 'Grisetten-Lied' adapted as 'Mein Freund aus Singapur', the waltz duet, a charming interpolation 'Ich hol' dir vom Himmel das Blau' (adapted from 'Gigolette' in Lehár's *Libellentanz*) plus Jahnkuhn alone in Danilo's entrance song. Massary was an alluring performer, but one much in the *diseuse* tradition. This Metropol production was obviously an individual one, and it would be interesting to know what Lehár made of it! There have, incidentally, been other recordings of 'Ich hol' dir vom Himmel das Blau', including one by Lotte Lehmann dating from 1928 (Od. 14805) and one of 'Mein Freund aus Singapur' by Trude Hesterberg, a cabaret singer and noted Widow of the 1930s, with piano accompaniment reissued on Telefunken HT–P 502.

The earliest LP of excerpts in German came from Decca, with Zurich forces. There is a curiously 'Heldentenorish' tinge to the whole proceedings and the atmosphere of a provincial German opera house populated with singers forced to devote their declining years to operetta. Nora Jungwirth's 'Vilja' is sweetly done, and Max Lichtegg sings pleasingly enough if sounding simply tired in his entrance song. Wanda von Kobierska gives a somewhat 'approximate' performance as Valencienne, and there is some lusty singing from Willy Schöneweiss as the Baron. There are some unexpected jumps in the score and even an unscheduled repeat in the first few bars.

The Philips disc offers just a few excerpts played in full, without a break, by seasoned Viennese operetta specialists under Heinz Sandauer. The items include a respectable 'Vilja-Lied' from Gerda Scheyrer and 'Ich bin eine anständ'ge Frau' sung utterly without feeling by Hedy Fassler. From Ariola Z 72021 E I have heard only an abridged waltz duet with Wilma Lipp an agreeable Hanna and Grundén as ever a stylish Danilo, but accompanied with exaggerated beat. Other German-language excerpt records I have heard include Saga 5365, with Mimi Coertse as Hanna, Friedl Loor as Valencienne and Karl Terkal singing not just Danilo and Camille but all the solo parts in the march septet! Another is Westminster WST 14145, agreeably done with Rudolf Christ his usual sensuous self as Danilo and Else Liebesberg as Hanna.

Electrola 1C 061–28194, recorded in June 1967, is a full-scale LP version

that proves disappointing. Anneliese Rothenberger produces a winning entrance song, and her 'Nein, ich will nicht!' in the first-act finale is startlingly
convincing; but she lacks the purity of tone for an outstanding 'Vilja'. Perhaps
the main interest lies in Gedda as Danilo; but by this stage of his career his
enunciation had become exaggerated – in the love duet for instance. Erika
Köth is a pale Valencienne, and Robert Ilosfalvy, as Camille, has something
of an edge to his voice – though he produces splendid, ringing top notes.
Willy Mattes directs at times a little brutally (the choral *allegretto* section of
the Act 2 introduction is taken unusually quickly), at other times with supreme sensitivity. The unfortunate aspect of the disc is the cuts made (notably
in the Act 1 introduction and finale) to avoid any contribution from the
ambassador, Cascada or Saint Brioche. At least it far outclasses a contemporary issue from Polydor (249 280), which is a collection of shorter extracts,
often tastelessly reconstructed and recorded with over-reverberant acoustic.
The Valencienne-Camille numbers are stylishly sung by Lucia Popp and
Heinz Hoppe, but Peter Alexander croons his way through Danilo's entrance
song with modernized orchestral accompaniment and Ingeborg Hallstein has
an added wordless chorus for her unremarkable 'Vilja-Lied'.

The very earliest recordings in English were of Eleanor Jones-Hudson
singing 'Vilja' (GC 3710) and (with Ernest Pike) the 'Maxim March' (GC
4431). Lehár himself, visiting London in June 1907, was happy to endorse
them with the message that they 'reproduce the fine musical points of my
own music in the most perfect manner'. From the first London cast, Elizabeth
Firth (Valencienne) and Robert Evett (Camille) recorded their three numbers (2, 5 and 11) on Odeon A–122, A–140 and A–128 respectively. Firth
sings with dignity and clarity, but Evett (later a distinguished theatre manager) is strained by the high notes. The tempi are slow, the interpretations
done with expression and feeling. Here, at least, is the operetta we know –
by contrast with Treumann's antics in Vienna. Anyone who believes the
notion that Lehár's concept was wholly debased in London should certainly
compare the original Vienna and London recordings!

In 1934 Hollywood laid its deadly hands on the score for a film version
with Jeannette Macdonald and Maurice Chevalier. Lyrics were by Lorenz
Hart, and excerpts from the soundtrack have been gathered on a limited
edition LP (La Nadine du Disco 260). 'Vilja' is sung sweetly by Macdonald,
but with exaggerated pauses and curious interjections from a Mario Lanza-
style tenor, while 'Girls, girls, girls' (the march septet) is sung in typical
Chevalier style with military band accompaniment. We are a million miles
from Lehár's operetta here, and to say that the 1952 MGM film version
(excerpts on MGM D 107) was more faithful is to say little. The French
accent of Chevalier is replaced by that of Fernando Lamas, who appropriates
virtually all the main numbers including 'Vilja' and the Pavilion duet. Trudy
Erwin (the singing voice of Lana Turner) appears but briefly, in the waltz
duet.

Meanwhile there had at least been more faithful versions of the operetta on LP in America. I have not heard the version with Risë Stevens, but Brunswick LAT 8003 turns out, after a brash Hollywood-style orchestral prelude, to be a most acceptable recording of Adrian Ross's original English version, sung with undoubted style by Kitty Carlisle as Hanna, Wilbur Evans as Danilo, Felix Knight as Camille and Lisette Verea as Valencienne. Seemingly on a higher plane still are the CBS excerpts, again offering the Ross version. Unfortunately I have heard only an EP of excerpts (numbers 4, 7, 9, 10 and 15), with Robert Rounseville an ardent Danilo and Dorothy Kirsten offering a sweetly phrased, expressive 'Vilja' and Lehman Engel providing authentic accompaniments.

With Capitol LC 6564 one might be forgiven for thinking that one had strayed into something from the Rodgers and Hammerstein canon, an impression created by the orchestrations and general style of singing and heightened by the presence of Gordon MacRae, who delivers 'Girls, girls, girls' as though it were the Soliloquy from *Carousel*. The selection again uses the 1907 Ross version and is of interest for the only recording I have come across of the female chorus 'Butterflies'. This was one of two numbers that Lehár provided for London in 1907 rather than have songs by other composers interpolated into his score. No such redeeming feature is to be found, alas, in another short LP of excerpts (CDN 1006), which is reasonably well sung by Donald Richards (Danilo), Elaine Malbin (Hanna) and, briefly, Nino Ventura (Camille), but which is sunk by the dance-band orchestration, the gratuitous wordless chorus and the regular beat of Al Goodman.

From 1961 comes a single LP side of excerpts (Reader's Digest RDS 9331) with full-scale forces and a new translation by Norman Sachs and Mel Mandel. The selection concentrates on the Hanna, Anna Moffo, who sings a fine 'Vilja'. William Lewis is a really impressive Danilo – rousing, forthright and commanding. On the other hand, the grisettes' song is very American, and Lehman Engel tends to pull the tempo around unnecessarily. The subordinate characters make little contribution. The full note of authenticity perhaps comes through for the first time in an excellent excerpts disc from 1962, in another new translation by Merl Puffer and Deena Cavalieri. Lisa Della Casa seems utterly at home as the widow, a little inclined to exaggeration in her pinched high notes but generally singing quite beautifully. John Reardon is a fluent Danilo, and 'Such a silly soldier boy', with some added pauses, is quite captivatingly done. The supporting singers are all good, and Franz Allers conducts idiomatically.

Equally good in its own way is the 1964 'original cast album' of the Musical Theatre of Lincoln Center production (RCA LSO 1094), which uses a modified version of the Christopher Hassall translation. It opens with Lehár's 1940 overture, most winningly played (as is the whole) – again under Allers. It reveals itself as no ordinary *Widow* with some re-allocation of vocal parts in the opening number and words added to the ballroom music. This is, however, a musical-theatre version in the best sense, and if the singing would not always pass in an opera house there is a rare and compelling vitality about the whole enterprise. Patrice Munsel's sing-speak entrance song does not augur well; but later she sings admirably, and her 'Vilja' (tastefully reconstructed) is one of the most effective on record. Bob Wright is a most personable Danilo. Not a version for purists, perhaps, but a refreshingly different one.

The remaining American LP recording (ASD 3500) is one of the 1978 New York City Opera production with Beverly Sills in the title role. Her broad vibrato may ruin the performance for many; but she brings the widow splendidly to life. The Danilo, Alan Titus, likewise has a vibrancy about his voice that brings a sparkle to the first-act finale as well as to his entrance song. The subsidiary couple, Glenys Fowles and Henry Price, sing in ringing tones, and Julius Rudel provides a genuine Viennese lilt. There is yet another new translation – by Sheldon Harnick – and a good one too, though the rhyming of 'clerk' with 'work' will grate on British ears. The excerpts include Njegus's song, the second of the 1907 additions for London.

Reassessment of Lehár's operetta in Britain had meanwhile been aroused by the Sadler's Wells Opera production of 1958. The new English version of Christopher Hassall cleverly adapted 'Zauber der Häuslichkeit' as a duet for Hanna and Danilo, thus removing its tendency to hold up the action, but otherwise stuck more faithfully to the original than the previous English version. The 1958 cast recording (CSD 1259) still conveys the air of excitement that was aroused by a great theatrical occasion. Howell Glynne is a splendidly rounded ambassador, and Marion Lowe makes a credible character of Valencienne. Hanna, June Bronhill, has the right touch of character and an attractive freshness in the voice. Appealing, too, is Thomas Round, by no means always on the note but displaying the right touch of abandon for Danilo and vocally caressing each of his girls at Maxim's. William Reid conducts, inheriting the theatre interpretation of Alexander Gibson, who was under contract elsewhere. Lehár's marvellous counter-themes come out especially well.

There are three further British excerpt records that use the Hassall lyrics. On World Records ST 60 Jacqueline Delman is a Hanna with commanding presence, pure and lyrical tone and an excellent 'Vilja'; but her Danilo (John Larsen) is thin-voiced, and the supporting singers are likewise not in the top flight. The orchestra sounds underweight, and John Hollingsworth's conducting is tentative and plodding. Much better is a second version with Bronhill – this time a little less secure of voice – in a studio recording under the baton of the experienced Vilém Tausky (HMV NTS 103). Particular interest lies in the Danilo of Jeremy Brett. He is not a singer; but he puts across the songs well and is the ladies' man to perfection. 'Jogging in a one-horse gig' is most fetching. The subsidiary couple are well chosen; they are David Hughes and Ann Howard. The Hassall version crops up again in the Scottish Opera production from Classics for Pleasure (CFP 40276), with an especially generous helping of excerpts. There are some beautiful high notes from Catherine Wilson, and Alexander Gibson caresses the score lovingly; but the whole is too studied and unexciting, without the natural passion and gaiety of the 1958 recording.

Of slightly more recent date is a Decca recording (SET 629), which is basically of the Hassall version (unacknowledged), but with a little Ross (the 1907 number for Njegus, attractively delivered by John Fryatt) and many anonymous alterations. The recording is announced as in 'Richard Bonynge's performing version', which covers some touching up of the orchestration, an overture by Douglas Gamley that owes almost as much to Mantovani as to Lehár, and the third-act can-can adapted to accommodate Regina Resnik as an unlikely but amusing grisette. The centre of attraction, though, is very much Joan Sutherland. Her notes are produced with typical ease and brilliance – but utterly soullessly. For his part, Werner Krenn seems too concerned with mastering the English language to make much of Danilo. The high points in stylishness come from Valerie Masterson and John Brecknock as Valencienne and Camille; but all is lost in Bonynge's unsympathetic conducting – mercilessly destroying the lilt and flow of the music to emphasise the entries of La Sutherland. A sadly misguided affair.

Moving on, we must pass swiftly over various low-budget excerpt records in English on the Embassy, Wing and Marble Arch labels. Likewise, the 'vocal snippets' type of presentation, originally ideally suited to two sides of a 78 and latterly extended to a whole LP side, need not detain us long. Of many 78 versions I would mention just Peter Anders and Anita Gura (Telef. E 1866; TS 3141–2), a selection appealingly sung and played, if over-seriously by Anders, who makes a night at Maxim's sound like a day at work. Moving into the LP era, we find a tasteless twenty-minute medley (Telefunken TS 3482–1/2), with Anneliese Rothenberger and Herbert Ernst Groh treated to a smoochy, strict-tempo accompaniment with harp glissandi, singing strings and wordless chorus in all the most inappropriate places. A much better two-singer medley is by Melitta Muszely and Rudolf Schock (Electrola STE 41161). From Polydor have come two LP selections – a brief one from 1951 with Elfriede Trötschel, Willy Hofmann, Valerie Bak and Walther Ludwig showing that even snippets may be done with style (478 107) and a longer one from the 1960s with Herta Talmar, Franz Fehringer, Rita Bartos and Sándor Kónya (46 555 LPHM). Also meriting attention is London International TW 91099, for it presents Grundén seeming, if anything, even more at home as Danilo in his native Swedish, with Sonja Sternquist as Hanna.

As far as individual excerpts are concerned, the 1940 overture has been recorded several times, including twice by Lehár himself – in 1940 with the VPO (DB 5579; 1C 147–30 639–40 M) and in 1947 with the Zurich Tonhalle Orchestra (Decca K 1708; ECS 2012). Stylistically incongruous as prelude to the operetta, it works well enough as a separate concert item. As far as vocal items are concerned, these must be dealt with selectively. From Act 1, 'Ich bin eine anständ'ge Frau' has been recorded separately once or twice; but the first excerpt that need detain us is Danilo's entrance song. Carl Brisson, Danish ex-boxer and British stage Danilo of the 1920s, sings it in a charmless, poker-faced 1932 recording accompanied by Alfredo Campoli and piano (Decca F 2820; ACL 1200). He moves on to the Act 2 finale for 'There once were two Princes' children', leading (with a contribution from an unnamed Hanna) into the reprise 'I'll go off to 'Maxim's' – a sensible arrangement. A later stage Danilo was Johannes Heesters, a Viennese favourite for many years. The version of his Maxim's song that I have heard is a film performance (Ariola 27 633 XDU) – a spirited and free, cabaret-style interpretation – but he apparently also recorded it with 'Lippen schweigen' for Polydor (47467) and with 'Es waren zwei Königskinder' for EMI (1C 134–32 812/13 M).

A total contrast is Thomas Stewart – gruff, matter-of-fact but entertaining in a recital with piano accompaniment recorded live in Pasadena in 1978. Evelyn Lear goes on to sing an excellent 'Vilja', before the two join in a waltz duet sung with real feeling (Pelican LP 2012). Max Lichtegg (K 1864) is deliberate and serious in Danilo's entrance song but shows more feeling in a verse of 9, as a bonus. I have not heard versions of Danilo's entrance song by Max Hansen (Poly. 21964), Herbert Ernst Groh (Parlo. R 2651), Reinhold Bartel (Telef. 6.22225 AF) and Marco Bakker (1A 125–53 586/87).

Of the 'Vilja-Lied' there are, of course, countless recordings, none of which obviously outclasses versions in the 'complete' recordings. In German there is Marie Dietrich with laboured, heavy delivery (Homochord 1446), Anni Frind sweet and expressive but with an untidy final note (EG 3640), Emmy Bettendorf with mezzo-ish tones (Parlo. E 10974; Rococo 5376), Ljuba Welitsch dramatic but with an appealing touch of tenderness (Decca X 534; BR 3053), Lotte Rysanek slightly rushed (CFP 40091), Irmtraud Kruchten sound enough, if without strong voice or personality (Telef. GMA 55), Anna Moffo, coarse-voiced (Telef. 6.22294) and Rita Streich (Pye TPLS 13064) typically charming. I particularly liked Aulikki Rautawaara, with her careful phrasing and good build-up (Telef. E 2496; HT 28). Dusolina Giannini (DA 4446; OASI 545) sings faithfully and straightforwardly, but on the reverse engages in extra wordless vocalizing in the waltz duet before being joined by Marcel Wittrisch, singing with engaging *mezza voce*. German versions of the 'Vilja-Lied' that I have not heard include Elfie Mayerhofer (Decca K 28103), Anneliese Rothenberger (1C 061–28802) and Cristina Deutekom (1A 125–53 586/87).

From many versions in English I would mention the Australian musical comedy doyenne Gladys Moncrieff (HMV NTS 208), Gwen Catley late in her career (Pye CEC 32013), Anna Moffo tending to croon in the lower reaches (RCA LSC 2794), Bronhill with spreading notes at a sentimental public performance in 1975 (M7 MLF 118), and Moira Anderson in an excellent operetta recital with the Royal Opera House Orchestra (St Michael MS 101). Jeannette Macdonald couples it with the waltz song (B 8247) as do Florence George (Brunswick 04106) and Eleanor Steber (Victor 11–9218; ARL1 0436) in what is perhaps the best English-language 'Vilja' I have come across – a dramatic, confident performance, but with lightness of touch and expression. Men tackling it (and why not?) are Derek Oldham, somewhat constricted of tone (B 4291), and John Hendrik sounding remarkably like Tauber (Parlo. R 2020) – both coupling it with the waltz song. Tauber himself sings 'Vilja' in English (Parlo. RO 20188; several reissues). Breaking the language rule, mention must be made of Renata Tebaldi's Latin-sounding 'Vilja' in Italian for Decca's *Fledermaus* 'Gala Performance' (SET 203), and also worthy of special treatment are full and sensitive performances of 'Vilja' and the waltz duet in French by Andréa Guiot and Jean-Christophe Benoit (Pathé-Trianon CTRY 7135). Sylvia Sass has recorded 'Vilja' in Hungarian (Hungaroton SLPX 16607).

Continuing through Act 2, the 'Lied vom dummen Reiter' is coupled with the waltz duet (Poly. 90042) in a 1928 record by Else Kochhann and Helge Rosvaenge – the former pleasantly relaxed, the latter forced and exaggerated. The Pavilion duet has been recorded several times, or at any rate the tenor solo 'Wie eine Rosenknospe'. I have not heard F. E. Engels (Poly. 10999), Max Hansen (Poly. 21965) or Peter Anders and Aulikki Rautawaara (Telef. E 3706; HT 9), but Rosvaenge does it with suavity of expression and intensity of feeling (Decca K 2235; LM 4520) and Charles Kullmann with attractive lyricism in Ross's English version (Col. DB 1597; SED 5528). Two sound LP versions are by Sonja Knittel and Heinz Hoppe, who also do the waltz duet (Telef. 6.22225 AF), and Murray Dickie and Emmy Loose (CFP 40091).

Recordings of the third-act waltz duet not already mentioned include Julia Moor and Marcel Wittrisch (Decca K 2234), Anna Moffo and Rudolf Schock (Eurodisc 85 109 TE), Adele Leigh and Nigel Douglas (an *echt*-Viennese version by two British singers who made good in Vienna – Philips SGL 5842), Marjon Lambriks and Alois Aichhorn (Telef. 6.22606 AF) and, perhaps best of all, by Renate Holm and Werner Krenn (SPA 595–6) – an enchanting version including the introductory spoken exchanges. Complementing the duet versions are adaptations for solo voice, the oldest going back to 30 January 1908 when Marcella Sembrich recorded it in Italian with easy coloratura and sweetly held notes but much adornment and heavy accompaniment (Victor 88107; Rococo R 23). Other versions backing the 'Vilja-Lied' have already been mentioned.

These solo versions of the waltz duet should not be confused, though, with sung versions of the 'Merry Widow ' waltz, which consists of 'Lippen schweigen' leading into 'O kommet doch, o kommt ihr, Ballsirenen' from the first-act finale and sometimes other themes. Examples are by Richard Tauber (Parlo. RO 20175), Richard Crooks (DB 2336; CDN 1019), Eleanor Steber (Victor 11–9218; ARL1 0436) and Helen Traubel (RCA VIC 1228). That, of course, is just the thin edge of the wedge of arrangements of music from *The Merry Widow* for all manner of ensembles that testifies to the remarkably widespread popularity of this classic among twentieth-century operettas.

DIE LUSTIGE WITWE

This listing includes only recordings sung in German and English

Z Zeta; V Valencienne; D Danilo; H Hanna; C Camille; Cas Cascada; B St
Brioche

1953 Niessner Z; Loose V; Kunz D;
Schwarzkopf H; Gedda C; O.
Kraus Cas; Schmidinger B /
chorus, Philharmonia /
Ackermann
HMV © SXDW 3045 ④ TC–
SXDW 3045
Angel ⓜ 3501BL

1958 Dönch Z; Loose V; Grundén D;
Gueden H; Kmentt C; Klein Cas;
Equiluz B / Vienna State Opera
Chorus and Orch. / Stolz
Decca DPA 573–4
Richmond SRS 62518

1962 Knapp Z; Steffek V; Waechter D;
Schwarzkopf H; Gedda C; Equiluz
Cas; Strohbauer B / Philharmonia
Chorus and Orch. / Matačić
HMV SLS 823
Angel SBL 3630

1965 Kusche Z; D. Chryst V; Schock
D; Schramm H; Jennings C; C.
Nicolai Cas; Katona B / German
Opera Chorus, Berlin SO / Stolz
Ariola-Eurodisc XD 27184
Everest S471 (2)

1972 Kélémen Z; Stratas V; Kollo D;
Harwood H; Hollweg C; Grobe
Cas; Krenn B / German Opera
Chorus, Berlin PO / Karajan
DG 2725 102 ④ 3374 102
DG (US) 2707 070 ④ 3370 003

1980 Kusche Z; Donath V; Prey D;
Moser H; Jerusalem C; Orth Cas;
Lenz B / Bavarian Radio Chorus,
Munich Radio Orch. / Wallberg
EMI SLS 5202
Angel SZBX 390

1949 (excerpts – in English) Stevens H;
V; Morgan D; C / chorus and
orch. / Rudolf
CBS (US) ⓜ ML 2064

1950 (excerpts) Schöneweiss Z;
Kobierska V; Lichtegg D; N.
Jungwirth H; Hopf C; Ferenz Cas;
Bratz B / Zurich State Theatre
Chorus; Zurich Tonhalle Orch. /
Reinshagen

Decca ⓜ ACL 185

1950 (excerpts – in English) Richard
D; Malbin H; Ventura C / Guild
Choristers, Al Goodman and his
Orch.
RCA (US) ⓜ CAL 397
(UK) ⓜ CDN 106

1950 (excerpts – in English) Verea V;
Evans D; Carlisle H; Knight C /
chorus and orch. / Van Grove
Brunswick ⓜ LAT 8003
Decca (US) ⓜ DL 8004

1952 (excerpts – in English) Rogier Z;
Warner V; Rounseville D;
Kirsten H; Dalton C; Harvuot
Cas; Geyans B / chorus and
orch. / Engel
CBS (US) ⓜ CL 838

1952 (excerpts – in English: from
MGM film soundtrack) Lamas
D; Erwin H / chorus, MGM
Studio Orch. / Blackton
Polydor (UK) ⓜ 2353 077
MGM (US) ⓜ MGM–E157

1952 (excerpts – in English) Norman
V; H; MacRae D; C / chorus
and orch. / Greeley
Capitol (UK) ⓜ LC 6564
(US) ⓜ T437

1955 (excerpts) Fassler V; Roland D;
Scheyrer H; Dotzer C / Vienna
Academy Chamber Choir,
Vienna Radio Orch. / Sandauer
Philips ⓜ 6593 012 ④ 7178 017

c.1955 (excerpts – in English) Embassy
Light Opera Company / Gregory
Embassy ⓜ WEP 1006

1957 (excerpts – in English) Hanson
D; Logan H / chorus and orch.
Embassy ⓜ WLP 6016

1957 (excerpts) Loor V; Terkal D; C;
Coertse H / Vienna Volksoper
Chorus and Orch. / Hagan
Saga © 5365
(US) ⓜ VX21400

1958 (excerpts – in English) Glynne
Z; Lowe V; Round D; Bronhill
H; McAlpine C; Dowling Cas;

Kentish *B* / Sadler's Wells Opera
Chorus and Orch. / Reid
EMI CSD 1259
Angel S35816

1960 (excerpts) Mottl *V*; Grundén *D*;
Lipp *H*; Christ *C* / chorus and
orch. / Paulik
Ariola-Eurodisc Z72021E

1960 (medley) Muszely; Schock/
Günther Arndt Choir, FFB
Orch. / Schmidt-Boelcke
EMI STE 41161

1961 (excerpts – in English) Pracht *V*;
W. Lewis *D*; Moffo *H*; Rubin *C*;
K. Smith *Cas*; Nagy *B* / chorus
and orch. / Engel
RCA Reader's Digest (UK)
RDS 9331

1961 (excerpts) Machera *V*; Christ *D*;
Liebesberg *H*; Equiluz *C* /
Vienna Volksoper Chorus and
Orch. / Bauer-Theussl
Westminster (UK) WPS 121
(US) WST 14145

1961 (excerpts – in English)
Wakefield *Z*; Elsy *V*; Larsen *D*;
Delman *H*; Brooks *C*; Bowman
Cas; Price *B* / chorus, Sinfonia
of London / Hollingsworth
World Records ST60

1962 (excerpts – in English) Franke
Z; Hurley *V*; Reardon *D*; Della
Casa *H*; C. Davis *C*; Kahl *Cas*;
Richards *B* / American Opera
Society Chorus and Orch. /
Allers
CBS (UK) 61833
(US) OS2280

1964 (excerpts – in English) Auer *Z*;
Weldon *V*; Wright *D*; Munsel
H; Porretta *C* / Music Theater of
Lincoln Center Chorus and
Orch. / Allers
RCA (US) LSO1094

*c.*1964 (excerpts) Vogel *Z*; Wenglor *V*;
Ritzmann *D*; Vulpius *H*;
Neukirch *C*; Hellmich *Cas* /
Leipzig Radio Chorus, Dresden

PO / Neuhaus
Philips 6593 004 ⓒ 7178 017

1965 (excerpts – in English) Thomas *V*;
H; Philips *D*; *C*; / chorus and
orch. / Braden
Fontana SFL 13026

1965 (excerpts) Shaw *V*; Dixon *D*; Carr
H; Waters *C* / chorus and orch. /
Fuggle
Pye Marble Arch ⓜ MAL 779

1967 (excerpts) Köth *V*; Gedda *D*;
Rothenberger *H*; Ilosfalvy *C* /
Bavarian Radio Chorus, Graunke
SO / Mattes
EMI 1C 061 28194

1968 (excerpts – in English) Fyson *Z*;
Howard *V*; Brett *D*; Bronhill *H*;
Hughes *C*; Howlett *Cas*; Fleet *B* /
McCarthy Singers, orch. / Tausky
EMI NTS 103

1968 (excerpts) Kusche *Z*; Popp *V*;
Alexander *D*; Hallstein *H*; Hoppe
C / Kallmann Chorus, Grand
Operetta Orch. / Marszalek
Polydor 249 280

1976 (excerpts – in English) McCue *Z*;
Hay *V*; Blanc *D*; Wilson *H*;
Hillman *C*; Sandison *Cas*;
Fieldsend *B* / Scottish Opera
Chorus, Scottish Philharmonia /
Gibson
CFP CFP 40276 ④ TC–CFP 40276

1977 (excerpts – in English) Masterson
V; Krenn *D*; Sutherland *H*;
Brecknock *C*; Fryatt *Cas* /
Ambrosian Singers, National PO /
Bonynge
Decca SET 629 ④ KCET 629
London OSA 1172 ④ OSA 5–1172

1978 (excerpts – in English) D. R.
Smith *Z*; Fowles *V*; Titus *D*; Sills
H; Price *C* / New York City
Chorus and Orch. / Rudel
HMV ASD 3500 ④ TC–ASD 3500
Angel S375000 ④ 4XS–37500 (8)
8XS–37500

Il trittico

EDWARD GREENFIELD

'As long as a transatlantic cable,' said Puccini, jaundiced after a performance of *Il trittico*. That was in the early 1920s, several years after this triptych of one-act operas had first been heard at the Met. in New York in December 1918. The three operas together, he reluctantly came to feel, were too long for a single evening, and at close on an hour each they certainly extend the limits normally set by this master of operatic timing.

Yet experience on record – where by chance the size of each panel is ideally suited to LP format – has amply confirmed that the sharp contrasts among the three add to the effect of the whole, as the composer planned from the start. Puccini's elemental themes in opera are here cleanly divided – respectively into melodrama, sentiment and high comedy – and though each opera has its essential internal contrasts, the Puccinian mix is complete only with all three together, a point one registers if anything more certainly on record than in the opera house. If at the New York première, and at other early performances, the degree of success was sharply tiered – with *Gianni Schicchi* immediately accepted as a comic masterpiece, *Il tabarro* regarded as Puccini repeating himself, and *Suor Angelica* considered as little more than a weak failure – then later experience has placed them much more evenly, all three of them in their way masterpieces.

IL TABARRO

The very start of *Il tabarro*, the prelude setting the scene on Michele's barge on the Seine in Paris, is among the most atmospheric passages in any Puccini opera. Daringly he asked for sound effects to be superimposed on his lapping water music, tugboat hooters and a motor-horn, though one of the most successful of the recordings completely ignores that instruction, the HMV version made in Rome with Vincenzo Bellezza conducting and Tito Gobbi in the role of the bargemaster deceived by his wife. In that 1955 record (mono) one can almost say that the mistiness of the sound actually adds to its atmosphere, like a gauze across a stage scene, and Bellezza's expressive warmth at a relatively slow tempo sets a pattern of sympathy that has not fully been matched in later accounts. In both the Decca version of 1962 conducted by Lamberto Gardelli and the CBS account of 1976 conducted by Lorin Maazel the faster tempi go with much greater clarity of detail, and the result is far less menacing. Erich Leinsdorf on the RCA set, like Bellezza, takes a measured view of the prelude, but unlike him runs the risk of seeming sluggish when he is reluctant ever to press ahead. It is noticeable that the two Italian conductors, Gardelli as well as Bellezza, are more successful in building up the big emotional moments, and it is largely a question of their using *rubato* or gently pressing a *stringendo* towards a climax. By contrast both Maazel and Leinsdorf have their moments of stiffness even though the actual playing (from the New Philharmonia Orchestra in both instances) is more refined than on the Italian sets.

The scene of the organ-grinder, who passes by on the bank while Giorgetta pours wine for the stevedores, is another that clearly establishes atmosphere, and though Bellezza on HMV is rhythmically understanding, the absence of laughter or any attempt to set the scene contrasts with all later versions. Maazel with his sharp clean textures brings out the *Petrushka*-like quality of the writing most effectively, but Leinsdorf on RCA conveys more of the jollity, and Gardelli on Decca (at a brisker tempo with rougher laughter) is the most abrasive.

Such contrasts are typical, with the 1955 HMV rather set apart from the others. In the balance of the three principal characters it also provides a distinctive approach, for here the soprano and tenor roles, well characterized as they are by Margaret Mas as the wife, Giorgetta, and Giacinto Prandelli as the young stevedore, Luigi, are clearly subsidiary to that of the barge-master, Michele, taken by Gobbi. Though Prandelli made a major appearance on record as Rodolfo in the Decca *Bohème* of 1950 opposite Tebaldi, Mas is otherwise hardly known on record. Yet with distinctive timbres, Mas mature, Prandelli light and still young-sounding, they together present the character-contrast against the frustrated bargemaster more convincingly than do a conventionally matched *prima donna* and *primo tenore*. The hint of vulnerability and nervous apprehension in Prandelli's portrayal is entirely convincing.

Most disappointing is the regular partnership of Tebaldi and del Monaco then nearing the end of its run on record, in the Decca version, for not only does del Monaco sing with little understanding of the character, virile of tone but regularly falling into coarseness, Tebaldi too is well below her best. Under pressure the voice hardens into rawness. The tenor in the other versions is Placido Domingo, remarkably consistent in both, a shade fresher of tone in 1970 than in 1976, but in detail often showing how experience in the studio had turned him away from histrionic devices – the glottal half-sob an obvious example – which are entirely acceptable on stage but can be distracting on record. At the point when the seeming confidence of the young stevedore is turned in a flash into fear during their second duet on the words 'E lui', Domingo's vocal acting in both performances vividly conveys apprehension.

Opposite him both Leontyne Price and Renata Scotto sing powerfully. Price's is the more beautiful rendering with fine contrasts of tone, veiled and smoky. Scotto's is the more positive and detailed, though unlike Price she is sorely taxed in the upper register, and the top C in the first duet is ugly. But Scotto outshines all her rivals when, after the second duet, she is about to face her husband as he emerges from the cabin and she utters in a monotone the line, 'Come è difficile esser felice' ('How hard it is to be happy'). One might liken it – in dramatic effect if not in meaning – to Tosca's monotone after Scarpia's death, 'E avanti a lui tremava tutta Roma', and Price, effective enough, treats is as a watered-down version of the great moment. Margaret Mas is more intense, but it is Scotto who turns it into a great and revealing statement, memorably dramatic.

When it comes to the bargemaster, Michele, Gobbi's portrayal of the deceived husband tormented into impulsive murder is by far the most individual and compelling on record. Even among Gobbi's many fine performances it stands out as a classic, with the menace of the character never weakened, but with sympathy roused all the more compellingly when in the key duet with Giorgetta he asks with heartfelt feeling 'Per chè non m'ami più' and then affectingly remembers the evenings when with their child he would wrap them both in his cloak. Line after line here is so distinctively sung by Gobbi, that one cannot ever hear them without thinking of his voice. So, too, with his snarl on the spoken comment 'Sgualdrina!' ('Slut!'), and equally in the final aria on the line 'Ma chi dunque? Chi dunque?'

Other performances almost inevitably bring their disappointments. Matching Gobbi most closely is Sherrill Milnes in Leinsdorf's version. He has plainly learnt much from his predecessor, passionately inflecting words and phrases and, unlike Gobbi who in the final aria, 'Nulla! Silenzio', presses his tone into roughness, the young Milnes provides rich tone even in the topmost register up to a magnificent, culminating top G. In the duet with Giorgetta his final cries of 'Resta vicina a me. La notte è bella!' in their power convey the agony of the bargemaster if anything even more compellingly than Gobbi's. By comparison Robert Merrill on Decca for all his stream of firm tone sounds uninvolved, the distinctiveness of the character largely missed. On the CBS set Ingvar Wixell is certainly distinctive, if only because his gritty timbre with its characteristic flutter sounds so un-Italianate in this music. Though it is an intelligent, plainly felt performance, the tone-colour itself implies stiffness, a lack of passion, a bank manager translated to the Seine. Though in 'Nulla! Silenzio' he points the dotted rhythms crisply – helped by Maazel's incisive direction – his performance sounds too drilled, too controlled, the culminating top G attacked and quitted too easily.

This is not an opera that has invited much recording of individual items. The Russian tenor Dimitri Smirnov with characteristically clean attack and fine detail recorded an excerpt labelled 'Hai ben ragione' hardly amounting to an aria at all (VA 49; Club 99.31), and towards the end of the 78 rpm era Giovanni Inghilleri recorded the Michele–Giorgetta duet 'Per chè non m'ami più' with Emma Tegani and the Philharmonia Orchestra under Alberto Erede (C 3772). His singing is firm and well phrased, though on the reverse in 'Nulla! Silenzio' he is more obviously taxed. In both items the limitations of 78 rpm side-length means that the music seemed to be rushed a little.

Otherwise it is Michele's culminating aria that alone has attracted singers, in two totally contrasted versions. It was only on second thoughts that Puccini wrote the dramatic 'Nulla! Silenzio' with its vigorous questioning over who might be Giorgetta's lover. Before that came the more lyrical 'Scorri fiume eterno', what Puccini called Michele's river song, less apt dramatically. Dinh Gilly recorded it much cut (DA 559), pouring forth a stream of dark, finely focused tone but making little variations in dynamics. In fuller form 'Scorri fiume eterno' was recorded by Lawrence Tibbett towards the end of his career, the voice still magnificent with its bass-like quality, the interpretation sharply rhythmic with snapping dotted rhythms (Rococo 5266). Tibbett can be heard too in an 'off-the-air' performance of the whole opera given at the Met. in New York, and there the top G in 'Nulla! Silenzio' is splendid too, but otherwise the singing is not so well sustained.

'Scorri fiume eterno' was also included as a fill-up on both the Decca and RCA versions of the opera sung by Merrill and Milnes respectively. As in the opera proper Milnes is the more expansive and resonant, almost convincing one (as few singers do) that the meandering vocal line is a real Puccini melody.

Curiously in a complete performance recorded in January 1938 by Clemens Krauss with Stuttgart Radio forces, 'Scorri fiume eterno', or rather its German translation 'Fliesse echtes Wasser', was included instead of the substitute aria. That the composer's revision was not respected is strange at so late a date, but it may have been because the baritone taking the role of Michele, Mathieu Ahlersmeyer, was more successful in lyrical music than dramatic. His is a fine performance, making the bargemaster a wise old Hans Sachs figure who suddenly turns nasty. As Luigi – or Henri as he becomes with the German translation adopting the names of the original French play of Didier Gold, *La Houppelande*, from which Puccini took the subject – Peter Anders is also excellent; though with crisply enunciated German words, when he sings opposite Hildegard Ranczak (who in the early scenes overacts in the role of vamp) the two soprano/tenor duets sound disconcertingly like Lehár. Ranczak sounds too old for the role, making things worse by sliding up to notes, but then in her duet with Ahlersmeyer she tries less hard and one begins to understand why she had a high reputation in Germany with many discerning opera-goers. The overtones of Lehár are encouraged by the conductor, for on this occasion Krauss sounds self-indulgent, letting rhythms sag rather than pressing ahead with any sort of Italianate ardour.

In the Cetra version of 1949, which like other complete opera recordings from this source is taken from a radio performance, the conducting of Giuseppe Baroni is much more idiomatic, though the playing of the Turin

Orchestra is hardly refined and the singing cast poor. Clara Petrella is the least unsatisfactory but her singing is unsubtle and generally squally under pressure. The role of Luigi is taken by an unpleasantly tight-toned tenor, Glauco Scarlini, and as Michele Antenore Reali is wobbly and uncertain, frequently pushing himself off the note so far as he focuses on one at all. The one good point about this version is that like the 1938 Stuttgart set the recording is surprisingly clear, far more so than is usual on Cetra at this period. Both those early versions, recorded live, include sound effects, though the barge hooter in the Stuttgart performance sounds like a transatlantic liner leaving for New York.

SUOR ANGELICA

It is hardly surprising that *Suor Angelica* was the last of the three *Trittico* operas to be fully appreciated. It used to seem bizarre that the composer himself counted this his favourite of the trio, but records have confirmed that the seeming flatness of the musical landscape is deceptive, with melodies moving by step and with a predominance of slow-moving ideas in common time. Even if those qualities make it harder for interpreters to achieve variety, *Suor Angelica* is planned in just as careful detail as *Il tabarro* and *Gianni Schicchi*.

Even the first complete version, dimly recorded in a dry studio in 1950 by Cetra, makes an effective case for the opera, and that is largely to the credit of the conductor, Fernando Previtali, whose pacing of the score is always convincing. Rosanna Carteri gives an under-characterized performance as the heroine, the voice usually firm and bright, but she shows relatively little concern for detail. Similarly Mití Truccato Pace gives a conventional account of the role of the Zia Principessa, producing much powerful tone so that the call for repentance on the word 'Espiare' shines out commandingly.

The next version appeared in 1957, recorded in Rome with Victoria de los Angeles as the luckless heroine and Tullio Serafin conducting most persuasively. Though for los Angeles the *tessitura* is sometimes uncomfortably high, this remains on balance the most moving and beautiful rendering of the part on record. The poise and warmth of her opening solo 'I desideri sono i fiori dei vivi' – 'Wishes are the flowers of the living' – establishes the weighty, tragic tone which yet allows a light and flowing account of the opening of the big aria, 'Senza mamma', the tender tone ever more golden, finely contrasted in the closing phrases of the passage sung 'come in estasi' with a tone drained of colour.

Tebaldi's rendering of the aria in the Decca set conducted by Lamberto Gardelli in 1962 brings a disappointingly unspecific performance, always felt but with generalized emotions, for Tebaldi too readily falls into a lachrymose style, and the voice under pressure goes hard, losing its golden tone. Best in this version is the Zia Principessa of Giulietta Simionato, formidably effective with words sharply articulated. A sort of Gigli pout, less intrusive than outright sobbing, afflicts the young Katia Ricciarelli in the recording she made of the complete opera for RCA in 1972 with Bruno Bartoletti conducting, but there the voice is so apt for the role that for the most part the flaw is forgivable. Ricciarelli more than her rivals conveys the vulnerability of Sister Angelica, shading the tone most beautifully and rarely allowing even a moment of hardness under pressure. So at the start of 'Senza mamma' the notes are more detached than is common – the score has no phrase marks over the separate quavers – and the *portamento* from the end of the second line on the word 'fredde' to the beginning of the next on 'E chiudeste' is exquisite, far more delicate than in other complete sets.

The atmospheric glow of the Rome recording helps the voices, Fiorenza Cossotto in the role of the Zia Principessa as well as Ricciarelli. The firmness and velvety richness of Cossotto's singing are a constant joy to the ear, and the contrasts between the two characters are superbly underlined, but unlike her two immediate predecessors in the role on record – Fedora Barbieri with Victoria de los Angeles as much as Simionato with Tebaldi – she has surprisingly poor diction with words often swallowed to give a generalized unspecific impression, albeit consistently powerful.

The Zia Principessa of Marilyn Horne is one of the glories of the CBS version made with Lorin Maazel taking a strongly characterful view of the score. With the voice close – so bringing out a hint of Supervia-like *vibrato* – the impact could hardly be more formidable right from her first entry. In effect she is too tough too soon and too consistently with no hint of patrician reserve, but her performance is well matched by the powerful contribution of Renata Scotto as Angelica. The size of Scotto's voice is an increasing asset as the opera progresses, and there are few of the moments of shrillness on top which have latterly afflicted this singer. There is hypnotic concentration in the repeated phrases of the heroine's solo as the Zia Principessa departs, and no one more movingly conveys the tragedy of Angelica as she takes poison: religious ecstasy gives way to tormented despair as she realizes the meaning of what she has done.

Maazel's conducting, concentrated and intensely individual, is strangely unatmospheric, for at the very start the metrical steadiness has one concentrating purely on musical qualities, rather than any scene-painting. Maazel later in the opera is masterly at grading the developing climaxes to give an architectural balance important in a work seemingly so slow and uneventful. More than any other version this one presents a third character as a genuine principal; Ileana Cotrubas as Sister Genovieffa gives a delightful, living portrait, full of magical detail.

Even Isobel Buchanan in her first recorded role cannot match Cotrubas as Genovieffa, beautiful as the voice is, but she is one of an unusually strong team of supporting singers assembled for the most recent version of *Suor Angelica* conducted by Richard Bonynge with Dame Joan Sutherland in the name part. It is a pity that Sutherland did not record the role earlier, for the beat in the voice is at times obtrusive, above all in the opening solo; but even more than Scotto, Sutherland commands a weight that brings satisfying climaxes in the second half. Her voice easily rises above a full ensemble, as in the final solo, which in other versions is almost always disappointing, whatever the balancing of the soprano's voice by the engineers. The Decca recording makes this easily the most atmospheric version with Bonynge's sympathetic conducting amply and aptly pauseful. Christa Ludwig as the Zia Principessa gives a beautifully detailed reading, never exaggerated, with dynamics kept down so that the climax of her big solo on 'Espiare' flashes out with sudden Wagnerian power, a superb moment, the more telling when the pace is so slow and concentrated.

The only separate passage from *Suor Angelica* recorded at all frequently is the aria 'Senza mamma'. Tina Poli-Randaccio in 1919, within months of the first production in New York, made a record of it which in its combination of easy flowing legato at a steady tempo and unexaggerated warmth of feeling has rarely been matched. It was good to have it included in HMV's second volume of 'The Record of Singing' (DB 181; RLS 743), for though the acoustic recording technique catches a distracting flutter, the singing amply confirms Poli-Randaccio's reputation as an outstanding verismo soprano of her day, renowned above all as Minnie in *La fanciulla del West*. Comparing the perfectly even flutter in Poli-Randaccio's voice with the much more uneven production of a latter-day singer such as Pilar Lorengar (SXL 6923) makes it clear why the ear accepts one rather than the other. Lorengar's reading too is on the fast side, but unlike Poli-Randaccio – who at the end pauses before her beautifully floated top A – Lorengar rushes at it and the result sounds tentative. Despite the flaws, Lorengar's is a fresh, girlish portrait. The antithesis of that lightweight view is that of Maria Callas, who in her recital disc (ALP 3799) added a totally distinctive portrait of Sister Angelica to her uniquely individual Puccini gallery. Characteristically – with Serafin an understanding accompanist – Callas chooses a tempo altogether slower, adopting a manner far weightier even than Poli-Randaccio's. It is a fine lesson in Callas's art to note the way that with spontaneous-sounding *rubato* she completely avoids any hint of squareness, an obvious danger in this aria at such a speed, and the touching-in of one or two half-sobs, mere catches in the voice, contrasts strongly with the exaggeration of others. On the last floated top A the attack is perfectly clean, but on the long *diminuendo* the unevenness always recognizable in Callas's voice grows ever more obtrusive to mar what is otherwise a classic reading. In the rapt codetta Callas flagrantly ignores the instruction to make each repeated 'Parlami' softer than the last but the suppressed urgency she conveys amply justifies it.

Between those extremes of lightness and weight comes such a reading as the young Mirella Freni's recorded on a recital disc of 1965 (World Records CM 19). The voice is fresh, but perhaps understandably at the beginning of her recording career Freni seemed too intent on conveying emotion, upsetting the legato line with heavy agogic pauses and little upward scoops. She might have taken a lesson from Poli-Randaccio's surprisingly straight rendering, but then so might the great Rosa Ponselle who, in 1954, nearly two decades after she had officially retired, was caught at the piano accompanying herself informally in this aria. Except for a hint of raucousness under pressure the tone is still glorious, and though in floating her final top A there is no question of a *pianissimo* the precision of attack and the expansion in *crescendo* are a marvel. Of the inter-war generation Magda Olivero (Cetra BB 25271; LPC 55011) is both subtle and moving.

GIANNI SCHICCHI

Maria Callas's portrait of young Lauretta, daughter of Gianni Schicchi, pleading for her beloved father to help in 'O mio babbino caro', is the least convincing of her sharp characterizations on her Puccini recital record (ASD 3799). It is very individual like the rest but totally misses charm. The whole approach is too heavy, treating the tragedy for real with sobs and a big *rallentando* at the end. Elisabeth Schwarzkopf in her 1966 version (SXDW 3049), underlines words in detail just as Callas does, but is yet all lightness and charm at a flowing speed. Though one knows that this is not the voice of a young girl (Schwarzkopf was over fifty at the time of the recording) the characterization is deliciously girlish. Such readings, detailed and thoughtful, contrast with those which treat the aria as though it comes from an operetta. Ursula Farr (SXL 6598) provides an extreme instance, but even the version (in English) which first made this a popular item with the British public outside the opera house, Joan Hammond's, is generalized in its warmth (Col. DB 2052; HQM 1186) hardly related to the situation in the opera. Among the earliest versions of the aria, that of Frances Alda, recorded in 1919 (DA 136; RLS 743) is characteristically fresh with beautiful clean phrasing and graceful *portamenti*. Florence Easton at the same period, the original Lauretta opposite Giuseppe de Luca (Vocalion H&D 30025; GV 520), is comparably fresh and straightforward with sweet firm tone, but the Italian is less convincing ('Peeaytah!' she sings) and the emotions less intense. Olivero (LPC 55011) is special for delicacy and feeling.

Whether heard separately (ASD 2274) or as part of the complete HMV recording conducted by Gabriele Santini, the performance of 'O mio babbino caro' by Victoria de los Angeles stands out in every way. It is the antithesis of Callas's, for wide-eyed charm brims from every note and though the pleading is intense, the golden tone (marred only by a slight thinning on the top A) tells of a girl who by habit smiles. The tone of loving reproach on 'Sì, sì' is irresistible. By comparison Renata Tebaldi on the rival Decca version treats the aria very much as a set piece unrelated to the drama. The tone is characteristically rich, clearly too mature for the role, but at least she is more characterful than Grete Rapisardi on the Cetra version conducted by Alfredo Simonetto, very ordinary and tremulous. On the most recent complete version conducted by Lorin Maazel, Ileana Cotrubas, fresh and charming at other points, sounds effortful in this aria, the manner breathy and too overtly emotional with the microphone exaggerating a flutter in the voice which still further prevents the simple purity of the vocal line from coming over.

'O mio babbino caro' stands apart from the rest of *Gianni Schicchi*, a brief reversion to Puccini's earlier, simpler manner, but the tenor too has a set-piece. That is his solo commending Gianni Schicchi, 'Avete torto', sometimes on record begun halfway through, where the dotted march rhythm develops on 'Firenze é come un albero fiorito'. An early version dating from 1923 has Antonio Cortis (Parlo. P 1598; GV 567) coping superbly with the high *tessitura*, the manner lithe and forward with the disjointed, conversational lines at the start finely characterized. In 1964 Mario del Monaco (who had failed to contribute to the complete Decca recording of 1962) included the second half of the aria on a recital disc (SXL 6140), pouring out thrilling tone in abundance but sounding raw and even strained in places. By contrast one marvels at Giovanni Martinelli who in his eighties in 1965 recorded the second half with throaty production but amazingly firm trumpet tone, defiantly emphasizing consonants (Celebrity CEL 500).

For the complete Decca set a choice was made for the role of Rinuccio which provided no rivalry whatever for del Monaco. The distant recording balance – with Agostino Lazzari barely audible against the orchestra in his first solo – merely underlines the feebleness of the singing, matched only by Giuseppe Savio on the Cetra Turin version, who sounds even more strained. In the HMV account Carlo del Monte is just as clearly a lyric tenor stretched to the limit, but with the help of crisply rhythmic conducting from Gabriele Santini (the dots of the march rhythm in the aria nicely exaggerated) he conveys boyish urgency effectively, arguably presenting a more convincing figure than Placido Domingo on what by a fair margin is vocally the most satisfying rendering of the role on record in the CBS version conducted by Lorin Maazel. Domingo not surprisingly is presented as a star rather than one of the team, and the relative ease with which he copes with the aria, pointing rhythms and phrases with a swaggering confidence, is fair justification, though he of all tenors did not need the sort of close balance provided by the CBS engineers.

It is a paradox that though this superbly constructed operatic farce revolves round Gianni Schicchi himself, there is no set-piece for him comparable with those for the soprano and tenor. Once Schicchi arrives on stage well over a third of the way through the piece, no one begins to compete with him, and we are fortunate that the most dominant Schicchi of his generation recorded the role twice, Tito Gobbi, first in 1958 for HMV and then in 1976 for CBS. The consistency between the two performances is amazing. In the later version the voice occasionally betrays signs of age, and undeniably the 1958 version has a wider range of tone-colour, but some of those differences are more the result of closer microphone placing in the later recording, which exposes the voice more. Even in the earlier version on the top Fs and the top G of the solo beginning 'Ah vittoria' one can already detect that the voice in that register loses some of its colour.

Both recordings present a classic rendering full of delicate vocal acting, the illumination of the face present in every line. It would be interesting to compare both these readings with a Gobbi live performance, for one suspects that for recording he shrewdly modified his comic acting, giving it something of lieder-style rather than opera-style. Certainly the performance of Giuseppe Taddei in the Cetra Turin set, recorded live, and for that matter the much less effective performance from Fernando Corena on Decca, might suggest that, for they are both broader in their effects. On his very first entry Taddei certainly scores, for with his big, dark, resonant voice he conveys sardonic scorn the more tellingly when he deduces from the gloomy faces of the relatives that Buoso Donati must be getting better. At that point Gobbi adopts a throwaway manner in both versions, lightness an essential part of his characterization leading up to the spoken address to the audience at the very end. There the earlier version is certainly preferable with its light chuckle and confidential tone of voice, but the later one presents a superb pay-off, where Corena on Decca sounds clumsy, adopting a heavy, public manner. Corena's exaggeration when impersonating the ailing Buoso is also disappointing, and Gobbi with characteristic finesse adopts a timbre that is comic in its tremulous whine without totally losing credibility. It is a mark of his virtuosity that in both his versions he adopts entirely different inflections for his repetitions of 'Sta bene!' when the relatives in turn are trying to bribe him, and the five contrasted inflections on CBS are quite different from those on HMV. Taddei on Cetra also provides marked contrasts – using a comic falsetto for example on the last 'Sta bene!' – but the effect is broader, again reflecting a live performance.

When *Gianni Schicchi* is very much an ensemble opera, those two versions inevitably suffer in comparison with the studio-made ones, though Simonetto's pacing of the score is most convincing, whatever the roughness of detail. Lamberto Gardelli, in this opera more than the others in the Decca set, is disappointing, often too intense and unyielding. The poor ensemble can hardly be excused and the flaws are exaggerated by the clarity of the recording. Santini's conducting in the HMV version is altogether more refined, often lightly pointed, never sounding hectic, always idiomatic. There are touches in Maazel's reading for CBS which are hardly idiomatic – the *appoggiature* for the weeping motif at the start do not droop as they should – but the very fact that the textures are so clearly presented in crystalline precision (not just a question of recording quality) brings out the modernity of many of Puccini's effects, notably his unexpected cribbings from Stravinsky in the energetic *tutti*. Then after the thrust of the motoric passages Maazel's sympathy and understanding come out the more affectingly each time the music relaxes into the lovers' motif.

It is the conducting of Francesco Molinari-Pradelli on a rare Philips version, dating from 1957 – in mono only, recorded just a year ahead of the HMV Gobbi and never issued in Britain – that stands as its most distinctive feature. Like Maazel, Molinari-Pradelli takes a motoric view of the score, more consistently so with a sharply metrical rendering of the passage of the relations weeping at the start. Though the recording is dim, the textures are light and – so far as the sound quality allows it – clean. Here, as Rinuccio, Lazzari makes quite a different impression from the disappointing one he was to give five years later in the Decca version, light and fresh, coping splendidly with the high *tessitura* of the aria 'Avete torto'. Opposite him as Lauretta, Bruna Rizzoli is similarly fresh-toned if with a noticeable flutter. 'O mio babbino caro' is plain and fresh, sweet enough but without much feeling, and all told, with Renato Capecchi a Schicchi with little bite in the voice, the whole performance sounds under-characterized. Capecchi's voice is not an easy one for the microphones to capture attractively, for at times it loses focus, and though he has plainly thought about the role closely, providing much good detail, the personality does not come over strongly. At the end there is an attempt at stage production with Schicchi chasing the relatives into the distance off-stage, but then Capecchi comes back and his spoken address to the audience is so light and fast it sounds like an Italian radio announcer.

Maybe the final lesson of this whole body of *Trittico* recordings – a point on which stage producers might also reflect – is that though the sharply contrasted character of each panel of the triptych is beautifully balanced against its fellows, the demands of each are so widely different that it is hard to achieve consistency among all three. The HMV series was collected into a box, with Gobbi in both *Il tabarro* and *Gianni Schicchi*, and Maazel has recorded all three operas for CBS (if with two different orchestras), but it was only in 1962 that Decca attempted a fully consistent cycle, and then it was less than a success. The outlook is hardly hopeful now or within the foreseeable future for getting a complete recording of *Trittico* that is both sharply characterized and consistent.

IL TRITTICO

IL TABARRO

M Michele; *L* Luigi; *G* Giorgetta; *T* Il Tinca; *F* La Frugola

1938   (in German) Ahlersmeyer *M*; Anders *L*; Ranczak *G*; Buchta *T*; Waldenau *F*/Stuttgart Radio Chorus and Orch./C. Krauss
Acanta ⓜ BB 22365

                     Opera Chorus and Orch./ Bellezza
EMI ⓒ SLS 5066 ④ TC–SLS 5066
Angel ⓒ SCLX 3849E

1949   Reali *M*; Scarlini *L*; Petrella *G*; Nessi *T*; Ticozzi *F*/Italian Radio Chorus and Orch., Turin/Baroni
Cetra ⓜ LPO 0259
Everest ⓒ 464

1962   Merrill *M*; Del Monaco *L*; Tebaldi *C*; Ercolani *T*; Danieli *F*/Florence Festival Chorus and Orch./Gardelli
Decca SET 236–8
London OSA 1151 or OSA 1364

1955   Gobbi *M*; Prandelli *L*; Mas *G*; De Palma *T*; Pirazzini *F*/Rome

1970   Milnes *M*; Domingo *L*; L. Price

G; De Palma T; Dominguez F/
Alldis Choir, New Philharmonia/
Leinsdorf
RCA (UK) SER 5619
(US) LSC 3220
1976   Wixell M; Domingo L; Scotto

G; Sénéchal T; Knight F/
Ambrosian Opera Chorus, New
Philharmonia/Maazel
CBS (UK) 79312
(US) M34570 ④ MT 34570

SUOR ANGELICA

SA Suor Angelica; P Principessa

1950   Carteri SA; Truccato Pace P/
Italian Radio SO, Milan/Previtali
Cetra ⓜ LPO 0259
Everest ⓔ 464
1957   De los Angeles SA; Barbieri P/
Rome Opera Orch./Serafin
EMI ⓔ SLS 5066 ④ TC–SLS
5066
Angel ⓔ SCLX 3849E
1962   Tebaldi SA; Simionato P/
Florence Festival Orch./Gardelli
Decca SET236–8
London OSA 1152 or OSA 1364
1972   Ricciarelli SA; Cossotto P/Santa

Cecilia Academy Orch./
Bartoletti
RCA (UK) RL 12712
(US) ARL 2712 ④ ARK 1 2712
1976   Scotto SA; Horne P/New
Philharmonia/Maazel
CBS (UK) 79312
(US) M 34505 ④ MT 34505
1978   Sutherland SA; Ludwig P/
National PO/Bonynge
Decca SET 627 ④ KCET 627
London OSA 1173 ④ 0SA 5–
1173

GIANNI SCHICCHI

GS Gianni Schicchi; L Lauretta; R Rinuccio; Z Zita

1949   (live performance –
Metropolitan Opera House, New
York) Tajo GS; Albanese L; Di
Stefano R; Elmo Z/Metropolitan
Opera
Orch./Antonicelli
Cetra ⓜ LO65
1949   Taddei GS; Rapisardi L; Savio
R; Dubbini Z/Italian Radio
Orch., Turin/Simonetto
Cetra ⓜ LPO 0259
c.1953   Anonymous soloists/Berlin SO/
Balzer
Royale ⓜ 1527
1957   Capecchi GS; Rizzoli L; Lazzari
R; Palombini Z/ San Carlo
Opera Orch./Molinari-Pradelli
Philips 6540 032
1958   Gobbi GS; De los Angeles L;
Del Monte R; Canali Z/Rome

Opera Orch./Santini
EMI SLS 5066 ④ TC–SLS
5066
Angel SCLX 3849E
1962   Corena GS; Tebaldi L;
Lazzari R; Danieli Z/Florence
Festival Orch./Gardelli
Decca SET 236–8
London OSA 1153 or OSA
1364
c.1972–3   (in German) Rupf GS;
Tomova-Sintov L; Teodorian
R; Härtel Z/Leipzig Radio
SO/Kegel
Eterna 826 296
1976   Gobbi GS; Cotrubas L;
Domingo R; Di Stasio Z/New
Philharmonia/Maazel
CBS (UK) 79312
(US) M 34534 ④ MT 34534

The Operas of Janáček

MICHAEL KENNEDY

The seven major operas of Leoš Janáček are among the principal glories of twentieth-century music. For an English writer to have made that dogmatic assertion would have been highly unlikely, if not unimaginable, only twenty years ago. That it is now almost a cliché is attributable not only to the crusading of such conductors as Rafael Kubelik, Sir Charles Mackerras, Edward Downes and Richard Armstrong, who have directed moving and compelling performances of these works in English translation, but equally to the availability of complete recordings of the operas by the Czech company, Supraphon. Through listening at home and then seeing the mind's vision realized on the stage, thousands of English-speaking opera-enthusiasts have come to know that in Janáček's operas they may find a combination of the dramatic impact of Puccini, the reality of Mascagni, the nobility of Verdi, the psychological insight into character of Britten, the ferocity of Shostakovich, all expressed in music that has irresistible vitality, melodic fertility, lyric splendour, savage cruelty, highly original orchestration and, surpassing all else, a profound sense of compassion for human beings and their involvement with their destinies. 'In every creature a spark of God', Janáček wrote beneath the title of his last opera *From the House of the Dead*, but it might well be the motto-theme of all his work. As one who is ever-ready to man the barricades in defence of all Strauss's operas and who yields to few in admiration of Britten's achievement, I believe nevertheless that Janáček's operas are the greatest contributions to the lyric theatre made by a composer since the death of Verdi. That four of them were written within the space of nine years after he had passed his sixty-fifth birthday was an example of protean creativity on a Verdian and Straussian scale as well as a tribute to the power of Janáček's apparently unrequited passion for the young Mrs Kamilla Stoesslová.

Yet, surprising as it may seem in the twentieth century, the textual problem of performing Janáček's operas involves musicological considerations almost as daunting as those which affect Handelian and other baroque works. One glance at a Janáček autograph score is enough to indicate the source of most of the confusion; by comparison the manuscript of a Vaughan Williams symphony is as copperplate. And a damaging effect of this illegibility is the lack of authentic editions of the scores. Sir Charles Mackerras has described how even Janáček's 'fair copies' look more like sketches; often it is hard to tell which pages are part of a full score and which are discarded. Correct and abandoned material exist on alternate pages. To make matters worse, Janáček composed straight into full orchestral score which he then gave to a copyist who wrote out the whole work, mistakes included. This copy Janáček then 'corrected' and revised in his inimitable way. It is not, then, very surprising that conductors, faced with this mess and not too sure that what Janáček seemed to want made sense, themselves began to 'edit' the scores. Many instrumental effects, considered to be either clumsy and eccentric or too austere, were extensively rescored (as happened to Bruckner). Recent Janáček scholars such as Kubelik, Mackerras and the Englishman John Tyrrell have taken immense trouble to vindicate Janáček's original ideas and one may happily and safely assume that within the next decade their views will prevail totally. Four of the recordings under review here incorporate the results of this scholarship, but the rest, made with what one may call 'impure' scores, nevertheless still demand serious consideration, for it should be remembered that they are in substance if not in detail faithful to Janáček and that through them hundreds of record-buyers have been converted to lifelong admiration for this exciting and moving music.

So far no recording has appeared of Janáček's first completed opera, the three-act *Šárka* (1887–8, revised 1924). The second, the one-act *Beginning of a Romance* (1891), was recorded in Czechoslovakia, but I have not heard it. The rest are all available and will be discussed in chronological order.

JENŮFA

Janáček began to make an opera in 1894 from a play about Moravian peasant life by Gabriela Preissová but did not complete it until 1903 – it is even possible that he destroyed the first draft in 1897. The play – and, in Czechoslovakia, the opera – is called *Her Stepdaughter* (*Její pastorkyňa*) and this title neatly contrives to imply that there are two heroines of equal status, the stepdaughter (Jenůfa) and the stepmother, the Kostelnička (sexton's wife). Admirers of the opera will know that both roles are superb vehicles for great singer-actresses, witness the sopranos who have sung them since 1920 (in several cases a Jenůfa has later in her career sung the Kostelnička). They include: Maria Jeritza, Maria Müller, Marta Fuchs, Ljuba Welitsch, Helena Braun, Gré Brouwenstijn, Tiana Lemnitz, Amy Shuard, Sylvia Fisher, Sena Jurinac, Elisabeth Söderström, Astrid Varnay, Josephine Barstow, Lorna Haywood, Pauline Tinsley. This roll-call is sufficient to give the lie to the astonishing criticism, sometimes still made, that Janáček wrote ungratefully and crudely for the female voice.

Jenůfa is the most frequently performed of Janáček's operas and has been commercially recorded three times by Supraphon. The dramatic love-story of the village girl Jenůfa who is deserted by her lover Števa, bears his son secretly while hidden by her stepmother, and finds happiness with the lover's half-brother Laca only after the child has been murdered by the stepmother, is the most obviously operatic of all the subjects Janáček tackled and it enabled him to anticipate Puccini's *Butterfly* and Strauss's *Salome* with deep character-studies of haunted and obsessed women. The four principal parts are meaty and rewarding both vocally and dramatically; there are excellent smaller parts; and the chorus in Acts 1 and 3 has important and attractive work to do. Janáček's technique of melodic themes based on the rhythms and cadences of the Moravian dialect and his frequent use of repetition of certain words and phrases (a characteristic of Slovakian folk music) are applied with all the technical and psychological subtlety of Wagnerian *Leitmotiv*. No original folk-songs are quoted, but the score is pervaded by the spirit of folk-music; even more strongly is it pervaded by a truly astonishing sympathy for human frailties. Janáček's music passes no moral judgements but shows both the good and the bad in the make-up of each character. After listening to this opera, one leaves the theatre or one's armchair enriched from contact with a great spirit.

The *Jenůfa* recordings use, in the main, the score as edited for the first Prague performance in 1916 by the conductor Karel Kovařovic. (Although the opera had been a great success on its first performance at Brno in 1904, it was repeatedly refused for Prague by Kovařovic whom Janáček had deeply offended by some outspoken criticism several years earlier.) Some recent public performances have restored a narration for the Kostelnička in Act 1 which Janáček cut before the vocal score was published in 1908, but none of the recordings includes it. Supraphon's first recording was issued in mono in 1952. Jaroslav Vogel, a distinguished Janáček scholar, conducts the Prague National Theatre Chorus and Orchestra in a performance which wonderfully blends and contrasts the mixed elements of the score – its lyricism, drama, melodrama and rhythmical impetus. By today's standards, though, the choral singing and orchestral playing are palely recorded, climaxes being underpowered and distant. Nevertheless the performance is classic by reason of the solo singing.

Štěpánka Jelínková's Jenůfa remains, for me, the loveliest I have heard, young-sounding, pure, ineffably touching in the Act 2 aria when, delirious, she searches for her baby and prays to the Virgin Mary for mercy and protection, profoundly moving in the last act when she forgives the Kostelnička, and radiant in the concluding duet with Laca when the music achieves a poetic spirituality rare in opera. Her voice has no trace of the excessive vibrato often, and (as will be seen) not unjustly, associated with Eastern European sopranos. Marta Krásová sings the Kostelnička, a powerful but not overwhelming interpretation. She is, as every Kostelnička must be, at her best in the Act 2 monologue when, driven half-mad by a combination of her hatred for Števa and of the baby as representative of the wrong he has done Jenůfa with her family pride and her strict religious outlook, she convinces herself that God will understand her motives in murdering the child. This aria is a formidable test of a dramatic soprano's range and control. The stepbrothers Števa and Laca are both finely sung, the former by Ivo Žídek whose light but strong tenor conveys the lad's fecklessness, his randy charm and his inability to cope with an emotional situation outside his shallow nature. Laca needs a more heroic tenor, for this character, like Jenůfa herself, develops in each act: jealous, surly and aggressive at first, contrite and loyal in the second act, strong, tender and noble in the last act. In that memorable artist Beno Blachut the part finds its ideal interpreter, and the sensitive treatment of the text in its original language is apparent even to a non-Czech.

When Supraphon recorded *Jenůfa* in stereo in 1969 only Žídek remained from the cast of seventeen years before. His Števa was remarkably little affected by the passage of time and gained, as of course did the whole performance, from the increased atmospheric vividness available from stereo. Again this is the Prague National Theatre company, conducted by Bohumil Gregor, who turns the screw throughout with the skill needed to enhance the music's intrinsic tension – the Dvořákian lyricism of the start of Act 2, in particular the beautiful orchestral passage when Jenůfa says goodnight before going to bed, is played with a rapturous élan. Gregor modifies the Kovařovic score in places. In Naděžda Kniplová, the role of the Kostelnička acquires the kind of interpreter who retains on records the dramatic flair of her stage performance yet contains it within musical bounds. The Kostelnička is a larger-than-life character and the singer is easily tempted to go 'over the top'. Kniplová is too much of an artist to do that; by sheer vocal technique allied to consummate delivery of the text, she freezes the marrow in our bones during her big Act 2 aria and brings tears to our eyes with her Act 3 confession. Disappointingly, the Jenůfa is not up to this standard; if she were, this recording would be difficult to surpass. But Libuše Domanínská employs excessive vibrato and though she is often quite appealing, she does not have the necessary lustre and purity of tone. Blachut's Laca is succeeded by that of Vilém Přibyl, more menacing in Act 1, equally inspired in Act 3. Přibyl's voice is of distinctive quality; if one does not like it there is nothing that can be done except to admire his superb application of its colours and timbres. I do like it, and it is particularly suited to the ejaculatory ecstasy of Janáček's melodic recitative.

Přibyl is Laca again, but less effectively, in the latest Supraphon *Jenůfa*, issued in Britain in 1980 and recorded in 1977–8. This is not a Prague performance. That excellent Janáček specialist František Jílek conducts the Orchestra and Chorus of the Brno Janáček Opera in what is easily the best technical recording of the three: balance, immediacy and dynamic range are alike admirable. Kniplová is again the Kostelnička, but, like Přibyl's, the voice shows signs of wear and tear, and in Act 2 she is obviously reluctant (or unable) to place the dramatic strain upon it which is such a feature of her earlier performance. However, the set contains a lovely Jenůfa from Gabriela Beňačková, a performance in the Jelínková mould and only slightly less to be preferred because of occasional loss of clarity of diction, and a strong Števa from Vladimír Krejčík. In all three recordings the smaller parts are more than adequately sung. The ideal cast would, I suppose, be the young Žídek as Števa, Blachut as Laca, Jelínková as Jenůfa and Kniplová as the Kostelnička, with Jílek conducting. One awaits the Vienna-Mackerras version with impatience, not only to hear what differences his editorial researches may make to an already marvellous score but to hear Elisabeth Söderström in the title role matched with Eva Randová as the Kostelnička.

Another complete *Jenůfa* is an 'off-the-air' recording of a live performance at the Vienna State Opera in October 1972. The balance is awry – orchestra in the foreground and voices far back on stage – but this is worth enduring for the sake of Sena Jurinac's ardent and lyrical Jenůfa and the fearsome splendour of Astrid Varnay's Kostelnička, which she once sang unforgettably at Covent Garden (the audience on the first night applauded throughout the interval after her big scene, but she steadfastly refused a curtain). The conductor is Janos Kulka and in the small roles of Jano, the cowhand Jenůfa teaches to read, and the Mayor's wife are, respectively, the youthful Edita Gruberova and the elderly Hilde Konetzni. The Števa and Laca are Jean Cox and William Cochran, acceptable repertory performances. The opera is sung in a revision of Max Brod's German translation.

Among solo excerpts from *Jenůfa*, two are of outstanding historical interest. Gabriela Horvátová, the Kostelnička in the first Prague production on 26 May 1916, recorded the Act 2 aria with piano accompaniment. It was first issued on Czech Radio Records RJ 152 and was transferred to LP, as part of a collection of historic performances by Czech singers, on Supraphon DV 6205. The singing is impressive and spontaneous, the voice a higher soprano than we are accustomed to hear in the role and strong in dramatic declamation. The 1921 recording (Parlo. P 1799; RLS 743) by Zinaida Yuryevskaya of Jenůfa's prayer in Act 2 (in German) is supremely beautiful, with a superbly played violin solo (could it be Rosé?). This singing, so controlled in its technique, so abandoned in its emotional range from terror to religious devotion, encourages the assertion that Yurievskaya must have been the Jenůfa of one's dreams. Domanínská, more moving and less wobbly than in the 1969 complete set, sings this same aria on a disc of excerpts from *Jenůfa*, *The Makropulos Affair* and *The Cunning Little Vixen* issued on Supraphon LPV 450. Milan Sachs conducts the Prague National Theatre Orchestra. With it is a shrill but powerful account of the Kostelnička's Act 2 aria by Marie Steinerová with Jílek conducting the Brno Janáček Opera Orchestra.

FATE (OSUD)

If *Jenůfa*, a village tragedy, is potent illustration of my belief that Janáček was the only composer who, had he known the book, could have made a convincing opera, worthy of the subject, from Hardy's *Tess of the d'Urbervilles*, it is reinforced by *Fate*. The power of *Jenůfa* lies in its claustrophobic evocation of a closed, narrow society dominated by almost incestuous relationships and by the strict interpretation of religious belief – a society familiar to Hardy in Wessex and still not extinct in remote parts of Britain even today. Yet when Janáček moved into the middle-class milieu of the spa town (based on Luhačovic) in which Act 1 of *Fate* is set, he again reminds the English listener of those scenes in Hardy novels where the characters' tragic dilemmas are played out against a background of Victorian Bournemouth or Weymouth. *Fate* was written between 1903 and 1907 but was not staged until 1958 and then in rearrangements which Janáček would have repudiated. It still awaits a British production. So it is the least-known of the mature operas and is often left out of consideration.

Gramophone listeners have no excuse, for the only recording, made by Supraphon in 1975–6, is outstandingly good and the conductor, Jílek, follows Janáček's original order of scenes and is faithful to the musical text. The result is incontrovertible proof of the music's greatness and of the viability of the opera dramatically. The plot, like *Jenůfa*, concerns lovers with an illegitimate child and a mother who goes mad, but the special interest is that the hero is an opera composer and Janáček is concerned to show the relationship between art and life in the stage-composer's unfinished opera – a subject which would have appealed strongly to Hofmannsthal and Strauss. It is Janáček's most full-bloodedly romantic opera; there are fascinating echoes of *Jenůfa* and anticipations of both *The Cunning Little Vixen* and *From the House of the Dead* (the latter coming to mind especially in the noble writing for male chorus in Act 2 of *Fate*). Janáček's evocation, by means of a bandstand waltz tune, of the spa, his depiction of the actual process of composing, and his final scene set at the rehearsal of an opera are splendid theatre. As he was to do again in *Káťa Kabanová*, he conveys the flavour of a provincial town with a musical sociologist's sureness of touch.

Jílek is obviously a devout believer in the genius of this score. He inspires the Brno company to a blazing performance, with impeccable orchestral playing and choral singing. Among the lesser roles, the baritone Jaroslav Souček is a strong Verva (the conductor) and Jarmila Palivcová, an impressive mezzo, sings the heroine Míla's mother. Míla herself is lyrically sung by Magdaléna Hajóssyová, proving herself a true Janáček soprano in her long and taxing Act 1 monologue. But the set is memorable above all for Přibyl's singing of the role of Živný. He infallibly suggests the romantic artist *par excellence* in a performance full of subtle nuances which rises to the heights in the Act 3 monologue in which, Wotan-like, he retells the events of Acts 1 and 2 and brings the opera to its climax.

The Act 1 arias of Živný and Míla are sung by the lyrical and cultured tenor Jaroslav Ulrych and by Domanínská, again in good voice, on a ten-inch Supraphon (SUF 20011) with the Brno Radio Symphony Orchestra conducted by Břetislav Bakala. These are drawn out more romantically than by Jílek.

THE EXCURSIONS OF MR BROUČEK

Janáček began Part I, *Mr Brouček's Excursion to the Moon*, in 1908. In fact he began it several times, as one librettist after another failed to provide what he wanted. Finally he wrote most of the text himself and, in 1912, put the uncompleted music in a drawer, discouraged by the abandonment of a production of *Fate* and by Prague's continued rejection of *Jenůfa*. But in 1916, after the long-delayed Prague triumph of *Jenůfa*, he found new hope and energy, completed the *Moon* episode and added a second part, *Mr Brouček's Excursion into the 15th Century*. The opera was completed in 1917 and staged in Prague in 1920. Its first British performance was in London in 1978, conducted by Mackerras. Some books on Janáček have described *Brouček* as a failure or, at the least, unsatisfactory. That will not have been the opinion formed by those who saw the English National Opera production at the London Coliseum and certainly not by those who possess the Supraphon recording by the Prague National Theatre company under Václav Neumann. The more one hears this unusual, original and courageous work, the more it slips into place as a necessary and important stage in Janáček's development. It is really two operas in one and is not properly described as a 'comic' opera. Fantastic and satirical, with comic moments, would be nearer the mark. It is based on two satirical novels by Svatopluk Čech (1846–1908) with, as central character, a hero – or anti–hero – called Matěj Brouček, a Prague property-owner, drinker, trencherman and philistine. In one book he dreams he visits the moon. The people he meets there represent Čech's satire both on the petit-bourgeois element's attitude to art and artists and on the bogus, ingrowing, effete aestheticism of some ivory-tower artists. In the second book Brouček encounters the rigidly nationalist Hussites of the fifteenth century. Janáček's uncanny ability to change mood almost from bar to bar and yet to impose a stylistic and organic unity on his composition is evident throughout *Brouček*. The love duet, the moonlight episodes in the streets of Prague, the extraordinary music depicting the flight to the moon – these, in Part 1, are Janáček highlights. In Part 2 it is impossible to be unaware of the composer's ambitions and fears for the new state of Czechoslovakia (the opera is dedicated to Thomas Masaryk, the first president) – all tragically ironic today. The patriotic fervour of the fifteenth-century excursion strikes the most overtly nationalist note in all the operas.

The recorded Prague performance (1962) is a splendid example of the merit of these Supraphon sets – even if there is no absolutely first-class or world-class singing (with one exception), there is throughout a sense of teamwork, of the cast thoroughly knowing, understanding and loving the music and its composer, and of having played the piece on the stage, which is compensation for the lack of specifically virtuoso or exceptional vocal virtues. Not that these performances fall below a pretty high standard. Bohumír Vích is a memorable Brouček, for example, arousing sympathy or affectionate mockery by the skilful use of tone-colour in his rich, mellow tenor voice. Other Prague stalwarts, some of them playing several roles (or rather the same role in different incarnations), include Domanínská, Ivo Žídek, and Helena Tattermuschová with her childlike high soprano. There is an unforgettably vivid piece of singing by Blachut as the apparition of Čech himself, singing in Part 2 a great hymn to Czech independence. At this point in the score, the composer of *Taras Bulba* and the *Glagolitic Mass* steps in front of his music, as it were, to direct our gaze to the plight of his homeland, a plea which is doubly moving because we know – as, thank goodness, he did not know – about 1938, 1948 and 1968.

A recording on Supraphon (SUF 20011) of the final scene of the Moon episode by the Brno Janáček Opera under Jílek with Ulrych, Domanínská and Josef Kejř, among others, is altogether sharper and more humorous in its pointing of the satire and magically poetic in the love-duet at the end. If you play the Neumann performance of this scene and then the Jílek, you will hear exemplified the difference between the smoother, more comfortably romantic Prague style of performing Janáček, deriving from Václav Talich, the conductor who applied cosmetic touches to the scores, and the Brno style, which keeps more strictly to Janáček's original scores.

Supraphon's stereo recording of the complete opera, made in the summer of 1980, was issued in Britain in 1982. The conductor is Jílek, with the Czech Philharmonic Orchestra and Chorus. With the extra spaciousness afforded by stereo, the most thrilling feature of this issue is the expressive orchestral playing and the fervent choral singing. Jílek's interpretation brings home more forcefully than Neumann's the poetry and power of this opera and its crucial place within Janáček's output. The music's backward glances to the lyricism of *Jenůfa* are evident enough, but Jílek stresses the anticipations of the works still to come. Most obvious of these is the foretaste at the end of Part 1 of the wonderful love duet which closes the second act of *Káťa Kabanová*, but there are hints too of *The Cunning Little Vixen* and even of *The Makropulos Affair*.

The opera is generally well sung, but it would be misleading to conceal the prevalence of East European wobble in some of the lesser roles. Brouček is sung by Vilém Přibyl with all his characteristic intensity and with a vivid sense of the ridiculous. As Mazal and his other materializations, Miroslav Švejda is a much less versatile and reliable tenor, but Vladimír Krejčík (in seven roles) is superb. Richard Novák's baritone is a firm asset, as is the singing of the soprano Jana Jonášová as the three heroines (contemporary lunar and fifteenth century). René Tuček sings the Čech aria, but there can be no comparison here with Blachut's noble 1962 performance. The set as a whole is better than the sum of its parts. This comes about, I am sure, because Jílek believes in the magic of the music and he conveys this belief to the listener with irresistible appeal.

KÁŤA KABANOVÁ

This opera, composed from 1919 to 1921, comes nearest to *Jenůfa* as a 'conventional' subject – the plot, briefly, concerns a young married woman, Káťa, imaginative and gentle, married to a weak merchant, Tichon, who is under the thumb of his monstrous bully of a mother (Kabanicha). While Tichon is away on business, Káťa, helped by her unmarried sister-in-law Varvara, has nightly meetings with Boris, a kindred spirit. On Tichon's return, Káťa's conscience gives way during a storm and she publicly admits her adultery. Boris is banished and Káťa drowns herself in the Volga. Janáček, a Russophile and admirer of Russian literature, wrote his own libretto as an adaptation of Ostrovsky's play *The Storm* (*Groza* in Russian, which also means 'terror', highly significant in this context). In 1907 he had pondered an opera based on Tolstoy's *Anna Karenina* (among operatic might-have-beens, this is surely in the same class as Verdi's *King Lear*), and *Káťa* shows us how completely he could be absorbed by an author so that he projects in music not only the characters but the social atmosphere of the original. The music of *Káťa* flows relentlessly and logically from the prelude, in which several of the opera's themes, or the germs of them, are first heard. One melodic cell merges into the next. Any lingering idea that Janáček was a kind of hit-and-miss primitive is dispelled by this wonderfully wrought score. Yet in 1951 Ernest Newman informed his readers that Janáček was 'rather a scrap-by-scrap composer, finding it difficult to think consecutively for more than two or three minutes at a time'. Difficult, forsooth!

Many will have a warm regard for the 1959 Supraphon set. Through this Prague National Theatre performance under Jaroslav Krombholc many came to know that *Káťa Kabanová* was a masterpiece of tragic opera, fiercely beautiful and truthful. The singing of the heroine by Drahomíra Tikalová is often touching and always sympathetic, but at full stretch her tone loses body. As the Kabanicha, another of Janáček's formidable matriarchs but with none of the redeeming features of the Kostelnička in *Jenůfa*, Ludmila Komancová is surprisingly lightweight. Varvara, a mezzo role, is sung by Ivana Mixová who sounds appropriately young and carefree – the relative freedom enjoyed by unmarried girls compared with their locked-away role in marriage was noted in the Russian provinces by Ostrovsky. With the exception of Kudrjáš, Varvara's boyfriend, all the men in *Káťa* are in varying degrees despicable or negligible. Even Boris is an equivocal kind of 'hero'. As Kudrjáš, a lyric-tenor role, Viktor Kočí sings the folk-song in Act 2 with unforced naturalness. The Boris is Beno Blachut, finding a poetry in all his phrases which makes up for a certain lack of ardour in his love scene with Káťa.

But that set is completely superseded by the first of the Mackerras-Vienna Philharmonic recordings, made for Decca in December 1976. Whereas Krombholc stuck to the touched-up Talich edition, Mackerras uses his own edition, which gets as close as is humanly possible to what Janáček intended.

The result is a vivid and strong interpretation which is no less beautiful than the Talich. Indeed, so superbly do the Vienna Philharmonic strings play, and so faithfully are they recorded, that, paradoxically, there are moments when the Mackerras version sounds almost more consciously beautiful than the impure versions he seeks to replace. His conducting of the work is of an intensity that springs only from impassioned and utter conviction – he is clearly the inspirer of the whole enterprise. There should be no surprise that the Vienna Philharmonic sound so much at home in this music – the Vienna Janáček tradition began with *Jenůfa* in 1918 and has been maintained.

The only non-Czech in the Decca cast is the singer of Káťa, the Swedish soprano Elisabeth Söderström. Hers is one of the most distinguished operatic performances on record, infallibly conveying every emotional inflection of Káťa's plight by means of rare vocal artistry, high notes perfectly placed, phrases coloured with delicacy and subtlety. Her long aria in Act 1, when she tells Varvara of her youthful upbringing and her religious feelings and then confesses to the carnal desires which are overwhelming her, is a *tour de force*, its eroticism almost palpable. Equally, her last aria, when her mind has given way and she hears 'voices' (wordless chorus) is heart-rending in its poignancy. She is opposed – it is the right word – by a powerful and hateful Kabanicha, sung by Naděžda Kniplová with whiplash sarcasm and spite. Her hard tone may not be pleasing, but it is right and it is superbly and accurately controlled. Petr Dvorský's Boris is more ardent and youthful than Blachut's; Krejčík is the wretched Tichon and the younger lovers, sung by Zdeněk Švehla and Libuše Márová, are well matched, the mezzo weightier in tone than in the Supraphon set. The thunder effects in the storm are overdone, but one can be ungrudgingly grateful to the microphone for enabling Janáček's use of the viola d'amore at several points in the score to be realized – in the theatre it is usually replaced by a viola because its sound is too weak. Mackerras also includes two short entr'actes composed to cover scene-changes for a production in Prague in January 1928 and used only rarely since then. These occur after Act 1, scene i and after Act 2, scene i. The latter, a march, is obviously related to the opera on which Janáček was working at the time, *From the House of the Dead*.

THE CUNNING LITTLE VIXEN

Janáček's ability to fashion the least likely material into a viable stage work is demonstrated again in *The Cunning Little Vixen* as this opera (1921–3) is known in English, though *Adventures of the Vixen Bystrouška* would be nearer the mark. Mixing the world of animals and humans, insects and birds, is a notoriously difficult procedure, full of sentimental pitfalls, and successes in staging this opera have varied considerably. But these considerations do not trouble the gramophone listener, who is free to supply mental pictures to match the poetry of the score. The opera is virtually plotless, comprising a cinematic succession of scenes based on a novelette by Rudolf Těsnohlídek.

The symbolic relationship of the Vixen and the Forester is the 'plot', as such. It is Janáček's most nostalgic opera, filled with the sounds of nature (is there a more evocative orchestral picture of a summer night?) and imbued with raw eroticism, yet with an element of political satire that is a reminder of the Europe of the 1920s. Echoes of *Káťa Kabanová* and pre-echoes of *From the House of the Dead* soon become evident as one comes to know the music intimately. So does the intricate structure of the score, its close dovetailing of themes and rhythms into a flowing narrative giving unity to the short and almost fragmentary scenes. The wordless chorus, used so eerily in *Káťa*, here symbolizes the voice of nature, a pagan timeless hymn to the life-force.

Supraphon first recorded *The Cunning Little Vixen* in 1957 in mono and remade it in 1971 in stereo, both in Prague National Theatre performances. The earlier set should be sought out by admirers of this composer because it is one of those recordings in which the true spirit of the music is captured, in this case a spirit which can prove tantalizingly elusive. The Vixen is sung almost to perfection by Hana Böhmová. She is roguishly rather than stridently women's-libbish as she leads the foolish hens up the farmyard path to their fate at her teeth, demurely but not coyly passionate in her love scenes with the Fox, sung (as Janáček wished) by a soprano, Libuše Domanínská, rather than by the tenor often used in stage productions. Rudolf Asmus, a warm, rich, characterful baritone, is well cast as the Forester, excellent in his good-humoured banter with the Parson, the Schoolmaster and the Pedlar and powerfully moving in his final apostrophe to the joys of young love and to the changing seasons, one of the most ecstatic arias in all Janáček. Much credit is due to the conducting of Václav Neumann and to the Prague orchestra's wonderful playing of a score in which the lengthy instrumental episodes are of prime significance.

The later set has the virtue of being better recorded, but Bohumil Gregor seems so worried that sentimentality might creep in that he gives the music less room to make its points, driving the singers so that none of them, with the exception of Jan Hlavsa's Schoolmaster, really fills out each character as their predecessors did. Helena Tattermuschová is a harsh-voiced Vixen, rarely suggesting the feminine allure which attracts the Forester so that she attains a womanly status for him even though he kills her. Nor is Zdeněk Kroupa in his best voice as the Forester. The part lies high for him and the strain often shows, though he is always sensitive to the text and the musico-verbal rhythms. He gives a much more convincing and better sung performance of the final scene in the extract on Supraphon LPV 450, with the Brno Janáček Opera Orchestra conducted by Bohumír Liška.

In 1982 two further complete recordings were issued, a reflection of the growing popularity of this opera. There is still room for a version in English. Decca's issue, in digital sound, is the fourth of the Mackerras-Vienna Philharmonic series and was recorded in March 1981. It presents the most accurate version of the score, so far as that can be ascertained. From the very first pages, it is clear that Mackerras sees the work in anything but a sentimental or winsome light – the repeated chattering figure on the strings is almost aggressive in its sharply edged contours. So it continues throughout the opera – note the fierce and deliberate opening to Act 3 – with many examples of Janáček's inspired orchestration being illuminated by a combination of brilliant conducting and playing with superb recording – as an instance there is the flash of trumpet-tone in Act 2 as the Vixen cries 'Tyrane'. The richness and lustrous tone of the Vienna strings and the rounded sonority of the brass ensure that no suggestion of coldness or austerity creeps into Mackerras's interpretation. Paradoxically, his tendency towards severity makes the music even more touching and poetic, so clearly is it presented. The prelude to Act 2, with its foreshadowing of the *Sinfonietta* and the *Glagolitic Mass*, is a marvellous example of the high quality of this set.

But the third Supraphon set, recorded in Prague between December 1979 and June 1980 in stereo, is a very strong contender for the title of first choice. Václav Neumann's interpretation has deepened in a quarter of a century, losing nothing in subtle insights and gaining in authority and precision. The Czech Philharmonic is marginally less polished than the Vienna, but this is still highly distinguished playing. Some will prefer Neumann's slower and more sensuous treatment of the off-stage wordless voices, though Mackerras's voices are magically more distant. Supraphon's recording tends to favour the solo voices better than Decca's. When it comes to individual performances, much will depend on personal preference. Both casts are principally Czech; the Supraphon singers sound more like a theatre ensemble while Decca's are individuals assembled for the occasion, but too much should not be made of this. Mackerras's Vixen is Lucia Popp, full of lively charm and especially impressive in the more dramatic passages, but her performance as a whole is less fully characterized, less vixenish, than Supraphon's Magdaléna Hajóssyová, who is as close a rival as could be wished to Böhmová and has the benefit of better recording. Popp's voice is richer and fuller, nearer in tone-colour to her Fox, Eva Randová, and their courtship tends to sound like that of two Straussian mezzos. Hajóssyová's Fox is none other than Gabriela Beňačková, whose voice is no less rich and vibrant but higher than Randová's. Hajóssyová's final amorous submission is more touching than Popp's. Supraphon boasts the stronger Forester (or Gamekeeper) in Richard Novák. Good as Decca's Dalibor Jedlička is, he sounds under pressure in the upper reaches of his voice and this detracts from the full effect of the wonderful final aria. Neither singer can match Asmus at any point. Decca's Harašta, Václav Zítek, on the other hand, is superior to Supraphon's Jaroslav Souček on every count. In both sets there are beautiful, closely observed and memorably sung performances of the scene in the inn in Act 3, the music shadowed with regret but nothing overstated, nothing sentimentalized. There are few more poignant musical expressions of the onset of age than the Forester's description of how his dog no longer presses him to go for a walk. In both sets, too, the fox cubs are entrancingly sprightly and amusing.

Fortunate the opera that attracts two such irresistible performances as these. Decca's album-notes maintain the high level of scholarship which has distinguished the Mackerras issues. John Tyrrell's long essay on the opera is the best study of it yet written, and there is the additional advantage of the reproductions of Staníslav Lolek's strip-cartoons of the Vixen's adventures which accompanied the newspaper tale by Rudolf Těsnohlídek that was the basis of Janáček's libretto. Deryk Viney has provided a spunky new translation although, as John Warrack pointed out in *Gramophone*, it is incorrect to render Terynka as Theresa.

THE MAKROPULOS AFFAIR (VĚC MAKROPULOS)

Karel Čapek's comedy about a woman who lives for 337 years (1585–1922) through having taken a magical elixir becomes a tragedy in Janáček's hands. In yet another triumph of making an opera (composed 1923–5) out of the most unlikely material – a scene in a lawyer's office, for instance – Janáček's libretto caters for his special musical needs with a sure touch. In the central character of a woman who has dried up emotionally after centuries of love and decides that she cannot bear to continue her existence even though the opera begins with her ruthless attempts to gain possession of the secret formula, he perceived that he could create the greatest of his female roles by combining the gentle, betrayed natures of Jenůfa and Káťa with the harsher personalities of the Kostelnička and the Kabanicha. Whereas Čapek was interested in the subject of longevity, Janáček was intrigued by the human dilemma. Čapek's heroine does not die at the end; Janáček's does (although the stage direction does not specifically say so). When one remembers that *Káťa*, the *Vixen* and *Makropulos* were written one after the other without a break, it is tempting to regard them as one huge operatic-symphonic trilogy. Play them through successively, and you will hear how Janáček's style develops and changes to suit the special demands of each work, yet how the musical personality behind each work remains constant in its search for truth and depth. For *Makropulos* the style becomes epigrammatic, the orchestration is harsher (brilliant trumpet writing), the chorus is used only marginally. There are no instrumental entr'actes, no conventional arias or duets. Yet to assert that the score lacks lyricism is to show oneself impervious to the stream of small thematic motifs which coalesce into an unbroken orchestral fabric of melody. It is thus that Janáček makes Act 1, where legal detail is the substance of the plot, into a *tour de force* of composition by overcoming obstacles most writers of opera would regard as insuperable.

Equally impressive is his exploitation of his fascinating opera-singer heroine, born Elina Makropulos and concealing her longevity by changing her name but not her initials – Ekaterina Myshkin, Else Müller, Elian MacGregor, Eugenia Montez, and finally Emilia Marty. The interpreter of this part must encompass the emotional range of prima donna, spoilt child, vindictive bitch, tender romantic and, at the end, must convey longing for spiritual redemption. British audiences will long remember the late Marie Collier's superb assumption of this demanding role in the Sadler's Wells Opera production first staged in 1964. The conductor then was Charles Mackerras, and he is the conductor of Decca's sumptuous recording made, as the second of the series, in Vienna in 1978 with Elisabeth Söderström getting as close to the heart and soul of Emilia as she did to Káťa's. For most of the opera Emilia's part comprises no more than one short line of dialogue at a time, but it gradually builds to the final act, which is virtually a *scena* for her alone. To have established so vivid a portrayal of this multi-faceted character on record, without the striking visual presentation possible in the theatre, is proof enough of Söderström's artistry. Her singing is vibrantly beautiful and impassioned from start to finish.

Nor is there a weakness in the supporting cast. Petr Dvorský's impulsive Gregor is a more mature performance than his Boris and a more thankful part anyway; Václav Zítek is a formidable Prus; Dalibor Jedlička sings the lawyer Kolenatý with a perception rivalled by Vladimír Krejčík as his clerk Vítek; and Anna Czaková and Zdeněk Švehla as the doomed young lovers Kristina and Janek are ideal. There is also a touching portrayal by the veteran Blachut of Hauk-Šendorf, Emilia's lover when she was Eugenia Montez in Spain. The music in which they recapture momentarily their old feelings for one another is among the most colourful and poignant in the opera and is only one place among many where the playing of the Vienna Philharmonic under Mackerras's inspired baton makes the listener gasp in astonishment at its power, passion and precision.

The 1967 Prague National Theatre set, brilliantly and comprehensively conducted by Bohumil Gregor, is the best of the Supraphon stereo series of Janáček operas. The Decca set is only marginally to be preferred because Mackerras goes closer to the original score and because the Vienna Philharmonic's playing is so magnificent. But it is arguable that Gregor's interpretation is nearer to the ambiguous spirit of the opera in its realization of its tragi-comic elements. His extra abrasiveness, which does not exclude lyricism and tenderness, is particularly telling in Act 2, which comes over as especially powerful. (I do not agree that this opera is flawed by a weak libretto. Indeed, the libretto seems to me to be admirably constructed.)

The singers' individual performances are on a high level, particularly the Marty of Libuše Prylová. She is not as lustrously beautiful a singer as Söderström, for at the top of her register she has a Slavonic soprano shrillness, but the larger (and older)-than-life personality of the heroine is conveyed with the same vivid, occasionally vulgar, often strident and always compelling magnetism which was the hallmark of Collier's performance. (Both these singers, Collier and Prylová, call to mind, by their interpretations, that Edith Evans expressed interest in playing this part in the play.) Prylová also conveys the tenderness and seductiveness where Janáček gives them prominence, and her final scene is both thrilling and terrifying – a splendid performance, even if it lacks Söderström's exposure of Emilia's vulnerability. The frantic, sinister side to Albert Gregor is well brought out by Ivo Žídek, and Přemysl Kočí's

Prus has a menacing authority. Milan Karpíšek is more decrepit but no less poignant than Blachut as Hauk-Šendorf and the roles of the Charwoman and Machinist (Slávka Procházková and Jiří Joran) are more fully characterized than in the Decca recording. The Kristina is Helena Tattermuschová, whose voice is an acquired taste.

Three extracts, one from each act, were recorded by Supraphon on SUA 10340. The interest here is Blachut's Gregor, a characteristically intense portrayal as far as one can tell from the Act 1 extract, which is from Gregor's cry of 'Konečně!' ('At last!') to the end of the act. I am not much impressed by Zdeňka Hrnčiřová's Emilia Marty, imperious but very wobbly. The Act 2 extract is the short scene mainly between Kristina and Janek, mellifluously sung by Milada Musilová and Rudolf Vonásek, from Kristina's 'Janku, pojd'sem' ('Come along, Janek') to Janek's cry of 'Tata!' ('Father!') when Emilia and Prus (Teodor Šrubař) enter. The third extract runs from Emilia's final entry at 'Cítila jsem že smrt na mne sáhala' ('Now I am sure death laid a hand on me') to the end. Vogel conducts the Brno Janáček Theatre Orchestra. This recording was a brave and precious venture in the 1950s but the later performances have diminished its value except for the preservation of a fragment of Blachut's Gregor.

FROM THE HOUSE OF THE DEAD

Janáček's last, and perhaps his greatest, opera was written in 1927–8. He completed it in July 1928, a month before he died at the age of seventy-four. Of all his strange choices of subject this is the most eccentric. It has less plot than *The Cunning Little Vixen*, it has no central character, and with the exception of a boy sung by a soprano and a few lines for a prostitute, there are no female voices. It is as if Emilia Marty had summed up and exhausted all he had to say in music about the character of woman (and of one particular woman, Mrs Stoesslová). The libretto, again by Janáček himself, is a skilful compilation and elision of extracts from Dostoyevsky's *Memoirs from the House of the Dead*, a novel based on the Russian writer's experiences of a Siberian prison-camp from 1850 to 1854. In each of the three acts a different captive sings a long narrative about the events which brought him to prison – we don't even know if they are telling the truth. In the second act the prisoners enact some theatricals. No character is developed; their relationships are haphazard. But, as those who have seen the opera will testify, it is a gripping theatrical experience, and the essentially dramatic nature of the music comes over strongly in a recording. Of all Janáček's scores, this is at once the most 'progressive' and the most characteristic.

The 1980 Mackerras-Vienna digital recording for Decca is unrivalled not only in the realism of its sound and the high quality of the singing, playing and conducting but in its fidelity to Janáček. The autograph score is a nightmare, for Janáček drew his own staves on small, oblong pieces of paper, adding extra staves when he brought in other instruments. So sparse and sketchy (not to mention illegible) did this appear that it misled two of Janáček's pupils, Bakala and Chlubna, to think it was unfinished. For the first performance at Brno in 1930 they prepared a version in which the scoring was thickened and romanticized and a new ending added. This version was later published and became standard. In the early 1960s, however, Kubelik began the process of reclaiming Janáček's original ideas. Mackerras, for his recording, not only used a score based by John Tyrrell on Janáček's original but also incorporated the many changes and additions the composer made to his copyist's final score. Thus innumerable points of orchestral detail, in its essentially chamber-music textures, are played by the Vienna Philharmonic for the first time as Janáček intended them to sound. (The interested listener is referred to Dr Tyrrell's marvellous notes which accompany this recording; he did the same service for Decca's *Káťa, Vixen* and *Makropulos*.) The libretto had also been altered for the Brno performance and this too is restored to its original form. The result, to those who already know the Supraphon set, is comparable to seeing a well-loved painting after cleaning – we always knew it was a masterpiece, now we can see even more clearly, through all kinds of fresh detail, just why. Nothing is more conclusive proof of Janáček's towering stature than the success of this opera. It has everything against it. It is grim, dissonant and disconnected. Yet it uplifts the spirit and gladdens the heart. Why? Because it incorporates, in a culminating display of virtuoso composing, the operatic skills learned in a lifetime by one man, as *Falstaff* did in Verdi's case and *Capriccio* in Strauss's; and because it is music not only of genius but of unrelenting intensity in its tribute to the unconquerability of the human spirit. 'I feel so excited,' he wrote while composing it, 'that my blood wants to gush out.' That excitement is behind every note. Also, thanks to Mackerras and the Vienna Philharmonic, the sheer beauty of the score is here revealed.

I need add little about the Decca set except to praise the uniformly splendid singing of the cast, led by Jiří Zahradníček as Luka, Ivo Žídek as Skuratov, Václav Zítek as Šiškov and Zdeněk Souček and Zdeněk Švehla in other roles, with Blachut as the Old Prisoner (very touching how Mackerras has retained this link with a great Janáček tradition through the use of this valiant veteran), who also sings the Innkeeper in *The Cunning Little Vixen*.

The 1964 Supraphon set, conducted by Gregor, purged some of the 1930 accretions to the score and restored the original ending, but compared with Decca it is not an *Ur*-text. One has only to hear the Prelude in the Prague set, with its harps still not edited out, and then to play the Vienna performance, to understand what Tyrrell and Mackerras have achieved, not least in showing how close to its origin as a violin concerto this music remained. (The solo violin has an important part in the score of several of the operas and clearly suggested operatic images to Janáček.) The Supraphon set is worth its place in any collection, however, for several memorable individual performances by singers. Splendid as is the tense performance by Zahradníček of Luka's Act 1 narration for Decca, it does not efface the even more moving and haunted singing of Blachut on Supraphon, a terrifyingly vivid interpretation. It is hard, too, to choose between Šiškov's Act 3 narration as sung by the lighter, reined-in but infinitely varied baritone of Přemysl Kočí for Supraphon and the deeper, firm and no less intense performance by Václav Zítek under Mackerras (who provides a much more dramatic and poetic accompaniment).

There was an earlier complete mono *From the House of the Dead*, a brave issue in its day, from Philips. This, sung in German, was a recording of a live performance given at the Holland Festival on 25 June 1954 by the Netherlands Opera under Alexander Krannhals. This is, of course, the 'old', spurious version and its historical value now is that it uses the 'optimistic' Bakala-Chlubna ending in which the prisoners' cries of 'Freedom' as they let their eagle fly away are combined with another of the work's main themes. (The flight of birds is another pervasive Janáček image, as in Káťa's Act 1 aria.) It also has the boy Aljeja sung by a mature-sounding tenor instead of the soprano Janáček specified, thereby destroying the planned contrasts of tenderness and innocence. Nevertheless, the spirit of the work comes over and there is a good Šiškov in Caspar Broecheler. It is incontrovertible, however, that where this of all the operas is concerned there is no alternative to the historic Mackerras performance which, for the first time, and forty years after the composer's death, put all this amazing work's cards on the table and finally established the case for Janáček to be regarded as the outstanding humanitarian composer of the twentieth century.

JENŮFA

L Laca; *S* Števa; *Jen* Jenůfa; *KB* Kostelnička Buryja; *M* Mayor; *J* Jano; *OM* Old Man

1952   Blachut *L*; Žídek *S*; Jelínková *Jen*; Krásová *KB*; Jedenáctik *M*; Subrtová *J*; Kalaš *OM*/Prague National Theatre Chorus and Orch./Vogel
Supraphon ⓜ SUA 10243–5
Artia (US) ⓜ ALP 080C/L

1969   Přibyl *L*; Žídek *S*; Domanínská *Jen*; Kniplová *KB*; Kroupa *M*; Tattermuschová *J*; Jindrák OM/ Prague National Theatre Chorus and Orch./Gregor
EMI 1C 165 01992–3
Angel SBL 3756

1977–8 Přibyl *L*; Krejčík *S*; Beňačková *Jen*; Kniplová *KB*; Halír *M*; Janská *J*; Berman *OM*/Brno Janáček Opera Chorus and Orch./Jílek
Supraphon SUP 2751–2

1982   Ochman *L*; Dvorský *S*; Söderström *Jen*; Randová *KB*; Zítek *M*; Jonášová *J*/Vienna State Opera Chorus, VPO/ Mackerras
Decca D267D3 ④ K267K33
London LDR 73009

KÁŤA KABANOVÁ

D Dikoj; BG Boris Grigorjevič; MK Marfa Kabanová (Kabanicha); T Tichon;
KK Káťa Kabanová; VK Váňa Kudrjáš; V Varvara; K Kuligin; G Glaša; F Fekluša

1959	Kroupa D; Blachut BG; Komancová MK; Vích T; Tikalová KK; Kočí VK; Mixová V; Jedlička K; Hlobilová G; Lemariová F/Prague National Theatre Chorus and Orch./ Krombholc Supraphon 50781–2	Márová V; Souček K; Pavlová G; Jahn F/Vienna State Opera Chorus, Vienna PO/Mackerras Decca D 51D2 ④ K51K22 London OSA 12116 ④ OSA 5–12116
1976	Jedlička D; Dvorský BG; Kniplová MK; Krejčík T; Söderström KK; Švehla VK;	c.1948 (excerpts) Šíma D; Válka BG; Zachardová KK; Pelc VK; Spurná V/Chorus, Brno Radio SO/Bakala Ultraphon H 24215–7

THE MAKROPULOS AFFAIR (VĚC MAKROPULOS)

EM Emilia Marty; AG Albert Gregor; V Vítek; K Kristina K; JP Jaroslav Prus;
J Janek; Kol Kolenatý

1967	Prylová EM; Žídek AG; Vonásek V; Tattermuschová K; P. Kočí JP; V. Kočí J; Berman Kol/Prague National Theatre Opera Chorus and Orch./Gregor Supraphon 50811–2 · CBS (US) B 2 C 167	Mackerras Decca D144D2 ④ K144K22 London OSA 12116 ④ OSA 5–12116
1978	Söderström EM; Dvorský AG; Krejčík V; Czaková K; Zítek JP; Švehla J; Jedlička Kol/Vienna State Opera Chorus, Vienna PO/	1950s (excerpts) Hrnčiřová EM; Blachut AG; Musilová K; Šrubař JP; Vonásek J; Asmus Kol/ Prague National Theatre Chorus and Orch./Vogel Supraphon ⓜ SUA 10340

THE ADVENTURES OF MR BROUČEK

B Brouček; M Mazal; TS The Sexton; Mál Málinka; W Würfl

1962	Vích B; Žídek M; Kočí TS; Domanínská Mál; Berman W/ Prague Smetana Theatre Chorus, Prague National Theatre Orch./Neumann Supraphon 50531–3	1980 Přibyl B; Švejda M; Maršík TS; Jonášová Mal; Novák W/Czech Philharmonic Chorus and Orch./ Jílek Supraphon 1116 3291–3

THE CUNNING LITTLE VIXEN

F Forester; HW His Wife; B Bystrouška; TS The Schoolmaster; TP The Parson;
Fox

1957	Asmus F; Belanová HW; Böhmová B; Votava TS; Halír TP; Domanínská Fox/Kühn	Children's Chorus, Prague National Theatre Chorus and Orch./Neumann

Supraphon ⓜ 10343–4
Artia (US) ©️ ALS 508
1971–2 Kroupa F; Procházková HW;
Tattermuschová B; Hlavsa TS;
Jedlička TP; Zikmundová Fox/
Prague National Theatre Chorus
and Orch./Gregor
Supraphon 112 1181–2
1981　Jedlička F; Zikmundová HW;
Krejčík TS; Novák TP; Popp B;
Randová Fox /Vienna State

Opera Chorus, Vienna PO/
Mackerras
Decca D257D2 ④ K257K22
London LDR 72010
1979–80 Novák F; Buldrová HW;
Frydlewicz TS; Prusa TP;
Hajóssyová B; Beňačková Fox/
Kühn Children's Chorus,
Czech PO/Neumann
Supraphon 1116 3471–2
Pro Arte (US) 2 PAL 2012

FATE (OSUD)

DS Doctor Suda; M Míla; Z Živný

1975–6 Krejčík DS; Hajóssyová M;
Přibyl Z/Brno State Theatre

Opera Chorus and Orch./Jílek
Supraphon SUP 2011–2

FROM THE HOUSE OF THE DEAD

G Gorjančikov; A Aljeja; FM Filka Morozov (Luka); S Šiškov; Sk Skuratov;
T Tchekunov; C Commandant

1954　(in German: live performance –
Holland Festival) Jongsma G;
Scheffer A; Van Mantgem FM;
Broecheler S; Wozniak Sk;
Genemans T; Holthaus C/
Netherlands Opera Chorus and
Orch./Krannhals
Philips ⓜ ABL 3119–20
Epic ⓜ SC 6005
1964　Bednář G; Tattermuschová A;
Blachut FM; Kočí S; Žídek Sk;
Heriban T; Horáček C/Prague
National Theatre Chorus and
Orch./Gregor
Supraphon 50705–6
CBS (US) 32 21 0006
1979　Novák G; Jirglová A; Přibyl
FM; Souček S; Žídek Sk;Jindrák

T; Horáček C/Czech
Philharmonic Chorus and Orch./
Neumann
Supraphon 1116 2941–2
1980　Jedličká G; Janská A;
Zahradníček FM; Zítek S; Žídek
Sk; Souček T; Švorc C/Vienna
State Opera Chorus, Vienna PO/
Mackerras
Decca D224D2 ④ K224K22
c.1960 (excerpts) Steinerová A; Plačar
FM; Bauer S; Ulrych Sk;
Mikulica T; Halír C/Brno
Janáček National Chorus and
Orch. Brno State PO/Bakala and
Vogel
Supraphon ⓜ SUA 10095

THE BEGINNING OF A ROMANCE (POČÁTEK ROMÁNU)

1970s　Hladík Jurasek; Janská Poluška;
Krejčík Tonek; Caban Mudroch;

Přibyl Adolph/Chorus and
Orch./Jílek
Voce ⓜ 54

The Operas of Stravinsky

DAVID MURRAY

There are composers, and there are opera-composers; everybody recognizes the distinction, though whether anything follows from it is hotly disputed. Haydn, Beethoven, Berlioz, Debussy, Ravel and Schoenberg were composers who happened to write the odd opera; Donizetti, Bellini, Wagner, Bizet, Verdi and Puccini were opera-composers who wrote some other pieces as well. Handel, Mozart and Berg straddled the notional line so confidently that it would be Procrustean to fix them to one side or the other. Janáček is more vexatious: the expressive inflections of the human voice inform all his music, but not always to an essentially dramatic purpose. Stravinsky is harder still: theatre-music and potential theatre-music loom large in his *oeuvre* – but which are the operas?

It is not that Stravinsky's theatrical vein was balletic as against operatic; the vocal components of even *Les Noces* and *Perséphone* are genuinely operatic (unlike, say, the choral contributions to Ravel's *Daphnis* and Florent Schmitt's *Tragédie de Salomé*). The trouble is rather that every Stravinsky theatre-piece was conceived as a spectacle enacted in a certain manner, and when he assigned a dramatic role to voices it was within a deliberate aesthetic *cadre* – specifically visual – that denied them the self-sufficient expressive force of nineteenth-century opera. From *The Nightingale* to *The Flood* (conceived as a television piece, and thus especially difficult to place) Stravinsky wrote a sort of vocal choreography; the executive virtues proper to it are matters of style, address, attack – nuances of 'feeling' and word-colour are generally beside the point, for the dramatic effects are generated from the calculated theatrical plan. Even *The Rake's Progress*, Stravinsky's nearest approach to standard opera, goes badly awry if heartfelt singing has to compensate for subfusc playing and a naïve production: the dramatic events seem too long and too short, under-prepared and under-represented in the music. And the key to the visual style of the one-act *opera buffa, Mavra* (1921), has never yet been discovered – Stravinsky wrote of its failed première that 'the real trouble was that the singers were unable to execute Mlle Nijinska's choreographic ideas'.

THE NIGHTINGALE

If we set *Mavra* and *The Flood* aside with respectful apologies, there are arguably three Stravinsky 'operas' on record. (Let us pretend that though *Renard, Les Noces* and *Perséphone*, to Gide's text, are certainly sung, they are primarily *danced* – they match respectively the voiceless *Soldier's Tale, Rite of Spring* and *Orpheus*; and let us not queer the pitch by remarking how closely related *Oedipus Rex* is to the *Symphonie des Psaumes*.) The earliest is *The Nightingale* (1907–14), formally a miniature Rimsky-Korsakov opera, but with the edges of the numbers blurred. Stravinsky and his old school friend Stepan Mitusov drew their libretto from Hans Christian Andersen's 'The Emperor's Nightingale'. It is well known that its short first act was composed even before *Firebird*, and the rest after *The Rite*; in the opera house, however, the obvious discrepancy of musical style is never felt as a weakness, for Stravinsky turned it to brilliant theatrical advantage.

The opera, or opera-pantomime, has been twice recorded: by André Cluytens in Calvocoressi's French translation, very sympathetically, and more recently by the composer with an American cast singing in Russian. (There have been many more recordings of the symphonic poem Stravinsky made from the opera in 1917, *Le chant du rossignol*, but it singularly fails to convey the effect of the opera.) They place the score in different lights. The French recording brings out the melting *fin de siècle* side of the music – Scriabin springs to the ear early in Act 2 (compare his op. 24 *Rêverie*); in Stravinsky's stereophonic recording, sharper and brighter, one hears Debussy's *Nuages* more candidly in the prelude, and the *Firebird* echoes when the stricken Emperor is menaced by the spectres of Act 3. The experimental mock-*chinoiserie* is more vividly realized by the composer.

Janine Micheau is a more womanly, vulnerable Nightingale than Stravinsky's Reri Grist, but Grist's authentic coloratura – a floated, seductive sound without depth – marvellously suggests an alien being. So does the eerily white tenor of Loren Driscoll as the Fisherman whose verses frame the chapters of the tale, where the tender and intimate tone of Jean Giraudeau indicates some mysterious involvement in the action. There is little to choose between the excellent Emperors, Donald Gramm and Lucien Lovano, or Elaine Bonazzi and Christiane Gayraud in the brief role of Death (who is bought off by the Nightingale); Marina Picassi and Geneviève Moizan both make much of the Cook. Either recording will serve as a persuasive reminder that *The Nightingale* belongs in the live repertory – genuine stage magic is too rare to let slip.

OEDIPUS REX

The 'opera-oratorio' *Oedipus Rex* works almost infallibly, granted a production that does not introduce more movement than the music envisages. Though it was first given in 1927 in concert form, Stravinsky intended it for the stage; the alienation-effect of its vernacular narrator in evening dress – the main text is in Latin, Jean Cocteau translated by Jean Daniélou – belongs to the dramatic plan. Cocteau's own flamboyance in his French narration can be treasured in the composer's first recording, but the dramatic point is really the contrast between direct explanation and ritual enactment in a dead language. In Stravinsky's second recording, John Westbrook reproduces Cocteau's slightly preening delivery; in the other versions the narrators – Sir Ralph Richardson, Alec McCowen and the American Michael Wager in English, Paul Pasquier and Jean Desailly in French – find their own voices. Leonard Bernstein's Wager cannot bring himself, understandably, to copy the school Latin of his singing colleagues: he says 'trivium' defiantly where they sing 'treeweeum' and 'serwa', and 'Wa-lay'. Stravinsky cannot have intended that (and probably never dreamt that anyone might do it: the vocal score sedulously replaces cs by ks to pre-empt Latinist speculations, but does not expressly rule out the school w); it is rhythmically limp as well as distracting. No other recording repeats the mistake.

Bernstein's performance is none the less among the strongest, though it suffers – like Ernest Ansermet's – from another small aberration: a deadly tempo for the great opening and closing chorus. At Stravinsky's marked speed, it sounds at once implacable and lithe; a few metronome points less and it becomes ponderous (in Stravinsky's second recording, in fact, he lets the later recurrences of the music run a notch faster). A heavily awestricken chorus cannot plausibly frame solo dramatic music as quick and elegant as that of *Oedipus* – it makes the arias seem dandyish. But Bernstein aims at full-blooded operatic effect, and has the right cast to achieve it: René Kollo a young, fiery Oedipus (impressively accurate), Tatiana Troyanos a svelte Jocasta full of grand forebodings – their fast duet is a virtuoso display – and Tom Krause as a splendidly forceful Creon. All this passion is a little superfluous, but while it lasts it is exciting. There are numerous deliberate 'operatic' devices in *Oedipus*, very much in inverted commas, and Bernstein plays them for full face value.

Ansermet is more discreet, less convinced. His refined Oedipus (Ernst Häfliger) and placid, efficient Jocasta (Hélène Bouvier) are flurried in the duet. James Loomis is a lightweight Creon and a dull Messenger – this version is one of the few to make the suggested doubling, which has only the negative point of presenting the characters as impersonal masks; the Messenger's tremendous report of the final catastrophe is here multiply sung, apparently because Ansermet read the Narrator's trailer – the chorus will help the Messenger when his speech fails – quite literally. That is a mistake, and in the end there is too much haphazard ensemble between Ansermet's chorus and orchestra to sound inevitable.

The Czech performance under Karel Ančerl is again operatically impassioned, with a strong Creon and a strikingly beautiful bass voice for Tiresias – though he takes his aria well above the prescribed tempo (as does Stravinsky's Chester Watson in his later recording). Ančerl's tempi are otherwise more faithful than Bernstein's, and his powerful Jocasta – Věra Soukupová – has the advantage over Troyanos in ripe maturity, something which the plot makes hard to ignore. At the centre of this excellent account of the work is a curate's egg, Ivo Žídek's Oedipus: youthful and even frail, he is by turns oddly detached from the action – his last aria is strangely mild – and acutely sensitive. His unsupported upper register is sometimes immediately affecting, sometimes just unheroic. The whole performance has a distinctive grip.

Colin Davis's Oedipus, Ronald Dowd, is variable too. Too generalized at the start and too bland about the discovery at 'Nonne monstrum', he is brilliantly suave with 'Invidia fortunam' (one of the best 'operatic' strokes of the piece). He has a sound Jocasta in Patricia Johnson, hobbled to a stolid one-two-one-two in her aria. Raimund Herincx makes an urgent Creon and a lachrymose Messenger; his climactic narration, like Benjamin Luxon's for Solti, is slightly foxed by a repeated B flat that edges toward B. Harold Blackburn's Tiresias is hard-hitting, and vague about phrase shapes. The chorus is alert but intermittently rough. Despite Davis's explosive dramatic sense – he regularly ignores Stravinsky's rhetorical comma-breaths – the performance is inclined to trundle.

At the time of writing, Solti's 1976 recording is the most recent in the catalogue. The Oedipus of Sir Peter Pears is a lesson in interpretation, but decidedly too fragile to convey the full impact of the role; Kerstin Meyer's veteran expertise as Jocasta has its executive limits too. These insightful sketches are uncomfortably juxtaposed with robust supporting voices – Donald McIntyre's blustering Creon (curiously ineffectual with the pronouncements of 'Thebis peremptor latet'), Stafford Dean's suggestively fraught Tiresias, a superb Messenger by Luxon (until his final narration). The sharp, reedy sound of the score is played down: the relentless triplets of the opening are melted into a sinuous throbbing, for example, while every potentially lyrical phrase is hauled up into the foreground. The result is febrile in the East European manner; the tough Slav roots of Stravinsky's choral style are obscured, and the constructive pastiche of the solo writing glossed as Art without irony. I do less than justice to Solti's virtues, probably, but heard next to the composer's recordings his performance sounds remarkably alien.

Both of Stravinsky's versions are indispensable. If the Oedipus Pears did with Solti offers still more discerning subtleties, the Oedipus he sang twenty-five years earlier with Stravinsky has the heroic gleam of voice that the music expects. The rest of the cast was solidly distinguished, with Heinz Rehfuss's authority lent to Creon and the Messenger, and a grand tragedy-queen from Martha Mödl. The performance has a monumental tread, which is not to say that any of it is or seems slow; these singers bring their experience in a ripe tradition to bear on the music. That throws Cocteau's insistently modern rhetoric into relief.

In respects mentioned earlier, Stravinsky's 1962 *Oedipus Rex* is slightly more adventurous and free, with a drier, brighter sound. The cast is American and younger, all just beginning their distinguished careers (which this recording enhanced). Not only are the principal voices clean-edged and vividly stylish, but they seem to take their style strictly from Stravinsky's writing: when the music makes a point of invoking statutory operatic devices, it is not underlined by traditional histrionics. The performance has, however, been brilliantly cast by timbre and temperament, with George Shirley's impassioned, fearful Oedipus matched with a magisterial Creon by Donald Gramm and Shirley Verrett's fiercely elegant Jocasta. Though John Reardon finds less in the role of the Messenger than Solti's Luxon, he rings out securely in the final narration, where the powers of a *Lohengrin* Herald are needed. It is a little unnatural to speak of this recording as a 'version', for it renders the work quite transparent; if in doing so it nudges it toward opera and away from oratorio, that has the force here of a fresh insight. We may recall that Stravinsky originally intended his chorus to be invisible. An oratorio is in its own way a staged event, and that was not the sort of event he envisaged: comparisons of *Oedipus Rex* with Handel's dramatic oratorios were always misplaced.

THE RAKE'S PROGRESS

Few representations of *Oedipus* satisfied Stravinsky (and certainly not those which pursued post-Nietzschean notions of how ancient tragedy must have looked). His 'melodrama' *Perséphone* of 1934, for the dancer-mime Ida Rubinstein and her company, casts an operatic shadow. Despite its speaking heroine, its detached solo tenor (with chorus) and its choreographic formality, and Stravinsky's refusal to let Gide include any diversionary episodes, we recognize it as a words-and-music drama: the dance is decorative illustration, as it was not in the *Apollo* of six years earlier. In fact *Perséphone* is a species of elevated masque (but *sui generis*), impersonally gentle where *Oedipus* had been impersonally grim. It becomes clearer that the 'monumentality' of *Oedipus* did not strive after massive mythic power, but rather the aspect of the personages on Keats's Grecian urn, timelessly captured at expressively elegant moments. Moments of action, not – generally – moments of feeling: Stravinsky's quasi-operas make small room for the 'aria of feeling' which dominates in Classical and much later opera. Where eighteenth-century composers raided the classics for dramatic occasions of sentiment, Stravinsky attends to what his legendary figures *do*, be it ever so symbolical. A Stravinsky aria typically represents a contained stance, not an affecting posture: hence the athletic poise required of his singers. But *Perséphone* evaded the operatic challenge by grace of the terms of the commission, and it was not until 1947 that the composer discerned a clear operatic opening at the Chicago Art Institute, where he saw Hogarth's cycle *A Rake's Progress*.

The stages of the decline of Hogarth's anti-hero are shown in stop-frame, fatal steps snapped with one foot in the air, betraying gestures frozen. It was just what Stravinsky needed – cartoon archetypes for characters, picturesque action without continuous development, no psychology. A librettist was needed to fill in the details, and on advice an invitation was successfully extended to Auden (who accepted it a second time on behalf of his friend Chester Kallman). The librettists' exact appreciation of their task is shown by their main new invention – the bearded lady Baba, a creature of gesture above all. *The Rake's Progress* was premièred in Venice on 11 September 1951, with a notable cast; though they made no studio recording, the first-night performance was broadcast and has now appeared as a recorded 'document'. It does not invite direct comparison with the more modern recordings, and will be discussed later.

Both of the modern recordings were conducted – like the première – by Stravinsky himself. The earlier one (1953) stemmed from the Metropolitan Opera production; Stravinsky came to England, bringing three American singers with him, to make the later one. Neither version, then, displays Auden's text in all-English accents (Hilde Gueden's Anne in the first version is Americo-Teutonic) – but of course the diction of the musical setting is purely Stravinskian, too cosmopolitan to need a national identity. When singers bend his prosody into colloquial lines, in fact, it does not gain but loses theatrical force. There is point and irony in its angularity. *The Rake* was precisely conceived as a number-opera; Stravinsky's music makes the dramatic function of each number clear, but specifically verbal effects are left to make their own points, not imitated in the vocal line.

In accuracy there is little to choose between the two recordings, and they reveal no interesting changes in the composer-conductor's opinions about how the music should go. The casting of Anne Trulove makes some difference: Stravinsky came to regret the close parallel between her and the Micäela of *Carmen*, and where Gueden was naïvely sweet and passive – often moving, though distressingly flat in the poignant falling thirds of her last aria (a Verdi reminiscence: cf. the *Otello* 'Salce, salce') – Judith Raskin cuts a cool, energetic figure. It is a dashing performance, slightly at odds with the action (for each of Anne's interventions is utterly ineffectual, except her accidental prompting of Tom in the climactic card game) but properly lithe in the music. The whole sound of the later recording, as with *Oedipus Rex* too, is more astringently vivid.

The Toms and the Nick Shadows are differently contrasted. Mack Harrell's bass-baritone Nick had a weight of menace denied to John Reardon's lighter voice, and in all respects a grander scale. (Would that Donald Gramm's impeccably baneful Nick had been ready for the second recording!) Reardon is livelier, and Stravinsky may have valued that. As for the feckless Tom, Eugene Conley's eager, combative youth makes at least as strong a dramatic centre as Alexander Young's subtler study – but it is evident everywhere why Stravinsky should have fixed upon Young as his ideal Tom. His lyrical line is delicately incised; there are passages in which he sounds reedy and abstracted (at the very outset, for example), but they are crisply juxtaposed with stretches of taut involvement (beginning with his first monologue). The operatic character is captured by strictly musical means – there is no independent suffering self. Young's faultless manners may even make him too unshakeably a gentleman for the ultimate catastrophe to seem pitiful enough. By Stravinsky's formal standards, that can hardly be a serious complaint.

Tom's role, like the rest of the opera, answers to two stylistic models, as much distinguished by operatic technique as the parts of *The Nightingale* are by harmonic flavour. For most of two acts, *The Rake's Progress* consists of accompanied arias and ensembles *à la* Gluck, number-opera pure and simple; but as the action grows darker, Stravinsky draws more and more upon Bach's cantatas as his model. (His flirtation with old English music, continued in the 'Cantata on old English Texts', is rather abruptly dropped in the *Rake* as the drama takes hold.) For the austere intensity of that manner, Young is a magnificent exponent, and luckily he has a Baba – Regina Sarfaty – who does not sabotage it by playing her just-preceding scenes too broadly. There is a large *Svensk Operaantologi*, on many records, in which can be found Baba's breakfast scene (an excerpt from a Swedish performance in Montreal), with Barbro Ericson grossly, expansively comic – more like most stage Babas than Stravinsky's own scrupulous performers: one wonders what her shrinking Tom, Ragnar Ulfung, can possibly have done to restore sobriety for Act 3.

Baba the Turk is less of a problem in *The Rake* than a substantial asset, all things considered, and the role is written *con amore*. Babas generally come in one or another of two kinds, corresponding to the favoured contralto-types: there are majestic, maternal Babas (including superannuated *monstres sacrés*), and seductive, volatile Babas. Jennie Tourel, the original Baba, captured both aspects. Blanche Thebom, in the Metropolitan cast, was of the first sort, kindly and dignified; Sarfaty is more the glamorous cosmopolite, able to make her exacerbated vocal line seem part of her circus *persona*, where with heavier Babas it is liable to seem a joke at the expense of the voice. In the unexpectedly moving duet with Anne, the Baba-types naturally sound either consoling mother-figures or worldly elder sisters; perhaps the psychological difference has no further significance. It is amusing to discover how much of Baba's music parodies Creon's music in *Oedipus*, whereas she echoes Jocasta not at all.

Tourel's ripe creation for the first production is one of several reasons for treasuring the recently released 'document', despite its variety of small first-night mishaps and the patchy reproduction. Accidents aside, there was nothing provisional or tentative about that performance except the La Scala chorus's comical English (evidently learned from someone who aspired to the refinement of postwar BBC-ese). Otakar Kraus's relentless Shadow rivals Harrell's, and Robert Rounseville lends a heroic ring to Tom – less subtle than Young, but vital and effective. The orchestra of La Scala plays bravely and creditably; the important harpsichord part is assigned, sadly, to a piano. No audience-noise intrudes, though there is applause – sometimes bemused – after each scene.

Above all there is the Anne of Elisabeth Schwarzkopf. She never took up the role again, but she had prepared it superbly, to the point where she can be heard to guide the ensembles firmly through passing uncertainties. She relishes the neat rhythmic displacements that stud the vocal line, and she brings the character to strong, vulnerable life. Anne's Act 1 *scena* is decisively shaped and paced (though her final C defeats the microphones), and her Bedlam lullaby lovely; in the duet with Baba, her 'He loves me still!' is radiantly amazed – as if such a thing were beyond her expected deserts – and thus heart-wrenching.

One would expect the *scena*, at least, to appear on record separately from time to time. Only the Swedish soprano Margareta Hallin (singing in English, Swedish EMI 4E 061 34616) seems to have done it; in some respects she is more at ease with the high-flying music than either of Stravinsky's later Annes, lighter and more secure.

It is characteristic of *The Rake's Progress* that despite its number-shape, scarcely any other excerpt proposes itself; the great moments are locked into the action, and involve two or three people at once. (Or more: the surefire Auction scene goes well on all the recordings.) Besides, what this opera shows off legitimately and best is virtuosity of line – and that is not, these days, a specially prized virtue.

LE ROSSIGNOL

R Le Rossignol; *C* La Cuisinière C; *P* Le Pêcheur; *E* L'Empereur; *Ch* Le Chambellan; *B* Le Bonze; *M* La Mort

1955 Micheau *R*; Moizan *C*; Giraudeau *P*; Lovano *E*; Roux *Ch*; Cottret *B*; Gayraud *M*/French National Radio Chorus and Orch./Cluytens
Columbia ⓜ 33CX1437
Angel ⓜ 35204

1961 (in Russian) Grist *R*; Picassi *C*;

Driscoll *P*; K. Smith *Ch*; Gramm *E*; Beattie *B*; Bonazzi *M*/ Washington Opera Society Chorus and Orch./Stravinsky
CBS (US) KS 6327
(UK) 72041

OEDIPUS REX

O Oedipus; *J* Jocasta; *C* Creon; *T* Tiresias; *S* Speaker; *Sh* Shepherd; *M* Messenger

1951 (narration in French) Pears *O*; Mödl *J*; Rehfuss *C*; *M*; Von Rohr *T*; Cocteau *S*; Krebs *Sh*/Cologne Radio Chorus and SO/Stravinsky
CBS (UK) ⓜ 61131
(US) ⓜ Y33789

1954 (narration in French) Häfliger *O*; Bouvier *J*; Loomis *C*, *M*; Vessières *T*; Pasquier *S*; Cuénod *Sh*/Brassus Chorale, Suisse Romande Orch./Ansermet

Decca ⓜ LXT 5098
London ⓜ A 4106

1955 (narration in German) Häfliger *O*; Töpper *J*; Engen *C*; *M*; Sardi *T*; Deutsch *S*; Kuen *Sh*/Berlin RIAS Chamber Choir, Berlin Radio SO/ Fricsay
DG ⓜ 2535 723

1962 (narration in English) Dowd *O*; Johnson *J*; Herincx *C*; *M*; Blackburn *T*; Richardson *S*;

Remedios *Sh*/Sadler's Wells Opera
Chorus, RPO/C. Davis
HMV ASD 518
Angel S35778
1962 (narration in English) Shirley *O*;
Verrett *J*; Gramm *C*; Watson *T*;
Westbrook *S*; Driscoll *Sh*;
Reardon *M*/Washington Opera
Society Chorus and Orch./
Stravinsky
CBS (UK) 72131
(US) M 31129
1966 (narration in French) Žídek *O*;
Soukupová *J*; Berman *C*; Haken
T; Desailly *S*; Zlesák *Sh*; Kroupa
M/Czech Philharmonic Chorus and

Orch./Ančerl
Supraphon 50678
Turnabout (US) TV 34179S
1975 (narration in English) Kollo *O*;
Troyanos *J*; Krause *C*; Flagello *T*;
Wager *S*; Hoffmeister *Sh*; Evitts
M/Harvard Glee Club, Boston
SO/Bernstein
CBS (UK) 76380
(US) M4X–33032
1976 (narration in English) Pears *O*;
Meyer *J*; McIntyre *C*; Dean *T*;
McCowen *S*; Davies *Sh*; Luxon *M*/
Alldis Choir, London PO/Solti
Decca SET 616 ④ KCET 616
London OSA 1168 ④ OSA 5–1168

THE RAKE'S PROGRESS

T Trulove; *A* Anne; *Tom* Tom Rakewell; *N* Nick Shadow; *S* Sellem the
Auctioneer; *B* Baba the Turk

1951 (live performance – Teatro La
Fenice, Venice) Schwarzkopf *A*;
Rounseville *Tom*; O. Kraus *N*;
Tourel *B*; Arié *T*; Cuénod *S*/
Teatro La Fenice Chorus and
Orch./Stravinsky
Cetra/Documents ⑩ DOC 29
1953 Scott *T*; Gueden *A*; Conley *Tom*;
Harrell *N*; Franke *S*; Thebom *B*/
Metropolitan Opera Chorus and
Orch./Stravinsky
Philips ⑩ ABL 3055–7
CBS (US) ⑩ SL 125

1964 Garrard *T*; Raskin *A*; Young
Tom; Reardon *N*; K. Miller *S*;
Sarfaty *B*/Sadler's Wells Opera
Chorus, RPO/Stravinsky
CBS (UK) 77304
(US) M3S–710
1967 (Act 2 Scene iii in Swedish: live
performance – Salle Wilfred
Pelletier, Montreal) Ulfung *Tom*;
Ericson *B*/Royal Opera House
Orch., Stockholm/Varviso
EMI 7C 153 35350–8

The Operas of Schoenberg

PETER STADLEN

Expressionist opera marks one of the rare points in history when the arts reached corresponding stages in their development. This is so, provided one accepts that Schoenberg's arrival at an atonal as well as non-thematic style derived not only from a need he felt to progress beyond Wagnerian and Straussian harmony but, as he himself believed, from a concern – short-lived and period bound – with psychological contents more extreme and violent than could be conveyed by traditional means. During this phase his music not only showed a close affinity with the expressionism of the visual arts, as instanced by the sacrifice of realism for the sake of extreme emotion in, say, Munch's *Der Schrei* and, in due course, by the non-representational style of Kandinsky (though this, like Schoenberg's atonality, was before long to serve very different artistic aims).

ERWARTUNG

Schoenberg's early free atonality found a perfect counterpart in the text of *Erwartung*, a monodram written for him by Marie Pappenheim not long after the young medical student had moved from her native Pressburg (Bratislava) to Vienna in 1908. Later in life Marie recalled how Schoenberg had asked her to do an operatic libretto for him, which she declined. Instead she offered to write a monodram and proceeded to complete it within three weeks, not having disclosed to him the topic which had been entirely her own idea.

A solitary 'Woman', having waited all night in vain for her lover, sets out to look for him. During her wanderings through a dark forest, terrifying hallucinations alternate with wistful yearning until, horrified, she discovers his body. She is overcome by nostalgic memories and tormented by jealousy, suspecting 'that white-armed whore and witch . . . over there at that house' to have caused the murder. Dawn breaks . . .

It has remained a matter for speculation whether the monologue is intended to represent a realistic account of the woman's thoughts and feelings during her search. Schoenberg himself tentatively suggested, some twenty years later, that the piece 'can be understood as a nightmare' and, on another occasion, that 'the aim is to represent in slow motion everything that occurs during a single second of maximum excitement, stretching it out to occupy half-an-hour'.

Here it seems relevant that, as I have recently established, not only was Marie a second cousin of Berta Pappenheim, the 'Anna O' whose treatment for hysteria, under hypnosis, by Dr Josef Breuer in Vienna marked the starting point of psychoanalysis and whose case history was published under that celebrated pseudonym jointly by Breuer and Sigmund Freud in 1895. Marie's Vienna-based son and daughter-in-law, Professor and Mrs Frischauf, told me the other day that their mother had been well aware of being related to Berta who had become a prominent feminist in Germany and continued to visit both Vienna and Pressburg. Moreover, Marie and her elder brother Martin, a psychiatrist, had been moving in psychoanalytical circles at the time of *Erwartung*; they can safely be assumed to have known the identity of the famous 'Anna O'.

To convey the unique ambiguity of the monologue, suspended between reality and hallucination, is a prime prerequisite of the soprano soloist in this first and quite possibly last psychoanalytical opera. Of the two singers who were the first to record this masterpiece of free atonality, Dorothy Dow collaborated with Dmitri Mitropoulos and the New York Philharmonic in 1952. The distinctly personal timbre of this singer's small, attractive voice benefits the brief lyrical moments of the part; but an element of *bel canto*, which is felt from the very beginning and never quite abandoned, tends to restrict the part within too conventional limits. Again, this approach precludes a careful observance of the more than a hundred instructions found in the vocal part of Schoenberg's score. These go well beyond frequent differentiations between *piano* and fourfold *pianissimo*, and demand a constant change of sharply contrasted and often violent moods – tempestuous, tender, distressed, dreamy, horrified, yielding, demented with fear. . . . Too often these vital fluctuations of expressive content are sacrificed in the misguided search for a primarily melodic significance of the vocal line, a wrong priority that also operates against creating the essential impression that the heroine is haunted by ever-changing, terrifying vistas of the forest.

Hermann Scherchen and the Hamburg Radio Orchestra are Helga Pilarczyk's partners on her first recording of the work, made in 1960, after she had given the first post-war stage performance in Hamburg in 1954. In 1962 she recorded *Erwartung* again, this time with Robert Craft and the Washington Opera Society Orchestra. What needs to be stressed first of all is the identical conception behind this singer's performances, with differences hardly ever amounting to more than the minor detail of emphasis, such as is bound to happen from one occasion to the next. This implies that the view of the role is the singer's own and owes little if anything to her very different conductors.

Curiously, while one instantly recognizes a voice of more heroic format than the lyric soprano of Dorothy Dow, this coincides with a much wider range both of volume, and, particularly important here, of expressive nuance.

Thus not only is the scream at the discovery of her lover's body truly shattering (even more so on the Wergo record) and the subsequent contrast between the lyrical *piano* of a momentarily confused 'the moonlight' but the aghast *pianissimo* 'here, the dreadful head' is also immensely gripping. The seamless transition, in mid-sentence, from a loud 'the moon radiates' to the whispered 'terror' is a proper feat of virtuosity, particularly effective on CBS. Even within the same range of decibels, the swift change of mood between the attempt to control fear: 'Don't be silly, it's a shadow' and tender memories thus evoked: 'Oh, how your shadow lingers on the white wall' testifies to the singer's affinity with the work's technique of free association. Above all, she responds instinctively to Schoenberg's conception of 'the Woman' as a singing actress as well as an acting singer: the whispered 'Is there someone?' repeated with increased anxiety. 'Is there someone?' is composed to reflect the contours of a spoken question – though not, to be sure, in the manner of Schoenberg's *Sprechgesang* that was to pose such problems in due course. Rather does it remind one of Janáček shaping a vocal line to resemble the curve of the spoken Czech.

At one spot, towards the end, Pilarczyk lapses into speech on both re-cordings: 'O you will not wake again'. This is one of four instances where the singer gets some notes wrong in the same passage on both recordings, though in two of these cases a single wrong note on the Scherchen record corresponds to batches of respectively sixteen and seven wrong notes under Craft. In addition, there are another sixteen slips under Scherchen and forty-two under Craft, none of which coincide, and it is worth noting that while under Scherchen six passages are too high and ten too low (by up to three semitones) with Craft all the wrong notes, with one exception, are too low (by up to two semitones).

Of Dorothy Dow's fourteen instances of wrong notes, all are too high by one or two semitones; only one spot corresponds to a wrong note of Pilar-czyk's, though this one is not too high but a semitone too low. Strange that a further twenty years of respect for Schoenberg's art and of familiarity with his idiom should not have prevented the even more widespread inaccuracies of pitch in the solo parts of two recent recordings of *Erwartung* by Anja Silja and Janis Martin; they collaborate with such celebrated modernists as Christoph von Dohnányi who is in charge of the Vienna Philharmonic and, respectively, the even more awe-inspiring Pierre Boulez who conducts the BBC Symphony Orchestra.

Maybe the haphazard diversity of these mistakes implies that in the immensely complex textures of *Erwartung* the distance between the lines merely represents an optimum and that this music no longer consists of right notes but of best notes. How responsibility for such flaws is to be apportioned as between the reliability of a conductor's sense of absolute pitch (which Scherchen, I happen to know, did possess) and the economics of rerecording, opponents of atonality will have to argue out among themselves.

Wrong notes apart, neither 'Woman', in the two recent recordings, is ideally equipped to project the psychological crisis symbolized by that role, what with Silja re-creating the part in terms of grand opera and relying on victorious high notes, while Martin, with her pleasant lyrical voice of limited dimension, never really transcends the expressive niceties of lieder singing. Yet, in fact, the vocal line throughout this work amounts to an accompanied recitative, extended to encompass the entire drama; it represents a producer's – Schoenberg's – minutely pitched view as to how to express the meaning of the text from bar to bar, directly and without providing any autonomous musical meaning to run parallel to the words. Indeed, without the words the vocal line would lack all significance. There does exist, however, a polarity between the vocal line and the instrumental texture, whose non-thematic but expressive polyphony provides a unique, specific equivalent to the conceptual contents.

Considered from this strictly 'musical' point of view, Mitropoulos's version is again the least idiomatic. This performance is no more than reasonably competent and certainly no less subject to an occasional moment of stress than is Scherchen's on Wergo. Not surprisingly, given that Scherchen was a member of the Schoenbergian inner circle, his reading betrays a closer familiarity with the style and spirit of this music and it is also more accurate if only up to a point. The chief disadvantage is the impression of a flat surface of sound observed from an unvarying distance which, respectively, fails to do justice to the score's colouristic inventiveness and is unsuggestive of a harrowing search.

Both with Craft and with Boulez, one instantly feels enveloped by the nocturnal forest. Yet Boulez's recording is distinctly superior to Dohnányi's as well as to Craft's in clarity of texture and plasticity of detail – for instance during the obsessive *ostinato* when the scene changes and becomes a moonlit path, or take the very last bar with its chromatic tutti slides in either direction, four-fold *pianissimo* variously metered and suggesting extinction unless it be the end of a nightmare. To what extent such ethereal subtlety is due to the skill of the conductor and his players or to that of the recording engineers, I find it difficult to tell. Nonetheless, given Pilarczyk's uncannily dramatic re-living of the Woman's experience, her recording with Craft remains the most authentic.

MOSES UND ARON

In contrast to the dramatized neurosis of *Erwartung*, Schoenberg's *Moses und Aron* – his other major contribution to the operatic repertory – is that untypical phenomenon, a philosophical opera or, as he himself put it one month before his death in 1951, religious-philosophical. Born a Jew, he became a (non-opportunist) Protestant in 1898, at the age of twenty-four. In 1922 he referred to his text for the unfinished oratorio *Die Jakobsleiter* of 1917 as testifying to 'a religious faith without any organizational fetters'. But in the same year a personal confrontation with anti-semitism – increasingly virulent in Austria at that time – and rumours of his one-time fellow-expressionist Kandinsky having turned racialist – started him off on a politically orientated return to Judaism which he formally rejoined after his emigration in 1933. A spoken drama, *The Biblical Way*, preceded the libretto of *Moses und Aron* which he wrote in 1928. Two of its three acts were composed between 1930 and 1932; the work has remained a torso.

Proceeding from thoughts and incidents recorded in the Old Testament, Schoenberg's Moses goes beyond the Bible's injunction against the making of an image. His unprecedentedly austere conception of the deity as a transcendent God – 'omnipresent, omnipotent, unimaginable' – is defended against the distortion and corruption through Aron's utilitarian, anthropomorphic, transient notions. Miracles, decreed by the Lord himself in the Bible and worked by Aron in the opera, are castigated by Schoenberg's Moses as symbols of Aron's soliciting opportunism. Even divine punishment and reward are in the neo-Moses's opinion deemed incompatible with the majesty of a supreme being that must not be thought of as prompted into action by human behaviour.

If at the end of the second act the Children of Israel plump for Aron's de luxe God rather than for Moses's starkly abstract notion, this is attributed to Moses's lack of oratorical gifts. No doubt Schoenberg was prompted by the Bible's 'heavy tongue', yet here he fails to distinguish tidily between a message that cannot be communicated and a message that is understood but rejected: 'O word, thou word that I lack' Moses exclaims at the end of Act 2. In fact, Schoenberg's Moses is brilliantly articulate as he explains what he does, and particularly what he does not mean by God.

However, Schoenberg's belief in the role played by the biblical brothers' unequal endowment with oratorical charisma has given rise to the dramatically effective idea to symbolize the difference between Aron's eloquence and Moses's introvert philosophizing through the confrontation of song and speech-song. I have elsewhere discussed in some detail Schoenberg's gradual disillusionment with speech-song* – an idea he had taken over from Humperdinck's melodrama *Die Königskinder* – whereby an impression of speech is combined with the adherence to prescribed pitches as well as durations. I have traced his progress from an undoubting confidence in the validity of this novel mode of delivery at the time he composed *Pierrot Lunaire* in 1912 to some remarks made shortly before his death when, as his late brother-in-law Kolisch told me, he stressed the need to avoid the vocal pitches he had notated in *Pierrot* since, he said, they do not fit the music.

As can be shown, Schoenberg's dwindling confidence in the possibility of correctly conveying the pitches of these spoken notes was due to his reciters failing to do so precisely because they attempted to comply with his mistaken instructions. In speech, as distinct from song, he declared, the sound of a

---

* 'Schoenberg und der Sprechgesang', 1. Congress of the International Schoenberg Society, Vienna 1974, pp. 202–12. Cf. also 'Schoenberg's Speech-Song', Music and Letters, Oxford University Press, January 1981.

syllable starts off at a given pitch but instantly leaves it by rising or falling. Now it is true that in a spoken syllable the pitch does not remain stationary so that the ear must be content with registering a kind of average pitch – perfectly possible, as we know from the performance of priests, actors and auctioneers. If their declamations yet remain safely distinct from song, this is due to differing modes of voice production. As for the pitch impression created by a syllable in speech-song, it is not so that the initial frequency occupies a privileged position. By acting as if it did, the *Pierrot* reciters, anxious to conform with Schoenberg's instructions, came to engage in those grotesque *glissando* howls that disfigure the music and caused his haphazard renunciation of the notes he had actually composed.

By the time he wrote the fully-fledged twelve-tone opera *Moses and Aron*, his attitude to the pitches of speech-song parts had reached the height of confusion. At the very start of Moses's part, a footnote states that 'the differences in pitch are merely to characterize the declamation', and only a few bars later those members of the chorus engaged in speech-song (often heard simultaneously with their singing colleagues) are instructed to approximate the indicated pitches as closely as possible; in fact, this time the word used is 'Lagen', registers, a far less specific term. If here he adds the warning, in brackets: 'not to be sung!!!', the cautioning is elaborated at bar 752: 'Here, as everywhere else, please do not ever sing the speech-notes, they do not correspond to the rows'. On consideration, what this cryptic remark amounts to is not that the notated pitches should be disregarded or even avoided and replaced by others, since any improvised substitutes would be equally unlikely to conform to the system. This instruction can only mean that he regarded spoken pitches as less assertive than sung pitches. This is of course true, the more so the shorter the notes are, and a good thing too, since otherwise some choral sequences of common chords and other tonal formations would sound as wrong here as a wrong note does in *Aida*; they would thus render the opera unperformable. Yet on the other hand, one part of Schoenberg's split personality did mean the spoken music as he composed it; this is surely proved by his frequent recourse to imitative writing. Though again, it must be admitted that one of these leitmotifs – the people's anxious 'where is Moses?' – is sometimes to be whispered, a mode of utterance which really does exclude any perception of pitch. Yet again, why should he have written the notes of a few speech passages without heads, merely with stems of equal length, if he did not thereby mean to contrast them with the majority of spoken notes where the pitch is intended? Above all, to introduce Moses's intricately differentiated atonal speech-song part by invocations of God that consist of repeated Cs in words of respectively 3, 3, 4 and 6 syllables clearly amounts to a purposeful compositional act.

All the more remarkable, then, that on the four recordings of the opera not a single Moses should observe a feature that is so striking and so easily realized. On Hans Rosbaud's live recording of the first-ever concert performance in Hamburg, 1954 (with the North German Radio Chorus and Orchestra on CBS), Hans Herbert Fiedler intones 'Einziger' on D, 'ewiger' on E flat, and both 'allgegenwärtiger' and 'unsichtbarer' back on D; ('Unique one, eternal, omnipresent, invisible'). Günter Reich, with Pierre Boulez and the BBC Singers and Symphony Orchestra on CBS in 1974, renders the first two words on D, only to descend to C sharp and B. Hard to believe that the same artist, on his Philips recording of the same year, with Michael Gielen and the Austrian Radio Chorus and Orchestra, should start not *above* Schoenberg's C but a whole fourth lower, on G, and only rise by a semitone thereafter. Oddest of all, Werner Haseleu with Herbert Kegel and the Leipzig Radio Chorus and Orchestra on Eterna in 1979 abandons Schoenberg's monotone for a repeated descent from D flat to B, followed by semitonal oscillations. On all recordings the speakers do observe the telling rise at the first two syllables of the following 'und unvorstellbarer Gott' ('and unimaginable God'), though again not on the authentic levels, and with the largest discrepancy again found between the two Reich versions, while Fiedler is the only one correctly to move upwards for the very last of these syllables.

Yet even if one were to accept that Schoenberg's purpose was merely to indicate a rough outline, a contour of speech, one is faced throughout these recordings at best with approximations. Interestingly enough, there are no hard and fast rules about the distorting effect of a given deviation. In Moses's next phrase, 'Gott meiner Väter, Gott Abrahams, Isaaks and Jakobs, der Du ihre Gedanken in mir wiedererweckt hast' ('. . .who hast reawakened their thought in me'), Rosbaud's Fiedler and Gielen's Reich come closest to the intended shape, an impression that remains unaffected by Fiedler's 'I' in Isaak being way out too high. Under Boulez, Reich deviates substantially while Kegel's Haseleu starts off altogether differently. Yet all four observe the conceptually significant upward leap at 'wieder', just as they do much later when Moses angrily interrupts Aron with a mocking, exaggerated repeat of his brother's 'Darfst?' ('dare not?') – a steep ascent and, in the case of Reich under Boulez, within the correct limits of D and C sharp.

Even landmarks such as these are liable to be ignored by the speaking choruses, most strikingly so when the group of Old Men offer their last moments of life as a gift to the Golden Calf: the Rosbaud version is the only one to sport at least a modest token of what should be a rise of an octave-plus-a-third up to 'nehmt sie als Opfer' ('accept them as a sacrifice'), even if their 'nehmt' is a G minor chord, instead of the higher E minor. Rather significantly, one spot to be done correctly by everyone is Moses starting a phrase on the same B natural that had just concluded Aron's sung phrase.

If Schoenberg's inconsistent, ambiguous attitude in the matter of spoken pitches must be blamed for the amazing permissiveness prevailing among these specialist conductors, he went out of his way to ensure the right notes in the sung choruses. With regard to a group of six singers, representing the Voice from the Burning Bush, he demands each line to be doubled by a different, named instrument, though he does not write these security parts into his score. Yet with the full singing choruses, too, one can almost invariably detect a helpful doubling somewhere or other in the orchestral textures; consequently there remain few problems in this sphere.

But here, as in *Erwartung*, Schoenberg overestimated the marksmanship of his singing soloists. There prevails a striking difference in this respect between the Arons of Kegel's Reiner Goldberg and Gielen's Louis Devos on the one hand and, on the other, Rosbaud's Helmut Krebs and Boulez's Richard Cassilly. Taking scene ii, for instance, with its prolonged dialogue between the brothers, Goldberg's intonation is simply faultless and only one solitary blemish can be detected in Devos's rendering. This compares with Krebs's ten spots of one, two or three wrong notes and Cassilly's twelve, including one sequence of fourteen, and another of six wrong notes.

Presumably Schoenberg, who did not live to hear a performance of this work, would have been particularly distressed by these faults since they distort not only his thought but his system; no disrespect is intended if one none the less proceeds to consider other aspects.

The confrontation between abstract notion and anthropomorphic image of the Deity, as symbolized by the speaking of Moses and the singing of Aron, needs to be further emphasized by characteristics of voice and interpretation. For Moses, referred to in the cast list merely as a Speaker, Schoenberg demanded, in a footnote, a very low, resonant voice. In the case of the live Rosbaud recording, inadequate engineering is no doubt to blame if both Fiedler and his antagonist Krebs are so fatally relegated to the background and deprived of contrasted plasticity as to be virtually disqualified. Günter Reich certainly lives up to Schoenberg's specifications, sounding even darker on Gielen's recording than on Boulez's and not only because he happens to start off on lower notes. Here also his words come across more clearly – a point of fundamental importance. If his cultured style of declamation has a contemplative quality and suggests an actor in the part of Moses speaking about God, Kegel's Haseleu appears to be addressing God directly. With a voice that is mightier still and less artful, he brings to mind the horned Moses of Michelangelo. We may note in passing that none of these four speakers ever engages in *glissandi* such as can be so distressing in *Pierrot*, no doubt because in the operatic score Schoenberg did not repeat his misleading instructions, while presumably none of the artists bothered to look them up in the earlier work.

As for the Arons – other than the acoustically handicapped Krebs – Boulez's Cassilly overshoots the mark in conveying Aron's subservience to the people's every whim, assuming a hypocritical, almost Mime-like tone of voice in a performance that is in any case marred by frequent wobbles, in addition to the so-often faulty intonation. Gielen's Devos belongs to a different class vocally and musically, but it is Goldberg who brings out even more fully Aron's seductive charm through the beauty of his tenor and the loveliness of phrasing that is not above a sly touch of humour in '. . . not expect of children what's hard for grown-ups'.

Of the minor parts, Rosbaud has a particularly strong Ephraimite in Hermann Rieth, while Felicity Palmer, in Boulez's version, is the nicest Young Girl. In the important role of the Priest, Werner Mann and Leonard Mroz are both good value on the recordings of respectively Gielen and Kegel. If Kegel rather than Gielen finally wins the day it is because the orchestral textures – unexpectedly wanting in clarity under Boulez – are even more lucid than with Gielen, and the playing more brilliant and sharply defined, particularly during that show-piece, the 'Dance round the Golden Calf' which on this issue is, moreover, preceded by offstage noises, remarkably suggestive of a rebellious mob.

DIE GLUCKLICHE HAND

Die Glückliche Hand ('The blessed Hand'), a 'Drama with Music', lasting twenty-three minutes, was composed between 1910 and 1913, respectively one year after *Erwartung* and *Pierrot*. But Schoenberg had started writing his own libretto in October 1908, at a time when his first marriage passed through a crisis which, I suggest, widens the autobiographical significance of the parable. For not only does The Man – the solitary baritone soloist – symbolize the creative artist who, with his bare hands, transforms a piece of gold into a jewelled diadem; he is betrayed by The Woman who deserts him for The Gentleman, both of them mimed parts. This lends a double meaning to the comments of a quasi-Greek Chorus, six men and six women who alternately speak, whisper and sing as they advise him to renounce his worldly ambitions for the sake of his art.

Two decades again separate the recordings by Craft, with the Columbia Symphony Orchestra and Chorus and by Boulez, with the BBC Symphony Orchestra and Chorus, the only extant versions. Chiefly no doubt because the solo part is shorter as well as less complex than in *Erwartung*, Craft's Robert Oliver and Boulez's Siegmund Nimsgern both remain loyal to the printed page, as well as to the dramatic sense, though Nimsgern commands that extra bit of vocal allure. The sung choruses are on the whole correct in both cases, but when it comes to notated speech or indeed whispering, both conductors aim at the prescribed pitches though with varying success. It is odd to find that with Boulez, of all people, the penultimate speech-song phrase of the chorus's Prologue – 'Und kannst nicht bestehn' – where men and women proceed chromatically in open octaves, the first four syllables sound merely somewhat indistinct yet the final one is not the prescribed E but clearly an E flat, presumably on account of the E flat that occurs here in the first double-bass. To cite just one pendant in Craft's performance, his choral Epilogue starts with the unison male speech-song – 'musstest Du's wieder' – too high by as much as four and even five semitones.

Otherwise he presents a truthful account, except for the puzzling omission of the taunting bursts of laughter by an offstage crowd. But it is Boulez whose lucidly articulate reading makes one experience the full impact of a work which, along with *Erwartung* and *Pierrot*, completes the trilogy of masterpieces from Schoenberg's free atonal period. Except that we are still, of course, waiting for a videotape version of *Die Glückliche Hand*, since that will re-create Schoenberg's minutely detailed scheme of coloured lighting that is synchronized in score with the musical events.

VON HEUTE AUF MORGEN

Von Heute auf Morgen was composed in 1928 to a libretto by Schoenberg's second wife Gertrud, hiding behind the pseudonym Max Blonda. A one-act satire on fashionable trends in sex and, by implication, in art, it tells of a happily married young husband who casts an eye on another girl until the wife retaliates by flirting with a tenor friend. Reconciled once again, the couple pour scorn on the spirit of a time where promiscuity is considered smart. 'Mummy,' asks the little girl as the curtain comes down, 'what does this mean: modern people?' The intended parallel is suggested by a letter where Schoenberg castigates changes of style 'from one day to the next, just for modernity's sake'. One is made to think of his *Satire*, op. 27, on the neo-classicism of 'the little Modernsky', if also of hopes that may have been raised in him by the recent global success of Krenek's *Johnny spielt auf*. Hard to believe that Schoenberg should have sent a copy of this strictly twelve-note operetta to his friend Franz Lehár. The recording by the Royal Philharmonic under Robert Craft, with Erika Schmidt, Derrik Olsen, Herbert Schachtschneider and Heather Harper (CBS 77223), whatever its merits, cannot gloss over the truth – Schoenberg was no Mozart when it came to a sense of humour.

ERWARTUNG

1952 Dow/New York PO/Mitropoulos
Philips ⓜ ABL 3393
CBS (US) ⓜ ML 4524
1960 Pilarczyk/North German RO/
Scherchen
Wergo WER 50001
Véga C35A175
1962 Pilarczyk/Washington Opera
Society Orch./Craft

CBS (UK) 72119–20
(US) M2S–679
1977 Martin/BBC SO
Boulez
CBS (UK) 79349
1980 Silja/Vienna PO/Dohnányi
Decca SXDL 7509 ④ KSXDC
7509

DIE GLUCKLICHE HAND

1961 Oliver/Columbia SO and Chorus/
Craft
CBS (UK) 72119–20
(US) M2S–679

1977 Nimsgern/BBC
Singers, BBC SO/
Boulez
CBS (UK) 79349

VON HEUTE AUF MORGEN

1964 E. Schmidt *Wife*; Olsen *Husband*;   CBS (US) M2S–780
Schachtschneider *Singer*; Harper   (UK) 77223
Friend/RPO/Craft

MOSES UND ARON

M Moses; *A* Aron; *YG* Young Girl; *YM* Young Man; *AM* Another Man;
E Ephraimite; *P* Priest

1954 (concert performance) Fiedler *M*;
Krebs *A*; Steingruber *YG*;
Kretschmar *YM*; Günter *AM*;
Rieth *P*; *E*/North German Radio
Chorus and Orch., Hamburg/
Rosbaud
CBS (Europe) ⓜ 78213
(US) ⓜ K3L241

1974 Reich *M*; Devos *A*; Csapo *YG*;
Lucas *YM*; Salter *AM*; Mann *P*;
Illavsky *E*/Austrian Radio Chorus
and Orch./Gielen
Philips 6700 084

1974 Reich *M*; Cassilly *A*; Palmer *YG*;
Winfield *YM*; Noble *AM*; Angas
P; Herrmann *E*/BBC Singers,
Orpheus Choir, BBC SO/Boulez
CBS (UK) 79201
(US) M2–33594

1976 Haseleu *M*; Goldberg *A*; Krahmer
YG; Ude *YM*; Polster *AM*; Mroz
P; Stryczek *E*/Dresden Catholic
Church Boys' Choir, Leipzig
Radio Chorus and Orch./Kegel
Eterna 826889–90
Supraphon 1416 2611–2

Wozzeck and *Lulu*

ROBIN HOLLOWAY

Berg's operas are the only two from a tradition of self-conscious radicalism that have (however precariously) entered the repertory and (however tenuously) caught the imagination of a wider audience. Both are notoriously difficult to perform and to listen to; notorious above all for the complex constructivistic schemes which have given scholastic commentators such heady exercise over the years. If these works were only known from their learned descriptions one would wonder how such wilfully aesthetical complication could ever hold or even reach the stage. Yet the advanced composer's perpetual plea that his listeners forget the technical scaffolding and go for the expression is in Berg's case without self-deception. *Wozzeck* and *Lulu* work in the theatre with a directness and power that the academic critic is unable to define so long as he remains content with the easier task of unravelling their compositional knitting. This, while in itself fascinating, obscures and evades the central issue of communication – of why and how the two operas produce their overwhelming effect.

WOZZECK

Once the ice was broken, *Wozzeck*'s compelling stage presence was recognized from the start; and nowadays there can hardly be a serious opera company that fails to rise to the challenge of a production once in a while. Recordings however have been surprisingly infrequent, and there is still no single one which does the work justice. The earliest, taken from a pair of concert performances conducted from memory by Dmitri Mitropoulos in Carnegie Hall in April 1951, remains in some important ways the best after three decades. Not for its singing to be sure, but for its grasp of and commitment to not only the letter of the score but also to its melodrama and human intensity – precisely those qualities that used to elicit sneering references to Berg as 'the twelve-tone Puccini' and which we now see to be one of the chief constituents of his complex genius. In rightness of speed, in naturalness of transitions, in placing of climaxes, we feel always that the man knows absolutely where the music has come from and where it is going to.

Mitropoulos's plasticity and fire exhibit an unsurpassed understanding of the score's fusion of letter and spirit.

This understanding, evident from the very first pages and continuing without remission to the last, can be demonstrated by a few examples from Act 1. The accompaniment to the Captain's paean to 'Moral Sense' really registers for once as the required gavotte. The following interlude, perhaps the most astonishing of this work's many hallucinatory flashbacks, concentrating and reconstituting material already taken in as if to illustrate Freud's theoretical account of 'dream-work' is superbly wrought. Scene ii is remarkable for its quality of fantasy; as Marie muses by the fire we hear the distant echoes of military music (by some inexplicable alchemy known only to the greatest interpreters) as somehow innocent rather than culpable in its powers of unconscious insinuation. And Mitropoulos makes a marvellous end to the act, a dangerous place often spoilt; the final bars of swelling accelerating *tutti* trill as Marie and the Drum-Major are pulled by force of lust into her bedroom are kept within bounds, and of course make an impact all the more horrible.

In Act 2 one begins to worry more about the poor singing. The Doctor seems to get no notes at all and the Captain very few. The Wozzeck is neutral and unmemorable. Marie on the other hand is, without much of a voice, one of the role's most sympathetic interpreters. Worthy of special mention here is the masterly way the first interlude grows out of the first scene. Mitropoulos excels at bringing out latent dance-feeling, or when the dance becomes blatant, at curbing its violence or parody to make something complex and equivocal out of it. In scene ii the movement from the slow waltz of the Doctor's assessment of the Captain – 'Hm! bloated features. . . fat thickish neck . . . apoplectic constitution . . .' to the *schwungvoller Walzer* a few pages later prepares us for his high-point of involvement, fluidity and control in the dance music of scene iv – the *rubati*, the fire, the sense of crazed bestial *immer zu*, are extraordinary, as also is the nightmarish waltz-blow-up that ends the scene. There is a red-hot edge to this conductor whatever he does and however messily. Thus the fugue in scene ii lives dangerously and does not avoid untidiness, while at the same time giving a better sense of overall direction – especially in the gradual unwind from Wozzeck's outburst of 'Gott in Himmel' when he can no longer bear the taunts, right down to the *Kammermusik* – than any other performance. Thus in the final scene the drunken music, after weirdly beautiful snoring-music, is more fully, disgustingly drunk than in any other performance.

And so it continues in Act 3. Marie's fairytale of the poor orphan boy is perhaps the most affecting to be heard on disc in its balance of flow and *lagrimoso*. The omnipresent B in the first lakeside scene shows that other conductors, before Boulez makes such a fuss about it, have also managed to embody in their performances a few salient points about this score (the same goes for the ubiquitous rhythm in scene iii); and the pages where Wozzeck, already intent on murdering his mistress, and quivering with the proximity of her beauty – all heaven for one more kiss – are charged with sense-enhancing intoxication. Later the drown-and-ripple music is harmonically clear as well as atmospherically suggestive, and is followed by a superb account of the Adagio; on the fast side, which produces the right effect of what Kerman with prim distaste calls 'a slow waltz in the lachrymose tradition of Gustav Mahler'. This in turn produces a sense, equally right, of the final scene's being an appendix not only to the Adagio but to the complete opera; an afterthought, outside the finished cycle, even while it initiates, in its voices of children, another cycle all over again. Mitropoulos conducts the best ending; and this most literal rendition of the notes is also the most suggestive of a range of puzzling further thoughts and feelings.

The masterly German music-making of Karl Böhm's recording has two complementary effects. The work is normalized; shown of course as congruent with Strauss and Mahler, and also taken back further into earlier epochs of Austro-German music. Yet just because of this solid grounding, we see as nowhere else the extraordinary violence of what Berg does to his inheritance. All the other conductors under review take it as a starting point that *Wozzeck* is a work of revolutionary modernism; their interpretations are all under the sign of the expressionistic aesthetic of extreme-as-extreme. Thus Act 2, scene ii is never such a riot of grotesque and fantastic invention as here; when the Captain accuses Wozzeck of running by 'like a razor slicing the world' we wince at the sharp edge all the more keenly for the material firmness of its surroundings. Again the extreme bizarreness of the *Kammermusik* in scene iii is realized to the full because of the implicit contrast with the mellifluousness of Mozart's serenades and Schubert's octet.

This quality of Böhm is most clearly heard in his handling of the all-important dance strain. Just because he has Haydn minuets, Beethoven scherzos and Bruckner *Ländler* in his blood, he can render the full beastliness of the waltz blow-ups in scene iv, revealing something truly terrifying about the way the ultra-refined Berg goes over the top in this music. It is like Ravel's *La valse*; it must, to convince, be based upon the real thing, not be from the start a mere expressionistic horror-piece. The same goes for the military music throughout *Wozzeck*, and the general emotional overkill exemplified for instance in the 'gigantification' of the theme after Marie's Bible scene (the first of Act 3). Such exaggeration is the essence of Berg's 'artistic manners' in this work, and depends upon our being shocked by its violation of norms and balances to come off properly. In the crux of this assault upon taste and decorum – the Adagio after Wozzeck is drowned – Böhm's brassiness, rhetoric and pathos go straight to the point (which is what 'centrality' means after all).

Such straightforward love of the score and of fine music-making is evident everywhere; one example among many is the first scene of Act 2, with Marie and her new necklace. It underpins the entire performance, making this the most satisfactory overall recording. Balance slightly favours the voices, producing some painful moments, like the Captain's horrid 'maus' in the very first scene. But this fault also reveals the best actual singing of any recorded *Wozzeck*. Of the minor roles the Andres of Fritz Wunderlich is predictably outstanding: the Drum-Major is suitably bellicose; and the Doctor, though in fast music he hardly attempts to find the notes, is excellently characterized and at least offends only negatively. Evelyn Lear makes a more sympathetic Marie than *Erdgeist* in *Lulu*, and occasionally produces singing of real beauty, as in the lullaby of Act 1 scene iii. Fischer-Dieskau is a 'natural' for the visionary aspects of Wozzeck; his hallucinations (eg. Act 1, scene ii) are wonderful, also the droll humour with which he imagines, in heaven, being put to work on the thunder. Occasionally he badly overdoes the *expression-ismo*, as on the word 'Tot', searching for the murder knife in the penultimate scene – but a few pages later he is fantastic as he evokes Marie with her hair hanging loose, and in his self-accusing cries of murder. As with another great visionary artist, Pears in *Peter Grimes*, there is a problem of credulity when they have to descend into low-life. Fischer-Dieskau as a humble illiterate soldier just doesn't convince; the exchanges with Marie in Act 1 do not ring true, and the great outburst of 'Wir arme Leute' sounds like the articulate anxious-conscience of the middle-classes rather than a cry from the beast of burden at the base of the whole base system. Fischer-Dieskau *cannot* be dumb, flat, inexpressive; it is his genius, and his fate, to be eloquent and explicit.

The high reputation enjoyed by Boulez's 1966 recording is curious. It lacks the solid musicality of Böhm and the fiery commitment of Mitropoulos. Boulez as a rule is clear, precise to the verge of nattiness, and flattened out, as if resisting the opera's unambiguous instructions to its performers and its 'palpable designs' upon its listeners. The recording is crude, with artificial highlighting and no atmosphere. The artifice is obtrusively unmusical throughout, except for the success of the onstage band in Act 2 scene iv. The *other* band (the offstage soldiers in scene iii of Act 1) is disastrously close and the window-closing that cuts it off badly mismanaged.

Only the grotesque and crazily heightened seem really to fire this conductor. Thus Act 1, scene iii and Act 2, scene i – scenes with Marie at her tenderest – are emotionally null; but what follows in each case (1 iv; 2 ii) – scenes between the Doctor and the Captain – are nervously alive rather than antiseptically clear. The mad Doctor, the sadistic Captain, the extravagant weirdness of texture Berg surrounds them with; these raise the temperature and sometimes the hair. So anything 'advanced' does better than anything 'retrograde'; and so also with 'objective' and 'heart-on-sleeve'; with an important and surprising exception – the final interlude, done with warmth and unstinted pathos. Another success is the waltz-bomb ending of Act 2, scene iv, a real lava-iceberg of extravagant but dispassionate violence. Indeed Boulez is good with all the *Ländler*, except for the pedantic dance-band tuning-up.

But so much else goes for nothing: The soldiers' snoring-chorus is well-tuned but blank atmospherically, while the crowd scene just before had been blank of pitch too. And while both pondside scenes in Act 3 are given with exceptional clarity, their unnervingly direct physical beauty is only realized in tiny flickers (for example the three solo violas in the first as Wozzeck praises Marie's lips, and in the second as he stumbles on her corpse – 'what is that crimson necklace around your neck?') – incomplete compensation for so much prose in this of all music. To study 'the fugue in *Wozzeck*', reach out for Boulez; but the brutal ugliness of the ends of the first two acts are not to be studied – or only as examples of what to avoid.

The singing is extraordinarily poor – almost nothing yields vocal pleasure or truth. Of the minor characters only the apprentices are good. Andres, Captain, and Drum-Major are dull, the Doctor even more (or less!) approximate than usual. Marie is unsympathetic with her dry tight little voice, and has no sense of line, whether in lullaby or march-trio, for the opera's only melodious role. Walter Berry's Wozzeck, unlike all this, is clearly the work of a distinguished artist. One has only to hear his 'wind' in the first scene (his first word not just 'ja ja, Herr Hauptmann') to know this man is strange, possessed – and he can rise to a grand explosion turning against his tormentors in Act 2, scene iii. Elsewhere he veers between pedantry in interpreting the *Sprechgesang* (as in the mushroom-gathering, Act 1, ii) and a ruinous *expressionismo* exceeding even Fischer-Dieskau's faults in this direction. In fact everyone's *Sprechgesang* is not only unconvincing (except, marginally, Marie's in the Bible scene, Act 3, i) but frequently simply repulsive. Boulez favours us with some *pensées* on the subject in the programme-book; but surely the gradual evolution over the years of empirical solutions to this tricky difficulty are greatly preferable to the fundamentalism which can result in noises so horrible as to make long stretches unlistenable-to with enjoyment. I haven't located the Kegel set.

The latest *Wozzeck*, under Christoph von Dohnányi, fails to establish itself so positively as Boulez or Böhm in their different ways, while achieving greater perfection than either. The singing falls somewhere between the two. Though it keeps higher standards of accuracy than *chez* Boulez, no one here is what one might call 'pitch-inevitable'; there is never the sense in any given place that it *has* to be just *these* notes. The Doctor doesn't try (as a rule) for the admittedly extravagant demands of his part. When it is not difficult he is good – witness the passage counting his pulse 'at its usual sixty'. Andres is tone-and-note-less throughout; the Captain unmemorable. The Drum-Major is not fierce enough (nor is his orchestral support). Anja Silja is among the better Maries. Her *Sprechgesang* in the Bible scene is none too convincing, but the cries of 'Heiland' are intense without strain. The big drawback is Eberhard Waechter's Wozzeck: colourless and ineffectual below *mezzo forte*; above it, notable only for his hollow-voiced raving, all the way from the thunder passage in Act 1, ii to his last scene.

The Vienna Philharmonic is of course wonderfully idiomatic and a graceful easer of difficulties – particular praise for the extraordinarily delicate trumpets. All instrumental *obbligati* are outstandingly musical – witness the *sentimental* (Berg's instruction) viola in the first scene, and the series of tiny solo parts in the Act 2 *Kammermusik* that surround the fatal first insinuation of 'knife' (pp. 250–1). Von Dohnányi knows the score inside-out (Berg is probably the only composer for whom this silly phrase makes sense!). Outstanding in Act 1 are the final variations of the scene iv passacaglia as the Doctor mounts towards his burst of megalomaniac joy; the interlude following; and the whole of the fifth scene with Marie and the Drum-Major.

In Act 2 reservations creep in. The fugue is admirably clear, but does not build towards Wozzeck's great outcry. The aforementioned *Kammermusik* is excellent; but the Waltz-interlude that blows up the insinuation of a knife into a nightmare of blood-crazed jealousy is simply not drastic enough. And so in Act 3 – the murder of Marie (scene iii) is so lucid and refined that we no longer *feel* it along the pulses – a far cry from the flesh-creeping onomatopoeia of yesteryear! And so the last interlude does not beat the breast or assault the wailing wall, but reserves its feeling, in the spirit of the whole performance – coolish though far from cold. In this spirit the last scene is tonally ravishing, the little ebbs and flows of tempo just before the strictly non-*rubato* end are especially good.

With such nuancing, the expressionistic immediacy of the work, the way in which it has up to now been played and heard, is abandoned. Much of the score is so delicate here that it hardly seems palpable any more. One wonders if this music has not become, after all the struggles to master it, a little too smooth. The result is so effortless and weightless that it doesn't *hurt* any more; and in not hurting, neither does it stir the depths as it once did, and surely ought to always.

The *Three fragments from Wozzeck*, prepared by Berg as a trailer for the complete opera, make an unsatisfactory concert item, neither a fair view of the whole nor well balanced in itself. The coupling (issued only in the USA) of the fine performance by Heather Harper with Boulez of the *Seven Early Songs* with Act 3 complete seems a tacit admission of the non-viability of the *Fragments* as a shape – for CBS presumably *intended* an all-soprano record. Or perhaps Berg has acted with characteristic duplicity – whetting appetite for the work in its entirety by the unsatisfactoriness as well as the quality of his extracts.

There have been several recordings, none of them (unlike Miss Harper's frequent concerts and broadcasts) adding anything significant to the small and imperfect coverage of Marie's role in the complete sets. First comes a pair of 78s from the mid-forties (Artist ⓜ 500). The orchestra under Werner Janssen is sometimes careful, sometimes exciting, and Charlotte Boerner's crisis of 'Heiland!' in the Bible scene are second to none. Gertrude Ribla and Ormandy in 1947 are utterly useless and dull, and cut the first nine bars of the Bible scene, as if Berg were a Handel or a Donizetti. In 1960 comes something worth hearing, Helga Pilarczyk, under Dorati. The beautifully atmospheric opening leads to a splendidly raucous Ives-Mahler march, cut off by an unusually convincing window-slam. The orchestra tends to be more fully characterized than the singer with her all-purpose anguish/ecstasy modern-music voice that sounds worn out with too much extremity. The Adagio flows faster than usual, which sounds better in the context of the *Fragments* than it would in the whole work, where the huge emphases and pathetic climax are needed. Dorati's handling of tempo fluctuations after the child's last words is exquisite, and allows him to get away with making a slight *ritenuto* at the very end against Berg's explicit instruction.

Leinsdorf four years later is the steadiest 'non-ritter', but the orchestra is pedestrian, the march fast but without zing, the Adagio slow but its vehemence and passion sedulous rather than deeply felt. Phyllis Curtin is nothing special, and her *Sprechgesang* in the Bible scene is particularly unconvincing. The 1967 version under Herbert Kegel is more like Dorati; a magical sunset, a sizzling march, and a strong sense of melancholy waltz about the final Adagio. Hanne-Lore Kuhse is good but lacks simplicity for such music as the lullaby, and in speech has a coyness worthy of La Schwarzkopf herself – the least suitable tone possible for this of all roles. Marie has still to be really well sung on disc.

LULU

Lulu, 'the second opera', has been slower to advance in the world than the first. For over forty years there was the many-edged problem of a missing third act. The work in its two-act form was already profoundly troubling; the recent restoration of Act 3, while closing many questions, poses new ones just as hard to answer. It is much longer than *Wozzeck*, much more difficult to hear in passing detail or to grasp as a whole; its story is still more squalid but lacks the unmistakeable human breadth of its predecessor. He must have a heart of stone who can sit through *Wozzeck* unmoved; but in *Lulu* events at an extreme of horribleness and emotional heightening are presented casually. Berg seems to take pleasure in disassociating – to take pains to disassociate – his effects (never more fervent in their aching, late-romantic beauty than here) from their causes.

Yet in spite of difficulties, both technical and stylistic, something of a tradition for playing *Lulu* has developed over the last few decades. Above all, it is realized that this is not an attempt to overtop the expressionistic plenitude of *Wozzeck*. The first opera is all intensity and directness: *Lulu* is nothing if not oblique; overkill makes it ludicrous ('gory, gory, gory' as Stravinsky said); the norm of the music and the action is fast, bubbly, almost comical.

Such lessons are learnt slowly, and one listens to the complete set of 1949, wondering how anyone who heard it could ever venture to give the work a second try, and how any company could bear to perpetuate six sides of unrelieved ordeal. Yet its very awfulness is historical, bringing back with acute nostalgia what it felt like to listen to modern music in the fifties – how in eager pursuit of the new and the rare one would put up with *anything* in the way of performance, poring over the score, vainly struggling to relate sight to sound and love the result. *Tristan* and *Parsifal* must also have seemed interminable and meaningless for decades after they were written; and in spite of half a century or so of outstanding Wagner interpretation there is still a sense of ordeal in every performance (or in oneself as one steals oneself to withstand a performance). It is the nature of these works; and *Lulu* is another such. Though standards have improved dramatically upon the risibility of the non-solutions in this earliest version, there is no guarantee, thirty years after, that the better can be infallibly relied upon.

And in a funny way there are some positive points. Being all so fast and with such light voices, the effect is operetta-like. In Act 1 the first scene, the Catechism, and the Letter-duet all show this quality; still more, the early stages of Act 2, where Lulu enters as a kind of Merry Widow presiding over the *jour fixe* of her many admirers – the toast of the underworld. This is done quite without understanding – indeed obviously accidental, the performers being concerned only to get through the nightmare as quickly as possible. Yet much of this work *should* froth and fizz like operetta; it just needs to be done supremely well! The overall impression is of people trying to make sense of a hieroglyphic script – 'do we go from left to right or from right to left?' The *Monoritmica* for instance is absolutely meaningless, and some of the noises here and elsewhere are indescribably dreadful, notably the English Waltz and the Ensemble that follows (though this last is *always* horrible – no performance has ever made it otherwise).

The singing, too, has its moments. Here is the only Athlete to achieve the low C; and Alwa, though patently drowning in molten lead, actually preserves a fresher voice than almost all his successors. And Dr Goll is a real piece of history, a speaking survivor from the silent heyday of the German expressionist cinema. In general, *speech* is more natural and convincing here, closer to a tradition of lofty diction that in later performances is preserved only in the Ringmaster of the prologue. And at least two crucial moments would have rewarded the patient listener of the fifties with the conviction that a great work does exist within the nightmare; Schön's death and Lulu's return both make an impact that not even *this* can totally efface.

The next *Lulu*, a live recording of the famous Hamburg production of the sixties, is still something of an ordeal. This is the 'electric bell' version where instead of the delicate vibraphone 'urinating' (Stravinsky again) in the ear for each exit and entrance, they (and one soon realizes their frequency) are marked by a sort of domestic fire alarm. In fact the 'official' percussion, as well, is dreadful altogether; the orchestra otherwise is dim and fuzzy, but plays with gumption and is directed by Leopold Ludwig with a certain understanding. The conspicuous new feature is the dramatic pacing. Moreover, there is a sense of team-work, and that this dauntingly difficult score is both a repertory piece and not entirely without fun and beauty. Everyone who saw this production must remember how well it worked theatrically; something of this comes over in the records, and remains instructive even now, when the performance has obviously become outclassed on purely musical grounds.

Even so, the advance on 1949 is enormous. From desperation in which anything goes, we have here a *Monoritmica* that really builds, however shaggy the details; an Adagio that is truly *appassionato*, jazzy 'jazz' and a dancy 'English waltz' (not always true in later, more accomplished performances); altogether a sense of purposefulness and shape. Act 2 is less good – grit and patience are needed to get through what should be tripping and transparent. Yet a sense of pace still survives, even when there is little actually to enjoy. The Lulu-Alwa duet is rough and his *Hymne* hurried; but they go to it with a will, and it is possible, from this performance, to *imagine* one that sounded beautiful.

Little delight, as usual, from the singers. Schön is dreadful; most of Act 2 is such a bawl that one is thankful when Lulu shoots him at last, and understands why. The Athlete is also dismal, though at least there is verisimilitude in the bear being his emblematic beast. Schigolch, is, suitably, a little hazy; Alwa as usual is tight and dry; the Geschwitz is not bad; the Schoolboy is the one vocal pleasure in the long stretch after the *ostinato* centre-point before Lulu's return. Anneliese Rothenberger has a good crack (sometimes literally) at the central role. But from her first chance (the *pussi*-song in Act 1) to her last gasp she is fatally charmless; sensible and hardworking, utterly not sexy, utterly not voluptuous. In *Lulus Lied* there is no vibration of involvement with the vital creature impelled in her distress to utter her credo – merely strain without ecstasy. And in general these discs betray their epoch in their ubiquitous range of old-style 'modern' vocal beastliness; everything ugly, coarse, exaggerated, inaccurate, is enshrined here, whether denying real gifts (or just raving on, giftless) in the interests of 'dramatic expression'. When six such voices are at it simultaneously (as in the Act 1, scene iii ensemble) one wants to call for the police; it is worse even than the electric bell.

With Karl Böhm's performance of 1968 (taken from another stage production, that of the Berlin Opera), musical pleasures at last begin to equal cultural duties, and we have the first intimations, whatever the shortcomings, of real mastery of the complex monster.

The big drawback is the heroine of Evelyn Lear. She seems to have the part all wrong – Lulu as brassy flirt, a Musetta without the heart of gold. It is obvious that she is trying intelligently to get under the skin of the part; but in the very seriousness of her intention she misses more than earlier contenders who attempt less or nothing. Thus her 'jetzt bin ich reich' after the death of Dr Goll essays childlike unconsciousness but achieves only unnaturalness. Her 'innocent little girl' relation to the Painter is marred by similar stiltedness. Even when the pleasure of intelligibility is added for the first time to the intrinsic pleasure of Berg's notes, as in the morning-bath duet with the Painter, the letter duet with Schön, and the love duet with Alwa, the voice in itself cannot please. One feels that what she actually produces is against the grain of what she can really do. And occasionally there are real mistakes of characterization. Her laughter throughout the second episode with the infatuated waiter is a case in point, and another is her too fruity response to Schön's death. Saddest is *Lulus Lied*. Böhm gives the music the breadth appropriate to an apologia, but Lear cannot cope with the long phrases; and this crucial moment is ruined by would-be expression, sloppiness and a cutting edge.

Her husbands and lovers include the too-frequent clutch of dry, tight tenors. Loren Driscoll's Painter is musical and intelligent – only the *sound* is unlovely; even so his address over the fresh corpse of his predecessor reveals the nobility of this passage for the first time on record, one example among dozens of music that had before to be endured and can now be anticipated, and experienced, with pleasure. The fervour of his orchestral support carries Alwa even in the duet and *Hymne* where we long for warmth and ease; where he needs to be strangulated, as in the cries of 'schweig . . . schweig . . .' which close Act 2, he has no difficulty. The Prince provides yet a third dried-up tenor. Of the deeper men, Schigolch is unmemorable, the Athlete memorable only for the ravishing evocation of his new pink knickers, and the Geschwitz really not mannish enough – a Brangäne-voice rather than the requisite sexless throb, though beautifully sung, especially in the dying bars at the end of the Act 2 Adagio.

Fischer-Dieskau (Dr Schön) is incomparably the most interesting artist here. He never loses sight of his animal image from the Prologue (well characterized, incidentally, by orchestra and Ringmaster alike), and one is always aware of the tiger beneath the polished capitalist. Sometimes to a fault; he is so consistently emphatic as to be occasionally counter-productive. But at its best – the repressed savagery of the opening of the Act 1 *Monoritmica* with the odd pounce on a salient word (as 'Blindheit', p. 178); the ferocity of the five-strophe aria in Act 2 (with a marvellous 'lacht wild', p. 444) – this was the most distinguished interpretation recorded up to this time, and remains so still.

Böhm's mastery is shown in two respects. First the attention to local detail (as for instance, in the two passages singled out already for Fischer-Dieskau's excellence, the omnipresence of their respective *Haupt*-rhythmic construction); and its large-scale corollary, control of dramatic architecture. This is the first performance with any grasp of such things, and an awareness of the intimate dependence of great upon small. So the ineluctable momentum of the letter duet that closes Act 1 – a mantrap for all its surface of silky deliciousness – comes as the inevitable goal of the entire act, not just as its piquant finale. The second aspect of Böhm's mastery is the superb warmth and sweep of the late-romantic ambience of the score. As a good Wagnerian and great Straussian, he retains a sensibility impervious to undermining irony and alienation. When Berg indicates a Mahlerian *adagio*, Böhm does just that. Such directness flowers best when unrestrained by the variously unsatisfactory voices, in the Adagio from Act 3. But the duet ending Act 2 is also very fine if one can blot out the singing, the *Hymne* especially with at last a real *dolce vibrando* in the marvellous orchestral simulation of a gigantic harp. The orchestra in general is plump and warm, good for *tutti* harmony and line, less so for colour and chamber-scoring. All these qualities come together in the Act 1 Sonata; powerful energy, sharp rhythmic pointing, no scrabbling or scrambling, the sections well demarcated by different tempi; and then a glow of late-romantic ardour in the coda.

All the same the great new joy of the 1976 recording under Christoph von Dohnányi is the spectacular advance in beauty and refinement of sound. This is of course partly due to a superior recording and the care that can be lavished upon details in a studio, as opposed to the hurly-burly of a live performance of a work so full of violent deaths and disasters. It is no denigration that one listens to this superb recording with an enhanced regard for Berg the musician; for the extraordinary range of his invention, from the highest elegance and voluptuousness, through a torrential let-rip of excitement, and horror, to deep sentiment whether vulgar, sensational, tender or elegiac; all composed with the tightest and most impersonal control. The music flourishes as never before, while the story and its characters are all held at a remove. This would be no denigration anyway; and, whether by accident or design, happens to fit in well with the shift in vantage that makes *Lulu* so different from *Wozzeck*. The relative coolness of von Dohnányi and his cast is the first indication on record that 'expressionism' as a performing style is superseded.

The virtuosity and refinement of the orchestra are astonishing. The first horn in particular performs feats of delicate athleticism in the Act 2 *Kammermusik* that one would scarcely have believed possible; and his colleague on the first trombone is not inferior. The trumpets produce throughout a dulcet *dolce*, whether muted or open, that shows the horrible 'Second Viennese Sound' of yesteryear, the searing and raucousness apparently inseparable from this style, need never be heard again. Naturally the high points of the super-silky sonority occur when the voices cease – in Act 1 the ravishing interlude after the first scene, with its *Wozzeck*-like summary of events just heard and *Wozzeck*-unlike grace, sparkle, and suavity; in Act 2 the outstanding brilliance and clarity of the film music, and in the extracts from Act 3 the absolutely unfaultable Variations.

The sumptuousness and accuracy given their head in these set-pieces can be enjoyed in virtually every bar of the vocal music also – but all too often by not concentrating too carefully upon the singers. There is a general problem of synchronization. Alwa is particularly prone to getting out with the orchestra, and the fault is heard also with the Prince in Act 1 and the Athlete in Act 2 (though he is excellent in every other respect, with outstanding command of transition between speech and song). Nor is the heroine immune, and her closing love duet with Alwa (Act 2 closing, that is) almost sounds as if they've been recorded separately, or far apart, from the orchestra. The best of Anja Silja is very good; the *pussi*-canzonetta and the 'jetzt bin ich reich' so unconvincing *chez* Lear are well-nigh perfect, as also the seductive wiles and comforts that delay Schön's weekly visit to the Bourse early in Act 2. Her account of *Lulus Lied* is one of the best in an episode that never seems quite as good as it should. Elsewhere, especially later on, some parts of the role are a bit much for her.

After Fischer-Dieskau, the Schön of Berry sounds a little mild. The tremendous last line of Act 1 goes comparatively for nothing, and though he bursts out well early in Act 2 – 'Das mein Lebensabend' – he lacks rage in the song that precedes his death. Stronger authority proceeds from the ex-Wotan; an inspired thought, to cast Hans Hotter as Schigolch.

Better than any individual performance is the sense of ensemble; the rapt concentration of Lulu, Schön, the Geschwitz, in the unearthly beauty of the opening pages of Act 2; a bit later the sense of Circe (rather than Merry Widow) among her enthralled menagerie as Lulu steps into the clustering circle of her admirers. This set in fact recaptures the operetta-lightness and comedy present by accident in the 1949 version. Elsewhere some of the fast speeds come as a revelation. The Act 2 *Kammermusik* has already been mentioned; in Act 1 the pace and turbulence of 'In Paris ist Revolution ausgebrochen' gives an entirely new feeling to the music. Von Dohnányi controls it all the way down to the Adagio with superb aplomb.

In short, while there is still a long way to go in respect of the singing, this is incomparably the best orchestral performance to be heard.

The latest recording of *Lulu* is strictly speaking not comparable with anything earlier since it is the only one to include Act 3. It would therefore be an indispensable document even if the performance were indifferent. But in fact virtually everything to do with these records is admirable, a tribute worthy of a great occasion, to be valued permanently when the visual impertinences of the first complete production are nothing but a bad memory. Which is not to say that it is the last word. Though there is as yet no rival, it is none the less possible to find room for improvement in Act 3, and the other two receive a performance to complement rather than replace the best features of Böhm and von Dohnányi.

As so often in Pierre Boulez's performances, the losses go in different ways; we miss on the one hand lightness of rhythm, charm, and sparkle; and on the other, ardour and intensity of expression. He keeps the music under strict rein, with occasional exceptions that can disconcert more than they please. And there is the perennial problem, in such harmonic music, of his lack of a feeling for how harmony moves – how it can make climax and relaxation irrespective of the music's dynamic and colouristic surface. In matters of balance and colouristic clarity he remains outstanding; anything in *Lulu* that relies on a vivid realization of sheer sonority is always extraordinary. A small example (out of hundreds) is the music for woodwinds throughout the Schigolch scene in Act 1, especially when it renders his asthma and his harmonica. This slithy stuff (Schigolch's counterpart in the menagerie is the worm) is something of an ordeal even with Hotter to sing – except here, where it is so weird and fascinating just as *noise* that one is captivated in spite of oneself.

Boulez tends towards a certain uniformity of speed. The 'operetta' sections of Act 1, in particular the comic-capers canon in the first scene, are a trifle lumpy (though there is a splendid *echt*-French trumpet for this music's return in the following interlude). He is short on *allegresse* – a quality much needed in this work as its full range is gradually understood. Thus Schön's *Musette* is undelicious, while the later stages of the Sonata are positively wooden. Moments of melodrama, on the other hand, are bloodcurdling, witness the first sight of the Doctor's body, or the trombones at Schön's 'Quick . . . away . . . but where . . . to my bride? my house?' And there are moments of delight: the morning bath duettino is enchanting, also the offstage Ragtime and English Waltz (the third dance – Hungarian Rock? – is powerfully obliterated by the full orchestra in the pit – an excellent piece of management). The horrible sextet, finely cordoned off with expert and sensitive *fermate* before and after, sounds about as well as it *can*. Yet there is an indefinable lack throughout the whole first act; the *Monoritmica* does not take off, the Adagio is brisk and clipped, and in spite of the extensive stage-exposure of this same cast and conductor, there is no great sense of musico-dramatic architecture.

And so it continues with Act 2. The Geschwitz music is excellent; but the later *parlando* scenes are too fast. (One passage, however, must be singled out as a model of absolute just-so perfection – the first, apparently innocuous converse between Alwa and Lulu in her Mignon role.) The feel of pantomime comedy is good, but the five-strophe aria less pointed and powerful than with Fischer-Dieskau and Böhm. Superb by any standards is the excitement of the shooting, the dying vehemence, the living appeals, the tumble into the film music *ostinato*, and the film music itself. Thereafter, the music is again too fast. Time should hang heavy here, after so many tumultuous thrills; we should wait and feel that we are waiting – it is oddly more tiring (and more dull) to get through this stretch too quickly. Then speed is again right for the whirl of ensemble as Lulu's return becomes imminent. But then the final *Hymne* to her beauty needs to be relaxed, and here, again, he hurries. The musing, wondering eroticism of Alwa's address to his mistress's thighs is despatched with particular refusal to relish; maybe Boulez does not approve of music being made to evoke thighs in an *andante amoroso*.

And so it continues in Act 3; the early stages in particular are exhausting in their unceasing density of scrambled activity. Obviously some of this music is meant to be a babble, especially the three ensembles with their twelve excited voice parts. But the all-important conversations – Lulu and the Marquis; Lulu and the Athlete; Lulu and Schigolch; Lulu, Geschwitz and the Athlete – are just as hectic; and here we have to cope not only with their spiderishly complex musical activity but a network of allusion across the entire range of the earlier acts, plus new words vital to the forwarding of the plot. These duos and trios should surely go more gently – and if they did, the full ensembles would also make more of an effect. In particular Boulez seems to have mistaken the musical character of the string phrase that accompanies the Countess. It seems to *want* to be a gentle *affetuoso*, but is rushed, like everything else, into a meaningless flurry. The music does not breathe; it is all surface movement with no background.

The second half of this new act is altogether more convincing. Though the impression is still paramount of areas of familiar music over which alien voice parts have been none-too-convincingly draped, no doubt the gradual growth of a tradition of performance will gradually dispel most qualms, as in the case of the complete tenth symphony of Mahler. And, as the area well-known from the *Lulu-Symphony* and the last track on all the two-act sets is reached, so the work itself, and its performance, gain in conviction. Yet I cannot feel that the conductor is the chief instigator of the effect – hear for instance the vigorous no-emotional nonsense reprise of the Adagio. The terror and deep pathos of these scenes between Lulu and her clients is achieved almost entirely through the singers.

A great deal of Teresa Stratas's physical fascination comes over in her voice. This includes her speaking voice which is quite different from any other Lulu's which all smack of the elocution class and sound embarrassedly eager to get singing again. She is full of personality even when telling the story of her imprisonment and escape. More heightened speech is more memorable – calling on Alwa when threatened with arrest, calling upon the Countess (the only use of her name – Martha – in the entire work) to help her out of her still more appalling trouble in Act 3. Intenser again, the passion of her spoken exclamation of love for Schön in Act 1. There is no froth or *pussi* here – this is the living anguish of a complete and vibrant woman. She excels also in the indeterminate area between speech and song; the growth from one to the other road from simulated sickness and exhaustion to full-voiced *Freiheit* in Act 2 is quite wonderful. This power of projecting many facets of personality by means of the voice comes over into her singing. She is the only Lulu who fascinates in herself, not just because of the fascination produced in everyone around her, and the aura of sax, vibe and *volupté* that halo her every utterance. She is the opposite of a flirt, or a gold-digger; she is anxious, nervous, fragile; delicious in animal laziness, able to imbue the 'Du . . .' during the Painter's momentary absence in their Act 1 duettino with something rapt and visionary; able to realize the coquettish and offhand equally with the passionate and the agonized. The voice can be unsteady, and she frequently sounds strained and easily tired. But we never lose sight of the character grasped whole and rounded. She is the first Lulu who can do what D. H. Lawrence found the highest tribute he could pay to a woman – appeal to the imagination.

In fact this is a woman-heavy *Lulu*, not only because of the three new female roles in Act 3. Hanna Schwarz's Schoolboy is outstanding in all his contributions, and Yvonne Minton's Geschwitz is nobility personified. The men are less distinctive, though Robert Tear's Painter is certainly the best yet. But Schigolch is wooden and dull, and the Athlete so-so. Alwa is, as ever, a bit dry; also too consistently loud, especially in the duet. Franz Mazura makes a strong Schön, excellent in the *Monoritmica*'s difficult graduations between speech and song, but lacking the tigerish demon of Fischer-Dieskau.

This version eclipses all rivals in its power of depicting close relationships (which was the one admirable feature of the Paris production, seen to best advantage on the television film with its use of close-ups). We feel this as early as the Catechism between the Painter and Lulu in Act 1, scene i. Something significant is going on here between two people – it is as simple, and new, as that – we remember it, and get the point when, hours later, Lulu the prostitute is visited by her second client, the Painter reincarnated as the Negro. The opera's central relationship is powerfully present whenever Lulu and Schön are on stage together. This also culminates in the final scene of Act 3 where the pillar of the establishment is reincarnated as Jack the Ripper. Here Mazura comes into his own. He is terrifying, and succeeds in showing the truth behind the apparent exigency or mere surrealism of the Schön/Ripper identification; the tiger of the Prologue is now released from all bourgeois decorum and the trammels of civilized self-sacrifice. Far from paying Lulu for her favours he even extorts his bus fare home before taking her then murdering her. Stratas is deeply pathetic in this dreadful scene. We realize through her that this too is a real relationship – that she is pleased (somehow) to be treated thus. When she says in a voice trembling with torment 'I'm really drawn to you, . . . don't keep me waiting' she shows she recognizes, in spite of everything, that this is, again, the man of her life. The very different close exchanges between Lulu and Martha are also deeply affecting. The circumstance, that Lulu can persuade her long-suffering admirer to beg a lout to sleep with her whatever her aversion, and the pathos, that the Countess is touchingly ready to oblige for the sake of a crumb of love, are obviated in the tender warmth of their music together. In all these close encounters these records reveal something of the paradox of Lulu the character – the beauty, the allure, the innocence, that survive disease and depravity; and in doing so, something of the same paradox of *Lulu* the opera, where squalor and horror are rendered in constructivistic contrivances of the utmost sophistication and are transfigured by a sound-world of angelic radiance.

The *Lulu-Symphonie*, unlike the fragments from *Wozzeck*, does make some sense as a whole, and provides a picture however partial of the whole opera. We must always be grateful that its compilation drew from Berg the incomparable orchestration of the Variations and Adagio from Act 3. But it remains a tricky work to bring off, and perhaps will (as the *Wozzeck* extracts now tend to) disappear as it outlives its usefulness in promoting the complete work. A pity; for while the singing continues to be the least satisfactory feature in performances of Berg's second opera, it is actually more enjoyable to follow the Lulu/Alwa duet in a good voiceless performance as the Symphony's first movement – to say nothing of the ravishing eight bars he added as introduction. And if he had, as he first intended, added a purely orchestral version of Schön's Sonata, the work would be a strong and substantial concert-piece.

Unlike the recordings of the *Three fragments from Wozzeck*, there are versions of the *Lulu-Symphonie* that do really add to what can be learnt from the complete sets. Dorati's famous record for instance, gives the best-shaped of all performances of the Rondo, and the fullest realization of the *grandioso* marking for the first of the Variations. The Adagio, though as always exceptionally clear and controlled, is less good. Helga Pilarczyk has the occasional true note but as a whole can stand as a classic instance of the false pathos and interpretative overkill that used to give 'expressionism' in modern vocal music such a bad name. Robert Craft's performance of four movements only is raucous in sound, fierce and blurred in character, but always shows his curious combination of understanding without feeling-for, whereas Ormandy shapes the music with constant awareness of its submerged vocal lines, especially in the *Hymne*, where the lovers' voices are transferred without change to saxophone and horn. Louisa de Sett pitches gutsily into Lulu's *Lied* – one certainly cannot fail to realize that this is a true testament of youth.

Ormandy is crude but ardent; Claudio Abbado by contrast is over-refined. His Rondo is a long iridescent swoon; sweet, shapeless and, in the end, dull. Yet such languishing elegance has its place – it is certainly true to one facet of the work, the one moreover that is the first to disappear in the stresses of the complete opera. Much the same can be said for Margaret Price's version of the *Lied* – beautifully sung, with the best coloratura on disc – but with no passion, no sense of *apologia pro modus vivendi*; and so with her Geschwitz; cool in her death-pangs, not yearning with *Liebestod*. The best features of Abbado's versions are the eloquent trumpet in the Variations, and the Italianate quality both of the organ-grinder music, and the *appassionato* of the Adagio.

The most comprehensive overall account comes from the husband and wife team of the best (in)complete set – Anja Silja under Christoph von Dohnányi. The Rondo for instance is at once delicate and gorgeous in sound (al'Abbado), and beautifully shaped (alla Dorati). In the *Lied* we really feel the symmetrical structure; and though Silja is a little unsafe up high, causing the occasional blench with strain and vibrato, her commitment to the role, and sense of this aria as the key to it, are unmistakeable.

The most recent *Lulu-Symphonie*, under Boulez, is undistinguished at best, and now and again really bad – witness the mechanized *ritenuti*, the coarse sonority, the general feeling of anti-harmony, anti-line, anti-gorgeous. Judith Blegen's *Lied* is mediocre; the most memorable characterization is produced by the first trumpeter – already nasty in the Rondo, cruder still in the Variations, and searingly horrible in the Adagio. It is extraordinary that this perfunctory affair could come from the man who presides with such success over the first recording of the complete opera in its entirety.

WOZZECK

W Wozzeck; *M* Marie; *D* Doctor; *DM* Drum Major; *C* Captain; *A* Andres

1951 (live performance – Carnegie Hall, New York) Harrell *W*; Farrell *M*; Herbert *D*; Jagel *DM*; Mordino *C*; D. Lloyd *A*/New York Schola Cantorum, New York PO/ Mitropoulos
Philips ⓜ ABL3388–9
CBS(US) ⓜ Y2-33126

1965 Fischer-Dieskau *W*; Lear *M*; Kohn *D*; Melchert *DM*; Stolze *C*; Wunderlich *A*/German Opera Chorus and Orch./Böhm
DG 2707 023

1966 Berry *W*; I. Strauss *M*; Dönch *D*; Uhl *DM*; Weikenmeier *C*; Van

Vrooman *A*/Paris Opéra Chorus and Orch./Boulez
CBS 79251

1974 Adam *W*; Schröter *M*; Rupf *D*; Goldberg *DM*; Hiestermann *C*; Klotz *A*/Leipzig Radio Chorus and Orch./Kegel
Eterna 826656–7

1980 Waechter *W*; Silja *M*; Malta *D*; Winkler *DM*; Zedník *C*; Laubenthal *A*/Vienna Boys' Choir, Vienna State Opera Chorus, VPO/ Dohnányi
Decca D231D2 ④ K231K22
London LDR 10046–7

Three Fragments

*c.*1947 Boerner, Janssen SO of Los Angeles/Janssen
Artist ⓜ 500

1947 Ribla, Philadelphia/Ormandy
Columbia (UK) LX1158–8*
CBS (US) ⓜ ML2140

1953 Anonymous artists
Allegro ⓜ ALL3144

1960 Pilarczk, LSO/Dorati

Mercury (UK) AMS16117
(US) SRI 70566

1964 Curtin/Sacred Heart Boychoir, Boston SO/Leinsdorf
RCA (UK) SER5518–9
(US) LSC7031

1967 Kuhse, Leipzig Radio SO/Kegel
Vanguard (US) VCS10011–2
Eterna 825538

LULU

L Lulu; *DS* Dr Schön; *A* Alwa; *S* Schigolch; *CG* Countess Geschwitz

1949 (radio broadcast) Steingruber *L*; Wiener *DS*; Libert *A*; Siegert *S*; Cerny *CG*/Vienna SO/Häfner
Philips ⓜ ABL 3394–6
CBS(US) ⓜ SL 121

1967 (live performance – Hamburg State Opera House) Rothenberger *L*; Blankenheim *DS*; Unger *A*; Borg *S*; Meyer *CG*/Hamburg State

Opera PO/Ludwig
EMI SME91714–6
Angel SCL3726

1968 (live performance – German Opera House, Berlin) Lear *L*; Fischer-Dieskau *DS*; Grobe *A*; Greindl *S*; Johnson *CG*; German Opera Orch./Böhm
DG 2709 029

1976 Silja *L*; Berry *DS*; Hopferwieser
      A; Hotter *S*; Fassbaender *CG*/
      Vienna PO/Dohnányi
      Decca D48D3 ④ K48K3
      London OSA13120 ④ OSA5–
      13120

1979 (with Act 3 – completed Cerha)
      Stratas *L*; Mazura *DS*; Riegel *A*;
      Blankenheim *S*; Minton *CG*/Paris
      Opera Chorus and Orch./Boulez
      DG 2740 213 ④ 3378 086
      DG 2711 024 ④ 3378 086

Lulu-Symphonie

1960 Pilarczyk, LSO/Dorati
      Mercury (UK) AMS16117
      (US) SRI–75066
1967 De Sett, Philadelphia/Ormandy
      CBS (US) MS7041
      (Europe) 72848
1969 Brink, Nürnberg SO/Maga
      Colosseum SM533

1970 M. Price, LSO/Abbado
      DG 2530 146
1974 Silja, Vienna PO/Dohnányi
      Decca SXL6657
      London OS26397
1975 Blegen, New York PO/Boulez
      CBS (UK) 76575
      (US) M35849

Index